Systems and Human Science
—for Safety, Security, and Dependability—

Selected Papers of the 1st International Symposium
SSR2003
Osaka, Japan, November 2003

Systems and Human Science
— for Safety, Security, and Dependability —

Selected Papers of the 1st International Symposium
SSR2003
Osaka, Japan, November 2003

Cosponsored by
Graduate School of Engineering Science, Osaka University
Society for Instrumentation and Control Engineers (SICE)
Robotics Society of Japan (RSJ)

Edited by

Tatsuo Arai
Shigeru Yamamoto
Kazuhisa Makino

2005

ELSEVIER

Amsterdam • Boston • Heidelberg • London • New York • Oxford
Paris • San Diego • San Francisco • Singapore • Sydney • Tokyo

ELSEVIER B.V.
Radarweg 29
P.O. Box 211, 1000 AE Amsterdam
The Netherlands

ELSEVIER Inc.
525 B Street, Suite 1900
San Diego, CA 92101-4495
USA

ELSEVIER Ltd
The Boulevard, Langford Lane
Kidlington, Oxford OX5 1GB
UK

ELSEVIER Ltd
84 Theobalds Road
London WC1X 8RR
UK

First edition 2005

Library of Congress Cataloging in Publication Data
A catalog record is available from the Library of Congress.

British Library Cataloguing in Publication Data
A catalogue record is available from the British Library.

ISBN: 0-444-51813-4

♾ The paper used in this publication meets the requirements of ANSI/NISO Z39.48-1992 (Permanence of Paper). Printed in The Netherlands.

Preface

Our society keeps growing with a large number of complicated machines and systems while we are spending our diverse lives. The number of aged people has been increasing in the society. It is more likely than ever that we are involved in dangers, accidents, crimes, and disasters. Securing and supporting our daily life, building reliable infrastructures against large-scale disasters, and preventing unexpected human errors are crucial issues in our highly developed complex society. The current safety engineering may provide definite tools and criteria to design fail-safe, fool-proof machines and systems; however, it does not always ensure our "sense of security" or "feeling of easiness". If the human nature is analyzed and treated properly in the process of designing machines and systems, we may create safer, more reliable, and more intelligent machines and systems that can support our society and give us neither anxiety nor uneasiness. The systems science deals with the analysis and synthesis for large-scale complex systems, while the human science covers various aspects of the human nature, such as human behavior, psychology, and communications. These two sciences should meet together to become a powerful tool for safe, secure, and reliable systems to achieve peaceful society (**SSR society**).

The First International Symposium on Systems and Human Science was successfully held in November 19 and 20, 2003, at Osaka University. The symposium brought together researchers and engineers with different backgrounds but with a common interest to create a new science to share their knowledge and address the latest challenges.

This volume is edited by selecting excellent papers from those presented at the symposium. The submitted papers were reviewed and screened by the symposium program committee and the peers, and finally 39 papers, including four invited, appear in this volume. We would hope that the book could contribute to the creation of a new science and indicate the right direction of the concerned researches.

Acknowledgments:

The editors are grateful to the speakers, the session organizers, the committee members and all other participants of SSR2003. They are also pleased to acknowledge the sponsoring institutions whose support has made the symposium possible.

Finally, they would like to thank Ms. Keiko Kobayashi for all her hard work in assembling the volume.

Tatsuo Arai
Shigeru Yamamoto
Kazuhisa Makino

SSR2003 Symposium Committees

Honorary Chair
Seiji Inokuchi (Hiroshima International University, JAPAN)

Advisory Committee
Hiroyuki Tamura (Chair) (Kansai University, JAPAN)
Carlos Balaguer (Universidad Carlos III de Madrid, SPAIN)
Norman Caplan (NSF, USA)
Susumu Fujii (Kobe University, JAPAN)
Toshio Fukuda (Nagoya University, JAPAN)
Keith W. Hipel (University of Waterloo, CANADA)
Kazuhiro Kosuge (Tohoku University, JAPAN)
Yoshimitsu Kurosaki (KHI, JAPAN)
Toshiaki Miura (Osaka University, JAPAN)
Toshiro Noritsugu (Okayama University, JAPAN)
Eiichi Ohno (Mitsubishi Elec. Co., JAPAN)
Tsuneo Yoshikawa (Kyoto University, JAPAN)

Organizing Committee
Tatsuo Arai (Chair) (Osaka University, JAPAN)
Takao Fujii (Osaka University, JAPAN)
Kazuo Furuta (University of Tokyo, JAPAN)
Sadao Kawamura (Ritsumeikan University, JAPAN)
Tetsuo Kotoku (AIST, JAPAN)
Marek Makowski (IIASA, AUSTRIA)
Shogo Nishida (Osaka University, JAPAN)
Takeo Oomichi (Meijo University, JAPAN)
Toshi Takamori (Kobe University, JAPAN)
Toshimitsu Ushio (Osaka University, JAPAN)

Technical Committee
Shigeru Yamamoto (Chair) (Osaka University, JAPAN)
Yoshinori Hijikata (Osaka University, JAPAN)
Shinsaku Hiura (Osaka University, JAPAN)

Kenji Inoue (Osaka University, JAPAN)
Yoshio Iwai (Osaka University, JAPAN)
Osamu Kaneko (Osaka University, JAPAN)
Yasushi Mae (Osaka University, JAPAN)
Kazuhisa Makino (Osaka University, JAPAN)
Takanori Masuda (Mie Pref. Institute of Science & Technology, JAPAN)
Tomohito Takubo (Osaka University, JAPAN)
Haruyuki Yoshida (Osaka Electro-Communication University, JAPAN)

Sponsors

Cosponsored by
Graduate School of Engineering Science, Osaka University
Society for Instrumentation and Control Engineers (SICE)
Robotics Society of Japan (RSJ)

Cooperation with
IEEE Robotics and Automation Society (IEEE RAS)
IEEE Systems, Man, and Cybernetics Society (IEEE SMC)
Institute of Systems, Control and Information Engineers (ISCIE)
Japan Society of Mechanical Engineers (JSME)
Japan Robot Association (JARA)

List of Referees for Paper Selection

Katsuhiro Akazawa
Tatsuo Arai
Liping Fang
Jiro Gyoba
Kiyotada Hayashi
Yoshinori Hijikata
Shinsaku Hiura
Koh Hosoda
Youji Iiguni
Kenji Inoue
Masahiro Inuiguchi
Jun Ishikawa
Yoshimichi Ito
Yoshio Iwai
Ichiroh Kanaya
Osamu Kaneko
Eizo Kinoshita
Tetsuo Kotoku
Takatsune Kumada
Yasushi Mae
Kazuhisa Makino
Marek Makowski
Nobuto Matsuhira
Fumitoshi Matsuno
Jun Miura
Toshiaki Miura
Hiroshi Morita
Hajime Nagahara
Mie Nakatani
Hirotaka Nakayama
Dragomir N. Nenchev
Masahiko Nishimoto
Kenzo Nonami
Tsukasa Ogasawara
Hiroshi Oku
Takeo Oomichi
Kosuke Sato
Motoyuki Sato
Noboru Sebe
Tatsuya Suzuki
Satoru Takahashi
Kunikatsu Takase
Tomohito Takubo
Hiroyuki Tamura
Keishi Tanimoto
Tetsuzo Tanino
Keiji Tatsumi
Tomohiro Umetani
Takeaki Uno
Shigeru Yamamoto
Tatsuhisa Yamamoto
Katsu Yamane
Kazumasa Yamazawa
Kazuhito Yokoi
Yeboon Yun

Contents

PART I

Invited Papers

CHAPTER 1

Multiple Participant Decision Making in Societal and Technological Systems

K.W. Hipel

Department of Systems Design Engineering, University of Waterloo, Waterloo, Ont. N2L 3G1, Canada
E-mail: kwhipel@engmail.uwaterloo.ca

L. Fang

Department of Mechanical and Industrial Engineering, Ryerson University, Toronto, Ont. M5B 2K3, Canada
E-mail: lfang@ryerson.ca

Contents

SYSTEMS AND HUMAN SCIENCE – FOR SAFETY, SECURITY, AND DEPENDABILITY
Edited by Tatsuo Arai, Shigeru Yamamoto and Kazuhisa Makino

Abstract

A unique perspective on multiple participants interacting within societal and technological systems is presented for harnessing both the cooperative and competitive sides of conflict needed for making wise decisions to foster a safe, secure, reliable, sustainable and fair society. To appreciate the great import of the role of multiple stakeholders within different kinds of systems, the world is classified in terms of environmental (natural world), societal (real life), intelligent (artificial life) and integrated (mixed life) systems. For each type of system, basic kinds of multiple participant decisions are explained and illustrated. Systems methodologies developed to address key problems for a specific system are referred to and areas where further research is needed are identified. The authors believe that a multidisciplinary, unifying and comprehensive systems approach to multiple participant decision making is urgently needed for appropriately addressing many complex challenges confronting society. Of prime importance is designing and operating systems in which multiple participants' value systems and rules governing their interactions are based upon ethical principles, including the prioritization of societal well-being, environmental protection and sustainable development, in order to create and maintain beneficial consequences for society.

1. Motivation

1.1. *The Great Electrical System Failure of August 14, 2003*

At 4:11 p.m. on Thursday, August 14, 2003, the electrical supply system suddenly and unexpectedly shut down in the Canadian province of Ontario as well as seven nearby American states in the northeastern part of the United States [41,54]. Without warning, 10 million Canadians and 40 million Americans were blacked out—a huge complex energy system had dramatically collapsed. People living in cities such as Toronto and New York were trapped inside of subway cars and elevators in apartment buildings and skyscrapers. Society was suddenly unplugged from its energy sources, thereby causing industrial, commercial, transportation and other systems to cease to function. A complex infrastructure system that was designed, built, operated and maintained by human beings proved to be highly unreliable and failed in its mission to supply electricity to its customers. The electrical system would be out of commission for up to 30 h. This stark system failure was worse than the Great Blackout of November 9th and 10th, 1965, when 30 million people living in the Northeastern United States and Canada were without power for about 12 h.

This dramatic energy system failure was supposedly caused by a series of huge back-and-forth power surges that persisted for only 9 or 10 s on an antiquated system of electrical transmission lines that encircle Lake Erie. When the oscillating surges started to spread from their probable source in Ohio, the cascading effects prompted computerized safety systems to shut down 22 nuclear-generating facilities and 80 fossil-fuel-fired plants in Canada and the United States. The only overall advisory body for the failed electrical system is a voluntary organization called the North American Electric Reliability Council set up by major utilities in Canada and the United States after the 1965 debacle.

The physical causes of this great energy system collapse are being investigated but the real underlying reasons for creating catastrophe are based upon an ongoing conflict of fundamental values among powerful lobby groups, governments, political parties, industrialists, concerned citizens groups and other stakeholders. Consider the case of the Canadian province of Ontario. In 1906, the government of Ontario founded the Hydro-Electric Power Commission which later became known as Ontario Hydro. Its mandate was to provide the citizens of Ontario with a reliable supply of electrical energy. Overall, Ontario Hydro successfully fulfilled its mission and by the 1990s it operated a complex system of nuclear, hydroelectric, oil, gas and coal generators having a capacity of over 30,000 MW. However, poor political decisions and outright greed severely handicapped Ontario Hydro. In particular, in the early 1990s the New Democratic Party, a left-wing political party, cancelled Ontario Hydro's plans for expansion, froze the rates charged for electricity and laid-off approximately 10,000 people. When an extreme right-wing government formed by the Progressive Conservative Party assumed office starting in 1995, the situation deteriorated even further. Specifically, this government started on the path of deregulation and privatization of electrical supply infrastructure—an approach that failed miserably in California and had mixed results in Great Britain.

The concept of allowing the marketplace to control the economy is founded upon the economic philosophy of F.A. Hayek and others and was heartily embraced by the Conservative Government of Margaret Thatcher of Great Britain in the early 1980s, followed by President Ronald Reagan of the United States [59]. However, the value system of maximizing profits for corporations is in direct conflict with the value system of providing citizens with a reliable and safe infrastructure for furnishing water, electricity, transportation and other basic societal needs as well as maintaining a healthy environment. The mindset to deregulate public infrastructure created a monster like Enron that destroyed infrastructure in countries throughout the world because of its unethical value system of profit maximization with no controls, which was in direct conflict with the basic values of the common good. In the province of Ontario, the Progressive Conservative government started on the road to electrical prioritization by breaking the once reliable Ontario Hydro into three companies—transmission, generation and marketing corporations. The value system was changed from furnishing a reliable supply of energy to Ontario citizens to selling electricity to the highest bidder in the marketplace in order to maximize profits.

Besides raising ethical questions, a deregulated electrical system is in conflict with the physical properties and constraints of an electrical supply system. More specifically, to obtain the highest prices for their products, generating firms were moving power over long distances to take advantage of higher prices at faraway locations. This not only potentially overloaded the system at certain points in the grid but also certainly caused higher electrical losses due to longer transmission distances. Accordingly, the market-based economic values of deregulation were also in direct conflict with the forces of basic physics or nature. Consequently, to create a reliable electrical system in North America, two serious conflicts must be carefully studied and ethically resolved. The first is the conflict of values between profit maximization in the marketplace and societal values—a huge moral dilemma. The second is the conflict between the market forces and the physical capabilities and constraints of the electricity supply system. It is interesting to note that only the American state of Texas and the Canadian Province of Quebec have purposely chosen to insulate themselves from the rest of the eastern North American grid. Since ice storms destroyed large sections of its long distance transmission lines in 1998, Hydro Quebec has conscientiously and purposefully spent significant amounts of money to upgrade its entire electrical supply system—a system that is clearly highly reliable and responsibly serves Quebec residents.

1.2. *Complex adaptive systems*

The electrical supply system in North America is an example of a complex adaptive system—in this case a system created entirely by human beings. Within the societal realm, the system consists of many different kinds of agents interacting with one another within a competitive marketplace for electricity supply and consumption. The agents which supply electricity include people and organizations that generate, transmit and market electricity. These agents may be privately run generating plants, government-owned transmission companies or individuals who take energy from the electrical grid when their private solar energy units cannot produce enough electricity but can contribute electricity to the grid when they have a surplus of solar-generated energy. The consuming or buying agents of electricity include individual households, large industrial firms, cities and agricultural enterprises. All these agents are intelligent, can adapt to changing situations and can learn from their experiences. The behavior of these agents is often based upon local information, such as the price of electricity in a given region at a particular time of day, or it may be influenced by how protocols are dictated at a more macro-level in which politicians continuously change the overall rules as to how the electricity game should be played.

In addition to individuals and human-designed institutions representing them, the electricity system contains a vast array of physical system components ranging from an advanced Candu nuclear reactor producing large amounts of electricity to a single switch in a home that turns on a light. Within this complex physical system, there may be automated intelligent systems that control how the system operates in an automatic mode and immediately shuts down parts of the system when a problem arises. Consequently, the electricity supply system is indeed a very complex dynamic system containing large numbers of agents within both the societal and physical subsystem components that are interacting in varying and sometimes unexpected ways.

The study of complex adaptive systems is a relatively new area of research that is now receiving widespread attention. As pointed out by Axelrod and Cohen [3], the origins of this discipline arise from three distinct fields: evolutionary biology, computer science and social design. The objective of the work by Axelrod and Cohen is to assist managers and policy makers to harness complexity. Because of the great import of complex adaptive systems, research has been carried out in a wide range of fields [3] including condensed matter physics, evolutionary biology, evolutionary competition [27], social science modeling of heterogeneous populations of people interacting with one another [49], cellular automata [42] and mathematical research in complexity [37].

Casti [8] points out that theorists in complex adaptive systems are in about the same position that physicists were in at the time of Galileo, who experimented with simple physical systems. However, Galileo's work furnished background information from which Sir Isaac Newton could develop a general theory of such processes. Presently, the complex systems community is in the process of carrying out interesting work largely using computer simulations to study a rich range of complex adaptive systems as it awaits the arrival of a Newton to provide an overall encompassing theory. Much of the research in complex systems is being done under the umbrella of what is called multiagent systems which is discussed further in Section 5 of this chapter.

The authors' objectives in this chapter are to make contributions to the development of complex adaptive systems theory and multiagent systems that can be employed for studying important types of world systems described in Section 2.1. The authors are particularly interested in better modeling and understanding complex adaptive systems for the ultimate purpose of devising decision making techniques that can actually be employed operationally for satisfying the conflicting aspirations of agents living in these systems in a fair and sustainable manner. Accordingly, the unifying concept of multiple participants existing and interacting in these various kinds of systems, as well as across systems, is one main emphasis of this research. A second key contribution is that these participants should behave ethically and make fair decisions according to ethical protocols when competing or cooperating with one another.

In Section 2, the four general types of world systems existing on planet earth are put forward, interrelationships among them are mentioned, the omnipresence of conflict within and across these systems is pointed out and the importance of agents adhering to ethical principles when competing and collaborating with others is stressed. These four systems—environmental, societal, intelligent and integrated systems—are then discussed in more detail in Sections 3–6, respectively, especially with respect to their multiple participant characteristics and the great import of participants interacting with others according to ethical value systems and protocols. As pointed out, the latter three systems can only exist within a global environmental system and, hence, participants living in these systems must follow ethical conduct that does not cause significant harm to the environment. For instance, as discussed and illustrated in Section 5, participants or agents participating in the economy must practice real sustainable development throughout all their economic activities. Formal approaches to multiple participant–multiple objective decision making are mentioned in Section 4.1 and the graph model for conflict resolution is applied to a serious conflict over the proposed export of Canadian water in bulk quantities in Section 4.2. It is recommended that some of these decision technologies in multiple participant decision making could be transferred for employment in advancing the fields of intelligent systems and multiagent systems as well as integrated systems. Challenges and opportunities mentioned throughout the chapter for research on multiple participant decision making in complex systems are summarized in the final section. These and other research projects should assist humanity in designing safe, secure and reliable societies in which multiple participants compete and cooperate in an ethical fashion to create a sustainable world that benefits everyone.

2. World systems

2.1. *General types of systems*

Multiple participants form a common component of key systems existing on planet Earth. Figure 1 portrays how systems containing multiple participants can be categorized into four main types of systems: environmental, societal, intelligent and integrated systems. Environmental systems refer to the set of all natural systems within which the other three kinds of systems survive. Examples of environmental systems include hydrological, atmospheric, zoological, botanical, ecological and geological systems. Societal systems comprise the broad range of activities carried out by human beings for serving both individuals and groups of people. Illustrations of societal systems include economical, political, agricultural, industrial, governmental, infrastructure and urban systems. Innovative humans and organizations within societal systems design, construct and maintain intelligent systems, such as robotic, mechatronic and automated production systems for satisfying human demands and needs. Integrated systems, like humans and software agents bidding for products over the Internet using eBay, constitute a combination of societal and intelligent systems. In fact, the North American electrical system mentioned in Section 1.1 is a mixed system because power generation facilities automatically shut down and detached themselves from the power transmission grid when sensors detected the huge power surges at the start of the Great Blackout of August 14, 2003.

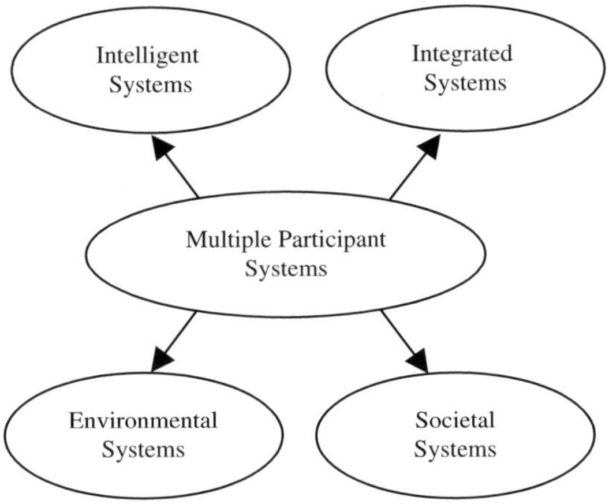

Fig. 1. Types of multiple participant systems.

The Venn diagram in Fig. 2 depicts how these systems are interconnected with one another. As can be seen, societal, intelligent and integrated systems can only exist within environmental or natural systems. Even though societal or real life systems create intelligent systems or artificial life, some of these created systems could exist on their own and hence, artificial life is not shown as a subset of real life. For instance, a well-constructed mechatronic system powered by solar radiation could be programmed to operate on its own and perhaps survive for a long period of time without maintenance by human beings. Integrated systems or mixed life arise where societal and intelligent

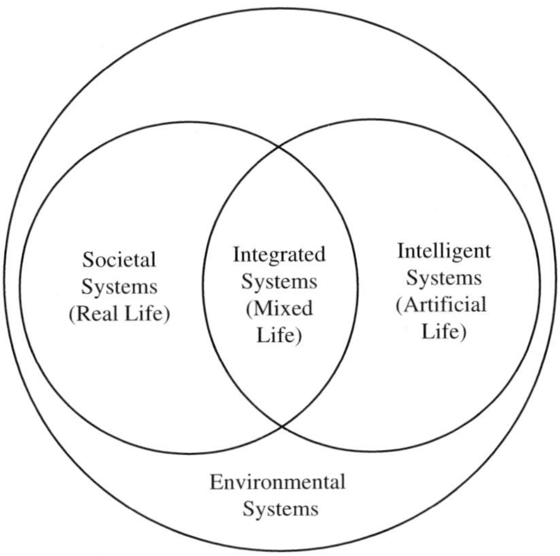

Fig. 2. World systems: competition and cooperation among systems agents.

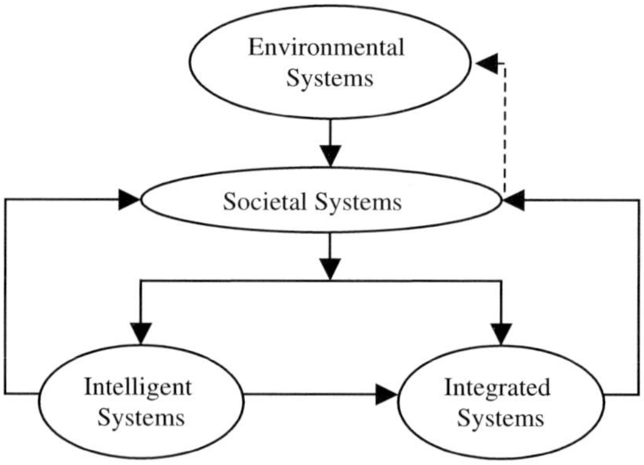

Fig. 3. Systems control.

systems overlap. An aircraft, for instance, having fully automated control systems, can be guided to a safe landing even if the pilot were incapacitated by a stroke.

It has often been jokingly said that God created the world and everything within it while the Dutch people made Holland. After building systems of containment dykes, dams and pumping stations, the Dutch pumped seawater from areas previously covered by the North Sea to create what are called polders. In fact, Dutch hydraulic engineers assisted Japanese engineers after the Meiji Restoration to build dyking systems along rivers in Japan to prevent flooding, and, in the year 2000, Japan and the Netherlands celebrated the 400th anniversary of the establishment of cooperation between the two countries, including joint hydraulic work in Japan starting in 1873 when the Dutch engineer Johannis de Rijke helped to improve shipping in the Yodo River [32]. These examples of building hydraulic infrastructure to serve societal needs demonstrate that humans can exercise some control over nature.

The flowchart displayed in Fig. 3 shows the control structure existing among the types of systems portrayed in Figs. 1 and 2. From Fig. 3, it is clear that other types of systems are completely reliant upon environmental systems. In a sense, human beings play the role of God, since intelligent and integrated systems were created by them. Feedback arrows in Fig. 3 point out that intelligent and integrated systems can influence societal systems. Furthermore, a dotted feedback arrow on the top right in Fig. 3 indicates that societal systems can affect environmental systems, usually in negative ways via soil, air and water pollution. Nonetheless, in the long run, nature is in control and too much human abuse of the environment can cause a catastrophic collapse of society and perhaps even the extinction of humans. Consequently, nature is the dominant player in any conflict that may take place across the systems portrayed in Figs. 1–3.

2.2. *Conflict, ethics and value systems*

Conflict arises in a given situation because of differences of objectives or value systems among the participants involved in the conflict. Figure 4 illustrates how this interaction

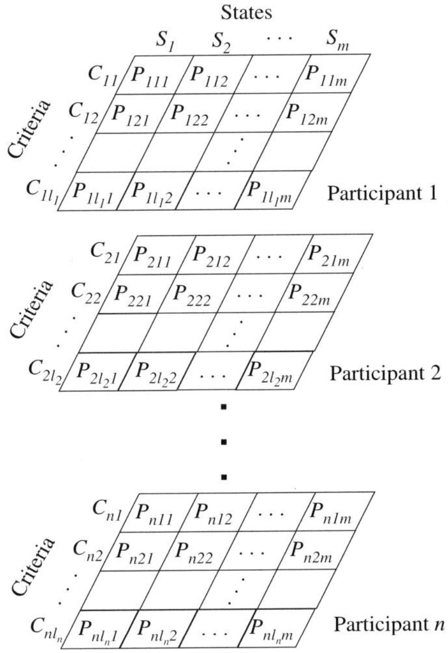

Fig. 4. Multiple participant–multiple criteria decision making.

may occur [25]. Each participant or decision maker has its own criteria for deciding upon its preferences among the states or possible scenarios that could occur. A state, S_i, is denoted by the *i*th column in each matrix, a criterion is given by a row in a matrix, and a payoff or preference value is contained in a matrix cell for the indicated criterion, state and participant. For a particular participant, the criteria may consist of non-quantitative factors, such as aesthetics, ethical issues and some types of environmental impacts, as well as quantitative criteria like cost and monetary benefits. An ethical or moral participant would prefer to see states and eventual resolutions that, for example, cause minimum damage to the environment and are equitable and fair to all stakeholders. In other words, an ethical person would prioritize criteria, such as sustainability, fairness and equitability when developing its preferences among the possible states. Hence, as depicted in Fig. 4, each participant has a multiple criteria decision analysis (MCDA) problem to analyze when ranking states according to its preference.

When interaction occurs among or across decision makers in Fig. 4, a conflict takes place and conflict analysis methods can be used to study the dispute. A key point to keep in mind is that differences in value systems and underlying ethics and beliefs provide the basic fuel for igniting and maintaining conflict. Accordingly, society has a duty to encourage and propagate ethical value systems among its citizens. Additionally, these citizens and their associated organizations should only create agents within intelligent and integrated systems that are pre-programmed to have ethical objectives and behave in a moral fashion. Only through purposeful and ethical design of systems, coupled with adhering to personal ethical principles, can human beings create a robust and reliable society that will persist for millennia to come. All this must be done within the constraint of the finite resources provided by Mother Nature and in a fashion that is sustainable in the long run.

Conflict can arise among multiple participants having different objectives separately within each system in Figs. 1–3 or across systems. For example, within a societal system, a company producing chemical products may be attempting to grab the largest possible market share for itself to the detriment of its competitors. The dumping of untreated pollutants by chemical plants into the natural environment constitutes a frontal attack by society against nature, which may react by closing down ecosystem activities that support life. In another situation, agents within a software system may be programmed to produce results that support specified human endeavors in a positive way. Hence, the spectrum of conflict types can range from pure competition among participants to full cooperation. Moreover, these different kinds of conflict can be studied using theoretical or analytical models and simulation.

In the subsequent four sections, the four types of systems displayed in Figs. 1–3 are discussed separately. For each kind of system, illustrative conflicts are mentioned, tools for systematically assessing conflict are discussed, ethical issues are highlighted and future research is suggested. Overall, challenges to overcome within and among systems are put forward in the final section for creating a better society and world in which all of us can live meaningful and creative lives.

3. Environmental systems

Biology is the study of living organisms consisting of animal life (zoology) and plant life (botany). Together, these living organisms exist with the rest of the natural environment at a given location in a unit called an ecological system. One or more ecological systems form an environmental or a natural system. Intensive competition for survival exists within each of the two main subdivisions of biology as well as among them. Moreover, natural factors such as local climatic conditions can have both positive and negative effects upon living organisms. Finally, humans, along with the societal, intelligent and integrated systems they have created, are now the main enemy of virtually all environmental systems. Humans have the ability to improve, degrade or, in some cases, completely destroy environmental systems.

In the great Serengeti plain of East Africa, the lion struts around as the supreme ruler at the top of the ecological food chain. The lion has the ability to consume other animals, such as zebra and wildebeest, whenever it gets hungry. For all the animal species, except the lion, the name of the game appears to be eaten or not be eaten—devour other living organisms and avoid being gobbled up by competitors in the food chain. Even though the lion may appear to be the king within the Serengeti ecological system, a Masai's spear may pierce its heart or agricultural expansion may decrease the size of its domain. Even man, the great hunter and destroyer, can be felled to the ground by a microscopic AIDS virus or killed in warfare by one of his own species or die from exposure to toxic pollutants that he so recklessly dumped into the natural environment.

The foregoing description of the survival game appears to be highly competitive and in some cases a zero-sum game—either devour or be devoured. However, studies about the survival of species indicate that organisms that know how to cooperate with others both within and outside of their own species, often dominate in the long run, and the meanest and toughest animals may lose in the natural selection process. Evolutionary biology uses game theory techniques to predict selection of mates and genetic evolution of a species (see, for example, [43,51]) and, quite often, it employs Prisoner's Dilemma to describe interactions of organisms over time. Prisoner's Dilemma is a basic game that models a situation in which one organism or person must decide whether or not to cooperate with another. In his landmark book on the *Evolution of Cooperation*, Axelrod [1] uses repeated two-player Prisoner's Dilemma to show that cooperation based upon reciprocity can evolve and maintain itself under the prospect of long-term interaction. In his 1997 book, Axelrod [2] carries the concept of collaboration much further. Game theory has even been used to predict responses of populations to environmental change [52] which, of course, may have been precipitated by human-related activities such as intensive industrial and agricultural enterprises coupled with urban growth.

As just noted, the greatest threat to living organisms and ecological systems are humans. Previously, the natural environment was considered to be an infinite source of raw materials for use in production and consumption, and an infinite sink in which society can dispose of massive quantities of waste. In an attempt to overcome this type of societal behavior, the concept of sustainable development was put forward in the famous 1987 report entitled *Our Common Future* [58]. Under sustainable development, the economic needs of the society are met in a manner, which maintains a healthy environment for present and future generations. As pointed out by Hipel [19], this important ideal explicitly recognizes the direct conflict between the objective of satisfying the materialistic requirements of society and the wise goal of protecting the natural environment. Accordingly, controversies over sustainable development have pitted environmentalists against industrial and other kinds of developers in many locations throughout the world. What is of particular interest in the ongoing negotiations over making trade-offs between development and the environment is that most of the potentially affected stakeholders, namely future generations, are not even sitting at the negotiation table. In fact, sustainable development can be viewed as a perpetual struggle between society and the environment. However, if society does not collaborate with nature and treat it with the respect it deserves, nature can permanently halt negotiations by closing down the life support system for humans and other living organisms.

The Tragedy of the Commons is a situation in which irresponsible utilization of a common resource due to individual greed causes the destruction of the resource [18]. For example, one nation may continue to harvest an endangered species of fish when there is no restriction on countries to reduce their catch. The ultimate result is the extinction of the fish species. In a sense, societies are participating in innumerable versions of this great travesty throughout the globe as human populations explode and common resources are depleted or severely degraded. Hence, as argued in Sections 2.2, 4.2, 4.3, 5.2 and 5.3, ethical behavior is desperately needed by society, especially in the great ongoing battle being played out between society and nature. In the long run, there is no choice, but for the society to behave in a sustainable manner, hopefully within the confines of enforceable international agreements closely connected to trade agreements.

To properly understand the complexity of sustainable development and the myriad of conflicts it invokes, a wide range of systems tools from the physical sciences as well as conflict resolution and other decision technology tools [23,48] will have to be used together in order to arrive at wise and sustainable decisions (see [20] for a description of the joint employment of physical systems and decision science tools in water resources). Society should not forget that the destruction of the natural environment of Easter Island located in the South Pacific, precipitated by cutting down all the trees, caused the great Moai culture to disappear just before the Dutch explorer Jacob Rogereen arrived on Easter Sunday, 1722 [16]. Hundreds of large stone statues of grotesquely shaped humans still ominously stand on the barren Easter Island landscape like tombstones recording the results of human folly and society's failure to play a cooperative, sustainable game with nature.

4. Societal systems

4.1. *Classification of societal conflict models*

Conflicts or differences of opinion inevitably arise whenever human beings interact with one another. For example, because Canada possesses the world's largest quantity of fresh water, private companies would like to consider water the same as any other commodity and export it in bulk quantities to other countries. Accordingly, environmentalists are in direct conflict with these companies at various locations in Canada, as exemplified by an example given later in this section. In other situations, there may be a relatively large degree of agreement and cooperation among disputants. For instance, owners of high-tech companies can avert nasty labor disputes over wages by adopting innovative policies such as granting ownership to employees by issuing shares to them and by sharing profits with employees. As can be appreciated from the foregoing, and many other illustrations, this interactive phenomenon called conflict arises in virtually every domain of human activity.

Because of the ubiquitous nature of conflict, research on conflict resolution has taken place in a wide range of disciplines. As explained in an overview paper by Hipel [19] and in articles contained within the theme on Conflict Resolution in the Encyclopedia of Life Support Systems (EOLSS), a wide range of psychological, sociological, operational research, game theory, systems engineering [23,48] and other kinds of models have been developed for systematically studying conflict and its resolution. Figure 5 shows the genealogy of formal mathematical models for analyzing conflict founded upon various underlying assumptions. The field of game theory was firmly established in 1944 with the publication of the landmark book by Von Neumann and Morgenstern entitled *Theory of Games and Economic Behavior* [53].

One way to categorize a game theoretic method is according to the type of preference information needed to calibrate the model. In a social situation, for instance, a person may ask a visitor if she would like to have a cup of tea or coffee. The guest may reply that she would prefer to consume a cup of coffee—she would certainly not say that she prefers to have coffee 1.9673 times as much as tea. In Fig. 5, the techniques listed in the left column are categorized as being non-quantitative approaches since they only assume relative preference information, such as one object being more preferred or equally preferred to another—there is no need for knowing exactly how much one object is preferred over another. Techniques falling under the right column generally assume cardinal preference information, such as coffee being worth 1.9673 and tea having a preference value of 1.0000. Because real numbers, such as those generated by cardinal utility functions, are used for modeling preferences for a decision maker, these techniques are labeled as being quantitative. Nonetheless, it should be emphasized that all the methods listed in both the columns in Fig. 5 constitute formal mathematical models. However, besides being axiomatic, the techniques in the left column are also qualitative and these methods are especially relevant for formally studying social conflict because of their inherent non-quantitative nature.

The aforementioned book by von Neumann and Morgenstern [53] dealt mainly with quantitative game theory methods. Immediately after World War II, most researchers worked in the development of quantitative game theory methods and this trend is still largely true up to the present time. Nonetheless, in 1971 Howard [28] published a pioneering book on metagame analysis. Fraser and Hipel [17] expanded the scope of metagame analysis in a procedure called conflict analysis while Fang *et al.* [11] made significant contributions through the development of the graph model for conflict resolution. As can be seen in the left branch, Howard [29] developed another useful method of non-quantitatively modeling dynamic aspects of conflict based upon the metaphor of a drama.

Conflict models have been developed for describing a rainbow of conflict situations from purely competitive or non-cooperative disputes to those having a high level of cooperation. For instance, the approaches listed in the left column of Fig. 5 can readily handle a conflict in which each decision maker has independent control of a specific set of options or actions when it interacts with others during the evolution of the dispute.

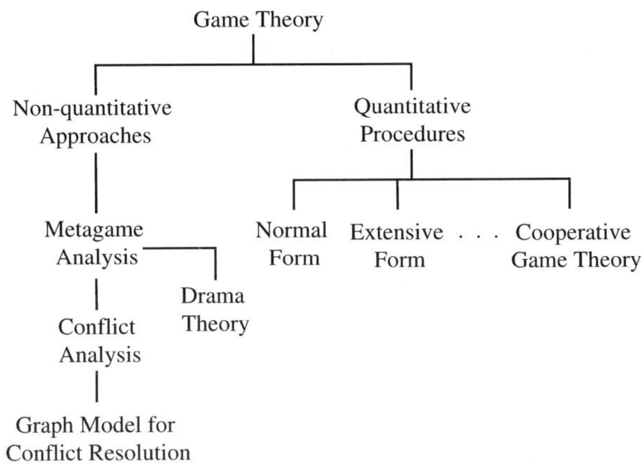

Fig. 5. Genealogy of formal conflict models.

In cooperative game theory shown in the right column in Fig. 5, parties to an agreement have decided to share in the division of a "pie" or resource but the size of the piece that should be allocated to each participant must be decided by following a rule for fair division or resource allocation. In another situation, two or more parties in a conflict may form a coalition to benefit coalition members when interacting with parties outside the coalition. Within the graph model paradigm and conflict analysis, algorithms are available to identify and model potential coalitions [35]. Based upon the construct of iterated Prisoner's Dilemma, Axelrod [1] shows that cooperation based on reciprocity can be maintained among competitors under long-term interaction.

4.2. *Bulk water export conflict*

The objective of this subsection is to use a water export conflict as an illustration of how unethical policies and behavior by decision makers within a societal system can potentially cause great harm against the environment and its complex ecosystems. Consider the case of the proposed export of water in bulk from Lake Gisborne which is located in a pristine wilderness area on the south coast of Newfoundland, Canada, approximately 10 km upstream from the nearest community, Grand Le Pierre, a small town. Lake Gisborne is spring-fed, has a surface area of 28 km^2, and a depth of 40 m. In June 1995, Canada Wet Incorporated, a division of the McCurdy Group of Companies based in Gander, Newfoundland, proposed to pump water from Lake Gisborne, and to ship the water to foreign markets. The development would be comprised of a water supply intake, pipeline and marine loading facility for ultra large crude carrier vessels. In addition, a bottling plant would be constructed in an accessible area close to the pipeline. The maximum water usage was estimated to be 300,000 m^3 per week. Fang *et al.* [14] employed the decision support system GMCR II [12,13,22] to apply a methodology called the graph model for conflict resolution, shown on the left-hand side of Fig. 5, to the Gisborne dispute for the situation in October 1999. They concluded that the company would not be allowed to export water in October 1999, and this strategic balance is still the case up until the present time. Nonetheless, Hipel *et al.* [21] utilized GMCR II to investigate in a dynamic fashion strategic aspects of future water exports from Lake Gisborne when the price of water is higher. Part of their study is summarized in this subsection to explain how human decision making under conflict can be harmful to the environment if it is not done in an ethical fashion to reflect environmental values and societal well-being.

The left column in Table 1 lists the four decision makers involved in the future Lake Gisborne conflict while the middle column gives the option or course of action that falls under the control of each decision maker. The right column lists the *status quo* at a future date when the price of water has risen. In this column, a Y means "yes", the option opposite a decision maker is selected, while an N means "no", it is not taken. Therefore, for this *status quo*, Canada would continue its prohibition of bulk water exports and the Provincial Government of Newfoundland and Labrador would select its option to maintain the ban on bulk water removals from basins under its jurisdiction. The Canadian Support, consisting of the private company and other supporters that would like to export water in bulk quantities, is not choosing its option to appeal for continuing the Gisborne project.

Table 1. Decision makers and options for the future Gisborne conflict

Decision makers	Options	*Status quo*
Federal Government of Canada	1. Continue a Canada-wide accord on prohibition of bulk water removals (prohibition)	Y
Provincial Government of Newfoundland and Labrador	2. Maintain the ban on bulk water removals from basins (maintain)	Y
Canadian Support	3. Appeal for continuing the Gisborne project based on the NAFTA (appeal)	N
Canadian Opposition	4. Petition for prohibition of water export (petition)	N

Finally, the Canadian Opposition, comprised of environmental groups and concerned citizens, is not currently putting forward a petition for prohibition of exports.

In general, the graph model methodology can handle any finite number of decision makers, each of whom can have a finite number of options. For the Gisborne conflict there are four decision makers, each of whom controls one option. After the decision makers and options are entered into GMCR II, the system generates all mathematically feasible states and has a number of ways (through dialog boxes) for removing infeasible states and combining indistinguishable states. Subsequent to removing infeasible states, there are 16 feasible states in the future Gisborne conflict, as shown in Table 2.

As explained in Section 4.1 and indicated in the left column of Fig. 5, the graph model for conflict resolution is a non-quantitative, yet axiomatic, approach for rigorously studying strategic conflict. The decision support system GMCR II requires only relative preference information over states such that states can be ranked from most to least preferred for each decision maker where ties are allowed. In other words, transitivity is assumed whereby if a decision maker prefers state s_1 to s_2 and state s_2 to s_3 this implies that it prefers s_1 to s_3. However, theoretically, the graph model for conflict resolution can also handle intransitive preferences in which a decision maker prefers state s_1 to s_2, s_2 to s_3 but s_3 to s_1, although the capability to take care of intransitive preferences is not incorporated into GMCR II. Currently, GMCR II has three flexible methods for eliciting relative preference information in which transitivity of preferences is assumed: option weighting, option prioritizing and direct ranking. When option prioritizing is employed, the preference statements for the Provincial Government are written in terms of option

Table 2. Feasible states for the future Gisborne conflict

State number	1	2	3	4	5	6	7	8	9	10	11	12	13	14	15	16
Federal																
1. Prohibition	N	Y	N	Y	N	Y	N	Y	N	Y	N	Y	N	Y	N	Y
Provincial																
2. Maintain	N	N	Y	Y	N	N	Y	Y	N	N	Y	Y	N	N	Y	Y
Support																
3. Appeal	N	N	N	N	Y	Y	Y	Y	N	N	N	N	Y	Y	Y	Y
Opposition																
4. Petition	N	N	N	N	N	N	N	N	Y	Y	Y	Y	Y	Y	Y	Y

numbers from most important on the left to least important on the right as: −2, −1, 3 IFF 1, −4, where the option numbers are given in Tables 1 and 2.

The −2 means that the Provincial Government most prefers to not maintain the ban on bulk water removals (as indicated by the negative sign). The next most preferred preference statement, −1, indicates that the Provincial Government prefers that the Federal Government not propose a Canada-wide accord on prohibition of bulk water removals from basins. The entry 3 IFF 1 means that the Provincial Government prefers that the Support appeals for continuing the Gisborne project (option 3) if and only if (IFF) the Federal Government proposes a Canada-wide accord on prohibition of bulk water removals (option 1). The least preferred preference statement, written as −4, means that the Provincial Government prefers the Opposition not make a petition to prevent water exports from Newfoundland. GMCR II takes the above option prioritizing information and quickly ranks the states from most to least preferred as shown in the line opposite Provincial in Table 3 where the numbers stand for states (see numbers given at the top in Table 2). The ranking of states according to preference is also given in Table 3 for the other three decision makers.

The manner in which GMCR II elicits preference information closely reflects the way people would express their preferences in English, or another language. For any formal decision-making model, one of the most crucial types of information that is required is the preferences, objectives or values of one or more decision makers. The preference capability of the graph model, as well as other techniques given in the left column of Fig. 5, makes them very powerful for employment in practical applications.

The conflict model for the Gisborne conflict given in Tables 1–3 provides a basic structure within which one can examine strategic interactions among the decision makers in detail. At the analysis stage, the stability of every state, for every decision maker, under all solution concepts implemented in the GMCR II system as listed in Table 4, is determined. A solution concept is a model of a decision maker's thinking in deciding whether or not to move unilaterally to a more preferred state. A state is stable for a decision maker if it is not advantageous for the decision maker to move away from the state unilaterally to a more preferred state. A state that is stable for every decision maker is called an equilibrium, which constitutes a possible resolution of the conflict.

For the future Gisborne conflict, state 10 is calculated by GMCR II to be a strong equilibrium because it is stable according to all the solution concepts in Table 4. As can be seen from Table 2, state 10 represents the situation in which the Provincial Government repeals the ban on bulk water removals from Newfoundland, disregarding the Federal Government's proposition to prohibit bulk water removals. The Opposition would make

Table 3. Ranking of states for the decision makers in the future Gisborne conflict

Preferences	Ranking of states from most preferred on left to least preferred on right															
Federal	4	12	8	16	10	2	14	6	3	11	7	15	9	1	13	5
Provincial	1	9	5	13	6	14	2	10	3	11	7	15	8	16	4	12
Support	1	9	2	10	5	13	6	14	7	15	8	16	3	11	4	12
Opposition	12	4	8	16	10	2	14	6	3	11	15	7	9	1	13	5

Table 4. Solution concepts of the graph model for conflict resolution

Solution concept	Stability description
Nash stability	DM (decision maker) cannot unilaterally move to a more preferred state
General metarationality (GMR)	All DM's unilateral improvements are sanctioned by subsequent unilateral moves by others
Symmetric metarationality (SMR)	All DM's unilateral improvements are still sanctioned even after possible responses by the original DM
Sequential stability (SEQ)	All DM's unilateral improvements are sanctioned by subsequent unilateral improvements by others
Limited-move stability L_h	All DMs are assumed to act optimally and a maximum number of state transitions (h) is specified
Non-myopic (NM)	Limiting case of limited move stability as the maximum number of state transitions increases to infinity

petitions in this case, but the Support would not appeal. Table 5 traces the evolution of the conflict from the *status quo* (state 4) in Table 1 to the final equilibrium (state 10). Starting at state 4 on the left, the Support makes a unilateral move to state 8 by appealing for continuing the Gisborne water export project. This change in option selection by the Support is indicated in Table 5 by the arrow from state 4 to 8. Then the Provincial Government can cause a unilateral movement to state 6 by removing the ban on bulk water exports. Next, the Support stops its appeal. Finally, the Opposition causes a unilateral change from state 2 to 10 when it decides to launch a petition.

The evolution of the Gisborne conflict from the *status quo*, state 4, to state 10 shows that, if the Provincial Government eliminated the ban on bulk water removals from basins under its jurisdiction, the Gisborne project would be continued and the Federal Government's proposition and the Opposition's petition would be disregarded. Accordingly, there is strategic risk inherent in the future water conflict.

When the water price in world markets rises so that it is possible to make significant profits from water exports, the government of Newfoundland and Labrador may choose its

Table 5. Moving from the *status quo* to an equilibrium in the future Gisborne conflict

Decision makers and options	*Status quo*		Intermediate states						Equilibrium state
Federal									
1. Prohibition	Y		Y		Y		Y		Y
Provincial									
2. Maintain	Y		Y	→	N		N		N
Support									
3. Appeal	N	→	Y		Y	→	N		N
Opposition									
4. Petition	N		N		N		N	→	Y
State number	4		8		6		2		10

strategy without prohibition on bulk water removals from basins under its jurisdiction, disregarding the Federal Government's proposition and the Opposition's petition. Subsequently, the Gisborne project would be continued, which would allow companies to argue under the terms of the North American Free Trade Agreement (NAFTA) that water is a commodity and, therefore, it can be exported from anywhere in Canada.

4.3. *Ethics in conflict behavior and policy design*

A person's or an organization's ethics or value system is reflected by its preferences and the actions it takes in a given decision situation. For the case of the Gisborne conflict, the Provincial Government most prefers not to maintain the ban on bulk water removals because of the economic benefits that could be garnered from higher priced water. Hence, the Provincial Government clearly prefers economic gain over environment protection and its associated ecosystems from the detrimental effects of large-scale water abstraction. Environmentalists, concerned citizens and many other groups would certainly view the Provincial Government's values as reflected in its preferences as being highly unethical. Protecting the environment from unwarranted economic activity can be interpreted as being a protected or held value that should be considered as an enduring moral principle. Baron and Spranca [4] believe that protected values are those that should not be traded off with other values, such as economic and political gains. Besides held values, Brown [7] defines assigned values as the worth of something to an individual or organization within a given context. Hence, assigned values may vary in importance according to the decision situation whereas held values must always be kept at the highest priority level in terms of preference. As depicted in Table 5, the strategic consequences of the Provincial Government's questionable preferences is a resolution in which the environment is potentially severely degraded. Human economic activities are clearly in direct conflict with nature which does not appear at the bargaining table for the conflict shown in Tables 1–3 and 5 for the societal systems component of the Gisborne dispute.

Agreements falling under the World Trade Organization (WTO) and NAFTA only stress the maximization of profits for corporations. Because environmental stewardship and societal well-being are ignored by these agreements, McMurtry [39] considers them to be unethical and immoral based on philosophical arguments. In fact, there is not a single binding clause regarding the protection of the environment in either of these trade agreements even though there are many binding clauses guaranteeing the rights of corporations and investors.

Based on an analysis of a generic conflict of values using GMCR II between the supporters of market-based economics, founded upon the unidimensional value of profit maximization, and proponents of principles for promoting a healthy environment, sustainable development and responsible social infrastructure, Hipel and Obeidi [24] conclude that the environment will continue to deteriorate. Clearly, international trade agreements must be radically reformed or replaced by ethical agreements that hold environmental and societal welfare values at a higher priority than bottom-line economics. Currently, the value system hardwired into treaties, such as WTO agreements and NAFTA, is in direct confrontation with the values encoded into international, national and provincial environmental and social welfare laws. For example, consider the case of the Boundary Waters Treaty of 1909 between Canada and the United States that has worked exceptionally well and in a very ethical fashion for almost a century. The International Joint Commission is an international operational body created by this treaty to investigate boundary water problems between the two countries in a non-partisan fashion [30]. The IJC completed a requested report on the removal of fresh water from the Great Lakes basin in March 2000 [31]. The report recommends that no Canadian province, American state or Federal Government should permit removal of water from the basin unless the proponents can demonstrate the removal will not endanger the integrity of the Great Lakes ecosystem. It also concludes that international trade obligations do not prevent Canada or the US from protecting fresh water supplies as long as there is no discrimination against individuals or corporations from other countries in the application of those measures. Because Lake Gisborne falls entirely within the Canadian province of Newfoundland and Labrador, it does not come under the jurisdiction of the Boundary Waters Treaty. If water were exported just once in bulk from Lake Gisborne, water-exporting companies could argue under Chapter 11 of NAFTA that they could export water from anywhere in Canada with no restriction on quantity.

Due to the aforesaid and other reasons, action is required now to design policies, laws, treaties and other agreements based upon ethical principles concerning the environment and people's well-being. These ethical values must be an integral part of any economic or trading agreement so that they can be properly enforced by economic incentives, a "carrot" approach, or by severe economic penalties, a "stick" approach. One way to design treaties is to carry out an MCDA study to compare a range of possible treaties according to both qualitative and quantitative criteria as is done for each participant in Fig. 4. The value-focused thinking approach of Keeney [33] could be employed to obtain the underlying values from stakeholders while constructing an MCDA model. Criteria reflecting held values or principles would be kept at a higher priority level than other criteria such as those solely reflecting monetary gain. Additionally, these agreements should be designed or revised in a completely open fashion with proper input from all stakeholders. One reason for the current trade agreements being so unfair to individual citizens and the environment is that they were entirely constructed behind closed doors under the direct influence of powerful lobby groups solely representing large corporations and powerful financial institutions. Moreover, any agreement should also contain a dispute resolution mechanism that is equitable, fair and effective for all stakeholders. Techniques given on the left in Fig. 5 may prove to be very helpful for use within negotiation processes that encourage progress in a positive direction towards win/win ethical resolutions.

5. Intelligent systems

5.1. *Description*

An intelligent system is an artificial, computerized world inhabited by agents that interact with one another as they strive to reach their objectives either independently or in cooperation with other agents. An agent may be a software program that represents someone's bidding strategy and objectives when purchasing a product on the Internet or it may be a mechatronic entity such as a robot working in cooperation with other robots assembling a car on a production line. Whatever the case, an agent plays the role of a person or citizen within a particular domain or environment in which it exists and operates. However, a specific intelligent system consisting of multiple interacting agents is entirely created by humans. A given agent living in the system is capable of independent or autonomous action on behalf of its user or owner and behaves according to the powers bestowed upon it in its software design as it strives to achieve its preprogrammed goals by following particular strategies it can control. Often agents are programmed to cooperate with one another in order to enhance the effectiveness of the intelligent system to achieve its goals [26,50]. A protocol constitutes the public rules by which agents can come to agreements within a given system or domain [45].

Although an intelligent system is the brainchild of human architects, it is purposely designed to survive on its own over a certain period of time without human interference. The current status of research in multiagent systems most closely describes what is meant by an intelligent system. However, multiagent systems are only in their infancy and many challenges remain to be overcome as the field develops. As pointed out by Wooldridge [57], the study of multiagent systems is a fairly recent sub-field of computer science that was initiated about 1980 and only achieved widespread international attention starting in the mid-1990s. The recent great expansion of work in multiagent systems is highly motivated by the popularity of the Internet, which can be envisioned as a huge open distributed system populated by large numbers of interacting agents. Nonetheless, as emphasized in Sections 1.2 and 2 and in Fig. 2, we believe that all major systems consist of agents or decision makers who compete and cooperate with one another as they strive to attain their goals. Hence, agents constitute one of the fundamental, if not paramount, ingredients of any overall major system and many of this system's subcomponents.

A number of excellent books have been written to explain the theory and practice of multiagent systems and point out research frontiers where innovative exploration is required (see, for example, [15,45,57]). Research on multiagent systems is quickly amassing a large vocabulary as researchers and practitioners coin new jargon to describe the phenomena of multiagents and their environments. Other related research fields that contribute to the development of the paradigm of an intelligent system include distributed artificial intelligence, concurrent systems [38], and artificial life and societies [10,40].

5.2. *Ethical intelligent systems design*

Just like the Dutch created the polders in Holland (see Section 2.1), human beings are the designers, builders and caretakers of intelligent systems. Accordingly, human beings have a great moral responsibility to construct intelligent systems having social environments in which agents behave ethically under appropriate domain protocols and strategies as they compete to obtain results, which in turn must be ethical and fair. As explained in Section 4.3 and illustrated by the bulk water conflict in Section 4.2, often humans and organizations do not abide by ethical principles which in turn can cause unethical consequences that can harm others and the environment. Even though it is clear that WTO agreements and NAFTA are fundamentally flawed and unethical, these policies are yet to be appropriately modified or replaced by ethical ones. Nonetheless, although human beings have a long way to go in properly fixing their own social systems, they currently hold the power to practice responsible social systems design engineering when creating intelligent systems.

One advantage of having an intelligent system to represent humans is that it has the capability to perform well in real time in the face of enormous amounts of information and different viewpoints concerning which decisions should be taken within a very short period of time, such as a microsecond. For example, in the great North American blackout of August 14, 2003, described in Section 1.1, if a fully automated intelligent system had been in place to manage a properly maintained electrical system, agents in this intelligent system could have worked in tandem to isolate the initial electrical problem and take instantaneous actions to stop it from spreading. Instead, there was system-wide confusion and panic, and operators tended to act according to their organizations' self-interests, thereby ignoring the integrity of the entire system, which soon ceased to function. As explained earlier, each unit in the electrical system behaved according to profit maximization and self-preservation rather than sustainably serving the safety and welfare of society as its top priority.

When formally modeling conflict that could take place among agents in an intelligent system, ethics can be responsibly handled in a number of related ways. Of paramount importance is that human beings design and build each agent in a system to have ethical objectives or preferences. For instance, an agent can be programmed to greatly not prefer states or situations in which the actions of itself and others will harm the environment or destroy basic social infrastructure. Each agent should only have actions or options at its disposal that can create positive results and not cause unethical behavior and consequences. Therefore, to avoid causing the stock market to collapse, agents who are buying or selling assets should not be allowed to collude in illegal fashions. Ethical protocols should be incorporated into an intelligent system to encourage agents to reach win/win solutions that do not cause environmental and social damage within or outside of the system.

Rosenschein and Zlotkin [45] mention that they directly import concepts from game theory for employment in their formal analyses of rules or protocols governing the high-level behavior of interacting computer systems or agents. In the past, it has been difficult to apply game theory to conflicts arising among decision makers in a societal context such as the bulk water export dispute outlined in Section 4.2. One reason for this is that game theory models require that players' preferences over states be represented cardinally by von Neumann–Morgenstern utilities [53]. However, people usually think in terms of relative preferences rather than cardinal numbers. Moreover, utility values are extremely difficult to measure. One should keep in mind that it is the objectives or preferences of an agent that ultimately dictate how it will behave. Therefore, designers can play the role of a benevolent and wise creator who responsibly designs, constructs, operates and maintains their intelligent systems.

Another drawback of game theory is that game theoretic models require players to act in a specific sequence (extensive-form game) or simultaneously (normal-form game).

However, in social conflicts as well as disputes among agents in a complex intelligent system like the Internet, players can choose to act in any sequence, at the same time or not at all. Because human beings design and program agents in intelligent systems, it may be possible to more realistically use concepts from classical game theory in multiagent systems than it is when studying social conflicts. Nonetheless, the authors of this chapter highly recommend that researchers consider incorporating into their systems design flexible concepts offered by the conflict analysis techniques given in the left column of Fig. 5 and referred to in Section 4.1. For example, they could create agents having responsible actions and relative preferences, as well as have them behave according to ethical solution concepts and negotiation protocols. In other words, a new discipline of ethical intelligent systems design engineering should be developed.

Table 4 lists solution concepts that can be employed for modeling human behavior under conflict within the paradigm of the graph model for conflict resolution. Under the assumption of transitivity, it can be proven mathematically that the solution concept of sequential stability always predicts at least one equilibrium or compromise resolution. When agents in a given intelligent system can only possess ethical options and preferences, the existence theorem guarantees that one or more reasonable equilibria will occur given the preferences and powers available to the agents. This analysis procedure is analogous to optimization in the sense that each agent tries to do as well as it can within the social constraints of the conflict. Whatever the case, given an agent knows how well it can do on its own, it may wish to cooperate with others through coalition formation to see if an even better result can be achieved (see, for example, the coalition algorithm designed by Kilgour *et al.* [35] for use with the graph model for conflict resolution). Other concepts that could be taken into account include misperceptions within the hypergame paradigm [56] and decision making in the presence of uncertain and partial preference information [36]. In summary, designers of intelligent systems should only program realistic, attractive and ethical human virtues into a given intelligent system. Ethical research from the social sciences as well as enhanced conflict modeling and analysis techniques (see the left column of Fig. 5) should be beneficial in establishing ethical intelligent systems design engineering.

5.3. *Designing ethical intelligent systems for an information economy*

Intelligent systems possess great potential to augment or even supplant human activities within many different kinds of societal systems ranging from hard systems production processes in industry to soft systems problems such as buying or selling. The underlying reason why intelligent systems may be ideal for modeling, analyzing and actually carrying out the functions of a rich variety of societal systems is that the theoretical characteristics that these modeling systems possess match key properties exhibited by actual societal systems. Specifically, real world societal systems are often composed of conflicting participants who are capable of interacting with one another in dynamic, often non-linear and unexpected ways. These agents can learn from one another as a result of these interactions and cause overall emergent properties in the system to evolve and change over time. Accordingly, intelligent systems founded upon the paradigm of complex adaptive systems and multiagent systems can be developed and implemented for studying the behavior of a specific societal system or replacing it.

Agent-based modeling and simulation in the social sciences was the focus of a colloquium sponsored by the National Academy of the Sciences held in Irvine, California, in the United States from October 4 to 6, 2001. In their introductory article presented at the conference, Berry *et al.* [5] pointed out that agent-based modeling assumes that social structure and overall societal behavioral characteristics are created from the bottom up as the result of interactions of individual agents. This form of world paradigm is fundamentally different from traditional social science, which usually assumes that social realities such as marketplaces exist and they produce various forms of social organization and structure. Articles published in the proceedings deal with a variety of social systems that can be modeled, simulated or constructed using concepts from intelligent systems and multiagent systems.

One example of an intelligent system which is now operational on the Internet is eBay in which people or their software surrogate agents can competitively bid for buying products from suppliers. In the limit, when software agents completely replace people, a pure intelligent system would be operating as an independent entity. Currently, when buying products on the Internet using eBay, people may not be sure whether they are dealing with people, software agents or some combination thereof.

eBay is one instance of what is called the Information Economy in which economically motivated software agents programmed according to algorithms for maximizing profits interact both competitively and cooperatively to fulfill their mandate for their human masters. As explained by Kephart [34] these economic agents, within a given economic system, have the potential to become another economic species on planet Earth along with people. These economic software agents could behave like businesses in which they buy information from other agents to produce informational goods and services for selling to other agents and human beings. In an attempt to optimize their preprogrammed goals, these agents can adapt their behavior according to the ever-changing demands of their customers and pressures from their competitors. Roth [46] suggests the development of an emerging discipline called Design Economics for creatively designing marketplaces for use as intelligent systems on the Internet. Roth believes that the proposed discipline could mature cumulatively in an analogous fashion to the development of bridge design by engineers as a result of vast experience and basic laws of physics.

As emphasized in Sections 2.2, 4.2, 4.3, 5.2 and 5.3, the authors of this chapter would like to encourage the design and implementation of ethical behavior by participants in any system to produce overall consequences or emergent phenomena that are just and sustainable. To illustrate how a specific intelligent system should be ethically designed as part of the information economy, consider the case of a bidding system to buy lumber for producing wood and paper products. Such a system could contain two key components. Of paramount importance would be rules and protocols embedded into the system that only permit ethical behavior and consequences. The second main component would encourage competitive behavior within appropriate social and environmental constraints in order to reduce the cost of a successful bid and thereby keep the price of finished products as low as possible. More specifically, any bidding company that has a record of producing severe pollution problems anywhere in the world would be outright prohibited from having an agent represent it in the bidding system, unless appropriate fines have been paid to an independent regulatory agency and the damaged environment has been restored by the company. Likewise, a selling company that participates in massive clear-cutting of forests anywhere in the world and does not practice reforestation that replaces all trees that are cut down, would not be permitted to sell harvested trees through its software agents within the intelligent system marketplace for lumber. Additionally, any organization that has violated international labor laws in the treatment of its employees would not be allowed access to the system. Whatever the case, companies and their surrogate software systems that are allowed to participate in the intelligent bidding system would then be able to bid according to rules that are competitive but are also fair, ethical and legal. There is no credible excuse why humans do not start now to design and build ethical intelligent systems on a global basis. After all, simulation can be used in advance to test the ethical and economic behavior of these complex adaptive systems before they are actually put in place. As noted in Section 4.3, we should also be modifying the unethical aspects of existing social and economic policies as well as designing and testing new societal policies that are socially and environmentally sound.

6. Integrated systems

As depicted in the Venn diagram in Fig. 2, an integrated or mixed system is a combination of societal and intelligent systems. In fact, as noted in Section 5.3, in some situations, a person may not know whether a software agent representing him or her in a bidding transaction using eBay is interacting with other software agents, people or some combination thereof. A software agent representing a client in an eBay auction on the Internet may employ a strategy to enter a bid less than a second before an auction closes in a process called "sniping" [47]. Bichler *et al.* [6] propose a structured design of electronic negotiations which could operate as an integrated system, consisting of human beings negotiating with each other and surrogate software agents, or a pure intelligent system in which only software agents negotiate on behalf of their clients.

Many of the modern airline passenger jets produced by Boeing, Airbus and Bombardier operate as integrated systems. In bad weather conditions or when the pilot is incapacitated, an aircraft can be flown entirely on automatic systems and can even land safely without intervention by people on the aircraft. However, in most situations the pilot and his crew exercise overall control of the airplane within an integrated systems framework.

The electrical supply system described in Section 1.1 is an illustration of a very large scale integrated system. When a serious problem does arise in a nuclear power generating plant, for example, intelligent systems can take over to automatically close down the system to prevent severe damage to the system and radiation leaks. Nonetheless, humans may have the ability to take over the safe shutdown of the nuclear plant once they have enough time to understand why the problem arose and what is happening.

The overall electrical supply system consists of numerous electrical generating plants driven by nuclear materials, coal, oil, water and natural gas, which produce huge quantities of electrical power that are delivered to customers via high-voltage transmission lines over long distances and also by local electrical networks. In the future, there is little doubt that more and more intelligent systems will be created to take over the daily operation of the system and to respond instantaneously in emergencies. Moreover, these intelligent and societal systems that manage and operate the electrical system must be founded upon ethical values that put the health, safety and welfare of society and the environment as their highest priorities. As is also explained in Section 1.1, the economic motivation propelling the electrical supply system must also be synchronized with the physical constraints of the system—selling electricity to the highest bidder anywhere in a huge electrical network simply does not make physical sense. Moreover, not providing electricity to poor people who cannot afford to buy it at exorbitant prices is immoral.

7. Great expectations

In Charles Dickens' famous 19th century novel, *Great Expectations*, the main character, Pip, goes through a complicated character development—from being self-centered and accepting society's empty values to having a much deeper maturity [9]. Likewise, the field of systems engineering and other associated systems science disciplines need a dramatic character transformation in order to create systems that truly benefit both individuals and society in humane and ethical ways. Only through the merging of values and philosophies from both the human and systems sciences, as well as other areas, can humankind approach the ideal goal of fostering a safe, reliable and equitable society in this challenging 21st century of Great Expectations.

The research contributions put forward in this chapter for advancing the field of systems engineering can be classified under two overarching and overlapping themes. The first realm of ideas reverberates with one clear message—multiple participants constitute an inherent and vital characteristic of virtually all major types of systems and, hence, should be considered in any comprehensive systems study. The second category of research suggestions contains a strong recommendation of how these participants who interact within and among systems should behave—ethically.

Under the umbrella of multiple participant decision making, a range of related observations, challenges and opportunities for future research can be made. Based upon real world illustrations such as the great North American electrical supply system failure of August 2003 in Section 1.1 and the ongoing dispute over the proposed export of water in bulk quantities from Canada in Section 4.2, the authors argue that conflict is omnipresent and, therefore, should be an integral part of any realistic systems study. By dividing the world into four main types of systems—environmental, societal, intelligent and integrated—as displayed in Figs. 1–3, the authors explain how each of these systems is fraught with interacting and conflicting agents who may also be in dispute with decision makers existing in other systems. Moreover, it is pointed out that participants taking part in a dispute could act in a highly competitive manner or exhibit cooperation via coalition formation and other means.

Within the domain of societal systems, the conflict analysis techniques listed on the left-hand side of Fig. 5 were scientifically developed for properly studying social conflict among real people and organizations. In fact, as explained in Section 4.1 and also mentioned by Raiffa *et al.* [44] in the preface of their recent book, classical game theory methods, shown on the right-hand side of Fig. 5, failed to work well to model and analyze societal conflict because these techniques contain many unrealistic assumptions that are incongruent with the basic properties of societal conflicts. As noted in Section 5 and also in the preface of the book by Rosenschein and Zlotkin [45], classical game theory methods are being widely employed for modeling and analyzing behavior of agents under conflict as well as designing high-level protocols in intelligent, integrated and complex adaptive systems. This is also the case, as pointed out in Section 3, for environmental systems. Accordingly, the authors highly recommend that researchers ensure that any game theoretic or other conflict methods utilized within a given system be scientifically tested for determining whether or not the models are appropriate. When necessary, suitable refinements and extensions can be made to the conflict models being entertained or a new class of models can be created.

One specific research topic that could be investigated now is whether or not the techniques given in the left branch of Fig. 5 could be used outside the domain of societal systems. For example, the graph model for conflict resolution, used in the bulk water conflict application in Section 4.2, along with its associated solution concepts listed in Table 4, may be useful for designing the behavior of agents living in a particular intelligent system in which the agents interact in a fashion that mimics human behavior under conflict. Such efforts would constitute a technology transfer of concepts from one area of systems engineering to another. Of course, appropriate changes can be made to these societal decision technologies when employed within another kind of system.

Dedicated research is required under the realm of ethics to design systems that harness the creative power of competition and cooperation among participants within an ethical structure that produces beneficial consequences that are fair and environmentally sound. Within an intelligent systems paradigm, one can design each agent to have a multiple objective framework similar to that shown in Fig. 4 such that criteria reflecting proper societal and environmental values are given priority over those connected to short-term financial gains, especially within the new era of an emerging information economy. This underlying value system would cause the agent to have overall preferences among states that would dictate responsible behavior when the agent interacts with others according to a specified solution concept. This should lead to enhanced types of equilibria that tend to produce win/win results for individual agents, but are also beneficial for society and the environment as a whole.

The authors firmly believe that humankind has a unique opportunity and challenge at this point in history to begin to design proper intelligent and integrated systems to create a safer and more reliable society. As already explained in Section 4.3, enormous changes are needed from the local to the global level to enhance or redesign our societal systems. Clearly, strong, equitable and reliable infrastructure is required to meet the basic needs of citizens. Such a solid infrastructure foundation consisting, for instance, of properly designed electrical supply systems, reliable water distribution systems, and policies and programs for societal well-being and safety, provides a high-level playing field upon which people and organizations can compete or cooperate to economically produce high-quality products and services that are sustainable. Associated with all of this are policies and rules that encourage ethical behavior to produce overall results which are beneficial to society and do not harm the environment. By appropriately reforming or perhaps replacing trade agreements such as the WTO agreements and NAFTA, which only take into account the one-dimensional goal of economic gain, society can prosper under policies that directly consider multiple objective needs that hold proper ethical values of both individuals and society at a higher level than profit maximization.

Because human behavior and the reaction of the environment to human activities cannot be completely controlled by society, there is, by definition, large uncertainty as to how societal and environmental phenomena will dynamically change over time. Hence, responsible redesign of societal and perhaps other systems could be done by following an adaptive management systems approach [55] whereby appropriate actions are taken as situations unfold but overall ethical considerations are maintained for continuing to guide these systems in a proper direction. Whatever the case, a clearly multidisciplinary and flexible approach will be needed to dynamically construct and maintain ethical systems to reliably serve society both now and for generations to come.

References

[1] R. Axelrod, *The Evolution of Cooperation*, Basic Books, New York (1984).

[2] R. Axelrod, *The Complexity of Cooperation: Agent-Based Models of Competition and Collaboration*, Princeton University Press, Princeton, NJ (1997).

[3] R. Axelrod and M.D. Cohen, *Harnessing Complexity: Organizational Implications of a Scientific Frontier*, Basic Books, New York (2000).

[4] J. Baron and M. Spranca, *Protected values*, Organ. Behav. Hum. Decision Processes **70** (1) (1997), 1–16.

[5] B.J.L. Berry, D. Kiel and E. Elliott, *Adaptive agents, intelligence and emergent human organization: capturing complexity through agent-based modeling*, Proc. Natl Acad. Sci. **99** (Suppl. 3) (2002), 7187–7188.

[6] M. Bichler, G. Kersten and S. Strecker, *Towards a structured design of electronic negotiations*, Group Decision Negotiat. **12** (2003), 311–335.

[7] T. Brown, *The concept of value in resource allocation*, Land Econ. **60** (3) (1984), 231–246.

[8] J.L. Casti, *Would-be Worlds: How Simulation is Changing the Frontiers of Science*, Wiley, New York (1997).

[9] C. Dickens, *Great Expectations*, Chatham River Press, New York (1982), First published in serial form in 1860–1861 in England.

[10] J.M. Epstein and R. Axtell, *Growing Artificial Worlds: Social Science from the Bottom Up*, Brooking Institution Press, Washington, DC (1996).

[11] L. Fang, K.W. Hipel and D.M. Kilgour, *Interactive Decision Making: The Graph Model for Conflict Resolution*, Wiley, New York (1993).

[12] L. Fang, K.W. Hipel, D.M. Kilgour and X. Peng, *A decision support system for interactive decision making. Part 1: model formulation*, IEEE Trans. Syst. Man Cybernet. Part C **SMC-33** (1) (2003), 42–55.

[13] L. Fang, K.W. Hipel, D.M. Kilgour and X. Peng, *A decision support system for interactive decision making. Part 2: analysis and output interpretation*, IEEE Trans. Syst. Man Cybernet. Part C **SMC-33** (1) (2003), 56–66.

[14] L. Fang, K.W. Hipel and L. Wang, *Gisborne water export conflict study*, Proceedings of the Third International Conference on Water Resources and Environment Research, I, G.H. Schmitz, ed., Dresden University of Technology, Dresden, Germany (2002), 432–436, July 22–25.

[15] J. Ferber, *Multi-Agent Systems: An Introduction to Distributed Artificial Intelligence*, Addison-Wesley, New York (1999).

[16] J.R. Flenley and S.M. King, *Late quaternary pollen records from Easter Island*, Nature **307** (5946) (1984), 47–50.
[17] N.M. Fraser and K.W. Hipel, *Conflict Analysis: Models and Resolutions*, North-Holland, New York (1984).
[18] G. Hardin, *The tragedy of the commons*, Science **162** (1968), 1243–1248.
[19] K.W. Hipel, *Conflict resolution*, Theme Overview Paper, in Conflict Resolution, Encyclopedia of Life Support Systems (EOLSS), EOLSS Publishers, Oxford, UK, http://www.eolss.net, 2002.
[20] K.W. Hipel, L. Fang and D.M. Kilgour, *Decision support systems in water resources and environmental management*, Keynote Paper, Proceedings of the Third International Conference on Water Resources and Environment Research, Vol. I, G.H. Schmitz, ed., Dresden University of Technology, Dresden, Germany, July 22–25, 2002, (2002), 287–300.
[21] K.W. Hipel, L. Fang and L. Wang, *Bulk water exports in Canada and the Lake Gisborne conflict*, Proceedings of the Second International Symposium on Integrated Water Resources Management (IWRM): Towards Sustainable Water Utilization in the 21st Century, held at the University of Stellenbosch, Stellenbosch, Western Cape, South Africa, January 22–24 (2003).
[22] K.W. Hipel, D.M. Kilgour, L. Fang and X. Peng, *Strategic support for the services industry*, IEEE Trans. Eng. Manage. **48** (3) (2001), 358–369.
[23] K.W. Hipel, D.M. Kilgour and S. Rajabi, *Chapter 27—Operations research and refinement of courses of action*, Handbook of Systems Engineering and Management, A.P. Sage and W.B. Rouse, eds, Wiley, New York (1999), 1077–1118.
[24] K.W. Hipel and A. Obeidi, *The battle of water to who*, Proceedings of the International Conference on From Conflict to Co-operation in International Water Resources Management: Challenges and Opportunities, S. Castelein, ed., at UNESCO-IHE Institute for Water Education, Delft, The Netherlands, November 20–22, 2002, (2002), 417–430.
[25] K.W. Hipel, K.J. Radford and L. Fang, *Multiple participant-multiple criteria decision making*, IEEE Trans. Syst. Man Cybernet. **SMC-23** (4) (1993), 1184–1189.
[26] F. Ho and M. Kamel, *Learning coordination strategies for cooperative multiagent systems*, Machine Learn. **33** (1998), 155–177.
[27] J. Holland, *Adaptation in Natural and Artificial Systems: An Introductory Analysis with Applications to Biology, Control, and Artificial Intelligence*, 2nd edn., MIT Press, Cambridge, MA (1992).
[28] N. Howard, *Paradoxes of Rationality: Theory of Metagames and Political Behavior*, MIT Press, Cambridge, MA (1971).
[29] N. Howard, *Confrontation Analysis: How to Win Operations Other Than War*, CCRP Publications, Pentagon, Washington, DC (1999).
[30] International Joint Commission, *Rules of Procedure and Text of Treaty*, Ottawa, Canada–Washington, DC, USA (1965).
[31] International Joint Commission, *Protection of the Waters of the Great Lakes: Final Report to the Governments of Canada and the United States*, Ottawa, Canada–Washington, DC, USA (2000).
[32] Y. Kamihayashi, *The background of G.A. Escher, Holland engineer who supported J. de Rijke for 40 years*, Historical Studies in Civil Engineering, Vol. 19, Japan Society of Civil Engineering (1999), 399–406.
[33] R.L. Keeney, *Value-Focused Thinking: A Path to Creative Decision-making*, Harvard University Press, Cambridge, MA (1992).
[34] J.O. Kephart, *Software agents and the route to the information economy*, Proc. Natl Acad. Sci. **99** (2002), 14.
[35] D.M. Kilgour, K.W. Hipel, L. Fang and X. Peng, *Coalition analysis in group decision support*, Group Decision Negotiat. **10** (2) (2001), 159–175.
[36] K. Li, K.W. Hipel, D.M. Kilgour and L. Fang, *Preference uncertainty in the graph model for conflict resolution*, IEEE Transactions on Systems, Man and Cybernetics, Part A **34** (4) (2004), 507–520.
[37] S. Lloyd, *Physical measures of complexity*, 1989 Lectures in Complex Systems, E. Jen, ed., Addison-Wesley, Redwood City, CA (1990).
[38] J. Magee and J. Kramer, *Concurrency*, Wiley, Chichester, UK (1999).
[39] J. McMurtry, *Value Wars: The Global Market Versus the Life Economy*, Pluto Press, London (2002).
[40] M. Mitchell, *An Introduction to Genetic Algorithms*, MIT Press, Cambridge, MA (1996).
[41] M. Mittelstaedt, *Why the lights went out*, The Globe and Mail (2003), pages A1 and A8, August 16, 2003.

[42] W. Poundstone, *The Recursive Universe*, Contemporary Books, Chicago (1985).
[43] J. Radcliffe and L. Ross, *Strategic and genetic models of evolution*, Math. Biosci. **156** (1999), 291–307.
[44] H. Raiffa, J. Richardson and D. Metcalfe, *Negotiation Analysis: The Science and Art of Collaborative Decision Making*, Harvard University Press, Cambridge, MA (2002).
[45] J.S. Rosenschein and G. Zlotkin, *Rules of Encounter: Designing Conventions for Automated Negotiation among Computers*, MIT Press, Cambridge, MA (1994).
[46] A.E. Roth, *The economist as engineer: game theory, experimentation, and computation as tools for design economics*, Econometrica **70** (4) (2002), 1341–1378.
[47] A.E. Roth and A. Ockenfels, *Last-minute bidding and the rules for ending second-price auctions: evidence from eBay and Amazon auctions on the Internet*, Am. Econ. Rev. **92** (4) (2002), 1093–1103.
[48] A.P. Sage and W.B. Rouse (eds.), *Handbook of Systems Engineering and Management*, Wiley, New York (1999).
[49] T.C. Schelling, *Micromotives and Macrobehavior*, W.W. Norton, New York (1978).
[50] E. Shakshuki, H. Ghenniwa and M. Kamel, *An architecture for cooperative information systems*, Knowledge-based Syst. **16** (2003), 17–27.
[51] J.M. Smith, *Evolution and the Theory of Games*, Cambridge University Press, Cambridge, UK (1982).
[52] W.J. Sutherland and K. Norris, *Behavioural models of population growth rates: implications for conservation and prediction*, Phil. Trans. R. Soc. Lond. B **357** (2002), 1273–1284.
[53] J. von Neumann and O. Morgenstern, *Theory of Games and Economic Behavior*, 1st edn., Princeton University Press, Princeton, NJ (1944), 3rd Edition (1953).
[54] T. Walkom, *Roots of Ontario's woes stretch well into the past*, Toronto Star (2003), pages F1, F4, and F5, August 23, 2003.
[55] C.J. Walters, *Adaptive Management of Renewable Resources*, MacMillan, New York (1986).
[56] M. Wang, K.W. Hipel and N.M. Fraser, *Modeling misperceptions in games*, Behav. Sci. **33** (3) (1988), 207–223.
[57] M. Wooldridge, *An Introduction to Multiagent Systems*, Wiley, Chichester, UK (2002).
[58] World Commission on Environment and Development (WCED). *Our Common Future*, Oxford University Press, Oxford, UK (1987).
[59] D. Yergin and J. Stanislaw, *The Commanding Heights: The Battle Between Government and the Marketplace that is Remaking the Modern World*, Simon and Schuster, New York (1998).

CHAPTER 2

Mathematical Modeling for Coping with Uncertainty and Risk

Marek Makowski[1]

International Institute for Applied System Analysis, A-2361 Laxenburg, Austria
E-mail: marek@iiasa.ac.at

Contents

Abstract

Coping with uncertainty in decision-making, especially for integrated management of risk, requires the analysis of various measures of outcomes resulting from applying alternative policy options. Policy options include various *ex ante* measures (such as mitigation, different arrangements for risk spreading) and *ex post* measures aimed at reducing and sharing losses. The outcomes of implementing a given set of policy measures are typically measured by various indicators such as *ex ante* and *ex post* costs, benefits from mitigation measures, welfare, quality of the environment, and indicators of risk exposure (value at risk, insolvency). The amount of data and the complexity of their relationships for any risk management problem are far too great to be analyzed based solely on experience and/or intuition.

[1]http://www.iiasa.ac.at/~marek.

SYSTEMS AND HUMAN SCIENCE – FOR SAFETY, SECURITY, AND DEPENDABILITY
Edited by Tatsuo Arai, Shigeru Yamamoto and Kazuhisa Makino

Therefore, mathematical models have become a key element of decision-making support in various policy processes, especially those aimed at integrated management of disaster risk.

This chapter outlines methodological, social, and technical problems related to the development of novel methods for such models, and illustrates applications of such methods by case studies done at IIASA.

1. Introduction

Everybody has to cope with uncertainty and to manage various risks in a world that is changing more and more rapidly and clearly stretching the social fabric. One of the dominant driving forces is efficiency, which has led to globalization, increased dependency among more diversified systems, a reduction in many safety (both technological and social) margins, and other factors which contribute to increased vulnerability.[2] However, faster development has its price. Traditional societies developed slower but in a more robust way, i.e., the consequences of wrong decisions or natural catastrophes were limited to rather small communities. Nowadays, the consequences of wrong decisions may be wider (even global and long term) and more serious. Even at the family level, faster development has its price. There is a great deal of stress caused by the demand to be the best, a much lower tolerance for failure, and by various risks (e.g., of a substantial decrease of future pension or of losing a single source of family income). Fewer people are successful in competitive societies than in egalitarian societies. This is not only a moral problem but in the longer term it reduces the security, safety, and reliability of three types of interlinked systems: human, economic, and technological.

A secure, safe, and reliable society requires rational and timely decision-making. However, decision-making is becoming more and more difficult because decision problems are no longer well-structured problems that are easy to solve by intuition or experience supported by relatively simple calculations. Even the same type of problems that used to be easy to define and solve are now much more complex because of the globalization of the economy and a much greater awareness of its linkages with various environmental, social, and political issues. Moreover, decision-making is done for the future, which always is uncertain. Thus, any decision-maker needs to cope with uncertainty in order to rationally manage various risks.

Rational decision-making typically requires

- a representation of relationships between decisions and outcomes (the consequences of applying a decision),
- an understanding of the uncertainties related to various representations of such relationships,
- a representation of preferential structures (measures of tradeoffs between various outcomes) of the stakeholders (persons and/or institutions affected by the consequences of implementing decisions),
- an assessment of the temporal and spatial consequences of implementing a selected decision,
- an assessment of various risks related to either implementing a (best at the moment) decision or postponing making a decision (until a possibly better decision can be made),
- a procedure (conventionally called DMP—Decision-Making Process) for selecting *the best* solution (decision), and
- a procedure for involving stakeholders in the DMP and for communicating decisions to stakeholders.

---

[2] A recent example is a faulty switch in a power station that resulted in a lack of electricity for dozens of millions of people.

It is not practicable to attempt to deal with all these issues for any given decision problem. Each of these elements has a large number of methods and corresponding tools and an attempt to fully exploit the capabilities of many of them is doomed to failure. Different decision problems and the associated DMP have different characteristics, which call for focusing on the implementation a selection of methods and tools. However, there are some common characteristics of model-based support for decision-making, and a selection of these are discussed in this chapter.

2. Context

2.1. *Common background*

Before focusing on coping with uncertainty and risk management issues in decision-making for complex problems, let us briefly consider a (theoretically simple) commonly known and well-structured problem: a decision by an individual to buy a car. From a methodological perspective, this is a multicriteria (with a small number of criteria) problem of a selection from a small set of alternatives. The alternatives are rather well defined and criteria are easily interpreted by a person making the decision. There are several methods for supporting decision-making in such situations, and yet the problem is typically solved using intuition and experience rather than any analytical tool. It is interesting to note that the same problem is solved in a different way by different future owners of a car and the same person may take very different decisions that even he/she cannot explain using the criteria that are believed to completely define the tradeoffs. Different approaches taken by different persons are explained by the concept of *Habitual Domain* introduced by Yu [1]. Different solutions (each believed to be *the best*) to the same choice problem show that even for a simple decision problem it may be impossible to precisely define a complete set of criteria and the tradeoffs between them.

While a choice of a car is typically done without using any analytical tools, intuition and experience alone cannot be used for the analysis of (a typically infinite number of) solutions to complex problems. Therefore, modern decision-makers typically need to somehow integrate knowledge from these various areas of science and practice, and practically this can be done only by using a mathematical model. Unfortunately, the culture, language, and tools developed for knowledge representation in the key areas (such as the economy, engineering, environment, finance, management, social, and political sciences) are very different. This observation is known to everybody who has ever participated in teamwork with researchers and practitioners who have backgrounds in different areas. Given the great heterogeneity of knowledge representation in various disciplines, and the fast growing amount of knowledge in most areas, the need for efficient knowledge integration for decision support remains a challenge that deserves to be addressed. More detailed discussion of these topics can be found in [2–4].

2.2. *Model-based decision-making support*

Safe, secure, and reliable societies cannot be realized without model-based support for analyzing and solving complex problems organized in a way that is transparent not only for scientists and experts. For any complex decision problem, models are necessary not only to support a decision-making process but also to enhance public understanding of problems and the proposed solutions. As this chapter focuses on supporting decision-making, we briefly comment only on the role of models in public information. By now it is commonly agreed that the provision of information is critical to public acceptance, and that in reality some commonly discussed problems are actually incorrectly understood. Selected issues of modeling for knowledge exchange are discussed in [3]. The relevance of this publication for policy-making is illustrated, e.g., by Sterman [5], who points out that although the Kyoto Protocol is one of the most widely discussed topics, most people believe that stabilizing emissions at near current rates will stabilize the climate. Current debates (some accompanied by strikes) on pension system reforms in several European countries also clearly show a wide misunderstanding of the consequences of population structure dynamics on economies in general and on pension systems in particular. These, and many other problems, can also be explained to the public by adapting relevant models for use in presentations that the public can understand. Unfortunately, various models developed for policy-making problems use different assumptions, and often different sets of data; therefore, a comparative analysis of their results can at best be done and understood by a small community of modelers. The need for public access to knowledge pertinent to policy-making will certainly grow; see, e.g., [6], which discusses access to environmental information; thus the role of models in public life will also grow accordingly. Multidisciplinary and interdisciplinary modeling will grow in importance for the next generation's society (see, e.g., [7]) for which a knowledge-based economy will become a major driving force for development. Models can represent knowledge as both synthesized and structured information, which can be verified by various groups of model users (see, e.g., [4,8–10]).

Making rational decisions for any complex problem requires various analyses of tradeoffs between conflicting objectives (outcomes) that are used for measuring the results of applying various policy options (decisions). There are three issues related to a proper model-based support: first, developing a model that represents the relations between decisions and outcomes; second, supporting analyses of tradeoffs between conflicting objectives; and third, organizing participation of stakeholders in selected activities of the whole modeling process.

Models, when properly developed and maintained, and equipped with proper tools for their analysis, can integrate relevant knowledge that is available from various disciplines and sources. While the substance of various environmental models is obviously different, many modeling methods and portable tools for model generation and analysis are applicable to problems of different origins. Many such models pose additional challenges owing to the large amount of data, complex relations between variables, the characteristics of the resulting mathematical programming problems, and requirements for comprehensive problem analyses. Such challenges have motivated the development of advanced modeling technology for supporting the whole modeling cycle. This includes model specification, data management, generation of model instances (composed of a selected model specification and data defining parameters and sets for compound variables), various methods of analyses of instances, and documentation of the whole modeling process. A modeling technology that supports this approach to model-based decision-making support is summarized in Section 3.1.

2.3. *Uncertainty and risk*

As outlined above, integration of knowledge for model-based decision support is a complex problem even without considering the two other elements of decision-making, which are the key characteristics of many problems, namely, uncertainty and risk.

About 200 years ago, Laplace argued that the world was completely deterministic, i.e., if we knew the current state of all the elements of the universe (from large bodies to atoms) and a set of scientific laws, then we could predict all events (including human behavior) with certainty. This implies that uncertainty is a consequence of our incomplete knowledge and will evaporate if knowledge becomes complete. This doctrine of scientific determinism was strongly resisted by many people, but it remained the standard assumption of science for over 100 years until a sequence of discoveries in physics proved that developments in science can increase uncertainty. In 1926, Heisenberg proved that the product of three attributes of a particle (the uncertainty in the position, the uncertainty in velocity, and the mass) can never be smaller than the Planck's constant. This was the first proof that uncertainty cannot be reduced below a certain level. Since 1933, Kolmogorov has developed probability theory in a rigorous way from fundamental axioms; in 1954, he published a fundamental work on dynamic systems, where he also demonstrated the vital role of probability theory in physics, and of apparent randomness in systems believed to be deterministic.

We should distinguish between two types of uncertainty related to a considered phenomenon:

- *epistemic uncertainty*: due to incomplete knowledge (which ranges from deterministic knowledge to total ignorance) of the phenomena,
- *variability uncertainty*: due to the inherent variability (i.e., natural randomness) of the phenomena, e.g., natural processes; human behavior; social, economic, technological dynamics; and discontinuities (or fast changes) in some of these processes.

While the epistemic uncertainty can be reduced provided that there are time and resources to do so, the variability uncertainty should be adequately addressed in any rational decision-making process. Further on, we will discuss *variability uncertainty* for which we will use the term *uncertainty*.

The most common treatment of the variability uncertainty is through one of the following three paradigms of probability defined as

- ratio of favorable events to the total number of *equally likely* events (Laplace),
- long-run frequency of the event, if the experiment were repeated *many* times (von Mises),
- a measure of a subjective degree of certainty about the event (Bayes, Keynes).

The first two paradigms assume that probability is an attribute of the corresponding event (or object), the third one is based on beliefs. However, a properly used probability is part of the additive set theory built by Kolmogorov on a set of mathematical axioms. Unfortunately, countless applications of probability theory do not conform to these axioms.

There are two pitfalls when using probability in decision-making under uncertainty:

- Incorrect calculation of probabilities (e.g., applying Laplace's paradigm to events that are not equally likely; or violating assumption of von Mises by counting frequency from observations of events that occurred under different conditions, by using a small sample of data, by interpreting as data results provided by various models based on related data, or by multiple use of the same data each interpreted[3] as independent events). Probability defined as the relative frequency is equal to the limit of an infinite sequence, and it is rarely proved to what extent it is related to the relative frequency inferred from a finite subset of the infinite sequence.
- Correct probabilities provide a good basis for frequently repeated decision-making provided neither the probability distribution nor payoffs change substantially (because this is a condition for a good approximation of an infinite sequence of decisions by a finite subsequence), and one wants to optimize a total expected outcome (defined as a sum of payoffs weighted by their probabilities). However, as demonstrated already in 1739 by Bernoulli's St Petersburg paradox (see, e.g., [11]), maximization of an expected outcome (or utility) is not rational for situations where a decision is made only once, or when for a sequence of decisions the consequences of each decision should be evaluated separately.

For rational decision-making under uncertainty one needs to evaluate the risks associated with implementing a decision. There is no common agreement (not to mention a lack of an underlying rigorous mathematical theory) on the definition of risk. We adapt here (after [12]) the following definition: *Risk is a situation or event in which something of human value (including humans themselves) has been put at stake and where the outcome is uncertain.* Risk has a wide range of connotations (e.g., related to fears, concerns, uncertainties, thrills or worries) but there are unifying features that portray the meaning of risk. Whatever the variation in connotation, risk implies the possibility (as opposed to a predetermination) of some outcome. Risk thus implies uncertainty about an outcome, and can only be measured if one knows all the possible outcomes and the probability of each outcome occurring.

However, measuring risk is still a challenging problem, especially for risks related to rare events with high consequences, conventionally called catastrophic risks that are characterized by the so-called heavy-tail distributions (moreover, such distributions are typically multimodal and often the expected value of losses corresponds to an event which cannot occur). To illustrate this problem, let us recall that investment risk is typically measured by a standard deviation (denoted by σ) of returns from that investment. Standard deviation is still commonly used as a primary measure of risk ignoring the facts showing that it is often not adequate. For example, the 1929, 1987 and 2000/2001 stock market crashes were each about a 10σ event; thus each would (under Gaussian statistics) happen only once in the lifetime of the Earth.

[3] Wittgenstein described this as buying several copies of a newspaper to increase the probability that a news is true.

Risk is not only difficult to measure but it is (especially low-probability risk) difficult for the public and most decision-makers to understand (see, e.g., [13]). Probably the most frequently asked question illustrating this is "Why have we had three 100-year floods during the last 10 years?". Hence building a common (for stakeholders with different habitual domains) understanding of risk is another challenging problem.

2.4. *Stakeholders, and temporal and spatial scales*

So far we have not considered the other three elements of decision-making, namely, stakeholders, and temporal and spatial scales. Due to space limitation we can only outline the scope of related problems by considering the problem of climate, which is a global common good. Climate change is driven by a combination of natural and anthropogenic processes, where the strongest impact of the latter is a function of the collective GHG emissions and sinks of all individuals and all human activities. Climate change is still far too complex a problem to be precisely modeled. However, there is strong evidence that anthropogenic activities may cause irreversible and abrupt climate change. Consequently, there is a growing understanding for the need for action aimed at limiting the anthropogenic impact on climate change.

Although the problem is global, responsibilities are place-specific and lie with all individuals, private and public organizations, and all nations. These stakeholders have different characteristics (e.g., assets, priorities, obligations) (see, e.g., [14]). Response policies and measures are local while the consequences are long-term and global, and therefore, a concerted effort by all stakeholders is necessary to achieve the global goal in a rational way. Moreover, there are many scientific uncertainties related to climate, and there are very diverse opinions on the scientific treatment of epistemic and variability uncertainties, and on the approaches for embracing it in the science–policy interface (see, e.g., [15,16]), and on assessing and communicating uncertainties to the public [17]. Generally, uncertainty may justify inaction until epistemic uncertainty is reduced, thus providing a better basis for making more efficient decisions. However, the time needed for reducing uncertainty may be (infinitely) long, and postponing some actions may either result in irreversible and abrupt changes or will require substantially more demanding solutions. While there are extremely different opinions on whether or not climate-related actions should actually be taken without any further delay, the consequences of embracing uncertainty as an excuse for inaction in other areas of decision-making are commonly known.

The long-time horizon and the global nature of the climate problem, together with the scientific uncertainties they present, pose special challenges for decision-makers who have to balance potentially demanding actions for averting global long-term risks against other more immediate (and typically local with a short-time horizon) human development demands. These three types of tradeoffs (global vs local, short-term vs long-term, uncertain vs perceived to be certain) are the major challenges for actual implementation of the necessary measures by politicians, whose constituencies have primarily local and short-term preferences. Model-based decision support is the only way to rationally identify various measures related to climate change, and to support various analyses of tradeoffs between the costs of the measures and their consequences for reducing the anthropogenic impact on global change. This is the only way to provide scientifically based and politically neutral input to policy-making processes, which need to be conducted in a participatory fashion, involving many research institutions interacting with potential users, i.e., decision-makers, various groups of experts, and stakeholders.

2.5. *Risk management*

Before discussing active risk management one should point out the alternative *wait-and-see* strategy, i.e., hoping that an unfavorable event will not occur, and reacting only if it indeed will be the case. Contrary to common beliefs such a strategy may have rational (see, e.g., [12] for arguments and case studies) explanations.

Active risk management is typically composed of two interrelated sets of actions:

- reducing the risk by mitigation, adaptation, and diversification measures,
- applying financial instruments (insurance, hedging, catastrophe funds, contingency credits, catastrophe bonds).

Reducing risk is well established in well-organized societies, and in the longer term it is the most rational action. However, its implementation requires resources and luck (to be able to implement the measures before the first catastrophe will occur). There is typically a limit beyond which a further reduction of risk is more expensive than the application of an appropriate combination of financial instruments. In addition to traditional financial instruments there are ideas of a new financial order [18] that aim at an integrated management of all types of economic risk.

Risk management requires the analysis of tradeoffs between outcomes (criteria) expressed in different units. The most common approach is to convert (typically for computations only) such a multicriteria problem into a single-criterion optimization problem. Such an approach has serious, but not commonly recognized, limitations (see, e.g., [19]). Therefore, it is worth mentioning a truly multicriteria optimization of decision-making under risk [20].

3. Model-based support for coping with uncertainty and risk

3.1. *Modeling for decision-making support*

Mathematical modeling for decision-making support is the process of creating, analyzing, and documenting a model, which is an abstract representation of a problem developed for finding possibly the best solution for a decision problem. The role of models in modern decision-making that is shared by the author of this chapter is discussed in detail in [21] along with the methodology and tools for model-based decision-making support, and several applications to complex environmental policy-making problems. A more diversified collection of methods and applications is presented in [22], and a more focused discussion of selected elements of modeling for decision support and an updated bibliography is provided in [19].

A mathematical model describes the modeled problem by means of variables, which are abstract representations of these elements of the problem, which need to be considered for the evaluation of the consequences of implementing a decision (typically represented by a vector composed of many variables). More precisely, such a model is typically developed using the following concepts:

- decisions (inputs) $\mathbf{x}$, which are controlled by the user;
- external decisions (inputs) $\mathbf{z}$, which are not controlled by the user;
- outcomes (outputs) $\mathbf{y}$, used for measuring the consequences of the implementation of inputs;
- relations between decisions $\mathbf{x}$ and $\mathbf{z}$, and outcomes $\mathbf{y}$; such relations are typically presented in the form:

$$\mathbf{y} = \mathbf{F}(\mathbf{x}, \mathbf{z}), \qquad (1)$$

where $\mathbf{F}(\cdot)$ is a vector of functions.

The concise formulation (1) of a model specification[4] may be misleading for those who are unaware of the complexity of the process of model specification. Each model represents a part of knowledge that is relevant for analysis of the given decision problem. Thus, the model must be confined to a well-defined area of interest, it can only be valid for a specific purpose, and the real phenomenon is always only partially to be represented by the model. Consider, for example, modeling a cup of coffee. Very different models are suitable for studying various aspects, e.g., how something (sugar, cream) is dissolved in the cup's content, or under what conditions the cup might break from thermal stresses, or what shape of cup is most suitable for use in aircraft, or how a cup of coffee enhances different people's productivity. An attempt to develop a model to cover all these aspects and represent all the accumulated knowledge on even such a simple topic would not be rational.

To define a purpose for modeling one needs to analyze if and how a model can contribute to finding a better solution than can be found without a model. This, in turn, implicitly sets the requirements for a selection of input and output variables, and a specification of functions (1) that define relations between variables. Because of the unquestionable success of modeling in problem solving, various modeling paradigms have been intensively developed over the last few decades. Thus, different types of models (characterized by types of variables and relations between them) were developed (e.g., static, dynamic, continuous, discrete, linear, non-linear, deterministic, stochastic, set-membership, fuzzy, soft constraints) with a view to best representing different problems by a selected type of model. Each modeling paradigm embodies a great deal of accumulated knowledge, expertise, methodology, and modeling tools specialized for solving various problems peculiar to each modeling paradigm.

Although several well-developed modeling paradigms exist, it is not easy to select the one that is best for the problem at hand. Moreover, for a selected paradigm a modeler must

[4] Actually any complex model contains also auxiliary variables (typically a vast majority of variables in a large model are the auxiliary variables) defined and used in order to make the model easier to develop, analyze, and maintain. However, for the sake of brevity we do not introduce auxiliary variables here.

find a way of avoiding too much detail while preserving the essential features of the specific problem. Finally, even for a selected set of variables and relations there are often several ways of introducing auxiliary variables and defining the relations, which might be equivalent (i.e., the results of the model analysis should be the same[5]) but different specifications may result in substantial differences in the efficiency of the whole modeling process (especially when difficult optimization problems are solved during the model analysis, see, e.g., [22,23]).

Thus, an appropriate model specification for any non-trivial problem requires a combination of knowledge, experience, intuition, and taste. Therefore, modeling remains and will remain an art. More discussion on the art of modeling can be found in [24].

However, not only model specification but also its use in decision-making processes is a more complex issue than typically perceived. In particular, model analysis is probably the least-discussed element of the modeling process. This results from the focus that each modeling paradigm has on a specific type of analysis. However, the essence of model-based decision-making support is precisely the opposite; namely, to support various ways of model analysis, and to provide efficient tools for comparisons of various solutions. Thus, we outline now a way in which a model that adequately represents the relations between the decisions and the outcomes (used for measuring the corresponding consequences) can be used for finding decisions that best fit the preferences of the decision-makers.

A typical structure when using models for decision-making support is illustrated in Fig. 1. The basic function of a Decision Support System (DSS) is to support the user in finding values of his/her decision variables that will result in a solution of the problem that best fits the preferences of the user.

A typical decision problem has an infinite number of solutions, and users are interested in those that correspond best to their preferences represented here by a preferential structure $\mathbf{P}(\mathbf{x}, \mathbf{y})$ of the user. A preferential structure takes different forms for different methods of model analysis, e.g.,

- classical simulation is composed of given values of input variables;
- soft simulation is defined by desired values of decisions, and by a measure of the distance between the actual and desired values of decisions;
- single criterion optimization is defined by a selected goal function and by optional additional constraints for other (than that selected as the goal function) outcome variables;
- multicriteria model analysis is defined by an achievement scalarizing function, which represents the tradeoffs between the criteria used for the evaluation of solutions.

A preferential structure typically induces partial ordering of solutions obtained for different combinations of values of inputs, and in a well-organized modeling process, preferential structure is not included in the model, but is defined during the model analysis phase, when users typically modify their preferences substantially. In fact, a

[5] The differences may, however, occur because of numerical characteristics of the underlying computational problems.

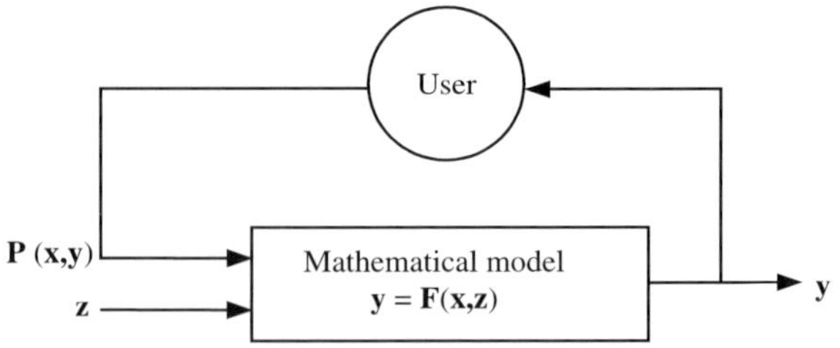

Fig. 1. A typical structure when using a mathematical model for decision-making support.

well-organized model analysis phase is composed of several stages (see, e.g., [19]), each serving different needs; thus, typically, not only are different forms of $P(\cdot)$ used for the same problem but also different instances of each of these forms are defined upon analysis of previously obtained solutions.

Such an approach of using models for supporting decision-making differs substantially from the (traditional) OR routine of representing a decision problem as a mathematical programming problem, e.g., in the form

$$\hat{\mathbf{x}} = \arg \min_{\mathbf{x} \in X_0} \mathcal{F}(\mathbf{x}), \tag{2}$$

which provides optimal decisions $\hat{\mathbf{x}}$. Countless number of actual applications show, however, that for most complex problems it is not possible to adequately define a $\mathcal{F}(\mathbf{x})$ (that represents preferences of decision-makers) nor a set of feasible solutions X_0. In fact, various types of mathematical programming problems are typically defined during the analysis phase; thus, optimization continues to play a crucial role in model-based decision support. However, optimization in supporting decision-making for solving complex problems has quite a different role from its function in some engineering applications (especially real-time control problems) or in very early implementations of OR for solving well-structured military or production planning problems. This point has already been made clear, e.g., by Ackoff [25] and by Chapman [26], who characterized the traditional way of using OR methods for solving problems as composed of the following five stages: describe the problem; formulate a model of the problem; solve the model; test the solution; and implement the solution. The shortcomings of such an approach are discussed in many other publications, some of which are overviewed in [21].

Thus, model-based support for decision-making for complex problems has to meet much more demanding requirements (than those adequate for problems of type (2), which are adequate for well-structured, relatively simple decision problems) for the underlying modeling process, which is far more complex than a process of model development for well-structured decision problems. These requirements demand also a new technology of modeling, such as the Structured Modeling Technology (SMT) discussed in detail in [27].

Models for the integrated management of catastrophic risk are not only complex but also possess specific features, which are discussed below. Thus, their presentation below serves two purposes. First, it illustrates the actual complexity of such models and justifies the reasons why the general-purpose modeling tools and the traditional OR approach to model analysis cannot be successful in such cases. Second, it provides enough details about such models and the corresponding modeling process to help in the development of this type of approach for supporting decision-making processes for similar types of problems.

3.2. *Integrated catastrophic risk management*

3.2.1. *Background.* Catastrophic risk management is a complex interdisciplinary problem requiring knowledge of environmental, natural, financial, and social systems. Their burden is unevenly distributed, debatable in scope, and yet not well matched to policy makers. A decision-making process requires the participation of various agents and stakeholders, individuals, governments, farmers, producers, consumers, insurers, investors, etc. The perception by all these actors of catastrophes, goals, and constraints with respect to these rare/high-consequence events is very diversified. The scarcity of historical data is an inherent feature and a major challenge in designing strategies for dealing with rare catastrophes. Thus, catastrophic risks create new scientific problems requiring integrated approaches, new concepts, and tools for risk management. The role of models enabling the simulation of possible catastrophes and estimating potential damages and losses becomes a key task for designing mitigation and adaptation programs.

Below we outline the model developed for supporting an integrated decision-making process. This model supports the analysis of spatial and temporal heterogeneity of various agents (stakeholders) induced by mutually dependent losses from extreme events. The model addresses the specifics of catastrophic risks: limited information, the need for long-term perspectives and geographically explicit models, and a multi-agent decision-making structure. The model combines geographically explicit data on the distribution of capital stocks and economic values in infrastructure and agriculture in a region with a stochastic model generating magnitudes, occurrences, and locations of catastrophes. Using advanced stochastic optimization techniques, the model, in general, supports the search for, and the analysis of, robust optimal portfolios of *ex ante* (land use, structural mitigation, insurance) and *ex post* (adaptation, rehabilitation, borrowing) measures for decreasing regional vulnerability measured in terms of economic, financial, and human losses as well as in terms of selected welfare growth indicators.

3.2.2. *The integrated catastrophe management model.* The model consists of three major submodels:

- a catastrophe module,
- an engineering vulnerability module, and
- an economic multi-agent module.

The catastrophe module simulates natural phenomenon using a model based on the knowledge of the corresponding type of event, which is represented by a set of variables and relations between them. For example, for a hurricane model the variables are the radius of the maximum winds or the forward speed of the storm. For an earthquake model that simulates the shaking of the ground these are epicenter location, magnitudes of earthquakes, Gütenberg–Richter laws, or attenuation characteristics. For a flood these are precipitation curves, water discharge, river characteristics, etc. The catastrophe models used in IIASA's case studies are based on Monte Carlo dynamic simulations of geographically explicit catastrophe patterns in selected regions (a discussion of these models is beyond the scope of this chapter but can be found, e.g., in [28–34]). A catastrophe model, in fact, compensates for the lack of historical data on the occurrence of catastrophes in locations where the effects of catastrophes may never have been experienced in the past.

The engineering module is used to estimate the damage that may be caused by the catastrophes. Shaking intensities, duration of standing water, water discharge speed or wind speeds are what engineering modules take from the catastrophe modules to calculate potential damage. The engineering modules use vulnerability curves and take into account the age of the building and the number of stories in order to estimate the damage induced by the simulated disaster.

The economic multi-agent model used in our case studies is a stochastic dynamic welfare growth model (see, e.g., [35]). This model maps spatial economic losses (which depend on implemented loss mitigating and sharing policy options) into gains and losses of agents: a central government, a mandatory catastrophe insurance (a catastrophe pool), an investor, individuals (cells or regions), producers (farmers), etc.

Catastrophe and vulnerability GIS-based modeling coupled with multi-agent models is still not widely used. However, it is becoming increasingly important

- to governments and legislative authorities for better comprehending, negotiating, and managing of risks;
- to insurance companies for making decisions on the allocation and values of contracts, premiums, reinsurance arrangements, and the effects of mitigation measures;
- for households, industries, farmers for risk-based allocation of properties and values;
- for scientific communities involved in global change and sustainability research.

A catastrophe can ruin many agents if their risk exposures are not appropriate. To design safe catastrophic risk management strategies it is necessary to define location specific feasible decisions based on potential losses generated by a catastrophe model. Some of these decisions reduce the frequencies (likelihood) and magnitudes of catastrophic events (say, land-use decisions) and redistribute losses and gains at local and international levels (say, pools, insurance, compensation schemes, credits). Different catastrophic scenarios, in general, lead to different decision strategies. The number of alternative decisions may be very large, and the straightforward *if–then* evaluation of all alternatives may easily require more than 100 years.

3.2.3. *Adaptive Monte Carlo optimization.* The important question is how to by-pass limitations of the *if–then* analysis and find a combination of strategies, which would be the "best" strategy for all possible catastrophes. In [35] it was shown that the search for "robust" optimal decisions can be done by incorporating stochastic Spatial Adaptive Monte Carlo optimization techniques into catastrophic modeling that enables the design of desirable robust solutions without evaluating all possible alternatives. The model is composed of elements with the following functionality:

- Initial values for policy variables are input into the Catastrophe Model.
- The Catastrophe Model generates catastrophes and induced direct and indirect damage.
- The efficiency of the policies is evaluated with respect to the performance indicators of the agents, e.g., insurers, insured, governments, etc.
- If these do not fulfill the requirements, goals, and constraints, they are further adjusted in the Adaptive Feedbacks submodel. In this manner, it is possible to take into account complex interdependencies between damages at different locations, available decisions, and resulting losses and claims.

The crucial question is the use of appropriate risk indicators (measures, metrics), e.g., to avoid bankruptcies of agents. Catastrophic losses often have multimodal distributions, and therefore, the use of mean values (e.g., expected costs and profits) may be misleading. Roughly speaking, we cannot think in terms of aggregate regional losses and gains as the sum of location specific losses and gains (e.g., if the mean value is substituted by the median). In our model, we apply economically sound risk indicators such as bankruptcy of insurers, expected shortfall of insurers' risk reserve, and overpayments and underpayments by individuals. These indicators are used together with the so-called stopping times to direct the analysis towards the most destructive scenarios.

3.2.4. *Case studies.* The adequacy of the outlined methodology was tested in a number of case studies. In its first application, the integrated model analyzed the insurability of risks in the Irkutsk region in Russia, which is exposed to the risk of earthquakes (see, e.g., [28,31]). Results demonstrated the model's capability of generating insurance strategies that are robust with respect to dependencies and uncertainties induced by the catastrophes, thus reducing the risk of bankruptcy to the insurers.

The second case study (see, e.g., [36]) in a seismic-prone Italian region illustrated the need for a joint effort by multiple stakeholders in managing the catastrophes. It emphasized that neither the market nor the government may be considered as the efficient mechanism for catastrophic risk management. Only some form of a public–private partnership would be appropriate. Also, it illustrated that the policy options suggested by stakeholders may often be misleading and result in even higher losses. Only comprehensive model-based analysis of dependencies between the timing of catastrophes occurrences, damages, claims, goals, and constraints of agents can assist towards loss-reduction management.

In the third case study [32], the integrated model evaluated an insurance program for mitigating and sharing losses due to severe floods in the Upper Tisza region in Hungary. In this study, special attention was given to the evaluation of strategies robust against a variety of floods. Such strategies are composed of a public multi-pillar flood loss-spreading program involving partial compensation to flood victims by the central government, the pooling of risks through mandatory public insurance on the basis of location-specific exposures, and a contingent *ex ante* credit to reinsure the pool's liabilities. A complementary (more focused on social and policy-making issues) description of this case study is given in [37].

4. Uncertainty, risk, and modern societies

After discussing the methodological background of model-based support for risk management, and presenting in more detail one selected approach and related applications, we summarize other IIASA's research activities pertinent to risk management.

The Risk, Modeling, and Society Project has a long history of research on the economic and social implications of technological, health, and other risks to modern societies. Major projects have been carried out on this broad, interdisciplinary topic, including the perception of risks to technological disasters, the institutional aspects of risk policy-making [38], the equity issues of siting locally unwanted facilities [39], and the role of expertise in risk policy-making [40].

Recent activities focus on the design of instruments and model-based democratic procedures for effectively and equitably reducing and redistributing the risks of extreme events, with special emphasis on transition and developing countries. A survey of global experience with respect to the financial aspects of disasters shows that the victims of extreme natural events, despite insurance and public solidarity, are primarily the households and businesses suffering the losses [38]. A project funded by the British Association of Insurers carried out seven case studies of major disasters in Asia, Europe, and the US, which showed that country practices differ greatly in how the financial risks are absorbed, whether privately through insurance arrangements and/or publicly through social solidarity. This study also investigated the incentive links between risk sharing and preventive measures to reduce the losses.

This theme of risk sharing and loss reduction for extreme events has now become topical at the global level, especially since the IPCC prediction that extreme weather events will worsen with climate change. A current concern is helping developing and transition countries adapt to weather extremes. Governments of many poor countries face budgetary restrictions in reducing disaster losses and providing post-disaster relief and reconstruction, and governments of very poor and highly disaster-prone countries, for example, Honduras, the Philippines, and China, face such enormous risks that regions can be set back years in their development. In collaboration with the Inter-American Development Bank, IIASA has contributed to the development of a proactive, integrated disaster risk management strategy [41] with special emphasis on developing tools for the financial management of these risks, and exploring whether disaster hedges could become a new form of assistance from the North to the South [42].

How risks are reduced and shared is a value-laden policy issue, which was addressed by the risk assessment project for managing flood risks in the Upper Tisza river basin. This activity combined information technology (presented in Section 3.2) with public participation through stakeholder interviews, surveys, and stakeholder workshops [43,44].

The work on risk financing in transition and developing countries has recently received recognition in the climate negotiations community and in particular in the UNFCCC activities on insurance and risk assessment in the context of climate change and extreme weather events. Moreover, the IIASA model-based research on financial risk management is now used in collaborative activities with the World Bank and the Inter-American Development Bank to take account of catastrophic events in country development plans.

IIASA has also promoted several activities addressing problems of social security. Here, we outline only the optimization-based analysis of social security under uncertainties and risks.

In most cases the social security system is the main determinant of population welfare. Dominating in major OECD countries the pay-as-you-go (PAYG) system is nowadays put under stress by rapidly changing demographic conditions—aging—characterized by lowering fertility and increasing longevity. Besides this, instabilities in financial markets, economic distress, inflation, and devaluation often produce grave impacts on sources financing retirement. Major questions to explore are

- What is essential for the efficient functioning of the system?
- Can the existing systems survive in the current demographic and economic environment?
- How can the transition from PAYG to funded pension systems work?

In many OECD countries a combination of the PAYG and funded pension systems is being discussed. Criteria for the evaluation of various combinations include the least cost for the transition, the least burden on various population groups (e.g., retirees and contributors to the systems), and the least costly financial measures to aid the transition, for example, through international/national borrowing.

The broad range of uncertainties inherent to social security problems necessitates the explicit introduction and treatment of uncertainties and risks into the social security simulation model, and the formulation and development of an optimization-based approach to the analysis of social security systems [45,46].

The social security simulation model [45] is a compromise between a purely actuarial model and an overlapping generations general equilibrium model. It deals with the production and consumption processes coevolving with birth-and-death processes of involved agents, e.g., region-specific households subdivided into single-year age groups, firms, governments, financial intermediaries, including pension systems and insurance. The production function of the model allows to track incomes expenditures, savings, and dissavings of agents, as well as intergenerational and interregional transfers of wealth. The stochastic optimization approach [46] combines this model together with a rolling horizon stochastic optimization procedure which allows to explicitly and realistically treat the underlying uncertainties with the goal of maximizing social welfare (consumption of workers and retirees) by fine-tuning the mix of the transfer-based PAYG and capital reserve finance funded social security schemes.

The social security simulation model of IIASA was applied in a multidisciplinary study of population aging in Japan [47]. This study was made possible by financial support from the Economic and Social Research Institute of the Japanese Cabinet Office as part of its Millenium Project. The general conclusions of the studies are slowing per capita growth, a declining national saving rate, rising social contribution rates (subject to the assumption of no change in labor force participation rates or the calculation of pension, health, and long-term care benefits), and reduction in net foreign assets. While the disposable incomes of both the elderly and the working-age population are expected to rise (i.e., living standards will continue to improve), the assumptions of the model translate into an eventual decline in the living standards of the young relative to those of the elderly. This is, of course, subject to our assumption that the main mechanism for adapting to the rising costs of pensions and health is increasing payroll contribution rates. This picture is typical for all rapidly aging regions of the world among which Japan may be leading the way, but other countries must surely follow.

We close this overview of selected IIASA's activities related to treatment of uncertainty and to risk management by providing references to selected publications (but not repeating publications already cited in this chapter) addressing pertinent methodological issues:

- An introduction to measuring risk [48]
- New measures of risk [49]
- Stochastic optimization for design of catastrophic risks portfolios [50–52]
- Tradeoffs between security and growth [53]
- *Ex ante* and *ex post* financial stabilization of long-term growth [54]
- Catastrophic risk management [55]
- The role of insurance in risk transfer [56]
- Modeling for financial optimization [57]
- Numerics of financial management [58].

5. Conclusions

Coping with uncertainty and rational risk management for any complex decision-making situation is a complex process, and there are no simple (and adequate) solutions to truly complex problems. Moreover, the impact of inadequate risk management may not only be significant but also global. Complexity and global impact require two types of cooperation:

- among stakeholders at different locations and of different types (central and local governments, enterprises, NGO's, individuals);
- between researchers from various fields that need to contribute to building objective, model-based support for decision-support.

There is a wealth of knowledge and experience that can contribute to rational risk management. However, these resources are fragmented and often in incompatible forms. Integrating such resources is part of a wider, and even more challenging problem, namely, integrating fragmented knowledge to appropriately serve the knowledge society. This new type of society can actually be safe, secure, and reliable only if decisions on various levels will be made in a concerted way using integrated knowledge.

Due to the unquestionable success of modeling in problem solving, various modeling paradigms have been intensively developed over the last few decades. In this, to a great extent case study-driven process, a growing tendency to focus on specific methodologies and tools was observed. Each modeling paradigm embodies a lot of accumulated knowledge, expertise, methodology, and modeling tools specialized for solving many of the problems belonging to each modeling paradigm. However, these resources are fragmented, and using more than one paradigm for a problem at hand is too expensive and time consuming in practice. The *Structured Modeling* of Geoffrion provides a methodology for unifying different paradigms and for structuring the modeling process, which is the necessary condition for effective modeling of complex systems. The SMT provides modular tools for structured modeling and supports also the key requirements for good modeling practice see, e.g., [5,21,22,25,27,59–62] for a discussion of various key elements of such practices and of some typical modeling pitfalls.

Modeling, especially of large and/or complex problems requires a combination of knowledge, craft, and art. Model-based support for policy-making issues is far more complex than modeling for solving better-structured problems, e.g., in engineering applications. Not only are models for policy-making more complex than models of well-structured problems, but there are more demanding requirements for the whole modeling process, which in turn needs to be transparent and well documented.

This chapter aims at sharing the knowledge and experience developed during the long-term development of several complex models, at providing basic information about several actual applications of model-based support for coping with uncertainty and risk, and about SMT which supports the whole modeling process for model-based decision-making support. SMT responds also to the challenging requirements for the modeling process, which will be growing in the near future when more and more policy-making processes will utilize model-based problem analysis and decision-making support.

Finally, this chapter provides an extensive list of references that aim to provide pointers for further reading for those new to some of the concepts presented and who may, therefore, find this presentation too sketchy.

Acknowledgments

The work reported in this chapter has been done by the Risk, Modeling and Society Project at IIASA in collaboration with other IIASA projects, and several institutions and colleagues, including the team led by Prof. Norio Okada of the Disaster Prevention Research Institute at Kyoto University. It is impossible to give credit to all colleagues who contributed to the reported research although the citations have been made whenever it was practicable to do so. However, the author would also like to acknowledge those contributions which had the largest impact on the reported research by mentioning in alphabetical order: A. Amendola, Y. Ermoliev, T. Ermolieva, J. Linnerooth-Bayer, and G. Pflug. Moreover, the author acknowledges the contributions of T. Ermolieva to the write-up for Section 3.2, and of J. Linnerooth-Bayer, T. Ermolieva, and G. Pflug for Section 4.

The author also thanks A. Beulens, A. Geoffrion, J. Granat, H. Scholten, H.-J. Sebastian and A.P. Wierzbicki for many discussions and joint activities on various modeling issues that have contributed also to the development of modeling methodology exploited in SMT.

References

[1] P. Yu, *Habitual Domains: Freeing Yourself from the Limits on Your Life*, Highwater Editions, Shawnee Mission, Kansas (1995).

[2] M. Makowski, *Knowledge integration in model-based decision support*, Proceedings of International Symposium on Knowledge and System Sciences: Challenges to Complexity, E. Shimemura, Y. Nakamori, J. Gu and T. Yoshida, eds, Japan Advanced Institute of Science and Technology, Ishikawa, Japan (2000), 43–56, ISBN 4-924861-09-X.

[3] A. Wierzbicki and M. Makowski, *Modeling for knowledge exchange: global aspects of software for science and mathematics*, Access to Publicly Financed Research, P. Wouters and P. Schröder, eds, NIWI, Amsterdam, The Netherlands (2000), 123–140.
[4] M. Makowski and A. Wierzbicki, *Modeling knowledge in global information networks*, Fourth Global Research Village Conference. Importance of ICT for Research and Science: Science Policies for Economies in Transition (Warsaw), KBN (the Polish State Committee for Scientific Research), and OECD (the Organization for Economic Co-operation and Development), Information Processing Centre, (2003), pp. 173–186, draft version available from http://www.iiasa.ac.at/~marek/pubs/prepub.html.
[5] J. Sterman, *All models are wrong: reflections on becoming a systems scientist*, Syst. Dyn. Rev. **16** (4) (2002), 501–531.
[6] M. Haklay, *Public access to environmental information: past, present and future*, Comput. Env. Urban Syst. **27** (2003), 163–180.
[7] P. Drucker, *The next society, a survey of the near future*, The Economist **361** (8246) (2001), 3–22.
[8] W. Borst, *Construction of engineering ontologies for knowledge sharing and reuse*, Technical Report, University of Twente Enschede, The Netherlands (1997).
[9] B. Funke and H. Sebastian, *Knowledge-based model building with KONWERK*, Working Paper WP-96-105, International Institute for Applied Systems Analysis, Laxenburg, Austria (1996).
[10] M. Mannino, B. Greenberg and S. Hong, *Model libraries: knowledge representation and reasoning*, ORSA J. Comput. **2** (1990), 1093–1123.
[11] P. Anand, *Foundations of Rational Choice under Risk*, Oxford University Press, Oxford (1993).
[12] C. Jaeger, O. Renn, E. Rosa and T. Webler, *Risk, Uncertainty, and Rational Action*, Earthscan Publications, London (2001).
[13] P. Stern and H. FIneberg, eds., *Understanding Risk: Informing Decisions in a Democratic Society*, National Academy Press, Washington DC (1996).
[14] A. Najam, ed., *Environment, Development, and Human Security: Perspectives from South Asia*, University Press of America, New York (2003).
[15] H. Pollack, *Uncertain Science...Uncertain World*, Cambridge University Press, Cambridge (2003).
[16] A. Kinzig and D. Starrett, *Coping with uncertainty: a call for a new science-policy forum*, AMBIO, J. Hum. Env. **32** (5) (2003), 330–335.
[17] A. Petersen, P. Janssen, J. van der Sluijs, J. Risbey and J. Ravetz, *RIVM/MNP guidance for uncertainty assessment and communication*, Technical Report IR-03-02, RIVM Bilthoven, The Netherlands (2003).
[18] R. Shiller, *The New Financial Order Risk in the 21th Century*, Princeton University Press, Princeton (2003).
[19] M. Makowski and A. Wierzbicki, *Modeling knowledge: model-based decision support and soft computations*, Applied Decision Support with Soft Computing, X. Yu and J. Kacprzyk, eds, Studies in fuzziness and soft computing, **124**, Springer, Berlin (2003), 3–60, ISBN 3-540-02491-3, draft version available from http://www.iiasa.ac.at/~marek/pubs/prepub.html.
[20] W. Ogryczak, *Multiple criteria optimization and decision under risk*, Control Cybernet. **31** (4) (2002), 975–1003.
[21] A. Wierzbicki, M. Makowski and J. Wessels, eds, *Model-based decision support methodology with environmental applications*, Mathematical Modeling and Applications, Kluwer, Dordrecht (2000), ISBN 0-7923-6327-2.
[22] M. Makowski, *Modeling techniques for complex environmental problems*, Natural Environment Management and Applied Systems Analysis, M. Makowski and H. Nakayama, eds, International Institute for Applied Systems Analysis, Laxenburg, Austria (2001), 41–77, ISBN 3-7045-0140-9.
[23] W. Ogryczak, *A note on modeling multiple choice requirements for simple mixed integer programming solvers*, Comput. Oper. Res. **23** (1996), 199–205.
[24] J. Paczyński, M. Makowski and A. Wierzbicki, *Modeling tools, Model based decision support methodology with environmental applications*, Mathematical Modeling and Applications, Kluwer, Dordrecht (2000), 125–165, ISBN 0-7923-6327-2.
[25] R. Ackoff, *The future of operational research is past*, J. Oper. Res. Soc. **30** (2) (1979), 93–104.
[26] C. Chapman, *My two cents worth on how OR should develop*, J. Oper. Res. Soc. **43** (7) (1992), 647–664.
[27] M. Makowski, *Structured modeling technology*, Eur. J. Oper. Res. **168** (3) (2005).

[28] A. Amendola, Y. Ermoliev, T. Ermolieva, V. Gitits and G. Koff, *A systems approach to modeling catastrophic risk and insurability*, Nat. Hazards J. **21** (2/3) (2000), 381–393.

[29] S. Baranov, B. Digas, T. Ermolieva and V. Rozenberg, *Earthquake risk management: scenario generator*, Interim Report IR-02-025, International Institute for Applied Systems Analysis, Laxenburg, Austria (2002).

[30] K. Christensen, L. Danon, T. Scanlon and P. Bak, *Unified scaling law for earthquakes*, Proceedings 99/1, National Academy of Sciences, US (2002).

[31] Y. Ermoliev, T. Ermolieva, G. MacDonald and V. Norkin, *Stochastic optimization of insurance portfolios for managing exposure to catastrophic risks*, Ann. Oper. Res. **99** (2000), 207–225.

[32] T. Ermolieva, Y. Ermoliev, J. Linnerooth-Bayer and A. Vari, *Integrated management of catastrophic flood risks in the Upper Tisza basin: a dynamic multi-agent adaptive Monte Carlo approach*, Proceedings of the Second Annual IIASA-DPRI Meeting Integrated Disaster Risk Management: Megacity Vulnerability and Resilience, International Institute for Applied Systems Analysis, Laxenburg, Austria (2002), http://www.iiasa.ac.at/Research/RMS.

[33] G. Walker, *Current developments in catastrophe modelling*, Financial Risks Management for Natural Catastrophes, N. Britton and J. Oliver, eds, Griffith University, Brisbane, Australia (1997), 17–35.

[34] K. Froot, *The Limited Financing of Catastrophe Risk and Overview*, Harvard Business School and National Bureau of Economic Research, Harvard (1997).

[35] T. Ermolieva, *The design of optimal insurance decisions in the presence of catastrophic risks*, Interim Report IR-97-068, International Institute for Applied Systems Analysis, Laxenburg, Austria (1997).

[36] A. Amendola, Y. Ermoliev and T. Ermolieva, *Earthquake risk management: a case study for an Italian region*, Proceedings of Second Euro Conference on Global Change and Catastrophe Risk Management: Earthquake Risks in Europe, International Institute for Applied Systems Analysis, Laxenburg, Austria (2000), pp. 267–295, http://www.iiasa.ac.at/Research/RMS.

[37] L. Brouwers, *Spatial and dynamic modeling of flood management policies in the upper Tisza*, Interim Report IR-03-02, International Institute for Applied Systems Analysis, Laxenburg, Austria (2003).

[38] J. Linnerooth-Bayer, R. Löfstedt, G. Sjöstedt, Transboundary Risk Management in Europe, Earthscan, London (2000).

[39] H. Kunreuther, J. Linnerooth-Bayer and K. Fitzgerald, *Citing hazardous facilities: lessons from Europe and America*, Energy Environment and the Economy: Asian Perspectives, P. Kleindorfer, H. Kunreuther and D. Hong, eds, Edward Elgar, Brookneld (1996), 145–167.

[40] J. Linnerooth-Bayer, *Climate change and multiple views of fairness*, Fair Weather? Equity Concerns in Climate Change, F. Toth, ed., Earthscan, London (1999), 267–295.

[41] P. Freeman, L. Martin, J. Linnerooth-Bayer, R. Mechler, S. Saldana, K. Warner and G. Pflug, *National systems for comprehensive disaster management: financing reconstruction. Phase II background study for the regional policy dialogue of the Inter-American Development Bank*, Technical Report, Inter-American Development Bank Washington, DC (2002). http://www.iadb.org/int/drp/ing/Red6/Docs/FreemanSistemasNatPhase2May20%02eng.pdf.

[42] H. Kunreuther and J. Linnerooth-Bayer, *The financial management of catastrophic flood risks in emerging-economy countries*, Risk Anal. **23** (2003), 627–639.

[43] A. Vari, J. Linnerooth-Bayer and Z. Ferencz, *Stakeholder views on flood risk management in Hungary's upper Tisza basin*, Risk Anal. **23** (2003), 583–601.

[44] J. Linnerooth-Bayer and A. Amenodla, *Special edition on flood risks in Europe*, Risk Anal. **23** (2003), 537–627.

[45] T. Ermolieva, A. Westlund and L. MacKellar, *On long-term forecasting of social security: a robustness analysis*, Qual. Quantity **35** (2001), 33–48.

[46] T. Ermolieva, *Optimization of social security systems under uncertainty Interim*, Report IR-02-077, International Institute for Applied Systems Analysis, Laxenburg, Austria (2002).

[47] L. MacKellar, T. Ermolieva, D. Horlacher and L. Mayhew, *Economic Impacts of Population Aging in Japan*, ESRI Series on Aging, Edward Elgar Publishing, Northampton, MA (2004).

[48] G. Pflug, *How to measure risk? Festschrift for F. Ferschl*, Physica Verlag, Berlin (1997).

[49] G. Pflug, *Some remarks on the value-at-risk and the conditional value-at-risk*, Probabilistic Constrained Optimization—Methodology and Applications, S. Uryasev, ed., Kluwer, Dordrecht (2000), 272–281.

[50] Y. Ermoliev, T. Ermolieva, G. MacDonald and V. Norkin, *Insurability of catastrophic risks: the stochastic optimization model*, Optimization **47** (3/4) (2000).
[51] Y. Ermoliev and S. Flam, *Finding pareto optimal insurance contracts*, Geneva Papers Risk Insurance Theor. **26** (2001), 155–167.
[52] Y. Ermoliev and V. Norkin, *On nonsmooth and discontinuous problems of stochastic systems optimization*, Eur. J. Oper. Res. **101** (1997), 230–244.
[53] P. Freeman and G. Pflug, *Infrastructure in developing and transition countries: risk and protection*, Risk Anal. **3** (23) (2003), 601–610.
[54] Y. Ermoliev, T. Ermolieva and V. Norkin, *Economic growth under shocks: path dependencies and stabilization*, Micro Meso Macro: Addressing Complex Systems Couplings, H. Liljenstrom and U. Svedin, eds, Abisco Book, Abisco, Sweden (2004), (forthcoming).
[55] Y. Ermoliev and V. Norkin, *Risk and extended expected utility functions: optimization approaches*, Interim Report IR-03-033, International Institute for Applied Systems Analysis, Laxenburg, Austria (2003).
[56] G. Pflug, *Risk reshaping contracts and stochastic optimization*, Central Eur. J. Oper. Res. **5** (3-4) (1998), 205–230.
[57] G. Pflug, E. Dockner, A. Swietanowski and H. Moritsch, *The AURORA financial management system: from model design to parallel implementation*, Ann. Oper. Res. **99** (2000), 189–206.
[58] G. Pflug and A. Swietanowski, *Selected parallel optimization methods for financial management under uncertainty*, Parallel Comput. **26** (2000), 3–25.
[59] A. Geoffrion, *An introduction to structured modeling*, Mgmt Sci. **33** (5) (1987), 547–588.
[60] M. Pidd, *Just modeling through: a rough guide to modeling*, Interfaces **29** (2) (1999), 118–132.
[61] Y. Nakamori and Y. Sawaragi, *Complex systems analysis and environmental modeling*, Eur. J. Oper. Res. **122** (2) (2000), 178–189.
[62] R. van Waveren, S. Groot, H. Scholten, F. van Geer, H. Wösten, R. Koeze and J. Noort, *Good Modelling Practice Handbook*, STOWA, Utrecht, The Netherlands (1999), http://waterland.net/riza/aquest/gmpuk.pdf.

CHAPTER 3

Managing Complex and Dynamic Systems for the Future

E.D. Jones

Lawrence Livermore National Laboratory, 7000 East Avenue, L-634, Livermore, CA 94551, USA
E-mail: jones37@llnl.gov

Contents

Abstract

The challenges of modern complicated systems regarding their design, analysis, and management are put in a historical context to better propose a framework for the future involving complementary uses of testing, modeling, and performance functions.

SYSTEMS AND HUMAN SCIENCE – FOR SAFETY, SECURITY, AND DEPENDABILITY
Edited by Tatsuo Arai, Shigeru Yamamoto and Kazuhisa Makino

1. Introduction

As scientists and engineers involved with complex and dynamic systems, we are at an important point in intellectual history, and we thus have a special responsibility to society. The unusual behavior of complicated engineered systems—with their attendant potential benefits and dangers—has been foreshadowed and anticipated for some time. Examples include solitary wave phenomena (e.g., Kortwieg de Vries and sine-Gordon models); hyper-sensitivity to initial conditions (e.g., weather models); nonlinear behavior of many-body simulations (e.g., Monte Carlo and cellular automata); and, more recently, system approaches to biological and earth sciences.

Closer to the public, over time we have built systems, such as energy, information, finance, communication, and physical infrastructure networks, with relatively simple component behaviors which in connection and interdependence with other elements have become complex systems capable of exhibiting unexpected phenomena and vulnerabilities to perturbations. A recent example is the failure of the Northeast American power grid in mid-August 2003, followed a couple of weeks later by the blackout of Italy. These power management systems were developed with hardware, software, and human operator components each well understood using traditional engineering practices. But their collective behavior and failure, in the American instance cited, are not understood to date despite the focused efforts of the best experts in the field. Failures of complex systems on which society has come to depend may be the difference between light and dark, or even life and death.

However, we do not need just large, extensive network systems to appreciate the problems and challenges we will face in this century regarding the design, analysis, and management of complex and dynamic systems. Smaller, more focused, semi-automatic or robotic systems also present laboratories for the investigation of complicated processes which typically involve a mixture of machine, software, and human factors. I will use my experience with the risk analysis of a semi-robotic medical radiation treatment device, the Gamma Knife, to illustrate the potential roles of measurement, simulation, and performance objectives in managing complex and dynamic systems in the future.

We now must rapidly learn to deal with such complicated systems, because they are becoming prevalent in our societies and present practical problems. Happily, we have techniques and tools, especially computational capabilities, to aid us. We also need paradigms or frameworks for thinking anew about systems in an increasingly nonlinear world. This chapter suggests a path forward based on complementary uses of system measurement, simulation, and performance functions.

2. Systems analysis and measurement

In order to foresee complex systems analysis, it is useful to put our predicament in a historical perspective. Since the beginning of the Age of Reason, Western thinkers have struggled with the respective roles and dilemmas associated with determinism and uncertainty. By the early 1800s, a synthesis of these ideas was obtained, as embodied in the work of Laplace [1,2]. Laplace's astronomical work was a completely mechanical explanation of the solar system based on Newtonian principles, i.e., it was the deterministic "celestial mechanics". However, astronomical measurements have discrepancies or errors among them and it is problematic to know which result is the usable one. The solution to this problem was the "law of errors" (i.e., errors are normally distributed such that the deviation from the mean is as predictable as the mean itself as a function of the number of observations) which arose out of two closely related ideas: probability theory, which sought to understand chance events, and statistics which sought to measure fluctuating phenomena. Laplace was explicit about the probabilistic nature of statistical calculations: we can never know with absolute certainty; we can only know with greater or lesser degrees of probability. With the "law of errors", statistics and probability theory allowed scientists to achieve far greater degrees of precision than they had imagined possible.

In general, the concepts of that era have propagated forth to inform systems thinking today. They are embedded in powerful conventional constructs of analysis: linear causality, precision certainty, reversibility, reductionism, and induction/deduction. Unfortunately, some or all of these concepts may not apply to evaluations of the complicated phenomena of modern complex and dynamic systems.

For instance, statistics can conquer uncertainty, but statistics needs proper measurements or tests to be made. Proper measurement involves the assumption that a piece of the system can be partitioned and isolated to be measured; the component measurement is independent of the other parts of the system; and the results can be placed back in the aggregated system without prejudice. This is a lot to take for granted with modern systems, which typically contain hardware, software, and human elements coupled together. To illustrate this, Fig. 1 summarizes the nature of errors or failures for such components.

We are familiar with hardware or machine failures, where the failures are random but their rates can be determined through statistically rigorous testing regimes. All software errors are pre-determined—they are encoded—but their occurrence depends on a conspiracy of circumstance which may not be anticipated by stochastic sampling. Unintentional human errors occur for both mechanistic and random reasons and can, in principle, have rates established through statistical tests; but all relevant conditions or environments may not be available. Intentional human acts, such as criminal or terrorist acts, are neither deterministic nor random and hence beg the use of probability. These error problems are compounded when different components interact in unexpected ways. So, in a complicated system the value of measurement is conditional.

	Deterministic	Stochastic
Hardware	No	Yes
Software	Yes	No
Human (unintentional)	Yes	Yes
Human (intentional)	No	No

Fig. 1. Nature of errors or failures associated with system components.

We had to deal with such problems for a risk-based evaluation of the Gamma Knife semi-robotic medical device [3]. Decomposing or partitioning of the system process into steps was aided by the linear process procedure from lesion identification, treatment planning, pre-treatment setup, to treatment. But each step contained a mix of hardware, software, and human activities and potential failure modes for which very little information was available (the Gamma Knife was a new device that had been used for a limited number of treatments and had few failures). Statistical samples with confidence levels for failures during each step were out of the question and we thus used qualitative probability distributions constructed from sparse manufacturer, operational, anecdotal, and expert information. The data were compared in a risk profiling method that allowed us to compare the relative risk (based on mean values) of each process step, independent of the other steps. This provided a first-order view of where important risk may lie in the performance of the system.

The bottom line of this discussion is that reductions for measurement or testing of a complex system are not adequate: they only provide an incomplete representation of the system's real state of affairs. Other aspects of system analysis are needed.

3. System simulations

Another way to represent the behavior of a system is through modeling or simulation. This, of course, requires another type of abstraction, and partial view, of the complex system involving a choice of mechanisms to model and preferences for the generation of certain types of system data or behaviors. But the coordination of the nature of the simulations with the system features testing and measurement capabilities can lead to a more faithful representation of the system as a whole. Computer simulations are a powerful way of gaining insight into complex system processes and are substantially aided by modern developments in high-performance computing, visualization tools, and the rise of interdisciplinary research.

System simulations can be profitably used in different ways. One approach is to look at many solutions at once to develop a sophisticated understanding of the global structure of an ensemble of system solutions with respect to its underlying mechanisms. This may entail looking for specific patterns in the system performance data, or using the "geometry" of the solutions to guide optimal performance strategies against several competing constraints. This approach is used in planning spacecraft trajectories in celestial mechanics, and in some forms of weather prediction. Another application is sensitivity studies where fluctuations or perturbations are introduced to study oscillations or limit cycles of the system, from which it is possible to design strategies that ensure stable operation. Example arenas are manufacturing processes and transportation networks. The computer modeling may be direct, in the sense of starting from basic mechanisms to develop system states of affairs or outcomes. On the other hand, as demonstrated by Lawrence Livermore fusion scientists, codes can be developed where the performance outcomes are provided as inputs and the optimal system design to meet those requirements is generated.

In the case of the Gamma Knife study, sequential Monte Carlo simulations were employed to generate a multitude of treatment scenarios in order to explore the risk space of the system. Each system process steps had qualitative (using relative scales) probability distributions for both equipment and human errors or failures and also distributions for the magnitudes of the errors. A Monte Carlo sampling technique was applied to each step distribution to determine if an error occurred in that step, and if so, what was its sampled magnitude; and then the errors were aggregated probabilistically using the logical relations among the system components. Thus, for each scenario the aggregate likelihood of error and its magnitude (i.e., its consequence) was recorded along with the risk contributors. Through 100,000 such simulations to reach convergence, a picture of the distribution of risks emerged along with the identification of the most significant contributors to the highest risks. The results of these simulations revealed different significant risk contributors than the relative point risk estimates mentioned in Section 2. This was due to the unexpected conspiracy effects of the interactions among process events, especially with respect to the tails of their distributions. In other words, the shape of the distributions turned out to be more important then their mean values, through nonlinear interactions which were only realized upon simulation. These effects were later validated by real events.

As mentioned above, the important science and art of complex systems analysis is to coordinate both system testing and simulation to achieve a more robust understanding and management of the system. Simulation can help direct what system features should be measured and to what extent; and, of course, system testing/measurement will inform the desired characteristics of the simulation model. The desirable goal is to achieve a high level of correlation among measurements, simulations, and phenomenological performance figures-of-merit. For complex systems, we probably cannot disentangle the nature of the correlations between deterministic and stochastic effects; but having confidence in the correlations themselves is extremely valuable regardless of their pedigree.

4. Bounding system performance

The third complementary aspect, in addition to measurement and simulation, needed for complex system evaluation and management is realistic performance bounds and associated figures-of-merit for system performance. Dynamic systems become problems when certain behaviors become unbounded or far exceed expected limits, and these can be facilitated if appropriate performance objectives are not employed and integrated with the design or analysis from the beginning. As an analogy, if nutrients and space are unlimited, bacteria will divide steadily and increase exponentially. But if resources are limited, the bacteria proliferation rate will drop or the death rate will increase, and the population will stabilize. Similarly, the scientist and engineer need to establish and impose limits for their systems to ensure that unwanted system excursions do not occur. These can be used to coordinate the measurement and simulation activities for system analysis so that the correlated representation of the system maps into performance figures-of-merit, and vice versa, to aid system control and management.

One useful approach to bounding system behavior is to delimit the risks, between residual risk of little or no interest and unacceptable risk; and to delimit performance, for example, between desirable performance objectives, such as throughput or maintainability, and available resources or options (money, equipment, people, etc.) which are always limited. One way to represent these bounds is in a risk-based framework as illustrated in Fig. 2.

The aim of the establishment of risk goals is to define the regions of prudent or acceptable risks, thus allowing systems to operate within them to maximize their benefits or utilities as resources and performance characteristics will permit. These risk goals should have both consequence and likelihood dimensions. Two limits are needed for the likelihood bounds: a "screening" frequency below which the unwanted high-consequence incident likelihood is considered negligible; and a "target" frequency above which the events for lower levels of consequence cannot be allowed to occur. Thus, for each risk goal the states of the system are managed (by the available options) such that the likelihood for any consequence is between the screening and target limits.

The region of "mutually acceptable equilibrium" (MAE) refers to common system scenarios and events that occur at frequencies high enough to make them statistically observable, but the consequences tend to be small. The statistics for MAE events allow a management balance which is continuously fine-tuned and has "preventive" qualities. Scenarios from this region might escalate into the region of "conservatively permissible risk" (CPR) where scenarios and events are highly improbable (beyond the design basis), but the consequences may be severe. Such system endpoints need to be examined to determine what design mechanisms or barriers are required so that their likelihood is limited. For CPR scenarios, if they occur, there needs to be mitigative management options. Emergency response is invoked if mitigation fails. The sequence of preventive, mitigative, and emergency response management constitutes a defense-in-depth against runaway system behavior. Of course, one always wants to move the risks, by cost-effective system design changes or management practices, from higher to lower risk regions.

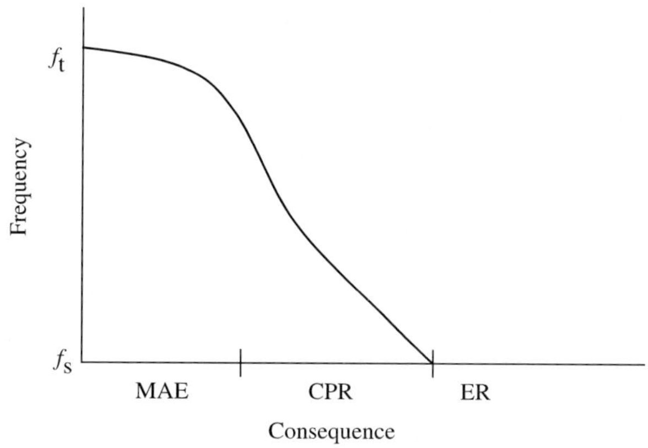

Fig. 2. Risk space defined and partitioned among screening (f_s) and target (f_t) frequencies and regions of mutually acceptable equilibrium (MAE), conservatively permissible risk (CPR), and emergency response (ER).

The risk goals, management options, and other objectives and constraints bound the complex system evaluation problem. They provide the endpoints of interest to scenarios and serve to reach problem closure by providing a quantitative feel for the magnitude of the risks relative to the various management strategies.

In the case of the Gamma Knife study, system component measurements were used in Monte Carlo simulations of a multitude of scenarios to delineate the risk space for the Gamma Knife system. The results indicated a relatively large population of scenarios in high-risk regions, which exceeded desirable risk goals. Inspection of these scenarios identified certain process tasks that are significant risk contributors. By making changes in procedures and design features associated with these tasks, subsequent simulations indicated a substantial reduction in potential high-risk scenarios. In terms of the discussion above, these methods exemplified how scenarios in the CPR regime could be moved to the MAE regime through system feature changes.

5. Summary

We are faced with managing emerging complex and dynamic systems in our societies, which we depend on for our well-being, safety, and security. Their mixed attributes of mechanics, software, and human factors give rise to complications and issues heretofore unaddressed in the history of system analysis. We may not be able to depend on traditional and reliable concepts such as reductionism or induction or even direct causality, and yet we must proceed.

This chapter has suggested that a science-based risk approach framework for analyzing, designing, and managing our complex systems entails a triad of complementary functions: measurement or testing, modeling or simulation, and risk-based objectives to bound performance. Probabilistic techniques play a fundamental role in combining and mapping information among these functions. Each function is inadequate in itself; but they can work together, synergistically, to help understand complex system behavior. This has been demonstrated in the case of the semi-robotic medical treatment device, the Gamma Knife. While the applications of these methods are contingent on the particular system of interest, the collection of principles they represent may be more universally applicable.

References

[1] I. Hacking, *The Emergence of Probability: A Philosophical Study of Early Ideas about Probability, Induction, and Statistical Inference*, Cambridge University Press, Cambridge, MA (1975).

[2] P.L. Bernstein, *Against the Gods: The Remarkable Story of Risk*, Wiley, New York (1996).

[3] E.D. Jones, W.W. Banks, T.J. Altenbach and L.E. Fischer, *Relative Risk Analysis in Regulating the Use of Radiation-Emitting Medical Devices: A Preliminary Application*, US Nuclear Regulatory Commission, (1995), NUREG/CR-6323.

CHAPTER 4

Characteristics of Visual Attention and the Safety

T. Miura, K. Shinohara and T. Kimura

Graduate School of Human Sciences, Osaka University, Suita, Osaka, Japan
E-mail: toshi@hus.osaka-u.ac.jp (T. Miura)

K. Ishimatsu

National Institute of Advanced Industrial Science and Technology, Tsukuba, Japan

Contents

Abstract

Characteristics of visual attention related to automobile driving safety are discussed from three aspects based on our research. The first concerns eye movements and useful field of view in a realistic setting, here in actual driving. The narrowing of the useful field of view with increasing demands and a trade-off between depth and width of processing were found. The second concerns a shift of attention in depth in a moving observer situation. Asymmetric characteristic of shift of attention in depth was more clearly found in moving observer situations than stationary situations. We call this asymmetry the rubber-band metaphor of visual attention. The third aspect concerns the time course of visual attention: The before and after effect of use of car navigation on attention to the forward traffic environment. A deteriorative effect was demonstrated. It should be stressed that it is important for safety to conduct psychological experiments on visual attention in behavior oriented situations.

SYSTEMS AND HUMAN SCIENCE – FOR SAFETY, SECURITY, AND DEPENDABILITY
Edited by Tatsuo Arai, Shigeru Yamamoto and Kazuhisa Makino

1. Introduction

The growth of traffic flow and density causes more accidents, more severe traffic jams and increasing pollution. Information systematization of vehicles and road networks (Intelligent Transport Systems, ITS) can resolve these problems. However, lack of evaluation of the systems and devices addressing driving safety cannot be overlooked. The purpose of the present study is to examine the safety and efficiency of visual information to be presented to drivers. For this purpose, three characteristics of visual attention related to ITS were briefly reviewed from the viewpoint of basic visual psychology. The first is useful field of view, that is, the two-dimensional range of visual attention. This is essential for gathering visual information. The second is shift of visual attention in depth. This is especially important for moving observers. The third is the temporal characteristic of visual attention, that is, before and after effects. In introducing new information aids for drivers, we should consider carefully the characteristics of human visual attention.

2. Change of useful field of view and cognitive momentum

There are a lot of studies on the useful field of view under tachistoscopic and moving window conditions, but characteristics of the useful field of view with free eye movements in natural behavior have never been examined. Based on our previous eye movement studies in driving, it was hypothesized that the size of the useful field of view becomes smaller with an increase in demands [1,2]. In order to examine this hypothesis, both eye movements and useful field of view were examined at the same time. As the target, a small spot of light was presented spatially and temporally at random. The subjects' task was to detect a target and respond orally. As Fig. 1 shows, the reaction time and eye movements of target detection were measured. It was clearly shown that with an increase in demands, that is increasing complexity of the traffic environment, the useful field of view becomes narrower, and, correspondingly, reaction time for detection of peripherally presented targets becomes longer. Thus the hypothesis was confirmed.

Why does narrowing of the useful field of view occur with an increase in demands? Further examination revealed two active functions. One is the deeper processing at each fixation point, which causes narrowing of the useful field of view. The other is the stronger inclination towards acquiring information in the peripheral visual field [3]. Our previous studies [3] also found these two active functions by examining the rate of increase in reaction time as a function of the onset eccentricity of targets. Moreover, we have also demonstrated the product of response eccentricity with reaction time in foveal vision to be constant, indicating the amount of processing resources available to be limited [4]. These active functions found in more demanding situations have been called "cognitive momentum" by Miura [1].

It might be said that this cognitive momentum reflects an optimization of allocation of limited processing resources for coping with more demands. A trade-off between depth and width of processing can thus be interpreted [1]. Recently we have also examined the effects of aging and consumption of alcohol on the useful field of view [5,6].

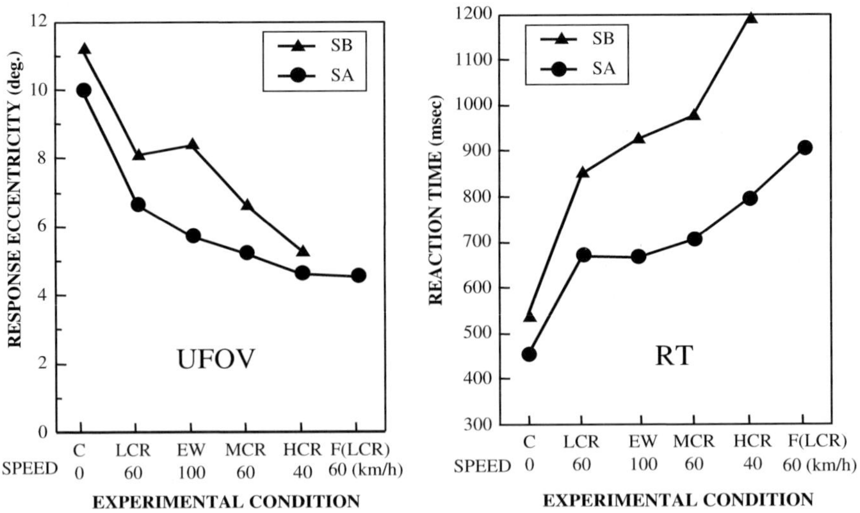

Fig. 1. Response eccentricity (size of useful field of view: left) and reaction time (right) as a function of situational demand. Note. conditions; C, control; LCR, low crowded route; EW, expressway; MCR, moderately crowded route; HCR, highly crowded route; F(LCR), fatigue on LCR; SA and SB, subject A and B.

Though these findings give a new perspective on visual attention, eye movement studies can tell a little about the shift of attention in three-dimensional space, and little research has been carried out in this area.

3. Attention in depth: the rubber-band metaphor

Shift of visual attention in depth (different distances) was examined in an observer moving situation [3,7–9], using a tunnel simulator. The simulator was 1/50 scale and 13 m in length and subjects were able to move as if in a real driving situation at various speeds (Fig. 2). The task of subjects was the judgment of relative distance of targets—farther, nearer or the same in comparison with a fixed point. Their reaction time was also measured. Targets were presented on the central sight line, at five apparent distances of 5–115 m (real sight distance of 0.2–4.6 m).

There were two independent variables. One was the observing condition of the subjects: Stationary and two moving conditions at apparent speeds of 40 and 80 km/h. These three conditions were conducted in separate sessions of 200 trials, and the order of the conditions was counterbalanced among subjects. One session lasted from 30 min to 2.5 h, depending on conditions.

The other variable was the validity of cues, that is, expectancy [10] of the appearance locations of the targets, relative to a fixed point. In each trial, subjects fixated on the fixed point, which indicated by color whether a target would be presented nearer to or farther from the fixed point. A green fixed point indicated nearer presentation, a red one indicated farther presentation, and when both green and red fixed points were presented, subjects

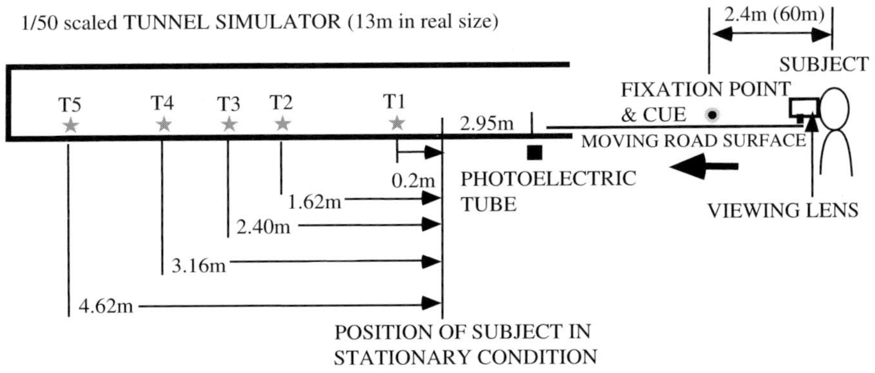

Fig. 2. The apparatus for experiments on attention in depth.

would not know the presentation location in advance. Within each session, 50% of trials were unknown (not cued), called neutral trials. The other 50% of trials were cued. Among cued trials, 80% of trials were cued correctly, called valid cue trials. The other 20% of trials were cued incorrectly, called invalid cue trials. In these trials, targets appeared at one of the other locations, that is if cued as nearer, the target appeared farther away or at the same location in comparison with the fixed point.

The results clearly showed that reaction times for nearer targets are shorter than those for farther targets under all conditions tested (Fig. 3). This supports a viewer centered representation of three-dimensional space [11]. Concerning the direction of shift (switching) of attention, the reaction time for a shift of attention from a distant location to a near location is shorter than the reverse (Fig. 4). This is called the "rubber-band

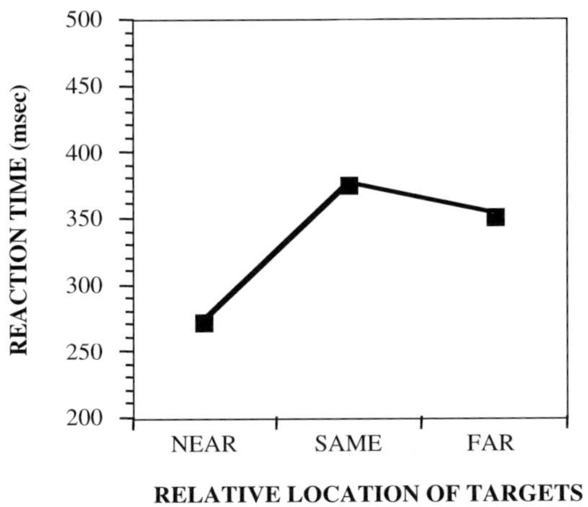

Fig. 3. Effect of location of targets relative to the fixation point.

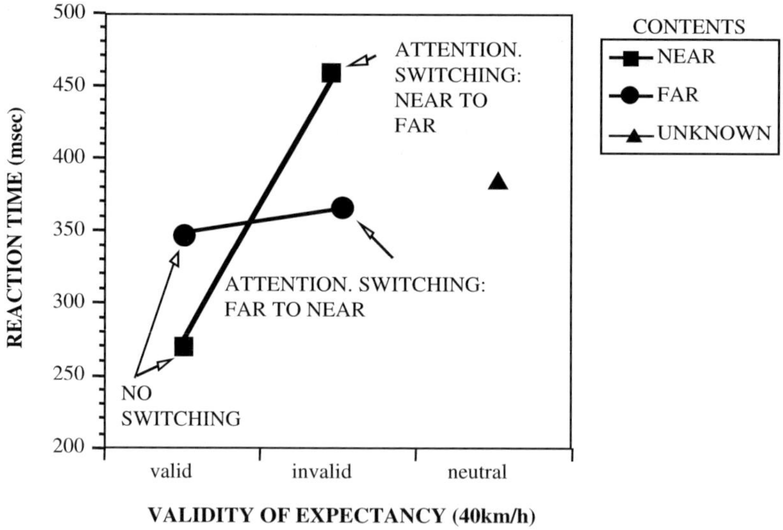

Fig. 4. Relation between validity and contents of cue (expectancy) in a moving situation (40 km/h): The asymmetry of attention switching is shown in invalid expectancy.

metaphor of attention" (asymmetrical viewer centered mode of attentional shift). The difference is greatest in high-speed situations, while almost no difference is found in stationary situations.

These results could not be explained by the characteristics of accommodation and vergence. This is because reaction times here are much shorter than the latency of those properties, and differences between subjects in moving and stationary situations cannot be fully explained by those. These findings are relevant to drivers' safety and are ecologically valid. Recently we have examined the relationship between the rubber-band phenomenon and depth perception [8,12,13]. Thus, two-dimensional and three-dimensional, that is, spatial characteristics of visual attention were clarified. Now we proceed to the temporal characteristics.

4. The temporal characteristics of visual attention: the before and after effects

The purpose of the present experiment is to examine the before and after effects of using a car navigation system on attention to the forward environment [14].

4.1. *Method*

Under control conditions, two slides of a forward traffic environment taken from the driver's perspective were successively presented. The subjects' task was to judge whether a dangerous change appeared in the second slide. Under the navigation conditions, subjects were required to observe a navigation display before or after presentation of the second slide.

4.1.1. *Procedure and experimental conditions (see Fig. 5).* Control and navigation conditions were conducted in separate sessions.

4.1.1.1. *Control conditions.* Under control conditions, the two alternative forced choice responses (dangerous or safe judgments of the second slides) were required as soon as possible. The second slides were presented successively to the first slides. Three kinds of dangerous change were shown: Lighting of brake lamps of a preceding vehicle, shortening of head way to a preceding vehicle, and jutting out of an oncoming vehicle towards the subjects'. In half the trials, these dangerous changes appeared. The presentation duration of the first slide varied between 2 and 5 s. The inter-stimulus interval between the first and the second slide was almost 0 s. The second slides disappeared with the subjects' response.

4.1.1.2. *Navigation conditions.* Under navigation conditions, subjects were required to observe a navigation display before or after the appearance of the second slide. So, the dangerous situation appeared after observing a navigation display (after effect case), or before observing a navigation display (before effect case). In the latter case, subjects were preparing to observe a navigation display.

In the after effect case, a signal tone cueing observation of a navigation display was presented during observation of the first slide. At the same moment as the signal tone, a navigation display was presented. Subjects had to identify the position of their own vehicle, the name of the next intersection and the direction of travel at the intersection shown by an arrow at the lower right corner of the display. After this observation, they returned their lines of sight to the slide of forward scenery as soon as possible. The second slides were presented 2, 3 or 5 s after presentation of the navigation display. After responding to the second slides, subjects answered questions about

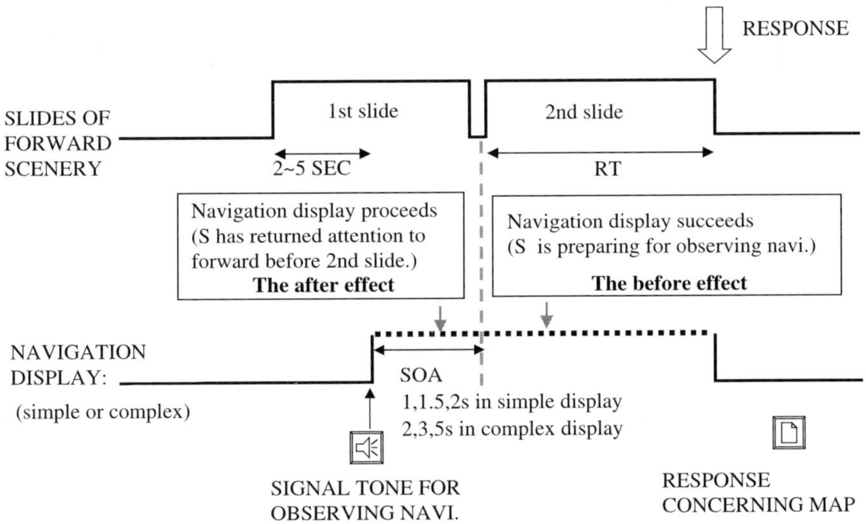

Fig. 5. Time course of stimulus presentation.

navigation information. The navigation display disappeared with the subjects' response to the second slides.

The subjects' head and eye movements were captured by a video camera in zoom mode. If the line of sight did not return to the first slide, the data were excluded from analyses.

In the before effect case, the second slides were presented during observation of the first slide. This presentation was the same as under control conditions, but the difference was that subjects were preparing to observe the navigation display in this case. The proportion of these trials was one quarter of all trials.

4.1.2. *Presentation of navigation display.* The navigation display was 6 in. in size, and presented at a position which was easy to observe and similar to a navigation display on the market. The map was a particularly simple one.

4.1.3. *Subjects.* Four undergraduate students participated in five sessions under control conditions and six sessions under navigation conditions. One session contained 60 trials. The total number of trials was 2640.

4.2. *Results and discussion*

In the following results, trials in which subjects were still observing the navigation display when the second slide was presented, and trials in which reaction times were over 2000 ms and under 100 ms were excluded from analysis.

4.2.1. *Reaction time and ratio of incorrect responses to forward dangerous events.* Figure 6 shows the results. Mean reaction times are 812 and 716 ms and mean ratio of incorrect responses (miss) are 7.57 and 3.35%, under navigation conditions and control conditions, respectively. These results confirm that attention to the forward situation deteriorates before and after observing a navigation display (the before and the

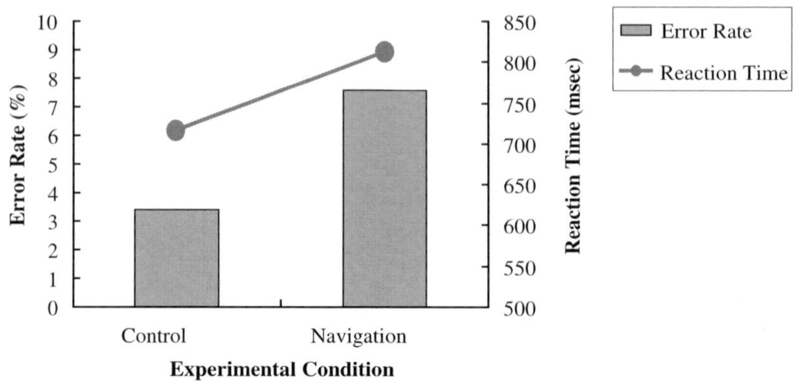

Fig. 6. Reaction time and error rate.

after effects). The same deterioration was demonstrated with every kind of danger and every subject.

4.2.2. *Temporal range of the after effect.* Figure 7 shows the time course of the effect. This demonstrates that attention to the forward situation deteriorates before observing a navigation display and the deterioration persists for around 5 s after the beginning of observation of a navigation display. The problem lies not only during direct observation of navigation but also before and after the observation when lines of sight are directed forward.

4.2.3. *Factors affecting deterioration of attention caused by observation of a navigation display*

4.2.3.1. *Factors of the before effect.* The following two factors may contribute to the effect.

(a) Firstly, the rubber-band characteristic could be a cause. That is, switching from preparing to pay attention to a nearer position causes the late detection of farther forward events. The present experiment was a stationary one, so a larger delay would be expected in moving situations. This is a factor of visual attention.
(b) Secondly, the deterioration of general primary attention was caused by preparation for subsidiary attention to other tasks. This is not restricted to visual matter.

4.2.3.2. *Factors of the after effect.* The following three factors may play a part.

(a) Interference between retention of a visual image of the navigation display and visual processing of the forward scenery [15,16]. This concerns the problem of visual presentation of navigation information.
(b) General load retention of navigation information. This is not restricted to visual presentation.
(c) Effect of residue of attention for other tasks. This would not be caused by intentional retention of information.

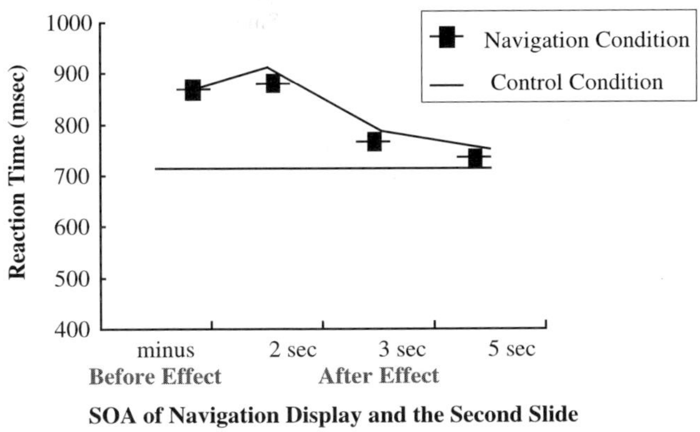

Fig. 7. Time course of deteriorative effect of using a navigation system.

4.2.4. *Conclusion and suggestions.* The effect of using automobile navigation systems on attention to the forward traffic environment was examined in laboratory experiments. These demonstrate that reaction times become longer under navigation conditions than under control conditions in which observation of a navigation display is not necessary. The deterioration begins before the observation (before effect), and the deteriorative effect persists for 5 s (after effect) in the present experiment. It could be said that it is almost self evident that visual attention will deteriorate during observation of navigation displays because sight lines deviate from the forward environment. However, this research shows that visual attention deteriorates both before and after observing navigation displays even when sight lines do not deviate.

5. Concluding remarks

Firstly, some characteristics and functions of the distribution of attention resources in a two-dimensional space, the useful field of view, were clarified. It was suggested that in-vehicle displays should not be demanding, especially in crowded situations. Secondly, characteristics of shift of attention in depth for moving observers were clarified. The cost of attending to closer locations is large. This suggests problems of safety in allocation of attention to in-vehicle displays and head-up displays. Thirdly, temporal characteristics of visual attention were clarified. Use of car navigation systems cannot have environmental validity with regard to safety, because their use makes drivers pay dual attention. In introducing information technology to automobiles, a balance among safety, convenience and comfort should be considered. Safety is the primary factor in driving, so, in introducing new technology, basic mechanisms of attention should be examined as in the present study.

References

[1] T. Miura, *Coping with situational demands: a study of eye movements and peripheral vision*, Vision in Vehicles, A.G. Gale, M.H. Freeman, C.M. Haslegrave, P. Smith and S.P. Taylor, eds, Elsevier, Amsterdam (1986), 205–216.

[2] T. Miura, *Active functions of eye movement and useful field of view in a realistic setting*, From Eye to Mind, R. Groner, G. D'Ydewalle and R. Parham, eds, North Holland, Amsterdam (1990), 119–127.

[3] T. Miura, *Behavior and Visual Attention*, Kazama Publishers (1996) (text in Japanese).

[4] T. Miura, *Visual search in intersections: an underlying mechanism*, IATSS Res. **16** (1992), 42–49.

[5] T. Miura, T. Ishida, Y. Nishida and K. Ishimatsu, Peripheral vision performance at low blood alcohol level. *Abstract of the ninth International Conference on Vision in Vehicles*, Vol. 22, (2001).

[6] K. Ishimatsu, T. Miura and L. Sugano, *Effects of aging on the useful field of view: predictability of target location and the distribution of attentional resource*, Perception **31** (suppl.) (2002), 169.

[7] T. Miura, M. Yano, M. Takahashi and R. Sugano, Research on presentation of information and traffic safety. *Research Report of the International Association of Traffic Safety Science* (1994) (text in Japanese).

[8] T. Miura, K. Shinohara and K. Kanda, *Shift of attention in depth in a semi-realistic setting*, Jpn. J. Psychol. **44** (2002), 124–133.

[9] T. Miura, K. Shinohara and K. Kanda, *Attentional shift in three-dimensional space for moving observers*, Perception **23** (suppl.) (1994), 43.

[10] M. Posner, M.J. Nissen and W.C. Ogden, *Attended and nonattended processing modes: The role of set for spatial location*, Modes of Perceiving and Processing Information, H.L. Pick and E. Saltzman, eds, Erlbaum, Hillsdale, NJ (1978), 137–157.
[11] G.J. Andersen and A.F. Kramer, *Limits of focused attention in three-dimensional space*, Percept. Psychophys. **53** (1993), 658–667.
[12] T. Kimura and T. Miura, *Attention in depth modulates spatial perception: the comparison between depth perception and distance perception*, Jpn. J. Psychon. Sci. **22** (2003), 39–40.
[13] T. Kimura, T. Miura, S. Doi and Y. Yamamoto, *Top-down and bottom-up allocation of attention in three-dimensional space when observers are moving forward*, Tech. Rep. Atten. Cogn. **16** (2002), 1–4.
[14] T. Miura and K. Shinohara, *Characteristics of visual attention related to ITS*, Traffic Sci. **28** (1,2) (1998), 53–59 (text in Japanese).
[15] L.R. Brooks, *Spatial and verbal components in the act of recall*, Can. J. Psychol. **22** (1968), 349–368.
[16] A.D. Baddeley and K. Lieberman, *Spatial working memory*, Attention and Performance, R. Nickerson, ed., Vol. VII, Erlbaum, Hillsdale, NJ (1980), 521–539.

PART II

Modeling, Decision Analysis and Management for Realizing an SSR Society

CHAPTER 5

An Agent-Based Rules Discovery from Complex Database

Mina Ryoke

Graduate School of Business Sciences, University of Tsukuba, 3-29-1 Otsuka, Tokyo 112-0012, Japan

Yoshiteru Nakamori

School of Knowledge Science, Japan Advanced Institute of Science and Technology, 1-1 Asahidai, Tatsunokuchi, Ishikawa 923-1292, Japan

Contents

Abstract

In this chapter, an agent-based approach to complex systems modeling is proposed. The requirement for complex systems modeling techniques is increasing in order to plan a safe, secure and reliable society, because more recently, most systems are becoming complex. This chapter describes agent-based clustering and an expression of the character of the obtained clusters. Each agent has a role to collect data points (objects) based on similarity, which is defined so that each agent can treat a mixed database. The interaction between the agents focuses on discussing the objects to consider all the attributes. The agent identifies an

SYSTEMS AND HUMAN SCIENCE – FOR SAFETY, SECURITY, AND DEPENDABILITY
Edited by Tatsuo Arai, Shigeru Yamamoto and Kazuhisa Makino

if–then rule based on the collected data and tries to determine variables for rule description. There is no objective function differing from the conventional mining methods, however, by taking this approach, there are some advantage points of the proposed method. One of the advantages is that it is not necessary to determine the number of the clusters before performing the process.

1. Introduction

The requirement for complex systems modeling techniques is increasing in order to plan a safe, secure and reliable society (SSR), because, more recently, most systems are becoming complex. A knowledge discovery method based on observed databases from complex systems has been investigated and has been applied to complex systems modeling. One well-known complex system is the environmental problem. Complex types of behavior often appear here, and make modeling difficult. These complex types of behavior often demand complex mathematical modeling based on a variety of professional knowledge to describe them. However, it is not easy for most political decision makers to understand the complex mathematical model and/or its behaviors, since they are usually not familiar with the techniques based on multiple professional fields. In such a case, rule based modeling is a promising modeling style, because the if–then rule description is familiar to human beings. The extracted information allows non-professional people to understand the decision-making process. In an interdisciplinary domain such as the environmental problem, people from different main fields have to work together to discuss and make strategies for society. Therefore, it is very important to express the work in a way everyone can understand.

We have been engaged in construction of rule-based models and faced up to a difficult problem of selecting variables (or attributes) used in the model in addition to the data partition problem. In order to perform them successfully, we are trying to develop an agent-based system in which many agents will compete to discover the local system substructures, and finally express the whole system structure in harmony. This chapter proposes an agent-based modeling technique that treats a complex database. A complex database means here that all data points in the database have the same attributes and some attributes are categorical and others are numerical. Cases when all attributes are categorical or numerical are not excluded.

Clustering analysis is an important technique in knowledge discovery from database [1]. Among non-hierarchical clustering methods, the k-means algorithm [2] is a powerful tool for partitioning a dataset into several disjointed clusters. In fuzzy versions of the k-means algorithm [3,4], each object is allowed to have memberships of all clusters rather than having a disjoint membership of exactly one cluster. However, most k-means-based methods require expensive distance calculations to converge, and moreover, working only on numeric data prohibits it from being used to cluster real world data containing categorical values. Another feature of the non-hierarchical clustering method is that an objective function is optimised to obtain a desired set of clusters [5,6]. As a result, a local optimal solution is obtained based on the necessary condition of optimality. The most important point here is that we have to define an objective function prior to the clustering, without knowing the nature of the dataset. This creates the challenge of defining better objective functions that become more complicated.

In order to treat categorical data without any predetermined objective function, we have attempted to use the idea of agent technology in this chapter. The definition of an agent is introduced in [7]. The definition varies according to the applied field. The most common definition of the agent is that the agent has its own criteria or internal model and acts following its own criteria depending on the situation. It should be noted that there are many papers that claim to use agent-based data mining, but most of them call the modules of techniques the agents, referring to them as "software agents" [8,9]. In [10], a similar concept about clustering is proposed. However, our approach is quite different from these in the sense of developing a model for the consequence part of if–then rules.

Agents are expected to find sub sets and to appropriately express the obtained sub sets. A number of agents are sent into a complex database. Each agent has its own territory, and begins at one data point in its territory, which is called the representative data point. Agents follow the territory-expanding algorithm that is the main proposal in this chapter. The representative data point varies when the agent expands or reduces its territory. Thus, agents do not expand their territories monotonically. In this sense this is not hierarchical clustering, but it is not non-hierarchical clustering either because there is no global criterion for clustering.

An agent has the ability to express a feature of its territory, which is called a rule or a local model from the global viewpoint. At the beginning the similarity measure is given by the distance between data points. As the agent expands its territory, it will adopt a linearity measure. At this stage, the linearity measure is used to determine the shape of territory while the similarity measure is used to determine the field of view.

The agent identifies an if–then rule based on the collected data and tries to determine variables for rule description. It differs from conventional mining methods in that there is no objective function. Taking this approach, there are some advantages of the proposed method. One of the advantages is that it is not required to determine the number of clusters before performing the process.

2. Definition of similarity

Here, an object means a data point, and an attribute is sometimes called a variable to explain an aspect of the object. The degree of similarity between objects is defined in order to treat the complex mixed database. Let the object set and the attribute set be O and X, respectively. Denote by z_{ix} the value of attribute x of object i.

We define the similarity between z_{ix} and z_{jx} as follows:

- In cases where the attribute x is numerical:

$$\mathrm{Sim}(z_{ix}, z_{jx}) = 1 - \frac{|z_{ix} - z_{jx}|}{\max_{l \in O}\{z_{lx}\} - \min_{l \in O}\{z_{lx}\}}, \qquad i,j \in O, \qquad x \in X. \tag{1}$$

- In cases where the attribute x is categorical:

$$\mathrm{Sim}(z_{ix}, z_{jx}) = \begin{cases} 1, & \text{if } z_{ix} = z_{jx} \\ 0, & \text{if } z_{ix} \neq z_{jx} \end{cases}, \qquad i,j \in O, \qquad x \in X. \tag{2}$$

There are several definitions of the similarity on an axis in [1] depending on the situation. If the modeler knows something about the target problem, he/she may define another similarity measure.

Whatever the similarity in each attribute axis, the similarity between two objects is defined as:

$$\mathrm{SIM}(i,j) = \frac{1}{|X|} \sum_{x \in X} \mathrm{Sim}(z_{ix}, z_{jx}), \qquad i,j \in O. \tag{3}$$

3. Behavior of each agent

Before describing the design of the agents, the behavioral outline of this approach is explained. From global information for all agents, a response attribute is given; a parameter $p_1 (0 < p_1 < 1)$ is also given. This parameter is referred to as an acceptable minimal similarity between objects. As for the data distribution which an agent has, it is highly continuous when the value of a parameter is large. This can be expressed as a view of the agent.

Each agent has several phases, which change according to the condition of the agent.

In the first phase, the criterion of the agent is the similarity between the object and the representative of the agent. When all objects are assigned to agents, the phase goes on. If the number of agents is too high, or each agent has only a small number of objects, the parameter of acceptable minimal similarity p_1 may be replaced by a smaller value. The basic idea of this phase is to develop small sets depending only on the similarity between the objects. In this chapter, the basic criterion is assumed to be the distance in the first phase.

In the second phase, an agent tries to find another agent. The criterion in this phase is the similarity between the representative of these agents. If the number of the objects belonging to a certain agent increases, then, naturally the representative object of the agent is replaced, and then the agent goes on to make a regression model as a conclusion part of the rule. The reason why there are two phases is the sensitivity of the criterion. For instance, we do not like to develop a linear model which covers selected objects by accident only for the correlation. The agent identifies some sets for rule expression in each phase. After developing the linear model, the agent tries to collect other objects which can be applied into the model.

4. Design of agent

In this section, the design of the agent is described. The agent has several types of sets in order to define the condition of itself.

After introducing a representative object which can be considered as a center, the internal model of the agent, which consists of several parts, is described.

4.1. *Representative object*

Each agent has an object which is called the representative object of the agent. As is shown later, the agent consists of a data set. The representative object of the agent is defined as one of the pair which has the greatest similarity in the set. The representative object is determined dynamically when the territory changes. When the number of data points which an agent has is three or more, the representative object is determined as one of the two objects with the greatest similarity in the territory. In other cases, an arbitrary object is assigned as the representative object.

The representative of the agent can be considered as a center. When the agent finds another object and the pair of objects which has the largest similarity is changed inside the agent, the representative of the agent is replaced with one of them. According to the replaced representative of the agent, some objects may be released, because of the limitation of the agent's view as described later. The released object becomes the representative of another agent and tries to find other objects in the first phase. When no agents change their members, this procedure will be terminated.

4.2. *View of agent*

Each agent has a limited field of view. Here we introduce a parameter called the acceptable minimal similarity. The field of view of an agent consists of objects each of which has similarity with the representative object greater than or equal to the acceptable minimal similarity. The agent tries to obtain those objects in its field of view.

As mentioned in the above section, each agent explores and holds the other object under the parameter p_1 in the beginning of the process. p_1 is defined as the acceptable minimal similarity between objects.

Assume that A denotes Agent A and i_A denotes the index of the representative object.

$$\mathrm{View}(A) = \{i \in O | \mathrm{SIM}(i, i_A) \geq p_1\} \quad (4)$$

This set View(A) denotes the objects which are held by Agent A.

The character based on the objects-set View(A) is described by attributes sets. When i_A is changed for some reason, that means the view of Agent A is changed. View(A) is also re-identified to be the definition. As a result, some objects may be released.

4.3. *Character of agent*

In order to get the picture of Agent A, some sets are identified. At first, the condition of Agent A is considered. Let a set Char(A) be defined as follows:

$$\mathrm{Char}(A) = \{x | \min_{i,j \in \mathrm{View}(A)} \mathrm{Sim}(z_{ix}, z_{jx}) \geq p_2\} \quad (5)$$

where, the parameter p_2 plays the same role as the parameter p_1 for the similarity between two objects in the property defined on the axis x. p_2 is expected to find the attributes which have greater similarity on the considered axis than the similarity between the two objects in the space consisting of all attributes, if $p_2 \geq p_1$. p_2 is referred to as the acceptable minimal similarity between objects with respect to the attributes.

In cases that the response variable is included in the set Char(A), the consequence part is described as a set. The rule of Agent A is expressed as follows:

$$\text{if}\{x \in \text{Char}(A)\}, \qquad \text{then } y \text{ is } A_y \tag{6}$$

where, A_y is identified as a set in the axis of the response variable y, if the number of the objects included in the set View(A) is greater than 3. Otherwise A_y is an interval or a singleton set. The expression is dependent on the number of the objects in the objects set View(A).

In cases that the response variable is not included in the set Char(A), the objects do not concentrate on the response axis. In such a case, the parameter p_1 should be increased, because the current parameter p_1 is strictly for the given database (or agents) for developing the rules. In particular, p_1 should be increased further if the response variable has symbolic value.

4.4. *More exploration of character depending on circumstance*

4.4.1. *Candidates of consequence attributes.* When the response variable has a numerical value and the response variable is included in the attribute set Char(A), there is a possibility that the consequence part may need to include a linear model. In such a case, an attributes set Survey(A) is identified in order to check other attributes.

$$\text{Survey}(A) = \{k| \min_{i,j \in \text{View}(A)} \text{Sim}(z_{ik}, z_{jk}) < p_3\} \tag{7}$$

When some attributes are included in the attribute set Survey(A), these are extensions of each attribute axis. Therefore, there is a possibility of developing a linear model using these attributes. Thus, the correlation between each attribute and the response attribute is checked. Considering that these attributes may have symbolic values, the correlation between each attribute and the response attribute is determined by several steps.

4.4.2. *Identification of correlation.* As the attributes may have symbolic values, the correlation between each attribute and the response attribute is determined by several steps as follows:

$$(i^*, i'^*) = \arg \min_{(i,j)|i,j \in \text{View}(A), i<j} \text{Sim}(z_{iy}, z_{jy}) \tag{8}$$

Equation (8) determines a pair of objects. The pair of objects has the smallest value of similarity between them on the response attribute axis y.

First, set i_1 and $i_{|\text{View}(A)|}$ as follows:

$$i_1 = i^*, \qquad i_{|\text{View}(A)|} = i'^* \tag{9}$$

Here, $|\text{View}(A)|$ denotes the number of objects included in View(A). In addition, the objects in the object set View(A) are re-labeled. The re-labeled sequence is $i_1, i_2, \ldots, i_j, \ldots, i_{|\text{View}(A)|}$.

$$i_{j+1} = \arg \max_{i | i \notin i_1, \ldots, j_j} \text{Sim}(z_{iy}, z_{i_j y}), \qquad j = 1, 2, \ldots, |\text{View}(A)| - 1 \tag{10}$$

Assume that the objects are re-arranged in order of number. By comparing the order with the other attributes, the correlations with the response attribute are determined.

$$\text{Mon}(x) = \frac{\sum_{m=2}^{|\text{View}(A)|-1} \text{Sig}(\text{DS}_m)}{|\text{View}(A) - 2|} \tag{11}$$

Here, DS_m is defined by the following equations:

$$\text{DS}_m = \text{Sim}(z_{i_m x}, z_{i_1 x}) - \text{Sim}(z_{i_{m+1} x}, z_{i_1 x}) \tag{12}$$

Sig(x) is defined by the following equations:

$$\text{Sig}(x) = \begin{cases} +1 & \text{if } x > 0 \\ 0 & \text{if } x = 0 \\ -1 & \text{if } x < 0 \end{cases} \tag{13}$$

The value of Mon(x) denotes the index of monotonicity in the attribute x when compared with the response attribute. When the order of the objects on the response attribute the same as the order of another attribute x, Mon(x) = 1.

4.4.3. *Exploration of modeling.* In this chapter, the monotonicity between the response attribute and each other attribute is determined, although there are some methods to determine the explanatory attributes.

$$\text{Space}(A) = \{x | \text{Mon}(x) \geq p_4,\ x \in X\} \tag{14}$$

where, p_4 is a parameter which is determined by experience at this moment.

An attribute set Space(A) is determined according to the above equation. The attribute set Space(A) denotes the candidates of the explanatory attributes for the linear model in the consequence part of the rule. In the current approach, the attributes included are assumed to be the explanatory attributes, although there are some ideas to determine them. The procedure to identify these attributes will be included in future work.

In the case of defining a model, the rule of Agent A is expressed as follows:

$$\text{if}\{x \in \text{Char}(A)\}, \qquad \text{then } y \text{ is } f(\text{Space}(A)) \tag{15}$$

4.5. *Expanding territory by agent*

In this section, the definitions of two sets are described. These sets are used for expanding the territory of the agent. Agent A identifies the object set Front(A) as follows:

$$\text{Front}(A) = \{i \in \text{View}(A) | \text{Sim}(z_{ix}, z_{i_A x}) \leq p_5,\ x \in \text{Space}(A)\} \tag{16}$$

The objects that are included in the object set Front(A) are located around the border of the territory. This indicates that the objects which have been checked for the possibility of expanding the territory and keeping the obtained model are identified. At this moment, the parameter p_5 is determined so that at least one object can be included in the object set Front(A) by the agent.

The view from the object set Front(A) is included in the object set FrontView(A), which is defined by:

$$\text{FrontView}(A) = \{i | \text{Sim}(z_{ix}, z_{jx}) \geq p_6 | i \notin \text{View}(A),\ \ j \in \text{Front}(A)\} \tag{17}$$

A parameter p_6 is the threshold for the view from the objects in Front(A). At this moment, the agent has the same value as the parameter p_1, otherwise a value so that at least one object is included in the object set FrontView(A). The decision whether each object in FrontView(A) is added to the agent or not depends on the regression model. The regression model has been developed with attributes belonging to the attribute set Space(A). The candidate objects are applied to the regression model, and the squared error is estimated for each object.

Let the current squared error be determined using the objects belonging to the object set View(A). If the error of the object is smaller than the current squared error, then they are taken. The parameter p_1 then becomes smaller so that all objects are included in View(A).

5. Experiment

In this section, an experiment using artificial data is shown to illustrate how the proposed method works.

This dataset contains 20 objects (data points). Each object has three attributes, one of which is categorical. The proposed clustering technique is applied to this artificial data and the result is shown in Fig. 1 in which the figures are the smallest similarities in the

Object	Attributes			Object	Attributes		
	x_1	x_2	x_3		x_1	x_2	x_3
1	1.46	5.45	II	11	1.80	5.82	II
2	1.50	5.47	II	12	1.85	5.96	II
3	1.54	5.65	I	13	1.90	5.92	II
4	1.59	5.87	I	14	1.94	5.88	II
5	1.63	5.96	I	15	1.99	5.91	II
6	1.68	6.09	I	16	2.04	6.11	II
7	1.72	6.25	I	17	2.09	6.11	II
8	1.77	6.28	I	18	2.14	6.08	II
9	1.81	6.52	I	19	2.18	6.14	II
10	1.86	6.66	I	20	2.23	6.15	II

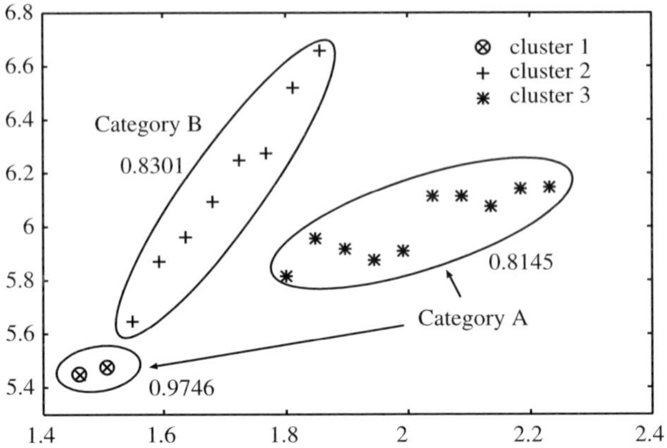

Fig. 1. Clustering result.

respective clusters. In this example, we set p_1 and p_2 at 0.75 and p_4 is given so that *Survey* is not empty. The other parameters are tuned by each agent.

The rules obtained are described as follows:

- Cluster $\times$: The condition attributes are x_1 and x_3, the consequence part is expressed by attribute x_3. The consequence is the term of attribute x_3 which consist of two objects.
- Cluster $+$: The condition attribute is x_3, the consequence part is described $x_2 = 0.9090 + 3.085 \times x_1$.
- Cluster $*$: The condition attributes are x_1 and x_3, the consequence part is described by the equation, $x_2 = 4.477 + 0.7593 \times x_1$.

6. Conclusion

In this chapter, the design of agents which identify rules from a complex database is proposed. In order to grasp the characters based on the objects kept by the agent, several sets are determined. The agent identifies these sets, then express their character as rules according to these sets. Future work includes trading of objects or attributes between agents in order to find better rules.

The methodology of the modeling technique described in this chapter is expected to contribute to realizing an SSR (Safe, Secure and Reliable) society such as solving a problem in an interdisciplinary domain in collaboration with various professional people. One of the advantages of using this technique is to be able to provide the if–then proposition based on observation data from complex systems like the environmental problem in an interdisciplinary domain. In order to contribute to realizing an SSR, it is necessary to apply this technique to observed data which has a much larger number of attributes. This will be included in future works.

References

[1] J. Han and M. Kamber, *Data Mining: Concepts and Techniques*, Morgan Kaufmann, Los Altos, CA (2001).

[2] J. MacQueen, *Some methods for classification and analysis of multivariate observations*, Proceedings of the 5th Berkeley Symposium on Mathematics Statistics and Probability, Vol. I, (1967), 281–297.

[3] J. Dunn, *A fuzzy relative of the ISODATA process and its use in detecting compact well-separated clusters*, J. Cybern. **3** (1974), 32–57.

[4] J.C. Bezdek, *Pattern Recognition with Fuzzy Objective Function Algorithms*, Plenum, New York (1981).

[5] R.N. Dave, *Use of the adaptive fuzzy clustering algorithm to detect lines in digital images*, Intelligent Robots and Computer Vision VIII, Vol. 1192, No. 2, (1989), 600–611.

[6] R.J. Hathaway and J.C. Bezdek, *Switching regression models and fuzzy clustering*, IEEE Trans. on Fuzzy Systems **1** (3) (1993), 195–204.

[7] J. Epstein, *Agent-based computational models and generative social sciences*, Complexity **4** (5) (1999), 41–60.

[8] T.B. Ho, T.D. Nguyen and N.B. Nguyen, *An agent-based architecture in knowledge discovery and data mining*, Proceedings of the first Asia-Pacific Conference on Intelligent Agent Technology Systems, Methodologies, and Tools, (1999), 259–263.

[9] J.S. McGormack and B. Wohlschlaeger, *Harnessing agent technology for data mining and knowledge discovery*, Data Mining and Knowledge Discovery: Theory, Tools, and Technology II, (2000), 393–400.

[10] G.D. Ramkumar and A. Swami, *Clustering data without distance functions*, Data Engng. Bull. **21** (1) (1998), 9–14.

CHAPTER 6

Additional Learning in Computational Intelligence and its Applications to Risk Management Problems

H. Nakayama

Konan University, 8-9-1 Okamoto, Higashinada, Kobe 658-8501, Japan
E-mail: nakayama@konan-u.ac.jp

K. Kuramoto

Chuden Engineering Consultants Co. Ltd, Deshio 2-3-30, Minami-ku, Hiroshima 734-8510, Japan
E-mail: kkuramot@cecnet.co.jp

M. Arakawa

Kagawa University, 2217-20 Hayashi-cho, Takamatsu, Kagawa 761-0396, Japan
E-mail: arakawa@eng.kagawa-u.ac.jp

K. Furukawa

Yamaguchi University, 2-16-1 Tokiwadai, Ube 755-8611, Japan
E-mail: furukawa@jim2.civil.yamaguchi-u.ac.jp

Contents

SYSTEMS AND HUMAN SCIENCE – FOR SAFETY, SECURITY, AND DEPENDABILITY
Edited by Tatsuo Arai, Shigeru Yamamoto and Kazuhisa Makino

Abstract

Learning machines should grow up in order to adapt to the environment changing over time. It has been observed that additional learning plays an effective role to this end. Since the rule for classification becomes more and more complex with only additional learning, however, some appropriate forgetting is also needed. It seems natural that much old data are forgotten as time elapses. On the other hand, it is expected to be more effective to forget unnecessary data actively. In this chapter, several methods for active forgetting including Radial Basis Function networks and the potential method are reviewed. The effectiveness of additional learning with active forgetting is shown by some risk management problems in stock portfolio problems and in land-slide disaster forecasting problems.

1. Introduction

In analogy to the growth of human beings, machine learning should make additional learning in order to adapt to the changeable environment, e.g., in financial investment problems and natural disaster forecasting problems. So far, machine learning has been mainly studied as "static" in the sense that its learning is just for pre-given teacher's data. However, teacher's data are usually not fixed over time in many practical problems. Therefore, we can consider the additional learning as a "dynamic" learning.

Since the learning in artificial neural networks is usually time consuming in many practical problems, we mean by additional learning to calculate only the increment between the current status and the new one without restarting from the beginning. It is not so easy to make additional learning by the multi-layer perceptron type of artificial neural networks, because the structure of networks should be changed as a number of new data are added. Instead, the authors reported that other kinds of machine learning techniques, e.g., mathematical programming approaches, Radial Basis Function (RBF) networks and the potential method, are effective for this purpose [5–10].

On the other hand, if we make only additional learning, the resulting decision rule becomes more and more complex, which leads to poor generalization ability. Therefore, it is also necessary to remove unnecessary data. This is called "forgetting" in this chapter. How do human beings forget unnecessary data? In general, whether some data are necessary or unnecessary is decided on the basis of the degree of importance of data. There are two ways for forgetting. One is passive forgetting. The other is active forgetting. It seems natural that the degree of importance of data reduces as time passes. Like this, a way for passive forgetting is to reduce the importance of old data. On the other hand, it seems more effective to forget data that give bad influences to the current judgment. We call this way of forgetting "obstacle data" actively "active forgetting". In this event, it is our aim to find "obstacle data". In the following sections we review additional learning and forgetting in RBF networks and the potential method. To show their effectiveness in risk management problems, both methods are compared in financial problems. In addition, RBF networks are applied to natural disaster forecasting problems, since the data sets are too large for the potential method in those cases.

2. Review of RBF networks and the potential method

2.1. *RBF networks*

Artificial neural networks with RBF try to follow the teacher's patterns $(\mathbf{x}_i, \hat{y}_i)$ $i = 1, \ldots, N$ by a function with the form of

$$f(\mathbf{x}) = \sum_{j=1}^{m} w_j h_j(\mathbf{x}), \tag{1}$$

where h_j $(j = 1, \ldots, m)$ are RBFs, e.g.,

$$h_j(\mathbf{x}) = \mathrm{e}^{-\|x-\mu_j\|^2/r_j}. \tag{2}$$

Usually, networks with RBFs are constructed by solving

$$E = \sum_{i=1}^{N} (\hat{y}_i - f(\mathbf{x}_i))^2 + \sum_{j=1}^{m} \lambda_j \omega_j^2 \rightarrow \text{Min}, \tag{3}$$

where the second term is introduced for the purpose of regularization.

Letting $A = (H_N^{\mathrm{T}} H_N + \Lambda)$, we have as a necessary condition for the above minimization

$$A\omega = H_N^{\mathrm{T}} \hat{y}. \tag{4}$$

Here

$$H_N^{\mathrm{T}} = [\mathbf{h}_1 \cdots \mathbf{h}_N], \tag{5}$$

where $\mathbf{h}_j^{\mathrm{T}} = [h_1(\mathbf{x}_j), \ldots, h_m(\mathbf{x}_j)]$, and Λ is a diagonal matrix whose diagonal components are $\lambda_1, \ldots, \lambda_m$.

Finally, our problem is reduced to finding

$$A^{-1} = (H_N^{\mathrm{T}} H_N + \Lambda)^{-1}. \tag{6}$$

Here, it is important to decide the parameter r. Slightly modifying the formula given by [3], the value of r may be determined by

$$r = \frac{d_{\max}}{\sqrt[n]{nm}},$$

where $d_{\max}$ is the maximal distance among the data; m is the dimension of data; n is the number of data.

2.2. *The potential method*

The potential method was suggested by one of the authors [8]. The idea of the potential method originated from the static electric theory. Another similar method is the Restricted Coulomb Energy (RCE) Classifier by Cooper [2] and Reilly *et al.* [12]. RCE tries to increase the ability of classification by adjusting the radii of hyperspheres which approximate the region of influence of data.

Unlike RCE, however, the potential method adjusts "charge" associated with each data in order to increase the ability of generalization. Each hidden unit corresponds to each teacher's pattern $\mathbf{x}_j$ $(j = 1, \ldots, N)$, which has some amount of charge c_j in which the sign depends on which category it belongs to. Letting $D(\mathbf{x}, \mathbf{x}_j)$ denote the distance between $\mathbf{x}$ and $\mathbf{x}_j$, the output unit is connected to

$$z(\mathbf{x}) = \operatorname{sgn} P(\mathbf{x}), \tag{7}$$

where

$$P(\mathbf{x}) = \sum_{j=1}^{N} \frac{c_j}{D(\mathbf{x}, \mathbf{x}_j)}. \tag{8}$$

Here, P is the well-known potential function, and the category a given test pattern belongs to is decided by the sign of this potential function.

Note that the potential method can classify each teacher's pattern $\mathbf{x}_j$ $(j = 1, \ldots, N)$ correctly without doing anything, because $P(\mathbf{x}_j) = +\infty$ for $c_j > 0$ and $P(\mathbf{x}_j) = -\infty$ for $c_j < 0$. This means that the potential method can make the perfect learning for given teacher's data without doing anything. If we use the potential method as it is, however, it yields several small isolated influence regions just like "islands" in many problems. Clearly, this phenomenon causes poor generalization ability. Therefore, in order to obtain as smooth a discriminant surface as possible, we adjust the charges of data. This is the learning of the potential method.

A way of learning in the potential method can be summarized as follows:

Step 0 At the beginning, all teacher's data have an equal amount of charge except for the difference in its sign (suppose that each pattern of class $\mathcal{A}$ has a positive charge, while each pattern of class $\mathcal{B}$ has a negative charge).

Step 1 Consider the ith pattern $\mathbf{x}_i$ $(i = 1, \ldots, N)$. Examine whether it is categorized correctly or not on the basis of the sign of output of

$$\tilde{P}(\mathbf{x}_i) = \sum_{j \neq i}^{N} \frac{c_j}{D(\mathbf{x}_i, \mathbf{x}_j)}. \tag{9}$$

If the pattern $\mathbf{x}_i$ is not categorized correctly, then add the index i to the set I_{error}. If I_{error} is empty, then stop the iteration. Otherwise go to the next step.

Step 2 Find the pattern $\mathbf{x}_p$ with the highest error, namely

$$|\tilde{P}(\mathbf{x}_p)| = \max_{i \in I_{\text{error}}} |\tilde{P}(\mathbf{x}_i)|. \tag{10}$$

Step 3 Find the pattern $\mathbf{x}_q$ in the other category than of $\mathbf{x}_p$ nearest to the pattern $\mathbf{x}_p$. Change the charge c_j of pattern $\mathbf{x}_j$ $(j = 1, \ldots, N)$ in such a way that the potential at $\mathbf{x}_m = (\mathbf{x}_p + \mathbf{x}_q)/2$ becomes zero. Namely, suppose that the new charge c'_j is given by

$$c'_j = c_j \exp(\mp \tilde{P}(\mathbf{x}_j)\gamma), \qquad j = 1, \ldots, N, \tag{11}$$

where denoting $q_j = c_j/D(\mathbf{x}_m, \mathbf{x}_j)$, $(j = 1, \ldots, N)$, γ solves

$$q_1 \exp(-\tilde{P}(\mathbf{x}_1)\gamma) + \cdots + q_{N'} \exp(-\tilde{P}(\mathbf{x}_{N'})\gamma)$$
$$+ q_{N'+1} \exp(\tilde{P}(\mathbf{x}_{N'+1})\gamma) + \cdots + q_N \exp(\tilde{P}(\mathbf{x}_N)\gamma) = 0. \tag{12}$$

Here, $\mathbf{x}_1, \ldots, \mathbf{x}_{N'}$ have positive charges, while $\mathbf{x}_{N'+1}, \ldots, \mathbf{x}_N$ negative charges. The sign $\mp$ in (11) means that $c_j > 0$ takes "−" and $c_j < 0$"+".

Replace the charge of each pattern by the new one given by (11), and go to Step 1.

3. Additional learning

3.1. *Additional learning by RBF networks*

For additional learning by RBF networks, we have the following simple algorithm.

3.1.1. *Adding a new training pattern.* As an additional learning, we can take a new training data into the matrix inversion (6) by a simple update formula

$$H_{p+1} = \begin{bmatrix} H_p \\ \mathbf{h}_{p+1}^{\mathrm{T}} \end{bmatrix}, \tag{13}$$

where $\mathbf{h}_{p+1}^{\mathrm{T}} = [h_1(\mathbf{x}_{p+1}), \ldots, h_m(\mathbf{x}_{p+1})]$.

$$A_{p+1}^{-1} = A_p^{-1} - \frac{A_p^{-1}\mathbf{h}_{p+1}\mathbf{h}_{p+1}^{\mathrm{T}}A_p^{-1}}{1 + \mathbf{h}_{p+1}^{\mathrm{T}}A_p^{-1}\mathbf{h}_{p+1}}. \tag{14}$$

3.1.2. *Adding a New Basis Function.* In cases in which we need a new basis function to improve the learning for a new data, we have the following update formula for the matrix inversion:

$$H_{m+1} = [H_m \quad \mathbf{h}_{m+1}], \tag{15}$$

where $\mathbf{h}_{m+1}^{\mathrm{T}} = [h_{m+1}(\mathbf{x}_1), \ldots, h_{m+1}(\mathbf{x}_p)]$.

$$A_{m+1}^{-1} = \begin{bmatrix} A_m^{-1} & 0 \\ 0^{\mathrm{T}} & 0 \end{bmatrix} + \frac{1}{\lambda_{m+1} + \mathbf{h}_{m+1}^{\mathrm{T}}(I_p - H_m A_m^{-1} H_m^{\mathrm{T}})\mathbf{h}_{m+1}} \times \begin{bmatrix} A_m^{-1}H_m^{\mathrm{T}}\mathbf{h}_{m+1} \\ -1 \end{bmatrix}\begin{bmatrix} A_m^{-1}H_m^{\mathrm{T}}\mathbf{h}_{m+1} \\ -1 \end{bmatrix}^{\mathrm{T}}. \tag{16}$$

3.2. *Additional learning by the potential method*

We can show that the additional learning can be easily made by using the potential method. Let $\mathbf{x}_t$ be a pattern newly added to the existing teacher's data. The procedure of additional learning can be divided into (1) the case in which $\mathbf{x}_t$ is classified correctly by the present rule, and (2) the case in which $\mathbf{x}_t$ is misclassified by the present rule. The details are as follows.

CASE 1. When the new data $\mathbf{x}_t$ is classified correctly by the present rule, find a data $\mathbf{x}_a$ closest to $\mathbf{x}_t$ but in the different category of $\mathbf{x}_t$. In addition, find a data $\mathbf{x}_b$ closest to $\mathbf{x}_a$ but in the different category of $\mathbf{x}_a$. Let $\mathbf{x}_{\mathrm{abm}}$ be the middle point of $\mathbf{x}_a$ and $\mathbf{x}_b$, i.e., $\mathbf{x}_{\mathrm{abm}} = (\mathbf{x}_a + \mathbf{x}_b)/2$. If the potential of $\mathbf{x}_{\mathrm{abm}}$ has a different sign from that of $\mathbf{x}_t$, then put the charge c_t on $\mathbf{x}_t$

in such a way that we have

$$P'(\mathbf{x}_{\text{abm}}) := P(\mathbf{x}_{\text{abm}}) + c_t/D(\mathbf{x}_t, \mathbf{x}_{\text{abm}}) = 0. \tag{17}$$

Namely, we put

$$c_t = -P(\mathbf{x}_{\text{abm}}) \times D(\mathbf{x}_t, \mathbf{x}_{\text{abm}}). \tag{18}$$

However, if the potential of $\mathbf{x}_{\text{abm}}$ has the same sign as that of $\mathbf{x}_t$, then we do not put any charge on $\mathbf{x}_t$ (i.e., $c_t = 0$).

The purpose of considering the potential of $\mathbf{x}_{\text{abm}}$ is to check whether the discriminant surface can be made correctly by adding $\mathbf{x}_t$. Also, by excluding unnecessary data from additional learning, the computation time can be reduced.

CASE 2. When the new data $\mathbf{x}_t$ is misclassified by the present rule, find a data $\mathbf{x}_a$ closest to $\mathbf{x}_t$ but in a different category from $\mathbf{x}_t$. Let $\mathbf{x}_{\text{atm}} = (\mathbf{x}_t + \mathbf{x}_a)/2$. Then put the charge c_t on $\mathbf{x}_t$ in such a way that we have

$$P'(\mathbf{x}_{\text{atm}}) := P(\mathbf{x}_{\text{atm}}) + c_t/D(\mathbf{x}_t, \mathbf{x}_{\text{atm}}) = 0. \tag{19}$$

Namely, we put

$$c_t = -P(\mathbf{x}_{\text{atm}})D(\mathbf{x}_t, \mathbf{x}_{\text{atm}}). \tag{20}$$

4. Forgetting

If we make only additional learning, the classification rule becomes more and more complex, which gives a poor generalization ability in general. It seems that human beings avoid this by forgetting unnecessary data. Whether a data is necessary or unnecessary can be reflected by taking into account the degree of importance of the data. For the moment, consider cases in which this degree of importance takes a value of either 0 or 1. We shall consider cases with a real number value for the degree of importance of data later in this chapter.

4.1. *Forgetting by RBF networks*

4.1.1. *Removing an old pattern.* As a kind of forgetting, consider a case in which an old pattern $\mathbf{x}_i$ is removed from the data set $\{\mathbf{x}_1, \dots, \mathbf{x}_p\}$. In this case also, we have the following matrix inversion formula ([11]):

$$A_{p-1}^{-1} = A_p^{-1} + \frac{A_p^{-1}\mathbf{h}_i\mathbf{h}_i^{\mathrm{T}}A_p^{-1}}{1 - \mathbf{h}_i^{\mathrm{T}}A_p^{-1}\mathbf{h}_i}. \tag{21}$$

4.1.2. *Removing an old basis function.* If we remove only unnecessary data, we might have a situation in which there are too many basis functions in our dynamic learning.

In such a case, although the weight of the redundant basis function is expected to be zero, we should remove the redundant basis function in order to save the computing time of matrix inversion and to increase the generalization ability.

$$\begin{bmatrix} A_m^{-1} & \mathbf{0} \\ \mathbf{0}^{\mathrm{T}} & 0 \end{bmatrix} = A_{m+1}^{-1} - \frac{1}{\lambda_m + \mathbf{h}_m^{\mathrm{T}} P_{m-1} \mathbf{h}_m} \begin{bmatrix} H_{m-1}^{+}(I_p - P_{m-1})\mathbf{h}_m \\ -1 \end{bmatrix}$$
$$\times \begin{bmatrix} H_{m-1}^{+}(I_p - P_{m-1})\mathbf{h}_m \\ -1 \end{bmatrix}^{\mathrm{T}}. \tag{22}$$

Here, P_{m-1} can be obtained from P_m by [11]

$$P_{m-1} = P_m + \frac{P_m \mathbf{h}_m \mathbf{h}_m^{\mathrm{T}} P_m}{\lambda_m - \mathbf{h}_m^{\mathrm{T}} P_m \mathbf{h}_m}. \tag{23}$$

According to [1], H_{m-1}^{+} can be obtained from H_m^{+} by

$$[\,(H_{m-1}^{+})^{\mathrm{T}} \quad \mathbf{0}\,] = (H_m^{+})^{\mathrm{T}} - \frac{\mathbf{h}_m \mathbf{h}_m^{\mathrm{T}} (H_m^{+})^{\mathrm{T}}}{\mathbf{h}_m^{\mathrm{T}} \mathbf{h}_m}. \tag{24}$$

4.2. *Forgetting by the potential method*

In the potential method, the degree of importance for each data is considered to be given by the value of kernel function $K_i(\mathbf{x}, \mathbf{x}_i) = c_i / D(\mathbf{x}, \mathbf{x}_i)$.

In many situations, it seems natural that the degree of importance of data reduces as time passes. A method for forgetting may be given by

$$c_f' = c_f \exp(-\alpha t), \tag{25}$$

where t denotes the time elapsed, α the coefficient of forgetting, c_f the original charge, and c_f' the charge after time t. Additionally, it is supposed that the data $\mathbf{x}_f$ is extracted from the set of teacher's data, if t is beyond a threshold (the forgetting period).

4.3. *Active forgetting*

The above method for forgetting depends only on the time elapse. However, it seems more effective to forget more active data which give bad influences to correct judgment. We call the way of forgetting depending on the time elapse "passive forgetting", whereas the one of actively forgetting data with bad influence "active forgetting".

A key for active forgetting is to find data giving a bad influence to correct judgment. We call such data "obstacle data". One way of finding obstacle data is given as follows.

Suppose that a test pattern $\mathbf{x}_t$ is misjudged by the potential method. Let I_F denote the set of data in the other category from $\mathbf{x}_t$. Removing a data $\mathbf{x}_i \in I_F$, judge the category of test data $\mathbf{x}_t$ on the basis of its potential. If the judgment is correct, the data $\mathbf{x}_i$ is considered an obstacle data. Find such obstacle data by checking all data $\mathbf{x}_i \in I_F$.

Several ways for forgetting obstacle data for RBFN and the potential method have been discussed in [10].

5. Stock portfolio problems

Our problem is to judge whether a stock is to be purchased or not. Seven economic indices are taken into account. We have the data in the 119 periods in the past for which it is already known if it has been purchased or not. We made a test of discrimination ability of RBFN and the potential method taking the first 50 data as the teachers' ones, and examined the ability of classification for the other 69 data. Note that the training data are in the period of bubble economy in Japan and the test data in the period after its collapse. This implies that unless additional learning is made, we have poor discrimination for test data. Figure 1 compares the results with/without additional learning and forgetting by RBFN. Flags represent misclassified data.

Figure 2 compares the effect of additional learning with/without forgetting by RBFN and the potential method. Both in RBFN and in the potential method, one can see that we have a much better classification by additional learning than by the initial learning only, and a slightly better classification by additional learning with forgetting than by additional learning without forgetting.

6. Natural disaster forecasting problems

There are many mountains, and therefore, very many slopes in Japan. Every year, we have many land-slide disasters. It is an important task to decide when we announce to the populace to evacuate. To this end, we have to forecast exactly when slopes fail [4]. Otherwise, local governments waste much money in the case of no failure after the announcement of evacuation, and on the other hand, are blamed for failure without any announcement.

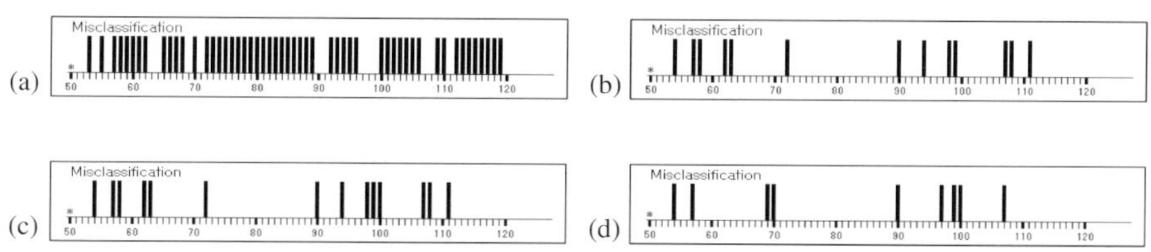

(a): initial learning only (#errors:53)
(b): with additional learning and without forgetting (#errors:13)
(c): with additional learning and passive forgetting (#errors:14)
(d): with additional learning and active forgetting (#errors:9)

Fig. 1. Misclassification for test data by RBFN.

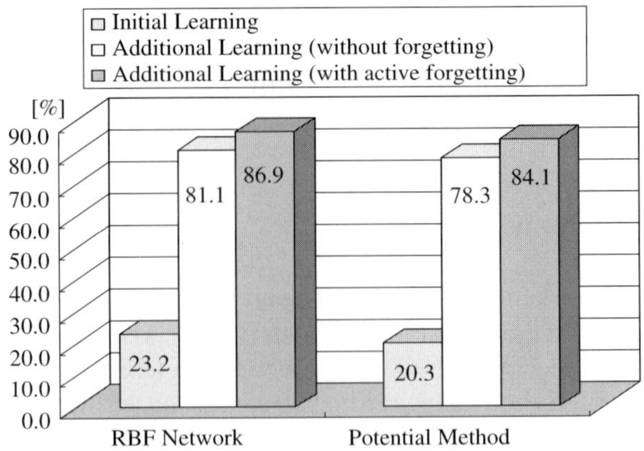

Fig. 2. Correct classification rate of additional learning with/without forgetting by RBFN and the potential method.

So far, the forecast of slope failure is made on the basis of a critical line on a two-dimensional space of rainfall indices, usually a short-term index of rainfall (here we used "hourly rainfall depth") and a long-term index of rainfall (here we used "effective rainfall"). Conventionally, since such a critical line is linear, it has poor precision of forecasting. Authors, therefore, tried to apply RBFN to obtain a nonlinear critical line (i.e., curve). Figure 3 shows a nonlinear critical line obtained by using RBFN, where T is the "half-life" representing the decay characteristic of a particular recession. Under the same condition for failure, the accuracy of classification by RBFN and the conventional linear CL for training data are, respectively, 95/111 (i.e., 85.6%) and 80/111 (i.e., 72.1%). Since these results are just for the past data, we studied the precision of forecasting several unknown data. Figure 4 shows the snake line (curve) of June 29, 1999.

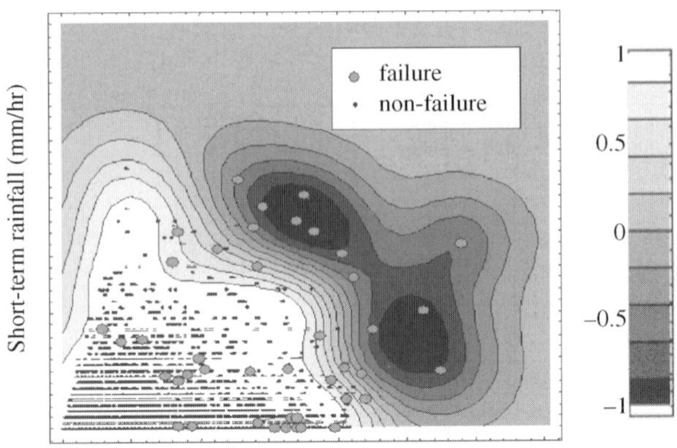

Fig. 3. Nonlinear critical line.

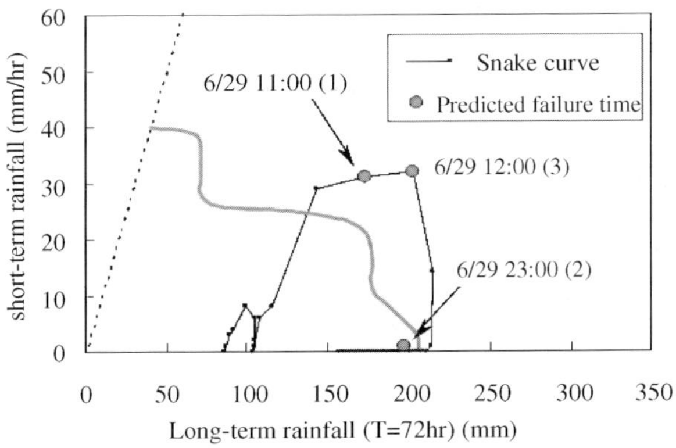

Fig. 4. Snake line.

The snake line (curve) is given by plotting the time history of rainfall. The dots (●) in the figure show failures that actually occurred. In fact, there was one slope failure at 11:00 and three slope failures at 12:00, which are all correctly forecasted, because they are all in the region of failure decided by the nonlinear critical line. In addition, we had two more failures at 23:00, which are also correctly forecasted.

7. Concluding remarks

In this chapter, we discussed additional learning along with forgetting in computational intelligence. We considered in particular RBFN and the potential method as effective methods in machine learning. It has been observed that additional learning provides much better performance than just initial learning, and moreover, we can improve the performance by forgetting. Since the environment of risk management problems such as financial investment problems and natural disaster forecasting problems changes over time, additional learning with forgetting is expected to work well.

References

[1] A. Ben Israel and T.N.E. Greville, *Generalized Inverses: Theory and Applications*, Wiley, New York (1974).

[2] P.W. Cooper, *The Hypersphere in Pattern Recognition*, Information Control **5** (1962), 324–346.

[3] S. Haykin, *Neural Networks: A Comprehensive Foundation*, Macmillan College Publishing Company (1994).

[4] K. Kuramoto, H. Tetsuga, H. Higashi, M. Arakawa, H. Nakamaya and K. Furukawa, *A study on a method for determining non-linear critical line of slope failures during heavy rainfall based on RBF network*, Trans. Soc. Civ. Eng. Jpn **672/VI-50** (2001), 117–132.

[5] H. Nakayama, *Growing learning machines and their applications to portfolio problems*, Proceedings of the International ICSC Congress on Computational Intelligence Methods and Applications (CIMA'99) (1999), 680–683.

[6] H. Nakamaya and A. Hattori, *Additional learning and forgetting by support vector machines and RBF networks*, Proceedings of the ICONIP'02 (in CD-ROM) (2002).

[7] H. Nakamaya and N. Kagaku, *Pattern classification by linear goal programming and its extensions*, J. Global Optim. **12** (1998), 111–126.

[8] H. Nakamaya and M. Yoshida, *Additional learning and forgetting by potential method for pattern classification*, Proceedings of the ICNN'97 (1997), pp. 1839–1844.

[9] H. Nakamaya, M. Yoshida and S. Yanagiuchi, *Incremental Learning for pattern Classification*, Proceedings of the ICONIP'97 (1997), pp. 498–501.

[10] H. Nakayama and K. Yoshii, *Active forgetting in machine learning and its application to financial problems*, Proceedings of the International Joint Conference on Neural Networks, (in CD ROM) (2000).

[11] M.J.L. Orr, Introduction to Radial Basis Function Networks http://www.cns.ed.ac.uk/people/mark/intro/intro.html (1996).

[12] D.L. Reilly, L.N. Cooper and C. Elbaum, *A neural model for category learning*, Biol. Cybern. **45** (1982), 35–41.

CHAPTER 7

Integrated Assessment of Global Warming Stabilization Scenarios by the Asia-Pacific Integrated Model

Toshihiko Masui, Kiyoshi Takahashi and Mikiko Kainuma

National Institute for Environmental Studies, 16-2 Onogawa, Tsukuba 305-8506, Japan

Yuzuru Matsuoka

Kyoto University, Yoshida, Sakyo-ku, Kyoto 606-8501, Japan

Contents

Abstract

This paper analyzes the economic and climatic impacts of greenhouse gas (GHG) emission scenarios. The profiles of energy consumption and economic losses of policy scenarios are compared to the reference scenario. The model estimates the global mean temperature increase, the sea level, and impacts on food productivity and malaria infection under the policy scenarios targeting 550 ppmv atmospheric CO_2 concentration.

SYSTEMS AND HUMAN SCIENCE – FOR SAFETY, SECURITY, AND DEPENDABILITY
Edited by Tatsuo Arai, Shigeru Yamamoto and Kazuhisa Makino

1. Introduction

It is predicted that global warming will have significant impacts on the society and economy of the Asia-Pacific region, and that adoption of measures to tackle global climate change will force the region to carry a very large economic burden. Also, if the Asia-Pacific region fails to adopt such countermeasure, it has been estimated that its greenhouse gas (GHG) emissions will increase to over one-half of total global emissions by the year 2100 [1]. In order to respond to such serious and long-term threats, it is essential to establish communication and evaluation tools for policy makers and scientists in the region. The Integrated Assessment Model provides a convenient framework for combining knowledge from a wide range of disciplines, and is one of the most effective tools to increase the interactions among these groups [2].

The Asia-Pacific Integrated Model (AIM) is a large-scale computer simulation model developed to promote the integrated assessment process in the Asia-Pacific region. The main goal of this model is to assess policy options for stabilizing the global climate, particularly in the Asia-Pacific region, from the two perspectives of reducing GHG emissions and avoiding the impacts of climate change [1].

We have evaluated the economic impacts of the Kyoto Protocol using the AIM model [3]. Although the Kyoto Protocol is very important as a milestone in climate policy, it is necessary to reduce emissions by more than the reduction target specified by the Protocol to achieve the long-term goals of the Framework Convention. Considerable efforts have been devoted to estimating the different stabilization pathways for contributing to the third assessment report of Intergovernmental Panel on Climate Change (IPCC) [4].

The objective of this research is to evaluate economic impacts for reducing GHG emissions and climatic impacts on vulnerable sectors (agriculture and health) simultaneously under plural stabilization pathways by using AIM model and to compare the consequences of the different pathways. The emission model examines several important variables such as GDP changes, energy consumption, carbon emissions, and marginal costs. Outputs of the emission model are fed as input to the climate model. Estimated climate changes under different scenarios are used to estimate the climatic impacts on food production and infectious diseases focusing on the Asia-Pacific region.

2. Structure of the AIM model

AIM comprises three main models: the GHG emission model (AIM/emission), the global climate change model (AIM/climate), and the climate change impact model (AIM/impact).

The AIM/emission model consists of country-level, bottom–up type energy models and global-level, top–down type energy and land-use models. A variety of global and regional assumptions, such as population and economic trends as well as government policies, are entered into the emission model to provide estimates of energy consumption, land-use change, etc., and provide predictions of GHG emissions. Emissions of SO_2, NO_x, and Suspended Particulate Matter (SPM) are also calculated within the AIM/emission model, and they are input into the AIM/climate model and a regional environmental model that was developed in order to reinforce the interaction with local atmospheric pollution problems.

With the exception of CO_2, GHG emitted into the atmosphere are gradually transformed by chemical reactions, which are calculated within the AIM/climate model. We divided these chemicals into two groups based on their reaction rates: long-life chemicals such as Chloro Fluoro Carbons (CFCs), and short-life chemicals such as ozone and OH radicals. A pseudo-equilibrium state is assumed for the latter group, and the oxidation and photochemical reactions of CH_4 and other molecules are represented by simple kinetic equations. The absorption of CO_2 and heat by the oceans is calculated using an upwelling-diffusion model (part of the AIM/climate model) with the oceans divided into a surface mixed layer and an intermediate layer that extends down to about 1000 m.

Global mean temperature changes are calculated with an energy balance/upwelling-diffusion ocean model, and used as input into the regional models. Data from the General Circulation Model (GCM) experiments are used in order to estimate the regional distribution of climate parameters. They are coupled with the global mean temperature change calculated in the AIM/climate model. The interpolated climate distributions are used in the AIM/impact model, which calculates global and regional climatic impacts. The AIM/impact model mainly treats the impact on primary production industries, such as water supply, agriculture, forest products, and human health. It can also be used to assess higher-order impacts on the regional economy.

3. Long-term mitigation scenarios

Atmospheric stabilization scenarios were used to limit the atmospheric concentration of CO_2 at 550 ppmv. As a reference scenario the driving forces used by the Special Report on Emissions Scenarios (SRES [5]) B2 scenario were taken. It is assumed that carbon emissions can be traded without quantitative limitations on trading cases within the allowable emissions. The global allowable emissions are specified in the 550 ppmv scenarios and they are allocated according to the population.

Figure 1 shows a projection of the world GDP from 2000 to 2100. In Fig. 1, ROW denotes "Rest of the World" and EEFSU denotes "East Europe and Former Soviet Union", respectively. World growth rates during this period vary from 1.25 to 3.16%/year, with an average of 2.1%/year. The highest is that of China, which varies from 1.5 to 6.4%/year. Figure 2 shows a projection of world CO_2 emissions. It is projected that China will become the top CO_2-emitting country after 2020. The growth rate in world CO_2 emissions will follow a downward curve, whereas that of China will increase. The growth rate in CO_2 is much higher than the growth rate of the GDP in China under this reference scenario. This is because energy efficiency in China is estimated to be lower than that of the developed countries in this case.

The results of the reference scenario are compared with three 550 ppmv scenarios. The three 550 ppmv scenarios examined are WRE 550, WGI 550, and MID 550. The WRE scenario was proposed by Wigley *et al.* [6] to find the optimal path to 550 ppmv from the economic point of view. WGI 550 is a scenario proposed by IPCC Working Group I [7].

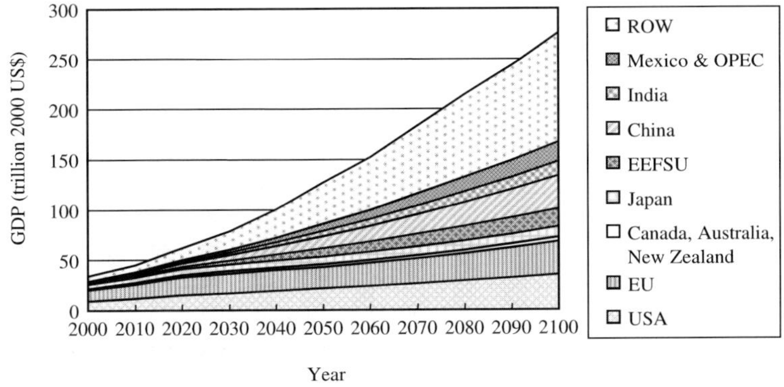

Fig. 1. Projection of the world GDP under the reference scenario (trillion 2000 US$).

It is a path aimed at avoiding an abrupt change in emissions in achieving the 550 ppmv target. The MID 550 scenario is proposed, representing the mean of these two scenarios.

Figure 3 shows world energy demand in enduse sectors in the reference scenario and Fig. 4 shows the results of the WRE 550 scenario. In the reference scenario, the use of solid energy increases from 18% in 2000 to 48% in 2100, and more than half is used in China in 2100. The world final energy demand in the WRE 550 scenario decreases to nearly half that in the reference scenario in 2100. This reduction comes about mainly from cutting coal use. The share of coal in the WRE 550 scenario becomes 29% in 2100. Electricity demand will increase in the policy scenarios. The share of electricity will increase from 17% in 2000 to 29% in 2100 in WRE 550.

4. GDP changes until 2100

Figure 5 shows the projections of the marginal costs for reducing emissions. The marginal costs for the WGI 550 scenario are the highest through the year 2060, those of MID 550

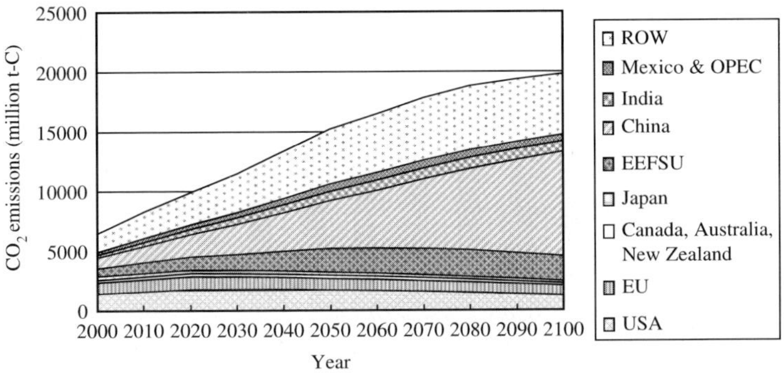

Fig. 2. Projection of CO_2 emissions under the reference scenario (million t-C).

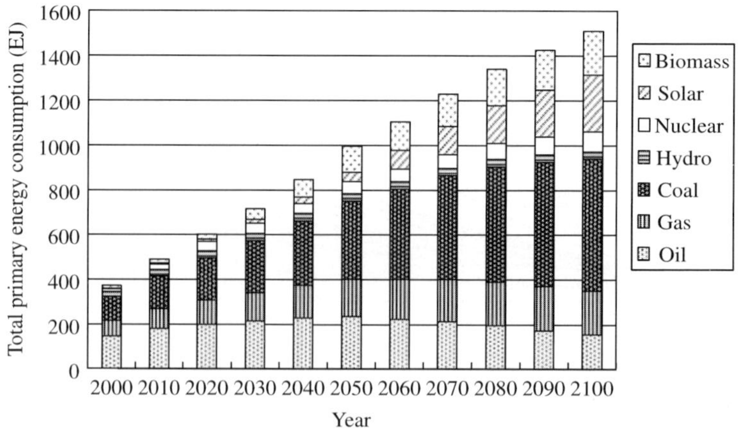

Fig. 3. World energy demand in enduse sectors under the reference scenario (EJ).

become the highest from 2060 to 2080, and then those of WRE 550 become the highest from 2090 onwards. Although the constraint of the WGI 550 scenario is the severest until 2070, the marginal costs become the second highest in 2070. The restructuring of the energy system at an early stage will decrease the marginal costs after 2050.

Figure 6 shows the projections for GDP changes compared to the reference scenario. The GDP loss in the WGI 550 scenario increases until 2050 and then recovers, while that of WRE 550 increases until 2070. The GDP loss in WRE 550 is the highest among the three 550 scenarios in 2100. This means that even if the impact of WRE 550 is minimal for the first three decades, it will become large later. The environmental impacts that will be discussed below show that if the timing of reductions is early, this will reduce the impacts compared to scenarios in which action is taken later.

Figure 7 shows the consumption changes relative to the reference scenario. The values shown are the present discounted values for macroeconomic consumption change with

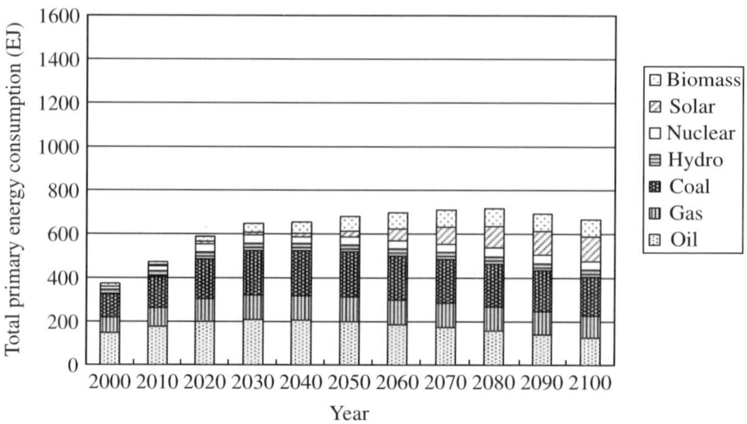

Fig. 4. World energy demand in enduse sectors under the WRE 550 scenario (EJ).

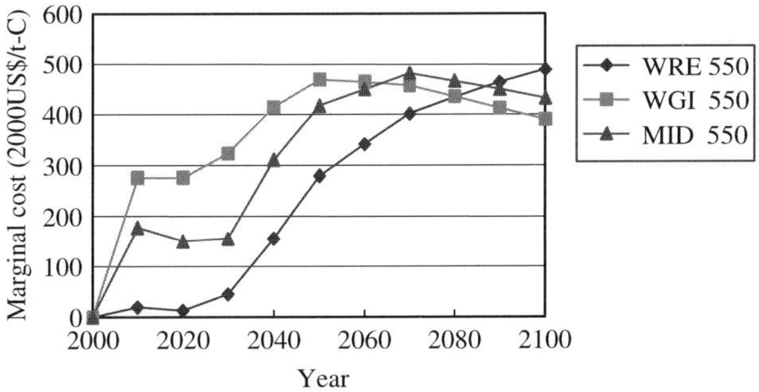

Fig. 5. Projection of marginal costs to reduce emissions (2000 US$/t-C).

respect to the reference scenario in trillions of 2000 US dollars through 2050. The discount rate is 5%/year. Consumption in India will grow at the highest level, especially in the WGI 550 scenario. Consumption will decline in Annex B countries and China. The greatest decline is in the US, followed by China, under the assumptions of the policy scenarios.

5. Global climate change

The impact on the global mean temperature is shown in Fig. 8. By 2100, the temperature rises by 2.77 °C compared with the 1990 value in the reference scenario. The results of the IPCC SRES range from 1.4 to 5.8 °C [8]. As the economic assumptions of the reference scenario are taken from the SRES B2 scenario, it is lower than the average of the SRES range. While the SRES B2 emissions range from 10.8 to 21.8 Gt-C in 2100, the result of the reference scenario is 21.9 Gt-C. This is because the reference scenario uses the assumptions of population and GDP from SRES B2, but does not focus so much on environmental sustainability.

The temperature increase in the WGI 550 scenario is the lowest, at 1.79 °C in 2100. The increase in the WRE 550 scenario is 2.02 °C. Although the targets of these two scenarios

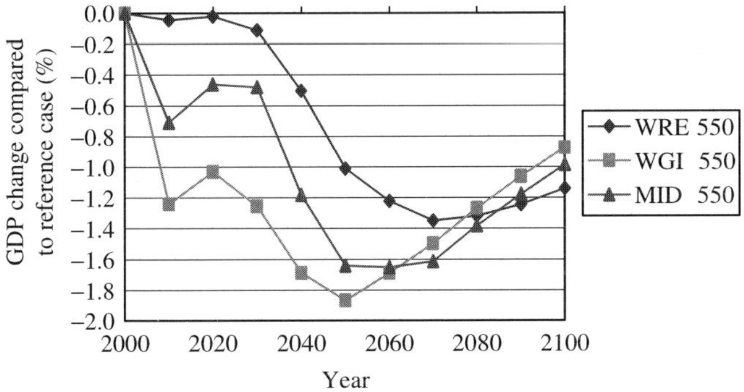

Fig. 6. Projection of GDP changes compared to the reference scenario (%).

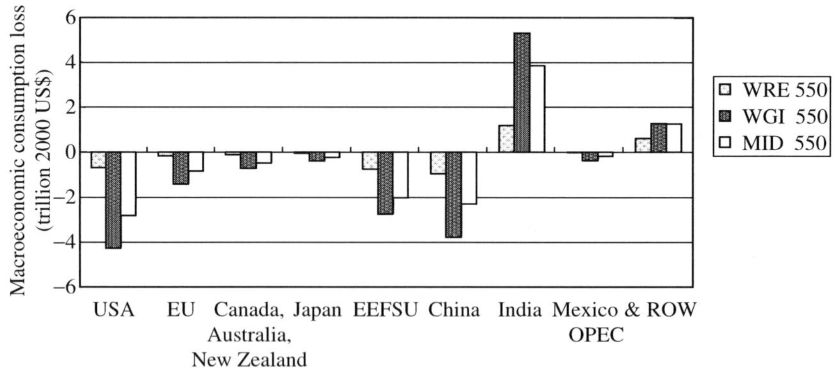

Fig. 7. Present discounted value of macroeconomic consumption loss with respect to the reference scenario (trillion 2000 US$).

are the same, there is a 0.23 °C difference in the temperature increase in 2100. These 550 ppmv scenarios can decrease the temperature by 0.75–0.98 °C in 2100 compared to the reference scenario. Although the macro economic consumption loss of the WRE 550 scenario is lower than that of the WGI 550 scenario, its impact on climate change is greater.

The globally averaged sea level rise relative to that of 1990 is shown in Fig. 9. It ranges from 40 to 52 cm. The global sea level in 2100 is projected to rise by 9–88 cm for the full range of SRES scenarios. The sea level in the WRE 550 scenario rises higher by 3.9 cm than that in the WGI 550 scenario.

6. Potential impacts in the Asian region

Climate change has direct or potential impacts on water resources, agricultural production, natural ecosystems, and human health, even if socioeconomic interactions are ignored. In the real world, global trade, immigration, and measures for adaptation modify the direct impacts. Hence, there are two stages of the impact study: the direct

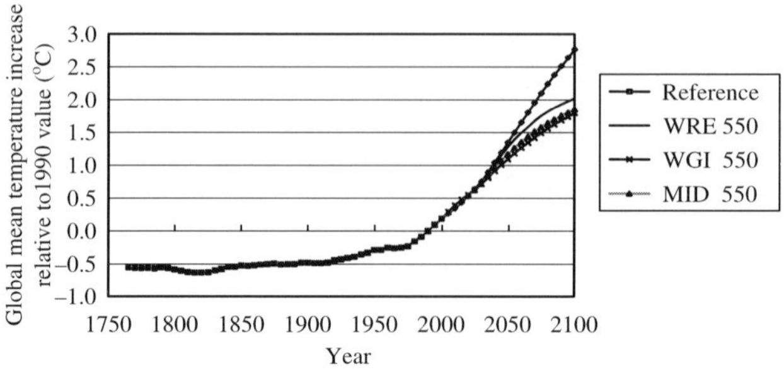

Fig. 8. Temperature increases relative to the 1990 value (°C).

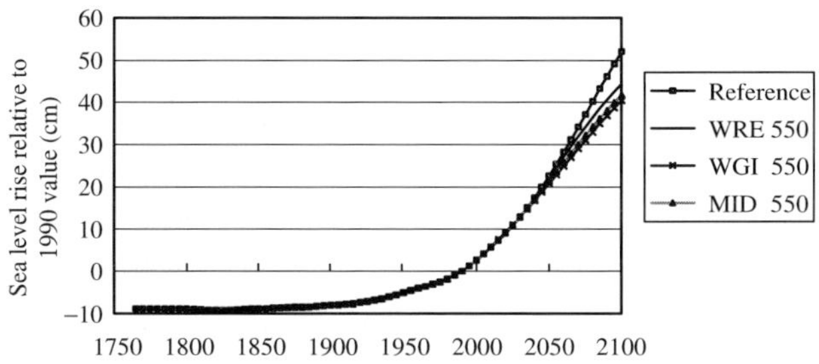

Fig. 9. Rise in the sea level relative to the 1990 value (cm).

and indirect stages. In this study, the direct impacts in Asia under the reference and 550 ppmv scenarios were considered.

Figure 10 shows the changes in winter wheat productivity (yield per unit area) in 2100 compared to 1990. The productivity of wheat will decline significantly in Sri Lanka, Malaysia, Korea-PDR, Burma, and other tropical countries.

Figure 11 shows changes in rice productivity in 2100 compared to 1990 under the reference and 550 ppmv scenarios. A slight decrease in rice production is expected in most countries, while a slight increase is expected in Bhutan and Taiwan. The productivity decline in India is projected to be the highest.

Air and water pollution, as well as solid and hazardous wastes, affect human health directly. Global climate change will also affect human health in the future in many ways.

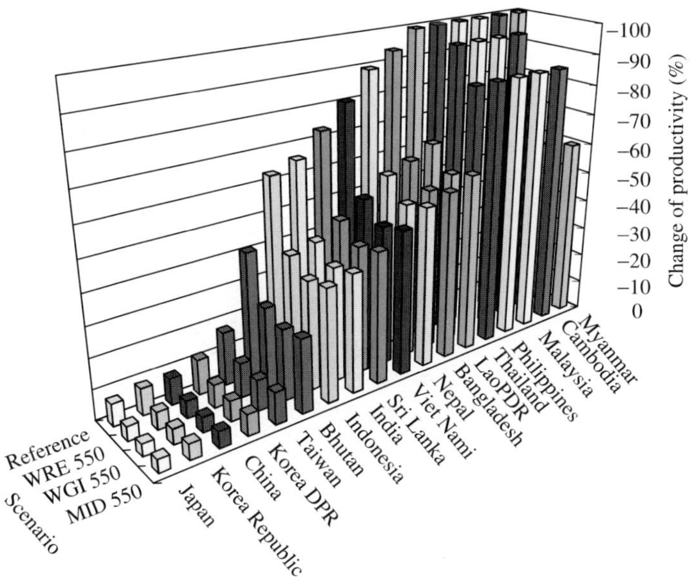

Fig. 10. Change in winter wheat productivity from 1990 to 2100 (%).

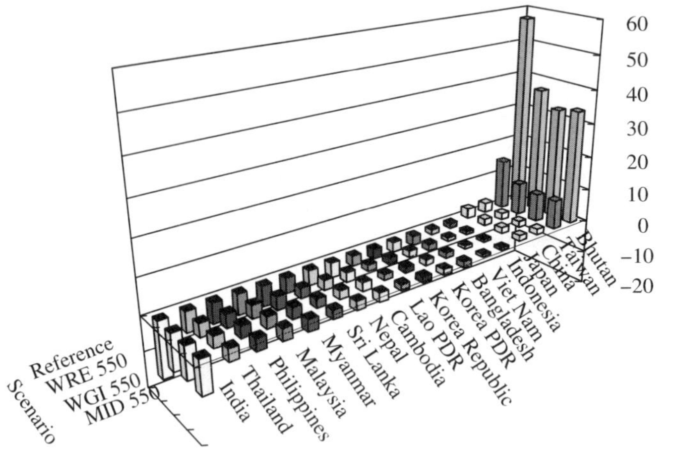

Fig. 11. Change in rice productivity from 1990 to 2100 (%).

For example, global warming will result in increasing temperatures and changing vegetation close to the ground. This will allow expansion of the habitat of the anopheles mosquito, which is the malaria vector. In addition, the development period of the malaria protozoa will shorten and their reproductive potential will increase. As a result, it is expected that the global risk of a higher incidence of malaria will increase.

Figure 12 shows the changes in the populations living where there is endemic malaria. The risk of a higher incidence of malaria in China, Nepal, Taiwan, Indonesia, and

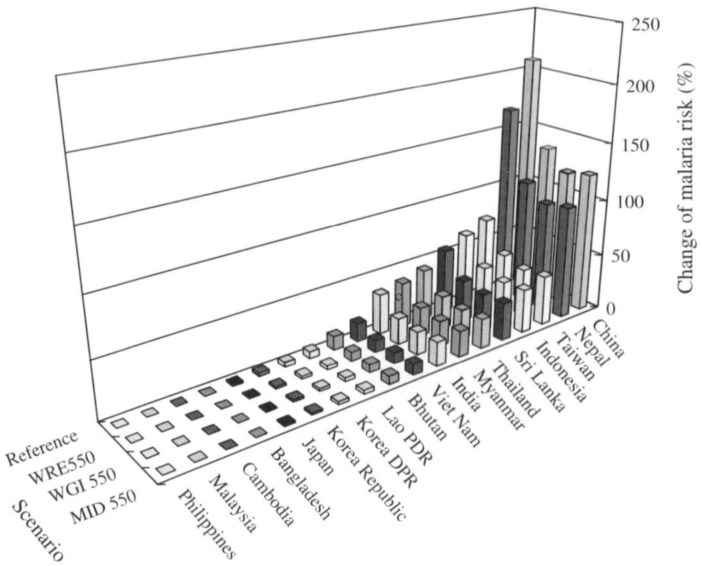

Fig. 12. Change in population living in areas at high malaria risk from 1990 to 2100 (%).

Sri Lanka will increase due to the environmental changes. Although China may be little affected by climate change in terms of food productivity, the impact it will experience in terms of malaria risk will be the greatest in the Asian region. Even under the 550 scenarios, the population living in areas at risk will double in 2100 compared to 1990.

Through the comparison of estimated impacts under the three stabilization scenarios (Figs. 10–12), it is found that negative impacts of climate change on agriculture and human health is greater under WRE550 scenario than under WGI550 scenario, though macro economic consumption loss of the WRE 550 scenario is lower than that of the WGI 550 scenario (Fig. 6).

7. Concluding remarks

Several climate change stabilization pathways are examined by the AIM model. An urgent task is to take action to combat global warming as it is an irreversible process and, once it occurs, the probability is very high that it will have multiplier effects that will further expand its impact. It is necessary to consider the many uncertainties involved in human activities such as population growth, economic development, and technological innovation, as well as uncertainties in natural processes to estimate future CO_2 emissions and to make plans for climate stabilization. The scenario approach is a practical means of analyzing the policy options under such uncertainties.

Although the emissions of developing countries were lower than those of developed countries in 2000, it is expected that they will grow much faster than those of developed countries in the future. The estimated impacts on developing countries in the Asian region are serious. The model projects that the early implementation of emissions reductions can minimize the scale of such impacts in the future.

References

[1] Y. Matsuoka, M. Kainuma and T. Morita, *Scenario analysis of global warming using the asian-pacific integrated model (AIM)*, Energy Policy **23** (4/5) (1995), 357–371.

[2] IPCC. *Costing methodlogies, Climate Change 2001, Mitigation*, Cambridge University Press, Cambridge, MA (2001).

[3] M. Kainuma, Y. Matsuoka, T. Morita, Analysis of Post-Kyoto Scenarios: the Asian-Pacific Integrated Model, Special Issue of the Energy Journal, The Costs of the Kyoto Protocol: A Multi-Model Evaluation, (1999), 207–220.

[4] IPCC. *Greenhouse gas emission mitigation, Climate Change 2001, Mitigation*, Cambridge University Press, Cambridge, MA (2001).

[5] IPCC. *Special Report on Emissions Scenarios*, Cambridge University Press, Cambridge, MA (2000).

[6] T.M.L. Wigley, R. Richels and J.A. Edmonds, *Economic and environmental choices in the stabilization of CO_2 concentrations: choosing the right emissions pathway*, Nature **379** (1995), 240–243.

[7] IPCC. *Climate models-projections offuture climate, Climate Change 1995, The Science of Climate Change*, Cambridge University Press, Cambridge, MA (1995).

[8] IPCC. *Projections of future climate change, Climate Change 2001, The Scientific Basis*, Cambridge University Press, Cambridge, MA (2001).

CHAPTER 8

Trust and Acceptance of Risks

Satoshi Fujii

Tokyo Institute of Technology, 2-12-1, Ookayama, Meguro-ku, Tokyo 152-8552, Japan

Toshiko Kikkawa

Keio University, 2-15-45, Mita, Minato-ku, Tokyo 108-8345, Japan

Kazuhisa Takemura

Waseda University, 1-24-1, Toyama, Shinjyuku-ku, Tokyo 162-8644, Japan

Contents

Abstract

This study sought to understand the determinants of risk acceptance. Thus, we implemented a survey ($n = 200$) to ask participants which policy measures would make accept each of the following risks: nuclear power plants, traffic accidents, food safety, electrical appliances, and medical mishaps. These results indicate that risk acceptance cannot be fully explained only by objectively achieved security, but other factors, such as scientific understanding and trust in workers and organizations, were also found to be important for increasing risk acceptance.

SYSTEMS AND HUMAN SCIENCE – FOR SAFETY, SECURITY, AND DEPENDABILITY
Edited by Tatsuo Arai, Shigeru Yamamoto and Kazuhisa Makino

1. Introduction

Daily life incurs many risks. For example, a large earthquake may strike Japan in the next 20–30 years, traffic accidents occur daily, and human error has led to nuclear power plant disasters, such as at TMI or Chernobyl; furthermore, no one knows when the next infectious disease, such as SARS, will emerge. Unfortunately, few Japanese have the option of living in a place without earthquakes; we cannot drive a car without traffic accident risks, and our energy-consuming lifestyles lead us to rely on nuclear power plants. Even eating the food we need to survive incurs the slight risk of food poisoning. We can never truly free ourselves from risk.

There is a growing concern with risk and safety in Japan. This concern has been attributed to an increase in technological accidents that have occurred in recent years, as well as to scientific uncertainty over the probability of risks. While we must assiduously work to reduce technological risks, we still have to accept these risks, to some extent, because it is impossible to eliminate such risks completely.

Therefore, the practical problem with which this research was concerned was to understand how people accept risks, given the impossibility of achieving zero-risk status. To examine determinants of risk acceptance for several risk events, we surveyed 200 Tokyo residents to find their response to a variety of risks.

2. Risk acceptance

When do people accept risks? Researchers have investigated this question for decades [1]. The simplest answer is that people do not accept risks and, instead, work to eliminate risk. If all risks are eliminated, security is guaranteed and a zero-risk state is achieved. Although risk-reduction efforts are necessary, society will always face some risks. Achieving zero-risk status might not be a realistic aim to strive for.

Another answer is that people rationally accept risks if they expect the expected benefit of an activity to exceed the expected cost [2]. For example, people may drive a car, knowing the risk of a traffic accident, if they believe that car use is beneficial. People may also accept nuclear plants, as long as the energy produced improves the quality of their lives.

However, many empirical studies (c.f. [3–6]) have contradicted the above claims. These studies have found that personal decision making frequently deviates from theories such as the "expected utility theory" [7], or the "subjective expected utility theory" [8], which assume rational decision making based on cost and benefit. Cost and benefit expectations can be important determinants of risk acceptance, but they do not fully explain the process. No one yet knows the probabilistic distribution of some risks, such as endocrine-disrupting chemicals. Other risks, such as those from electromagnetic fields, remain controversial. We cannot evaluate these risks by science, or by costs and benefits, alone.

We compared the relative weight of two components of risk: the possibility of risk and the damage from risk. These two possible determinants are closely related to cost expectation, which is assumed to determine decision making in rational choice models, such as the expected utility theory. We also investigated the effects of compensation after risk events have occurred. Compensation is expected to reduce or eliminate the cost of risks. Additionally, we examined how understanding the scientific causes of a risk affected risk acceptance. Scientific understanding may reduce the extent of unknown risks [2] and may lead to risk acceptance.

3. Trust and risk acceptance

We presumed that trust in workers and regulatory agencies constitutes another important determinant of risk acceptance. Instead of controlling risks by themselves, individuals may trust in, and delegate power to, organizations or institutions. This situation can be represented through the "Trust Game" [9].

The Trust Game has two players: Player A (the truster) and Player B (the trusted). Player A can "trust" Player B by sending a monetary endowment X (see Fig. 1). Player B then receives double what player A has sent (i.e., $2X$). Player B must choose between "reciprocating" (returning $1.5X$ and taking $0.5X$ for himself) and "betrayal" (taking all he has received, i.e., $-2X$). In this game, if Player A trusts Player B, the total monetary amount that Player A and Player B have increases by X. However, if Player A does not trust Player B, there is no collective increase. In this situation, trusting behavior is collectively beneficial. However, if Player B betrays Player A, Player A loses X. If Player A fears this risk, he does not trust Player B, which results in no collective benefit.

The basic structure underlying risk problems in our society may be seen as resembling that of the Trust Game, assuming that lay people represent Player A and risk experts represent Player B. Social benefits may increase if lay people "trust" risk experts by asking them to administer risks. Risk experts may "reciprocate" by successfully managing the risk, or "betray" by failing to effectively manage risks. If people expect experts to reciprocate, trust and social benefits may increase. However, if people expect betrayal by the experts, trust and social benefits may not increase. For example, people's benefits could increase if electricity companies repay the trust of the public by managing

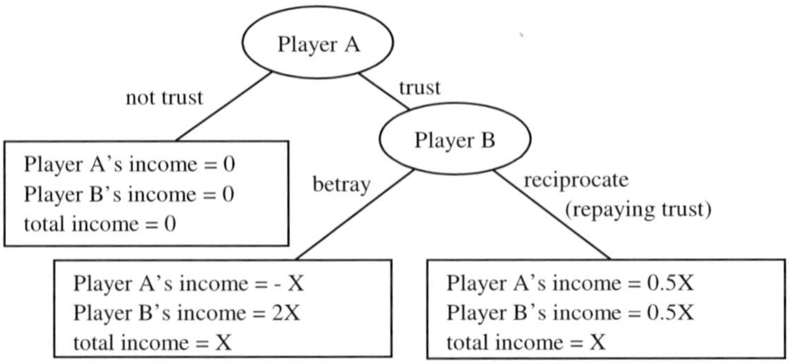

Fig. 1. An example of the Trust Game.

nuclear plants successfully. people's benefits would not increase if nuclear plants ceased operations due to a lack of people's trust. If electricity companies fail in repaying public trust due to a serious nuclear plant problem, people's benefits will decrease.

4. Methods

4.1. *Sample*

Tokyo residents living within 50 km of the city center were randomly selected as participants for the August 2002 survey. A surveyor first visited the residents to ask them if they would participate in the survey. If the resident agreed to participate, a questionnaire was left at the home. After a few days, the surveyor again visited the home and collected the questionnaire.

4.2. *Measures*

As discussed above, we assumed that risk acceptance is determined by factors beyond subjective expectations of costs and benefits. We assumed that trust in persons and regulatory agencies in charge of risk would be another important determinant. Thus, we asked respondents to evaluate political policies or decisions implemented by administrators and the government. In the questionnaire, we asked respondents to consider six risk management measures and to choose three out of the six measures that would increase their risk acceptance for each of the following risks: nuclear power plants, traffic accidents, food safety, electrical appliances, and medical mishaps. The six choices were as follows:

(1) decrease the probability that the risk occurs;
(2) minimize the damage when the risk occurs;
(3) compensate for damage when the risk occurs;
(4) know that the government adequately manages the risk;
(5) know that workers and regulatory agencies are trustworthy;
(6) know that scientific mechanisms of accidents and mishaps are well understood.

These six measures correspond to determinants of risk acceptance, as discussed in Section 1. In the questionnaire, the following phrasing framed the question related to each risk:

> With respect to (type of risk inserted here), how do you achieve a feeling of "*an-shin*"? Of the following six statements, which do you consider the first-, second-, and third-most important factors in creating a sense of "*an-shin*"?

An-shin in Japanese corresponds to "security" in English, but connotes, additionally, peace of mind. People may lack *an-shin* even when they are guaranteed security. People may have peace of mind, even when they are not guaranteed security from risks.

To ask participants directly whether they would be willing to accept certain risk events might not be appropriate, as almost all risks in our society exist *as if* they have already been accepted. Therefore, we measured *an-shin* instead of directly asking about risk acceptance. Note that in Section 5, we use the term "risk approval" for this measure of *an-shin*.

5. Results

Table 1 shows the distributions and mean ranks of the six risk management measures, according to perceived effectiveness with regard to increased risk approval. The table shows that measures to decrease the probability of risk occurrence and measures to minimize damages from risk were evaluated as effective in increasing risk approval for the risks listed in the questionnaire. The former was the most effective in increasing risk approval for electrical appliances and traffic accidents, while the latter was the most effective in increasing risk approval for nuclear plants.

Respondents indicated that measures that decrease the expected cost of the risks (i.e., measures minimizing the damage and probability of the risks) were also effective for medical mishaps and food risks. However, increasing trust in workers and regulatory agencies was evaluated as more effective than decreasing expected costs. Thus, increasing trust is the most effective risk management measure with regard to food risks and medical mishaps. Regarding electrical appliance and nuclear power plant risks, respondents chose scientific understanding and explanation of accident mechanisms. These two risks differ from the other risks, such as traffic accidents, food, and medical mishaps, in that they are caused by more advanced technologies, which are less likely to be understood, even by risk experts.

Compensation for risk damages was not chosen as effective in increasing risk approval, except for the traffic accident risk. Respondents indicated that risk approval for traffic accidents may increase with the compensation measure. This may be because damage from traffic accidents is generally less than the damage from the other risks presented in the questionnaire. Additionally, it is likely that many people will actually face traffic accidents in their lives.

6. Discussion

This study sought to understand the determinants of risk acceptance. Thus, survey participants were asked which policy measures would make them feel *an-shin* as an indicator of risk approval. The results showed that the risk management measures that would increase risk approval depended on the respective risks. The following three findings emerged from the survey.

(1) For traffic accidents, nuclear power plants, and electrical appliance risks, the most effective measure for risk approval was that of minimizing the damage or the probability of accidents.

Table 1. Distributions and means of ranks of the six policy actions according to perceived effectiveness to increase risk approval

		Medical mishaps		Food		Electric appliance		Nuclear plants		Traffic accidents	
		Frequency	%	Frequency	%	Frequency	%	Frequency	%	Frequency	%
Decrease the probability that the risk occurs	1st	46	23.0	55	27.5	51	25.5	49	24.5	103	51.5
	2nd	49	24.5	43	21.5	55	27.5	24	12.0	45	22.5
	3rd	44	22.0	39	19.5	43	21.5	48	24.0	29	14.5
	≥4th	61	30.5	63	31.5	51	25.5	79	39.5	23	11.5
	Mean rank	2.91[a]		2.87[a]		2.73[b]		3.18[a]		1.98[b]	
Minimize the damage when the risk occurs	1st	23	11.5	19	9.5	36	18.0	42	21.0	31	15.5
	2nd	37	18.5	45	22.5	49	24.5	57	28.5	79	39.5
	3rd	48	24.0	31	15.5	47	23.5	40	20.0	30	15.0
	≥4th	92	46.0	105	52.5	68	34.0	61	30.5	60	30.0
	Mean rank	3.51[c]		3.64		3.08[c]		2.91[b]		2.90[a]	
Compensate for the damages when the risk occurs	1st	6	3.0	3	1.5	8	4.0	1	0.5	15	7.5
	2nd	18	9.0	10	5.0	28	14.0	10	5.0	26	13.0
	3rd	37	18.5	39	19.5	40	20.0	24	12.0	66	33.0
	≥4th	139	69.5	148	74.0	124	62.0	165	82.5	93	46.5
	Mean rank	4.24		4.40		4.02		4.59		3.65[c]	
Know that the government adequately manages the risk	1st	7	3.5	38	19.0	11	5.5	40	20.0	18	9.0
	2nd	17	8.5	28	14.0	8	4.0	21	10.5	13	6.5
	3rd	18	9.0	23	11.5	8	4.0	28	14.0	21	10.5
	≥4th	158	79.0	111	55.5	173	86.5	111	55.5	148	74.0
	Mean rank	4.43		3.59[c]		4.58		3.61		4.24	

Table 1. (*Continued*)

		Medical mishaps		Food		Electric appliance		Nuclear plants		Traffic accidents	
		Frequency	%	Frequency	%	Frequency	%	Frequency	%	Frequency	%
Know that workers and regulatory agencies are trustworthy	1st	99	49.5	74	37.0	30	15.0	38	19.0	20	10.0
	2nd	45	22.5	47	23.5	30	15.0	34	17.0	19	9.5
	3rd	23	11.5	30	15.0	26	13.0	20	10.0	26	13.0
	≥4th	33	16.5	49	24.5	114	57.0	108	54.0	135	67.5
	Mean rank	2.12[b]		2.52[b]		3.69		3.53		4.06	
Know that scientific mechanisms of accidents and mishaps are well understood	1st	19	9.5	11	5.5	64	32.0	30	15.0	13	6.5
	2nd	34	17.0	27	13.5	30	15.0	54	27.0	18	9.0
	3rd	30	15.0	38	19.0	36	18.0	40	20.0	28	14.0
	≥4th	117	58.5	124	62.0	70	35.0	76	38.0	141	70.5
	Mean rank	3.81		4.00		2.91[a]		3.19[c]		4.19	

Note. For calculating mean ranks, ranks for options that were not selected as top three options were assumed as "5.5", i.e., mean ranks between 4th and 7th.
[a]The second highest ranked policy.
[b]The highest ranked policy.
[c]The third highest ranked policy.

(2) For food and medical mishap risks, the most effective policy was that of increasing trust in workers and regulatory agencies, rather than that of minimizing the damage or the probability of accidents.

(3) Risk approval for electrical appliances and nuclear power plants could increase if people knew that the scientific mechanisms of accidents and mishaps were well understood.

A possible reason why trust in workers and organizations is so important for food and medical mishap risks is that medical and food workers, and their organizations, are assumed to have relatively more control over these risks, unlike the other risks presented here. Electrical appliances and nuclear accidents, on the other hand, are assumed to stem more from mechanical error than from human error. This explanation also agrees with the finding that better understanding of scientific mechanisms is important for electrical appliance and nuclear plants risks. Conversely, the mechanisms of food and medical mishaps may be simpler than problems associated with nuclear power and electrical appliances. Thus, people may believe that increasing accident prevention among workers and organizations is most effective in this case. Traffic accidents were assumed to be less under the control of workers and organizations (such as the police in charge of traffic) than accidents from medical mishaps and foods. We believe this is why trust was not considered as an important determinant for traffic accident risk approval.

These results indicate that risk acceptance cannot be fully understood by adopting a rational choice theory, which assumes that people maximize the expected benefits and/or minimize the expected costs. Minimizing damage and the probability of accidents were assumed to be just two examples of effective risk management measures for increasing risk approval or, in more commonly used words, risk acceptance. In other words, the feeling of *an-shin*, or risk approval, cannot be explained only by objectively achieved security. Other factors, such as scientific understanding and trust in workers and organizations, were also found to be important for increasing risk acceptance.

This indicates that those who wish to increase the public's risk acceptance should appear trustworthy and try to understand the scientific mechanisms of accidents; they should also try to minimize risk damage and probability. Trust is important, especially for risks where accidents can be prevented relatively easily by workers and/or organizations. These risks include those associated with food and medical mishaps. Scientific understanding of risk mechanisms is also important for risk acceptance, especially for risks involving mechanisms that are relatively complex, such as nuclear power and electrical appliance risks.

References

[1] P. Slovic, B. Fischhoff and S. Lichtenstein, *Cognitive processes and societal risk taking*, Cognition and Social Behavior, J.S. Carroll and J.W. Payne, eds, Lawrence Erlbaum, Potmac, MD (1976).

[2] B. Fischhoff, P. Slovic, S. Lichtenstein, S. Read and B. Combs, *How safe is safe enough? A psychometric study of attitudes toward technological risks and benefits*, Policy Sci. **9** (1978), 127–152.

[3] R.M. Dawes, *Behavioral decision making and judgment*, Handbook of Social Psychology, 4th edn., Vol. 1, D.T. Gilbert, S.T. Fiske and G. Lindzey, eds, McGraw-Hill, Boston, MA (1998), 497–548.

[4] D. Kahneman, J.L. Knetsch and R.H. Thaler, *Anomalies: the endowment effect, loss aversion and status quo bias*, J. Econ. Perspect. **5** (1991), 193–206.
[5] J.W. Payne, J.R. Bettman and E.J. Johnson, *The Adaptive Decision Maker*, Cambridge University Press, New York (1993).
[6] P. Slovic, *The construction of preferences*, Am. Psychol. **50** (1995), 364–371.
[7] J. von Neumann and O. Morgenstern, *Theory of Games and Economic Behavior*, 2nd edn., Princeton University Press, Princeton, NJ (1947).
[8] I.R. Savage, *The Foundations of Statistics*, Wiley, New York (1954).
[9] D. Kreps, *Corporate culture and economic theory*, Perspectives on Positive Political Economy, J. Alt and K. Shepsle, eds, Harvard Business School Press, Boston (1990).

CHAPTER 9

A Value Judgment for Evaluating the Sense of Security Provided by Nursing Care Robots Based on Cumulative Prospect Theory

Hiroyuki Tamura

Faculty of Engineering, Kansai University, 3-3-35 Yamate-cho, Suita, Osaka 564-8680, Japan

Yoshitomo Miura and Masahiro Inuiguchi

Graduate School of Engineering Science, Osaka University, 1-3 Machikaneyama, Toyonaka, Osaka 560-8531, Japan

Contents

Abstract

In this chapter, we deal with evaluating the sense of security provided by nursing care robots. The method involves collecting information by means of questionnaires from people who need care or who participate in nursing, then attempting to evaluate the value of the sense of security provided by nursing care robots using cumulative prospect theory with multiattribute value function and interpreting the results.

SYSTEMS AND HUMAN SCIENCE – FOR SAFETY, SECURITY, AND DEPENDABILITY
Edited by Tatsuo Arai, Shigeru Yamamoto and Kazuhisa Makino

1. Introduction

Japan currently has an aging society composed largely of elderly people, and the proportion of the aged in the population is increasing. This causes problems because the number of people who need care is increasing every year. It is estimated that more than 4% of Japanese will need care in 2025. However, the number of nurses is smaller than required. In such a society, people increasingly turn to machines and tools for nursing care or welfare and some are already put to practical use. A wheelchair, nursing care bed and others are already put to practical use and are becoming more popular. However, more research and development of nursing care robots is urgently required because of the diversification of people who need care.

In this chapter we assume certain types of nursing care robots are available and try to evaluate the sense of security they provide. For this purpose, we use a utility theoretic approach [1,2]. More specifically, we use cumulative prospect theory (CPT) [3,4] for modeling human psychological phenomena where CPT has been proposed as a revised version of prospect theory [5]. We then conduct an experiment and judge the value of the sense of security provided by nursing care robots.

2. Nursing care robots

Robots that make some contribution to caring for people are referred to as "nursing care robots". Some nursing care robots are already on sale and in practical use, but most of these have a mechanical shape that is entirely different from humans, and their abilities are limited to a particular function. For example, they help bedridden people to sit up in bed or take a meal. Moreover, they are too expensive for an individual to buy, so they are used only in some medical or nursing care institutions. On the other hand, more advanced nursing care robots are currently the subject of research. For example, some of them can perform a variety of actions and they are expected to respond to diverse needs. Others look like humans and can communicate with people, and they are expected to give people a sense of security.

For nursing care robots, giving us a sense of security is an important prerequisite. If a robot does not give us a sense of security, it needs to be improved. Though there have been some studies comparing the sense of security of a particular robot with that of another, or with conventional robots like [6], there are no reports comparing the sense of security provided by robots with that of humans. Here, we attempt to compare the sense of security provided by a nursing care robot with that of a human nurse. It is also useful to evaluate the sense of security of a society in which nursing care robots are already popular and evaluate the value to such a society.

3. Theory

We used the utility theoretic approach for evaluating the sense of security provided by nursing care robots. In preparation, we will introduce some theories used in this chapter.

3.1. *Cumulative prospect theory*

CPT was proposed by Tversky and Kahneman in 1992 [3]. Its characteristics are as follows:

- The value function in this theory shows risk averse values in the gain domain and risk prone values in the loss domain.
- The value function in the loss domain is steeper than in the gain domain.
- Probabilities for quite good outcomes and quite bad outcomes are more heavily weighted than the probabilities of other outcomes.
- The weighting function is defined for all probabilities.

This theory can explain people's decision-making as follows:

- People's attitude to risk is risk averse for gains and risk prone for losses.
- People are sensitive to changes in probability for the best or the worst outcome.

We denote the prospect that yields outcome x^j with probability $p_j, j = 1, \ldots, n$ by

$$l = (p_1, x^1; p_2, x^2; \ldots; p_n, x^n). \tag{1}$$

Throughout, for convenience of exposition, we arrange the prospect so that

$$x^1 \precsim x^2 \precsim \cdots \precsim x^n \tag{2}$$

where $a \succsim b$ denotes that a is preferred to or indifferent to b.

In CPT, the value of the prospect V is evaluated by the evaluation function

$$V = \sum_{j=1}^{n} \pi_j v(x^j) \tag{3}$$

where the value function v is convex and its curve is gentle in the gain domain, while it is concave and its curve is steeper in the loss domain, as shown in Fig. 1. This shows that people are risk averse in the gain domain and risk prone in the loss domain and that people in general are loss averse. The shape of the value function is common to prospect theory.

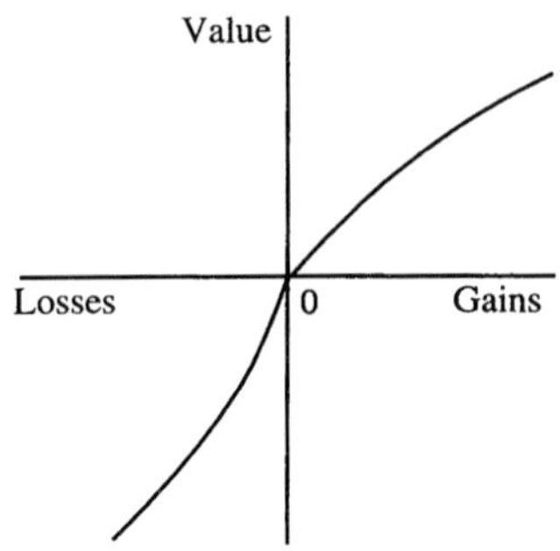

Fig. 1. Value function.

The decision weight π is different from prospect theory, and it is defined by weighting functions w^+ and w^-. Concretely, the decision weight π is defined as follows: For gains,

$$\pi_j = w^+(p_j + \cdots + p_n) - w^+(p_{j+1} + \cdots + p_n). \tag{4}$$

For losses,

$$\pi_j = w^-(p_1 + \cdots + p_j) - w^-(p_1 + \cdots + p_{j-1}). \tag{5}$$

A weighting function w^+ is defined for probabilities associated with gains, and a separate weighting function w^- is defined for probabilities associated with losses. Both w^+ and w^- are relatively sensitive to changes in probability near the end points 0 and 1 but they are insensitive in the middle region as shown by the solid line in Fig. 2. The shape of the two weighting functions are much the same, but w^- is straighter and higher than w^+. The dotted line shows the case for expected utility model.

Weighting functions w^+, w^- are both simple monotone increasing functions which satisfy $w^+(0) = w^-(0) = 0$, $w^+(1) = w^-(1) = 1$, and w^+, w^- both having the characteristics that alteration of weight for alteration of quite high or low probabilities is large and alteration of weight for alteration of middle probabilities is small, as shown in Fig. 2.

3.2. *Multiattribute value function*

In CPT [3], the value function is assumed to have a single attribute. Here we use a multiattribute value function [7] in CPT.

3.2.1. *Definition of multiattribute value function.* We define the outcome $\mathbf{x} \in X$ as characterized by m attributes $X_1, X_2, ..., X_m$. We can then denote the outcome as follows:

$$\mathbf{x} = (x_1, x_2, \cdots, x_m), \qquad x_i \in X_i, i = 1, 2, \cdots, m \tag{6}$$

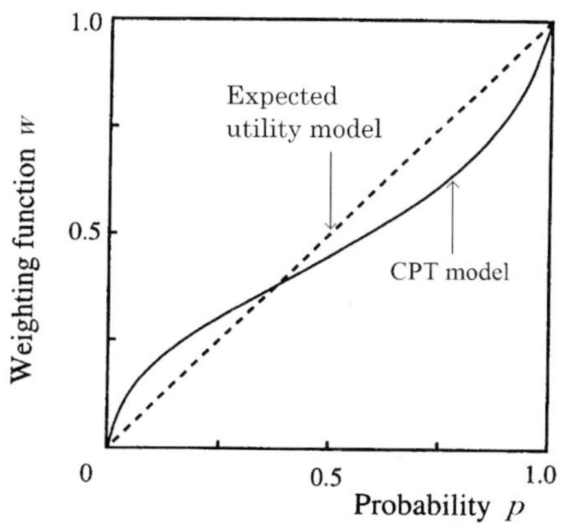

Fig. 2. Weighting function.

and the set of all outcomes X is denoted $X = X_1 \times X_2 \times \cdots \times X_m$. The m-attribute value function is defined as $v : X \rightarrow R$ upon $X = X_1 \times X_2 \times \cdots \times X_m$. It is almost impossible to find such an m-attribute value function without assuming independence of the multiple attributes, so we assume difference independence or weak difference independence among attributes as follows.

3.2.2. *Difference independence.* We denote that I is a subset of $\{1, 2, \ldots, m\}$ consisting of r elements ($1 \leq r < m$) and J is the complement of I consisting of $(m-r)$ elements. We divide the m elements of attributes into two sets $X_i, i \in I$ and $X_i, i \in J$ then we describe the r-attribute space made by $X_i, i \in I$ as X_I, the $(m-r)$-attribute space made by $X_i, i \in J$ as X_J and $X = X_I \times X_J$.

We can then fix the outcome $\mathbf{x}_J \in X_J$ at some level and discuss two prospects given at will upon X_I. We can then say that the r-attribute space X_I is difference independent of the $(m-r)$-attribute space X_J if the difference in strength of preference [7] upon X_I does not depend on the fixed conditional level $\mathbf{x}_J \in X_J$. We represent this property as $X_I(\mathrm{DI})X_J$.

Furthermore, we can say that the attributes $X_1, X_2, \cdots, X_m$ are mutually difference independent, if they satisfy $X_I(\mathrm{DI})X_J$ for all $I \subset \{1, 2, \cdots, m\}$ and its complement J.

3.2.3. *Weak difference independence.* We can say that the r-attribute space X_I is weak difference independent of the $(m-r)$-attribute space X_J if the order of difference in strength of preference does not depend on the conditional level $\mathbf{x}_J \in X_J$. We represent this property as $X_I(\mathrm{WDI})X_J$.

Here we define the normalized conditional value function as follows:

$$v_I(\mathbf{x}_I|\mathbf{x}_J) := \frac{v(\mathbf{x}_I, \mathbf{x}_J) - v(\mathbf{x}_I^0, \mathbf{x}_J)}{v(\mathbf{x}_I^*, \mathbf{x}_J) - v(\mathbf{x}_I^0, \mathbf{x}_J)} \tag{7}$$

where $\mathbf{x}^*$ is the best prospect and $\mathbf{x}^0$ is the worst prospect, so $v(\mathbf{x}_I^*, \mathbf{x}_J) > v(\mathbf{x}_I^0, \mathbf{x}_J)$.Then we obtain the property

$$X_I(\mathrm{WDI})X_J \Leftrightarrow v_I(\mathbf{x}_I|\mathbf{x}_J) = v_I(\mathbf{x}_I|\mathbf{x}_J^0), \qquad \forall x_J \in X_J \tag{8}$$

which means that the normalized conditional value function does not depend on the conditional level. So we can denote

$$v_I(\mathbf{x}_I) := v_I(\mathbf{x}_I|\mathbf{x}_J^0) \tag{9}$$

Furthermore, we can say that attributes $X_1, X_2, \ldots, X_m$ are mutually weak difference independent, if they satisfy $X_I(\mathrm{WDI})X_J$ for all $I \subset \{1, 2, \ldots, m\}$ and its complement J.

Difference independence is a special case of weak difference independence.

3.2.4. *Decomposition of multiattribute value function.* If we assume that all attributes are mutually weak difference independent, then we have either an additive model (10) or a multiplicative model (11) of the multiattribute value function.

$$v(\mathbf{x}) = \sum_{i=1}^{m} k_i v_i(x_i), \qquad \text{if } \sum_{i=1}^{m} k_i = 1 \tag{10}$$

$$kv(\mathbf{x}) + 1 = \prod_{i=1}^{m} \{kk_i v_i(x_i) + 1\}, \qquad \text{if } \sum_{i=1}^{m} k_i \neq 1 \tag{11}$$

where

- $v(x_1^0, x_2^0, \ldots, x_m^0) = 0, v(x_1^*, x_2^*, \ldots, x_m^*) = 1$
- $v_i(x_i) := v_i(x_i|x_{i^c}^0),\ i^c = \{1, \ldots, i-1, i+1, \ldots, m\}$
- $k_i = v(x_i^*, x_{i^c}^0)$
- k is the solution of $k + 1 = \prod_{i=1}^{m}(kk_i + 1)$

If we have an additive model, the property of difference independence is satisfied among attributes, where k_i is called the weighting coefficient for attribute X_i.

4. Algorithm

Using the theories introduced in Section 3, we propose an algorithm for evaluating the sense of security. In this algorithm we evaluate the prospect value that includes attributes of the sense of security, and we regard this as the value of the sense of security. The algorithm is described as follows.

Step 0

Determine the subject of evaluation, alternatives and outcomes $\mathbf{x}^j \in X(j = 1, \ldots, n)$ and the probability p_j of obtaining each outcome for each alternative.

Step 1

Prescribe attributes for sense of security $X_i(i = 1, \ldots, m)$, and measure the conditional value function under each attribute $v_i(x_i^j)$ of the alternative.

We can measure the conditional value function under each attribute individually because we assume mutual weak difference independence among all attributes and the function does not depend on the other attributes. In fact, we can determine the conditional value function by asking an individual about the value under each attribute because it is difficult to measure the conditional value function itself. However, $0 \leq v_i(x_i^j) \leq 1, v_i(x_i^0) = 0, v_i(x_i^*) = 1$ by definition of the normalized conditional value function (7).

Step 2

Measure weighting coefficient k_i for each attribute.

As we described in the previous section, $k_i = v(x_i^*, \mathbf{x}_{i^c}^0)$, we can determine k_i by asking an individual about the probability p which satisfies the relationship for two prospects

$$(1, \mathbf{x}) \sim (p, \mathbf{x}^*; 1 - p, \mathbf{x}^0), \qquad \mathbf{x} = (x_i^*, \mathbf{x}_{i^c}^0) \tag{12}$$

and calculating

$$k_i = v(x_i^*, \mathbf{x}_{i^c}^0) = pv(\mathbf{x}^*) + (1-p)v(\mathbf{x}^0) = p \tag{13}$$

because k_i represents the value on the vertex of the m-attribute space $X_1 \times X_2 \times \cdots \times X_m$.

Moreover, if we assume difference independence among the attributes, we can measure k_i by pairwise comparisons because $\sum_{i=1}^{m} k_i = 1$ is satisfied.

Step 3

Calculate the value of each outcome $\mathbf{x}^j$ using the additive model

$$v(\mathbf{x}^j) = v(x_1^j, x_2^j, \ldots, x_m^j) = \sum_{i=1}^{m} k_i v_i(x_i^j) \tag{14}$$

or the multiplicative model

$$kv(\mathbf{x}^j) + 1 = \prod_{i=1}^{m} \{kk_i v_i(x_i^j) + 1\}, \qquad k + 1 = \prod_{i=1}^{m} (kk_i + 1) \tag{15}$$

of the multiattribute value function. At this time, calculate value $v(\mathbf{x}^R)$ where $\mathbf{x}^R$ denotes the outcome for "preserving the status quo (present condition)".

Step 4

Arrange the outcomes, including the preservation of the status quo, in ascending order as follows:

$$v(\mathbf{x}^1) \le \cdots \le v(\mathbf{x}^R) \le \cdots \le v(\mathbf{x}^n) \tag{16}$$

Step 5

Calculate the decision weight π_j for each outcome using (4) and (5) in CPT, and evaluate the value of the sense of security by the evaluation function in CPT

$$V = \sum_{j=1}^{n} \pi_j v(\mathbf{x}^j) \tag{17}$$

Using this algorithm, we can quantitatively evaluate the sense of security provided by nursing care robots.

5. Experiment

We now attempted to evaluate the sense of security that people feel in two different societies and compared the results. One is a society in which nursing care robots do not exist and the other is a society in which they are popular. We also attempted to evaluate the sense of security provided by various types of robots and consider what type of robot brings the greatest value to people. Ideally we should evaluate the sense of security of people who need care, but for the purposes of our study we used university students as

Table 1. Probability of obtaining each outcome

Outcome	Society 1	Society 2
No care	0.35	0.25
Care by family	0.35	0.35
Care by nurse	0.30	0.30
Care by robot	0	0.10

experimental subjects. We evaluated the value of the sense of security of 12 students, and we show a typical example in this chapter.

Step 0

We designate outcomes and their probabilities in Table 1. The probabilities are assigned based on a variety of statistical data [8,9]. Society 1 denotes the society in which nursing care robots do not exist and Society 2 denotes the society where standard nursing care robots are widespread.

Step 1

We also designate the attributes for evaluation based on the concerns of individuals as follows:

(1) Care level
(2) Sense of intimacy
(3) Cost
(4) Effect on family

and we assume the value of outcomes under each attribute as shown in Table 2.

Step 2

Next we measure weight for each attribute both in the case that attributes are difference independent and in the case that they are not. This individual weight is set for each attribute as follows:

- In the case that attributes are difference independent, we measure weight k_i by pairwise comparison made by the subject. In this case the determined weight for "care level" $k_1 = 0.495$ and weight for "sense of intimacy" $k_2 = 0.117$, weight for "cost" $k_3 = 0.332$ and weight for "effect on family" $k_4 = 0.067$.
- In the case that attributes are not difference independent, we measure weight k_i by (12). This subject determined $k_1 = 0.6, k_2 = 0.2, k_3 = 0.5$ and $k_4 = 0.1$.

Step 3

Next, we calculate the value of each outcome. Calculating them using the additive model, we obtain the results in column DI of Table 3 and using the multiplicative model,

Table 2. The value under each attribute

Outcome	Care	Intimacy	Cost	Family
No care	0	0	1	1
Care by family	0.8	1	1	0
Care by nurse	1	0.7	0	1
Care by robot	0.5	0.2	0.4	1

Table 3. The value of each outcome

Outcome	DI	WDI
No care	0.3990	0.5652
Care by family	0.8350	0.8999
Care by nurse	0.6439	0.7341
Care by robot	0.4667	0.5517

we obtain the results in column WDI (where DI denotes difference independent and WDI denotes weak difference independent).

At this point, we can see some differences between the results obtained by the additive model and by the multiplicative model. In other words, we obtained different results in the case where difference independence is assumed than in the case where weak difference independence is assumed. In particular, the order of value of outcomes for "No care" and for "Care by robot" is inverted.

Step 4

We must next arrange the outcomes, including the preservation of the status quo, in ascending order (16), where the status quo depends on the individual. Then we assume that the subject receives no care at all at present. Now we obtain the following order of outcomes:

- For the case in which difference independence is assumed, the ascending order of values is "No care (status quo)", "Care by robot", "Care by nurse" and "Care by family".
- For the case in which weak difference independence is assumed, the ascending order of value is "Care by robot", "No care (status quo)", "Care by nurse" and "Care by family".

Step 5

Finally we calculate the decision weight and the value of the sense of security. When we calculate decision weight, we must take note of the order of outcomes arranged in Step 4. In this instance, we assume the weighting function $w(p) = p + \frac{1}{10}\sin(2\pi p^{2/3})$, and the value function is logarithmic. The result is shown in Table 4.

This result shows that:

- People feel anxious about nursing care robots such as those analyzed in this chapter in the case of WDI, though in the case of DI, people feel secure.
- The property of difference independence does not hold among attributes because the results of DI and WDI in Table 4 are different, and in fact this individual feels anxious about a society such as one in which the robots analyzed are popular. So this type of robot must be improved further in order to ensure a sense of security.

Table 4. Value of sense of security in each society based on DI and WDI

Case	DI	WDI
Society 1	0.5282	0.6229
Society 2	0.5469	0.6202

Table 5. Value of the sense of security of society with respect to various types of nursing care robot

Robots	Value of Sense of Security
Not exist	0.6229
Standard	0.6202
High ability	0.6695
Good design	0.6668
Reasonable price	0.6741

The robots postulated in this chapter do not ensure a sense of security. Therefore, we evaluated the alteration in the value judgment of the sense of security for different types of nursing care robots in order to find out what type of robot brings people a sense of security. In detail, we assume four types of robots including "Standard" (described above), "High ability", "Good design" and "Reasonable price". The parameters for each type of robot are assumed as follows:

- For a "High ability" robot, the value assigned to "Care level" is 0.6, and all other parameters are the same as for the "Standard" robot.
- For a "Good design" robot, the value assigned to "Sense of intimacy" is 0.4, and all other parameters are the same as for the "Standard" robot.
- For a "Reasonable price" robot, the value assigned to "Cost" is 0.6 and the probability of receiving "Care by robot" increases to 0.2 from 0.1, while all other parameters are the same as for the "Standard" robot.

The result obtained is shown in Table 5 where we assume that attributes are mutually weak difference independent.

This result shows that depending upon the robot's character, design or productivity, the value judgment of the sense of security provided by nursing care robots may change. When we want to increase the sense of security provided by nursing care robots, we tend to think that we need to improve the ability of the robots or to refine the design. However, we found that it is also important to decrease the price.

6. Conclusion

By using an algorithm based on CPT, we were able to evaluate quantitatively the value of the sense of security provided by nursing care robots. In general, for evaluating a multiattribute value function, it is common to use the weighted sum of each value function for each attribute without verifying the property of difference independence. However, in this chapter we found that the property of difference independence does not hold when we evaluate the sense of security provided by nursing care robots. Therefore, we cannot perform a value judgment simply using the weighted sum of each value function for each attribute. We need to postulate at least a weak difference independence among multiple attributes. We also found that people feel anxious about robots assumed as "Standard" in this chapter and feel secure about robots that have higher performance where we assume that multiple attributes are mutually weak difference independent.

For further study we need to compare our results with results analyzed by other methods based on other theories and judge which method is more appropriate for evaluating the value of the sense of security. In this chapter we dealt with value judgments of the sense of security for an individual, but value judgments for society will also be developed.

References

[1] J. von Neumann and O. Morgenstern, *Theory of Games and Economic Behavior*, 3rd edn., Wiley, New York (1953).

[2] P.J.H. Schoemaker, *Experiments on Decisions Under Risk*, Kluwer (Nijhoff Publishing), Boston (1980).

[3] A. Tversky and D. Kahneman, *Advances in prospect theory: cumulative representation of uncertainty*, J. Risk Uncertainty **5** (1992), 297–323.

[4] H. Fennema and P. Wakker, *Original and cumulative prospect theory: a discussion of empirical differences*, J. Behav. Decis. Making **10** (1997), 53–64.

[5] D. Kahneman and A. Tversky, *Prospect theory: an analysis of decision under risk*, Econometrica **47** (1979), 263–291.

[6] T. Kanda, H. Ishiguro and T. Ishida, *Psychological evaluation on interactions between people and robot*, J. Robotics Soc. Jpn **19** (1999), 78–87.

[7] H. Tamura, *Decision Analysis*, Handbook of Industrial Automation, K. Shell and E. Hall, eds, Marcel Dekker, New York (2000), 359–376.

[8] About architecture and welfare, http://www3.yomogi.or.jp/architec/kentiku&fukusi.html.

[9] Mainichi nursing care news, http://www.kaigo-fukushi.com/shakai/200212/shakai2002121303.html.

CHAPTER 10

A Case Study of Resolving Social Dilemma among Multiple Municipal Governments in Locating a Large-Scale Refuse Incineration Plant

Shinichi Fujita[1]

Environmental Management Technology Center in Kansai, 2-9-10 Kawaguchi, Nishi-Ku, Osaka 550-0021, Japan

Hiroyuki Tamura

Faculty of Engineering, Kansai University, 3-3-35 Yamate-cho, Suita, Osaka 564-8680, Japan

Contents

Abstract

In this study, we apply a method of group decision-making using the Descriptive Analytic Hierarchy Process, called D-AHP, to locating a large-scale refuse incineration plant. In this D-AHP model, the rank reversal phenomena are legitimately observed and are explanatory. The alternative sites of a new refuse incineration plant are settled in the existing two adjacent cities in Japan, and the alternatives are evaluated using the group preference between the representatives of two cities. The results of evaluations show the effectiveness of the method of D-AHP for resolving social dilemma between two conflicting municipal governments.

---

[1]Presently with Environmental Pollution Control Center of Osaka Prefectural Government, 1-3-62 Nakamichi, Higashinari-Ku, Osaka 550-0025, Japan.

SYSTEMS AND HUMAN SCIENCE – FOR SAFETY, SECURITY, AND DEPENDABILITY
Edited by Tatsuo Arai, Shigeru Yamamoto and Kazuhisa Makino

1. Introduction

The total amount of municipal waste which generally consists of the domestic waste and paper from kitchen and office was about 52 million ton per year in 2000 in Japan, and 77.4% was incinerated [1]. The responsibility for disposing of municipal waste lies with the mayor of the city. Therefore, the refuse incineration plant has to be constructed and operated by the municipal government itself or an organization that consists of several municipal governments.

In 2000, "the Basic Law for Establishing the Recycling-based Society Enacted" was established in Japan, and efforts to reduce the amount of waste have been made by municipal government, citizens and offices. But, the amount of municipal waste has not been decreased. It becomes a very important job for the municipal government to construct or reconstruct the refuse incineration plant. Therefore, it tends to be very difficult to get a consensus of the residents near the area intended to refuse incineration plant, because they fear and hate various environmental impacts due to construction and operation of the plant, especially dioxin emitted from the plant.

In recent years, a large-scale refuse incineration plant tends to be constructed by plural municipal governments, instead of one small plant in one city. In this case, to decide the location of a plant, it is required to obtain a consensus among the multiple municipal governments. There generally exists a conflict among these municipal governments, because it is a very difficult task for the municipal government to obtain a consensus of one's citizens who live in the region near the site intended for construction or reconstruction of the refuse incineration plant.

A method of modeling group decision-making among multiple municipal governments in locating a refuse incineration plant somewhere in two cities using AHP was proposed [2]. This model was developed using the Descriptive Analytic Hierarchy Process, called D-AHP [3]. The model was merely applied to the problems to construct a hypothetical new refuse incineration plant somewhere in the hypothetical two cities. Then, we proposed a group utility function approach for the same problem [4]. Although this model is able to reflect the ethical conflict resolution among multiple municipal governments, it was not easy for municipal officers to handle.

In this study, an approach using D-AHP is applied to two existing adjacent cities in Japan.

2. Two cities and an incineration plant for the case study

For inspecting a method of group decision-making based on D-AHP, the existing two cities in Osaka Prefecture in Japan are selected (see Fig. 1). The outline of the two cities is shown in Table 1. The organization to dispose of the municipal waste generated from the two cities has been established. A refuse incineration plant was constructed at the plane area in Kaizuka City, and it has been operated by the organization. However, it is required to reconstruct the plant, because a long time has passed since the current plant was constructed and it has deteriorated.

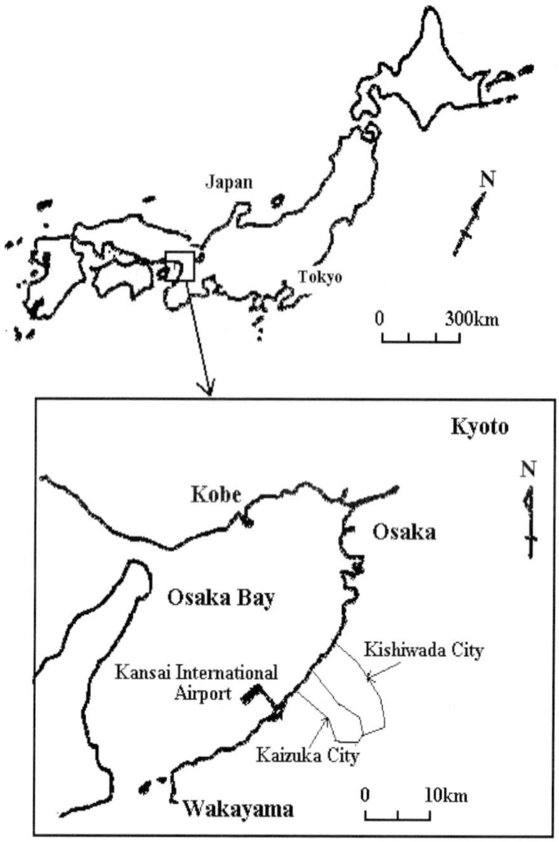

Fig. 1. The location of the two cities.

Five alternative sites for the refuse incineration plant are selected in the two adjacent cities (Kishiwada City and Kaizuka City). These sites are located at the new reclaimed land in Kishiwada City, at hilly and plain area in both the cities, and at the boundary of the two cities (see Fig. 2). These sites are selected from the possible places readily able to provide more than 6 ha of land.

Among the five alternatives, A4 is the place where the current plant exists and that means reconstructing here. However, since the current plant is small, it is necessary to enlarge the site by buying more than 3 ha in order to reconstruct a new plant while the current plant is working. The conditions of the refuse incineration plant are shown in Table 2.

Table 1. The outline of the census of the two cities

	Kishiwada City	Kaizuka City
Area (km^2)	72	44
Population	200,000	90,000
Amount of the municipal waste generated (ton per year)	89,630	45,310

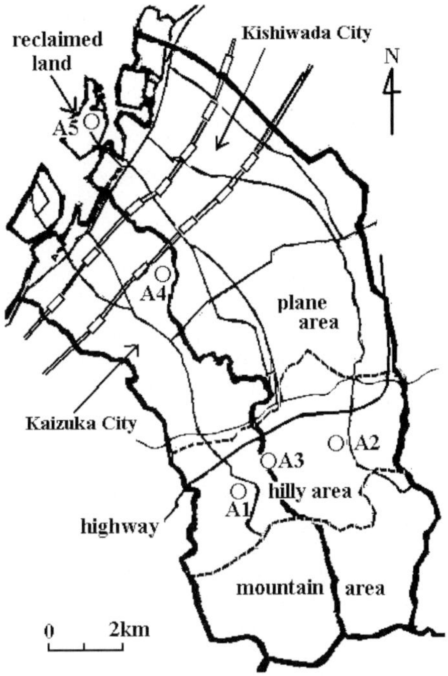

Fig. 2. The two cities and five alternative sites of the plant.

Table 2. The conditions of the refuse incineration plant

The area of the plant	6 ha
Incineration ability	600 ton per day
The height of the chimney	100 m
Exhaust gas temperature	200 °C
Gas emission volume (dry)	217,700 N m^3/h
Dioxin compound	0.1 ng-TEQ/N m^3
Sulfur oxides	10 ppm
Nitrogen oxides	30 ppm
Dust	0.01 g/N m^3

The items to evaluate the location of refuse incineration plant are shown in Table 3, where the items with no difference among the alternatives such as water resource, public sewage, and existing road near the site were excluded. Furthermore, the items are simplified in the same way as in the previous study [2].

3. The outline of D-AHP

Although AHP is a simple method and is valid to analyze the cases which include many items, to evaluate alternatives whose relation is complicated [5], it is known that AHP has a shortcoming if it comes across irrational rank reversal phenomena [6]. When a new copy

Table 3. The items to evaluate the location of the refuse incineration plant

Convenience of construction	Cost	Cost to buy the lot Cost to reclaim the land
	Impact to the natural environment	The area of deforestation
	Impact to the cultural asset	The possibility of the reserved culture asset
Convenience of operation	Commute of the workers	Distance from the nearest railway station
	Garbage transport	The average distance to carry the municipal waste
Resident consensus of Kishiwada City	Environmental impact to the residents living in Kishiwada City due to the facility	Air pollution (concentration of dioxin)
		Offensive odor Noise
	Environmental impact to the residents living in Kishiwada City due to the garbage truck	The average length of the road in the resident area where the garbage trucks go through
	Influence caused by the existence of the facility to the residents living in Kishiwada City	Obstruction of landscape (can see the facility from the resident area)
		Jamming
Resident consensus of Kaizuka City	Environmental impact to the residents living in Kaizuka City due to the facility	Air pollution (concentration of dioxin)
		Offensive odor Noise
	Environmental impact to the residents living in Kaizuka City due to the garbage truck	The average length of the road in the resident area where the garbage trucks go through
	Influence caused by the existence of the facility to the residents living in Kaizuka City	Obstruction of landscape (can see the facility from the resident area)
		Jamming

alternative is added to or when an alternative is removed from the existing set of alternatives, the rank of the remaining alternatives may change. D-AHP has an advantage that the rank reversal phenomena are legitimately observed and are explanatory [3].

D-AHP contains two characteristics: preference characteristics and status characteristics. The preference characteristics represent the degree of satisfaction of each alternative with respect to each criterion, and the status characteristics C represent the evaluated value of a set of alternatives, where C is calculated as follows:

$$C = \left| \log_{\rho} \left(\prod_{i=1}^{n} w_i \right)^{1/n} \right| \tag{1}$$

where w_i denotes the weighting coefficient for each criterion and ρ denotes a constant, usually $\rho = 9$.

The algorithm of D-AHP is shown as follows [3]:

Step 1 Multiple criteria and multiple alternatives are arranged in a hierarchical structure.

Step 2 The criteria pairwise which are arranged in one rank higher level than the alternatives are compared. Eigenvector corresponding to the maximum eigenvalue of the pairwise comparison matrix is normalized to sum to 1. The priority obtained is set to be preference characteristics that represent basic priority.

Step 3 For each criterion, the aspiration level is asked of the decision maker (DM). A hypothetical alternative that gives the aspiration level for all the criteria is added to a set of alternatives. Including this hypothetical alternative, a pairwise comparison matrix for each criterion is evaluated. The eigenvector corresponding to the maximum eigenvalue is normalized so that the entry for this hypothetical alternative is equal to 1. This is the procedure for the preference characteristics.

Step 4 If the consistency index (C.I.) = 0 for each comparison matrix, preference characteristics, i.e., basic priority, is used as the weighting coefficient for each criterion. If C.I. ≠ 0 for some criteria the priority for these criteria is revised by using

$$w_i = w_i^{\mathrm{B}} \times C^{f(\mathrm{C.I.})}, \qquad 0 \le C \le 1, \ 0 \le f(\mathrm{C.I.}) \le 1 \tag{2}$$

where w_i^{B} denotes basic weight for element i obtained from preference characteristics, and C denotes the status characteristics calculated by (1).

Step 5 If some priorities are revised taking into account the status characteristics, the priority for each criterion is normalized to sum to 1.

Step 6 Overall weight is evaluated. If there exists an upper level in the hierarchy, Step 7 is followed. Otherwise, the procedure stops.

Step 7 A pairwise comparison matrix of criteria with respect to each criterion in the higher level is evaluated. If some pairwise comparison matrices are not consistent, the status characteristics are evaluated and the priority revised. Step 6 is followed.

4. Evaluation using AHP

4.1. *Evaluation using Saaty's AHP*

In Fig. 3, we show the hierarchical structure for evaluating the location of the refuse incineration plant. By asking the municipal officers who work at the waste disposal plants to answer as if they represent each city (therefore we could regard them as representing Kishiwada City and Kaizuka City), pairwise comparison is performed.

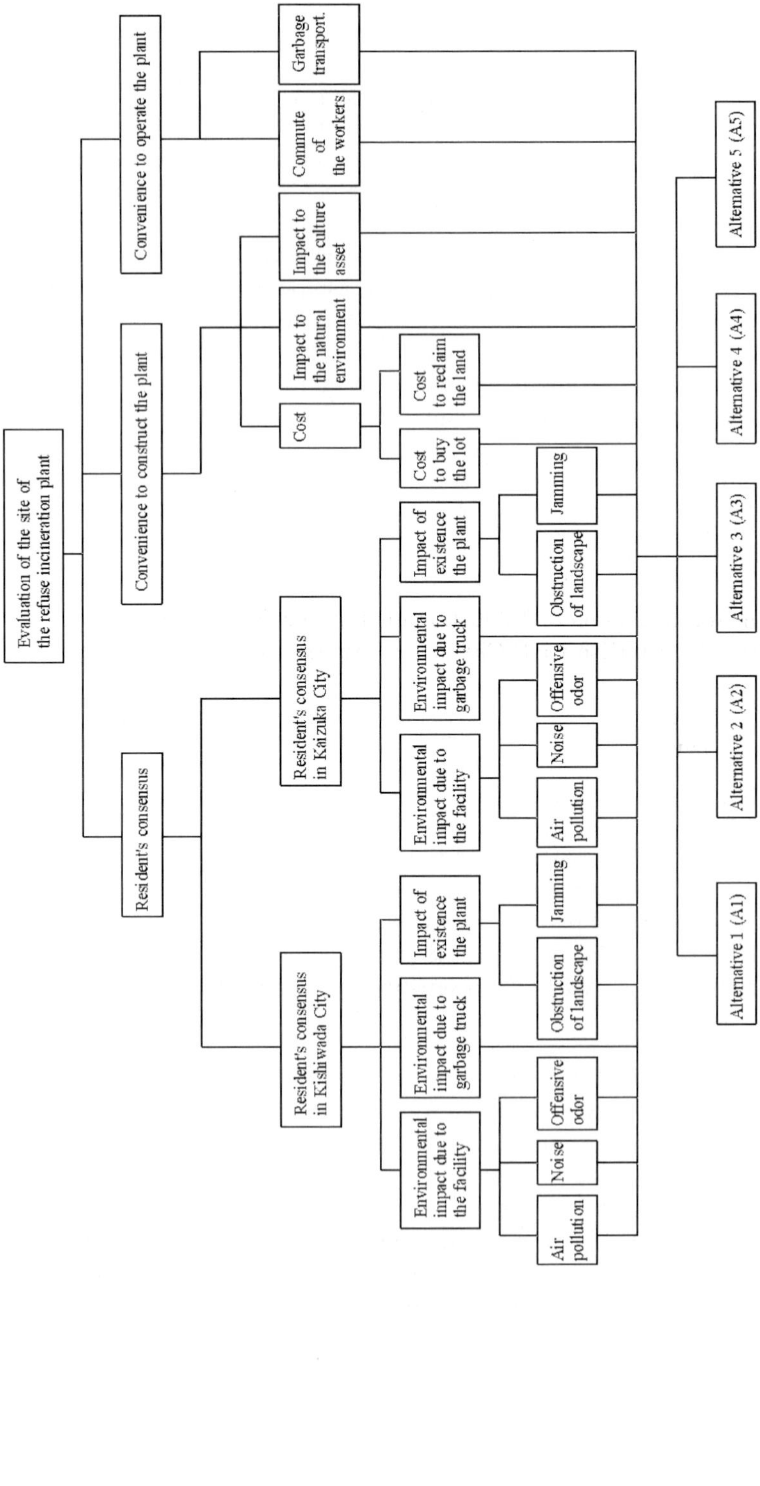

Fig. 3. The hierarchical structure to evaluate the location of the refuse incineration plant.

Table 4. The result of evaluation using Saaty's AHP

Alternatives	Kishiwada City		Kaizuka City		Geometric Mean		Excluding A5	
	Weight	Rank	Weight	Rank	Weight	Rank	Weight	Rank
A1	0.244	1	0.141	5	0.192	3	0.229	4
A2	0.135	5	0.240	1	0.187	4	0.235	3
A3	0.180	4	0.188	4	0.184	5	0.230	2
A4	0.226	2	0.207	3	0.216	2	0.306	1
A5	0.216	3	0.225	2	0.220	1	–	–

The result of evaluation is shown in Table 4, where the second column indicates the result for the representative of Kishiwada City and the third column indicates the result for the representative of Kaizuka City. In this result, a difference of the evaluation for both the decision makers was only found under the criterion of "resident's consensus". In the evaluation by the representative of Kishiwada City, pairwise comparison of "resident's consensus in Kishiwada City" was eight times more important than "resident's consensus in Kaizuka City", and in the evaluation by the representative of Kaizuka City, the result was entirely the opposite.

For deriving the group preference between two adjacent cities, the geometric mean of each element of the pairwise comparison matrices is simply calculated. The results for the geometric mean between the representatives of Kishiwada City and Kaizuka City are shown in the fourth column of Table 4. In the fourth column, alternative A5 located at the new reclaimed land at Kishiwada City is the most desirable site, and alternative A4 located at the place where the current plant exists is the second.

Next, the most desirable site A5 is excluded; the result for the geometric mean is changed as shown in the last column of Table 4. In this result, A3 is the second desirable site, while A3 was the most undesirable site in the results for the geometric mean shown in the fourth column. In this case, the irrational rank reversal occurs.

4.2. *Evaluation using D-AHP*

The same problem is analyzed by using D-AHP [3]. The alternatives are evaluated using the algorithm mentioned in Section 3, where the hierarchical structure is the same as the one used in Saaty's AHP (see Fig. 3). The pairwise comparison matrix is the same as the one used in Saaty's AHP except for the alternatives level. In the alternatives level, the aspiration level is asked for each criterion, and a hypothetical alternative that gives the aspiration level for all the criteria is added to a set of alternatives and pairwise comparison is performed.

The result of evaluation is shown in Table 5, where the second column indicates the result for the representative of Kishiwada City and the third column the result for representative of Kaizuka City. The result of the group preference between the representatives of both the cities is shown in the fourth column of Table 5 that is derived by the geometric mean of each element of the pairwise comparison matrix.

Table 5. The result of evaluation using D-AHP

Alternatives	Kishiwada City		Kaizuka City		Geometric Mean		Excluding A5	
	Weight	Rank	Weight	Rank	Weight	Rank	Weight	Rank
A1	2.306	3	1.638	5	1.970	5	1.855	4
A2	1.437	5	2.846	1	2.146	4	2.061	3
A3	1.965	4	2.355	3	2.161	3	2.147	2
A4	2.430	1	2.286	4	2.358	2	2.273	1
A5	2.348	2	2.609	2	2.479	1	–	–
Aspiration level	1.000	–	1.000	–	1.000	–	1.000	–

In the fourth column, alternative A5 is the most desirable site as obtained by Saaty's AHP, while alternative A4 is the second. Then, as in Section 4.1, the most desirable site A5 is excluded. The result for the geometric mean is shown in the last column of Table 5, where the rank for the remaining alternatives is not changed.

The results of evaluation show the effectiveness of the method based on D-AHP, because there are many cases in which the number of alternatives may change in the case of locating the refuse incineration plant.

In the hearing of the related persons, the fact that the present factory existed in Kaizuka City was a large factor from which the new plant was selected by Kishiwada City. To examine the possibility of expressing the fact, the priority of each city is changed.

In Table 6, the result of changing the priority of each city is shown. The result of the evaluation giving two times the priority to the weight of "resident's consensus in Kishiwada City" is shown in the second column. In contrast, the result of the evaluation giving two times the priority to the weight of "resident's consensus in Kaizuka City" is shown in the third column.

In Table 6, alternative A5 is the most desirable site just like the geometric mean in Tables 4 and 5. For the results of the evaluation giving two times the priority to Kaizuka City, alternative A4 becomes the third desirable site, and alternative A2 becomes the second, which is the most undesirable site for the representative of Kishiwada City. This fact may suggest the necessity to revise the model using the geometric mean.

Table 6. The result of evaluation using D-AHP changing the priority of each city

Alternatives	Giving two times the priority to Kishiwada City		Giving two times the priority to Kaizuka City	
	Weight	Rank	Weight	Rank
A1	2.113	3	1.827	5
A2	1.843	5	2.447	2
A3	2.077	4	2.245	4
A4	2.388	2	2.327	3
A5	2.423	1	2.535	1
Aspiration level	1.000	–	1.000	–

Table 7. The result of evaluation using group disutility functions

	Values of disutility functions		Values of the group disutility functions		
	Kishiwada City	Kaizuka City	Case 1	Case 2	Case 3
A1	0.412	0.501	0.457	0.366	0.313
A2	0.526	0.360	0.443	0.339	0.294
A3	0.417	0.412	0.415	0.320	0.271
A4	0.423	0.527	0.475	0.386	0.332
A5	0.444	0.382	0.413	0.315	0.268

4.3. *Comparison with the result of evaluation using disutility functions*

In Table 7, we show the result of evaluating the location of the refuse incineration plant between two cities using the group disutility function, where the property of utility independence and/or convex dependence between two decision makers is taken into account [4].

In Table 7, Case 1 means the case of mutual utility independence holds between the representatives of both cities, Case 2 means the first order convex dependence holds for the representative of one city and utility independence holds for the representative of another city, and Case 3 means mutual first order convex dependence holds between the representatives of both cities. In the table, the smaller the value of the group disutility function, the more desirable this alternative is. Then alternative A5 is the most desirable site for all cases, the same result obtained by using both AHP. Furthermore, the second desirable site is alternative A3, which is located in a hilly area at the boundary of both the cities. The disutility function based on convex dependence property could describe the ethical conflict resolution between the two decision makers.

In contrast, AHP has the advantage of being able to analyze easily for the case where many items are included and their relation is complicated. However, the concept of ethical conflict resolution among decision makers is not included in this model.

5. Conclusion

In this chapter, a method of decision support based on D-AHP is applied to decide the location of a large-scale refuse incineration plant to dispose of municipal waste. The alternative sites are located in two existing cities in Japan. For evaluating the location of the refuse incineration plant, there are many cases in which the number of alternatives may change. Therefore, the model using D-AHP is considered effective in locating the plant, because in this model, the rank reversal phenomena are legitimately observed and are explanatory.

The most desirable site chosen by the model proposed in this chapter was alternative A5. In 2002, the land-use plan of the new refuse incineration plant for both the cities was decided. The location of the new plant is on the new reclaimed land at Kishiwada City (A5). The construction work is being performed now.

The case study in this chapter is carried out on the evaluation of the location of a new refuse incineration plant using actual geographical conditions and the conditions of the plant for the existing two cities. Instead of reproducing the real decision-making process between the two cities, the case study was performed by asking the municipal officers who work at the waste disposal since they represent "Kishiwada City" and "Kaizuka City". As a result of the evaluation, the site located at the new reclaimed land at Kishiwada City (A5) is selected and this is the actual site of the new plant. This fact may suggest the effectiveness of the method described in this chapter to support resolving social dilemma between two conflicting agents.

In the hearing of the related persons, the fact that the present factory existed in Kaizuka City was a large factor in the selection the new plant of the location of by Kishiwada City. We should improve AHP to reflect the concept of ethical conflict resolution among decision makers hereafter.

References

[1] Ministry of the Environment, Web site information (2003) (in Japanese).

[2] S. Fujita and H. Tamura, *A group decision making model among multi-municipals for siting a refuse incineration plant*, Proceedings of the Ninth IFAC/IFORS/IMACS/IFIP Symposium on Large Scale Systems, Bucharest, Romania, (2001), 103–108.

[3] H. Tamura, S. Takahashi, I. Hatono and M. Umano, *On a behavioral model of analytic hierarchy process for modeling the legitimacy of rank reversal*, Research and Practice in Multiple Decision Making, Y.Y. Haimes and R.E. Steuer, eds, Lecture notes in economics and mathematical systems 487, Springer, Berlin (2000), 173–184.

[4] S. Fujita and H. Tamura, *A case study of the ethical conflict resolution among multiple municipals for siting a refuse incineration plant*, CD-ROM Proceedings of the IEEE International Conference on Systems, Man and Cybernetics (SMC-2003), Washington, DC, USA (2003).

[5] T.L. Saaty, The Analytic Hierarchy Process, McGraw-Hill, New York (1980).

[6] V. Belton and T. Gear, *On a shortcoming of Saaty's method of analytic hierarchies*, OMEGA Int. J. Mgmt Sci. **11** (3) (1983), 228–230.

CHAPTER 11

Lifecycle Cost Evaluation of Maintenance Policy—The Case of the Water Transmission System in Kobe

K. Tanimoto

Department of Social Systems Engineering, Tottori University, 4-101 Koyama-cho Minami, Tottori, Japan

M. Matsushita

Kobe Municipal Waterworks Bureau, 5-3-23 Tanaka-cho, Higashi-Nada, Kobe, Japan

H. Tatano

Disaster Prevention Research Institute, Gokasyo, Uji, Kyoto, Japan

Contents

Abstract

This study aims to evaluate the reduction of the lifecycle cost (LCC) of both preventive and corrective maintenances in the case of the water transmission system in Kobe. We develop a Markov decision process model in order to derive the maintenance policy and the LCC under the policy. As a result, the reduction of the LCC by preventive maintenance in this case is

SYSTEMS AND HUMAN SCIENCE – FOR SAFETY, SECURITY, AND DEPENDABILITY
Edited by Tatsuo Arai, Shigeru Yamamoto and Kazuhisa Makino

not negligible. This suggests that cost reduction only by corrective maintenance, which can be easily evaluated in practice, may be an underestimate of the total cost reductions.

1. Introduction

Since the Hanshin–Awaji earthquake in 1995, the managers of lifeline systems such as the water supply system and the power supply system have been more motivated to reduce the risk of failure caused by disasters and accidents. It is important for them to elaborate on the maintenance policy and explain its cost-effectiveness to the users.

Maintenance that the managers can take on can be categorized into two major classes. Corrective maintenance (CM) is the maintenance that occurs when the lifeline system fails, and which as a result of the failure aims to restore the system to a specified condition. Preventive maintenance (PM) is the maintenance that occurs when the system is operating, and which aims to retain a system in a specified condition by providing prevention of incipient failure.

Currently, the managers are taking measures against failure and evaluating the reduction of losses. The loss reduction that the managers usually focus on is the reduction of the breakdown loss during CM, which can be given by constructing a backup system and upgrading the restoration system, for example. The reduction of such a loss can be evaluated easily by practical valuation techniques, for example, loss reduction during CM multiplied by the probability of failure. Conversely, loss reduction by PM—replacing the system before failure, for example—is often overlooked because it is not easily estimated. The reduction of loss by PM is a result of the reduction of failure risk, not only when undertaking PM but also thereafter. This implies that the reduction of loss by PM must be evaluated in terms of the lifecycle cost (LCC) reduction.

This study aims to develop a Markov decision process model by the use of dynamic programming to derive the maintenance policy, and separately, the "LCC reduction during CM" and the "LCC reduction by PM". As a case, we focus on the project of the water transmission system in Kobe city in Japan. We apply the model to show that the *LCC reduction by PM* is not negligible in this case. This suggests that evaluating only the *LCC reduction during CM* may be an underestimate of the total LCC reduction.

2. Water transmission system in Kobe

Because the water resource of Kobe depends on Lake Biwa, located 80 km east of Kobe, water is transmitted from the lake to the boundary of Kobe by the wholesaler, Hanshin Water Company. In Kobe city, the Kobe Municipal Waterworks Bureau (the water manager in Kobe) purchases the water from the wholesaler and transmits it through the existing transmission tunnel. If this tunnel fails, huge losses will occur because about 75% of the water resource comes through it. The tunnel may be deteriorated now because it is more than 40 years since its construction. Thus, undertaking PM is an important task to be carried out by the water manager.

However, there is no alternative water transmission tunnel. As a result, it is impossible for the water manager to perform PM because the transmission must halt during PM which incurs a prohibitory high social cost. With this in mind, an additional tunnel called the Large Capacity Transmission Main (LCTM) is to be built. With the LCTM, PM of the existing tunnel is possible because water can be supplied through the LCTM during PM. In addition, with the LCTM, the breakdown loss during CM of the existing tunnel can be reduced because the LCTM may work as a backup. Thus, the LCTM contributes to reduce the *LCC reduction during PM* and the *LCC reduction by CM.*

3. Formulation of lifecycle cost and maintenance policy

For a recent literature overview for maintenance policy, we refer to the review articles by Wang [1] and Cho and Parlar [2]. Following their models, we construct a discrete time Markovian deteriorating system with incomplete system observation; the water transmission system obeys a deteriorating process, which cannot be observed by the water manager without inspection since the system is underground. The water manager's problem in our model is to choose the policy, i.e., to choose the action, say replacing or doing nothing, for each state and the next inspection time, which minimizes the LCC in an infinite time horizon.

3.1. *Cost structure and deterioration process*

We represent the state of the water transmission system by (i, e, d). The grade of deterioration of the existing transmission tunnel is classified as one of $s+2$ discrete states, $0, 1, \ldots, i, \ldots, s+1$ in the order of increasing deterioration. State $s+1$ is a failure state. The state of the earthquake is denoted by discrete number e. The probability that the earthquake e occurs in one unit of time is denoted by $\mu(e)$. The state of the LCTM is represented by binary d where $d = 0(1)$ means without (with) the LCTM. The reason why we represent the state of the LCTM instead of its state of deterioration is that the LCTM will not be deteriorated because it is made of high deterioration-resistant material.

While the manager can observe the deterioration state if it is at failure state, he/she cannot observe if it is at i $(0 \leq i \leq s)$ without inspection because the system is under the ground. The states e and d can be observed by him/her without inspection.

The feasible options when observing i $(\leq s)$ is either to replace the system, in other words PM (action R), or to continue operation and inspect after T units of time (action $I(T)$, $(1 \leq T < \infty)$). Without the LCTM, neither PM action nor inspection is possible. If the system is in a failure state, the replacement of the system is compulsory, specifically CM.

Let us represent the construction cost of the LCTM by Δ. We represent the discount factor per unit of time by β $(0 < \beta < 1)$. The cost of replacement includes not only the cost of engineering works, but also social losses during replacement. The cost of engineering works may depend on the grade of deterioration and the social losses during maintenance may depend on both the availability of the alternative tunnel and the occurrence of an earthquake. Thus, we denote the cost of replacement by $r(i, e, d)$. The costs of CM and PM are given by $r(s+1, e, d)$ and $r(i, e, d)$ $(0 \leq i \leq s)$, respectively. The inspection cost is represented by c. The social loss under the system's operation at state (i, e, d) is denoted by $l(i, e, d)$. While l depends on e and d for the same reason of the cost of replacement, it depends on i because the deterioration may cause the leakage of water which incurs a loss for the water manager. We assume that

(1) For any e, $r(i, e, 1)$ and $l(i, e, 1)$ are nondecreasing in i.
(2) $l(i, e, 1) - r(i, e, 1)$ is nondecreasing in i.
(3) For any e, $r(s+1, e, 1) \geq c + r(i, e, 1)$ for $(0 \leq i \leq s)$ is satisfied.

(1) means that as the system deteriorates, the losses and the cost of replacement are more costly. (2) means that the merit of replacement becomes greater as the system deteriorates. (3) means that the cost replacement at the failure state is high enough to exceed the replacement cost in a nonfailed state plus inspection cost.

We represent $\tilde{f}(i, d) = \sum_e \mu(e) f(i, e, d)$ for all functions $f(i, e, d)$. Then the following equations can be easily derived from (1)–(3).

(1) $\tilde{r}(i, 1)$ and $\tilde{l}(i, 1)$ are nondecreasing in i.
(2) $\tilde{l}(i, 1) - \tilde{r}(i, 1)$ is nondecreasing in i.
(3) $\tilde{r}(s+1, 1) \geq c + \tilde{r}(i, 1)$ for $(0 \leq i \leq s)$, is satisfied.

The state of deterioration behaves stochastically. The transition probability when the current state is (i, e, d) is represented by p_{ij}^e where j denotes the state of deterioration in the next time. It is natural to assume that $p_{ij}^e = 0$ for all $j < i$ because the system cannot recover its function without replacement. We represent $p_{i,s+1}^e$, the probability that it fails in the next time, by α_i^e. The x-step transition probability from state i to j by $P_{ij}^e(x)$ is given by

$$P_{ij}^e(x) = \sum_{k=i}^{j} p_{ik}^e \tilde{P}_{kj}(x-1) \tag{1}$$

where $P_{ij}^e(0)$ is the identity matrix and $\tilde{P}_{ij}(x) = \sum_e \mu(e) P_{ij}^e(x)$. Let us denote $\tilde{\alpha}_i = \sum_e \mu(e)\alpha_i^e$, $\tilde{p}_{ij} = \sum_e \mu(e) p_{ij}^e$. We assume the totally positive for order 2 (TP_2) properties [3] hold for transition probability.

3.2. *Formulation*

The water manager's problem is to choose the policy, i.e., to choose the action for each state (i, e, d) and the next inspection time T, which minimizes the LCC. Such a policy is called an optimal policy. We let $V(i, e, d)$ denote the LCC when the system starts from (i, e, d) and an optimal policy is employed thereafter. Assuming that it takes one unit of time for replacement, the LCC when the system starts from (i, e, d) with action R is given by

$$u(i, e, d) = r(i, e, d) + \beta \tilde{V}(0, d) \tag{2}$$

We let $H(i, e, d; T)$ denote the LCC when the system starts from (i, e, d) with action $I(T)$ and an optimal policy is adopted after the next inspection time. Assuming that the inspection time is negligibly small, it is formulated by

$$H(i,e,d;T) = l(i,e,d) + \sum_{x=1}^{T-1} \beta^x \sum_{j=i}^{s} P_{ij}^e(x)\tilde{l}(j,d) + \beta^T \sum_{j=i}^{s} P_{ij}^e(T)(c + \tilde{V}(j,d)) + \sum_{x=1}^{T} \beta^x \sum_{j=i}^{s} P_{ij}^e(x-1)\tilde{\alpha}_j \tilde{u}(s+1,d) \quad (3)$$

3.2.1. *LCC reduction by PM.* The LCC, if reduced both by PM and during CM, can be given by the LCC of the water transmission system with the LCTM in place. Given the system at state $(i,e,1)$, the LCC with the LCTM is given by $V(i,e,1)$. Let us denote the LCC starting from state $(i,e,1)$ if the water manager could not take PM, say action R, by $v(i,e,1)$. Then the LCC reduction by PM can be given by $v(i,e,1) - V(i,e,1)$. The LCC, $V(i,e,1)$ and $v(i,e,1)$, can be formulated by

$$V(i,e,1) = \min[u(i,e,1), \min_T H(i,e,1;T)] \quad (4)$$

$$v(i,e,1) = \min_T \left[l(i,e,1) + \sum_{x=1}^{T-1} \beta^x \sum_{j=i}^{s} P_{ij}^e(x)\tilde{l}(j,1) + \beta^T \sum_{j=i}^{s} P_{ij}^e(T)(c + \tilde{v}(j,1)) + \sum_{x=1}^{T} \beta^x \sum_{j=i}^{s} P_{ij}^e(x-1)\tilde{\alpha}_j \left\{ \tilde{r}(s+1,1) + \beta\tilde{v}(0,1) \right\} \right] \quad (5)$$

3.2.2. *LCC reduction during CM.* Without the LCTM, the water manager has neither the LCC reduction by PM nor the LCC reduction during CM. Thus, the difference between $v(i,e,1)$ and the LCC without the LCTM, $V(i,e,0) - v(i,e,1)$, gives the LCC reduction during CM only. It is noted that without the LCTM the water manager can take action $I(\infty)$ only because the inspection is not feasible as stated above. Thus $V(i,e,0)$ is given by

$$V(i,e,0) = H(i,e,0;\infty) \quad (6)$$

Then the total LCC reduction at state $(i,e,0)$ is given by $[v(i,e,1) - V(i,e,1)] + [V(i,e,0) - v(i,e,1)] = V(i,e,0) - V(i,e,1)$. If we have $V(i,e,0) - V(i,e,1) \geq \Delta$, constructing the LCTM is cost-effective since the LCC reduction is greater than construction cost.

4. Structure of optimal maintenance policy

Let us define $L(i, e, 1)$ and $W(i, e, 1)$ by

$$L(i,e,1) = \begin{cases} l(i,e,1) & (0 \leq i \leq s) \\ (1-\beta)u(s+1,e,1) & (i = s+1) \end{cases}$$
$$W(i,e,1) = \begin{cases} c + V(i,e,1) & (0 \leq i \leq s) \\ u(s+1,e,1) & (i = s+1) \end{cases} \tag{7}$$

LEMMA 1. *If we have the next equation, $W(i, e, 1)$ is nondecreasing in i for any e*

$$l(i,e,1) \leq (1-\beta)r(s+1,e,1) \qquad (0 \leq i \leq s) \tag{8}$$

PROOF. We have

$$\begin{aligned}\sum_{j=i}^{s} P_{ij}^{e}(x-1)\tilde{\alpha}_j &= \sum_{j=i}^{s} P_{ij}^{e}(x-1)\left(1 - \sum_{k=j}^{s} \tilde{p}_{jk}\right) \\ &= \sum_{j=i}^{s} P_{ij}^{e}(x-1) - \sum_{j=i}^{s} P_{ij}^{e}(x) = 1 - P_{i,s+1}^{e}(x-1) - 1 \\ &\quad + P_{i,s+1}^{e}(x) = P_{i,s+1}^{e}(x) - P_{i,s+1}^{e}(x-1)\end{aligned} \tag{9}$$

Then $H(i, e, 1; T)$ can be rewritten as

$$\begin{aligned}H(i,e,1;T) &= l(i,e,1) + \beta^T \sum_{j=i}^{s} P_{ij}^{e}(T)(c + \tilde{V}(j,1)) \\ &\quad + \sum_{x=1}^{T-1} \beta^x \sum_{j=i}^{s} P_{ij}^{e}(x)\tilde{l}(j,1) \\ &\quad + \sum_{x=1}^{T} \beta^x (P_{i,s+1}^{e}(x) - P_{i,s+1}^{e}(x-1))\tilde{u}(s+1,1) = l(i,e,1) \\ &\quad + \beta^T \sum_{j=i}^{s+1} P_{ij}^{e}(T)\tilde{W}(j,1) + \sum_{x=1}^{T-1} \beta^x \sum_{j=i}^{s+1} P_{ij}^{e}(x)\tilde{L}(j,1)\end{aligned} \tag{10}$$

By using L and W, (4) can be given by

$$V(i,e,1) = \min\left[u(i,e,1), \min_T \left\{ l(i,e,1) + \beta^T \sum_{j=i}^{s+1} P_{ij}^e(T)\tilde{W}(j,1) + \sum_{x=1}^{T-1} \beta^x \sum_{j=i}^{s+1} P_{ij}^e(x)\tilde{L}(j,1) \right\}\right] \tag{11}$$

Because it holds $l(i,e,1) \leq (1-\beta)r(s+1,e,1)$ for any i and e from (8), we have $l(i,e,1) \leq (1-\beta)[r(s+1,e,1) + \beta\tilde{V}(0,1)] = (1-\beta)u(s+1,e,1)$. For any e, $l(i,e,1)$ is nondecreasing in i $(0 \leq i \leq s)$ from (1). Thus $L(i,e,1)$ is nondecreasing in i $(0 \leq i \leq s+1)$ for any e.

The algorithm to solve $V(i,e,1)$ by the value iteration method is given by

$$V^{k+1}(i,e,1) = \min\left[u^k(i,e,1), \min_T \left\{ l(i,e,1) + \beta^T \sum_{j=i}^{s+1} P_{ij}^e(T)\tilde{W}^k(j,1) + \sum_{x=1}^{T-1} \beta^x \sum_{j=i}^{s+1} P_{ij}^e(x)\tilde{L}(j,1) \right\}\right] \tag{12}$$

where k represents the step of the iterations. $u^k(i,e,1)$ and $W^k(i,e,1)$ are given by

$$u^k(i,e,1) = r(i,e,1) + \beta\tilde{V}^{k-1}(0,1)$$
$$W^k(i,e,1) = \begin{cases} c + V^k(i,e,1) & (0 \leq i \leq s) \\ u^k(s+1,e,1) & (i = s+1) \end{cases} \tag{13}$$

$V(i,e,1)$ is given by $V^{k+1}(i,e,1)$ in (12) when we let $k \to \infty$. Let us give the initial values, u^0 and V^0, as the LCC if it continues to be replaced from now to forever, which are represented by

$$V^0(i,e,1) = u^0(i,e,1) = r(i,e,1) + \frac{\beta}{1-\beta}\tilde{r}(0,1) \tag{14}$$

Then $W^0(i,e,1)$ is given by

$$W^0(i,e,1) = \begin{cases} c + V^0(i,e,1) & (0 \leq i \leq s) \\ u^0(s+1,e,1) & (i = s+1) \end{cases} \tag{15}$$

From assumption (3), we have $c + r(i,e,1) \leq r(s+1,e,1)$ for any i and e. Thus, it is easy to check that $c + V^0(i,e,1) \leq u^0(s+1,e,1)$ holds. Because $V^0(i,e,1)$ is nondecreasing in i for any e, $W^0(i,e,1)$ is nondecreasing in i $(0 \leq i \leq s)$. These lead us to the fact that

$W^0(i, e, 1)$ is nondecreasing in i $(0 \le i \le s+1)$ for any e. Because $u^0(i, e, 1)$, $l(i, e, 1)$ and $\sum_{j=i}^{s+1} P_{ij}^e(x)\tilde{L}(j, 1)$ are all nondecreasing in i for any e [3], $V^1(i, e, 1)$ given by (12) is nondecreasing in i for any e. By (13), $W^1(i, e, 1)$ is calculated by

$$W^1(i, e, 1) = \begin{cases} c + V^1(i, e, 1) & (0 \le i \le s) \\ u^1(s+1, e, 1) & (i = s+1) \end{cases} \tag{16}$$

Since the next equation holds, $c + V^1(i, e, 1) \le u^1(s+1, e, 1)$ is satisfied.

$$\begin{aligned} c + V^1(i, e, 1) &\le c + r(i, e, 1) + \beta\tilde{V}^0(0, 1) \le r(s+1, e, 1) + \beta\tilde{V}^0(0, 1) \\ &= u^1(s+1, e, 1) \end{aligned} \tag{17}$$

From (17) and the nondecreasing property of $V^1(i, e, 1)$ in i for any e, $W^1(i, e, 1)$ is nondecreasing in i $(0 \le i \le s+1)$ for any e. As iterating the calculation of (12), the same discussion can be applied for any k. Thus $\lim_{k\to\infty} W^k(i, e, 1) = W(i, e, 1)$ is nondecreasing in $i(0 \le i \le s+1)$ for any e. □

THEOREM 1. *If we have (8), the control limit policy [3] is optimal.*

PROOF. From Lemma 1 and $l(i, e, 1) - r(i, e, 1)$ is nondecreasing in i for any e, the next equation is nondecreasing in i for any e and T.

$$\begin{aligned} &H(i, e, 1; T) - u(i, e, 1) \\ &\quad = [l(i, e, 1) - r(i, e, 1)] + \beta^T \sum_{j=i}^{s+1} P_{ij}^e(T)\tilde{W}(j, 1) + \sum_{x=1}^{T-1} \beta^x \sum_{j=i}^{s+1} P_{ij}^e(x)\tilde{L}(j, 1) \end{aligned} \tag{18}$$

Therefore, the sign of (18) changes at most once and when change occurs it is from negative to positive. This completes the proof. □

By Theorem 1, if we have (8), it is optimal for the water manager to replace the system if it is observed that the state of deterioration is greater than the control limit state. Thus, with the LCTM, in order to minimize the LCC, PM (action R) should be undertaken when the state of deterioration is observed to be greater than the control limit state.

5. Numerical analysis

5.1. *Data*

5.1.1. *State.* Through a discussion with the practitioners in Kobe Municipal Waterworks Bureau, we classify the deterioration state under four states. That is to say, $i = 0$ represents like new, $i = 1$ is the state in which the structural strength of the tunnels is enough to transmit water, $i = 2$ is the state in which the structural strength of the tunnels is not enough and $i = 3$ represents fault. The state of the earthquake is $e = 0$ when no earthquake occurs, $e = 2$ when the earthquake with more than 300 (gal) occurs, and $e = 1$ otherwise.

5.1.2. *Probability of an earthquake.* According to Rikitake [4], the occurrence probability of an earthquake of more than 300 (gal) is 0.00517 ($= \mu(2)$). The probability $\mu(0)$ is 0.99185. Obviously, $\mu(1) = 1 - \mu(0) - \mu(2)$. One unit of time is given as a year.

5.1.3. *Loss when earthquake does not occur.* The loss is derived from the leakage of water. We assume that the percentage of leakage is 3% and the loss is the potential profit for the amount of leaked water.

5.1.4. *Loss when earthquake occurs.* When an earthquake occurs, the system will be stopped during check and recovery if it is damaged. Because the households have to save water in the interim, the loss is estimated by the reduction of consumer surplus when they save water. The industries also save water. When they save, their added value will be decreased. By using input–output analysis in Kobe city, we calculate the decrease in added value for each industrial sector [5,6]. As a result, we give the loss for each state as shown in Table 1.

5.1.5. *Maintenance cost.* We give the maintenance cost for each state as shown in Table 2. The cost of inspection is given as $c = 0.1$ (billion yen) and the construction cost of the LCTM is $\Delta = 500$ (billion yen). The discount factor per unit of time is given as $\beta = 0.96$.

5.1.6. *Transition probability.* Although the number of samples is insufficient, we estimate annual transition probability by experimental data in Japan. The estimated probability is referred to Ref. [6].

Table 1. Loss for each state, $l(i, e, d)$ (billion yen per year)

State	Loss	State	Loss	State	Loss	State	Loss	State	Loss	State	Loss
(0,0,0)	3	(0,1,0)	36	(0,2,0)	276	(0,0,1)	3	(0,1,1)	26	(0,2,1)	199
(1,0,0)	3	(1,1,0)	36	(1,2,0)	276	(1,0,1)	3	(1,1,1)	26	(1,2,1)	199
(2,0,0)	3	(2,1,0)	36	(2,2,0)	276	(2,0,1)	3	(2,1,1)	26	(2,2,1)	199

Table 2. Maintenance cost for each state, $r(i, e, d)$ (billion yen per year)

State	Cost	State	Cost	State	Cost	State	Cost
(3,0,0)	5960	(0,0,1)	400	(0,1,1)	424	(0,2,1)	597
(3,1,0)	5993	(1,0,1)	400	(1,1,1)	424	(1,2,1)	597
(3,2,0)	6233	(2,0,1)	400	(2,1,1)	424	(2,2,1)	597
		(3,0,1)	1650	(3,1,1)	1673	(3,2,1)	1846

Table 3. The LCC reduction during CM and that by PM in each state (billion yen)

State	During CM	By PM	Total	State	During CM	By PM	Total
(0,0,0)	1075	394	1469	(2,1,0)	1971	309	2280
(1,0,0)	1234	443	1677	(0,2,0)	1115	407	1522
(2,0,0)	941	363	1304	(1,2,0)	1153	420	1573
(0,1,0)	1105	403	1526	(2,2,0)	2313	291	2604
(1,1,0)	1186	429	1615				

5.2. *Results*

Because (8) is satisfied in this case, the control limit policy is optimal. Specifically, with the LCTM, the water manager should not replace the system if the deterioration state i is 0 or 1; however, it should be replaced if i is observed as 2. The optimal time for the next inspection is estimated as 1 year in any state when replacement is not necessary.

In Table 3, we show the result of the LCC reduction. The total LCC reduction is greater than the construction cost of the LCTM, 500 billion yen. Then constructing the LCTM is cost-effective in any state. Although the LCC reduction by PM is smaller than the LCC reduction during CM, about 20% of total LCC reduction is attributed to the reduction by PM. Note that the LCC reduction by PM is nearly equal to the construction cost for several states. This implies that the LCC reduction by PM is not negligible in this case and that the omission of evaluating the LCC reduction by PM may be an underestimate of the total LCC reduction.

6. Conclusion

We study the maintenance policy and the LCC under the policy with the case of water transmission system in Kobe. As a result, we can show the LCC reduction during CM and by PM separately. The model in this study should be further extended in terms of PM and by considering the number of the components of system. Although we assume that PM is only a replacement, the manager can make repairs which lead the state to a better state but not necessarily state 0. Considering that the manager takes on repairs in the evaluation, this may actually reduce the LCC. In addition, the manager does not always replace or repair the whole system, but only a part of the system. The evaluation when assuming the system consists of multi-unit components is the work to be studied.

References

[1] H. Wang, *A survey of maintenance policies of deteriorating systems*, Eur. J. Oper. Res. **139** (2002), 469–489.

[2] D.I. Cho and M. Parlar, *A survey of maintenance models for multi-unit systems*, Eur. J. Oper. Res. **51** (1991), 1–23.

[3] H. Kawai, J. Koyanagi and M. Ohnishi, *Optimal maintenance problems for Markovian deteriorating systems*, *Stochastic Models in Reliability and Maintenance*, S. Osaki, ed, Springer Verlag, Berlin, Heidelberg (2002), 193–218.

[4] T. Rikitake, *Zishin Yochi (Forecasting Earthquake)*, Nihon Senmon Tosyo Shuppan, (2001), 373–393 (in Japanese).

[5] M. Matsushita, K. Tanimoto, H. Tatano and N. Okada, *Upgrading Municipal Water Supply System: Kobe's Challenge*, the paper presented at Recent Challenges in Integrated Disaster Management, Kyoto University (2001).

[6] K. Tanimoto, M. Matsushita and H. Tatano, *Developing model to estimate the benefit by upgrading water transmission system—a case study in Kobe city*, Presented at Third DPRI-IIASA Meeting on Integrated Disaster Risk Management (2003).

CHAPTER 12

Securing Fair Water Allocation in the Aral Sea Basin

L. Fang

Department of Mechanical and Industrial Engineering, Ryerson University, Toronto, Ont. M5B 2K3, Canada
E-mail: lfang@ryerson.ca

L.Z. Wang and K.W. Hipel

Department of Systems Design Engineering, University of Waterloo, Ont. N2L 3G1, Canada
E-mail: L25wang@engmail.uwaterloo.ca (L.Z. Wang), kwhipel@engmail.uwaterloo.ca (K.W. Hipel)

Contents

Abstract

A comprehensive water allocation model is employed for equitably allocating initial water rights among demand sites located in the Aral Sea basin. The approach allocates water resources in two steps: initial water rights allocation, and subsequent water and net benefits reallocation. The Aral Sea basin lies within the newly independent states of Kazakhstan, Kyrgyzstan, Tajikistan, Turkmenistan, and Uzbekistan, which were founded after the breakup of the former Soviet Union in the early 1990s, and Afghanistan. The extraction of water draining into the Aral Sea by these states resulted in a massive shrinkage of the Aral Sea and a devastating ecological disaster. The water allocation application considered in this research investigates initial water allocation by a priority-based maximal flow programming method for the demand sites sharing the Amu Darya river basin area in the Aral Sea basin.

SYSTEMS AND HUMAN SCIENCE – FOR SAFETY, SECURITY, AND DEPENDABILITY
Edited by Tatsuo Arai, Shigeru Yamamoto and Kazuhisa Makino

1. Introduction

In order to achieve sustainable development and a secure society, institutions and methodologies for water allocation should be reformed for regions with water resources shortages, like the Aral Sea basin in Central Asia. Water allocation should consider three principles: equity, efficiency, and sustainability [1,2]. By equity, it is meant that water resources within river basins should be fairly shared by all the stakeholders. Efficiency means the economic use of water resources with respect to minimizing costs and maximizing benefits. Under sustainability, water is utilized economically both now and in the future such that the environment is not harmed. Wang *et al.* [1,2] propose a cooperative water allocation methodology to take into account the aforementioned three principles. The model allocates water resources in two steps: initial water rights allocation based on water rights systems or agreements, and subsequent water and net benefits reallocation.

The objective of this chapter is to apply the cooperative water allocation model to the Aral Sea basin. In particular, results of the initial water rights allocation based on the prior rights system are reported for the Amu Darya river basin in the Aral Sea basin. Challenges for achieving a fair, efficient, and sustainable water allocation are discussed. The Aral Sea basin lies within northern Afghanistan and the five independent states of the former Soviet Union including the area of two southern oblasts (regions) of Kazakhstan, three oblasts of the Kyrgyz Republic, the whole territory of Tajikistan and Uzbekistan, and four velayats (regions) of Turkmenistan [3].

The Aral Sea basin covers an area of about 1,510,000 km^2, having a sharply continental climate characterized by high evapotranspiration and severely arid conditions. Annual precipitation is less than 100 mm in the southwest deserts and about 200 mm approaching the foot-hills of the southeastern mountains [4]. The region provides favorable thermal conditions for the growth of cotton and other heat-loving crops: the noontime temperature during growing seasons (May–September) ranges from 20 to 45 °C and the average daily temperature in July is 35 °C [4].

The Amu Darya (2574 km in length) and Syr Darya (2337 km) rivers, with an average total annual flow of 116.5 km^3, are the two major rivers of the region and supply the Aral Sea with bulk water. The population in the basin has grown from 13 million in 1960 to more than 40 million at present. Annual water diversions have increased from 60 to 105 km^3 and irrigated lands rose from 4.5 million ha to just over 8 million ha [5].

The Aral Sea was once the fourth largest lake in the world by area. However, it is now facing a serious ecological crisis. The causes for the disaster date back to the introduction of advanced irrigation techniques in the region in the mid-1920s and the collectivization in the 1930s by then newly established Soviet government. Small-scale traditional irrigation systems were replaced by large state-run enterprises. The change led to destabilization of irrigation and lowered water-use efficiency. Irrigation efficiencies were further decreased by expansion and mechanization of irrigation in the 1950s. During this period, the potential shrinkage and damage of the Aral Sea were recognized. However, the large irrigation water diversions continued up to the 1990s [6]. As a result, the average annual flow to the Aral Sea dropped from over 50 km^3 before 1960 to 10 km^3 since 1975 [7]. Today, the Aral Sea is nearing half of its surface area and less than one-third of its volume that existed in 1960.

The significant reduction of inflows and the massive shrinkage of the Aral Sea created devastating ecological impacts.

2. Water uses and allocation in the Aral Sea basin

According to an estimate for 1987 by Raskin *et al.* [4], the total annual water demand in the Aral Sea region is 97.32 km^3, with 53.55 km^3 in the Amu Darya basin and 43.77 km^3 in the Syr Darya basin. The agricultural sector is the primary user of water resources, accounting for 82% of the total demand. The major crop is cotton, accounting for 51% of the agricultural water use in the Amu Darya basin and 34% in the Syr Darya basin. Fodder crops account for the second largest requirement, at 29 and 19% of the agricultural water demand in the Amu Darya and Syr Darya basins, respectively. Water-intensive rice production accounts for 19 and 12%, respectively, of the agricultural water demand. Industrial water uses are far less than agricultural uses, accounting for approximately 6% in the Amu Darya basin and 12% in the Syr Darya basin. The municipal water demands are about 6% of the total demand. Water demands for livestock are quite small, while fisheries account for some 3% of the total demand [4]. During the 1940s to 1970s, several agreements were reached between the Soviet Union and Afghanistan regarding the waters of the Amu Darya river, allocating an annual supply of 9 km^3 to Afghanistan. However, no more than 2 km^3 per year has been diverted to Afghanistan so far [5].

The International Fund for the Aral Sea (IFAS) and United Nations Environment Program (UNEP) [3] state that the average long-term surface water supply in the Aral Sea basin is about 116 km^3. The annual surface water supply in the Amu Darya river basin is about 80 km^3, about 8% of which is formed in Afghanistan. Only about 10% of the Amu Darya's surface water supply reaches the Aral Sea. In the Syr Darya river basin, the annual surface water supply is about 40 km^3. The Syr Darya river no longer reaches the Aral Sea. All of its discharge is now being used for irrigation and other purposes. Except for Uzbekistan, the available usable ground water resources are less than 1 km^3 per year. A deficit of water resources is observed in the whole region except Kyrgyzstan and Tajikistan, caused by an arid climate and water losses especially in irrigation systems [3].

Under the Soviet system, water allocation and conflict resolution in the basin were an intra-national issue and water-use strategies were developed to maximize the perceived benefits to the entire region, in which the cost of environmental damage was assumed to be minimal [8]. Dramatic changes took place after the breakup of the Soviet Union in 1991. Each independent republic of the region has been struggling to realize its full potential since then. The political conditions in this region make water resources management very complex and international treaties have been negotiated to resolve conflicts over water resources. The countries in the Aral Sea basin have recognized the need to develop fair and rational agreements for sharing and using their water and energy resources. Some progress has been made in achieving regional cooperation and attracting international financial and technical support for solving Aral Sea water problems, including: the creation of the Interstate Coordinating Water Commission (ICWC) in 1992, establishment of the Interstate Fund for the Aral Sea in 1993 [3], signing of the Syr Darya Water and Energy

Resources Framework Agreement in 1998 [9], and initiation of various Aral Sea basin studies and model developments for decision support.

Studies of the Aral Sea problem have found that the Aral Sea cannot be restored to its former grandeur without totally disrupting the economies of the basin states [5]. The main task facing the region is to preserve the Aral Sea's current size and ameliorate adverse impacts, which would require an inflow of 35 km^3 per year [6]. Another reality is that the present method of water allocation among the Aral Sea basin countries is still based on Soviet era rules, disregarding the emerging priorities of the independent republics. The present method is not suitable for interstate water allocation and thus inevitably creates resources management conflicts. Intrastate water allocation is also in a similar situation, leading to inefficient and wasteful delivery and use of water [10].

To achieve sustainable water use, the water allocation for competing uses in the Aral Sea basin should be carried out in an integrated and cooperative manner. Water resources policies in the Aral Sea basin need to be restructured. Equitable intrastate water rights systems, interstate agreements, and corresponding institutions must be developed. Proper decisions should be made on introduction of water conservation techniques, water pricing, how to account for water demands from various types of uses, and how water should be apportioned among competing users.

Regional water resources management tools may assist the republics in the Aral Sea basin in making better decisions. Mathematical simulation [4] and optimization [9,11] models of the Aral Sea water resource systems have been reported. While many factors are addressed in the current planning effort for this region, some aspects, such as stakeholder participation, water rights, and fairness of water allocation are not given enough consideration and not explicitly included in models.

3. Cooperative water allocation model: achieving equitable, efficient, and sustainable water resources utilization

Wang *et al.* [1,2] develop a comprehensive methodology for achieving equitable, efficient, and sustainable water allocation among competing water uses and stakeholders in a river basin. In the model, water allocation is based on a network representation of a river basin and is carried out in two steps: (1) allocation of initial water rights to water stakeholders and users based on existing water rights systems or agreements; and (2) reallocation of water and net benefits through water transfers to promote equitable cooperation of all stakeholders in a river basin and to achieve efficient use of water. Cooperative game theory is utilized to carry out the associated water transfers and net benefit reallocation.

In a node-link river basin network model, water users and uses are aggregated into stakeholders (water user associations) and water use (demand) sites, respectively, according to geographic location and ownership. A node is symbolized as a dot, circle, triangle, or rectangle, representing a physical component of interest such as inflow, natural or man-made junction, intake structure, water or wastewater treatment plant, aquifer, reservoir, natural lake, dam, weir, or water demand site. A link stands for a natural or man-made water conduit such as a river channel, canal, or pipeline between two different nodes, but can also represent any flow of water such as the seepage between a demand site and an aquifer. The links include river reaches, diversions, transmission, and return flow links. Because different types of nodes and links have different hydrological and economic properties, subsets of the general set of nodes are defined for the mathematical formulation of the model. In addition to the general mass balance equations for each node, there are other hydrologic constraints for some natural physical response processes. These include link losses, node inflow adjustments, node losses, consumption and pollutant discharges, and outflows. There are also policy and system control constraints in the water allocation model.

Three methods, prior water rights, modified riparian water rights, and lexicographic minimax demand shortage ratios, are proposed for the equitable initial water rights allocation [2]. The first method is devised for water allocation based on an equity concept called priority method, by which demands with a higher priority can obtain water before those with a lower priority. The method can be applied to many kinds of water rights systems including prior, riparian, and public allocation schemes. Under the prior (appropriative) rights regime, water is treated as private property. Water is appropriated according to "first in time, first in right". In cases of water scarcity, there is no sharing of the shortage in water. Junior uses are allocated after the senior uses have been satisfied. Thus, the priorities are assigned according to the starting time of water uses. Under a traditional riparian system, the water at a node is distributed to water demands immediately connected to it at every time step as fully as possible in an order from upstream to downstream. A special prior water allocation problem can be formulated for a traditional riparian water rights allocation problem, if higher priorities are strictly assigned to upstream demands and lower priorities to downstream demands. The public allocation regime treats water as public property, and the state is the owner of waters. In this system, water rights are administratively allocated to users through water permits from governments. As water demands increase and begin to compete for available water supplies during times of water scarcity, the priorities to get water are usually assigned by governmental authorities according to the importance of uses.

For prior water rights allocation problems, considering the difficulty in assigning proper unit cost coefficients for generalized network flow programming, a maximal network flow programming method for multiperiod water allocation is developed. The basic ideas of the method include: (1) The storage of every reservoir is divided into several subzones according to reservoir operation rules. Each subzone has a storage demand and corresponding priority. (2) Every inflow link to a demand node may have one or more inflow demands with various priorities. Thus, in prior water allocation method, each inflow link to a demand node is viewed as consisting of one or several dummy sublinks and each sublink has an inflow demand and corresponding priority. (3) If more than one sublink with the same supply priority are connected to an identical source node, flows are allocated simultaneously in proportion to their inflow demands in every time period. (4) For each inflow link to a stream flow requirement node, it is separated into a bypass sublink in addition to sublinks for stream flow requirements with various priorities. No demand and priority are assigned to bypass links and non-sublinks. (5) Water is allocated to meet inflow and storage demands according to priorities. The prior water allocation can be found by sequentially solving the maximal network flow program for each priority from the highest to lowest priority.

The traditional riparian water allocation system performs poorly in terms of fairness during water shortage times. To ensure reasonable water uses and no harm to downstream uses, the minimum demands of all uses in a river basin should be met as far as possible. A fairer method, called modified riparian water rights allocation, can be viewed as a special form of maximal network flow program [2]. Under the modified system, higher priorities are assigned to all minimum water demands in a river basin and lower priorities are given to all maximum water demands. During times of water shortage, another possible approach for allocating initial water rights fairly is to have equitable allocation of water among all demands in the sense that no shortage ratio can be decreased further without either violating a constraint or increasing an already equal or worse-off shortage ratio value that is associated with another demand. A lexicographic minimax multiperiod resource allocation problem can be used to formulate the equitable water sharing problem [2]. This method is not presented in detail here. The application given in this chapter focuses on application of the prior allocation methodology to the Amu Darya river basin.

4. Initial allocation of water rights in the Amu Darya river basin

Figure 1 portrays the network scheme of the Amu Darya river basin water resource system. This representation is based on the work of Raskin *et al.* [4] and McKinney and Karimov [11]. In the network, there are seven types of nodes: 9 inflow, 14 junction, 9 aquifer, 6 reservoir, 1 hydropower plant, 12 off stream demand, and 1 stream flow requirement nodes. The number of links is 87. Each off stream demand node aggregates water demands of the water users in a common geographic area with shared water sources and includes water for irrigation, livestock, municipal, and industrial uses. The off stream demand nodes are considered as agricultural nodes, since irrigation is the dominant use in this basin. The furthest node downstream represents the Aral Sea, which is modeled as a stream flow requirement node. Treating the Aral Sea as a demand node rather than an outlet of the network makes it possible to analyze the Aral Sea's water demands and their effects on water allocation.

Every type of node has its own hydrological characteristics. Reservoir evaporation, node losses, and inflow adjustments, seepages and return flows are considered as hydrological constraints in addition to the general water balance. Each reservoir is divided into four zones with different storage priorities according to the operation rules. Other assumptions made for the nodes include linear surface area–storage relationships for reservoirs, and the linear reservoir response sub-model for simulating seepages from the reservoirs and aquifers. Links between nodes represent river reaches, diversion pipes, seepages, and return flows. Capacity constraints, transmission losses as well as the node and link seepages to aquifers are also considered by utilizing various loss coefficients. Due to data limitations, salinity constraint is not included in the current model. The input data for surface water supply, ground water

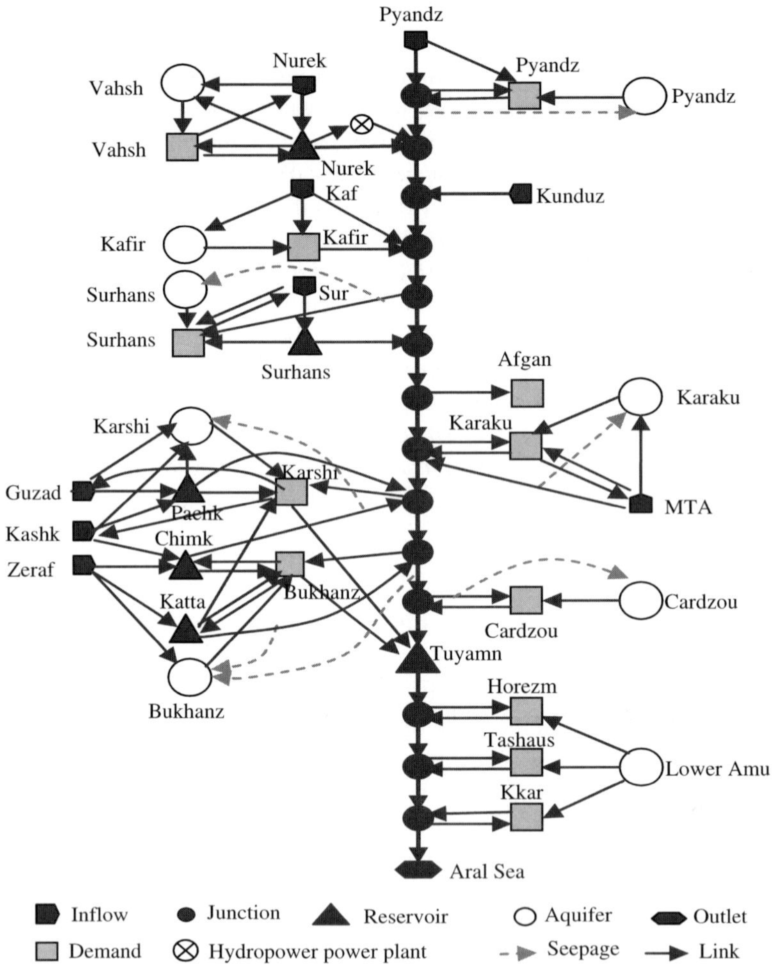

Fig. 1. Amu Darya river basin network.

supply, major reservoirs, and demands at various sites in the Amu Darya river basin mostly come from previous studies of the Aral Sea basin [4,11].

The estimated tributary inflows on a monthly basis for a typical dry year are taken from [4]. The total annual basin inflow is 39.2 km^3 in this scenario. Due to limited data, the initial available ground water volume of each aquifer is taken to be the one-twelfth of the total annual available ground water resources. The monthly inflow adjustments into aquifers are estimated by the proportions of the total annual available ground water resources according to the distribution of monthly inflows of the corresponding nearest tributaries. The initial storage volume of each reservoir is assumed to be corresponding to active operational storage. The monthly inflow adjustments for each reservoir or agricultural demand node are estimated by the proportions of the product of annual available precipitation and area with respect to the distribution of monthly inflows of the corresponding nearest tributary. The various loss coefficients are estimated according to common experience. For example, the water loss (consumption) coefficients at all agricultural demand nodes are assumed to be 70% in all the time periods; coefficients of node seepages are set to 1% where there are seepages from the nodes to aquifers; water loss coefficients of all links in the river basin are taken to be 5%, and all link seepage coefficients are set as 1%. The monthly total inflow water demands at various demand sites in the Amu Darya river basin are also taken from [4]. The Aral Sea's demand of water from the Amu Darya river is assumed to be 23 km^3 per year. Its monthly distribution is estimated as being proportional to the monthly total available water supply of the Amu Darya basin.

Utilizing the data described above, the maximal network flow problem, formulated as a linear program for prior water allocation, is used to find the optimal initial water rights allocations for demand nodes in this basin, where the non-linear salinity constraint is not considered. Although the public water allocation system terminated after the breakup of the former Soviet Union and there currently exist no formal and clear water rights systems in this basin, the situation among the independent states competing for water resources can be analyzed by using the prior water allocation method. As pointed out before, the prior water rights allocation method is very flexible. It can be applied not only under a strict priority water rights regime, but also under riparian water rights and even public allocation if the priorities are properly assigned according to the existing water rights system or agreements. In this study, the priorities are set as the follows: (1) The minimum water volume required by each reservoir to meet the water head for hydropower production, ecology, and the future needs is assigned the highest priority. (2) Off stream demands are assigned priorities in the order of upstream to downstream. All inflow links to a same demand node are set to be equal. (3) Two cases for the Aral Sea's inflow demand are considered. In case one, it is assigned the lowest priority while in case two it is given the second highest priority.

The model is coded in GAMS, a general algebraic modeling system, for mathematical programming problems [12], and solver MINOS 5 is utilized for solving the optimization problem. According to the report from MINOS, the search process consists of 18 iterations, and there are 1064 equations and 1556 control variables in every iteration. It costs about 5 computer seconds to run the program on a 1700 MHz Intel Pentium 4 CPU. As mentioned above, the program searches for an optimal flow control schedule and gets the initial water rights allocations for demand sites (including water-right inflows and reservoir storages) subject to hydrological constraints and priority assignments. Ratios of water supply to demand are used to represent the satisfaction of demand for each demand site under the water right allocation. Each ratio is determined by dividing the total value of inflow adjustment and water-right inflows or storages by the node water demand (inflow adjustment plus the total inflow demand) for cases 1 and 2, and each month of the year. Table 1 lists the results for the 12 agricultural demand sites, the hydropower plant, and Aral Sea. Keep in mind that, if a demands node has a ratio of one in a month, it means its demand is fully met in that period. The lower the ratio, the less is the satisfaction of the demand. As can be seen in Table 1 for case one, the demands upstream from the middle node Karakum are nearly fully satisfied, and the down stream demands are less satisfied except for Karshi and Bukharaz. This is because the upstream demands

Table 1. Water supply/demand ratios for both cases

Site	Case	Jan	Feb	Mar	Apr	May	Jun	Jul	Aug	Sep	Oct	Nov	Dec
Pyandz	Case 1	1.000	1.000	1.000	1.000	1.000	1.000	1.000	1.000	1.000	1.000	1.000	1.000
	Case 2	1.000	1.000	1.000	1.000	1.000	1.000	1.000	1.000	1.000	1.000	1.000	1.000
Vahsh	Case 1	1.000	1.000	1.000	1.000	1.000	1.000	1.000	1.000	1.000	1.000	1.000	1.000
	Case 2	1.000	1.000	1.000	1.000	0.431	0.158	0.131	0.094	0.604	1.000	1.000	1.000
Nurek HPP	Case 1	1.000	1.000	1.000	1.000	1.000	1.000	1.000	1.000	1.000	1.000	1.000	1.000
	Case 2	1.000	1.000	1.000	1.000	1.000	1.000	1.000	1.000	1.000	1.000	1.000	1.000
Kafir	Case 1	1.000	1.000	0.971	1.000	1.000	1.000	1.000	1.000	0.544	0.972	1.000	1.000
	Case 2	1.000	0.070	0.050	0.105	0.153	0.129	0.068	0.034	1.000	0.854	1.000	1.000
Surhans	Case 1	1.000	1.000	1.000	1.000	1.000	1.000	1.000	1.000	1.000	1.000	1.000	1.000
	Case 2	1.000	0.098	0.065	0.167	0.228	0.201	0.089	0.044	0.643	0.113	1.000	1.000
Afgan	Case 1	1.000	1.000	1.000	1.000	1.000	1.000	1.000	1.000	1.000	1.000	1.000	1.000
	Case 2	1.000	1.000	1.000	0.804	1.000	0.600	0.375	0.375	1.000	1.000	1.000	1.000
Karakum	Case 1	0.199	0.139	0.313	0.518	0.156	0.106	0.042	0.045	0.060	0.120	0.159	0.210
	Case 2	0.081	0.068	0.153	0.253	0.076	0.052	0.021	0.022	0.029	0.282	0.099	0.131
Karshi	Case 1	1.000	1.000	1.000	1.000	1.000	1.000	1.000	1.000	1.000	1.000	1.000	1.000
	Case 2	0.027	0.018	0.146	0.279	0.124	0.108	0.061	0.022	1.000	0.052	0.284	0.100
Bukharaz	Case 1	1.000	1.000	1.000	1.000	1.000	1.000	1.000	1.000	1.000	1.000	1.000	1.000
	Case 2	0.021	0.026	0.124	0.232	0.111	0.074	0.047	0.030	0.035	0.929	0.395	0.161
Cardzou	Case 1	1.000	0.364	0.242	0.464	0.212	0.166	0.124	0.111	0.219	0.363	1.000	1.000
	Case 2	0.167	0.037	0.033	0.051	0.042	0.059	0.060	0.393	1.000	1.000	1.000	1.000
Horezm	Case 1	1.000	0.217	0.059	0.219	0.111	0.197	0.213	0.199	0.554	1.000	1.000	1.000
	Case 2	0.231	0.043	0.027	0.099	0.051	0.091	0.098	0.091	0.252	1.000	1.000	0.444
Tashaus	Case 1	0.037	0.029	0.029	0.042	0.058	0.100	0.072	0.074	0.362	1.000	1.000	0.141
	Case 2	0.037	0.029	0.029	0.042	0.058	0.100	0.072	0.074	0.362	1.000	1.000	0.037
Kkar	Case 1	0.019	0.028	0.012	0.061	0.019	0.035	0.033	0.038	0.167	0.730	0.076	0.021
	Case 2	0.019	0.028	0.012	0.061	0.019	0.035	0.033	0.038	0.821	0.730	0.645	0.034
Aral Sea	Case 1	0.019	0.019	0.011	0.008	0.011	0.017	0.021	0.023	0.020	0.013	0.012	0.025
	Case 2	1.000	1.000	1.000	1.000	1.000	1.000	1.000	1.000	1.000	1.000	1.000	1.000

All agricultural demand node loss coefficients are set to be 70%.

are assigned higher priorities such that they have the advantage of being able to take the upstream source water. For case two, Pyandz, the farthest upstream demand, and the Nurek hydropower plant are satisfied, and the Aral Sea's satisfaction ratios amount to 100%; however, most of the others have very low supply/demand ratios. The relatively high ratios of Afgan are due to their low inflow demands and the contribution from its inflow adjustments. The inflows to the Aral Sea for both the cases are plotted in Fig. 2. Since the Aral Sea is given the lowest priority in the basin in case one, the Aral Sea can only get less than 2.5% of its monthly water demands. In case two, the Aral Sea gets much higher monthly ratios. However, the upstream demands get much lower monthly water supply to demand ratios.

The accuracy of input data also greatly affects the results of initial water rights allocations. A sensitivity analysis of various water loss coefficients shows that water loss (consumption) coefficients at agricultural demand sites play an important role in water allocation, because they are the major factors to determine how much return flow is available for downstream uses. Figure 3 shows the inflows to the Aral Sea from the

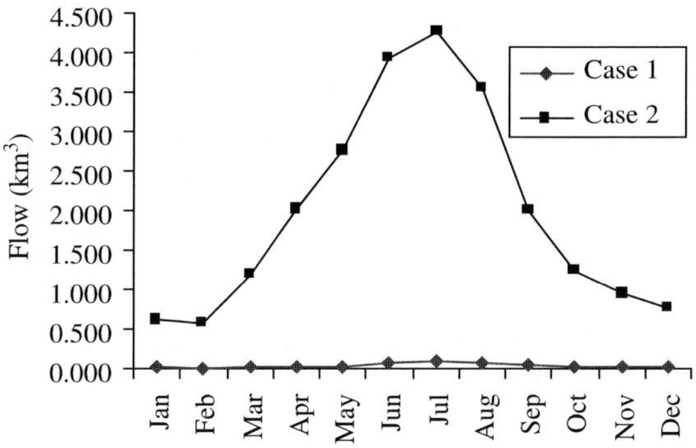

Fig. 2. Inflows to the Aral Sea from the Amu Darya River.

Amu Darya river with various water loss (consumption) coefficients used as inputs. An 8.33% increase of loss coefficients will result in a 75.96% decrease of the flow to the Aral Sea in July.

Although one cannot guarantee the accuracy of input data in this case study, the maximal network flow method can determine fair water rights allocation based on priorities. The study shows that the assignment of priorities directly affects the results of water rights allocation. Under the situations of water shortage in a river basin, the water rights system and associated priority assignments are key factors to consider in achieving fair water allocation for a secure society. The method developed can be utilized to test different water rights systems and priority assignments. Once a sound water rights system and the associated priority assignment are constructed, water can be allocated to users. The study also shows that the maximal network flow method can provide fair multiple period optimal water rights allocations under various rights systems. Based on the initial water rights allocation, the economic optimal water reallocation can be carried out in a cooperative and sustainable manner [1,2].

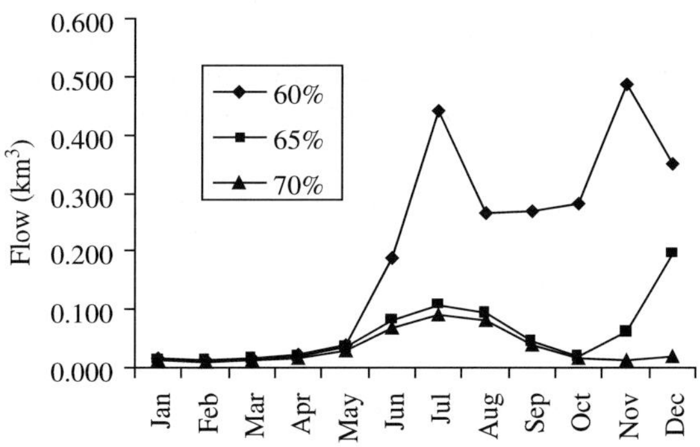

Fig. 3. Inflows to the Aral Sea from the Amu Darya River with various water loss (consumption) coefficients input at agricultural demand sites.

5. Conclusions

The Aral Sea ecological crisis demonstrates that the establishment of equitable intrastate water right systems and interstate agreements to facilitate regional cooperation on water resources management among the countries in a river basin is indeed a difficult challenge. The cooperative water allocation model developed in [1,2] is employed for equitably allocating initial water rights among demand sites located in the Amu Darya river basin of the Aral Sea basin. The modeling results show that it can be utilized for water rights allocation under various rights systems, and can provide fair results provided that sound water rights systems are constructed and priorities are assigned accordingly.

References

[1] L.Z. Wang, L. Fang and K.W. Hipel, *Water resources allocation: a cooperative game theoretic approach*, J. Environ. Informatics **2** (2) (2003), 11–22.

[2] L.Z. Wang, L. Fang and K.W. Hipel, *Cooperative water resources allocation based on equitable water rights*, Proceedings of the IEEE International Conference on Systems, Man and Cybernetics (2003), Held October, Washington, DC, USA, p. 4425.

[3] IFAS (International Fund for the Aral Sea) and UNEP (United Nations Environment Programme), State of the Environment of the Aral Sea Basin, Regional Report of the Central Asian States 2000. http://www.grida.no/aral/aralsea/english/water/water.htm, accessed on August 20, 2003.

[4] P. Raskin, E. Hansen, Z. Zhu, M. Iwra and D. Stavisky, *Simulation of water supply and demand in the Aral Sea region*, Water Int. **17** (1992), 55–67.

[5] D.C. McKinney, *Cooperative management of transboundary water resources in Central Asia*, http://www.ce.utexas.edu/prof/mckinney/papers/aral/CentralAsiaWater-McKinney.pdf, accessed on August 20, 2003.

[6] P.P. Micklin, *The Aral crisis: introduction to the special issue*, Post-Soviet Geography **33** (5) (1992), 269–282.

[7] P.H. Gleick, *Water in Crisis: A Guide to the World's Fresh Water Resources*, Oxford University Press, New York (1993).

[8] P.P. Micklin, *The water management crisis in Soviet Central Asia*, The Carl Beck Papers in Russia and Eastern-European Studies, No. 105, Center for Russian and Eastern European Studies, University of Pittsburgh, Pittsburgh, PA (1991).

[9] E. Antipova, A. Zyryanov, D.C. McKinney and A. Savitsky, *Optimization of Syr Darya water and energy uses*, Water Int. **27** (4) (2002), 504–516.

[10] D.C. McKinney, *Basin-scale integrated water resources management in Central Asia*, Presented at Third World Water Forum, Kyoto, Japan, March 18, 2003.

[11] D.C. McKinney and A.K. Karimov, *Report on model development: Aral Sea regional allocation model for the Amu Darya River*, Prepared for Central Asia Mission, US Agency for International Development, 1997, http://www.ce.utexas.edu/prof/mckinney/apersral/pt-on-Amudarya.html, accessed on August 20, 2003.

[12] A. Brooke, D. Kendrick, A. Meeraus and R. Raman, *GAMS—A Users Guide*, GAMS Development Corporation, http://www.gams.com/, December 1998.

PART III

Fault Detection and Reliable Control

CHAPTER 13

On Fault Detection Based on Recursive Subspace Identification

Hiroshi Oku

Department of Electronics, Information and Communication Engineering, Osaka Institute of Technology, 5-16-1, Omiya, Asahi-ku, Osaka 535-8585, Japan

Contents

Abstract

This chapter concerns detection of faults in systems. From the viewpoint of safety and security, fault detection schemes are essential for automation in industry, since quick alarms help to prevent the subsequent occurrence of complete failure of industrial machines and plants. Fault detection schemes based on subspace identification are promising since subspace identification algorithms are known as powerful tools for system identification. In this chapter, two fault detection schemes are briefly reviewed. One is to observe changes in system parameters by two recursive parameter estimation algorithms based on subspace identification in parallel. The other is a stochastic whiteness test on the so-called residual which is generated by a recursive subspace identification algorithm.

SYSTEMS AND HUMAN SCIENCE – FOR SAFETY, SECURITY, AND DEPENDABILITY
Edited by Tatsuo Arai, Shigeru Yamamoto and Kazuhisa Makino

1. Introduction

Recently, more and more factories have been automated in industry. It is no doubt that automation has provided improvements in efficiency at the factories, and that, as a result, companies have succeeded in greatly reducing costs. In fact, some large factories, which are open for 24 h a day, are managed by a small number of factory workers.

In the viewpoint of safety and security, fault detection schemes are essential for automation in order to prevent the subsequent occurrence of the complete failure of industrial machines and plants. Fault detection schemes are designed to raise the alarm as quickly as possible when machines and plants have faults. Without fault detection schemes, it is almost impossible for only factory workers to observe large factories without any pauses.

In general, a good fault detection scheme gives as quick an alarm as possible when a fault occurs, and as few false alarms as possible when no fault exists. In particular, which parameter estimation algorithm is chosen is one of the crucial factors behind the performance of fault detection schemes. Suitable candidates for parameter estimation algorithms are subspace identification methods (e.g., [14–16,18]). It is well known that subspace identification methods are numerically robust in comparison with conventional identification methods, for example, least squares and least mean squares. Recently, recursive algorithms of subspace identification have been proposed [5,9,11,12,17].

If we notice that faults in machines and plants can make their dynamics different, statistics-based change detection schemes (e.g., [1,4]) are applicable to fault detection. In this chapter, particularly, two change detection schemes based on recursive subspace identification, presented in [10,13], will be reviewed. In order to detect changes in the dynamics of the system, both the schemes observe input and output measurements of a system under surveillance to estimate statistics related to the parameters of the system by recursive subspace identification [9,11,17], and then statistical hypotheses testing is carried out.

In Section 2, a problem formulation considered here is presented. Section 3 is devoted to a brief review of recursive subspace identification according to [10]. In Section 4, a fault detection scheme based on parallel parameter estimation is reviewed [13]. In Section 5, a residual-based change detection scheme is reviewed [10]. A numerical example on the fault detection scheme based on parallel parameter estimation is presented in Section 6. For any square matrix M, tr M denotes the trace of M. $\|\cdot\|_2$ denotes the matrix two-norm [3].

2. Problem formulation

Let us consider a system modeled by a linear, finite dimensional, discrete time, time-invariant, state-space model, which is described by the following innovations form:

$$x_{t+1} = Ax_t + Bu_t + Ke_t, \tag{1a}$$

$$y_t = Cx_t + Du_t + e_t, \tag{1b}$$

where $t \in \mathbb{Z}$, $y_t, e_t \in \mathbb{R}^l$, $u_t \in \mathbb{R}^m$, $x_t \in \mathbb{R}^n$. e_t is assumed to be the Gaussian white noise with zero mean and covariance matrix equal to $\sigma_e^2 I$, i.e., $\mathbf{E}[e_t] = 0$ and $\mathbf{E}[e_s e_t^{\mathrm{T}}] = \delta_{\mathrm{st}}\sigma_e^2 I$, where $\mathbf{E}$ denotes expectation and δ_{st} the Kronecker's delta. The exogenous input u_t is assumed to be bounded, pseudo-stationary [8], relevantly persistently excited and independent of e_t in a relevant sense, which will be defined later. The matrices A and $A - KC$ are assumed to be stable throughout this chapter. (A, C) is assumed to be observable and $(A, [\,B \quad K\,])$ to be reachable.

In order to carry out the change detection schemes considered here successfully, a *fault* of the system is defined as follows. A fault is an abrupt and/or incipient change in the system, which makes the transfer function of the system different. Note that we do not mind whether changes in the spectral density of the input signal may occur, since sometimes a change of input is required in order to adapt for a changeable environment surrounding the system, or since, if necessary, it is possible to prepare another detection scheme in order to observe the input source independently. Therefore, these input changes are *not* our concern and should not be detected. The problem is *to detect a fault of a system under surveillance in real time, without being disturbed by changes in the spectral density of the input signal.*

3. Brief review of recursive subspace identification

In this section, a recursive subspace identification algorithm is reviewed according to [10]. For the rest of the chapter, capital calligraphic letters are reserved for denoting such structured matrices as Hankel and Toeplitz matrices and so on. For a sampled sequence of a signal $\{\ldots, w_0, w_1, \ldots, w_N, \ldots\}$, the Hankel matrices $\mathcal{W}_N$, $\mathcal{W}_{P,N}$ and the vector of the stack of finite successive samples $w(\cdot)$ are respectively defined, with two integers α and β, by

$$\mathcal{W}_N := \begin{bmatrix} w_1 & \cdots & w_N \\ \vdots & \ddots & \vdots \\ w_\alpha & \cdots & w_{N+\alpha-1} \end{bmatrix} =: [\, w_\alpha(1) \quad \cdots \quad w_\alpha(N)\,], \tag{2}$$

$$\mathcal{W}_{P,N} := \begin{bmatrix} w_{1-\beta} & \cdots & w_{N-\beta} \\ \vdots & \ddots & \vdots \\ w_0 & \cdots & w_{N-1} \end{bmatrix} =: [\, w_\beta(1-\beta) \quad \cdots \quad w_\beta(N-\beta)\,]. \tag{3}$$

It is assumed that $\alpha \geq n+1$ and $\beta \geq n$.

Definition 1. (Assumptions on exogenous input). *Given a positive integer N_0, the exogenous input u_t is called persistently exciting if the following relations hold for $\forall N > N_0$ including infinity:*

$$\frac{1}{N}\mathcal{U}_N\mathcal{U}_N^{\mathrm{T}} > 0, \tag{4}$$

$$\frac{1}{N}\begin{bmatrix} \Phi_N \\ \mathcal{U}_N \end{bmatrix}\begin{bmatrix} \Phi_N^{\mathrm{T}} & \mathcal{U}_N^{\mathrm{T}} \end{bmatrix} > 0, \tag{5}$$

where Φ_N is called the regressor matrix and it is chosen as $\Phi_N := \mathcal{U}_{P,N}$ if $K = 0$ in (1), otherwise $\Phi_N := [\mathcal{U}_{P,N}^{\mathrm{T}} \quad \mathcal{Y}_{P,N}^{\mathrm{T}}]^{\mathrm{T}}$.
The exogenous input u_t is called uncorrelated with the noise e_t if $\frac{1}{N}\sum_{t=1}^{N-\tau} e_t u_{t+\tau}^{\mathrm{T}} \to 0$ for $\forall\tau$ as $N \to \infty$ with probability 1.

Note that the word "uncorrelation" is used here with slight abuse of terminology [2,6]. Note also that, from (4), it is shown that $\forall N > N_0$ including infinity there exists a positive number $M < \infty$ such that

$$\left\| \left(\frac{1}{N}\mathcal{U}_N\mathcal{U}_N^{\mathrm{T}} \right)^{-1} \right\|_2 \leq M.$$

In this case, the exogenous input u_t will be called *inversely bounded*.

Taking into account that $(A - KC)^{\beta}$ with sufficiently large β becomes very small and negligible, from (1) the relation between the input and output Hankel matrices can be described by [7]

$$\mathcal{Y}_N = [\,\mathcal{O}\mathcal{L} \quad \mathcal{H}\,]\begin{bmatrix} \Phi_N \\ \mathcal{U}_N \end{bmatrix} + \mathcal{K}\mathcal{E}_N =: \Theta\mathcal{Z}_N + \mathcal{K}\mathcal{E}_N, \tag{6}$$

where $\mathcal{O}$ is the so-called *extended observability matrix* defined by

$$\mathcal{O} := [\,C^{\mathrm{T}} \quad \cdots \quad (CA^{\alpha-1})^{\mathrm{T}}\,]^{\mathrm{T}}, \tag{7}$$

while $\mathcal{L}$ is the reversed controllability matrix defined by $\mathcal{L} := \mathcal{L}_u$ if $K = 0$ in (1), otherwise $\mathcal{L} := [\,\mathcal{L}_u \quad \mathcal{L}_y\,]$, where $\mathcal{L}_u := [(A - KC)^{\beta-1}(B - KD), \ldots, (B - KD)]$, $\mathcal{L}_y := [(A - KC)^{\beta-1}K, \ldots, K]$. The lower triangular Toeplitz matrices, $\mathcal{H}$ and $\mathcal{K}$ are, respectively, defined by

$$\mathcal{H} := \begin{bmatrix} D & & \cdots & O \\ CB & D & & \\ \vdots & & \ddots & \vdots \\ CA^{s-2}B & \cdots & CB & D \end{bmatrix}, \quad \mathcal{K} := \begin{bmatrix} I & & \cdots & O \\ CK & I & & \\ \vdots & \ddots & \ddots & \vdots \\ CA^{s-2}K & \cdots & CK & I \end{bmatrix}. \tag{8}$$

From (6), an estimate of $\Theta_{\Phi} := \mathcal{O}\mathcal{L}$, denoted by $\hat{\Theta}_{\Phi,N}$, can be derived from the solution to the minimization with respect to Θ

$$\hat{\Theta}_{\Phi,N} := \arg\min_{\Theta} \frac{1}{N} \operatorname{tr} \mathcal{K}\mathcal{E}_N(\mathcal{K}\varepsilon_N)^{\mathrm{T}}$$
$$= \arg\min_{\Theta} \frac{1}{N} \operatorname{tr}(\mathcal{Y}_N - \Theta\mathcal{Z}_N)(\mathcal{Y}_N - \Theta\mathcal{Z}_N)^{\mathrm{T}}. \tag{9}$$

When solving the minimization (9), $\hat{\Theta}_{\Phi,N}$ is given by

$$\hat{\Theta}_{\Phi,N} = \frac{1}{N}\mathcal{Y}_N \Pi^{\perp}_{\mathcal{U}_N} \Phi_N^{\mathrm{T}} \left(\frac{1}{N}\Phi_N \Pi^{\perp}_{\mathcal{U}_N} \Phi_N^{\mathrm{T}}\right)^{-1}, \tag{10}$$

where

$$\Pi^{\perp}_{\mathcal{U}_N} := I - \frac{1}{N}\mathcal{U}_N^{\mathrm{T}}\left(\frac{1}{N}\mathcal{U}_N\mathcal{U}_N^{\mathrm{T}}\right)^{-1}\mathcal{U}_N. \tag{11}$$

Note that, if N is finite, (11) is equivalent to

$$\Pi^{\perp}_{\mathcal{U}_N} = I - \mathcal{U}_N^{\mathrm{T}}(\mathcal{U}_N\mathcal{U}_N^{\mathrm{T}})^{-1}\mathcal{U}_N. \tag{12}$$

Essentially, subspace identification is implemented by the singular value decomposition of $\hat{\Theta}_{\Phi,N}$ multiplied from both the sides by relevant weighting matrices, followed by solving linear equations with respect to (A, B, C, D) [14]. Therefore, the recursive update of the estimate $\hat{\Theta}_{\Phi,N}$ has been the most important issue of recursive subspace identification [11–13,17].

When the pair of the data $(u_{N+\alpha}, y_{N+\alpha})$ is sampled at the instant $N+\alpha$, the parameter Θ_Φ is estimated in a recursive manner by the following equation with the help of the auxiliary equations omitted here and found in [11,13]

$$\hat{\Theta}_{\Phi,N+1} = \hat{\Theta}_{\Phi,N} - \xi_{N+1}(r_{N+1} + \hat{\Theta}_{\Phi,N}q_{N+1})q_{N+1}^{\mathrm{T}}\Psi_N^{-1}, \tag{13}$$

where, with $u_\alpha(N+1)$ and $y_\alpha(N+1)$ being defined similarly to (2) while $u_\beta(N-\beta+1)$ and $y_\beta(N-\beta+1)$ similarly to (3), $\phi(N+1) := [\,u_\beta(N-\beta+1)^{\mathrm{T}} \quad y_\beta(N-\beta+1)^{\mathrm{T}}\,]^{\mathrm{T}}$,

$$\Psi_N := \Phi_N \Pi^{\perp}_{\mathcal{U}_N} \Phi_N^{\mathrm{T}}, \tag{14}$$

$$r_{N+1} := y_\alpha(N+1) - \frac{1}{N}\mathcal{Y}_N\mathcal{U}_N^{\mathrm{T}}\left(\frac{1}{N}\mathcal{U}_N\mathcal{U}_N^{\mathrm{T}}\right)^{-1}u_\alpha(N+1), \tag{15}$$

$$q_{N+1} := \frac{1}{N}\Phi_N\mathcal{U}_N^{\mathrm{T}}\left(\frac{1}{N}\mathcal{U}_N\mathcal{U}_N^{\mathrm{T}}\right)^{-1}u_\alpha(N+1) - \phi(N+1), \tag{16}$$

$$\zeta_{N+1} := \left(1 + \frac{1}{N} u_\alpha(N+1)^{\mathrm{T}} \left(\frac{1}{N} \mathcal{U}_N \mathcal{U}_N^{\mathrm{T}}\right)^{-1} u_\alpha(N+1)\right)^{-1},$$

$$\xi_{N+1} := \left(\frac{1}{\zeta_{N+1}} + q_{N+1}^{\mathrm{T}} \Psi_N^{-1} q_{N+1}\right)^{-1}.$$

Note that the above recursive algorithm (13) can easily be integrated with an exponential forgetting factor [9,11]. The recursive algorithm with the exponential forgetting factor will be used for the numerical example in this chapter.

4. Fault detection using parallel parameter estimation [13]

In this section we will restrict ourselves to the special case where $K = 0$ in (1), i.e., the system to be observed can be described by the so-called output error model. The change detection scheme based on parallel parameter estimation [13] is applicable to this case.

Suppose that we have two pairs of estimates $(\hat{\Theta}_{\Phi,N}, \hat{\Psi}_N)$ and $(\bar{\Theta}_{\Phi,N}, \bar{\Psi}_N)$ at the sampling instant $N + \alpha - 1$. The first pair is obtained with a recursive solution given by (13–16), while the second pair is obtained by solving a fixed windowed least squares problem

$$\bar{\Theta}_N = \arg\min_{\Theta} \operatorname{tr}(\bar{\mathcal{Y}}_N - \Theta \bar{\mathcal{Z}}_N)(\bar{\mathcal{Y}}_N - \Theta \bar{\mathcal{Z}}_N)^{\mathrm{T}} =: [\, \bar{\Theta}_{\Phi,N} \quad \bar{\Theta}_{U,N} \,],$$

where $\bar{\mathcal{Z}}_N := [\, \bar{\Phi}_N^{\mathrm{T}} \quad \bar{\mathcal{U}}_N^{\mathrm{T}} \,]^{\mathrm{T}}$,

$$\begin{aligned} \bar{\mathcal{U}}_N &:= [\, u_\alpha(N - L + 2\alpha) \quad \cdots \quad u_\alpha(N) \,], \\ \bar{\mathcal{U}}_{P,N} &:= [\, u_\beta(N - L + \beta) \quad \cdots \quad u_\beta(N - \beta) \,], \end{aligned} \tag{17}$$

$\bar{\Phi}_N := [\, \phi(N - L + \beta) \quad \cdots \quad \phi_s(N - \beta) \,] := \bar{\mathcal{U}}_{P,N}$, and the output Hankel matrix $\bar{\mathcal{Y}}_N$ is defined similarly to $\bar{\mathcal{U}}_N$ in (17). For the sake of convenience, the algorithm producing the estimates $\hat{\Theta}_{\Phi,N}$, $\hat{\Psi}_N$ will be named the accurate 4SID algorithm, while the algorithm producing the estimates $\bar{\Theta}_{\Phi,N}$, $\bar{\Psi}_N$ will be named the tracking 4SID algorithm.

According to Section 3.4 in [13], the quantity defined by

$$D(\bar{\Theta}_{\Phi,N}, \Theta_\Phi) := \operatorname{tr}(\bar{\Theta}_{\Phi,N} - \Theta_\Phi) \frac{1}{\alpha \sigma_e^2} \bar{\Psi}_N^{-1} (\bar{\Theta}_{\Phi,N} - \Theta_\Phi)^{\mathrm{T}},$$

is thought of as χ^2-distributed. This quantity can be regarded as the distance from the true value of the parameter Θ_Φ to its estimate $\bar{\Theta}_{\Phi,N}$ made by the windowed least squares, regularized by the covariance of the noise e_t. However, the true value Θ_Φ must be unknown in practice. To circumvent it, the true value will be replaced by its estimate $\hat{\Theta}_N$ made by the accurate 4SID as the reference value, and hence the proposed distance becomes

$$D(\bar{\Theta}_{\Phi,N}, \hat{\Theta}_{\Phi,N}) = \mathrm{tr}(\bar{\Theta}_{\Phi,N} - \hat{\Theta}_{\Phi,N})\frac{1}{\alpha\bar{\sigma}_{e_N}^2}\bar{\Psi}_N^{-1}(\bar{\Theta}_{\Phi,N} - \hat{\Theta}_{\Phi,N})^{\mathrm{T}}, \tag{18}$$

where $\bar{\sigma}_{e_N}^2$ denotes an estimate of the covariance of the noise e_t. Due to Lemma 1 in [13], note that the assumption on the knowledge of the covariance of the noise is not necessary for this case.

Consequently, the hypotheses test between the following two hypotheses will be carried out in the fault detection scheme:

$$\text{Hypotheses}\begin{cases}\mathbf{H}_0: & \mathbf{H}_1 \text{ is denied.}\\ \mathbf{H}_1: & \text{the system has a fault.}\end{cases}$$

Using the distance (18) as the decision function, the decision rule is described by

$$d = \begin{cases}0 \text{ if } D(\bar{\Theta}_{\Phi,N}, \hat{\Theta}_{\Phi,N}) \le a; & \mathbf{H}_0 \text{ is chosen,}\\ 1 \text{ if } D(\bar{\Theta}_{\Phi,N}, \hat{\Theta}_{\Phi,N}) > a; & \mathbf{H}_1 \text{ is chosen,}\end{cases} \tag{19}$$

where a is a threshold conveniently chosen according to the χ^2-distribution with $l\alpha$ degrees of freedom.

Remark 2. The windowed least squares can be replaced by the recursive subspace algorithm in Section 3 integrated with exponential forgetting as the tracking 4SID algorithm. According to Wellstead and Zarrop [19], an exponential forgetting factor, denoted by γ_L, is roughly associated with the window size $L = (1 - \gamma_L)^{-1}$ of the windowed least squares.

5. Residual-based fault detection [10]

The general case including $K \neq 0$ in (1) is considered in this section. A change detection scheme presented in [10] is applicable to this case. It is based on a hypotheses testing on the so-called residual, which is a by-product of the recursive subspace identification algorithm.

5.1. *Asymptotic property of a statistic*

If no change occurred in the dynamics of the system during sampling, the estimate $\hat{\Theta}_{\Phi,N}$ would converge to the value which satisfies (6) as N goes to infinity. In the case of no change of the system with a sufficient number of samples, the second term on the right-hand side of (13) must be very small or driven only by the noise signal e_t. In this section, an asymptotic property of a statistic which is useful for change detection is presented. It is summarized by the following theorem.

THEOREM 3. *[10] Let α and β be chosen sufficiently large but finite integers. Assume that the exogenous input u_t satisfies the aforementioned assumptions. Suppose that the system stays at an operating point and that there exists $\Theta^* := [\,\Theta^*_\Phi \quad \Theta^*_\mathcal{U}\,]$ such that $\forall N > N_0$*

$$\mathcal{Y}_N = \Theta^*_\Phi \Phi_N + \Theta^*_\mathcal{U} \mathcal{U}_N + \mathcal{K}\mathcal{E}_N, \tag{20}$$

$$y_\alpha(N+1) = \Theta^*_\Phi \phi(N+1) + \Theta^*_\mathcal{U} u_\alpha(N+1) + \mathcal{K}e_\alpha(N+1). \tag{21}$$

Define $e_\alpha(\infty) := [\,e^{\mathrm{T}}_{1\infty} \quad \cdots \quad e^{\mathrm{T}}_{\alpha\infty}\,]^{\mathrm{T}}$, where $e^{\mathrm{T}}_{i\infty} \in \mathbb{R}^l$, $i = 1, \ldots, \alpha$, are zero-mean Gaussian random vectors with the covariance matrix equal to $\mathbf{E}[e_{i\infty} e^{\mathrm{T}}_{j\infty}] = \delta_{ij}\sigma_e^2 I$. Then,

$$r_{N+1} + \Theta^*_\Phi q_{N+1} \rightarrow \mathcal{K}e_\alpha(\infty), \tag{22}$$

in probability as N goes to infinity.

This implies that the recursive subspace identification algorithm has the potential ability for a whitening filter since from (2) and (8) the top block row of the vector $\mathcal{K}e_\alpha(N+1)$ equals e_{N+1}. Θ^*_Φ on the left-hand side of (22) will be replaced by the estimate $\hat{\Theta}_{\Phi,N}$ since it must be unknown.

5.2. *Change detection using GMA*

Once the system has a fault, the recursive subspace identification algorithm (13) goes into a transient state and the theorem is not applicable for a while after detecting a fault. In the transient state, the statistics of the top block row of $r_{N+1} + \hat{\Theta}_{\Phi,N} q_{N+1}$ are dominated by those of the output and input signals. If the output y_t and the noise e_t has a reasonable signal-to-noise ratio, a significant behavior can be observed in the top block row of $r_{N+1} + \hat{\Theta}_{\Phi,N} q_{N+1}$ after detecting a fault. This notable property is expected to avoid false alarms. Moreover, it is empirically known that such behavior, as mentioned before, is irrelevant to changes in the dynamics of the input source. Hence, the discussion above explains the reason why the top block row of $r_{N+1} + \hat{\Theta}_{\Phi,N} q_{N+1}$ generated recursively by the recursive subspace identification algorithm is a promising test statistic for the detection of a fault in the dynamics of the system, without being disturbed by changes in the input signal.

For notational simplicity, let $\hat{\varepsilon}_{N+1}$ denote the top block row of $r_{N+1} + \hat{\Theta}_{\Phi,N} q_{N+1}$. Making use of the real-time observation of $\hat{\varepsilon}_{N+1}$, an online fault detection scheme is developed in this chapter. The key point of the fault detection scheme presented here is to decide *whether the covariance of the test statistic $\{\hat{\varepsilon}_t\}$ is significantly larger than that of $\{e_t\}$* (i.e.,$\sigma_0^2 I$) or not. In other words, the system concerned seems to stay an operating point if no significant difference in the covariance can be seen. Otherwise, it seems to jump from one operating point to another, and this is what we want to detect.

The fault detection scheme tests between the two following hypotheses:

$$\text{Hypotheses}\begin{cases} \mathbf{H}_0\text{:} & \mathbf{H}_1 \text{ is denied.} \\ \mathbf{H}_1\text{:} & \text{the system has a fault.} \end{cases}$$

Note that, as long as the noise e_t retains the constant covariance $\sigma_0^2 I$, the sampling and test can continue sequentially.

From now on, let us consider the single output case, i.e., $l = 1$ for ease of discussion. Note that it is straightforward to extend the discussion to the multiple output case. According to [1], the geometric moving average (GMA) algorithm in the case of a change in the variance *would* be given by

$$g_t = \sum_{i=0}^{\infty} \gamma_i s_{t-i}, \qquad s_t = \ln\frac{\sigma_0}{\sigma_1} + \left(\frac{1}{\sigma_0^2} - \frac{1}{\sigma_1^2}\right)\frac{\hat{\varepsilon}_t^2}{2}, \tag{23}$$

where $\gamma_i := \lambda(1-\lambda)^i$ for $0 < \lambda \le 1$, σ_1^2 denotes the *variance of $\hat{\varepsilon}_t$ in the transient state.* With $g_0 = 0$, g_t is rewritten in a recursive manner as

$$g_t = (1-\lambda)g_{t-1} + \lambda s_t. \tag{24}$$

However, σ_1^2 should be treated as an unknown variable since the knowledge of (A, B, C, D, K) is required in order to evaluate σ_1^2. To circumvent it, the maximum likelihood estimate of σ_1^2 is introduced to (23) and (24) as follows:

$$g_t = \sup_{\sigma_1}\left(\frac{\sigma_1^2 - \sigma_0^2}{\sigma_1^2\sigma_0^2}\tilde{g}_t + \ln\frac{\sigma_0}{\sigma_1}\right), \tag{25}$$

where $\tilde{g}_t := (1-\lambda)\tilde{g}_{t-1} + \lambda\frac{\hat{\varepsilon}_t^2}{2}$ with $\tilde{g}_0 = 0$. Note that $\tilde{g}_t$ can be computed in a recursive manner without the knowledge of σ_1^2. It is easy to show that $\hat{\sigma}_1^2 = 2\tilde{g}_t$ attains the supremum in (25), and then, we have

$$g_t = \left(\frac{\tilde{g}_t}{\sigma_0^2} - \frac{1}{2}\right) + \ln\frac{\sigma_0}{\sqrt{2\tilde{g}_t}}. \tag{26}$$

Consequently, the decision rule d is given by

$$d = \begin{cases} 0 \text{ if } g_t < h; & \mathbf{H}_0 \text{ is chosen,} \\ 1 \text{ if } g_t \ge h; & \mathbf{H}_1 \text{ is chosen,} \end{cases} \tag{27}$$

where h is a conveniently chosen threshold.

6. Numerical example

Due to page limitation, a numerical example on the fault detection scheme based on parallel parameter estimation, shown in Section 4, is presented in this section. On the residual-based scheme, a numerical example can be found in [10].

Consider a SISO system described by the following third-order output-error model [13]

$$y_t = \frac{B(q)}{A(q)} u_t + e_t,$$

$$A(q) := 1 - (\sqrt{3}r_1 + r_2)q^{-1} + (r_1^2 + \sqrt{3}r_1 r_2)q^{-2} - r_1^2 r_2 q^{-3},$$

$$B(q) := 0.2q^{-1} + 0.08q^{-2},$$

where q^{-1} is the backward shift operator and $(r_1, r_2) = (0.95, 0.75)$. The poles of the system are located at

$$\left(\frac{\sqrt{3}r_1}{2} \pm j\frac{r_1}{2}, r_2 \right) = (0.475(\sqrt{3} \pm j), 0.75).$$

In this simulation, a fault is given by an abrupt change of the parameters (r_1, r_2) to $(0.7, 0.9)$ at the sampling instant 4500. As illustrated in Fig. 1, there are several changes in the spectral density of the input signal, which are not to be detected by the fault detection scheme. For the interval, $[0, 1500]$, a zero-mean white sequence with unit variance is used as the input signal. For the interval $[1501, 3500]$, the input equals the sum of a zero-mean white sequence with unit variance filtered with a 10th-order Butterworth filter (cutoff 0.6 times the Nyquist frequency) and a zero-mean white sequence with variance 0.01.

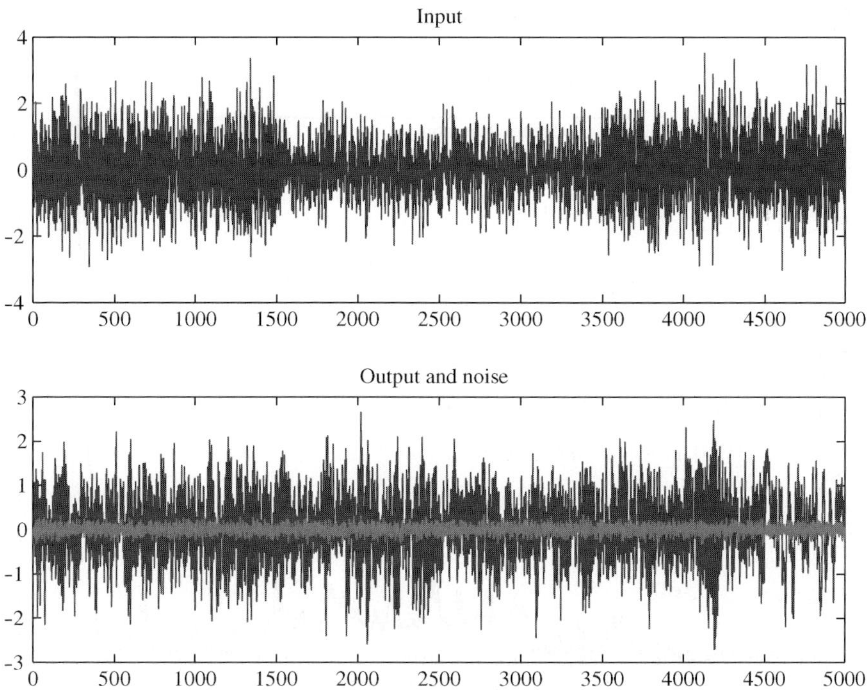

Fig. 1. Input, output and noise.

The output is contaminated by a zero-mean white noise e_k which is uncorrelated with the input signal. The SNR, y to e_t, is approximately 17.8 dB. We choose $\alpha = \beta = 12$. Since the dimension of the output is $l = 1$, the degree of freedom of the χ^2-distribution should be taken as $l\alpha = 12$. As mentioned in Remark 2, we use the recursive subspace algorithm with the exponential forgetting factor $\gamma_L = 0.99$ as the tracking 4SID. This choice of the exponential forgetting factor is roughly associated with the choice of the window size of $L = 100$ for the windowed least squares.

In Fig. 2, the solid line illustrates the decision function $D(\bar{\Theta}_{\Phi,N}, \hat{\Theta}_{\Phi,N})$, while the dotted line illustrates the threshold which is chosen according to 1% of the level of significance. This figure shows that the decision function begins to increase immediately after the sampling instant 4500 and then it exceeds the threshold. On the other hand, around 1500 and 3500, at which the spectral density of the input signal undergoes abrupt changes, no significant behavior of the decision function can be seen. This implies that the fault detection scheme has the ability to detect changes in the dynamics of the system without being disturbed by changes in the input source.

Figure 3 illustrates the singular values of the estimates of the parameter Θ_Φ, made by the accurate 4SID algorithm (located at the top in the figure), and by the tracking 4SID algorithm (located at the bottom), respectively. In the interval [1500, 3500], the estimate by the tracking 4SID does not seem very good. However, from Fig. 2, it does not affect

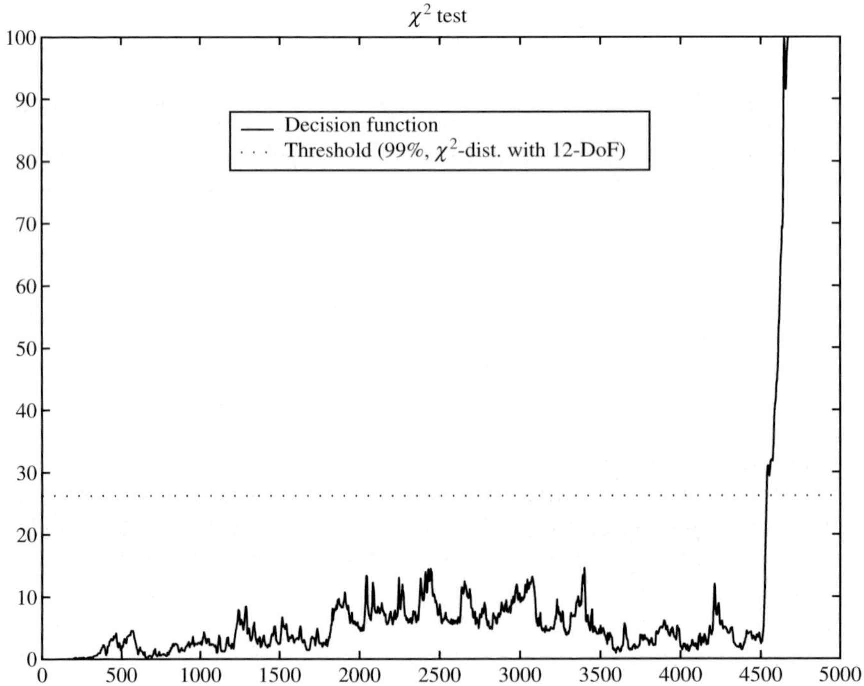

Fig. 2. Hypotheses testing.

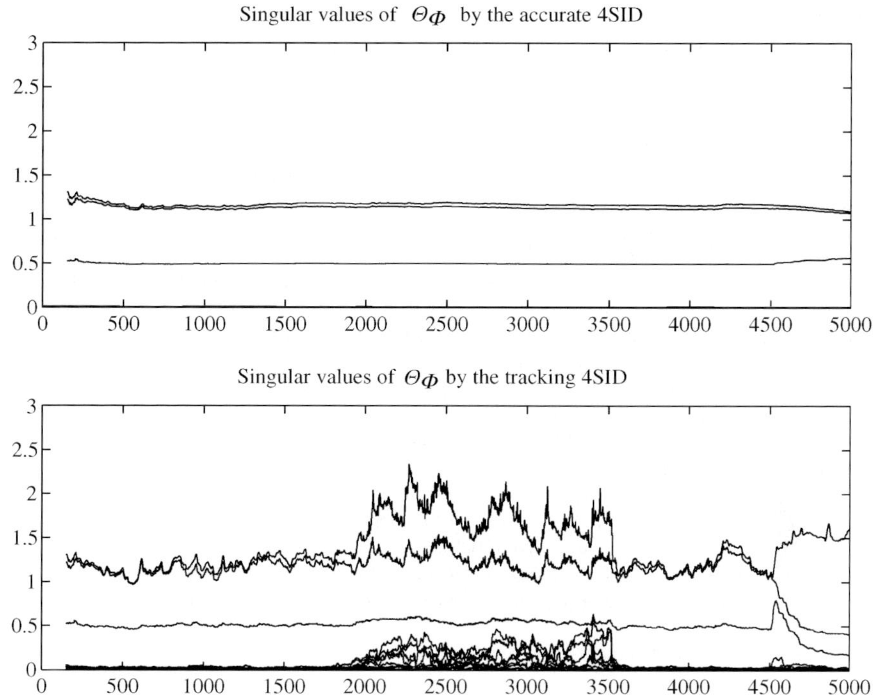

Fig. 3. Singular values of estimates of Θ_{Φ}.

the change detection scheme significantly, and as a result there is no false alarm in the simulation.

7. Concluding remarks

In this chapter, two fault detection schemes based on recursive subspace identification have been reviewed. Both schemes have the ability to detect a fault of a system under surveillance in real time, without being disturbed by changes in the dynamics of the input source. One scheme is based on a hypotheses testing on the distance between the two estimates of a parameter of a system, one of which is made by a (windowed or recursive) subspace identification algorithm having the ability to *fast* track the variation of the parameter, and the other of which is made by a recursive subspace identification algorithm without forgetting (or with relatively *slow* forgetting). This scheme is computationally more expensive than the other one, since it is required that two parameter estimation algorithms are activated in parallel. Nevertheless, it has great potential as a *fault isolation* scheme. The other scheme is based on a hypotheses testing on the so-called residual, which is a by-product of the recursive subspace identification algorithm. This scheme is computationally cheaper than the former one. Moreover, it can deal with systems represented by the so-called innovations form. The innovations form is a wide class of models, which includes, as a part, the output-error model. However, a reasonable signal-to-noise-ratio is desirable for this scheme.

References

[1] M. Basseville and I.V. Nikiforov, Detection of Abrupt Changes, Prentice-Hall, New Jersey (1993).

[2] D. Bauer and M. Jansson, *Analysis of the asymptotic properties of the MOESP type of subspace algorithms*, Automatica **36** (4) (2000), 497–509.

[3] G.H. Golub and C.F. Van Loan, Matrix Computations, 3rd edn., The Johns Hopkins University Press, Baltimore, MD (1996).

[4] F. Gustafsson, Adaptive Filtering and Change Detection, Wiley, Chichester (2000).

[5] T. Gustafsson, M. Lovera and M. Verhaegen, *A novel algorithm for recursive instrumental variable based subspace identification*, Proceedings of the 37th CDC (Florida), December 1998, (1998), 3920–3925.

[6] E.J. Hannan and M. Deistler, The Statistical Theory of Linear Systems, Wiley, New York (1988).

[7] M. Jansson and B. Wahlberg, *A linear regression approach to state-space subspace system identification*, Signal Process. **52** (1996), 103–129.

[8] L. Ljung, System Identification, 2nd edn., Prentice-Hall, New Jersey (1999).

[9] H. Oku, *Sequential subspace state-space system identification and state estimation of unknown multivariable systems*, Ph.D. Thesis, University of Tokyo (2000).

[10] H. Oku, *Application of a recursive subspace identification algorithm to change detection*, Proceedings of the 13th IFAC Symposium on System Identification (Rotterdam, The Netherlands), August 2003, (2003), 1399–1404.

[11] H. Oku and H. Kimura, *A recursive 4SID from the input–output point of view*, Asian J. Control **1** (4) (1999), 258–269.

[12] H. Oku and H. Kimura, *Recursive 4SID algorithms using gradient type subspace tracking*, Automatica **38** (6) (2002), 1035–1043.

[13] H. Oku, G. Nijsse, M. Verhaegen and V. Verdult, *Change detection in the dynamics with recursive subspace identification*, Proceedings of the 40th CDC (Orlando, Florida), December 2001, (2001), 2297–2302.

[14] P. Van Overschee and B. De Moor, Subspace Identification for Linear Systems, Kluwer Academic Publishers, Massachusetts (1996).

[15] M. Verhaegen, *Subspace model identification Part 3: analysis of the ordinary output-error state-space model identification algorithm*, Int. J. Control **58** (3) (1993), 555–586.

[16] M. Verhaegen, *Identification of the deterministic part of MIMO state space models given in innovations form from input–output data*, Automatica **30** (1) (1994), 61–74.

[17] M. Verhaegen and E. Deprettere, *A fast, recursive MIMO state space model identification algorithm*, Proceedings of the 30th CDC (Brighton), December 1991, (1991), 1349–1354.

[18] M. Verhaegen and P. Dewilde, *Subspace model identification Part I: the output-error state space model identification class of algorithms*, Int. J. Control **56** (5) (1992), 1187–1210.

[19] P.E. Wellstead and M.B. Zarrop, Self-tuning Systems, Wiley, Chichester (1991).

CHAPTER 14

Structure of Reliable Controllers

N. Sebe and A. Mochimaru

Department of Artificial Intelligence, Kyushu Institute of Technology, 680-4, Kawazu, Iizuka, Fukuoka 820-8502, Japan

Contents

Abstract

This paper is concerned with the fault-tolerant control based on the integrity. The integrity is the property that closed-loop systems remain stable in the presence of failures of sensors and/or actuators. This property is important for multivariable control systems. In this paper, the effectiveness of the simultaneous uncertainty modeling and controller design approach to design reliable control systems is demonstrated. This paper also investigates the rank deficiency of reliable controllers.

SYSTEMS AND HUMAN SCIENCE – FOR SAFETY, SECURITY, AND DEPENDABILITY
Edited by Tatsuo Arai, Shigeru Yamamoto and Kazuhisa Makino

1. Introduction

The reliable control becomes very important as control systems become larger and more complex. One reason is that there would be some failures of sensors and/or actuators in large systems because such systems have many components. Another reason is that centralized controllers transmit the effects of failures directly to the other parts of a controlled system. Some partial failures would make the closed-loop system unstable even if both the controller and the plant were stable. Thus, not only attaining the higher performance but also tolerating the outages of sensors and/or actuators is very important for designing large-scale systems.

In recent years, the reliable control system design has been studied. The integrity is one of the theories of the reliable control. The integrity is the property that closed-loop systems remain stable even if there exist some outages of sensors and/or actuators. Although integrity is a very important property, it may be too conservative because it ensures the stability of the open-loop systems. To avoid this drawback, some other problem formulations concerning the integrity have been proposed. Gündeş [1] proposes the k-out-of-m integrity, which allows the prespecified number k of failures out of m possible sensors and/or actuators. The condition proposed in [1] requires, however, to check the stability of the system for each possible case of failures; thus, the condition is not suitable for practical controller synthesis. For the k-out-of-m integrity problem, Hamada *et al.* [2,3] propose a robust control problem against Frobenius norm-bounded uncertainties and a reliable controller design procedure based on it.

One of the other works concerning the reliable control is the reliable controller design developed by Veillette *et al.* [4]. They propose the condition based on the Riccati equation for the reliable control problem.

This paper shows that the condition developed in [4] can be derived from the small gain theorem. This analysis clarifies the relation among the reliable control based on the Riccati equation and the integrity theories. Furthermore, this paper also investigates the relation between the robust stability conditions in [3] and in [5]. The robust stability condition for Frobenius norm-bounded uncertainties in [3] is shown to be a special case of the robust stability condition for uncertainties modeled by the LFT-scaling. The numerical example illustrates the effectiveness of the simultaneous modeling and designing procedure proposed in [5]. The example also shows the rank deficiency of reliable controllers. This paper also gives a discussion on this rank deficiency.

Notations

$\mathbf{R}$	the set of real numbers
$\lVert G(s) \rVert_\infty$	H_∞ norm of the system $G(s)$
$M \star N$	star product of M and N

2. Condition based on the Riccati equation

In this section, the reliable control problem considered in [4] is precisely reviewed. As the paper has been referred in many works, it might be worth clarifying the underlying

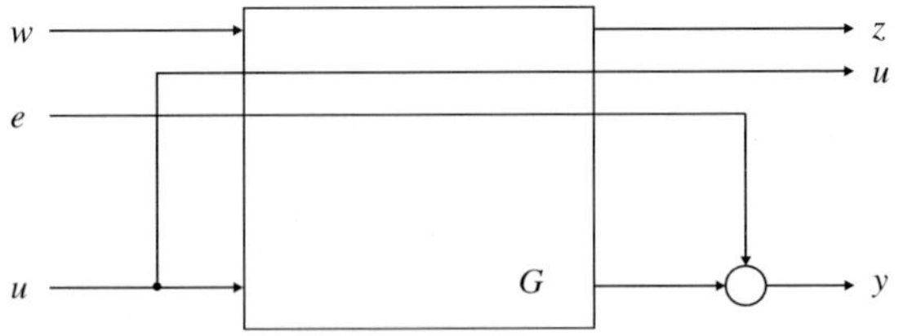

Fig. 1. Block diagram of the generalized plant.

properties behind the stability condition. Fig. 1 shows the generalized plant considered in [4]. Veillette *et al.* assume that the state space representation of the generalized plant is given by

$$\dot{x} = Ax + B_1 w + B_2 u, \qquad z = C_1 x, \qquad y = C_2 x + e. \tag{1}$$

Note that this generalized plant has a special structure that the external input e is directly added to y and u directly appears in the output. Furthermore, there is no direct term from w to the other signals and no direct term to z from the other signals. Accordingly, the so-called "orthogonal" and "normalized" conditions for the standard H_∞ control problem hold [6].

Suppose Ω corresponds to a selected subset of sensors susceptible to outages, and

$$C_2 = C_\Omega + C_{\bar{\Omega}}, \tag{2}$$

where C_Ω and $C_{\bar{\Omega}}$ denote the measurement matrices associated with Ω and the complementary subset, respectively.

Proposition 1. *[4] If there exist $X \geq O$ and $Y \geq O$ which satisfy*

$$A^{\mathrm{T}}X + XA + \frac{1}{\alpha^2} XB_1B_1^{\mathrm{T}}X - XB_2B_2^{\mathrm{T}}X + C_1^{\mathrm{T}}C_1 + \alpha^2 C_\Omega^{\mathrm{T}}C_\Omega = O, \tag{3}$$

$$AY + YA^{\mathrm{T}} + \frac{1}{\alpha^2} YC_1^{\mathrm{T}}C_1Y - YC_{\bar{\Omega}}^{\mathrm{T}}C_{\bar{\Omega}}Y + B_1B_1^{\mathrm{T}} = O, \tag{4}$$

then for any sensor outages in Ω, the closed-loop system is stable, and $\|T_w\|_\infty < \alpha$, where T_w is the transfer function from $\begin{bmatrix} w \\ e \end{bmatrix}$ to $\begin{bmatrix} z \\ u \end{bmatrix}$

From (2), (4) becomes

$$AY + YA^{\mathrm{T}} + \frac{1}{\alpha^2} Y(C_1^{\mathrm{T}}C_1 + \alpha^2 C_\Omega^{\mathrm{T}}C_\Omega)Y - YC^{\mathrm{T}}CY + B_1B_1^{\mathrm{T}} = O. \tag{5}$$

Let us consider the modified generalized plant shown in Fig. 2. The extra output $\alpha C_\Omega x$ is added to the generalized plant (1). Note that the "orthogonal" and "normalized" conditions still hold. Then, the Riccati equations (3) and (5) are exactly same as the conditions for the

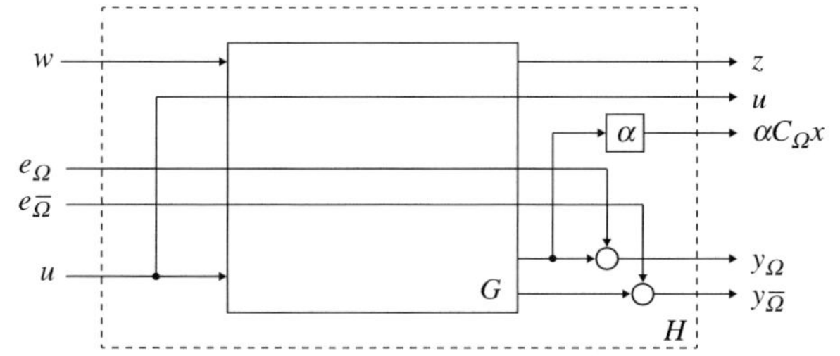

Fig. 2. Block diagram of the generalized plant considered in [4].

standard H_∞ control problem which is defined by Fig. 2, i.e., Proposition 1 is the condition for $\|T_{\text{mod}}\|_\infty < \alpha$, where T_{mod} is the transfer function from

$$\begin{bmatrix} w \\ e_\Omega \\ e_{\bar{\Omega}} \end{bmatrix} \text{ to } \begin{bmatrix} z \\ u \\ \alpha C_\Omega x \end{bmatrix}.$$

Furthermore, μ (the structured singular value) analysis [7,8] ensures that the closed-loop system remains stable if $\|T_{\text{mod}}\|_\infty < \alpha$ holds even when any uncertainties $(1/\alpha)\Delta$ ($\|\Delta\|_\infty \leq 1$) are connected between $\alpha C_\Omega x$ and e_Ω. (Note that the scaling matrix for this case is merely an identity matrix. From the viewpoint of robust performance analysis, the condition in Proposition 1 is too conservative.) As the outages are modeled as $-1/\alpha$, this robustness ensures the reliability of the closed-loop systems. From the above discussion, the condition developed in [4] can be derived from the small gain theorem.

Note that the performance should be evaluated without the additional inputs e, outputs u, $\alpha C_\Omega x$. Because these extra inputs and outputs are added to take into account the sensor outages, this formulation leads to the designed results being conservative.

Another disadvantage of Proposition 1 is that it cannot deal with simultaneous outages of actuators and sensors. Also, the proposed design method cannot deal with the k-out-of-m integrity [2]. Reducing these disadvantages is very important for practical designs.

Finally, the reliable control problem should be reformulated as a robust performance problem. As the failures can be modeled by a structured and parametric uncertainty, even the D-scaling would improve the performance. Furthermore, a more modern approach based on the simultaneous modeling and design technique [5] would attain higher performance with reliability.

3. Condition based on the LFT-scaling

In this section, the relation between the condition based on the LFT-scaling [5] and the integrity condition with the diagonal Frobenius norm-bounded uncertainties [3] is investigated. For the k-out-of-m integrity problem, the maximum number of failures can be specified by diagonal Frobenius norm-bounded uncertainties. Thus, the robust control for the system with diagonal Frobenius norm-bounded uncertainties is proposed for the reliable control problem in [2,3].

PROPOSITION 2. *[3] Suppose a given uncertain system:*

$$\dot{x}(t) = (A + B\Delta C)x(t), \tag{6}$$

where $x \in \mathbf{R}^n$ *and* $\Delta \in \mathbf{R}^{r\times r}$ *which satisfies*

$$\Delta = \mathrm{diag}\{\delta_1, \delta_2, \ldots, \delta_r\}, \qquad \|\Delta\|_F = \sqrt{\delta_1^2 + \delta_2^2 + \cdots + \delta_r^2} \leq 1. \tag{7}$$

The uncertain system (6) is quadratically stable if there exist $X > O$ *and* $F > O$ *which satisfies*

$$\begin{bmatrix} AX + XA^{\mathrm{T}} + B\mathcal{D}(F)B^{\mathrm{T}} & XC^{\mathrm{T}} \\ CX & -F \end{bmatrix} < O, \tag{8}$$

where $\mathcal{D}(\cdot)$ *denotes the function that reduces all the off-diagonal elements of* $(\cdot)$ *to zero.*

Figure 3 shows the relation between the modeled uncertainties and the matrix F in (8). The region in Fig. 3 is the modeled uncertainties described with the matrix F in (8), where

$$F = \begin{bmatrix} 1 & \alpha \\ \alpha & 1 \end{bmatrix} \qquad (|\alpha| < 1).$$

It is important to note that the singularity of F enables to eliminate the region near the point $(\delta_1, \delta_2) = (1, l1)$.

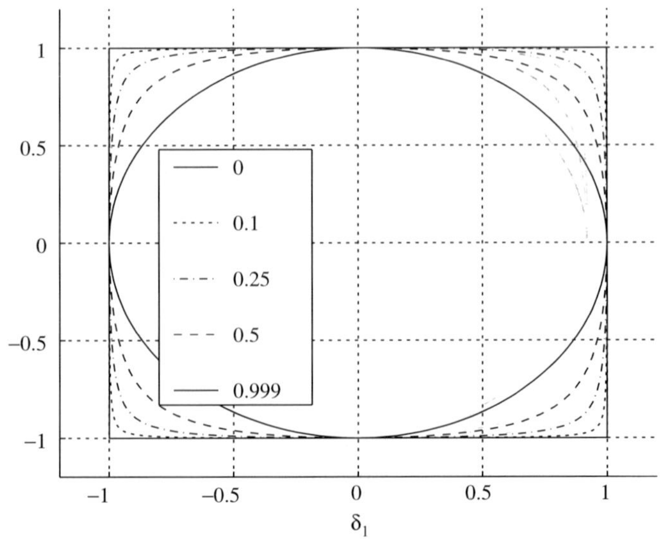

Fig. 3. The region $\|\Delta\|_F \leq 1$ $(r = 2)$.

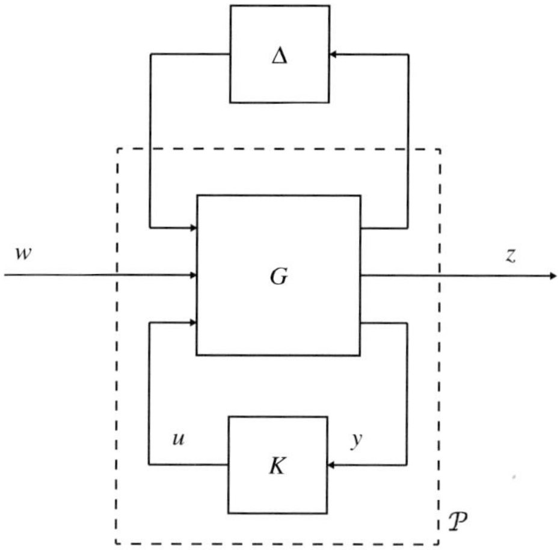

Fig. 4. Closed-loop feedback system $\mathbf{\Delta}\star\mathcal{P}$.

Let us consider the system depicted in Fig. 4, the state space realization of $\mathcal{P}$ and its corresponding data matrix $H_{\mathcal{P}}$ are as follows:

$$\mathcal{P} = \left[\begin{array}{c|c} \mathcal{A} & \mathcal{B} \\ \hline \mathcal{C} & \mathcal{D} \end{array}\right], \qquad H_{\mathcal{P}} = \begin{bmatrix} \mathcal{A} & \mathcal{B} \\ \mathcal{C} & \mathcal{D} \end{bmatrix} \in \mathbf{R}^{(n_{\mathrm{cl}}+(r+p_1))\times(n_{\mathrm{cl}}+(q+m_1))},$$

where n_{cl}, m_1 and p_1 denote the order of the matrix $\mathcal{A}$, the input w and the output z, respectively. Here, a compact set $\mathbf{\Delta} \subset \mathbf{R}^{q\times r}$ is given. Suppose the convex hull of the set $\mathbf{\Delta}$ includes O. Let $\mathbf{B}$ denote the set of matrices with norm less than or equal to 1, and the set of matrix $\mathbf{M}$ is defined as follows:

$$\mathbf{M} = \left\{ \begin{bmatrix} M_{11} & M_{12} \\ M_{21} & M_{22} \end{bmatrix} : \begin{array}{c} \bar{\sigma}(M_{11}) < 1, M_{12} = M_{12}^{\mathrm{T}} > O, \\ M_{21} = M_{21}^{\mathrm{T}} > O,\ M_{22} = O \end{array} \right\}. \tag{9}$$

PROPOSITION 3. *[5] The following statements are equivalent.*

(1) *There exists a matrix $M \in \mathbf{M}$ such that $\mathbf{\Delta} \subseteq \mathbf{B}\star M$ holds, and that the star product $M\star\mathcal{P}$ is well defined, internally stable, and satisfies the following inequality:*

$$\|\mathrm{diag}(I_r, \gamma^{-1/2} I_{p_1}) M\star\mathcal{P}\, \mathrm{diag}(I_q, \gamma^{-1/2} I_{m_1})\|_\infty < 1. \tag{10}$$

(2) *There exist positive-definite matrices $\mathcal{Y} \in \mathbf{R}^{n_{\mathrm{cl}}\times n_{\mathrm{cl}}}$, $Q \in \mathbf{Q}^{q\times q}$, $R \in \mathbf{R}^{r\times r}$ and a matrix $S \in \mathbf{S}^{r\times q}$ such that the following inequalities hold:*

$$[I \quad \Delta^{\mathrm{T}}] \begin{bmatrix} R & S \\ S^{\mathrm{T}} & -Q \end{bmatrix} \begin{bmatrix} I \\ \Delta \end{bmatrix} \geq O \qquad (\forall \Delta \in \mathbf{\Delta}), \tag{11}$$

$$[H_{\mathcal{P}}^{\mathrm{T}} \quad I]\begin{bmatrix} \mathrm{diag}(O, R, \gamma^{-1}I_{p_1}) & \mathrm{diag}(\mathcal{Y}, S, O_{p_1 \times m_1}) \\ \mathrm{diag}(\mathcal{Y}, S, O_{p_1 \times m_1})^{\mathrm{T}} & -\mathrm{diag}(O, Q, \gamma I_{m_1}) \end{bmatrix}\begin{bmatrix} H_{\mathcal{P}} \\ I \end{bmatrix} < O. \quad (12)$$

Note that the relation between the LFT-scaling matrix M and the IQC parameter matrices R, Q, S is given by

$$M = \begin{bmatrix} R^{-1/2}S(Q + Q^{\mathrm{T}}R^{-1}S)^{-1/2} & R^{1/2} \\ (Q + S^{\mathrm{T}}R^{-1}S)^{-1/2} & O \end{bmatrix}.$$

Formally, the conditions in Proposition 2 and that in Proposition 3 without performance evaluation are same, if the parameter matrices are selected as follows:

$$Q = F, \qquad R = \mathcal{D}(F) \qquad \text{and} \qquad S = O. \quad (13)$$

Contrarily, the uncertainties considered in Proposition 2 are diagonal matrices, while those in Proposition 3 are full matrices. If $r = 2$, Proposition 3 provides a robust stability condition for uncertainties

$$\Delta = \begin{bmatrix} \delta_{11} & \delta_{12} \\ \delta_{21} & \delta_{22} \end{bmatrix} \in \mathbf{R}^{2\times 2},$$

i.e., the uncertainty model is determined in four-dimensional space. And with (13), the section of the generalized ellipsoid with $\delta_{11} - \delta_{22}$ plane covers the unit circle on this plane, which derives the robust stability condition for diagonal uncertainties (6) described in Proposition 2.

Here, a question arises. Does the more generalized modeling technique described in Proposition 3 have any advantage for the reliable control problem over the condition in Proposition 2? It seems not. It seems natural to fix the off-diagonal elements of the center of the uncertainty $Q^{-1}S^{\mathrm{T}}$ to 0, as the off-diagonal elements of Δ in (6) are fixed to 0. This paper shows this conjecture is not true and demonstrates the effectiveness of the simultaneous modeling and designing technique for the reliable control problem.

4. Numerical example

In this section, the numerical example illustrates the advantage of the condition based on the LFT-scaling [5]. Let us consider the same example in [4]. The generalized plant is

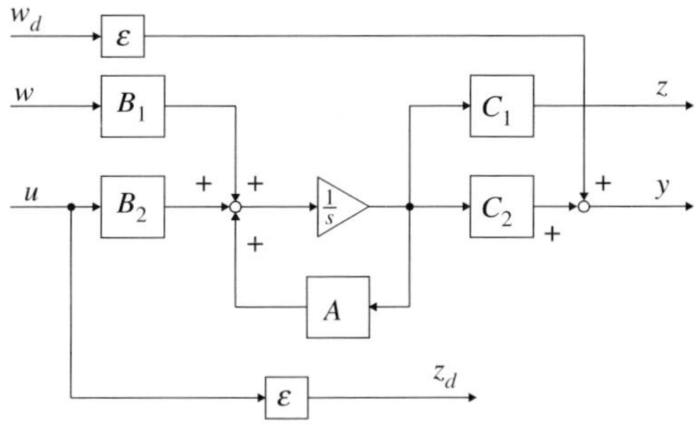

Fig. 5. Block diagram of the generalized plant.

shown in Fig. 5 where the matrices are given by

$$A = \begin{bmatrix} -2 & 1 & 1 & 1 \\ 3 & 0 & 0 & 2 \\ -1 & 0 & -2 & -3 \\ 2 & -1 & 2 & -1 \end{bmatrix}, \quad B_1 = \begin{bmatrix} 0 \\ 1 \\ 0 \\ 0 \end{bmatrix}, \quad B_2 = \begin{bmatrix} 0 & 0 \\ 1 & 0 \\ 0 & 0 \\ 0 & 1 \end{bmatrix},$$

$$C_1 = [1 \quad 0 \quad -1 \quad 0], \qquad C_2 = \begin{bmatrix} 1 & 0 & 0 & 0 \\ 0 & 0 & 1 & 0 \end{bmatrix}. \tag{14}$$

The generalized plant (14) has two sensors, and the problem is to design a controller which can tolerate either outage of the two sensors. Figs. 6 and 7 depict the modified block diagrams of the generalized plant (14) for the design method in [4,5], respectively. The extra input w_d and output z_d in Fig. 5 are added so that the problem satisfies the assumptions of the standard H_∞ problem [6] and avoids the numerical difficulties.

Note that both the conditions in [3,5] are formulated as bilinear matrix inequalities (BMIs) for output feedback problems. In this paper, the procedure called "dual iteration" proposed in [5,9] is applied to solve the example.

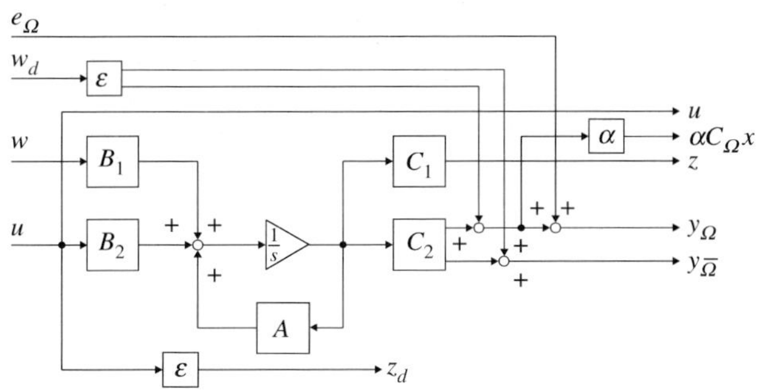

Fig. 6. Modified block diagram for the design method in [4].

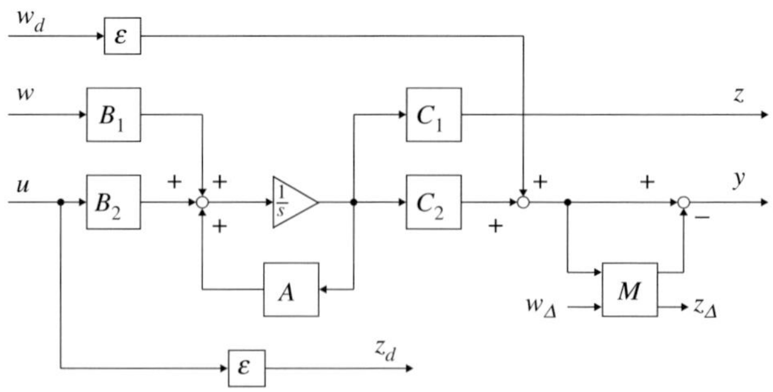

Fig. 7. Modified block diagram for the design method in [5].

4.1. *Integrity condition based on the Riccati equation*

For the reliable control problem stated in an earlier section, Veillette *et al.* consider two failure patterns described as follows:

- sensor 1 is susceptible to fail;
- sensor 2 is susceptible to fail.

Let us call the above designs Reliable Design 1 and Reliable Design 2, respectively.

Table 1 shows the achieved H_∞-norms from $\begin{bmatrix} w \\ w_d \end{bmatrix}$ to $\begin{bmatrix} z \\ z_d \end{bmatrix}$

The parameter α is the design specification. As mentioned before, α does not imply the achieved performances, it only gives the upper bound.

4.2. *Integrity condition based on the LFT-scaling*

In this subsection, a reliable controller is designed by the LFT-scaling method. For the reliable control problem, the set $\mathbf{\Delta}$ in Proposition 3 is defined as follows:

$$\mathbf{\Delta} = \left\{ \begin{bmatrix} \delta_1 & 0 \\ 0 & \delta_2 \end{bmatrix} : \begin{bmatrix} 0 & 0 \\ 0 & 0 \end{bmatrix}, \begin{bmatrix} 1 & 0 \\ 0 & 0 \end{bmatrix}, \begin{bmatrix} 0 & 0 \\ 0 & 1 \end{bmatrix} \right\}, \tag{15}$$

where each matrix corresponds to the normal system, the system with the outage of sensor 1, and the system with the outage of sensor 2, respectively.

Table 1. The achieved H_∞-norms with the reliable controller designed in [4]

	Reliable Design 1 ($\alpha = 3.20$)	Reliable Design 2 ($\alpha = 4.46$)
No failure	0.17	0.37
y_1 fails	0.32	0.30
y_2 fails	0.55	0.31

The obtained state space matrices of the controller are as follows:

$$A_k = \begin{bmatrix} -37.555 & 2.063 & -3.403 \\ -23.246 & -19.376 & -23.741 \\ 11.710 & 23.983 & -27.289 \end{bmatrix},$$

$$B_k = \begin{bmatrix} 1.2984 \\ 0.3954 \\ -0.2005 \end{bmatrix} \times 10^2 \times V_{B_1}^{\mathrm{T}}, \tag{16}$$

$$C_k = \begin{bmatrix} 1.2655 & -0.0525 & 0.0075 \\ 0.2906 & 0.3919 & 0.2004 \end{bmatrix} \times 10^2,$$

$$D_k = \begin{bmatrix} -4.4900 \\ -0.4302 \end{bmatrix} \times 10^2 \times V_{B_1}^{\mathrm{T}}, \qquad V_{B_1} = \begin{bmatrix} 0.6758 \\ 0.7371 \end{bmatrix}.$$

A fourth-order controller is obtained. By approximating a fast mode to a constant, a third-order controller is obtained, whose state space matrices are given by (16). Furthermore, it should be interesting to note that

$$\mathrm{rank}[D_k + C_k(sI - A_k)^{-1}B_k] = 1. \tag{17}$$

This special structure of the designed controller is investigated more precisely later.

Table 2 shows the achieved H_∞-norms with the controller design in [3,5] and the reduced-order controller (16). These reliable controllers achieve higher performance than that obtained in [4]. Furthermore, the controller obtained by Asai *et al.* [5] is the optimal controller for the reliable control problem, although the problem is a BMI problem. Table 3 shows achievable H_∞ norms for each failure pattern without any consideration for the reliability. The worst performance is 0.2154, which almost coincides with the performance with the obtained reliable controller (16). This fact shows the optimality of the designed controller.

Table 2. The achieved H_∞-norms with the reliable controller (1) designed by the method in [3], (2) designed by the method in [5], (3) rank reduced controller of (2)

	Design method		
	(1)	(2)	(3)
No failure	0.1326	0.1878	0.1906
y_1 fails	0.2602	0.2155	0.2170
y_2 fails	0.1194	0.0903	0.0787

Table 3. The achievable H_∞-norms without any consideration for the reliability

With y_1 and y_2	0.0123
Without y_1	0.2154
Without y_2	0.0123

The obtained IQC parameter matrices Q, R and S in Proposition 3 are as follows:

$$Q = \begin{bmatrix} 75.302 & 70.628 \\ 70.628 & 87.410 \end{bmatrix}, \quad R = \begin{bmatrix} 3.150 & -2.565 \\ -2.565 & 3.921 \end{bmatrix}, \quad S = \begin{bmatrix} 36.076 & 2.565 \\ 2.565 & 41.745 \end{bmatrix}. \tag{18}$$

Fig. 8 shows the generated uncertainty model, i.e., the section of the generalized ellipsoid described by the matrices (18). The region in Fig. 8 includes the uncertainties (15), but not all the diagonal Frobenius norm-bounded uncertainties. Note that the center of the ellipsoid $Q^{-1}S^{\mathrm{T}}$ has non-zero off-diagonal elements, although the off-diagonal elements of $\boldsymbol{\Delta}$ defined by (15) are fixed to 0. The non-zero off-diagonal elements of $Q^{-1}S^{\mathrm{T}}$ contribute to the improvement of performance.

Let us see the reason why the designed controller is not full rank. Before stating the reasons, remember that the technique called "loop shifting" ensures that the (1,1) element of the LFT-scaling M can be set as O, i.e., $M_{11} = O$.

Now, the reasons are stated below.

- M_{21}^{-1} becomes singular to eliminate the region near $(\delta_1, \delta_2) = (1, 1)$. Thus, M_{21} has very large singular values.
- For the robust stability, the given plant P, the designed controller K and the LFT-scaling M should satisfy $\|M_{12}(I + PKM_{22})^{-1}PKM_{21}\|_\infty < 1$.

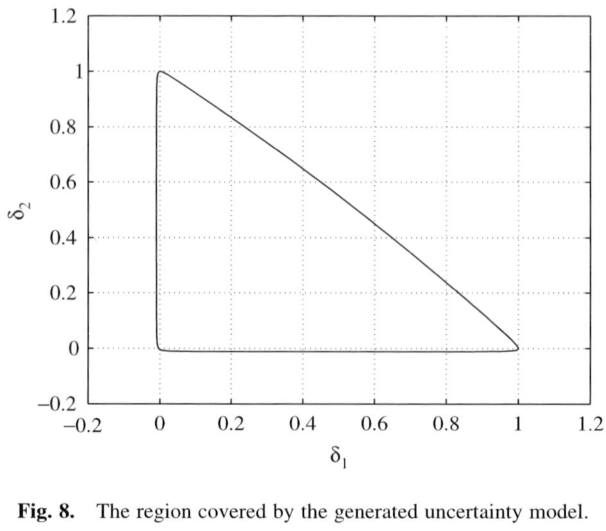

Fig. 8. The region covered by the generated uncertainty model.

- As M_{21} has very large singular values, each row vector of K should be orthogonal to the basis of M_{21} corresponding to its large singular values, i.e., the basis of the null space of M_{21}^{-1}.

Let us check the above reasons for this example. The generated LFT-scaling is

$$M = \begin{bmatrix} 0 & 0 & 7.1304 & -3.9738 \\ 0 & 0 & -3.9738 & 7.8313 \\ 0.2048 & -0.1136 & 1.8648 & -1.7091 \\ -0.1136 & 0.1853 & -1.4774 & 1.8586 \end{bmatrix}. \tag{19}$$

On the other hand, the matrices B_k and D_k of the full-order controller are

$$B_k = \begin{bmatrix} -0.0025 & -0.0090 \\ 0.0023 & 0.0013 \\ 0.5814 & 0.5937 \\ -2.0142 & -2.2079 \end{bmatrix} \times 10^2, \qquad D_k = O. \tag{20}$$

Let the singular value decompositions of B_k and M_{21} be $B_k = U_B \Sigma_B V_B^{\mathrm{T}}$ and $M_{21} = U_M \Sigma_M V_M^{\mathrm{T}}$, and decompose V_B and U_M as

$$V_B = [\, V_{B_1} \quad V_{B_2} \,], \qquad U_M = [\, U_{M_1} \quad U_{M_2} \,]. \tag{21}$$

The singular values of B_k are $\Sigma_B = \mathrm{diag}\{3.1019, 0.0286\} \times 10^2$. This implies that the designed controller is nearly singular. Furthermore, $V_{B_1}^{\mathrm{T}} U_{M_1} = 5.4695 \times 10^{-4}$. The fact implies that the major part of B_k and the major part of M_{21} are orthogonal to each other.

5. Conclusion

This paper investigates the integrity conditions from the viewpoint of the small gain theorem and the LFT-scaling. The numerical example shows that the method by Asai *et al.* achieves higher performance than that by Veillette *et al.* The effectiveness and the flexibility of the LFT-scaling approach to design reliable control systems are also demonstrated. The numerical example also shows that the designed controller is not full rank. This paper also investigates the reasons for the rank deficiency.

As decentralized controllers are always full rank, rank-deficient centralized controllers might have an advantage in integrity over decentralized controllers. This conjecture might affect the motivation to use decentralized control systems. Thus, further research should be made on this topic.

References

[1] A.N. Gündeş, *Stability of feedback systems with sensor or actuator failures: analysis*, Int. J. Control **56** (4) (1992), 735–753.

[2] Y. Hamada, S. Shin and N. Sebe, *A design method for fault-tolerant control systems based on H_∞ optimization*, Proceedings of 35th IEEE Conference on Decision and Control, Strony 1918–1919, Kobe, Japan, December 1996.

[3] Y. Hamada, S. Shin and N. Sebe, *Quadratic stability conditions of linear systems with Frobenius norm-bounded diagonal perturbations*, Trans. Soc. Instrum. Control Engrs **36** (8) (2000), 720–722.

[4] R.J. Veillette, J.V. Medanic and W.R. Perkins, *Design of reliable control systems*, IEEE Trans. Autom. Control **AC-37** (3) (1992), 290–304.

[5] T. Asai, S. Hara and T. Iwasaki, *Simultaneous parametric uncertainty modeling and robust control synthesis by LFT-scaling*, Automatica **36** (2000), 1457–1467.

[6] J.C. Doyle, K. Glover, P.P. Khargonekar and B.A. Francis, *State-space solutions to standard H_2 and H_∞ control problems,* IEEE Trans. Autom. Control **34** (1989), 831–847.

[7] G.J. Balas, J.C. Doyle, K. Glover, A. Packard and R. Smith, *μ-Analysis and Synthesis Toolbox*, MuSyn Inc., Minneapolis (1991).

[8] K. Zhou, A. Packard and J.C. Doyle, *Review of LFTs, LMIs, and μ*, Proceedings of 30th IEEE Conference on Decision and Control, December 1991.

[9] T. Iwasaki, *The dual iteration for fixed-order control*, IEEE Trans. Autom. Control **44** (4) (1999), 783–788.

CHAPTER 15

Simultaneous Stabilization and its Application to Reliable System Synthesis Within a Behavioral Framework

Osamu Kaneko and Takao Fujii

Graduate School of Engineering Science, Osaka University Machikaneyama 1-3, Toyonaka, Osaka 560-8531, Japan

Contents

Abstract

In this chapter, we consider reliable control system synthesis and address the problem of simultaneous stabilization within a behavioral framework. We provide a necessary and sufficient condition for the existence of a simultaneous stabilizing control law for two given plants.

SYSTEMS AND HUMAN SCIENCE – FOR SAFETY, SECURITY, AND DEPENDABILITY
Edited by Tatsuo Arai, Shigeru Yamamoto and Kazuhisa Makino

1. Introduction

Recently, many control systems are increasing in both complexity and scale in order to achieve higher quality specifications imposed on real plants. As a result, it is probable that a failure of a control device will lead to an accident sufficiently crucial to endanger the safety of people and society. Thus, a lot of concerns regarding safety and reliability have become focused on many process industries and it is necessary for control systems designed for real plants to retain stability and safety under such crucial failures. For the purpose of designing control systems fulfilling these requirements, control system synthesis taking into account the dynamics of the plant after failure, known as *reliable control system synthesis*, was proposed and developed (cf. [3,4,11–13,16] and so on). The standard reliable system synthesis can be illustrated in Fig. 1.

As shown in Fig. 1, a "feedback controller" Σ_c stabilizes not only a plant Σ_{P1} but also a plant Σ_{P2}. The former corresponds to the plant before faults occur while the latter corresponds to that after faults occur. Since reliable control system synthesis involves stabilizing more than two different plants using one controller, it can also be formulated as a *simultaneous stabilization* problem from a theoretical viewpoint. In standard system theory based on transfer functions or state space representations, although the simultaneous stabilization problem has already been solved for the case of two plants, some unsolved problems remain in this area with respect to system theory (cf. [1,2] and so on). Thus, simultaneous stabilization is also a challenging issue from a theoretical point of view.

Incidentally, in cases in which the main purpose of system synthesis is to design a system with increased robustness for expectable failures, it is natural to include design of the system itself as part of the "control system synthesis". This means that it is also natural to design a system in which the role of a failed sub-system must be complemented by another sub-system. On the other hand, the control system synthesis in a behavioral framework that is proposed by Willems (cf. [14,15]) is to impose additional constraint conditions on the behavior of a plant so as to restrict the behavior of such interconnected systems to the desired behavior. From the viewpoints of mathematical models that represent these additional constraint conditions, the behavioral control concept admits controllers described by improper rational functions, which means a larger class than that

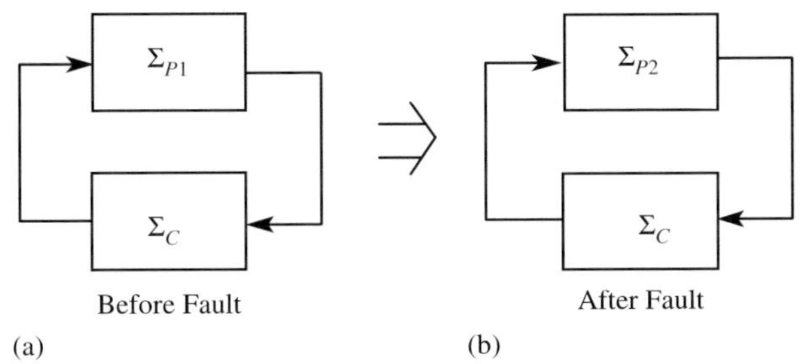

Fig. 1. A reliable control system (in the standard framework).

addressed in standard system theory, in which feedback controllers only are admitted, is regarded as "the controller set". Since controllers described by improper rational functions correspond to modifications of the structure of the system, tuning of the physical parameters and so on, the most preferred purpose of control system synthesis in a behavioral framework is to achieve the desirable specifications, different from that in a usual feedback control framework.

From these points of view, in this chapter, we consider reliable control system synthesis and address the simultaneous stabilization problem within a behavioral framework. Using this approach, we regard the simultaneous stabilization problem as shown in Fig. 2.

In Fig. 2, it can be seen that the connections have no direction, indicating that a subsystem Σ_C is not necessarily implemented by a feedback controller driven like a CPU, differently from the standard system control synthesis. In this chapter, we provide a necessary and sufficient condition for the existence of a simultaneous stabilizing control law for a pair of two given plants within a behavioral framework.

This chapter is organized as follows. In Section 2, we give a brief review of the behavioral system theory required in this chapter. In Section 3, we formulate the problem we address here, describing the problem of simultaneous stabilization in a behavioral framework. In Section 4, we provide the complete necessary and sufficient conditions for a pair of two given plants to be simultaneously stabilizable in a behavioral framework. In Section 5, we give a simple example in order to show the validity of our results. In Section 6, we draw our conclusions.

Notations. Let $\mathbf{R}$ and $\mathbf{C}$ denote the set of real numbers and complex numbers, respectively. Let $\mathbf{R}^q$ and $\mathbf{R}^{p\times q}$ denote the set of real vectors of size q and that of real matrices of size $p\times q$, respectively. Let $\mathbf{R}[\xi]$ denote the set of polynomials of real coefficients and $\mathbf{R}^{p\times q}[\xi]$ denote the matrix version of them of size $p\times q$. Similarly, let $\mathbf{R}(\xi)$ denote the set of rational functions of real coefficients and $\mathbf{R}^{p\times q}(\xi)$ denote the matrix version of them of size $p\times q$. In the case of $p \geq q (p \leq q)$, let $\mathbf{R}_{\mathbf{C}}^{p\times q}[\xi]$ denote the subset of $\mathbf{R}^{p\times q}[\xi]$ with full column (row, respectively) rank for all $\xi = \lambda \in \mathbf{C}$. Let $\mathbf{R}_{\mathbf{H}}^{q\times q}[\xi]$ denote the set of polynomial matrices whose determinants have no roots on the closed right half-plane. We call an element of $\mathbf{R}_{\mathbf{H}}^{q\times q}[\xi]$ *Hurwitz*. Note that a unimodular matrix on $\mathbf{R}^{q\times q}[\xi]$ is also referred to as Hurwitz.

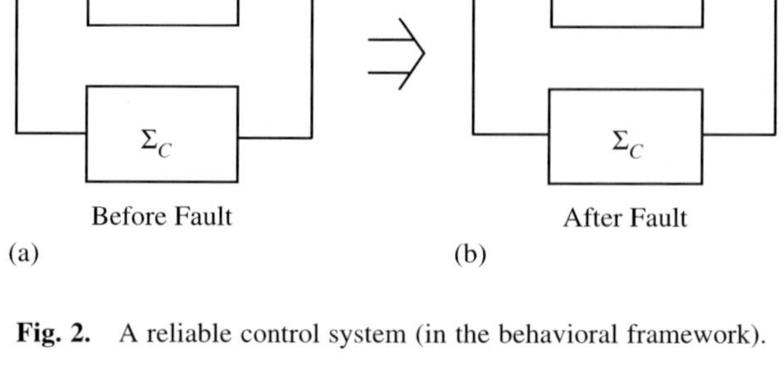

Fig. 2. A reliable control system (in the behavioral framework).

2. Preliminaries

In this section, we set out briefly the concepts and definitions required in the following sections. For more details, see [10,14,15] and so on.

2.1. *Behavioral system theory*

A dynamic system Σ is defined as a triple $\Sigma = (\mathbf{T}, \mathbf{W}, \mathbf{B})$, with time axis $\mathbf{T}$, signal space $\mathbf{W}$ and behavior $\mathbf{B}$. Consider a dynamic system $\Sigma = (\mathbf{R}, \mathbf{R}^{\mathrm{q}}, \mathbf{B})$. Moreover, assume that Σ is linear, time-invariant and differentiable. Then, a dynamic system Σ can be represented by

$$R_{\mathrm{L}} \frac{\mathrm{d}^{\mathrm{L}} w}{\mathrm{d}t^{\mathrm{L}}} + \cdots + R_1 \frac{\mathrm{d}w}{\mathrm{d}t} + R_0 w = 0 \tag{1}$$

where $R_i \in \mathbf{R}^{\bullet \times \mathrm{q}}$, $i = 0, \ldots, N$. This is called a *kernel representation* of Σ and the variable w is called a manifest variable. A kernel representation is written as $R(\frac{\mathrm{d}}{\mathrm{d}t})w = 0$ using a polynomial matrix $R(\xi) := R_0 + R_1\xi + \cdots + R_N\xi^N \in \mathbf{R}^{\bullet \times \mathrm{q}}[\xi]$. Since premultiplying a polynomial matrix $R(\xi)$ inducing a kernel representation by any unimodular matrix $U(\xi)$ has no influence on the behavior (i.e., the kernel of $R(\mathrm{d}/\mathrm{d}t)w = 0$ and that of $U(\mathrm{d}/\mathrm{d}t)\ R(\mathrm{d}/\mathrm{d}t)w = 0$ are the same), there are many kernel representations for the behavior of a system Σ. In particular, we refer to a kernel representation $R(\mathrm{d}/\mathrm{d}t)w = 0$ as *minimal* if $R(\xi)$ has normal full row rank. Let $\rho(\mathbf{B})$ denote the size of rows of a minimal kernel representation of $\mathbf{B}$ and note that $\rho(\boldsymbol{B})$ is independent from representations of $\mathbf{B}$. Throughout this chapter, we assume that a system is linear, time-invariant and differentiable.

A dynamic system $\Sigma = (\mathbf{R}, \mathbf{R}^{\mathrm{q}}, \mathbf{B})$ is said to be *controllable* if for all $w_1, w_2 \in \mathbf{B}$ there exist $w \in \mathbf{B}$ and $T_1, T_2 (\in \mathbf{R})$ such that $w(t) = w_1(t)$ for $t \leq T_1$ and $w(t) = w_2(t)$ for $t > T_2$. Σ is controllable if and only if a minimal kernel representation is induced by an element of $\mathbf{R}_{\mathbf{C}}^{\rho(\mathbf{B}) \times \mathrm{q}}[\xi]$. The controllability of a system $\Sigma = (\mathbf{R}, \mathbf{R}^{\mathrm{q}}, \mathbf{B})$ is also equivalent to saying that $\mathbf{B}$ can be described by

$$w = M_{\tilde{\mathrm{L}}} \frac{\mathrm{d}^{\tilde{\mathrm{L}}} \ell}{\mathrm{d}t^{\tilde{\mathrm{L}}}} + \cdots + M_1 \frac{\mathrm{d}\ell}{\mathrm{d}t} + M_0 \ell \tag{2}$$

where $M_i \in \mathbf{R}^{\mathrm{q} \times \bullet}, i = 0, \ldots, L$. This is called an *image representation* of Σ and ℓ is called a latent variable. Similar to kernel representations, we use the notation $w = M(\mathrm{d}/\mathrm{d}t)\ell$ by using a polynomial matrix $M(\xi) := M_0 + M_1\xi + \cdots + M_L\xi^L \in \mathbf{R}^{\mathrm{q} \times \bullet}[\xi]$. Moreover, since postmultiplying a polynomial matrix $M(\xi)$ inducing an image representation by a unimodular matrix $V(\xi)$ has no influence on the behavior (i.e., the image of $M(\mathrm{d}/\mathrm{d}t)\ell$ and that of $M(\mathrm{d}/\mathrm{d}t)V(\mathrm{d}/\mathrm{d}t)\ell'$ are the same), there are many image representations for the behavior of a controllable system Σ. In addition, ℓ is said to be *observable* from w if $w = 0$ implies $\ell = 0$. A latent variable ℓ in $w = M(\mathrm{d}/\mathrm{d}t)\ell$ is observable from w if and only if $M(\xi) \in \mathbf{R}_{\mathbf{C}}^{\mathrm{q} \times (\mathrm{q} - \rho(\mathbf{B}))}[\xi]$.

Contrary to the notion of controllability, we often have to consider cases in which behavior cannot be "touched" using the external free variables and any trajectory only follows its past. Formally, we call a system *autonomous* if for all $w_1, w_2 \in \mathbf{B}$ such that $w_1(t) = w_2(t) \forall t < 0$ $w_1(t) = w_2(t) \forall t \geq 0$ holds. A system $\Sigma = (\mathbf{R}, \mathbf{R}^{\mathrm{q}}, \mathbf{B})$ is autonomous if and only if a minimal kernel representation of $\mathbf{B}$ is induced by a non-singular polynomial matrix $R(\xi) \in \mathbf{R}^{\mathrm{q} \times \mathrm{q}}[\xi]$.

A dynamic system is said to be stable if for all $w \in \mathbf{B}$ implies $w(t) \rightarrow 0$ as $t \rightarrow \infty$. As can clearly be seen, the autonomy of a system is a necessary condition for the system to be stable. A system $\Sigma = (\mathbf{R}, \mathbf{R}^{\mathrm{q}}, \mathbf{B})$ is stable if and only if a minimal kernel representation of $\mathbf{B}$ is induced by a non-singular polynomial matrix $R(\xi) \in \mathbf{R}_{\mathbf{H}}^{\mathrm{q} \times \mathrm{q}}[\xi]$.

2.2. *Behavioral system synthesis*

Consider two dynamic systems, $\Sigma_1 = (\mathbf{T}, \mathbf{W}, \mathbf{B}_1)$ and $\Sigma_2 = (\mathbf{T}, \mathbf{W}, \mathbf{B}_2)$, which share common signal space. Then, the interconnection of Σ_1 and Σ_2 is described by $\Sigma_1 \cap \Sigma_2 = (\mathbf{T}, \mathbf{W}, \mathbf{B}_1 \cap \mathbf{B}_2)$, that is, the behavior of the interconnected system is constrained by physical laws of both Σ_1 and Σ_2. Now, consider two linear time-invariant and controllable systems $\Sigma_p = (\mathbf{T}, \mathbf{W}, \mathbf{B}_p)$ and $\Sigma_c = (\mathbf{T}, \mathbf{W}, \mathbf{B}_c)$. Each of the behaviors $\mathbf{B}_{\mathrm{p}}$ and $\mathbf{B}_{\mathrm{c}}$ are described by minimal kernel representations induced by polynomials $R(\xi) \in \mathbf{R}^{\rho(\mathbf{B}) \times \mathrm{q}}[\xi]$ and $C(\xi) \in \mathbf{R}^{\mathrm{m} \times \mathrm{q}}[\xi]$ with $m \leq (q - \rho(\mathbf{B}))$. Then, the interconnection of two dynamic systems can be described by

$$\begin{bmatrix} R\left(\frac{\mathrm{d}}{\mathrm{d}t}\right) \\ C\left(\frac{\mathrm{d}}{\mathrm{d}t}\right) \end{bmatrix} w = 0 \tag{3}$$

The interconnection described by (3) is said to be a regular interconnection if $p + m$ is equal to the row rank of $[R(\xi)^{\mathrm{T}}\, C(\xi)^{\mathrm{T}}]^{\mathrm{T}}$. Next, let $\nu(\Sigma_p)$ denote the largest degree of all $\rho(\mathbf{B}) \times \rho(\mathbf{B})$ minors of $R(\xi)$. Similarly, let $\nu(\Sigma_c)$ denote the largest degree of all $m \times m$ minors of $C(\xi)$. Moreover, define $\nu(\Sigma_p \cap \Sigma_c)$ as the largest degree of all $(\rho(\mathbf{B}) + m) \times (\rho(\mathbf{B}) + m)$ minors of $[R(\xi)^{\mathrm{T}}\, C(\xi)^{\mathrm{T}}]^{\mathrm{T}}$. The regular interconnection is said to be *regular feedback* if $\nu(\Sigma_p) + \nu(\Sigma_c) = \nu(\Sigma_p \cap \Sigma_c)$. Regular feedback means that the interconnection can be achieved by a proper controller (cf. [8,15]). On the other hand, in the case of $\nu(\Sigma_p) + \nu(\Sigma_c) > \nu(\Sigma_p \cap \Sigma_c)$, the regular interconnection is said to be *singular feedback* which means that the interconnection can be achieved by a non-proper controller.

Assume that $m = q - \rho(\mathbf{B})$ and the regular interconnection case. For the sake of stabilization of the plant, the controller must be designed so as to satisfy the case that $\Sigma_p \cap \Sigma_c$ is autonomous and $\Sigma_p \cap \Sigma_c$ is stable. That is to say, $[R(\xi)^{\mathrm{T}}\, C(\xi)^{\mathrm{T}}]^{\mathrm{T}}$ must be an element of $\mathbf{R}_{\mathbf{H}}^{\mathrm{q} \times \mathrm{q}}[\xi]$. Then, Σ_c is said to be the *stabilizer* of Σ_p.

Next, we prepare some useful lemmas in this chapter. The first lemma is a generalization of the well known doubly coprime factorization [5,13].

LEMMA 2.1. *Assume that $\Sigma = (\mathbf{R}, \mathbf{R}^{\rm q}, \mathbf{B})$ is linear, time invariant and controllable. Consider $R(\xi) \in \mathbf{R}^{\rm p \times q}[\xi]$ inducing a kernel representation of* **B** *and $M(\xi) \in \mathbf{R}^{\rm q \times (q-p)}[\xi]$ inducing an observable image representation of* **B**. *Then there exist $Q(\xi) \in \mathbf{R}^{\rm (q-p) \times q}[\xi]$ and $N(\xi) \in \mathbf{R}^{\rm q \times p}[\xi]$ such that*

$$\begin{bmatrix} R(\xi) \\ Q(\xi) \end{bmatrix} [\, N(\xi) \quad M(\xi) \,] = \begin{bmatrix} I & 0 \\ 0 & I \end{bmatrix} \tag{4}$$

Next, the following two lemmas are not only "lemma" but also important results with respect to theoretical points of view.

LEMMA 2.2. *Assume that $\Sigma_p = (\mathbf{R}, \mathbf{R}^{\rm q}, \mathbf{B})$ is controllable. Then $C(\mathrm{d}/\mathrm{d}t)w = 0$ induced by $C(\xi) \in \mathbf{R}^{\rm (q-p) \times q}[\xi]$ is a stabilizing controller for Σ_p if and only if $C(\xi)M(\xi)$ is Hurwitz, where $M(\xi)$ induces an observable image representation of* **B**.

PROOF. Premultiplying a non-singular matrix $P(\xi)$ by a unimodular matrix does not have any influence on the zeros of the determinant of $P(\xi)$. Using this well known fact and (4) yields

$$\det \begin{bmatrix} R(\xi) \\ C(\xi) \end{bmatrix} \det \begin{bmatrix} N(\xi) & M(\xi) \end{bmatrix} = \det \begin{bmatrix} I & 0 \\ C(\xi)N(\xi) & C(\xi)M(\xi) \end{bmatrix} = \det(C(\xi)M(\xi))$$

This completes the proof of the lemma. □

LEMMA 2.3. *Assume that $\Sigma_p = (\mathbf{R}, \mathbf{R}^{\rm q}, \mathbf{B})$ is controllable. Then all of the stabilizing controllers for Σ can be described by*

$$\begin{bmatrix} F\left(\dfrac{\mathrm{d}}{\mathrm{d}t}\right) & B\left(\dfrac{\mathrm{d}}{\mathrm{d}t}\right) \end{bmatrix} \begin{bmatrix} R\left(\dfrac{\mathrm{d}}{\mathrm{d}t}\right) \\ Q\left(\dfrac{\mathrm{d}}{\mathrm{d}t}\right) \end{bmatrix} w = 0 \tag{5}$$

where $B(\xi) \in \mathbf{R}_{\mathbf{H}}^{\rm (q-p) \times (q-p)}[\xi]$ is an arbitrary Hurwitz matrix and $F(\xi) \in \mathbf{R}^{\rm (q-p) \times p}[\mathbf{s}]$ is an arbitrary matrix.

PROOF. Assume that $C(\xi)$ is described by (5). Then, the calculation of $[\, R(\xi)^{\mathrm{T}} \quad C(\xi)^{\mathrm{T}} \,]^{\mathrm{T}}$ yields that the interconnected behavior is autonomous and stable due to the stability of $B(\xi)$. Conversely, let $C(\xi)$ induce a stabilizing controller for the plant. Then, from (4), we can observe that

$$\begin{bmatrix} R(\xi) \\ C(\xi) \end{bmatrix} = \begin{bmatrix} I & 0 \\ C(\xi)N(\xi) & C(\xi)M(\xi) \end{bmatrix} \begin{bmatrix} R(\xi) \\ Q(\xi) \end{bmatrix}$$

Since it follows from Lemma 2.2 that $C(\xi)M(\xi)$ is Hurwitz, defining $B(\xi) := C(\xi)M(\xi)$ and $F(\xi) := C(\xi)N(\xi)$ completes the proof the lemma. □

3. Problem formulation

In this section, we formulate the problem we address in this chapter. At first, for the sake of brevity of the discussion, we impose the following assumptions without loss of generality. Let $\Sigma_i = (\mathbf{T}, \mathbf{R}^{\mathrm{q}}, \mathbf{B}_i)$ $(i = 1, 2)$ denote two plants.

- All of Σ_i are linear, time-invariant, finite-dimensional, and controllable.
- $\rho(\mathbf{B}_i)$ $(i = 1, 2)$ are the same. We denote $\rho(\mathbf{B}_i) = \mathbf{p}$.
- Each of $\mathbf{B}_i$ of Σ_i are represented by kernel representations $R_i(\mathrm{d}/\mathrm{d}t)w = 0$, where $R(\xi) \in \mathbf{R}^{\mathrm{p}\times\mathrm{q}}[\xi]$. Moreover, we assume $R_i(\xi) \in \mathbf{R}_{\mathbf{C}}^{\mathrm{p}\times\mathrm{q}}[\xi]$.
- Let $M_i(\xi)$ denote a polynomial matrix inducing an image representation of Σ_i $(i = 1, 2)$. Moreover, we assume $M_i(\xi) \in \mathbf{R}_{\mathbf{C}}^{\mathrm{q}\times(\mathrm{q}-\mathrm{p})}[\xi]$.

Using the assumptions above, we consider the following problem.

PROBLEM 3.1. Assume that the above conditions hold. Then find a necessary and sufficient condition for the existence of a control law stabilizing Σ_i, i.e., $\Sigma_i \cap \Sigma_c$ are stable $(i = 1, 2)$.

4. Main result

The following theorem is a necessary and sufficient condition for the existence of a stabilizing controller for two given plants.

THEOREM 4.1. *Let $\Sigma_1 = (\mathbf{R}, \mathbf{R}^{\mathrm{q}}, \mathbf{B}_1)$ and $\Sigma_2 = (\mathbf{R}, \mathbf{R}^{\mathrm{q}}, \mathbf{B}_2)$ be two given plants. Assume that they are linear, time-invariant, and controllable. Let $R_i(\xi)$ and $M_i(\xi)$ $(i = 1, 2)$ denote polynomial matrices inducing a kernel representation and an observable image representation, respectively, of each system. Then there exists a simultaneous stabilizing controller for Σ_1 and Σ_2 if and only if there exist polynomial matrices $C_1(\xi) \in \mathbf{R}^{(\mathrm{q}-\mathrm{p})\times\mathrm{p}}[\xi]$ and $C_2(\xi) \in \mathbf{R}_{\mathbf{H}}^{(\mathrm{q}-\mathrm{p})\times(\mathrm{q}-\mathrm{p})}[\xi]$ such that*

$$\begin{bmatrix} C_1\left(\frac{\mathrm{d}}{\mathrm{d}t}\right) & C_2\left(\frac{\mathrm{d}}{\mathrm{d}t}\right) \end{bmatrix} w = 0 \tag{6}$$

is a stabilizing controller for the augmented system described by

$$R_2\left(\frac{\mathrm{d}}{\mathrm{d}t}\right)\begin{bmatrix} N_1\left(\frac{\mathrm{d}}{\mathrm{d}t}\right) & M_1\left(\frac{\mathrm{d}}{\mathrm{d}t}\right) \end{bmatrix} w = 0. \tag{7}$$

PROOF. (If) part: Firstly, it is clear that the augmented system described by (7) is controllable, thus it has an image representation. One of these can be described by

$$\begin{bmatrix} R_1\left(\frac{d}{dt}\right) \\ Q_1\left(\frac{d}{dt}\right) \end{bmatrix} M_2\left(\frac{d}{dt}\right)\ell = w. \tag{8}$$

Clearly, the above is also an observable image representation. Since the behavior of the interconnection of this augmented system and the controller described by

$$\begin{bmatrix} C_1\left(\frac{d}{dt}\right) & C_2\left(\frac{d}{dt}\right) \end{bmatrix} w = 0$$

with a Hurwitz polynomial $C_2(\xi)$ is stable, Lemma 2.2 allows us to observe that

$$\begin{bmatrix} C_1(\xi) & C_2(\xi) \end{bmatrix} \begin{bmatrix} R_1(\xi) \\ Q_1(\xi) \end{bmatrix} M_2(\xi) \tag{9}$$

is also Hurwitz. Now, since

$$\begin{bmatrix} C_1\left(\frac{d}{dt}\right) & C_2\left(\frac{d}{dt}\right) \end{bmatrix} \begin{bmatrix} R_1\left(\frac{d}{dt}\right) \\ Q_1\left(\frac{d}{dt}\right) \end{bmatrix} w = 0 \tag{10}$$

is a controller for the behavior described by an image representation $w = M_2(d/dt)\ell$, i.e., Σ_2, it also follows from Lemma 2.2 that this is also a stabilizing controller for Σ_2. Moreover, $C_2(\xi)$ is Hurwitz, so it follows from Lemma 2.3 that this is also a stabilizing controller for Σ_1. This completes the proof of the (If) part of the theorem.

Conversely, assume that there exists a simultaneous stabilizing controller for Σ_1 and Σ_2. From Lemma 2.3, the stabilizing controller for Σ_1 can be described by

$$\begin{bmatrix} F\left(\frac{d}{dt}\right) & B\left(\frac{d}{dt}\right) \end{bmatrix} \begin{bmatrix} R_1\left(\frac{d}{dt}\right) \\ Q_1\left(\frac{d}{dt}\right) \end{bmatrix} w = 0 \tag{11}$$

for some Hurwitz values of $B(\xi)$ and some polynomial values of $F(\xi)$. The above controller also stabilizes Σ_2, Lemma 2.2 allows us to obtain that

$$\begin{bmatrix} F(\xi) & B(\xi) \end{bmatrix} \begin{bmatrix} R_1(\xi) \\ Q_1(\xi) \end{bmatrix} M_2(\xi) \tag{12}$$

is also Hurwitz. By using Lemma 2.2 again, in this point, we can regard

$$\begin{bmatrix} F\left(\frac{d}{dt}\right) & B\left(\frac{d}{dt}\right) \end{bmatrix} w = 0 \tag{13}$$

as the stabilizing controller for the plant described by

$$w = \begin{bmatrix} R_1\left(\frac{\mathrm{d}}{\mathrm{d}t}\right) \\ Q_1\left(\frac{\mathrm{d}}{\mathrm{d}t}\right) \end{bmatrix} M_2\left(\frac{\mathrm{d}}{\mathrm{d}t}\right)\ell. \tag{14}$$

This is also an observable image representation of the augmented system stated in the theorem. This completes the proof of (Only If) part of the theorem. □

As can clearly be seen, by setting the input/output partition of the variable w, the above theorem says that the solvability of the simultaneous stabilization problem is equivalent to the existence of a stabilizing controller for the augmented systems described by (7). This condition can be formulated using Bezout equations and solutions as follows:

COROLLARY 4.1. *Let $\Sigma = (\mathbf{R}, \mathbf{R}^{\mathrm{q}}, \mathbf{B})$ be a linear, time-invariant, and controllable system. Let $V(\xi)$ and $D(\xi)$ denote left coprime factors such that $R(\xi) := [-D(\xi)V(\xi)]$ inducing a kernel representation of Σ such that $D(\xi)^{-1}V(\xi)$ is proper and $D(\xi)$ is non-singular. Moreover, let $\tilde{X}(\xi)$ and $\tilde{Y}(\xi)$ denote a solution of a Bezout equation of a right coprime factor $\tilde{V}(\xi)$ and $\tilde{D}(\xi)$ consisting in a polynomial $M(\xi) = [\,\tilde{V}(\xi)^{\mathrm{T}} \quad \tilde{D}(\xi)^{\mathrm{T}}\,]^{\mathrm{T}}$ inducing an observable image representation of Σ. Then there exists a stabilizing controller described by $[\,C_1(\mathrm{d}/\mathrm{d}t) \quad C_2(\mathrm{d}/\mathrm{d}t)\,]w = 0$ induced from $C_1(\xi)$ and $C_2(\xi)$ such that $C_2(\xi)$ is Hurwitz if and only if there exist Hurwitz $B(\xi) \in \mathbf{R}_{\mathbf{H}}^{(\mathrm{q-p})\times(\mathrm{q-p})}[\xi]$ and $F(\xi) \in \mathbf{R}^{(\mathrm{q-p})\times \mathrm{q}}[\xi]$ such that $F(\xi)N(\xi) + B(\xi)\tilde{Y}(\xi)$ is Hurwitz.*

5. Example

In this section, we show a simple example of simultaneous stabilization in a behavioral framework. Here, we consider the case of two plants and omit detailed discussion which can be found in [7].

Consider two plants $\Sigma_{Pi} = (\mathbf{R}, \mathbf{R}^2, \mathbf{B}_i)$ with the behaviors $\mathbf{B}_i$ described by minimal kernel representations induced by

$$R_1(\xi) = \begin{bmatrix} -(\xi+1)(\xi-1) & \xi - 2 \end{bmatrix} \tag{15}$$

and

$$R_2(\xi) = \begin{bmatrix} -(\xi+1)(\xi-2) & \xi - 1 \end{bmatrix}, \tag{16}$$

respectively. Define $[\,-d_i(\xi) \quad n_i(\xi)\,] := R_i(\xi)$. These two systems can then be described by the following transfer functions

$$g_1(\xi) = \frac{\xi - 2}{(\xi-1)(\xi+1)}, \qquad g_2(\xi) = \frac{\xi - 1}{(\xi+1)(\xi-2)}. \tag{17}$$

It can be seen that the above two plants satisfy the conditions stated in Theorem 4.1 (The detailed discussion is omitted here). Indeed, we can derive the following simultaneous stabilizer:

$$C(\xi) = \begin{bmatrix} -\frac{3}{4}(\xi+1)^2 & \frac{3}{4}\xi + \frac{1}{2} \end{bmatrix}. \tag{18}$$

while they are not simultaneously stabilizable in standard system theory (see [9]).

Of course, the above controller is described by an improper rational function with respect to input–output points of view, so it corresponds to modifying the structure of systems, among other aspects.

Incidentally, the above two plants are not simultaneously stabilizable in standard system theory (see [9]), because they do not satisfy the well-known p.i.p condition on infinite zeros [12,16], which implies that cancellation occurs on infinite zeros and poles. This means that we cannot use the controller described by improper transfer functions. However, behavioral control system synthesis allows the use of such a controller, so we do not have to take into account the cancellation on infinite zeros and poles. This is also another reason why there exists a simultaneous stabilizer for the above example within the behavioral framework.

6. Concluding remarks

In this chapter, we have addressed the simultaneous stabilization problem within a behavioral framework. We have provided a necessary and sufficient condition for a pair of given plants to be simultaneously stabilizable.

The detailed discussions omitted in this chapter will be found in our forthcoming papers [6,7].

References

[1] V.D. Blondel, Simultaneous Stabilization of Linear Systems, Springer, Berlin (1994).

[2] V.D. Blondel, *Simultaneous stabilization of linear systems and interpolation with rational functions*, Open Problems in Mathematical Systems and Control Theory, V.D. Blondel, E. Sontag, M. Vidyasagar and J.C. Willems, eds, Springer, London (1999), 53–60.

[3] B. Ghosh, *An approach to simultaneous system design, Part 1*, SIAM J. Contr. Optimiz. **24** (1986), 480–496.

[4] B. Ghosh, *An approach to simultaneous system design, Part 2*, SIAM J. Contr. Optimiz. **26** (1988), 919–963.

[5] T. Kailath, *Linear Systems*, Prentice-Hall, Englewood (1980).

[6] O. Kaneko, K. Mori, K. Yoshida and T. Fujii, *The behavioral approach to simultaneous stabilization for pairs of linear systems*, 16th International Symposium on Mathematical Theory of Networks and Systems (MTNS 2004) (2004), CD-ROM.

[7] O. Kaneko, K. Mori, K. Yoshida and T. Fujii, *Synthesis of reliable control systems based on simultaneous stabilization problem in a behavioral framework—a parameterization of the simultaneous stabilizers for simultaneously stabilizable pairs*, Trans. Soc. Instr. Contr. Eng. (2004), (in press).

[8] M. Kuijper, *Why do stabilizing controllers stabilize?*, Automatica **31** (1995), 621–625.

[9] H. Maeda and T. Sugie, *Systems and Control Theory for Advanced Control*, Asakura-Shoten, Tokyo (1990) (in Japanese).

[10] J.W. Polderman and J.C. Willems, Introduction to Mathematical Systems Theory—A Behavioral Approach, Springer, Berlin (1997).
[11] K. Suyama, *Reliable Control*, Measurement and Control **35** (1996), pp. 151–159 (in Japanese).
[12] M. Vidyasagar and N. Viswanadham, *Algebraic design techniques for reliable stabilization*, IEEE Trans. Autom. Contr. **AC-27** (1982), 1085–1095.
[13] M. Vidyasagar, *Control System Synthesis—A Factorization Approach*, The MIT Press, Cambridge, MA (1985).
[14] J.C. Willems, *Paradigms and puzzles in the theory of dynamical systems*, IEEE Trans. Autom. Contr. **AC-36** (1991), 259–294.
[15] J.C. Willems, *On interconnections, control, and feedback*, IEEE Trans. Autom. Contr. **AC-42** (1997), 326–339.
[16] D.C. Youla, J.J. Bongiorno, Jr. and C.N. Lu, *Single-loop feedback-stabilization of linear multivariable dynamical plants*, Automatica **10** (1974), 159–173.

CHAPTER 16

Fault-Tolerant Control Using Time-Sharing Multirate Controllers

Hiroaki Kawahara, Yoshimichi Ito and Noboru Babaguchi

Graduate School of Engineering, Osaka University, 2-1, Yamada-oka, Suita, Osaka 565-0871, Japan

Contents

Abstract

This chapter presents some methods to design fault-tolerant control system using a time-sharing multirate control scheme. In particular, we focus on the following three problems: to design the system possessing M-actuator integrity, to design the system possessing L-sensor integrity, and to design the system possessing one actuator or sensor integrity. The solvability condition is also derived for each case.

SYSTEMS AND HUMAN SCIENCE – FOR SAFETY, SECURITY, AND DEPENDABILITY
Edited by Tatsuo Arai, Shigeru Yamamoto and Kazuhisa Makino

1. Introduction

In designing feedback control systems, the influence of the possible actuator and/or sensor failures must be taken into account, and the system should be designed to be fault-tolerant against such failures. The notion of integrity is introduced from this viewpoint, and is defined as the property that the closed-loop system remains stable in the presence of actuator and/or sensor failures. In this chapter, a feedback control system is said to be "fault-tolerant" if the feedback system possesses the above property.

The integrity of the feedback system has been investigated by many researchers. Concerning the integrity condition, Fujita and Shimemura derive a necessary and sufficient condition for integrity by using U-matrix [1]. Gündes introduces m-actuator integrity and derives a necessary and sufficient condition, where m indicates the maximum number of tolerable failures of actuators [2]. Concerning the design problem, Fujita and Shimemura propose a method to design state feedback controllers which possess integrity against pre-specified actuator failures [3]. Hamada *et al.* present a design method for output feedback controllers which guarantee the l-partial integrity of the feedback system, where l is the maximum number of tolerable failures of actuators and/or sensors, and "partial" implies that only pre-specified actuators and sensors have the possibility to fail [4]. However, the following problem is not fully investigated despite the fundamental importance of the design problem: *under what condition do the controllers exist which make the feedback system fault-tolerant*? This problem would be very difficult if we used a linear time-invariant controller.

On the other hand, it is shown that many problems, which are hard to solve when linear time-invariant controllers are used,[1] can easily be solved by using *time-sharing multirate controllers*. The time-sharing multirate controller uses a multirate hold and multirate sampler acting at separate time intervals. The advantage of this control scheme is that the input matrix as well as the output matrix of the state space realization of the discretized plant can be assigned arbitrarily by appropriate choice of hold and sampling functions. By exploiting this useful property, we show that it is always possible to design a static feedback controller which makes the feedback system fault-tolerant provided that the plant satisfies some reasonable conditions.

This chapter is organized as follows: in Section 2, we first introduce some notations and definitions, together with some useful results for our study. Next, we briefly summarize the time-sharing multirate control scheme, which plays a fundamental role in this chapter. In Section 3, exploiting some useful properties of this control scheme, we consider the problem of designing the feedback system which possesses integrity against possible actuator and/or sensor failures, and show that such a design problem is always possible under reasonable conditions. The chapter concludes in Section 4.

---

[1] For example, strong stabilization, simultaneous stabilization, reliable stabilization, and exact model matching in the discrete-time sense.

2. Preliminary

2.1. *Mathematical preliminary*

In this section, we introduce some notations and definitions, together with useful lemmas for our study.

A square matrix X is referred to as a stability matrix if $\rho(X) < 1$ where $\rho(X)$ stands for the spectral radius of X. The set of stability matrices which belong to $R^{n\times n}$ is denoted by S^n. For $A \in R^{n\times n}$, $Q_i \in R^{n\times n}$ $(i = 1, \ldots, N)$, and $k \in \{0, \ldots, N\}$, the set $\mathcal{F}_k^n(A; Q_1, \ldots, Q_N)$ is defined as follows:

$$\mathcal{F}_k^n(A; Q_1, \ldots, Q_N) := \left\{ A + \sum_{p=1}^{N-k} Q_{i_p} | i_p \in \{1, \ldots, N\}, i_p \neq i_q (p \neq q) \right\}.$$

Furthermore, the set $\mathcal{E}_k^n(A; Q_1, \ldots, Q_N)$ is defined as follows:

$$\mathcal{E}_k^n(A; Q_1, \ldots, Q_N) := \bigcup_{i=0}^{k} \mathcal{F}_i^n(A; Q_1, \ldots, Q_N).$$

For example, $\mathcal{F}_0^n(A; Q_1, \ldots, Q_N)$ has only one element, i.e., $S_0 := A + Q_1 + \cdots + Q_N$. $\mathcal{F}_1^n(A; Q_1, \ldots, Q_N)$ has N elements which are described by the following matrices:

$$\begin{aligned} S_1 &:= A \qquad\qquad +Q_2 \cdots + Q_{N-1} \quad +Q_N, \\ &\vdots \\ S_N &:= A + Q_1 \quad +Q_2 \cdots + Q_{N-1}. \end{aligned}$$

Therefore, $\mathcal{E}_1^n(A; Q_1, \ldots, Q_N) = \{S_0, S_1, \ldots, S_N\}$.

The following three lemmas are quite useful for our study. The first one gives a sufficient condition for the existence of Q_i $(i = 1, \ldots, N)$ satisfying $\mathcal{E}_k^n(A; Q_1, \ldots, Q_N) \subset S^n$.

LEMMA 1. *[6] Suppose $A \in R^{n\times n}$, $N \geq 2$, and $1 \leq k \leq N$. Then, there exist $Q_i \in R^{n\times n}$ $(i = 1, \ldots, N)$ satisfying $\mathcal{E}_k^n(A; Q_1, \ldots, Q_N) \subset S^n$ if the following condition holds:*

$$\rho(A) < \frac{2N - k}{k}.$$

In the case of $k = 1$, we can obtain a necessary and sufficient condition.

LEMMA 2. *[5] Suppose $A \in R^{n\times n}$ and $N \geq 2$. Then, there exist $Q_i \in R^{n\times n}$ $(i = 1, \ldots, N)$ satisfying $\mathcal{E}_1^n(A; Q_1, \ldots, Q_N) \subset S^n$ if and only if the following condition holds:*

$$|\mathrm{trace}(A)| < (2N - 1)n.$$

Lemma 2 can be proved by Lemma 3, which is also useful in this chapter.

LEMMA 3. *[7] Suppose $A \in R^{n \times n}$ and $N \geq 2$. Then, A can be decomposed into the sum of N stability matrices if and only if* $|\text{trace}(A)| < Nn$.

2.2. *Time-sharing multirate controllers*

In this section, we give a brief summary about time-sharing multirate sample-hold controllers.

Let us consider the open-loop system as depicted in Fig. 1. Here, P is a single-input single-output linear time-invariant plant described by

$$\dot{x}(t) = Ax(t) + bu(t), \tag{1}$$

$$y(t) = cx(t). \tag{2}$$

$\mathcal{MH}$, $\mathcal{MS}$ are, respectively, the multirate holds and multirate samplers, and they act according to the following equations:

$$u(t) = f(t - kT)\rho[k], \qquad kT \leq t < (k+1)T, \tag{3}$$

$$\eta[k] = \int_{(k-1)T}^{kT} g(t - (k-1)T)y(t)\mathrm{d}t. \tag{4}$$

Here, T is some basic period for the control, which we call the frame period. In particular, in the following, we consider the hold function $f(t)$ and the sampling function $g(t)$ where

$$f(t) = \begin{cases} f_p, & (p-1)T_{\mathrm{I}} \leq t < pT_{\mathrm{I}}; \quad p = 1, \ldots, N_{\mathrm{I}} \\ 0, & L \leq t < T, \end{cases} \tag{5}$$

$$g(t) = \begin{cases} 0, & 0 < t < L \\ \sum_{q=1}^{N_{\mathrm{O}}} g_q \delta(t - (L + \mathrm{i}T_{\mathrm{O}})), & L \leq t \leq T, \end{cases} \tag{6}$$

which correspond to the multirate hold and multirate sampler, respectively (see Fig. 2).

It should be noted that these equations imply that the manipulation of the plant input and the detection of the plant output work on separate time intervals, i.e., $[kT, kT + L)$ and $[kT + L, (k+1)T]$, respectively. Hence, we call the above control scheme *the time-sharing multirate sample–hold scheme* [5].

As seen from the above equations, on each interval of their operations, the multirate holds change their output N_{I} times and the multirate samplers detect their input N_{O} times.

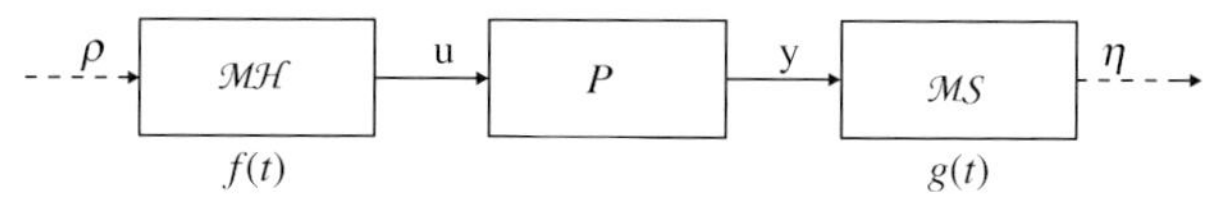

Fig. 1. Control system with time-sharing multirate sample-hold scheme.

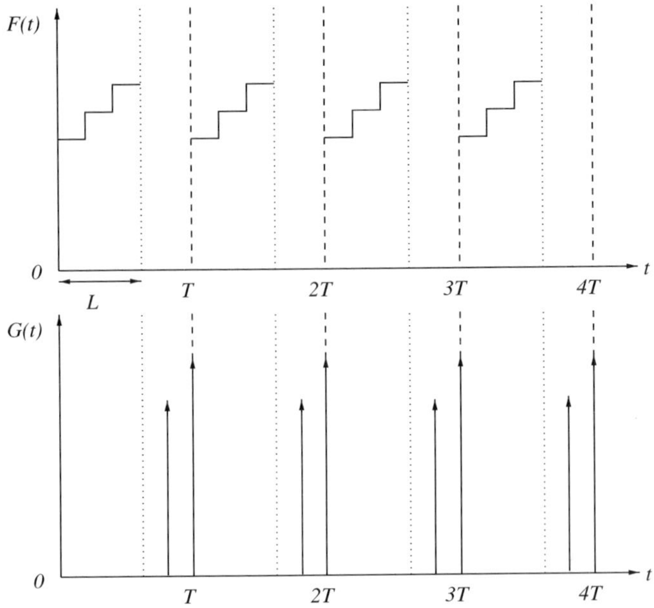

Fig. 2. Time-chart of the time-sharing multirate scheme ($N_{\mathrm{I}} = 3$, $N_{\mathrm{O}} = 2$).

The integers N_{I} and N_{O} are called, respectively, the input multiplicity and the output multiplicity. We assume that the period T_{I} for the multirate hold is given by L/N_{I}, and the period T_{O} for the multirate sampler is given by $(T - L)/N_{\mathrm{O}}$.

In [5], it is shown that the state equation of the discrete-time system with the multirate hold (5) and the multirate sampler (6) satisfying the time-sharing condition is given by

$$\xi[k+1] = \bar{A}\xi[k] + \bar{F}\rho[k], \tag{7}$$

$$\eta[k] = \bar{G}\xi[k], \tag{8}$$

where

$$\bar{A} = \mathrm{e}^{AT}, \qquad \bar{F} = \mathrm{e}^{A(T-L)}[\tilde{A}^{N_{\mathrm{I}}-1}\tilde{b}, \ldots, \tilde{b}] \begin{bmatrix} f_1 \\ \vdots \\ f_{N_{\mathrm{I}}} \end{bmatrix},$$

$$\bar{G} = [g_1, \ldots, g_{N_{\mathrm{O}}}] \begin{bmatrix} c \\ \vdots \\ c\hat{A}^{N_{\mathrm{O}}-1} \end{bmatrix} \mathrm{e}^{-A(T-L-T_{\mathrm{O}})},$$

$$\tilde{A} = \mathrm{e}^{AT_\mathrm{I}}, \qquad \tilde{b} = \int_0^{T_\mathrm{I}} \mathrm{e}^{A\tau} b \, \mathrm{d}\tau, \qquad \hat{A} = \mathrm{e}^{AT_\mathrm{O}}.$$

Here, note that if (A, b, c) is controllable and observable, it follows that the matrices $\bar{F}$ and $\bar{G}$ can be made to coincide with any prescribed matrices by suitably choosing the multirate hold and multirate sampler, provided that the input multiplicity N_I and the output multiplicity N_O are large enough.[2] Note in particular that the number of the columns of $\bar{F}$, as well as the numbers of the row of $\bar{G}$ can also be changed arbitrarily. Hence, the above result is very powerful, since the input and output matrices can be adjusted arbitrarily. We will exploit the above result in the problem of fault-tolerant control against sensor and/or actuator failures.

3. Fault-tolerant control using time-sharing multirate controllers

3.1. *Problem formulation*

The system of our concern is shown in Fig. 3. Here, P is a m-input l-output linear time-invariant plant given by

$$\dot{x}(t) = Ax(t) + Bu(t), \qquad y(t) = Cx(t), \tag{9}$$

where $A \in R^{n\times n}$, $B = [b_1, ..., b_m] \in R^{n\times m}$, $C = [c_1^\mathrm{T}, ..., c_l^\mathrm{T}]^\mathrm{T} \in R^{l\times n}$, and $m \geq 2$, $l \geq 2$. K is a static controller of appropriate dimension given by

$$\rho[k] = K\eta[k]. \tag{10}$$

$\mathcal{MH}$ and $\mathcal{MS}$ are, respectively, multirate holds and multirate samplers in which each element works according to the following equations:

$$u_i'(t) = f_i(t - kT)\rho[k], \;\; kT \leq t < (k+1)T; \;\; i = 1, ..., m, \tag{11}$$

$$\eta[k] = \sum_{j=1}^{l} \int_{(k-1)T}^{kT} g_j(t - (k-1)T) y_j'(t) \mathrm{d}t, \tag{12}$$

where

$$f_i(t) = \begin{cases} f_{ip}, & (p-1)T_\mathrm{I} \leq t < pT_\mathrm{I}; \;\; p = 1, ..., N_\mathrm{I}; \;\; i = 1, ..., m \\ 0, & L \leq t < T, \end{cases} \tag{13}$$

$$g_j(t) = \begin{cases} 0, & 0 < t < L \\ \sum_{q=1}^{N_\mathrm{O}} g_{jq} \delta(t - (L + qT_\mathrm{O})), & L \leq t \leq T; \;\; j = 1, ..., l. \end{cases} \tag{14}$$

---

[2] It is possible if we set $N_\mathrm{I} = N_\mathrm{O} = n$ where n is the state dimension of the plant.

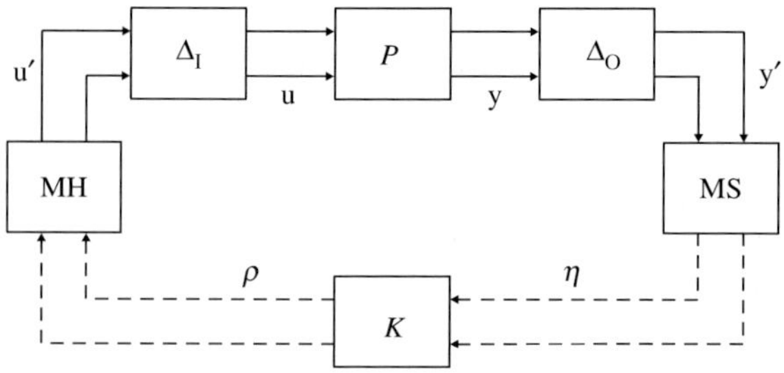

Fig. 3. Feedback system with possible actuator and/or sensor failures.

In Fig. 3, Δ_I and Δ_O represent, respectively, the models of the actuator failures and the sensor failures. They are expressed by the following equations:

$$\Delta_I = \text{block diag}\{\delta_1, \ldots, \delta_m\} \in R^{m \times m}, \tag{15}$$

$$\Delta_O = \text{block diag}\{\delta_{m+1}, \ldots, \delta_{m+l}\} \in R^{l \times l}, \tag{16}$$

where we assume that $\delta_i(\delta_{m+j})$ is 0 when the ith actuator (the jth sensor) fails, otherwise $\delta_i = 1$ ($\delta_{m+j} = 1$).

Next, we introduce some definitions. M-actuator integrity is defined as the property that the closed-loop system remains stable whenever the number of the actuator failures is less than or equal to M provided that no sensor fails. L-sensor integrity is also defined in a similar manner. In addition, we introduce l-sensor/actuator integrity, which is defined as the property that the closed-loop system remains stable even if any one of the actuators or sensors fails.

Here, note that when m-actuator integrity and l-sensor integrity are considered (the case of $M = m$ and $L = l$), there is a possibility that no manipulating input is generated. Therefore, it is required that the plant itself must be stable. In this case, there exists a trivial solution $K = 0$, which satisfies m-actuator integrity and l-sensor integrity. To avoid such a trivial case, we assume that $M < m$ and $L < l$. Here, we also assume the following:

Assumption 1. Each pair (A, b_i) $(i = 1, \ldots, m)$ is controllable and each pair (c_j, A) $(j = 1, \ldots, l)$ is observable.

It should be noted that this assumption is not quite restrictive because of the following reasons: if we were to design a feedback system possessing $(m-1)$-actuator integrity, the stabilizability of each pair (A, b_i) is required. Similarly, if we were to design a feedback system possessing $(l-1)$-sensor integrity, the detectability of each pair (c_j, A) is required. Thus, in those cases, the stabilizability of (A, b_i) and the detectability of (c_j, A) are necessary to make the feedback system fault-tolerant. In order to simplify the matter, we assume that the controllability of (A, b_i) and the observability of (c_j, A) instead of assuming the stabilizability and the detectability for each pair.

Now, we state the problems considered in this chapter.

PROBLEM 1. For given plant P satisfying Assumption 1, find multirate hold $\mathcal{MH}$, multirate sampler $\mathcal{MS}$, and static controller K which make the feedback system fault-tolerant possessing M-actuator integrity.

PROBLEM 2. For given plant P satisfying Assumption 1, find multirate hold $\mathcal{MH}$, multirate sampler $\mathcal{MS}$, and static controller K which make the feedback system fault-tolerant possessing L-sensor integrity.

PROBLEM 3. For given plant P satisfying Assumption 1, find multirate hold $\mathcal{MH}$, multirate sampler $\mathcal{MS}$, and static controller K which make the feedback system fault-tolerant possessing 1-actuator/sensor integrity.

3.2. *Solvability conditions for the problems*

In this section, we derive some solvability conditions for the problems stated in Section 3.1. To this end, we first derive the closed-loop equation of the system shown in Fig. 3.

Using (9), (15), and (16), the realization of $\Delta_{\mathrm{O}} P \Delta_{\mathrm{I}}$ is given by

$$\dot{x}(t) = Ax(t) + [\delta_1 b_1, \ldots, \delta_m b_m] u'(t),$$

$$y'(t) = \begin{bmatrix} \delta_{m+1} c_1 \\ \vdots \\ \delta_{m+l} c_l \end{bmatrix} x(t).$$

Applying the results of Section 2.2 to each element of the above system, we obtain

$$\xi[k+1] = \bar{A}\xi[k] + [\delta_1 I_n, \ldots, \delta_m I_n] \begin{bmatrix} \bar{F}_1 \\ \vdots \\ \bar{F}_m \end{bmatrix} \rho[k],$$

$$\eta[k] = [\bar{G}_1, \ldots, \bar{G}_l] \begin{bmatrix} \delta_{m+1} I_n \\ \vdots \\ \delta_{m+l} I_n \end{bmatrix} \xi[k].$$

Here, note that $\bar{F}_i$ and $\bar{G}_j$ can be arbitrary pre-specified matrices owing to Assumption 1, hence we can assign

$$\begin{bmatrix} \bar{F}_1 \\ \vdots \\ \bar{F}_m \end{bmatrix} = I_{nm}, \qquad [\bar{G}_1, \ldots, \bar{G}_l] = I_{nl} \tag{17}$$

by suitably choosing f_{ip} and g_{jq} in (13) and (14).[3] By this, together with (10), we obtain the closed-loop equation as $\xi[k+1] = A_{\mathrm{cl}} \xi[k]$ where

$$A_{\mathrm{cl}} = \bar{A} + [\delta_1 I_n, \ldots, \delta_m I_n] K \begin{bmatrix} \delta_{m+1} I_n \\ \vdots \\ \delta_{m+l} I_n \end{bmatrix}.$$

Now, partition K into $m \times l$ block matrices as

$$K = \begin{bmatrix} K_{11} & \cdots & K_{1l} \\ \vdots & \ddots & \vdots \\ K_{m1} & \cdots & K_{ml} \end{bmatrix}, \qquad K_{ij} \in R^{n \times n}, \quad i = 1, \ldots, m; \quad j = 1, \ldots, l$$

and introduce Q_i and R_j as follows:

$$Q_i = \sum_{j=1}^{l} K_{ij}, \qquad i = 1, \ldots, m, \tag{18}$$

$$R_j = \sum_{i=1}^{m} K_{ij}, \qquad j = 1, \ldots, 1. \tag{19}$$

Using the above notations, together with the ones introduced in Section 2.1, it is easy to see that Problems 1 and 2 can, respectively, be reformulated as follows:

Problem 1′. For given $\bar{A} \in R^{n \times n}$ and integer M $(1 \leq M < m)$, find Q_i $(i = 1, \ldots, m)$ satisfying the condition $\mathcal{E}_M^n(\bar{A}; Q_1, \ldots, Q_m) \subset S^n$.

---

[3] For this purpose, we chose $N_I = N_O = n$, $f_{ip} \in R^{1 \times nm}$ $(i = 1, \ldots, m;\ p = 1, \ldots, n)$, and $g_{jq} \in R^{nl \times 1}$ $(j = 1, \ldots, l;\ q = 1, \ldots, n)$.

PROBLEM 2′. For given $\bar{A} \in R^{n \times n}$ and integer L $(1 \leq L < l)$, find R_j $(j = 1, \ldots, l)$ satisfying the condition $\mathcal{E}^n_L(\bar{A}; R_1, \ldots, R_l) \subset S^n$.

Hence, we can apply Lemma 1 to obtain the solvability conditions for Problems 1 and 2.

THEOREM 1a. *Under Assumption 1, Problem 1 is solvable if the following condition holds:*

$$\rho(\mathrm{e}^{AT}) < \frac{2m - M}{M}.$$

THEOREM 2a. *Under Assumption 1, Problem 2 is solvable if the following condition holds:*

$$\rho(\mathrm{e}^{AT}) < \frac{2l - L}{L}.$$

For the computation of Q_i and R_j, an LMI-based method proposed in [6] is useful. The matrices K_{ij} can easily be obtained by Q_i and R_j.

When $M = 1$, we can obtain necessary and sufficient condition for the solvability of Problem 1 by applying Lemma 2.

THEOREM 1b. *Under Assumption 1, Problem 1 is solvable if and only if the following condition holds:*

$$|\mathrm{trace}(\mathrm{e}^{AT})| < (2m - 1)n.$$

Similarly, when $L = 1$, we can obtain a necessary and sufficient condition for the solvability of Problem 2.

THEOREM 2b. *Under Assumption 1, Problem 2 is solvable if and only if the following condition holds:*

$$|\mathrm{trace}(\mathrm{e}^{AT})| < (2l - 1)n.$$

For the computation of Q_i and R_j, see [5,7] details of.

From the above theorems, we can conclude that fault-tolerant control against M-actuator failures or L-sensor failures is always possible by choosing the frame period T to be small enough, provided that the time-sharing multirate scheme is used and the conditions of Assumption 1 are met.

Next, we consider Problem 3 which concerns the design of the feedback system possessing integrity against one actuator or sensor failure. This problem can be reformulated as follows:

PROBLEM 3'. For given $\bar{A} \in R^{n\times n}$, find Q_i $(i = 1, \ldots, m)$ and R_j $(j = 1, \ldots, l)$ satisfying the following conditions:

$$\mathcal{E}_1^n(\bar{A}; Q_1, \ldots, Q_m) \subset S^n, \tag{20}$$

$$\mathcal{E}_1^n(\bar{A}; R_1, \ldots, R_l) \subset S^n, \tag{21}$$

$$\sum_{i=1}^{m} Q_i = \sum_{j=1}^{l} R_j. \tag{22}$$

If we can find Q_i $(i = 1, \ldots, m)$ and R_j $(j = 1, \ldots, l)$ satisfying the above conditions, we can obtain K_{ij} satisfying (18) and (19). One of the easiest ways to obtain K_{ij} is as follows:

$$\begin{bmatrix} K_{11} & \cdots & K_{1l} \\ \vdots & \ddots & \vdots \\ K_{m1} & \cdots & K_{ml} \end{bmatrix} = \begin{bmatrix} S & R_2 & \cdots & R_l \\ Q_2 & 0 & \cdots & 0 \\ \vdots & \vdots & \ddots & \vdots \\ Q_m & 0 & \cdots & 0 \end{bmatrix}$$

where

$$S = Q_1 - \sum_{j=2}^{l} R_j = R_1 - \sum_{i=2}^{m} Q_i.$$

The solvability condition for Problem 3 is given by Theorem 3.

THEOREM 3. *Problem 3 is solvable if and only if the following condition holds:*

$$|\mathrm{trace}(\mathrm{e}^{AT})| < \min\{(2m-1)n, (2l-1)n\}. \tag{23}$$

PROOF. From Lemma 2, it is easy to see that condition (23) is necessary. In the following, we show that condition (23) is also sufficient. Here, we assume that $m \le l$. The case of $l \le m$ can be proved in a similar way.

When $m \le l$, condition (23) becomes $|\mathrm{trace}(\mathrm{e}^{AT})| < (2m-1)n$. Therefore, from Lemma 2, there exists Q_i $(i = 1, \ldots, m)$ satisfying $\mathcal{E}_1^n(\mathrm{e}^{AT}; Q_1, \ldots, Q_m) \subset S^n$. Now, fix Q_is and let S_i $(i = 0, \ldots, m)$ and S_{m+j} $(j = 1, \ldots, l)$ be as follows:

$$S_0 := \mathrm{e}^{AT} + \sum_{i=1}^{m} Q_i = \mathrm{e}^{AT} + \sum_{j=1}^{m} R_j, \tag{24}$$

$$S_i := S_0 - Q_i, \qquad i = 1, \ldots, m, \tag{25}$$

$$S_{m+j} := S_0 - R_j, \qquad j = 1, \ldots, l, \tag{26}$$

where S_i represents the transition matrix for the case that only the ith actuator fails, and S_{m+j} represents the case that only the jth sensor fails.
From (22) and (24)–(26), we obtain

$$S_{m+1} + \cdots + S_{m+l} = S_1 + \cdots + S_m + (l - m)S_0.$$

Since S_i $(i = 1, \dots m)$ are stability matrices, $|\text{trace}(S_i)| < n (i = 1, \dots, m)$. Therefore, $|\text{trace}(S_1 + \cdots + S_m + (l - m)S_0)| < ln$. By this, together with Lemma 3, we can decompose the matrix $S_1 + \cdots + S_m + (l - m)S_0$ into the sum of l stability matrices S_{m+j} $(j = 1, \dots, l)$. Thus, from (26), we can obtain R_j $(j = 1, \dots, l)$. This completes the proof. □

For details of the computation of Q_i and S_{m+j}, see [5] and [7].

4. Conclusion

In this chapter, we consider three types of fault-tolerant control problems of feedback systems under the condition that the time-sharing multirate sample–hold scheme is used, and derive their solvability conditions. These conditions are satisfied by suitably choosing the frame period T, and hence, it is always possible to design a fault-tolerant system possessing integrity. Generalization of Theorem 3 to the case of M-actuator–L-sensor integrity would be an interesting problem as a future study.

References

[1] M. Fujita and E. Shimemura, *Integrity conditions for linear multivariable feedback systems based on U-matrices*, J. SICE **23** (4) (1987), 379–385 (in Japanese).

[2] A. Nazli Gündes, *Stability of feedback systems with sensor or actuator failures*, Anal. Int. J. Control **56** (4) (1992), 735–753.

[3] M. Fujita and E. Shimemura, *A design method of a linear state feedback system possessing integrity against the specified actuator failure*, J. SICE **22** (1) (1986), 23–29 (in Japanese).

[4] Y. Hamada, S. Shin and N. Sebe, *A design method for fault-tolerant multivariable control systems*, J. SICE **34** (9) (1998), 1184–1190 (in Japanese).

[5] Y. Ito, T. Hagiwara, H. Maeda and M. Araki, *Time-sharing multirate sample-hold controllers and their application to reliable stabilization*, Dyn. Continuous, Discrete Impulsive Syst. Ser. B: Appl. Algorithms **8** (2001), 445–463.

[6] T. Ueno, *LMI-based method for reliable stabilization using time-sharing sample-hold controllers*, (in Japanese) Bachelor Thesis, Osaka University (1999).

[7] Y. Ito, S. Hattori and H. Maeda, *On the decomposition of a matrix into the sum of stable matrices*, Linear Algebra Appl. **297** (1999), 177–182.

CHAPTER 17

Fault Diagnosis for Robust Servo Systems

K. Suzuki, A. Murakami, K. Matsumoto and T. Fujii

Graduate School of Engineering Science, Osaka University, Toyonaka, Osaka 560-8531, Japan

Contents

Abstract

In this chapter, we propose two fault diagnosis methods for robust servo systems in the case of bias faults. First, we consider the case where only input bias faults occur, and show that the difference between the plant input and the model input possesses required functions as a residual generator for a stable plant. Second, we construct a fault diagnosis system in a general framework, where the residual generator is composed so as to respond to faults alone. The residual is evaluated by the estimation error of faults. The evaluation time is reduced by using data fitting. Numerical examples demonstrate the efficiency of our method.

SYSTEMS AND HUMAN SCIENCE – FOR SAFETY, SECURITY, AND DEPENDABILITY
Edited by Tatsuo Arai, Shigeru Yamamoto and Kazuhisa Makino

1. Introduction

The fault detection and isolation (FDI) problem has been widely studied since the 1980s, and many methods have been proposed from several viewpoints [1–5].

These approaches to the FDI problem are mainly separated into three types based on system identification, control design, and signal processing. In the system identification based approach, faults are taken as some model changes. This approach is very intuitive and reasonable on the one hand; on the other hand, it imposes many severe restrictions on online operations in terms of computational costs and the ability to diagnose faults. In the control design based approach, faults are considered as additive signals, and the aim is to extract the features of faults by appropriate control design. This approach is very practical in terms of computational costs, but tends to make the structure of the resulting fault diagnosis system more complex. In addition, it requires a long time to detect and isolate faults in the particular case where the response of the fault diagnosis system is slow. In the signal processing based approach, faults are similarly taken as additive signals. This approach is used mainly in process control systems, and is powerful to detect changes alone, but the fault occurrence positions are difficult to decide, and the running cost is huge.

In this chapter, we focus on a fault diagnosis system for robust servo systems which are widely used in practical situations. Existing diagnosis methods proposed in the above frameworks have such generality that include those methods applicable to robust servo systems considered here. Since different systems have their own features, the diagnosis system should be designed according to their features. Furthermore, if there are two methods with the same or almost the same performances, one with general and yet complex structures, and the other with less general and yet very easy structures, then it is reasonable from the practical viewpoint to choose the latter.

Juričić and Žele [6] took faults as some signals due to modeling uncertainty; the judgment whether faults occur or not is carried out based on the stochastic properties of the estimation error. This is a different framework from the system identification, but the applicability conditions are the same as those for the identification based methods. This means that the working plant is required to be shutdown temporarily when the method is applied. Xu and Kwan [7] first design a residual generator that reacts to fault signals alone, and then design a residual evaluator that maximizes the sensitivity of sensor faults by using a max–min design method. This method works online and is applicable to a real plant (water tank system). Our proposed method is slightly similar to this method in the framework,[1] but quite different in the design method of the residual generator and the evaluation method.

From the above viewpoints, first we consider faults as additive signals, and construct an online fault diagnosis system by utilizing the features of robust servo system in the case where only actuator faults exist. We then extend the diagnosis system to the case where both sensor faults and actuator faults exist. There we utilize the merits of design based approaches and signal processing based approaches in order to possibly simplify the diagnosis system structure.

[1] By the framework we mean that first, residual signals are generated based on input/output data, and then the signals are evaluated.

2. Preliminary

In this section, we introduce several definitions regarding faults. For discussion of fault diagnosis, the distinction between different levels of faults must be clarified, because the word is very ambiguous.

DEFINITION 1. *Event:* An internal or external occurrence involving equipment performance or human action that causes a system upset.
Fault: A change in the characteristics of a parameter component such that its mode of operation or performance is changed in an undesired way. Required specifications are no longer fulfilled.
Failure: The inability of a system or a subsystem to accomplish its required function.
The task of fault diagnosis is to first detect *event* occurrences before developing *faults*, and then give some information on the faults. The main purpose of this chapter is to construct such a fault diagnosis system for robust servo systems that performs the above tasks.

3. Problem formulation

In this section, we state the fault diagnosis problem for robust servo systems. The robust servo system considered here is a closed loop system with process noise and reference r_{ref} as in Fig. 1. Here, K is a controller and the plant P is described by

$$\begin{aligned} \dot{x}(t) &= Ax(t) + B(u(t) + f_u(t)) \\ y(t) &= Cx(t) + f_y(t) + w(t) \end{aligned} \tag{1}$$

where $x(t) \in \mathcal{R}^n$ is the state vector, $y(t) \in \mathcal{R}^p$ is the output vector, $u(t) \in \mathcal{R}^m$ is the input vector, $w(t) \in \mathcal{R}^p$ is the output disturbance, and $f_u(t) \in \mathcal{R}^m, f_y(t) \in \mathcal{R}^p$ are the input fault vector and the output fault vector of bias type, respectively. These are simulated by step signals. Here, we call the additive signals fault signals because the (event) signals may cause the fault and it is more intuitive. In addition, we assume the following:

- $f_u(t)$ and $f_y(t)$ do not occur simultaneously
- controllability and observability of the system both hold
- the system (A, B, C) is stable.

The problem is how to detect and isolate any fault occurrence of the robust servo system under the above conditions.

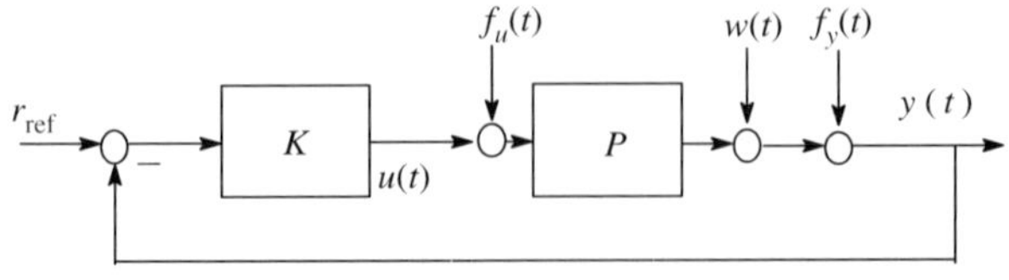

Fig. 1. Robust servo system with faults.

4. Fault diagnosis method

Fault diagnosis methods should be useful and efficient. Generality is important for any systems, but each system has specific properties. To utilize these specific properties for fault diagnosis, it is required to consider a specialized case and construct the corresponding fault diagnosis system. In the general framework of the approach to FDI problem, the procedure is first to design a residual generator such that it reacts only when faults occur, and then to construct an evaluator of the result. However, the procedure or the constructed system is general, and some redundancy exists. So we construct two fault diagnosis systems of robust servo systems in the following specific cases. We first consider the case where actuator faults alone exist. In this case, a more simple system can be constructed by using the properties of a robust servo system rather than using those general procedures. Second, when actuator and sensor faults exist, we develop the diagnosis system according to the general procedures since the properties of a robust servo system cannot be exploited to construct a fault diagnosis system. Nevertheless, our residual generator is constructed very simply and the succeeding evaluation can be performed in a short time by using data fitting.

4.1. *Method I—in the case where faults occur only at actuators*

We consider the case where $w(t) = 0$ and faults occur only at actuators, i.e., $f_y(t) = 0$. The plant model of the system (1) is described by

$$\begin{aligned} \dot{x}_m(t) &= Ax_m(t) + Bu_m(t) \\ y_m(t) &= Cx_m(t) \end{aligned} \tag{2}$$

where $x_m(t)$, $y_m(t)$, $u_m(t)$ are the state, the output, and the input vectors with suitable dimensions, respectively. Here, we define the error of the state vector as $x_f(t) = x(t) - x_m(t)$. Then we have

$$\begin{aligned} \dot{x}_f(t) &= Ax_f(t) + B(u(t) - u_m(t) + f_u(t)) \\ e(t) &= Cx_f(t) \end{aligned} \tag{3}$$

where $e(t) = y_m(t) - y(t)$ denotes *the output error*. Now, the signal we want is the detected value of the fault $f_u(t)$. Then, the detection problem of the fault $f_u(t)$ can be reduced to the well-known input observability problem [11] by noting the form of the above system as well as the availability of the signals $e(t)$, $u(t)$, and $u_m(t)$. Since it is proved in [11] that the detectability condition is fulfilled when the controllability and observability of the system hold, the detectability is guaranteed under this case. Furthermore, actuator faults can be detected in the following way.

4.1.1. *Design the fault detector.* Since the system in Fig. 1 considered here is a robust servo system, the error signal $e(t)$ in (3) becomes zero in steady state after enough time passes. In addition, if $e(t) = 0$, we have $x_f(t) = x(t) - x_m(t) = 0$, which implies $\dot{x}_f(t) = 0$ in (3), and thus $B(u(t) - u_m(t) + f_u(t)) = 0$. Therefore, we have the following relation in steady state:

$$f_u(t) = -u(t) + u_m(t). \tag{4}$$

Here we note that although the detector is very simple, it performs the required functions properly, i.e., (1) determination of the fault occurrence part and time, and the fault magnitude. However, the detected results based on the transient response are not precise because the results obtained do not reach steady-state values, and therefore this detector has a potential of enhancing the performance more. In this sense the proposed detector is one of the residual generators in the FDI problem. Thus, the required procedure is as follows:

Procedure 1

Step 1 Construct the error system (3).

Step 2 Design the fault detector (4).

4.2. *Method II—in the case where actuator and sensor faults exist*

The above fault diagnosis method is not useful when sensor faults exist because the structure changes. Therefore, another algorithm for the fault diagnosis is required in the case where both actuator and sensor faults exist. Simani *et al.* [8] proposed a fault diagnosis form in their article,[2] and its form consists of residual generation and evaluation as shown in Fig. 2. Here "residual" means the deviation between the measurements and the estimates.

A residual generator is required to have the following properties:

$$\begin{aligned} &(i)\ r(t) \le \beta \quad \text{if } f(t) = 0 \\ &(ii)\ r(t) > \beta \quad \text{if } f(t) \ne 0 \end{aligned} \tag{5}$$

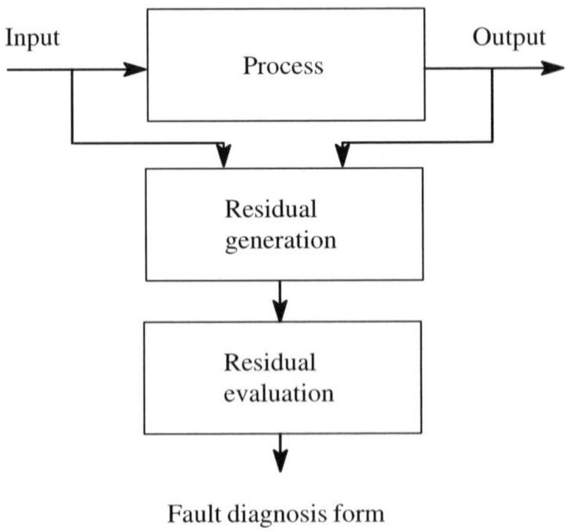

Fig. 2. Fault diagnosis form.

[2] Many other researchers have proposed and used this form, so we call this form as the general framework.

where $r(t) \in \mathcal{R}^p$ is a residual vector and β is a suitable threshold. These properties demand of the residual generator that its detected value is zero when a fault signal $f(t)$ exists, and non-zero otherwise. The main problem of fault diagnosis is how to design a generator with such properties and evaluate the residual.

In this framework, we discuss in Sections 4.2.1 and 4.2.2 how to construct the residual generator and evaluate the residual.

4.2.1. *Residual generation*

We denote how to design the residual generator $V_{ry}(s)$, $V_{ru}(s)$ in Fig. 3 based on the above discussions. Let us recall the plant (1) and denote $H(s) = C(sI - A)^{-1}B$. Then the residual $r(t)$ can be obtained as follows:

$$\begin{aligned} r(t) &= V_{ry}(s)(y(t) + f_y(t) + w(t)) + V_{ru}(s)u(t) \\ &= V_{ry}(s)(H(s)u(t) + H(s)f_u(t) + f_y(t) + w(t)) + V_{ru}(s)u(t) \\ &= (V_{ry}(s)H(s) + V_{ru}(s))u(t) + V_{ry}(s)(H(s)f_u(t) + f_y(t) + w(t)). \end{aligned} \tag{6}$$

Now we select I and $-H(s)$ as $V_{ry}(s)$ and $V_{ru}(s)$, respectively, in order that the generator has the properties (5), then we have

$$r(t) = V_{ry}(s)(H(s)f_u(t) + f_y(t) + w(t)) = H(s)f_u(t) + f_y(t) + w(t). \tag{7}$$

Thus, the residual depends on the fault signals alone. This is confirmed by calculation of the transfer functions from the reference r_{ref}, the actuator fault $f_u(t)$, the sensor fault $f_y(t)$, and the output disturbance $w(t)$ to the residual $r(t)$ (see Appendix).

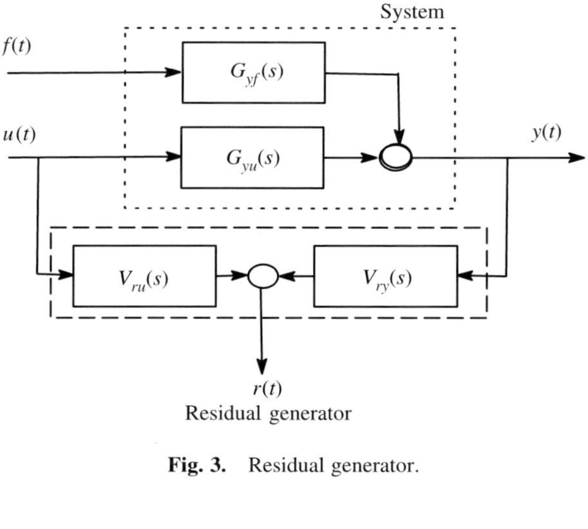

Fig. 3. Residual generator.

4.2.2. *Residual evaluation*

The residual $r(t)$ obtained in (7) is affected by actuator faults $f_u(t)$ and sensor faults $f_y(t)$. However, the effects of the actuator faults are observed as step responses of $H(s)$, and those of the sensor faults are observed as direct step signals, since we assume the faults are step signals in Section 3. The unit step responses are available because the nominal plant model $H(s)$ is known and stable. Comparing the step responses with residual signals gives us the information on the faults, i.e., fault occurrence times, positions, and magnitudes. Here we use a fitting based on the least square of the error of the residual.

First, the unit step responses of faults are obtained by using the nominal plant model $H(s)$, and we denote the sequences $rd(t)$ as follows:

$$rd(t) = (rd(1), rd(2), \ldots,)^{\mathrm{T}}. \tag{8}$$

Let the number of data used in the fitting be N. Assuming that the present time is k, the responses used in the fitting $rd_k(t)$ are a part of $rd(t)$ denoted by

$$rd_k(t) = (rd(k - N + 1), rd(k - N + 2), \ldots, rd(k))^{\mathrm{T}} \tag{9}$$

where the sequence $rd_k(t)$ is shifted recursively. Denote the sequences of a part of the residual $r(t)$ as $rs_k(t)$ in a similar way, where $rs_k(t)$ are a certain real number θ times of $rd_k(t)$ when $f_u(t)$ or $f_y(t)$ occurs. Here, we define the sum of square of the residual error in order to evaluate the existence of faults as follows:

$$e = (rs_k(t) - \theta rd_k(t))^{\mathrm{T}}(rs_k(t) - \theta rd_k(t)). \tag{10}$$

The value of e approaches to zero if the fitting works well. (10) is a convex downward quadratic function, so e becomes minimum when $(\mathrm{d}e/\mathrm{d}\theta) = 0$ holds. Then the optimal value of θ (denote θ^*) becomes as follows:

$$\theta^* = \frac{rs_k(t)^{\mathrm{T}} rs_k(t)}{rd_k(t)^{\mathrm{T}} rd_k(t)}. \tag{11}$$

Thus, the above operations make it possible to reduce the time period between the fault occurrences and evaluation of the detected faults.

Procedure 2

Step 1 Prepare all unit step responses of faults.
Step 2 Replace the sequences $rs_k(t)$ with new N pieces residual data.
Step 3 Calculate the values of e for all cases.
Step 4 Seek the minimum of the results obtained in Step 3, and decide the fault occurrence time, the magnitude, and the position.
Step 5 Repeat Steps 2–4.

5. Numerical examples

In this section, we show the simulations for the case where the fault diagnosis system designed above is applied to an Inverse Linear Quadratic (ILQ) servo system designed by the ILQ design method [9,10]. The bias faults $f_u(t)$ and $f_y(t)$ due to the actuator and sensor faults are simulated by step signals. Following the procedures given in the previous section we construct the fault diagnosis systems.

First, in Case 1, we construct a fault diagnosis system based on Procedure 1. In this case, the system is a fault detector rather than a diagnosis system because no designs are required. So construct the fault detector (4).

Second, in Case 2, we construct a fault diagnosis system following Procedure 2. The plant model (2) used here is given as follows:

$$A = \begin{pmatrix} -2 & 0 & 1 \\ 2 & -3 & 0 \\ 1 & 0 & -4 \end{pmatrix}, \quad B = \begin{pmatrix} 1 & -1 \\ 1 & 3 \\ 0 & 1 \end{pmatrix}, \quad C = \begin{pmatrix} 2 & 4 & 0 \\ 1 & -1 & 2 \end{pmatrix}.$$

The robust servo controller is designed for unit step reference signals.

Figures 4–10 show the time responses of the four kinds of signals in the two cases where the faults occur in different times.

Figs. 4 and 8 are the output responses, Figs. 5 and 7 are the control input responses, Figs. 6 and 9 are the residual signals, and Fig. 10 is the evaluated result in Case 2. Simulations setting is shown in Table 1, where sensor and actuator mean the names of the sensor and the actuator in which simulated faults occur, magnitude means the magnitude of the fault, and time means the fault occurrence time, respectively. In addition, "–" means that no faults occur in the part.

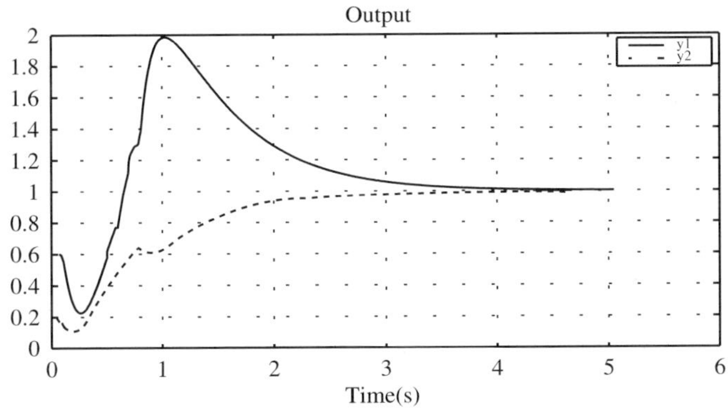

Fig. 4. Output in Case 1.

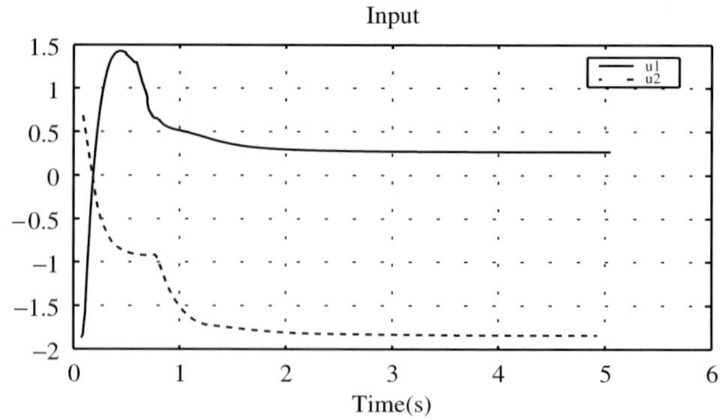

Fig. 5. Control input in Case 1.

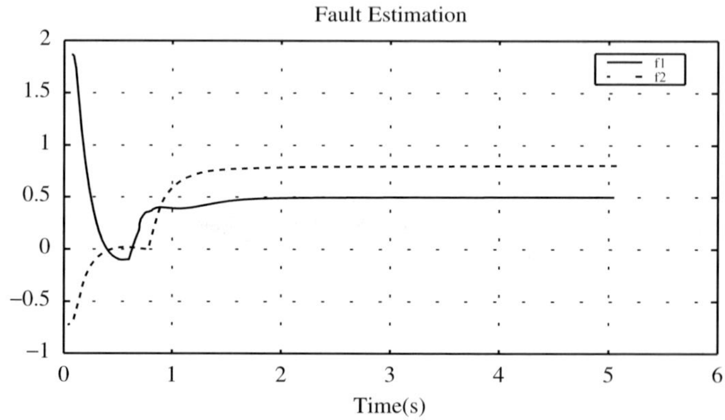

Fig. 6. Fault detection result in Case 1.

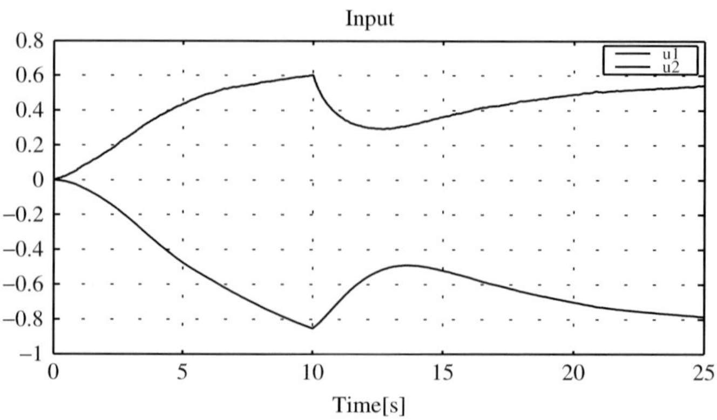

Fig. 7. Control input in Case 2.

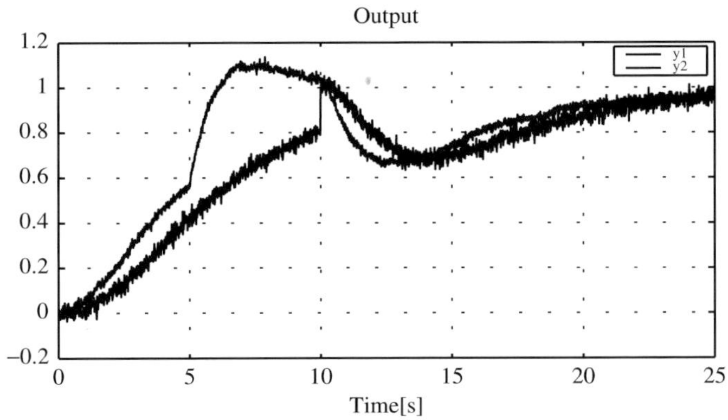

Fig. 8. Output in Case 2.

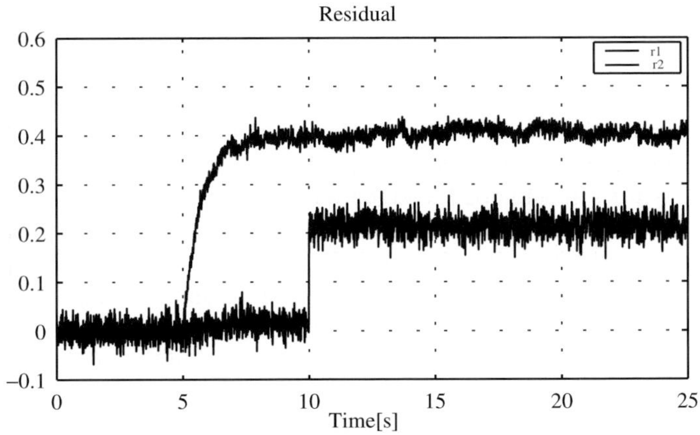

Fig. 9. Residual signal in Case 2.

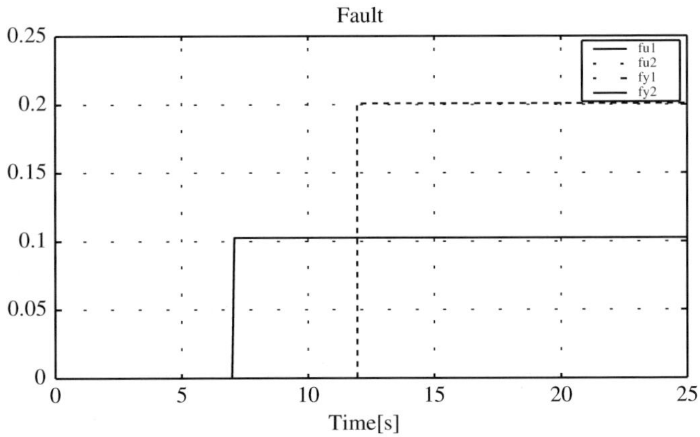

Fig. 10. Evaluated result in Case 2.

Table 1. Simulation setting

Case	Sensor	Actuator	Magnitude	Time (s)
1	–	1	0.8	0.7
	–	2	0.5	0.5
2	1	–	0.1	5
	–	2	0.2	10

The results for Case 1, in which the fault occurs only at actuators, are shown in Figs. 4–6; those for Case 2, in which the fault occurs both at an actuator and a sensor, are shown in Figs. 7–10.

In Case 1, the two actuator faults are added. One has the magnitude of 0.8 in 0.7 s at actuator 1, the other has the magnitude of 0.5 in 0.5 s at actuator 2. Observing the output response in Fig. 4 and the control input response in Fig. 5 does not necessarily provide all the fault information, but the detector detects the occurrence time, the position, and the magnitude with a good performance as in Fig. 6.

If both actuator and sensor faults occur, however, the detector cannot work normally because the structure changes. Then we construct the diagnosis system for Case 2.

In Case 2, one actuator fault and one sensor are added. The actuator fault has the magnitude of 0.1 in 5 s at actuator 1, and the sensor fault has the magnitude of 0.5 in 0.5 s at sensor 2. Observing the output response in Fig. 8 as well as the control input response in Fig. 7 does not provide information about faults, but the residual signal as shown in Fig. 9 provides effective information. One step response at 5 s and one direct step signal at 10 s are presented obviously. The evaluated result based on the residual as shown in Fig. 10 provides the fault occurrence positions and the magnitudes perfectly, although the occurrence time is not correct. It is because the comparison in Case 2 requires N data, so the evaluated results are delayed. However, it is not important because the residual indicates the correct occurrence time.

6. Conclusion

In this chapter, we have proposed two fault diagnosis methods for robust servo systems in the case of bias faults. First, in the case when faults occur only at the input, we derived simple conditions for fault detectability and proposed a simple design method for the fault diagnosis system which is based on the difference between the plant input and the model input. Second, in the case when faults occur both at the input and the output, we designed a residual generator and evaluator according to general fault diagnosis framework. The residual generator was designed such that it has sufficient functions, and yet its structure is simple. The evaluation is derived based on the sum of the square of the estimate error. The procedure made it possible to reduce the time period between the fault occurrences and evaluation of the detected faults. Last, the efficiency of our methods was confirmed by a numerical example.

Appendix A. Derivation of (7)

Assume that the robust servo system has the state feedback structure, and denote the reference, the actuator fault, the sensor fault, the output disturbance, and the residual as $r_{\text{ref}}, f_u(t), f_y(t)$, $w(t)$, and $r(t)$, respectively. The system we consider here is shown in Fig. 1 with an observer. It is assumed that the plant, the observer, and the integrator are stated as follows:

Plant:

$$\dot{x} = Ax + Bu$$

$$y_p = Cx, \qquad y = y_p + f_y + w.$$

Observer:

$$\dot{\hat{x}} = (A - LC)\hat{x} + Bu_p + Ly = (A - LC + BK_{\text{F}})\hat{x} + LCx + L(f_y + w) + BK_{\text{C}}x_c,$$

L: observer gain.

Integrator:

$$\dot{x}_c = r_{\text{ref}} - y = r_{\text{ref}} - (y_p + f_y + w) = r_{\text{ref}} - (Cx + f_y + w).$$

Here K_{C}, K_{F} are the integration gain and the feedback gain, respectively. The control input with the actuator fault u and the calculated input u_p are given as follows:

$$u = K_{\text{C}}x_c + K_{\text{F}}\hat{x} + f_u$$

$$u_p = K_{\text{C}}x_c + K_{\text{F}}\hat{x}.$$

Substituting V_{ry}, V_{ru} by I, $-H$, respectively, and denoting the state and the output vector of V_{ru} as x_r, y_r, respectively, yields:

$$y_r = -Cx_r$$

$$\dot{x}_r = Ax_r + Bu_p = Ax_r + B(K_{\text{C}}x_c + K_{\text{F}}\hat{x}).$$

The residual r is

$$r = y_r + y = Cx + f_y + w - Cx_r.$$

Considering the above descriptions and denoting $\tilde{x} = [x^{\mathrm{T}}, \hat{x}^{\mathrm{T}}, x_c^{\mathrm{T}}, x_r^{\mathrm{T}}]^{\mathrm{T}}$ yields the following system with the inputs $r_{\mathrm{ref}}, f_u, f_y$, w and the output r:

$$\dot{\tilde{x}} = \begin{bmatrix} A & BK_{\mathrm{F}} & BK_{\mathrm{C}} & 0 \\ LC & A - LC + BK_{\mathrm{F}} & BK_{\mathrm{C}} & 0 \\ -C & 0 & 0 & 0 \\ 0 & BK_{\mathrm{F}} & BK_{\mathrm{C}} & A \end{bmatrix} \tilde{x} + \begin{bmatrix} B \\ 0 \\ 0 \\ 0 \end{bmatrix} f_u + \begin{bmatrix} 0 \\ L \\ -I \\ 0 \end{bmatrix} f_y$$

$$+ \begin{bmatrix} 0 \\ L \\ -I \\ 0 \end{bmatrix} w + \begin{bmatrix} 0 \\ 0 \\ I \\ 0 \end{bmatrix} r_{\mathrm{ref}}, \tag{A1}$$

$$r = \begin{bmatrix} C & 0 & 0 & -C \end{bmatrix} \tilde{x} + f_y + w.$$

From (A1), the transfer functions $G_{rw} = G_{rf_y}$, G_{rf_u}, $G_{rr_{\mathrm{ref}}}$ are obtained as follows:

$$G_{rw} = \left[\begin{array}{c|c} A & 0 \\ \hline -C & I \end{array} \right] = I \tag{A2}$$

$$G_{rf_u} = \left[\begin{array}{c|c} A & -B \\ \hline -C & 0 \end{array} \right] = -H \tag{A3}$$

$$G_{rr_{\mathrm{ref}}} = \left[\begin{array}{c|c} A & 0 \\ \hline -C & 0 \end{array} \right] = 0. \tag{A4}$$

From (A2–A4), (7) is derived.

References

[1] A. Willsky, *A survey of design methods for failure detection in dynamic systems*, Automatica **12** (6) (1976), 601–611.

[2] R. Isermann, *Process fault detection based on modeling and estimation methods—a survey*, Automatica **20** (4) (1984), 387–404.

[3] T. Brinsmead, J. Gibson, G. Goodwin, G. Lee and D. Mingori, *Fault Detection—a Quadratic Optimization Approach*, Proceedings of Thirty Sixth Conference on Decision and Control, (1997), CD-ROM.

[4] D. Henry, A. Zolghadri, M. Monsion and S. Ygorra, *Off-line robust fault diagnosis using the generalized singular value*, Automatica **38** (8) (2002), 1347–1358.

[5] R. Patton, P. Frank and R. Clark, *Issues of Fault Diagnosis for Dynamic Systems*, Springer, Berlin (2000).

[6] D. Juričić and M. Žele, *Robust detection of sensor faults by means of a statistical test*, Automatica **38** (4) (2002), 737–742.

[7] R. Xu and C. Kwan, *Robust isolation of sensor failures*, Asian J. Control **5** (1) (2003), 12–23.

[8] S. Simani, C. Fantuzzi and R.J. Patton, *Model-Based Fault Diagnosis in Dynamic Systems Using Identification Techniques*, Springer, Berlin (2002).

[9] T. Fujii, *A new approach to LQ design from the viewpoint of the inverse regulator problem*, IEEE Trans. AC **32** (11) (1987), 995–1004.

[10] T. Fujii and N. Mizushima, *A new approach to LQ design: application to the design of optimal servo systems*, Trans. Soc. Instrum. Control Eng. **E-1-1** (2001), 43–50, http://srv01.sice.or.jp/~e-trans/.

[11] M. Hou and R.J. Patton, *Input observability and input reconstruction*, Automatica **34** (6) (1998), 789–794.

PART IV

Detection and Neutralization Technologies for Landmines and Other Abandoned Weapons

CHAPTER 18

A Small Reaction Manipulator for Maneuvering a GPR Sensing Head

H. Yabushita, Y. Hirata and K. Kosuge

Tohoku University, Aoba-yama 01 Aoba-ku, Sendai 980-8579, Japan

Contents

Abstract

In this chapter, we propose a small reaction manipulator for detecting anti-personnel mines. The small reaction manipulator realizes rapid and precise motion control, which are useful for improvement of sensor head maneuver ability. In particular, ground penetrating radar (GPR) requires precise position control to obtain underground information.

In order to realize precise and rapid motion control of a sensor head, it is necessary to restrict oscillations caused by end-effector motion. Such mechanical oscillations are produced by fluctuations of kinetic momentum. In order to reduce oscillations it is necessary to keep kinetic momentum constant. For this purpose we used counter weights mounted on a small reaction manipulator. By controlling the counter weights, the small reaction manipulator could precisely position the GPR at high-speed without oscillation.

This chapter presents some experimental results from the evaluation of the proposed manipulator.

SYSTEMS AND HUMAN SCIENCE – FOR SAFETY, SECURITY, AND DEPENDABILITY
Edited by Tatsuo Arai, Shigeru Yamamoto and Kazuhisa Makino

1. Introduction

In more than 70 countries, about 120 million anti-personnel mines have been buried. These mines injure 2000 people each month. Most of the injured people are civilians; especially 20% of them are children who are under 15 years old. Anti-personnel mines have been buried not only in battlefields but also in such areas as residential areas, community roads and gardens. Many deminers are working to remove mines, but the demining process consists of a series of dangerous tasks, which are a detection process, a prodding process and a digging process. One deminer is killed for every 1000 anti-personnel mines [1] removed.

Some reports say that the cost of removing one anti-personnel mine is over \$350, while in contrast the manufacturing cost of the cheapest anti-personnel mine is less than \$3. One deminer is only able to investigate a minefield less than 6 m^2 each day. It is estimated that the total period for demining all buried anti-personnel mines is over 500 years, under the assumption that no new mines will be buried. Furthermore, deminers are not able to detect all mines in a minefield. It is claimed that a deminer can detect and remove 99.6% of all mines, thus the probability of removing all mines is not high enough for utilizing the minefields as residential areas. In fact, some deminers have been injured in areas that had previously been demined. It is therefore imperative to improve the probability and the speed of mine detection.

Improving the speed of the demining process is the most important issue for the reconstruction battlefields that contain many mines. If we were able to increase demining speed, we could expand the detection area and decrease the cost of demining. In order to achieve high-speed detection, we propose a new robot system that has a small reaction manipulator.

2. Concept of proposed robot for high-speed mine detection

In the near future, robot technologies are expected to be applied to hazardous fields such as space, disaster sites, radioactive areas, and so on. Many robots have been developed to execute some dangerous tasks instead of humans. For example, robots could rescue people from disaster sites, or check the state of equipment in nuclear power plants. Minefields are also a dangerous area, where we could apply robotic technologies. In minefields, the utilization of robots is very safe and effective compared with the same processes performed by humans. In this section, we propose the concept of a high-speed mine detection robot.

The proposed mine detection robot is illustrated in Fig. 1. Its characteristics include low ground pressure tires, a small reaction manipulator, ground penetrating radar (GPR) and a camera. The robot has eight low ground pressure tires. These tires have great flexibility for making a broad contact surface between the ground and the tire. The broad contact surface makes the ground pressure less than the activating force of a mine. By using low ground pressure tires, the robot could drive on mine fields without triggering mines. Therefore, multiple robots could execute demining tasks in parallel. By using multiple robots, we could dramatically improve the time cost of the demining process.

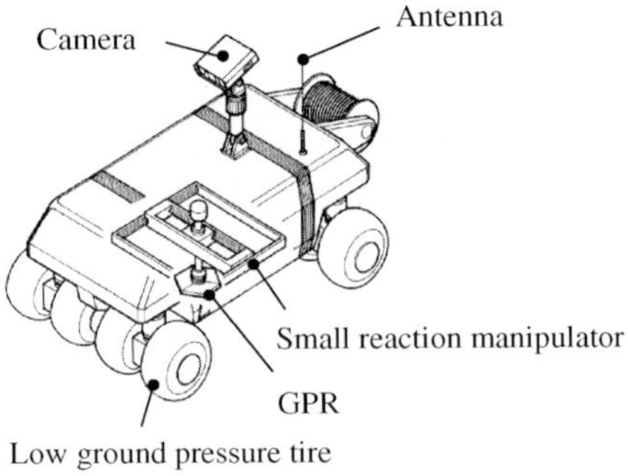

Fig. 1. Concept of proposed mine detection robot.

However, the tire oscillates easily due to its great flexibility when the robot operates the GPR. This characteristic makes accurate positioning of the GPR worse. It is necessary to reduce such oscillations in order to realize high precision and high-speed GPR maneuver.

In order to reduce oscillation, we propose a small reaction manipulator. Such a small reaction manipulator could operate to position the GPR precisely and rapidly even if the manipulator is mounted on a flexible structure such as low ground pressure tires.

The small reaction manipulator utilizes a small reaction control. The small reaction control has been studied, in relation to applications in space, at sea, in flexible base robots, and in macro- micro manipulators [2–5]. As traditional reaction control methods, the generalized Jacobian matrix method, the reaction null space method, and the method using counter weights are proposed. In a mine detection task, such methods have not been utilized. In this chapter, we utilize a linear mechanism that uses counter weights in order to realize a small reaction force control. Each linear mechanism independently realizes a small reaction motion. The independence of the small reaction mechanisms enables us to make a small reaction manipulator, which consists of several small reaction modules. If one axis of the manipulator is damaged, it will be easy to exchange the axis for a new modular one. The small reaction manipulator will be explained in detail in Chapter 4.

3. Effect of GPR maneuver

GPR is commonly used for detection of underground information. For example GPR detects leaks from water pipes, cracks in tunnel walls, cavities under railroads, and anti-personnel landmines. GPR could detect the depth of a buried object using the microwave reflection of anti-personnel landmines. Microwaves are reflected from the boundary between materials of different permeability. From the pattern of reflected microwaves, we could identify the depth of a buried object, and create a cross sectional diagram of the underground environment. GPR requires a constant height between the GPR and the ground surface, because fluctuation of the height of GPR creates complex ground-bounce. Such ground-bounce hides beneficial information about buried objects. To get clear underground information, we need to control the position of the GPR precisely.

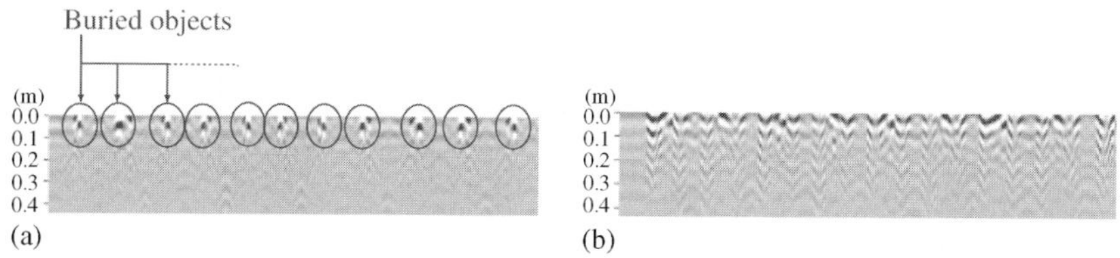

Fig. 2. Effect of maneuver of GPR. (a) Maneuver of GPR with linear guide; (b) Maneuver of GPR with free hand.

Two examples utilizing GPR are shown in Fig. 2(a) and (b), which show cross sectional underground diagrams. In Fig. 2(a), the data are measured by GPR mounted on a linear guide to keep the arc at a constant height. From Fig. 2(a) we can identify particular signals caused by buried objects easily. On the other hand, from Fig. 2(b), which is measured by GPR during a fluctuating maneuver, it is difficult for us to find buried objects. From these results obtained by GPR detection, we can see that precise position and orientation of the GPR is important for obtaining clear underground information.

The GPR used in this chapter has axial resolution of about 23 mm. The smallest anti-personnel mine used as a target in our project has a diameter of 55 mm. In order to recognize the shape of a mine it is necessary that the axial resolution should be less than 10 mm. Synthetic-aperture radar (SAR) techniques are commonly used for improvement of the axial resolution of GPR. The SAR technique which is applied to our system utilizes the positional information provided by the manipulator, therefore we do not need to discuss the accuracy of orientation of the GPR. To achieve 10 mm axial resolution, SAR requires, a 10 mm measurement interval. The manipulation of the GPR position should satisfy the accuracy of ± 5 mm.

4. Small reaction manipulator

4.1. *Small reaction modules*

The proposed mine detection robot system consists of a mobile base and a manipulator mounted on the mobile base. The mobile base has low ground pressure tires to enable it to drive on minefields without triggering mines. The manipulator is not fixed on an inertial coordinate system, because the mobile base's suspension system and the low ground pressure tires have high flexibility. In this case, when the manipulator operates the end-effector, a reaction force, which is generated by end-effector motion oscillates the manipulator itself. This characteristic makes the end-effector's position and orientation worse. In order to keep the positioning error small, the motion speed should be restricted in a traditional mobile manipulator.

In this section, we propose a small reaction module, which realizes a small reaction motion. The module has a straight motion mechanism. The small reaction module consists of an end-effector and a counter weight for preventing a reaction motion. A reaction force is produced by changing the kinetic momentum of a system. The counter weights can be controlled to maintain the kinetic momentum.

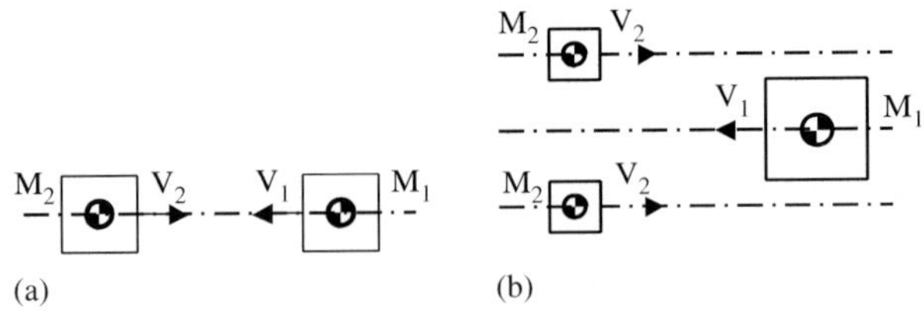

Fig. 3. Alternative configurations of small reaction manipulator. (a) Coaxial configuration; (b) Parallel axial configuration.

We propose two types of small reaction module. Configurations of an end-effector and counter weights are shown in Fig. 3. One is the coaxial configuration and the other is the parallel axial configuration. The coaxial configuration puts the end-effector and the counter weight on a coaxial. The parallel axial configuration puts the end-effector and two counter weights in parallel on the same plane.

In order to prevent reaction motion, we control the counter weight to keep the total kinetic momentum of the whole system constant. A constant kinetic momentum generates any reaction force on a system. The total momentum of the small reaction module with the coaxial configuration is expressed as follows:

$$m_1 v_1 + m_2 v_2 = P \tag{1}$$

where, m is a mass, v is a velocity, P is total kinetic momentum of the coaxial system. In this equation, the subscript 1 means the end-effector and the subscript 2 means the counter weight. In order to prevent any reaction force, it is necessary to keep the total kinetic moment P constant. From (1), we can derive the equation of motion of the module as follows:

$$m_1 \dot{v}_1 + m_2 \dot{v}_2 = 0 \tag{2}$$

where, $\dot{v}$ is acceleration of the end-effector and the counter weight. From (2), we can derive the desired acceleration of the counter weight as follows:

$$\dot{v}_2 = m_1/m_2 \times \dot{v}_1 \tag{3}$$

From (3), we can control the counter weight to reduce the reaction force. We call the module using counter weights for reducing the reaction force a small reaction module.

Similarly, the total momentum of the parallel axial configuration is expressed as follows:

$$m_1 v_1 + (m_2 + m_2) v_2 = P \tag{4}$$

In (4), it is assumed that two counter weights have the same mass and the same velocity. We can treat two counter weights in the same way as one counter weight. The system, which consists of two counter weights is the same as a coaxial configuration. From (4) we can obtain the desired acceleration of counter weights in the parallel configuration system as follows:

$$\dot{v}_2 = -m_1(2m_2) \times \dot{v}_1 \tag{5}$$

The small reaction control with respect to the parallel axial configuration system is almost the same as the coaxial configuration. Each of the two small reaction modules has respective advantages. The coaxial configuration is light and compact; the parallel axial configuration has a long range of movement. In addition, both these modules keep the center of gravity at a constant position. This characteristic is important, because changes in the center of gravity generates oscillation of the whole system.

4.2. *Small reaction manipulator*

In order to operate GPR over rough ground surfaces, we developed a manipulator that has three degrees of freedom. This manipulator consists of three small reaction modules, which are constructed with an orthogonal structure. The vertical axis called the z-axis uses the coaxial configuration module. The GPR is attached to the end-effector of the z-axis. Both the horizontal axes, called the x-axis and the y-axis, use the parallel axial configuration module.

This manipulator not only maintains kinetic momentum during dynamic motion but also keeps the center of gravity in static a situation. With these characteristics, the manipulator could achieve high precision and high speed sensor head maneuvers, even if the manipulator is mounted on a mobile base which has flexible structures such as low-pressure tires.

5. Experiments

5.1. *Prototype of manipulator*

The prototype of the small reaction manipulator is shown in Fig. 4. The base frame of the manipulator is mounted on the black support structure through the springs. This support structure imitates a mobile base's suspension. The coupled blocks on each axis are

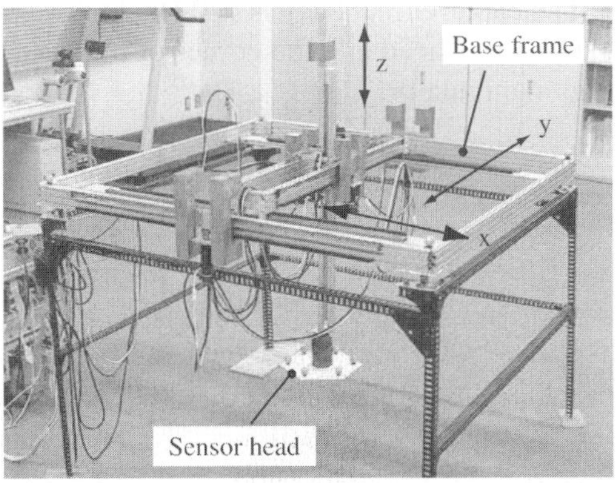

Fig. 4. Prototype of small reaction manipulator.

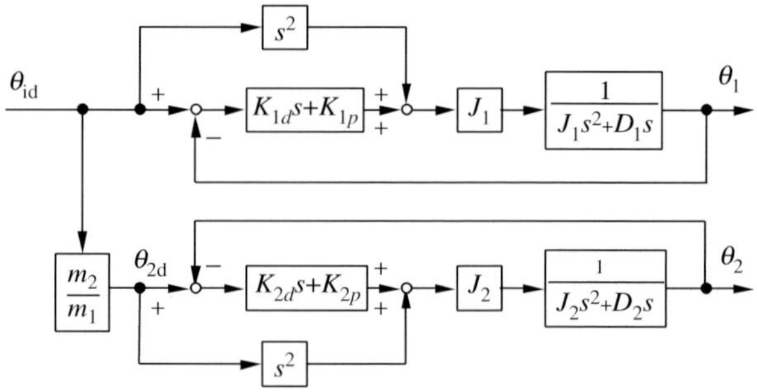

Fig. 5. Control block diagram for small reaction control.

counter weights. The sensor head is attached to the end-effector of the z-axis. The mass of the sensor head is about 1.0 kg. In the z-axis, the sensor head and the counter weight are controlled using a ball screw. In the x-axis and the y-axis, the sensor head and two counter weights are driven by a rack and pinion mechanism. The total mass of the manipulator is 40 kg. The total length of the manipulator is 1300 mm × 1300 mm × 1500 mm. With respect to each axis, the movable range of the x-axis is 900 mm, the y-axis, 800 mm, and the z-axis 400 mm. The maximum speed is 0.6 m/s for the x- and y-axis, and 0.4 m/s for the z-axis. The CPU for controlling the manipulator is a dual MMX Pentium 200 MHz, and the control frequency is 1000 Hz. A QNX is utilized for controlling the manipulator. The manipulator is controlled with a PD controller. The block diagram of the PD controller for a small reaction manipulator is shown in Fig. 5. In Fig. 5, m_1 is the mass of the end-effector and m_2 is the mass of the counter weight.

5.2. *Experimental conditions*

To validate the proposed small reaction manipulator, we evaluated the positioning error and tracking error of the sensor head and the oscillation of the base frame. To capture the behavior of the sensor head and the base frame, we used a motion capturing system. This system can measure the 3D position of marked points in real time. The capture resolution of the system is 1.7 mm. The capture frequency is 120 Hz. In this experiment, the captured points were attached to the sensor head and the corner of the base frame. Figure 6 shows the captured points on the manipulator.

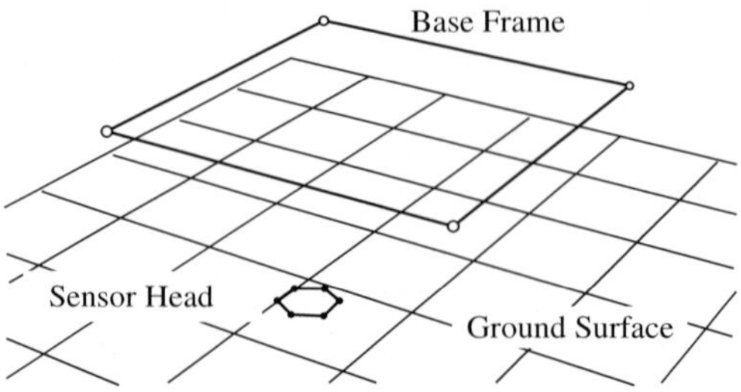

Fig. 6. Observed points on the manipulator captured by the motion captured system.

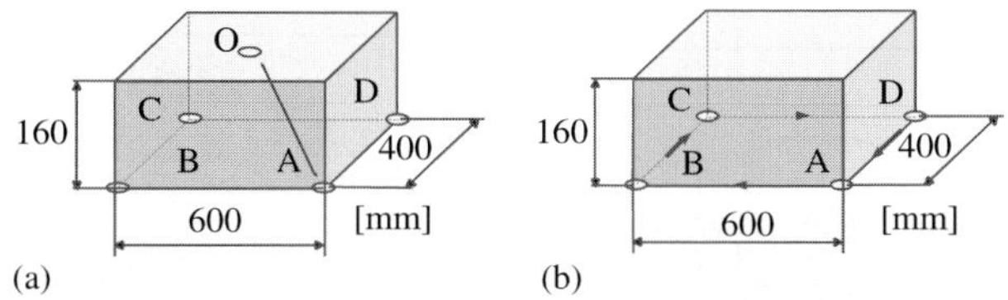

Fig. 7. Experimental trajectory of sensor head. (a) For positioning error; (b) For tracking error.

5.2.1. *Positioning error.* To evaluate the positioning performance of the sensor head, we measured the position of the sensor head and the frame, with the manipulator fixed on a desired point, which was designated by fifth order function. The desired path for evaluation of the positioning error is shown in Fig. 7(a). In this experiment, the sensor head moves straight from point O to point A over 1.0 s and moves straight back from point A to point O over 1.0 s then stays at point O for 0.6 s. Next, the sensor head moves from point O to point B, moves back, and stops, the same as before. The sensor head then moves to points C and D in the same way as points A and B. When the sensor head stops at point O, we measure its spatial position. To evaluate the performance of the small reaction manipulator, we did two experiments; one using small reaction control and the other not using small reaction control.

5.2.2. *Tracking error.* To evaluate the performance of path tracking, we measured the spatial position of the end-effector and the frame, when the sensor head traced a desired path, as shown in Fig. 7(b).

First, the sensor head moves straight from point A to point B over 1.4 s. Next, the sensor head moves straight from point B to point C over 1.2 s, straight from point C to point D over 1.4 s, and from point D to point A over 1.2 s. We compared the two experimental results; one experimental condition using the small reaction control and the other condition not using the small reaction control.

5.3. *Experimental results*

5.3.1. *Positioning error.* We evaluated the oscillations of the base frame and the positioning errors of the end-effector. The horizontal tracking errors are shown in Figs. 8 and 9. In these figures, dots show the displacement of the base frame and the sensor head from the desired position. In these figures, the circle has a radius of 5 mm. The origin of these figures shows the desired position. Obviously, the positioning error decreases when using the small reaction control. When we do not use the small reaction control, the maximum positioning error of the sensor head is 12.5 mm in the x-axis and 7.5 mm in the y-axis. These errors exceed the limits of required performance, discussed in Section 3. On the other hand, when we use the small reaction control, the maximum positioning error of the end-effector is 3.0 mm in the x-axis and 2.0 mm in the y-axis.

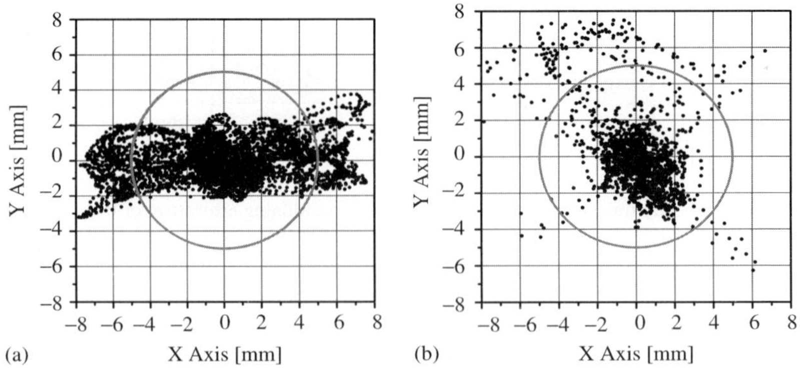

Fig. 8. Positioning error without small reaction control in the horizontal plane. (a) Base frame; (b) Sensor head.

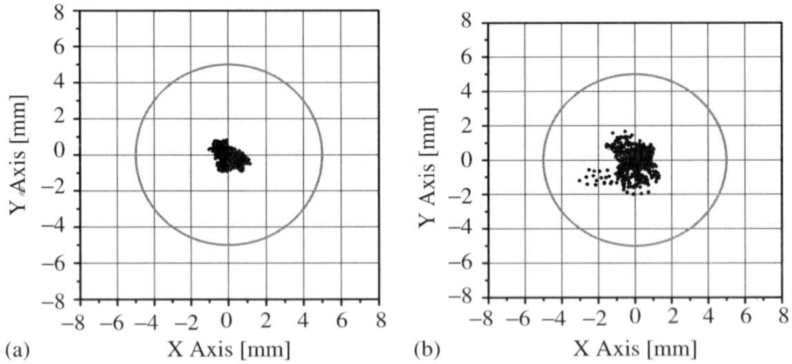

Fig. 9. Positioning error with small reaction control in the horizontal plane. (a) Base frame; (b) Sensor head.

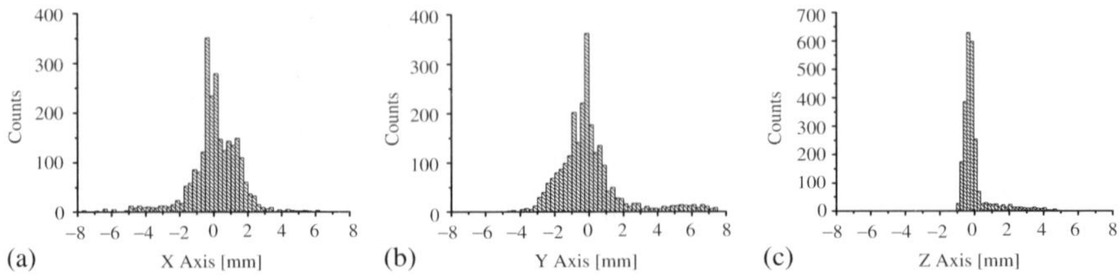

Fig. 10. Histogram of positioning error without small reaction control. (a) *X*-axis; (b) *Y*-axis; (c) *Z*-axis.

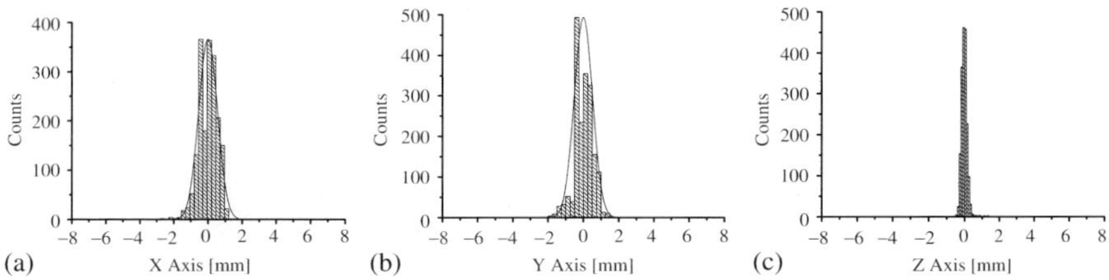

Fig. 11. Histogram of positioning error with small reaction control. (a) *X*-axis; (b) *Y*-axis; (c) *Z*-axis.

Histograms of the positioning error of the end-effector are shown in Figs. 10 and 11. These figures show the dispersion of the position of the sensor head with and without the small reaction control. The standard deviations of the *x*-, *y*-, and *z*-axis are 0.54, 0.52, and 0.21, respectively. These standard deviations mean that 99.99% of all data are included within ± 2.1 mm.

5.3.2. *Tracking error.* We evaluated oscillations of the base frame and tracking errors of the end-effector, when the end-effector traced the desired path shown in Fig. 7(b). The desired position consists of two sides along the *x*-axis and two sides along the *y*-axis. Figures 12 and 13 show the horizontal oscillations of the base frame and the tracking errors of the end-effector. The tracking error is calculated by subtraction of the captured position from the end-effector's desired position. In Figs. 12 and 13, the oscillations of the base frame show displacement from the initial position. The same as for the base frame, the oscillations of the sensor head show the displacement from the desired position. When the sensor head moves along *x*-axis, a positive error about the *x*-axis shows that the actual position of the sensor head is ahead of the desired position. A positive error about the *y*-axis shows that the actual position is shifted to outside of the manipulator's desired path. A positive error about the *z*-axis shows that the actual position is below the desired position. A negative tracking error has the

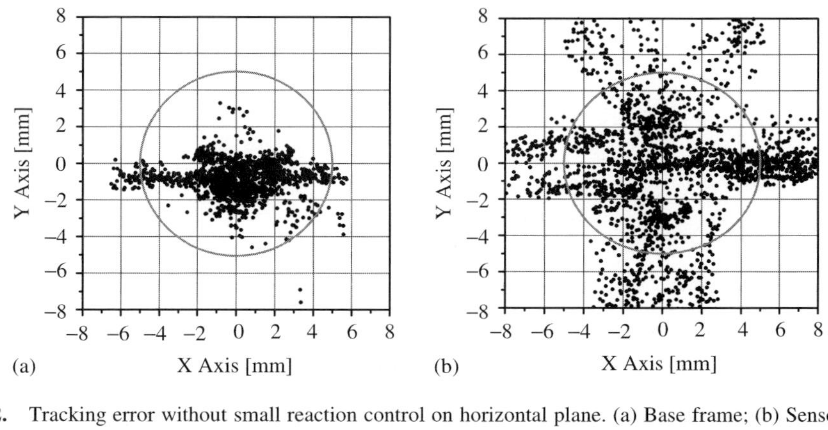

Fig. 12. Tracking error without small reaction control on horizontal plane. (a) Base frame; (b) Sensor head.

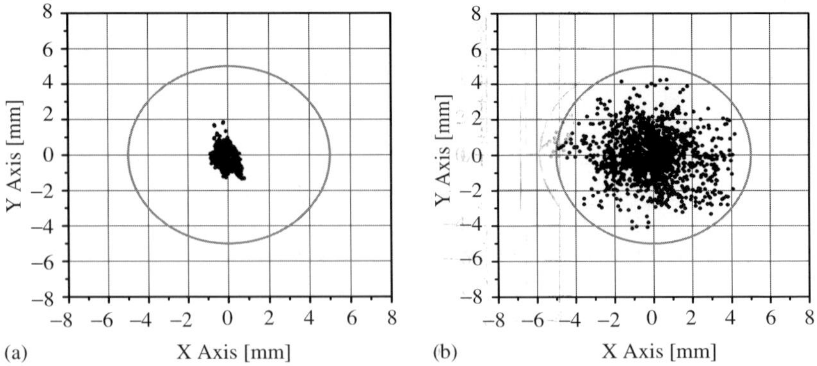

Fig. 13. Tracking error with small reaction control on horizontal plane. (a) Base frame; (b) Sensor head.

opposite definition. If the end-effector moves along the y-axis, the tracking errors along the x- and y-axis satisfy similar relationships. Figures 14 and 15 show histograms of the tracking error about the x-, y-, and z-axis. In Fig. 14, operation without the small reaction control makes the standard deviations about the x-, y-, and z-axis as 4.66, 5.42, and 0.90, respectively. On the other hand, standard deviations about the x-, y-, and z-axis are 1.42, 1.32, and 0.89 with the small reaction control. The standard deviations with the small reaction control mean that 99.73% of all data are included within ± 4.29 mm. Thus the tracking motion satisfies the required performance specifications.

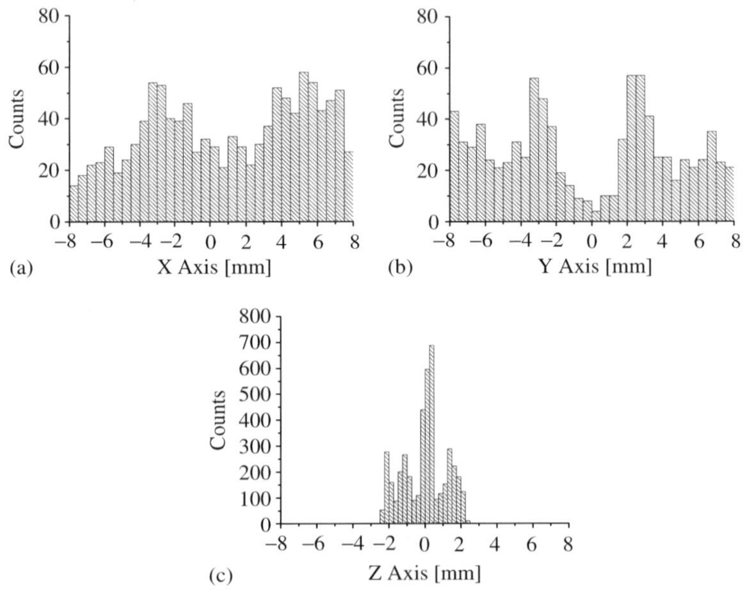

Fig. 14. Histogram of tracking error without small reaction control. (a) X-axis; (b) Y-axis; (c) Z-axis.

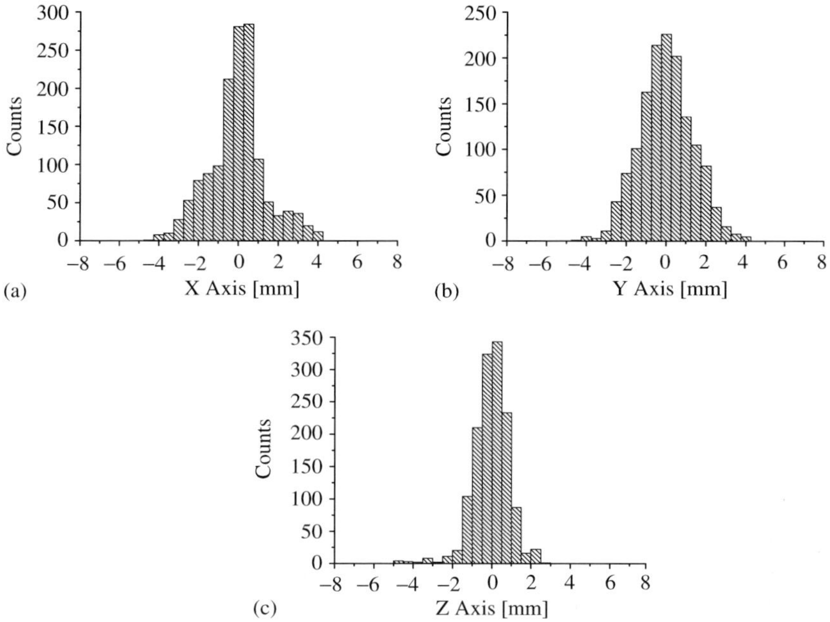

Fig. 15. Histogram of tracking error with small reaction control. (a) X-axis; (b) Y-axis; (c) Z-axis.

6. Conclusion

In this chapter, we proposed a small reaction manipulator able to realize high speed and precise sensor head maneuvers by reducing oscillations generated by sensor head motion. The proposed manipulator counteracts reaction forces using the counter weights. Some experimental results concerning positioning error and tracking error of the sensor head illustrate the validity of the proposed manipulator.

References

[1] J. MacDonald, J.R. Lockwood, J. McFee, T. Altshuler, T. Broach, L. Carin, R. Harmon, C. Rappaport, W. Scott and R. Weaver, *Alternatives for Landmine Detection*, RAND, Santa Monica, CA (2003).

[2] K. Yoshida, *Engineering test satellite VII flight experiments for space robot dynamics and control: theories on laboratory test beds ten years ago. Now in orbit*, Int. J. Robotics Res. **22** (5) (2003), 321–335.

[3] H. Kajita and K. Kosuge, *Velocity-based control of manipulator/vehicle system floating on water*, J. Robotics Mec. **9** (5) (1997), 318–323.

[4] D.N. Nenchev, Space robotics. Keynote lecture, Robomec, 96–2 (1996), 1493–1496.

[5] D.N. Nenchev, K. Yoshida, P. Vichitkulsawat and M. Uchiyama, *Reaction null-space control of flexible structure mounted manipulator system*, IEEE Trans. Robotics Autom. **15** (6) (1999), 1011–1023.

CHAPTER 19

Mine Detection Algorithm Using Pattern Classification Method by Sensor Fusion—Experimental Results by Means of GPR

Masaki Fujimoto

Graduate School of Science and Technology, Chiba University, 1-33, Yayoi-cho, Inage-ku, Chiba, Japan

Kenzo Nonami

Department of Electronics and Mechanical Engineering, Faculty of Engineering, Chiba University, 1-33, Yayoi-cho, Inage-ku, Chiba, Japan

Contents

Abstract

In this chapter, we propose a land mine detection algorithm using a sensor that combines ground penetrating radar and a metal detector. Pattern classification method is used for the algorithm to detect only dangerous objects. Features are extracted by using the statistics. Though our result was determined in an ideal environment, this proposed system indicates that the probability of false alarm is much lower than that in the existing system.

SYSTEMS AND HUMAN SCIENCE – FOR SAFETY, SECURITY, AND DEPENDABILITY
Edited by Tatsuo Arai, Shigeru Yamamoto and Kazuhisa Makino

1. Introduction

More than 100 million land mines worldwide are currently buried underground. These mines not only prevent economic development, but also cause much harm to local residents [1].

The present general detection method of humanitarian demining is the manual operation of a Metal Detector (MD) and probe by a skillful worker. In this traditional method, the probe is gently inserted into the ground, and the existence of a buried mine is judged by feel and by metal response. However, there are many places, such as a battlefield in an area where mines have been buried, which also contain scattered pieces of metal. Therefore, for every one detection by MD of an Anti-Personnel Mine (APM), which is made of plastic and contains hardly any metal, false alarms occur an average 1583 times [2]. This means that the Probability of False Alarm (PFA) is 99.94%. As a result, although the present detection technique is the cheapest and the most reliable system, it also has problems, such as the enormous labor and time necessary, and the excessive strain, and danger to the worker.

Therefore, a new technology for efficient mine detection is greatly needed to lower the PFA for as long as possible while also securing reliability beyond the present capability. Therefore, in this study, we discuss a sensor that combines Ground Penetrating Radar (GPR) and an MD. This sensor may be considered a next-generation mine detection sensor that will replace MD [3]. Pattern classification of the features obtained by the fusion of both the sensors is performed, and the Probability of Detection (PD) and decline in PFA are improved by detecting only dangerous objects. Furthermore, by using a manipulation robot to automate detection, exact positioning accuracy is acquired and the variation in a measurement state is suppressed by making the gap of the ground and sensor head constant. Also, the ground scanning speed based on robot manipulator becomes constant compared with the manual scanning. Therefore, PFA caused by gap and scanning speed change decreases and efficiency is improved. In the case of robotics-based operation, the database of mine detection will be made automatically and the classification of the detected data will be carried out using such a database. It seems that the reliability of mine detection will be totally improved.

In this chapter, a mine detection algorithm is proposed and the result, which verifies the pattern classification performance under an ideal environment, is shown by carrying out the feature extraction of the output of GPR using statistics.

2. Mine detection sensor

The mine detection sensor: SENCI-ONα^{pro}III used in this study is shown in Fig. 1. It is a compound-type mine detection sensor, which consists of an MD (Eddy Current Tester, ECT) coil in the circumferential part, and a transceiver antenna unit of GPR in the central part [3]. The specifications of SENCI-ONα^{pro}III are shown in Table 1.

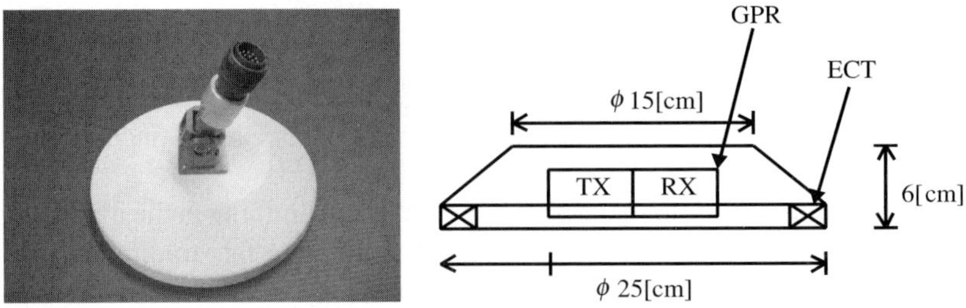

(a) Over view (b) Configuration

Fig. 1. Mine detection sensor: SENCI-ONα^{pro}III.

Table 1. Specification of SENCI-ONα^{pro}III

	Specification
GPR system	Impulse radar system
Design frequency of GPR	1.5 GHz
Inquiry depth of GPR	~800 mm
ECT system	Two phase detection system
Frequency range of ECT	1–100 kHz
Inquiry depth of ECT	~250 mm
Operating conditions	~50 °C ~95 (%RH)

3. Mine detection algorithm

The flow of the mine detection algorithm proposed in this study is shown in Fig. 2. In order to measure a regular interval pitch using the mine detection sensor, which is attached at the tip of the manipulator for tracking the earth surface, directions for measurement are sent to the CPU for mine detection sensor processing. If measurement instructions are received, measurements are performed by the ECT and GPR, and feature extraction is carried out in the analysis of the output data, and parameterization is performed as the value of the features. Our algorithm performs pattern classification based on the feature parameter, and detects only dangerous objects, such as an APM, Anti-Tank Mine (ATM), and Unexploded Ordnance (UXO).

4. Experimental conditions

In an experiment of the sample data acquisition, in order to minimize the influence of ground surface reflection as long as possible and to emphasize the reaction of the mine, the lift distance of the sensor head to the ground surface was set to 0 cm. In order to lose the influence of a soil boundary, the size of the experimental soil area

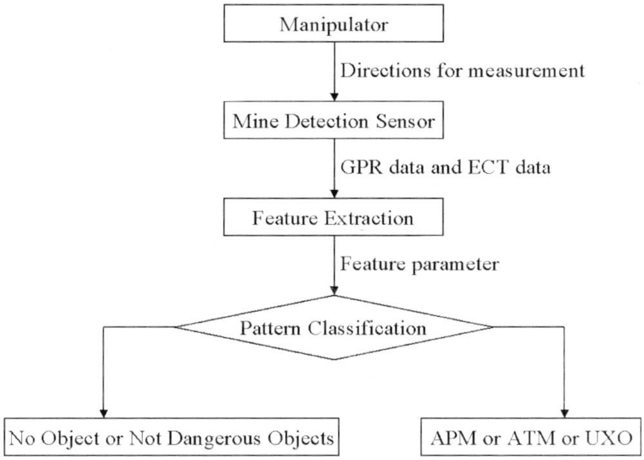

Fig. 2. Mine detection algorithm.

was set as follows: length 1.8 m, width 1.8 m, and depth 1.5 m. Dry, sandy soil, which had few impurities, was used.

The following are the sample objects: PMN and PMN2, which are a real APM made of plastic and rubber and filled with imitation powder; T72 and M14, which are an imitation APM in the form of a real mine; MVZ-57, which is a real APM made of metal; TM-57, which is a real ATM; and a stone, which is the same size as the APMs. PMN, PMN2, T72, M14, and stone were buried at a depth of 3 cm, which is a typical mine laying-under-the-ground depth. MVZ-57 was buried at a depth of 5 cm, and TM-57 was buried at a depth of 50 cm. A summary of the sample objects is shown in Table 2.

5. Signal processing

5.1. *Spectrum analysis*

In GPR measurements, when an electromagnetic wave is reflected by the buried object, a peculiar resonance frequency arises, and the frequency component is considered to affect

Table 2. Experimental sample

Sample	Size (cm)	Casing material	Laying depth (cm)
PMN	$\phi 11.2 \times 5.6$	Plastic and rubber	3
PMN2	$\phi 12.5 \times 5.4$	Plastic and rubber	3
T72	$\phi 7.6 \times 4.0$	Plastic and rubber	3
M14	$\phi 5.6 \times 4.6$	Plastic	3
Stone	$10 \times 10 \times 5$	Sandstone	3
MVZ-57	$\phi 8.0 \times 4.0$	Metal	5
TM-57	$\phi 30.0 \times 10.0$	Metal	50

the received waveform. A discrete time Fourier transformation is performed using

$$X(n) = \sum_{k=0}^{N-1} x(k) \exp\left(-j\frac{2\pi}{N} nk \right), \quad n = 0, 1, 2, \ldots, N - 1, \tag{1}$$

for a measured time domain waveform (A-scope) and the feature extraction of the received signal is carried out by analyzing the spectrum. The power spectrum is normalized by

$$\text{Power}(n) = |X(n)| / \sum_{m=0}^{N-1} |X(m)|. \tag{2}$$

In (1) and (2), N is the number of sampling data, $x(k)$ represents the time domain data and $X(n)$ represents the frequency domain data.

The A-scope waveform obtained by the experiment is shown in Fig. 3(a), and the power spectrum and phase are shown in Fig. 3(b) and (c). Three waveforms of Fig. 3 are measured for the same object and differ only by the measurement time.

5.2. *Phase compensation*

In Fig. 3, even when the three waveforms were measured in the same position, differences occurred with the waveform and spectrum due to measurement time. It is thought that, if the temperature changes with measurement time, these differences occur because of temperature drift in the analog circuit of the GPR system. Therefore, phase compensation was performed by arranging the position of the maximum peak value of the A-scope. The A-scope, power spectrum and a phase-after-phase compensation are shown in Fig. 4. By performing phase compensation, it was shown that the change due to temperature drift was reduced.

6. Feature extraction by statistical techniques

6.1. *Selection of feature point*

When the average power spectrum component for each measurement was compared, the difference in power was found by the frequency band of 1–2 kHz as shown, for example, in Fig. 5. This is due to the frequency reduction that is caused by sampling time: 1 μs to the design frequency of GPR: 1.5 GHz. Therefore, this frequency band is a zone where the feature peculiar to the buried object appears. As shown in Fig. 5, the feature point frequency in this domain is denoted as: FP1, FP2, FP3, FP4, FP5 and FP6.

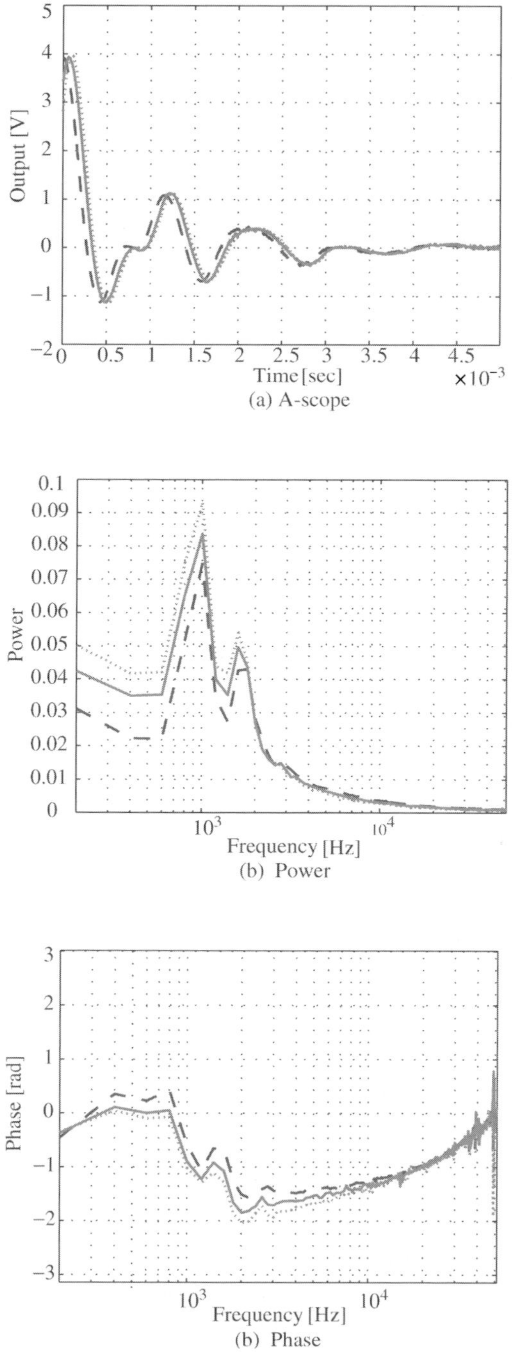

Fig. 3. Spectrum analysis for law data.

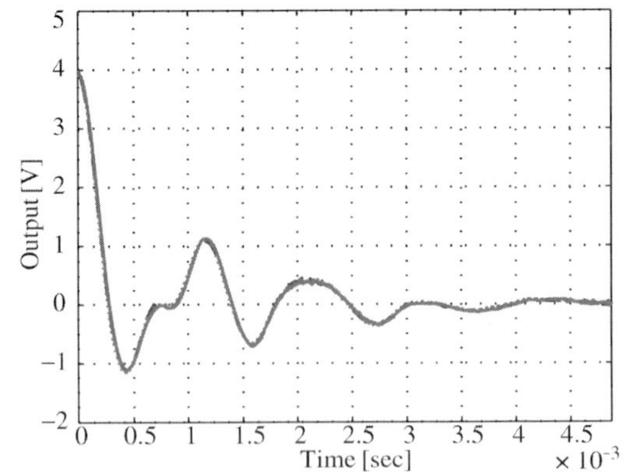

(a) A-scope

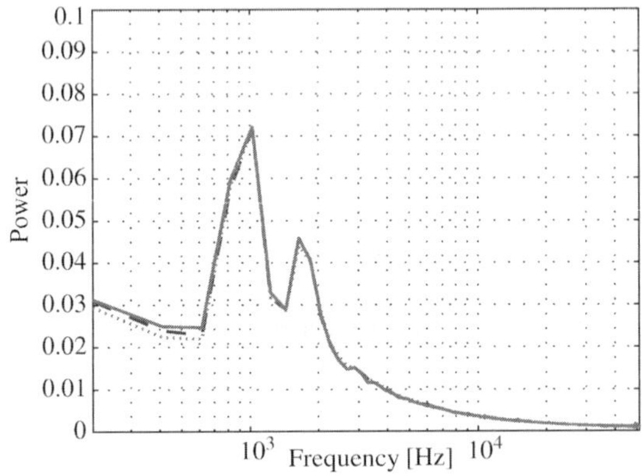

(b) Power

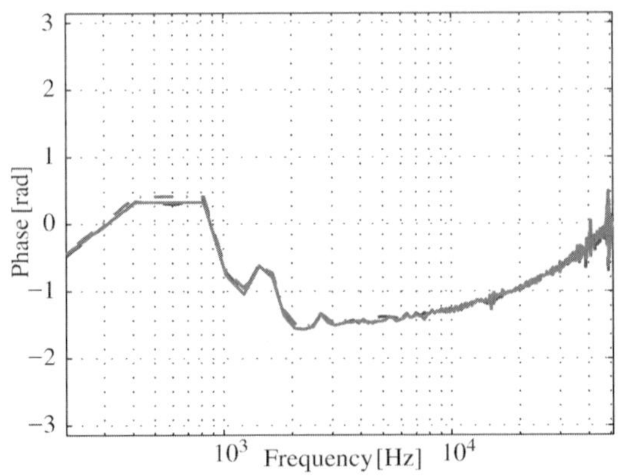

(c) Phase

Fig. 4. Phase compensation data.

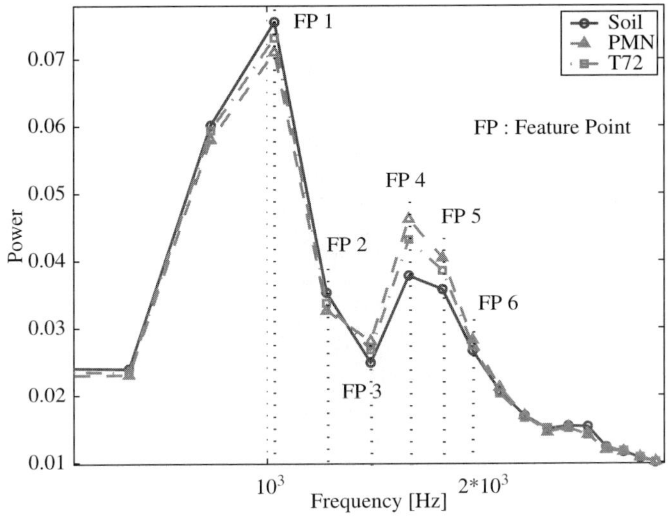

Fig. 5. Feature points of power spectrum.

6.2. *Sample feature point distribution*

The value of the feature point measured by the experiment was not a fixed value, but a certain amount of variance exists due to causes such as fluctuation, the noise of the waveform at the time of measurement and measurement error. So, in order to carry out a statistical comparison evaluation of the variance distribution of a sample point, the sample mean:$\bar{x}$ and sample variance:s^2 are calculated by

$$\bar{x} = \frac{1}{n} \sum_{k=1}^{n} x_k, \tag{3}$$

and

$$s^2 = \frac{1}{n-1} \sum_{k=1}^{n} (x_k - \bar{x})^2, \tag{4}$$

and a histogram expressed with the bar graph of Fig. 6 is generally used. In (3) and (4), n is the number of measurement samples, and x_k is the measured sample value.

When sample mean $\bar{x}$ is presumed to be equal to the population mean μ, the $100(1-\alpha)\%$ Confidence Interval (CI) to μ is calculated by

$$\bar{x} - t_{n-1;\alpha/2} \frac{s}{\sqrt{n}} \leq \mu \leq \bar{x} + t_{n-1;\alpha/2} \frac{s}{\sqrt{n}}. \tag{5}$$

In (5), $t_{n-1;\alpha/2}$ is a constant characteristic of a Student's t-distribution.

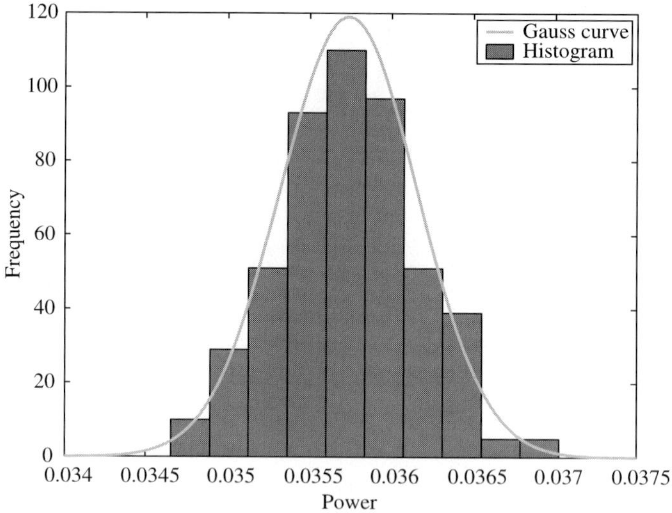

Fig. 6. Comparison of histogram with Gauss curve.

Furthermore, when the sample variance s^2 is presumed to be equal to the population variance σ^2, the $100(1 - \alpha)\%$ CI to σ is calculated by

$$\frac{\sqrt{n-1}s}{\chi_{n-1;\alpha/2}} \leq \sigma \leq \frac{\sqrt{n-1}s}{\chi_{n-1;1-\alpha/2}}. \tag{6}$$

In (6), $\chi_{n-1;\alpha/2}$ is a constant characteristic of a Chi-square distribution.

When we can assume from the histogram that the sample distribution is a normal distribution, the population distribution can be approximated with the normal curve calculated by [4]

$$f(x) = \frac{1}{\sigma\sqrt{2\pi}} \exp\left[-\frac{1}{2\sigma^2}(x-\mu)^2 \right], \tag{7}$$

and is expressed by the solid line of Fig. 6.

Since we could assume that the feature distribution of all measurement samples obtained in the experiment is a normal distribution, the subsequent feature point distributions are approximated and compared with the normal curve.

6.3. *Feature comparison*

The population mean and variance values of each measurement in each feature point and the 99% CI for them are shown in Tables 3–8. The distribution map of each feature point is shown in Figs. 7–12.

Table 3. Population parameters of feature point 1

Sample	μ	99%CI (μ)	σ	99%CI (σ)
Soil	7.55×10^{-2}	$[7.51 \times 10^{-2}, 7.59 \times 10^{-2}]$	1.05×10^{-3}	$[9.71 \times 10^{-4}, 1.14 \times 10^{-3}]$
PMN	7.10×10^{-2}	$[7.08 \times 10^{-2}, 7.12 \times 10^{-2}]$	1.30×10^{-3}	$[1.23 \times 10^{-3}, 1.37 \times 10^{-3}]$
PMN2	7.30×10^{-2}	$[7.29 \times 10^{-2}, 7.31 \times 10^{-2}]$	1.58×10^{-3}	$[1.50 \times 10^{-3}, 1.66 \times 10^{-3}]$
T72	7.31×10^{-2}	$[7.29 \times 10^{-2}, 7.33 \times 10^{-2}]$	1.06×10^{-3}	$[9.98 \times 10^{-4}, 1.13 \times 10^{-3}]$
M14	7.62×10^{-2}	$[7.54 \times 10^{-2}, 7.70 \times 10^{-2}]$	7.52×10^{-4}	$[6.75 \times 10^{-4}, 8.51 \times 10^{-4}]$
Stone	8.99×10^{-2}	$[8.90 \times 10^{-2}, 9.08 \times 10^{-2}]$	1.49×10^{-3}	$[1.34 \times 10^{-3}, 1.69 \times 10^{-3}]$
MVZ-57	1.05×10^{-1}	$[1.04 \times 10^{-1}, 1.06 \times 10^{-1}]$	1.01×10^{-3}	$[9.07 \times 10^{-4}, 1.14 \times 10^{-3}]$
TM-57	7.72×10^{-2}	$[7.64 \times 10^{-2}, 7.80 \times 10^{-2}]$	8.32×10^{-4}	$[7.47 \times 10^{-4}, 9.42 \times 10^{-4}]$

Table 4. Population parameters of feature point 2

Sample	μ	99%CI (μ)	σ	99%CI (σ)
Soil	3.53×10^{-2}	$[3.51 \times 10^{-2}, 3.55 \times 10^{-2}]$	7.43×10^{-4}	$[6.87 \times 10^{-4}, 8.10 \times 10^{-4}]$
PMN	3.26×10^{-2}	$[3.25 \times 10^{-2}, 3.27 \times 10^{-2}]$	1.13×10^{-3}	$[1.07 \times 10^{-3}, 1.19 \times 10^{-3}]$
PMN2	3.56×10^{-2}	$[3.55 \times 10^{-2}, 3.57 \times 10^{-2}]$	1.20×10^{-3}	$[1.14 \times 10^{-3}, 1.26 \times 10^{-3}]$
T72	3.37×10^{-2}	$[3.36 \times 10^{-2}, 3.38 \times 10^{-2}]$	8.32×10^{-4}	$[7.83 \times 10^{-4}, 8.88 \times 10^{-4}]$
M14	3.64×10^{-2}	$[3.60 \times 10^{-2}, 3.68 \times 10^{-2}]$	5.60×10^{-4}	$[5.03 \times 10^{-4}, 6.34 \times 10^{-4}]$
Stone	3.49×10^{-2}	$[3.45 \times 10^{-2}, 3.53 \times 10^{-2}]$	5.15×10^{-4}	$[4.62 \times 10^{-4}, 5.83 \times 10^{-4}]$
MVZ-57	6.60×10^{-2}	$[6.53 \times 10^{-2}, 6.67 \times 10^{-2}]$	1.45×10^{-3}	$[1.30 \times 10^{-3}, 1.64 \times 10^{-3}]$
TM-57	4.16×10^{-2}	$[4.12 \times 10^{-2}, 4.20 \times 10^{-2}]$	5.43×10^{-4}	$[4.87 \times 10^{-4}, 6.15 \times 10^{-4}]$

Table 5. Population parameters of feature point 3

Sample	μ	99%CI (μ)	σ	99%CI (σ)
Soil	2.49×10^{-2}	$[2.48 \times 10^{-2}, 2.50 \times 10^{-2}]$	1.05×10^{-3}	$[9.71 \times 10^{-4}, 1.14 \times 10^{-3}]$
PMN	2.81×10^{-2}	$[2.80 \times 10^{-2}, 2.82 \times 10^{-2}]$	1.22×10^{-3}	$[1.16 \times 10^{-3}, 1.29 \times 10^{-3}]$
PMN2	2.80×10^{-2}	$[2.79 \times 10^{-2}, 2.81 \times 10^{-2}]$	1.69×10^{-3}	$[1.61 \times 10^{-3}, 1.78 \times 10^{-3}]$
T72	2.68×10^{-2}	$[2.67 \times 10^{-2}, 2.69 \times 10^{-2}]$	1.19×10^{-3}	$[1.12 \times 10^{-3}, 1.27 \times 10^{-3}]$
M14	2.56×10^{-2}	$[2.53 \times 10^{-2}, 2.59 \times 10^{-2}]$	8.41×10^{-4}	$[7.55 \times 10^{-4}, 9.52 \times 10^{-4}]$
Stone	2.64×10^{-2}	$[2.61 \times 10^{-2}, 2.67 \times 10^{-2}]$	1.05×10^{-3}	$[9.42 \times 10^{-4}, 1.19 \times 10^{-3}]$
MVZ-57	4.06×10^{-2}	$[4.02 \times 10^{-2}, 4.10 \times 10^{-2}]$	9.13×10^{-4}	$[8.20 \times 10^{-4}, 1.03 \times 10^{-3}]$
TM-57	2.64×10^{-2}	$[2.61 \times 10^{-2}, 2.67 \times 10^{-2}]$	9.89×10^{-4}	$[8.87 \times 10^{-4}, 1.12 \times 10^{-3}]$

Table 6. Population parameters of feature point 4

Sample	μ	99% CI (μ)	σ	99% CI (σ)
Soil	3.78×10^{-2}	$[3.76 \times 10^{-2}, 3.80 \times 10^{-2}]$	1.05×10^{-3}	$[9.71 \times 10^{-4}, 1.14 \times 10^{-3}]$
PMN	4.62×10^{-2}	$[4.61 \times 10^{-2}, 4.63 \times 10^{-2}]$	1.21×10^{-3}	$[1.15 \times 10^{-3}, 1.28 \times 10^{-3}]$
PMN2	4.28×10^{-2}	$[4.27 \times 10^{-2}, 4.29 \times 10^{-2}]$	1.44×10^{-3}	$[1.37 \times 10^{-3}, 1.52 \times 10^{-3}]$
T72	4.31×10^{-2}	$[4.30 \times 10^{-2}, 4.32 \times 10^{-2}]$	1.31×10^{-3}	$[1.23 \times 10^{-3}, 1.40 \times 10^{-3}]$
M14	3.50×10^{-2}	$[3.46 \times 10^{-2}, 3.54 \times 10^{-2}]$	7.34×10^{-4}	$[6.59 \times 10^{-4}, 8.31 \times 10^{-4}]$
Stone	4.70×10^{-2}	$[4.65 \times 10^{-2}, 4.75 \times 10^{-2}]$	6.26×10^{-4}	$[5.62 \times 10^{-4}, 7.08 \times 10^{-4}]$
MVZ-57	2.85×10^{-2}	$[2.82 \times 10^{-2}, 2.88 \times 10^{-2}]$	1.10×10^{-3}	$[9.88 \times 10^{-4}, 1.24 \times 10^{-3}]$
TM-57	3.01×10^{-2}	$[2.98 \times 10^{-2}, 3.04 \times 10^{-2}]$	8.85×10^{-4}	$[7.94 \times 10^{-4}, 1.00 \times 10^{-3}]$

Table 7. Population parameters of feature point 5

Sample	μ	99% CI (μ)	σ	99% CI (σ)
Soil	3.57×10^{-2}	$[3.55 \times 10^{-2}, 3.59 \times 10^{-2}]$	4.19×10^{-4}	$[3.87 \times 10^{-4}, 4.57 \times 10^{-4}]$
PMN	4.04×10^{-2}	$[4.03 \times 10^{-2}, 4.05 \times 10^{-2}]$	5.05×10^{-4}	$[4.80 \times 10^{-4}, 5.33 \times 10^{-4}]$
PMN2	3.87×10^{-2}	$[3.86 \times 10^{-2}, 3.88 \times 10^{-2}]$	7.95×10^{-4}	$[7.57 \times 10^{-4}, 8.37 \times 10^{-4}]$
T72	3.85×10^{-2}	$[3.84 \times 10^{-2}, 3.86 \times 10^{-2}]$	6.06×10^{-4}	$[5.70 \times 10^{-4}, 6.47 \times 10^{-4}]$
M14	3.40×10^{-2}	$[3.36 \times 10^{-2}, 3.44 \times 10^{-2}]$	3.96×10^{-4}	$[3.55 \times 10^{-4}, 4.48 \times 10^{-4}]$
Stone	3.40×10^{-2}	$[3.36 \times 10^{-2}, 3.44 \times 10^{-2}]$	5.67×10^{-4}	$[5.09 \times 10^{-4}, 6.42 \times 10^{-4}]$
MVZ-57	1.82×10^{-2}	$[1.80 \times 10^{-2}, 1.84 \times 10^{-2}]$	6.53×10^{-4}	$[5.87 \times 10^{-4}, 7.38 \times 10^{-4}]$
TM-57	3.63×10^{-2}	$[3.59 \times 10^{-2}, 3.67 \times 10^{-2}]$	5.24×10^{-4}	$[4.70 \times 10^{-4}, 5.93 \times 10^{-4}]$

Table 8. Population parameters of feature point 6

Sample	μ	99%CI (μ)	σ	99%CI (σ)
Soil	2.66×10^{-2}	$[2.65 \times 10^{-2}, 2.67 \times 10^{-2}]$	3.93×10^{-4}	$[3.63 \times 10^{-4}, 4.28 \times 10^{-4}]$
PMN	2.82×10^{-2}	$[2.81 \times 10^{-2}, 2.83 \times 10^{-2}]$	4.80×10^{-4}	$[4.56 \times 10^{-4}, 5.07 \times 10^{-4}]$
PMN2	2.78×10^{-2}	$[2.77 \times 10^{-2}, 2.79 \times 10^{-2}]$	5.51×10^{-4}	$[5.25 \times 10^{-4}, 5.80 \times 10^{-4}]$
T72	2.74×10^{-2}	$[2.73 \times 10^{-2}, 2.75 \times 10^{-2}]$	4.69×10^{-4}	$[4.41 \times 10^{-4}, 5.01 \times 10^{-4}]$
M14	2.60×10^{-2}	$[2.57 \times 10^{-2}, 2.63 \times 10^{-2}]$	3.12×10^{-4}	$[2.80 \times 10^{-4}, 3.53 \times 10^{-4}]$
Stone	2.31×10^{-2}	$[2.29 \times 10^{-2}, 2.33 \times 10^{-2}]$	4.66×10^{-4}	$[4.18 \times 10^{-4}, 5.27 \times 10^{-4}]$
MVZ-57	1.62×10^{-2}	$[1.60 \times 10^{-2}, 1.64 \times 10^{-2}]$	6.16×10^{-4}	$[5.53 \times 10^{-4}, 6.96 \times 10^{-4}]$
TM-57	2.70×10^{-2}	$[2.67 \times 10^{-2}, 2.73 \times 10^{-2}]$	5.00×10^{-4}	$[4.49 \times 10^{-4}, 566 \times 10^{-4}]$

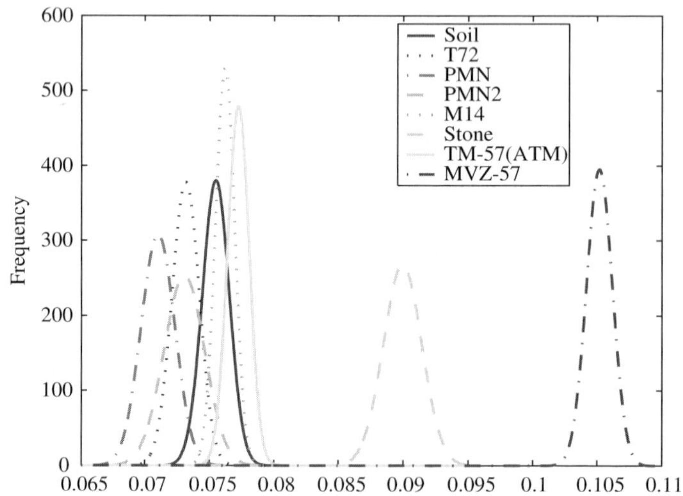

Fig. 7. Distribution map of feature point 1.

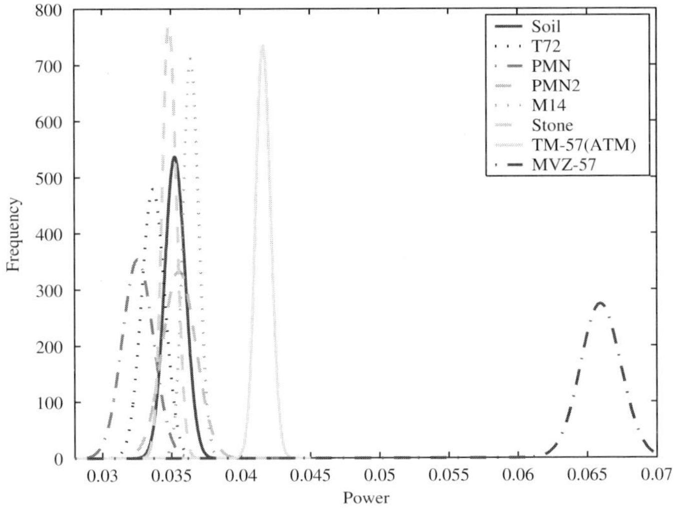

Fig. 8. Distribution map of feature point 2.

Each feature point shows that MVZ-57 has a feature which is completely different from the other candidates for measurement. Moreover, since the feature of stone appears distinguishable from feature points 1 and 6, it turns out that classification is easy. And, TM-57 can be easily classified from feature points 2 and 4.

On the other hand, feature point 5 appears most distinguishable from the soil and APM.

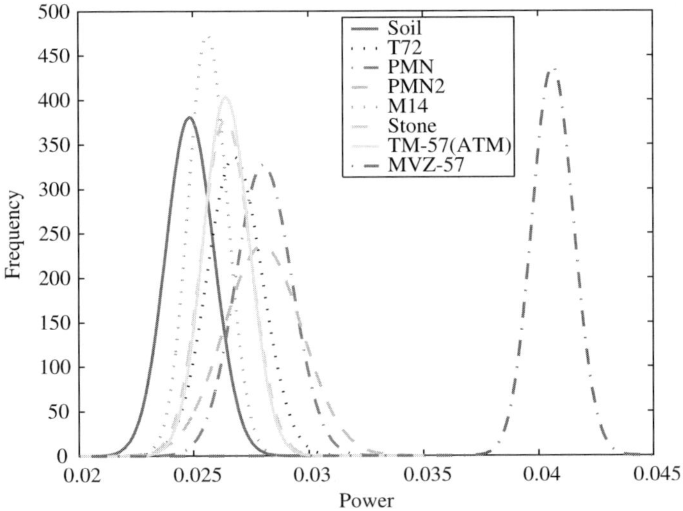

Fig. 9. Distribution map of feature point 3.

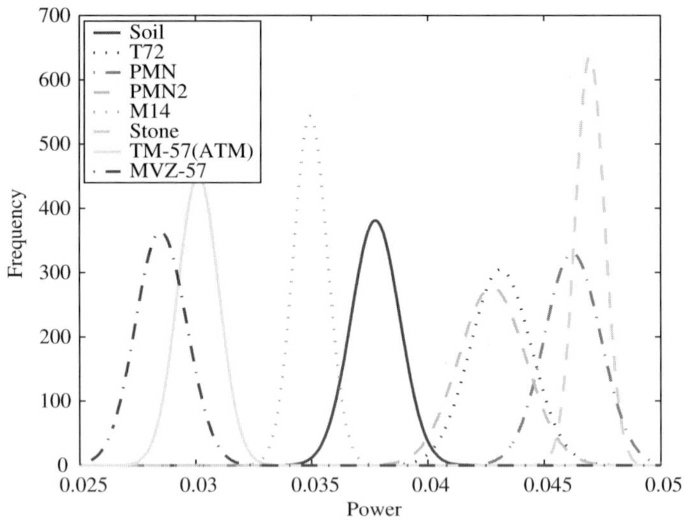

Fig. 10. Distribution map of feature point 4.

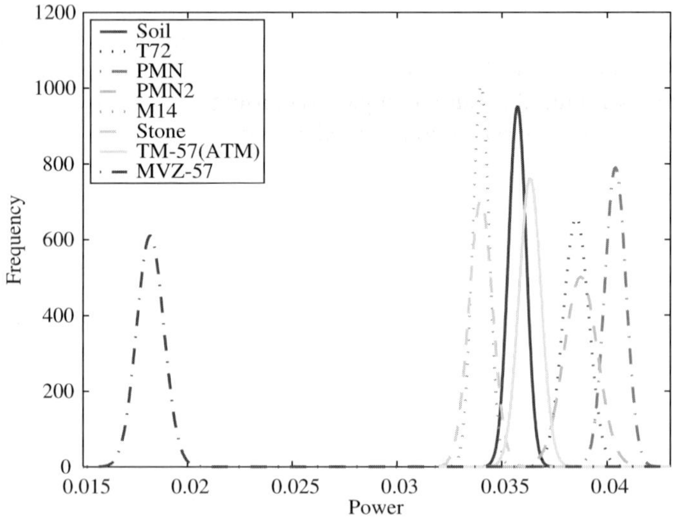

Fig. 11. Distribution map of feature point 5.

6.4. *Examination of classification possibility to APM*

In this section, based on the data of feature point 5 that the feature of APM appears most distinguishable, the detection and classification possibilities are examined. The feature point distribution map, with the removal of the feature distributions of metal-APM, stone and ATM, can be easily classified at other feature points, as shown in Fig. 13.

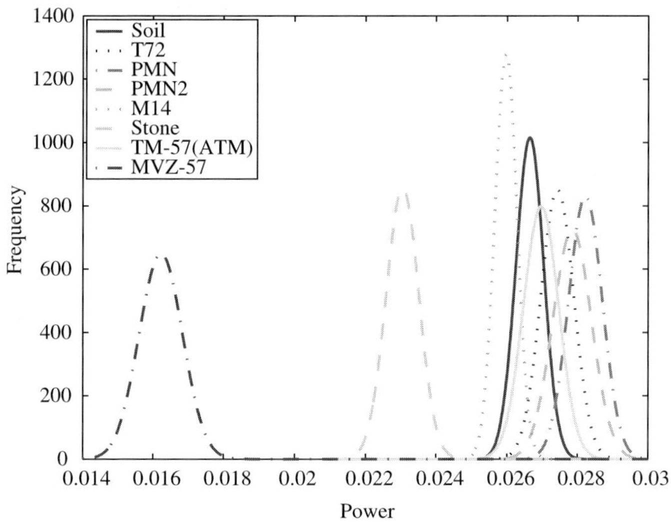

Fig. 12. Distribution map of feature point 6.

The most important consideration is whether the existence of a mine is distinguishable. Then, in order to classify soil, M14 and PMN2, which adjoin the soil distribution without the buried object according to the detection probability of 99.7%, the 3σ value classification boundary of each distribution is used. Two straight dashed lines show the 3σ value classification boundary for them in Fig. 13.

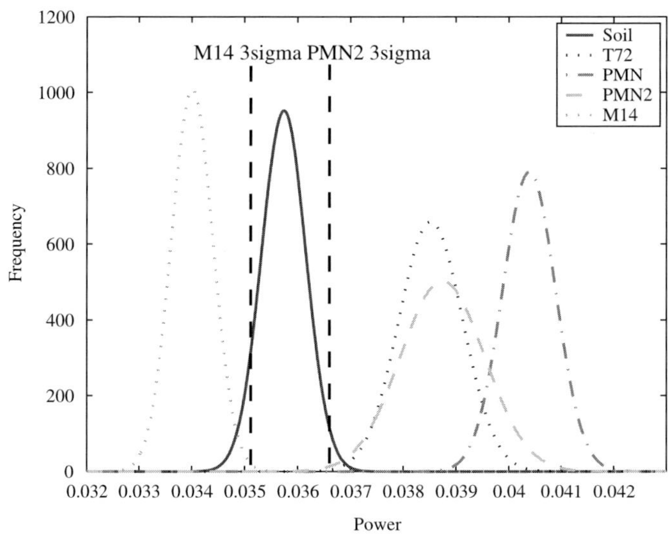

Fig. 13. Features of APM and 3σ boundary.

From Fig. 13, the critical region of the soil feature distribution determined by the 3σ boundary of M14 and the 3σ boundary of PMN2 becomes 18.2%. Therefore, a classification of PD 99.7% and PFD 18.2% is attained.

7. Conclusions

A mine detection algorithm by pattern classification using combined GPR and MD sensors was proposed.

The influence of temperature drift, which occurs with a temperature change at the time of data measurement, was sharply reduced by phase compensation signal processing. And, by statistical evaluation of experimental data, due to the peculiar features of buried objects, classification of APM, ATM, metal-APM, and stone was possible. Under ideal environment conditions, it was shown for APM that a 99.7% PD and 18.2% PFA are possible.

However, the data object represents ideal environmental data, and many problems exist in the application under real environmental conditions.

The influence of the laying-under-the-ground depth, ground lift of the sensor head and earth surface, soil containing impurities and the characteristic changes with the soil in which the dielectric constant characteristics differ should be considered. Furthermore, the feature extraction using the sensor fusion with MD should also be examined. Then, an optimal feature extraction algorithm and classification algorithm applicable to a real environment can be developed.

References

[1] M. Fujimoto and K. Nonami, *Study of mine detection algorithm and marking control to mine buried position by mine detection sensor*, The 20th Annual Conference of the Robotics Society of Japan in Osaka, 2J18 (2002).

[2] http://www.mext.go.jp/a_menu/kagaku/jirai/.

[3] M. Fujiwara, *Sensor for detection, application of combined sensor of ground penetrating radar and metal detector*, Workshop on Humanitarian Demining of Anti-Personnel Mines in Tokyo (2001) 78–83.

[4] I. Guttman and S.S. Wilks, *Introductory Engineering Statistics*, Wiley, New York (1965).

CHAPTER 20

Land Mine Detection Algorithm Using Ultra-Wide Band GPR

T. Fukuda and K. Yokoe

Nagoya University, Furo-cho, Chikusa-ku, Nagoya 464-8603, Japan

Y. Hasegawa

University of Tsukuba, 1-1-1, Tennodai, Ibaraki, Tsukuba 305-8573, Japan

T. Fukui

Nagoya University, Furo-cho, Chikusa-ku, Nagoya 464-8603, Japan

Contents

Abstract

In this chapter, we introduce a sensor-fusion-type mine detection system using a metal detector and a ground penetrating radar (GPR). In order to reduce the fault alarm rate of a metal detector in a conventional demining process, GPR is a promising tool as an additional sensor because it can observe the shape and depth of a buried object in a C-scan image

SYSTEMS AND HUMAN SCIENCE – FOR SAFETY, SECURITY, AND DEPENDABILITY
Edited by Tatsuo Arai, Shigeru Yamamoto and Kazuhisa Makino

when a sensor head of GPR is raster scanned precisely by a manipulator system. Therefore, it is possible to detect a land mine with a lower fault alarm rate based on not only metal detection but also the object shape. It enables shortening of the demining works. However, if two sensors are used for mine sensing, a worker has to synthesize multiple complicated information in addition to the precise raster scanning of the sensor head. Besides, an operator has to adjust the sensitivity of the metal detector and GPR according to its environment conditions such as the dielectric constant of a soil. Therefore, in this chapter we propose an automated mine detection algorithm based on a C-scan image and show some experimental results.

1. Introduction

A lot of land mines remain in hot-spots and in post hot-spots all over the world. It is said that the number of land mines is more than current mine actions with conventional tools can remove despite receiving support from many governments. The removal speed is important because people can come back and cultivate their land without risking being mutilated or killed.

There are three kinds of major demining approaches: manual mine clearance, animal detection such as dog and mechanical mine clearance. The manual approach can be applied everywhere. The mine dog detection is faster than the manual, but there are significant limitations to the applicable field. The mechanical mine clearance is the fastest. But there are also more significant limitations than the mine dogs and most machines are not easy to implement. The reason why the manual mine clearance is slow is that there is no appropriate sensor for mine detection. The detection rate of a metal detector that is the most popular detector is less than 1%. In almost all cases, a deminer has to dig and prod the area where a sensor responds but no mine is present [1–3]. Therefore, a purpose of our study is to improve this detection rate of the manual mine clearance by developing a mine detection system with a metal detector and ground penetrating radar (GPR).

One of the promising sensors for mine detection is GPR. GPR is used to find pipes of water, electricity and gas underground before construction. It can also find a big cavity underground before sinking. GPR provides a three-dimensional subsurface object image of a the scanning area by a precise raster scanning. From this image, we can get the shape of an object's upper side, which is very effective information for mine detection. We intuitively guess that the sensor fusion with a metal detector and the GPR can improve the detection accuracy by measuring not only metal response but also object shape. However, sensing data of GPR is enormous and dependent on the environmental conditions. Therefore, an automated adaptation system for the sensing conditions is required and furthermore an automated mine recognition system is desired to implement GPR for mine detection. Besides, a sensor fusion algorithm is also necessary since the system has more than two sensors for mine detection; otherwise an operator has to judge based on more than two kinds of information simultaneously in the mine searching process.

Therefore, we propose the concept of a sensor-fusion-type mine detection system with GPR and a metal detector, and propose the automated adaptation algorithm and the mine detection algorithm using GPR, which is a component of the sensor-fusion-type mine detection system. Finally we show measurement data in order to confirm the performance of the proposed algorithm.

2. Antipersonnel mine detection system

Our final objective is to develop an effective and safe mine detection system. This system can decrease fault alarm rate by using GPR and a metal detector and also decrease human work and its risk by an auto-mine-detector and robotic manipulator mounted on an unmanned vehicle shown in Fig. 1. This unmanned vehicle is equipped with low-contact-pressure tires so that it can move on a minefield receiving electric

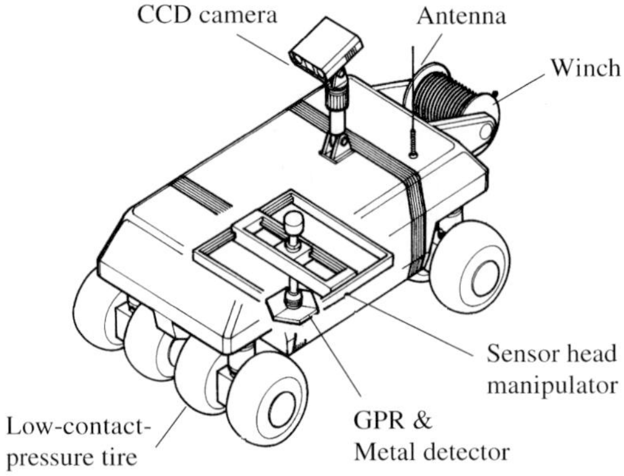

Fig. 1. Unmanned vehicle of antipersonnel mine detection system.

power and commands from a host system via a cable. A sensor head manipulator mounted on the vehicle can precisely control the sensor head's location and orientation of GPR and a metal detector keeping a certain gap to the ground surface and the orientation normal to the ground surface.

There are three categories of challenging technologies in order to develop the system: sensing, access-control and integration technology. The main technology is a sensing technology which consists of

(1) Integrated ultra-wide band GPR (UWB GPR) with a metal detector. UWB GPR has a high resolution, therefore the mine shape can be observed clearer. The integrated sensor is more effective than separated sensors because it can realize precise positioning of the responding point from two sensors.
(2) Sensor-fusion-type mine detection algorithm. Sensing data from GPR is not comprehensive for a user. Therefore, an automated mine recognition system is required to implement GPR for mine detection. Besides, a sensor fusion algorithm is also necessary since the system has more than two sensors for mine detection, otherwise an operator has to judge based on more than two kinds of information simultaneously.

In this chapter, we focus on the sensor-fusion-type mine detection algorithm in the sensing technology.

3. Mine detection algorithm

3.1. *Sensor-fusion-type mine detection system*

In this chapter, we propose the concept of a sensor-fusion-type mine detection system with GPR and a metal detector shown in Fig. 2. The metal detector not only detects the fuse part of a land mine but also detects a piece of metal such as a fragment or a bullet. They can be excluded based on the shape's difference in the three-dimensional image provided by GPR.

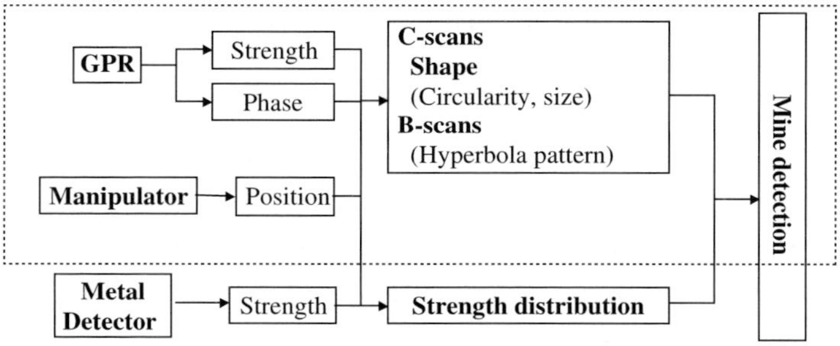

Fig. 2. Sensor-fusion-type mine detection algorithm.

The three-dimensional image is generated by synthetic aperture GPR and raster scanning. The process for the image is represented in Section 3.2. The sensor-fusion-type mine detection system decreases the fault alarm by using a metal detector and GPR including precise sensor head manipulation.

3.2. *C-scan image*

As for a display mode of sensing outputs of GPR, B-scan which shows a section picture of the underground is generally used. But we cannot guess the precise shape of an object from the B-scan image because it senses along only one traverse line. On the other hand, a C-scan image is the plane image at each depth which can show the shape of objects. As a signal processing for generating a C-scan image, synthetic aperture processing is used after selection of a necessary frequency component by gate processing.

3.2.1. *Gate processing.* When two objects P_1 and P_2 are buried at a depth of l_1 and l_2, respectively, a received signal φ at frequency ω is

$$\varphi = r_1 \sin \omega \frac{2l_1}{c} + r_2 \sin \omega \frac{2l_2}{c}, \tag{1}$$

where reflection rates of objects P_1 and P_2 are r_1, and r_2, respectively, and c is velocity of light. If the frequency ω is constant, these two objects cannot be divided from the observed signal φ. On the other hand, if ω is a function of time: $\omega(t) = at$, a received signal can be expressed by

$$r_1 \sin \frac{2l_1}{c} at + r_2 \sin \frac{2l_2}{c} at = r_1 \sin \omega_1 t + r_2 \sin \omega_2 t, \tag{2}$$

where

$$\omega_1 = \frac{2l_1}{c} a, \quad \omega_2 = \frac{2l_2}{c} a. \tag{3}$$

It is expressed by the sum of two signals of different frequency corresponding to each depth, and it can be separated by a low pass filter. In this way we can get a clear image by synthetic aperture processing after extraction of a necessary frequency component.

3.2.2. *Synthetic aperture processing.* Wave function φ is usually given by a function with four variables: x, y, z and k, but in this time, k can be treated as fixed because a specific frequency component with gate processing ($k = \omega/c$) is selected. Therefore, $\varphi(x, y, z, k)$ can be expressed by

$$\frac{\partial^2}{\partial t^2}\varphi(x,y,z) = c^2\left(\frac{\partial^2\varphi}{\partial x^2} + \frac{\partial^2\varphi}{\partial y^2} + \frac{\partial^2\varphi}{\partial z^2}\right). \tag{4}$$

If $e^{-2i\omega t}$ is substituted into (4), the equation is

$$\left(\frac{\partial^2}{\partial x^2} + \frac{\partial^2}{\partial y^2} + \frac{\partial^2}{\partial z^2} + 4k^2\right)\varphi(x,y,z) = 0. \tag{5}$$

When we apply Fourier extension for this $\varphi(x, y, z)$, it becomes

$$\varphi(x,y,z) = \int_{-\infty}^{\infty}\int_{-\infty}^{\infty} e^{ik_x x + ik_y y}\ Q(k_x, k_y, k, z)\ dk_x\ dk_y. \tag{6}$$

We substitute (6) for (5).

$$(-k_x^2 - k_y^2 + 4k^2)Q + \frac{\partial^2}{\partial z^2}Q = 0. \tag{7}$$

Therefore, a general solution for Q becomes the following expressions.

$$Q = \alpha\, e^{i\sqrt{4k^2 - k_x^2 - k_y^2}z} + \beta\, e^{-i\sqrt{4k^2 - k_x^2 - k_y^2}z}, \tag{8}$$

where α and β are coefficients that depend on the initial conditions. Here are two solutions. One is the solution when a target exists in a negative direction on z-axis, and the other is the solution when a target is in a positive direction. A solution with a physical meaning is the first item. In consequence a general solution of this $\varphi(x, y, z)$ becomes as follows:

$$\varphi = \int_{-\infty}^{\infty}\int_{-\infty}^{\infty} \alpha\, e^{i\sqrt{4k^2 - k_x^2 - k_y^2}z}\ e^{ik_x x + ik_y y}\ dk_x\ dk_y. \tag{9}$$

If we got measured data at $z = 0$, relational expressions of the measurement data

$\varphi(x, y, 0)$ and the coefficient α become

$$\varphi(x, y, 0) = \int_{-\infty}^{\infty} \int_{-\infty}^{\infty} \alpha(k_x, k_y)\, \mathrm{e}^{\mathrm{i}\sqrt{4k^2 - k_x^2 - k_y^2}0}\, \mathrm{e}^{\mathrm{i}k_x x + \mathrm{i}k_y y}\, \mathrm{d}k_x\, \mathrm{d}k_y, \tag{10}$$

and

$$\alpha(k_x, k_y) = \int_{-\infty}^{\infty} \int_{-\infty}^{\infty} \varphi(x, y, 0)\, \mathrm{e}^{-\mathrm{i}k_x x - \mathrm{i}k_y y}\, \mathrm{d}x\, \mathrm{d}y. \tag{11}$$

Therefore, we can derive the function by substituting α with a measured value of $z = 0$.

$$\varphi(x, y, z_0) = \int_{-\infty}^{\infty} \int_{-\infty}^{\infty} \left(\int_{-\infty}^{\infty} \int_{-\infty}^{\infty} \varphi(x, y, 0)\, \mathrm{e}^{-\mathrm{i}k_x x - \mathrm{i}k_y y}\, \mathrm{d}x\, \mathrm{d}y \right) \mathrm{e}^{\mathrm{i}\sqrt{4k^2 - k_x^2 - k_y^2} z_0}\, \mathrm{e}^{\mathrm{i}k_x x + \mathrm{i}k_y y}\, \mathrm{d}k_x\, \mathrm{d}k_y. \tag{12}$$

From this function, the data $\varphi(x, y, 0)$ which was measured at $z = 0$ is converted into the equivalent value $\varphi(x, y, z_0)$ measured at the top of a target shown in Fig. 3. In this case, Fourier expansion shortens the calculation time of FFT. Finally, we can get an image of the target by plotting on these two dimensions according to $\varphi(x, y, z_0)$.

In practice, the number of sampling signals is finite and the sampling area is also limited. Therefore, (12) is transformed into a discrete form as follows

$$\varphi(x, y, z_0) = \sum_{k_x=0}^{N_{k_x}-1} \sum_{k_y=0}^{N_{k_y}-1} \left(\sum_{x=0}^{N_x-1} \sum_{y=0}^{N_y-1} \varphi(x, y, 0)\, \mathrm{e}^{-\mathrm{i}k_x x - \mathrm{i}k_y y} \right) \mathrm{e}^{\mathrm{i}\sqrt{4k^2 - k_x^2 - k_y^2} z_0}\, \mathrm{e}^{\mathrm{i}k_x x + \mathrm{i}k_y y}, \tag{13}$$

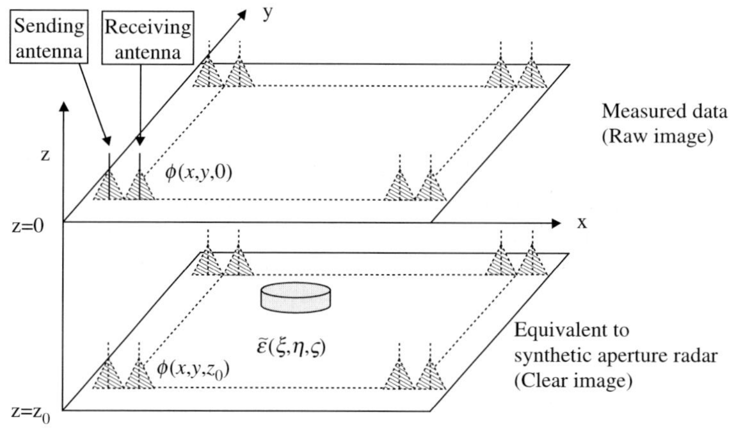

Fig. 3. Relationship between $\varphi(x, y, 0)$ and $\varphi(x, y, z_0)$.

where Δx and Δy are measurement intervals, and N_x and N_y are the number of sampling data in x and y directions, respectively. N_{kx}, N_{ky} are point numbers on Fourier expansion in x and y directions, and

$$N_{k_x} = \frac{2\pi}{\Delta x \Delta k_x}, \quad N_{k_y} = \frac{2\pi}{\Delta y \Delta k_y}. \tag{14}$$

The resolution depends on a measurement interval and on a wavelength of a radio wave. When the shorter measurement interval and the higher frequency of radio wave are realized, the higher resolution image of a buried object can be observed. These values should be carefully set, considering C-image resolution and the cost of signal processing in a real-time level. In this chapter, we use the intervals: $\Delta x = 10$ mm, $\Delta y = 10$ mm, and sampling numbers: $N_{kx} = 1024$, $N_{ky} = 1024$.

3.3. *Mine detection in C-scan image*

The C-scan image is obtained by the synthetic aperture processing and gate processing. In this subsection, the algorithm to detect a mine candidate in C-scan image is explained. It detects a mine based on shape features; circularity and size. In order to evaluate the circularity and the size of blocks in C-scan, we have to make a binary image from the gray-scale C-scan image. The threshold setting should be adaptive because the strength of the radio wave scattered from an object is dependent on the relative permittivity, profile of top surface of an object, object size, object depth, object orientation and so on. In other words, some mines are observed at a threshold, but some mines disappear at the same threshold. Besides, the strength of radio wave scattered from an object is also dependent on the frequency used by GPR. The power spectrum has a peak at a certain frequency like a resonance phenomenon. Therefore, the proper strength and frequency should be adjusted in order to generate binary C-scan images at each depth. In total we have three parameters: threshold, frequency and depth as shown in Fig. 4.

As one of the solutions for these parameter settings, we make binary images at all thresholds from a C-scan image and pick up all candidates which satisfy selection conditions in all the binary images. We consider two indices as a selection condition: circularity and size in order to eliminate small pieces of metal and large objects. A metal detector cannot distinguish those from a land mine. The circularity is calculated by

$$C_{\text{ircularity}} = 4\pi A_{\text{rea}}/(G_{\text{irth}})^2, \tag{15}$$

$$G_{\text{irth}} = N_x + N_y + 1.414 N_{xy}, \tag{16}$$

where A_{rea} is the pixel number of a candidate in C-scan image, and N_x and N_y are pixel numbers on the edge of the candidate in x and y directions, respectively. Besides, N_{xy} is the pixel number in bias directions of the edge of the candidate.

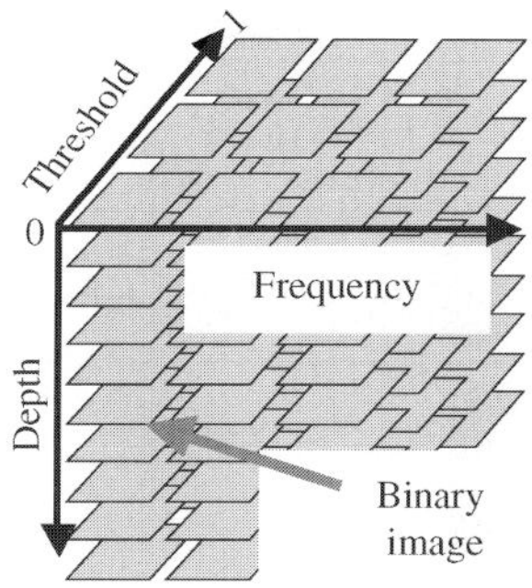

Fig. 4. Binary images made at every step of threshold, frequency and depth from C-scan image.

The flow of the mine detection task is as follows:

(1) Make C-scan image at every depth step and every frequency step.
(2) Normalize C-scan image after noise reduction by median filtering.
(3) Make binary images from C-scan image by changing strength threshold from 0.01 to 0.99 with 0.01 interval.
(4) Extract features of each block observed in the binary C-scan images: circularity and size.

4. Experimental results

We investigate the performance of our proposed mine detection algorithm in a test field. Two expanded polystyrene boxes are filled with sand or trass as shown in Fig. 5. The trass disturbs the radio field of GPR because it consists of volcanic ashes and stones with magnetic material. In these fields, two types of land mine mock-ups, two stones and a spherical expanded polystyrene are buried at the depth of 100 mm as shown in Fig. 6. We used commercially available GPR "UG-V33A" which is a product of Mitsui Engineering and Shipbuilding. Its transmitter is FMCW (frequency-modulated continuous wave) from 30 MHz to 1 GHz. The minefield dimensions are 660 mm × 320 mm and scanning interval is 20 mm.

As detection conditions, we set that the circularity should be more than 0.6 and that the area size is from 10 cm^2 to 100 cm^2. We investigate the performance of our algorithm on a

Fig. 5. Minefield (left: sand, right: trass).

Item	Photo	Feature	Item	Photo	Feature
Mock-up (M-14)		Plastic Φ 60 mm Height : 50 mm	Stone (spherical)	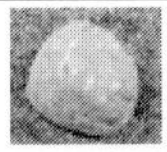	Φ 65~75 mm
Mock-up (TYPE72)	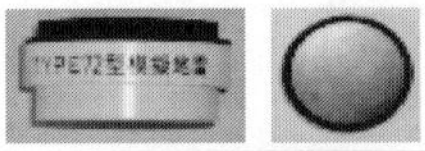	Plastic Φ 78 mm Height : 40 mm	Expanded polystyrene	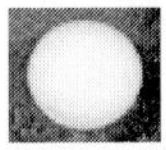	Expanded polystyrene Φ 70 mm
Stone (elliptic)		100 × 185 mm			

Fig. 6. Buried objects.

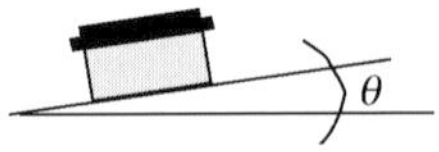

Fig. 7. Orientation of buried object ($\theta = 0, 15, 30, 45, 60, 75, 90$ in degrees).

mine detection rate defined by (17) when the angles of buried objects were changed from 0 to 90 at 15° steps as shown in Fig. 7.

$$P = \frac{n}{7}, \tag{17}$$

where P is detection rate and n is the orientation number from 1 to 7.

We show the measuring data of M-14 mock-up in the sand field in B-scan image and C-scan image in Fig. 8(a). The C-scan image is made when the mean frequency is 0.39 GHz, the threshold is 0.85 and the depth is 100 mm. In this case, all conditions for mine judgment are satisfied so that the detection system could recognize it as a mine. In another case where the elliptic-shaped stone is buried in sand in the same depth, the most circular image is observed when the mean frequency is 0.39 GHz, the threshold is 0.89 and

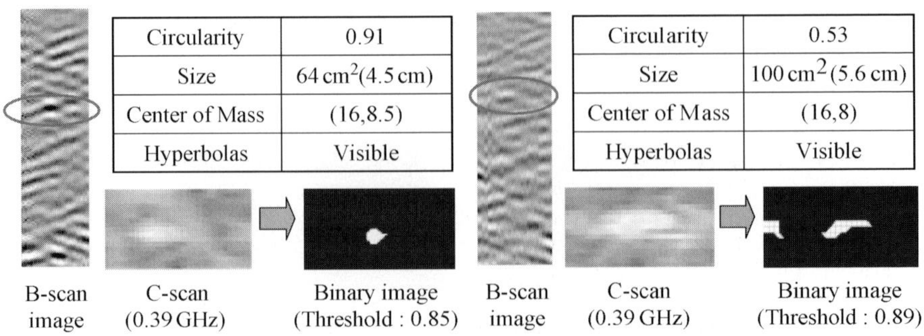

Fig. 8. Measurement results.

Table 1. Exploration results of the proposed mine detection algorithm

Environmental condition	M14	72AP	Expanded polystyrene	Stone (elliptic)	Stone (spherical)
			Sand		
10 cm	100	57	100	–	100
15 cm	100	57	100	–	100
20 cm	100	57	–	–	100
			Trass		
10 cm	100	57	100	–	100
15 cm	100	57	100	–	100
20 cm	100	57	–	–	–

Numeric values show identification rate, and "–" means that the system finds a candidate but rejects.

the depth is 100 mm as shown in Fig. 8(b). However, the circularity does not satisfy the condition. Therefore, the system does not recognize it as a land mine. The results of the other objects in both the fields are summarized in Table 1 using the detection rate. Numerical values in the table means the detection rate and "–" means the system finds an object but rejects the candidate. From these results, the proposed algorithm can detect the spherical objects which have almost the same radius as a land mine. But the system only with GPR cannot distinguish a land mine from spherical objects. Therefore, the sensor fusion system with other sensors such as a metal detector is required in order to reduce the fault alarm rate.

5. Conclusion

We introduced the sensor-fusion-type mine detection system and proposed the mine detection algorithm based on C-scan image of GPR. In this algorithm, we adaptively obtain the best C-scan image by finding the best parameter settings: frequency and strength of GPR and then evaluate the shape and size of each candidate observed in it. We experimentally confirmed the performance of the proposed algorithm. This algorithm could reduce the fault alarm rate by installing the sensor-fusion-type mine detection system.

As future works, we will investigate performance improvement of our algorithm in real minefields after development of the sensor-fusion-type mine detection system.

References

[1] (Geneva International Centre for Humanitarian Demining), Mine Action Equipment: Study of Global Operational Needs (2002).

[2] K.A. Moody and J.P. LeVasseur, *Current and Emerging Technologies for Use in a Hand-Held Mine Detector*, Land Force Technical Staff Course V, Department of Applied Military Science, The Royal Military College of Canada, (2000).

[3] J.P. Trevelyan, *Technology Needs for Humanitarian Demining*, Department of Mechanical and Materials Engineering, The University of Western Australia, (2000), February.

CHAPTER 21

Development of Highly Sensitive Biosensor for Explosive Substances*

T. Onodera

Japan Science and Technology Agency, Hon-cho 4-1-8, Kawaguchi, Saitama 332-0012, Japan

R. Harada

Art, Science and Technology Center for Cooperative Research, Kyushu University, Kasuga-shi, Fukuoka 816-8580, Japan

D. Ravi Shankaran

Japan Science and Technology Agency, Hon-cho 4-1-8, Kawaguchi, Saitama 332-0012, Japan

T. Sakai

Graduate School of Agriculture, Kyushu University, Hakozaki 6-10-1, Fukuoka 812-8581, Japan

J. Liang

Graduate School of Information Science and Electrical Engineering, Kyushu University, Hakozaki 6-10-1, Fukuoka 812-8581, Japan

K. Matsumoto

Graduate School of Agriculture, Kyushu University, Hakozaki 6-10-1, Fukuoka 812-8581, Japan

*This work has been supported by Japan Science and Technology Agency (JST).

SYSTEMS AND HUMAN SCIENCE – FOR SAFETY, SECURITY, AND DEPENDABILITY
Edited by Tatsuo Arai, Shigeru Yamamoto and Kazuhisa Makino

N. Miura

Art, Science and Technology Center for Cooperative Research, Kyushu University, Kasuga-shi, Fukuoka 816-8580, Japan

T. Imato

Graduate School of Engineering, Kyushu University, Hakozaki 6-10-1, Fukuoka 812-8581, Japan

K. Toko

Graduate School of Information Science and Electrical Engineering, Kyushu University, Hakozaki 6-10-1, Fukuoka 812-8581, Japan

Contents

Abstract

Explosive molecules which are leaking from a landmine may have extremely low concentrations in soil or air. In the present study, we aim at the development of a highly sensitive biosensor to detect explosive molecules for landmine detection. We realized the biosensor using a Surface Plasmon Resonance sensor and antigen–antibody reaction, and then the sensor detected 2,4,6-trinitrophenol, which is one of the explosives with high sensitivity of ppb level.

1. Introduction

There are more than 100 million landmines that have been buried in the world, and 3 million landmines are newly buried every year. It is a serious problem that anti-personnel landmines cause extensive damage to more than 20,000 people a year. However, only 100,000 landmines are removed a year [1].

Metal detectors are used to detect landmines. Landmines with plastic cases can be detected by increasing the sensitivity of metal detectors. However, there are many metal fragments on minefields. In this case, metal detectors will also react to metal fragments. If the metal detector sounds an alarm, a deminer must check the existence of landmines following manual procedures. Thus, it needs a lot of time to detect landmines using metal detectors.

On the other hand, dogs are the most reliable for detecting landmines. Trinitrotoluene and dinitrotoluene which are leaking from a landmine [2] may have extremely low concentrations in soil or air. Thus, dogs can detect landmines by sniffing over the field. However, training of dogs costs a lot of money, and also handlers need patient training for a long period. In addition, dogs cannot concentrate on detection for more than 2 h. Thus, a novel technology is desired for efficient landmine detection.

In recent years, various kinds of detecting landmine technologies have produced physical sensors such as ground penetrating radar (GPR); however, it is difficult to detect landmines using only a physical sensor. As chemical sensing technologies, gas chromatography–mass spectrometry, enzyme-linked immunosorbent assay (ELISA), and radioimmunoassay-based methods are sensitive for explosive substances. These methods are difficult to apply for landmine detection, because mine detection tools must have five conditions: low cost, portability, high throughput, operationality and high reliability. In order to overcome these conditions, Nomadics Inc. developed Fluorescence Impersonating Dog Olfaction (Fido) which is a highly sensitive and selective sensor for 2,4,6-trinitrotoluene (TNT) vapors emanating from a landmine, and is based on amplifying fluorescent polymers. The polymer was developed by Swager's group at Massachusetts Institute of Technology. Fido can detect TNT in the parts per quadrillion range [3]. However, the sensor has a lack of selectivity. Fido reacted to aromatic compounds, which do not have a nitro group [4]. Therefore, Fido has to be used with a gas chromatograph for obtaining actual selectivity to detect nitro aromatics for landmine detection [5,6]. Gas chromatography is difficult to use on the field from the viewpoint of portability.

One of the most sensitive sensors is a Surface Plasmon Resonance (SPR) sensor. Antigen–antibody reaction is used in immunoassay such as ELISA. Antibody has specificity to its antigen, and hence trace substances can be detected using antibody. In the present study, we aim at the development of an ultra super-sensitive biosensor to detect trace explosive molecules by combining the SPR sensor technology with antigen–antibody reaction. The SPR sensor and the antigen–antibody reaction are used for obtaining high sensitivity and high selectivity, respectively.

2. Experiments

2.1. *Principle of detection*

We use an SPR sensor, which has the highest sensitivity among various kinds of chemical sensors and biosensors. The principle of an SPR sensor is as follows.

An evanescent wave appears on the surface of Au thin film when light is irradiated to the film as shown in Fig. 1. Surface plasmon appears on the opposite side facing the sample solution. When the wave number of the evanescent wave is matched with that of the surface plasmon, the intensity of refraction is reduced because photon energies are used to excite the surface plasmon. This phenomenon is called an SPR. The resonance angle, which is the incident angle when the refraction intensity is most reduced, will be affected by the refraction indices of Au thin film modified with antibodies and the attached solution. The resonance angle is largely shifted by binding a tiny amount of measured samples, i.e., antigens, with antibodies.

The concentration of target samples can be estimated by obtaining a correlation between the analyte concentration and the resonance angle beforehand. For highly sensitive detection, we use an indirect competitive method, which is effective to detect chemical substances with low molecular weight [7–9]. The refraction index of Au thin film modified with antigen–protein conjugates depends on the concentration of antigen and the substances can be detected using the SPR.

The indirect competitive method is used to enlarge the angle shift, because the method is adopted to detect antibodies, which are bound to the Au surface, instead of antigens. In other words, the method detects antigens indirectly. The difference in molecular weight between antigen and antibody is more than 100 times. The method had been first introduced to the sensor technique by Miura *et al.* [10,11] in 1992 for the detection of small molecules. The schematic diagram of the indirect competitive method is shown in Fig. 2. In this method, antigen–proteins are immobilized on the Au thin film. Antigen causes the competitive immuno reaction with the antibody added to the sample solution. When antibody solution flows on the Au thin film immobilized with antigen–proteins,

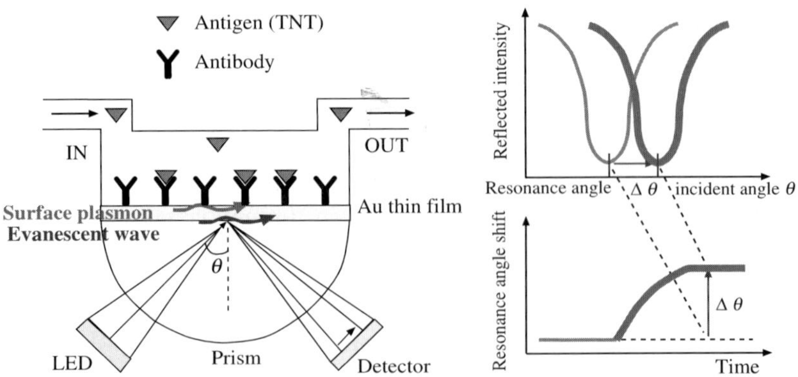

Fig. 1. Schematic diagram of the SPR sensor.

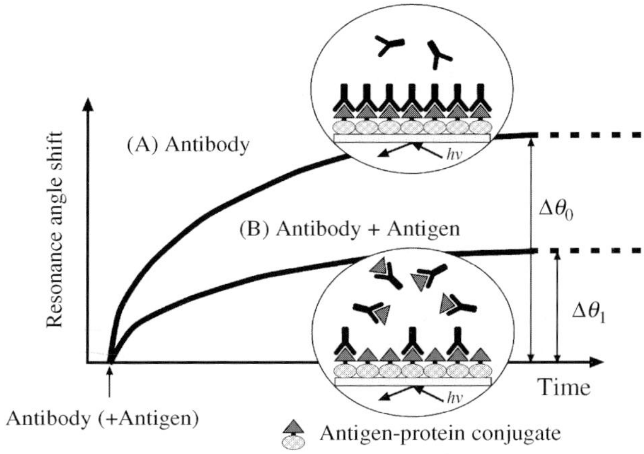

Fig. 2. Principle of TNP detection by SPR immunosensor.

immuno reaction occurs between immobilized antigen–proteins and antibodies, and then the resonance angle shift ($\Delta\theta_0$) will appear. When antigen exists in antibody solution, the immuno reaction between antigen–proteins and antibodies is inhibited by antigen, resulting in decline of the resonance angle shift by $\Delta\theta_1$. Quantitative determination of the antigen concentration can be made from the difference of $\Delta\theta_0$ and $\Delta\theta_1$.

2.2. *Materials*

Eighty percent of the landmines contain TNT as an explosive. Figure 3 shows the structure of TNT and 2,4,6-trisenitrophenol (TNP). Here, we selected TNP as a target substance instead of TNT as a first step to detect explosives with high sensitivity. TNP is similar to TNT, because they have three nitro groups and TNP is also an explosive. The difference is that each substance has either a methyl group or a hydroxyl group. In addition, the purchase of TNP is easy.

TNP has no immunogenicity due to its low molecular weight and thus, it should be modified into a conjugate with a protein such as bovine serum albumin (BSA). TNP–BSA

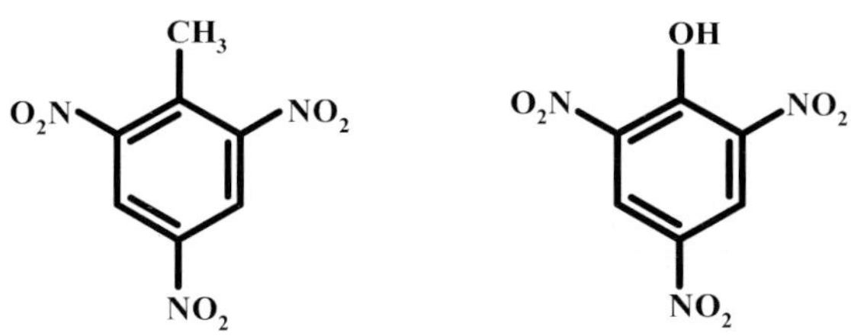

2,4,6-trinitrotolune (TNT) 2,4,6-trinitrophenol (TNP)

Fig. 3. Explosive substances.

conjugate (TNP–BSA) and anti–TNP antibody (TNP–Ab) were purchased from Cosmo Bio Co., Ltd.

Each of TNP–BSA, BSA, TNP–Ab and TNP was dissolved in phosphate buffer saline (PBS; pH 7.2) and the running buffer was PBS (pH 7.2). Pepsin was prepared in glycine/HCl buffer (0.2 M; pH 2.0). All the measurements were carried out at room temperature.

A sensor assembly used here was composed of a prototype SPR analyzer (provided by TOTO Ltd, Japan) working with the Kretschmann configuration, a flow cell and a microtube peristaltic pump. An Au thin film, prepared by sputtering gold on a glass prism with chromium as an adhesion layer, was used as the base for a sensor chip. The Au sputtered glass prism was attached to the flow cell of the SPR instrument. The thickness of the gold film was *ca.* 45 nm.

3. Results and discussion

TNP–BSA was physically immobilized on the gold surface of the sensor chip by the flow of 500 ppm TNP–BSA solution as shown in Fig. 4. Then, the resonance angle shift of the sensor increased rapidly and reached a steady state in about 15 min. The increment in resonance angle shift due to the adsorption of TNP–BSA was *ca.* 0.26°. Then the chip was exposed to the flow of BSA solution (1000 ppm) three times in order to block non-specific adsorption sites of the chip. Although the subsequent exposure to the flow of PBS was made following each flow of TNP–BSA or BSA, no change in the resonance angle was observed. The total angle shift by the three BSA treatments was *ca.* 0.14°.

TNP was added to the TNP–Ab solution to prepare the test solutions containing 50 ppm TNP–Ab and TNP of different concentrations (1000–0 ppb). The solutions were

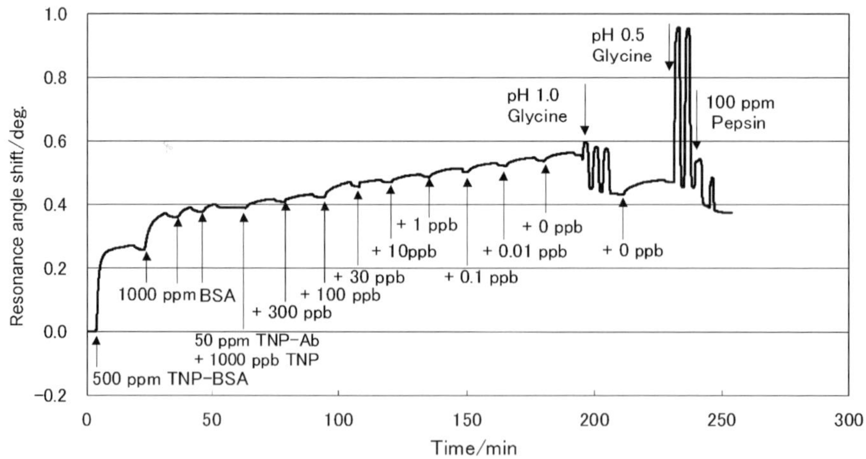

Fig. 4. Response transients of resonance angle of the TNP–BSA immobilized SPR sensor to TNP solutions of different concentrations.

injected sequentially. When 1000 ppb TNP added in 50 ppm TNP–Ab solution was circulated, the angle shift changed a little. In this case, most antibodies were inhibited from binding to TNP–BSA, and hence the resonance angle did not increase. In the case of 30 ppb TNP, the angle shift became larger than 1000 ppb TNP. The resonance angle shift due to 0 ppb TNP (TNP–Ab without TNP) following 0.01 ppb TNP indicates the maximum binding between antibody and immobilized TNP–BSA. It means $\Delta\theta_0$ as in Fig. 4.

We found that the flow of glycine did not completely remove anchored antibody. However, the antibody was removed on exposure to the flow of pepsin (100 ppm) glycine/HCl buffer solution for a few minutes. Pepsin is a proteolytic enzyme. The difference in refractive index between PBS and glycine/HCl buffer solution caused a peak-like drastic shift in the resonance angle of the sensor chip during the pepsin treatment. Use of pepsin solution has already been reported for the purpose of regenerating a sensor chip bound with anti-BaP–BSA antibody [9]. Then the sensor chip was reusable more than 20 times.

As shown in Fig. 5, the resonance angle shift was sensitive to the concentration of TNP in the range of 0.1–1000 ppb. The base line was fixed at 0.39° in Fig. 4; 0° as in Fig. 5 means the base line. The large difference in molecular weight between TNP–Ab and TNP and also the strong association of the antibody with the antigen seem to furnish such a high sensitivity. Using the currently developed SPR immunosensor, the concentration of TNP was determined as low as 0.1–1 ppb. Additionally, antibody has specificity to its antigen, and hence trace substances can be detected selectively using the antibody. The TNP–Ab does not bind to chemical substances, which exist in soil and air, except for nitro aromatics. Furthermore, the binding ability of the antibody to aromatics with two nitro groups is low. Therefore, the SPR immunosensor can distinguish its antigen exactly.

We also tried to detect TNP using an SPR angle measuring instrument (SPR-20, DKK, Japan) with displacement method, which is different from the indirect competitive method [12]. Protein G′ (SIGMA) was immobilized via a self-assembled monolayer on a sensor chip coated with Au thin film. The monolayer was created by 11-mercaptoundecanoic

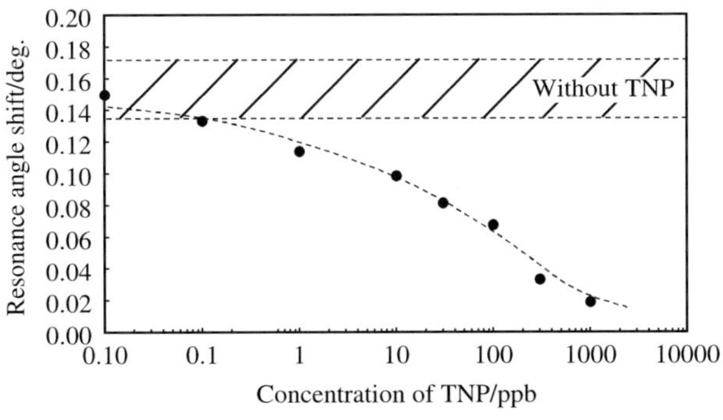

Fig. 5. Dependence of the resonance angle shift of TNP–BSA immobilized SPR sensor on the concentration of TNP.

acid (Aldrich). The sensor chip was exposed to the flow of anti-TNP–BSA antibody (TNP–BSA–Ab), which was made by our group. TNP–BSA–Ab bound to protein G′ with 0.4° of resonance angle shift. TNP–KLH (Biosearch Technologies) was introduced to the sensor cell, and TNP–KLH bound to TNP–BSA–Ab with 0.1° of angle shift. Then, 0.1 ppb TNP was injected into the cell. The decrease in the resonance angle was 0.007°. This result indicates that TNP–KLH was displaced with TNP and the method can be used to detect the ppb level of TNP.

4. Conclusion

A highly sensitive SPR-based immunosensor for detection of TNP functioning with indirect competitive method and displacement method was developed. The sensor detected TNP with the sensitivity of ppb level.

In future, monoclonal antibodies to TNT and 2,4-dinitrotoluene (DNT) and a high-performance sampling system will be developed for a landmine detection system. Then we are going to try to detect TNT and DNT using the developed methods with the sampling system and antibodies.

Acknowledgments

We would like to acknowledge valuable discussions with Prof. K. Ushijima, Prof. K. Hayashi, Prof. T. Matsui and Dr. M. Sou of Kyushu University and Mr H. Ohara of TOTO Ltd.

References

[1] J. MacDonald, J.R. Lockwood, J. McFee, T. Altshuler, T. Broach, L. Carin, R. Harmon, C. Rappaport, W. Scott and R. Weaver, Alternatives for Landmine Detection, Rand, California (2003), 1–13.

[2] T.F. Jenkins, D.C. Leggett, P.H. Miyares, M.E. Walsh, T.T. Ranney, J.H. Cragin and V. George, *Chemical signatures of TNT-filled land mines*, Talanta **54** (2001), 501–513.

[3] V.K. Pamula, Detection of Explosives, Handbook of Machine Olfaction: Electronic Nose Technology, Wiley-VCH, New York (2003), 547–560.

[4] J.-S. Yang and T.M. Swager, *Fluorescent porous polymer films as TNT chemosensors: electronic and structural effects*, J. Am. Chem. Soc. **120** (1998), 11864–11873.

[5] M. Grone, M. Fisher, C. Cumming and E. Towers, *Investigation of an area reduction method for suspected minefields using an ultra-sensitive chemical vapor detector*, Proc. SPIE **4742** (2002), 550–561.

[6] M. Fishe and J. Sikes, *Minefield edge detection using a novel chemical vapor sensing technique*, Proc. SPIE **5089** (2003), 1078–1087.

[7] K.V. Gobi, S.J. Kim, R. Harada and N. Miura, *Sub-ppb level detection of 2-hydroxybiphenyl using portable surface-plasmon-resonance immunosensor*, Electrochemistry **71** (6) (2003), 430–432.

[8] N. Miura, M. Sakai, G. Sakai and K.V. Gobi, *Regenerable surface plasmon resonance (SPR)-based immunosensor for highly sensitive measurement of sub-ppb levels of benzo(a)pyrene*, Chem. Lett. **31** (3) (2002), 342–343.

[9] N. Miura, M. Sakaki, K.V. Gobi, C. Kataoka and Y. Shoyama, *Highly sensitive and selective surface plasmon resonance sensor for detection of sub-ppb levels of benzo[a]pyrene by indirect competitive immunoreaction method*, Biosens. Bioelectron. **18** (2003), 953–959.

[10] N. Miura, H. Higobashi, G. Sakai, A. Takeyasu, T. Uda and N. Yamazoe, *Piezoelectric crystal immunosensor for sensitive detection of methamphetamine (stimulant drug) in human urine*, Technical Digest of the Fourth International Meeting on Chemical Sensors, (1992), 228–231.

[11] N. Miura, H. Higobashi, G. Sakai, A. Takeyasu, T. Uda and N. Yamazoe, *Piezoelectric crystal immunosensor for sensitive detection of methamphetamine (stimulant drug) in human urine*, Sensors Actuators B **13–14** (1993), 188–191.

[12] A.W. Kusterbeck, G.A. Wemhoff, P.T. Charles, D.A. Yeager, R. Bredehorst, C.-W. Vogel and F.S. Ligler, *A continuous flow immunoassay for rapid and sensitive detection of small molecules*, J. Immunol. Methods **135** (1990), 191–197.

CHAPTER 22

Complex-Valued Self-Organizing Map: A Framework of Adaptive Processing for Multiple-Frequency Millimeter-Wave Interferometric Imaging Systems

Akira Hirose

Department of Electrical and Electronic Engineering, The University of Tokyo, 7-3-1 Hongo, Bunkyo-ku, Tokyo 113-8656, Japan

Department of Frontier Informatics, The University of Tokyo, 7-3-1 Hongo, Bunkyo-ku, Tokyo 113-8656, Japan

Takahiro Hara

Department of Frontier Informatics, The University of Tokyo, 7-3-1 Hongo, Bunkyo-ku, Tokyo 113-8656, Japan

Contents

SYSTEMS AND HUMAN SCIENCE – FOR SAFETY, SECURITY, AND DEPENDABILITY
Edited by Tatsuo Arai, Shigeru Yamamoto and Kazuhisa Makino

Abstract

An adaptive system needs to possess a framework of adaptability that reflects properly its object and circumstances. This chapter describes a complex-valued self-organizing map (C-SOM), which is a class of complex-valued neural networks, for imaging plastic landmines with an electromagnetic wave radar front-end. A transmitted electromagnetic wave propagates, being diffracted and reflected by changes in medium properties, and interferes to generate an image at a receiver surface. Thereby, the basic variables are amplitude, phase and frequency. The information space constructed by phase and/or frequency has a specific periodic topology that depends on the objectives of observation. An adaptive mine imaging system should have a framework that reflects such signal properties. The C-SOM is one of the adaptive systems that satisfy the requirement. The feature vector extractor of the C-SOM determines the fundamental metric and constructs an information space so that the space is appropriate for the coherent radar image treatment. In this chapter, we report that a C-SOM based mine imaging system performs successfully the segmentation of plastic mines buried near the ground surface.

1. Introduction

To construct safe, secure and reliable systems, we need to deal with objective phenomena by building proper models of them. Neural network systems are expected to realize adaptive treatment in various applications. However, even in the neural network cases, the proper *a priori* modeling is equally important because the network behavior reflects strongly the adaptability framework of the network.

Assume that we construct a radar system using the electromagnetic wave. The wave possesses the amplitude and phase as its entity. It generates a radar raw image after wave-attributed physical phenomena such as propagation, diffraction, reflection and interference. We have to prepare a framework of adaptive signal processing with which the system can treat the raw image properly.

This chapter proposes a complex-valued self-organizing map (C-SOM), a class of complex-valued neural networks [1], to perform the imaging of buried mines. The C-SOM provides the radar image clustering system with an appropriate adaptive framework. The main reason is that the feature vector generator of the C-SOM extracts a set of features in such a manner that the metric reflects the wave nature of the radar image yielding process.

Ground penetrating radars (GPRs) which observe underground nondestructively are applied to many fields such as underground target detection, ruin exploration and underground stream investigation [2,3]. The GPRs will possibly be applied also to landmine detection because of their possibility to detect nonmetal mines [4–6]. However, plastic anti-personnel mine detection is a difficult task for them because of the small size, low reflectance, influence of ground surface and inhomogeneity of soil. In addition, lack of mine disposal experts and danger of demining make it necessary to support and automate the mine detection.

This chapter proposes multi-frequency interferometric radar imaging system using the C-SOM [7,8]. We construct an interferometric millimeter front-end with a Vector Network Analyzer (VNA) that observes amplitude and phase simultaneously at multiple frequencies. The observed data is processed adaptively by the C-SOM [1,9]. We report successful experimental results on visualization of plastic mine buried near the ground surface.

2. System construction

Plastic mine detection by GPRs is difficult for some reasons in general. The first reason lies in the profile of plastic mines. The reflectance of a plastic mine is very low since it is made of as little metal as possible. In addition, its size is often smaller than the wavelengths of conventional GPRs.

The other reason is the influence of surroundings. The reflection at the ground surface is unavoidable in measuring underground with the GPRs. It is difficult to distinguish a reflection at the ground surface and that at shallowly buried mines. Moreover, variation of dielectric constant of soil affects the propagation of the electromagnetic wave since its

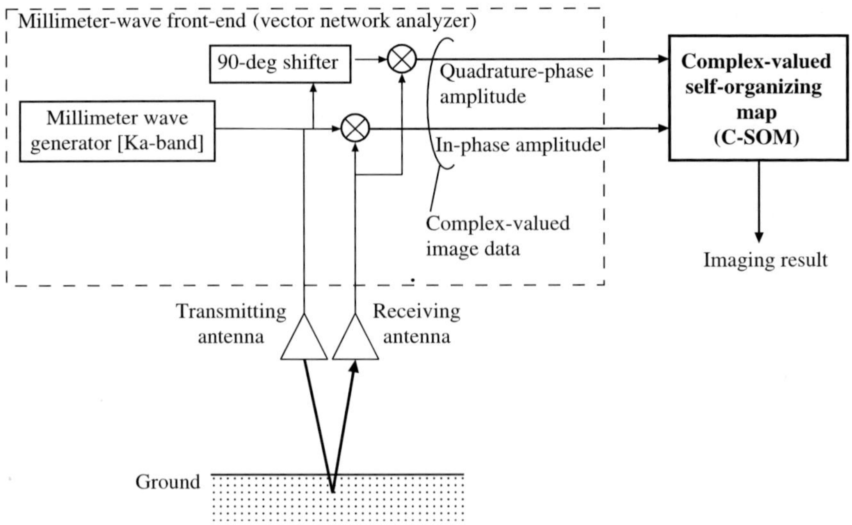

Fig. 1. Construction of the interferometric radar system.

velocity depends on the soil composition and moisture. The roughness of the ground surface also influences the signals to be detected.

Figure 1 shows the system construction. We construct an experimental millimeter wave front-end with a VNA. Millimeter wave generated in the VNA is transmitted at a transmitting horn antenna targeting an object. The wave propagates and is reflected at the object. The system receives it at a receiving horn antenna. Then the VNA yields the detection/transmission ratio of amplitude and phase through homodyne detection. The system performs the observation at multi-frequency points so that the observation data reflect the object property and the range. We deal with the multi-frequency data adaptively with the C-SOM mentioned in the following section.

The sensing part (antennas) consists of two square horn antennas. We carried out our observation in millimeter band (30–40 GHz). We filled a 70 cm × 70 cm container with soil and placed an object on/in it. In the present experimental system, the sensing part is mechanically scanned translationally. A personal computer (PC) controls the system and obtains image data. We perform adaptive clustering using C-SOM on the PC.

3. C-SOM signal processing

The adaptive signal processing of the C-SOM is performed as follows.

3.1. *Feature vector extraction*

In the system, we conduct multi-frequency observation. Fourier analysis confirms the fact that frequency-domain data and time-domain one (depth direction data in the system) are equivalent in nature. We adopt a nonlinear adaptive signal processing method to deal with the frequency-domain data. That is, we propose a feature vector extraction from complex-valued information in the frequency domain.

A pixel in the image has complex-valued data constructed by in-phase and quadrature-phase amplitudes observed at multiple frequencies. In the radar image clustering system using the C-SOM, a small area block is assigned to every pixel, including the pixel itself at the top-left, in an overlapping manner. Then a feature vector of the pixel is calculated for each pixel based on the block data. Radar image clustering is performed based on the distribution of the feature vectors in a high-dimensional feature-vector space.

Figure 2 presents the block diagram of the nonlinear adaptive clustering system based on the C-SOM. The system consists of two parts: a feature vector extractor and a self-organizing map. First, we prepare a $L \times L$ small block for each pixel by centering the pixel itself in the block. The blocks therefore overlap with neighbors. Feature extractor calculates a feature vector that reflects the statistical property of each block data. We adopt a complex-valued mean and covariances as described below. The feature vector is extracted at block after block, i.e., repeatedly for all the image pixels. Then they are fed to a SOM which classifies each pixel into an appropriate class adaptively.

In the system, we define the feature vector so that the metric that determines the distance between resulting information data reflects the wave nature of the interferometric radar. The wave has a 2π periodicity in its phase, which should be maintained in the processing. We construct a complex-valued data at each pixel point (i,j) at frequency f as $z(i,j,f) =$ (in-phase amplitude) $+ \sqrt{-1}$(quadrature-phase amplitude) so that the requirement is satisfied.

In the present system, we choose mean M and quadratic covariances $K(\xi, \eta, f_\zeta)$ as the feature vector elements. The covariance part consists of spatial covariances K_s at a base

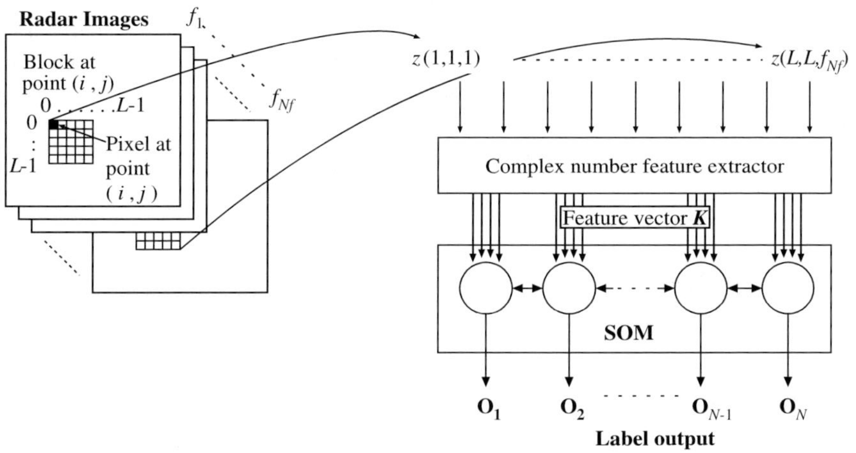

Fig. 2. Relation between the images and the blocks which is fed to the C-SOM illustrated as block diagram.

frequency f_b and frequency-domain covariances K_f at each spatial point (i,j). That is to say,

$$M = \frac{1}{L^2}\sum_{i'=0}^{L-1}\sum_{j'=0}^{L-1} z(i+i',j+j',f_b) \tag{1}$$

$$K(\xi,\eta,f_\zeta) = \frac{1}{L^2}\sum_{i'=0}^{L-1}\sum_{j'=0}^{L-1} z(i+i',j+j',f_b)\, z^*(i+i'+\xi,j+j'+\eta,f_b+f_\zeta). \tag{2}$$

We take into consideration the spatial shift up to one in the present experiment. That is, we consider mean M, variance $K(0,0,0)$, covariances $K(0,1,0)$, $K(1,0,0)$, $K(1,1,0)$ for simplicity, as well as the covariances in frequency domain $K(0,0,f_\zeta)$. Then we consider only the slope steepness in the space by neglecting the higher order properties such as curvature. After all, the feature vector $\mathbf{K}$ is chosen as

$$\mathbf{K} \equiv [\mathbf{K}_s, \mathbf{K}_f] \tag{3}$$

$$\mathbf{K}_s \equiv [M, K(0,0,0), K(0,1,0), K(1,0,0), K(1,1,0)] \tag{4}$$

$$\mathbf{K}_f \equiv [K(0,0,f_1), K(0,0,f_2), \ldots, K(0,0,f_{N_f})] \tag{5}$$

where $\mathbf{K}_s$ and $\mathbf{K}_f$ correspond to spatial and frequency-domain components. In (4) and (5), $K(0,0,0)$ is always real number while the others are complex numbers.

Incidentally, here we modify the spatial–domain correlation $\mathbf{K}_s$ as follows. Assume a clustering of an airborne earth surface imaging [9]. We observe the earth surface from an airplane with an interferometric radar. If there is a volcano below, we will observe a circular contour in the phase image. Thereby, we intuitively cluster the phase circles into a single area as a mountain. In other words, it is better to consider only the gradient magnitude by neglecting the slope direction [9]. The present case of the landmine imaging is similar to the mountain observation case. Hence, considering the insensitiveness to the gradient, we make the gradient parameters in space nondirective. If we express $K(\xi,\eta,0) \in \mathbf{K}_s$ as

$$K(\xi,\eta,0) = |K(\xi,\eta,0)| e^{j\varphi(\xi,\eta,0)} \tag{6}$$

then the gradient information is included in the argument $\varphi(\xi,\eta,0)$. Therefore, we define a new feature element that is insensitive to direction K'_s as

$$K'(\xi,\eta,0) = |K(\xi,\eta,0)| e^{j|\varphi(\xi,\eta,0)|}. \tag{7}$$

Finally (7) gives a new definition of the feature vector $\mathbf{K}'$ as

$$\mathbf{K}' \equiv [\mathbf{K}'_s, \mathbf{K}_f]. \tag{8}$$

In the following experiments, we adopt the modified feature vector $\mathbf{K}'$ to realize a desired clustering.

3.2. *C-SOM clustering dynamics*

The C-SOM classifies each pixel at (i,j) in the image according to the corresponding feature vector $\mathbf{K}'(i,j)$ calculated for the block at the point (i,j). The dynamics is the same as that in literature [8] except for the inclusion of frequency-domain correlations. After the pixels at all the points are classified adaptively, they yield a new image sheet showing the clusters of pixels. The adaptive classification is performed by the C-SOM that takes into account the block texture in the spatial and frequency domain.

Figure 3(a) is a schematic diagram of the SOM dynamics. Reference vectors representing prospective data clusters self-organize as follows. First, we determine the number of

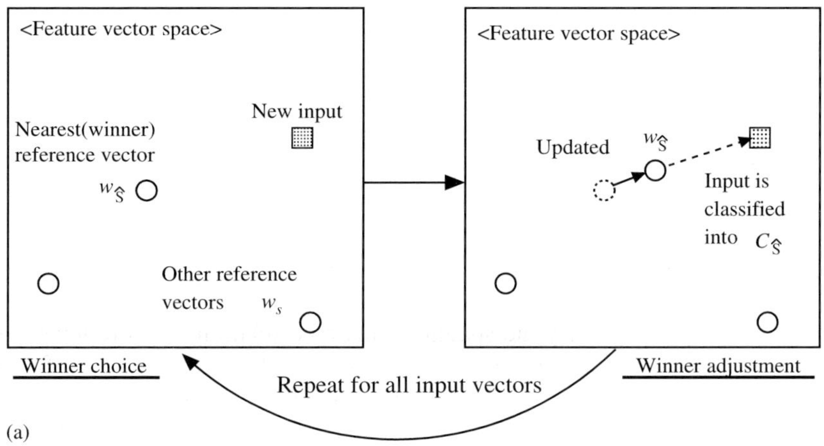

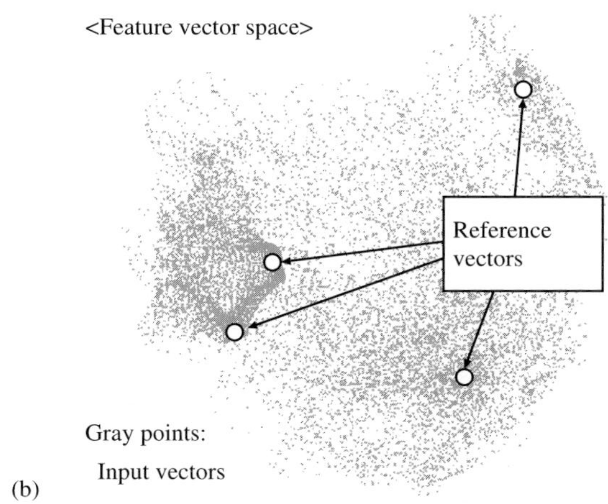

Fig. 3. Schematic diagram of the SOM dynamics: (a) winner reference vector choice and the reference adjustment and (b) reference vector distribution example after the self-organization.

classes. We choose the class number according to the application and profile of input images. We put them at random around the origin (center) of the complex feature-vector information space. Then we start to feed data points to be classified sequentially. For each input, the SOM determines a winner, i.e., the nearest reference vector. We classify the input into the class represented by the determined winner reference vector. At the same time, the winner reference value is adjusted so that it approaches slightly to the input data value. We repeat the above process for all the input data.

Figure 3(b) shows a typical result after the repetition. Open circles are the reference vectors, while the gray dots show the input signal distribution. It is found that the reference vectors are arranged at the dense input regions with a moderate sparseness. That is to say, the input property is represented by the distribution of the reference vectors. We find that an adaptive clustering (vector quantization) is performed successfully. The above algorithm is described as follows.

The Dynamics:

(1) Initialize the state: We map initial reference vectors $\mathbf{w}_s(t)$ $(t = 0)$ at random.

(2) For input feature vector $\mathbf{K}'$ calculated for (i, j)-point block:

(a) Find the class $C_{\hat{s}}$ to which $\mathbf{K}'$ should belong:

$$\mathbf{K}' \in C_{\hat{s}} \qquad \text{if} \qquad \|\mathbf{K}' - \mathbf{w}_{\hat{s}}(t)\| = \min_{s} \{\|\mathbf{K}' - \mathbf{w}_s(t)\|\} \tag{9}$$

where $C_{\hat{s}}$ is the winner class, $\mathbf{w}_{\hat{s}}$ is the winner vector and $\|\cdot\|$ denotes Euclidean distance.

(b) Update the reference vectors $\mathbf{w}_s$ as

$$\mathbf{w}_s(t+1) = \begin{cases} \mathbf{w}_s(t) + \alpha[\mathbf{K}' - \mathbf{w}_s(t)], & s = \hat{s} \\ \mathbf{w}_s(t), & s \neq \hat{s} \end{cases} \tag{10}$$

where α is learning parameter in the range of $0 < \alpha < 1$.

Repeat (2) for all the input feature vectors $\mathbf{K}'$ obtained by scanning i and j in the image.

In the C-SOM, the distance and the migration in (9) and (10) reflect the metric of phase- and amplitude-information space as mentioned in Section 3.1. Therefore, though the procedure expressions (9) and (10) are identical with those of conventional SOM, the combination of the complex-valued feature vector extractor and the SOM leads to the C-SOM specific dynamics.

4. Experiments and results

This section presents the experimental conditions and obtained results.

4.1. *Parameters in the experiments*

The features of the experimental target objects are listed in Table 1. We adopt a mock mine imitating Chinese TYPE72 as well as a metal can instead of metal mine.

Table 1. Features of target objects: metal can and mock mine

	Metal can	Mock mine
Diameter	100 mm	78 mm
Height	45 mm	40 mm
Materials	Metal	Synthetic rubber, steel, plastic, infilling with the same dielectric constant of explosive

The mock mine is genuinely designed except for explosive. It is filled with a material that has the same dielectric constant as that of explosive. Experimental parameters are shown in Table 2. The frequency sampling point of 81 results in 125 MHz interval. The theoretically corresponding measurable range is about 1.2 m in the air and about 30 cm in soil with refractive index of 4, for example, though the index largely depends on soil constituent and moisture. If we calibrate the zero distance at the antenna surface, and assume the typical distance between antennas and the ground surface as 30 cm, then the penetration depth is about 20 cm. The value is appropriate for the present measurement.

4.2. *Metal can on the ground surface*

First, we observe a metal can put on the ground surface. We show raw data observed at 30 GHz as an example on the left-hand side of Fig. 4. In the image, we show amplitude and phase in grayscale separately. We recognize a circular pattern in the phase image. Then we estimate that there exists something without any signal processing, besides that of our brain.

The right-hand side image shows the clustering result obtained by using the C-SOM. Each level in grayscale corresponds to a class (cluster). If neighboring pixels belong to an identical class, the resulting image presents a spatial cluster at the area. The image shows that the central pattern is classified in a single area, even though the raw phase image has a concentric pattern. The metal can imaging is successful.

Table 2. Parameters in the experiments

Sweeping start frequency $f_{\min}$	30 GHz
Sweeping stop frequency $f_{\max}$	40 GHz
Basis frequency f_b	35 GHz
Sampling number in frequency N_f	81
Frequency interval Δf	125 MHz
Antenna–ground surface distance	$\approx$ 30 cm
Scanning area size $X \times Y$	381 mm $\times$ 381 mm
Scanning interval ΔX, ΔY	3 mm, 3 mm
Sampling number in space $N_x \times N_y$	128 $\times$ 128
Block size $L \times L$	12 $\times$ 12
Reference vector number	16

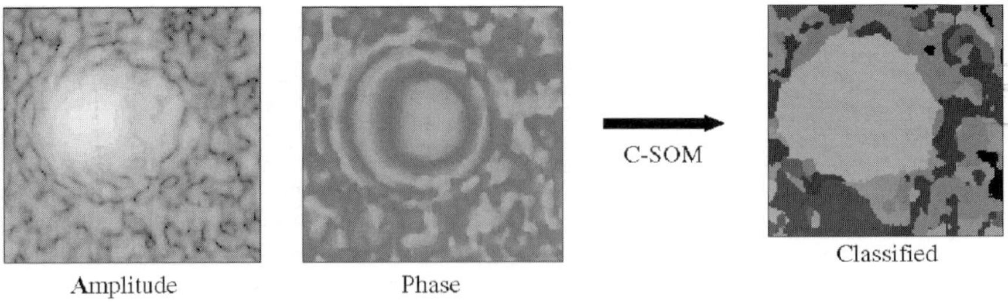

Fig. 4. Classification result of metal can put on the ground surface.

We can see something circular in the central area whereas the surrounding area is speckled at random. This fact suggests that the clustering by the complex-valued SOM is appropriately done as we would do if we had phase sensitive eyes and a brain.

4.3. *Metal can buried near the ground surface*

Next, we observe a metal can buried 3 mm below the ground surface. We show the observed data on the left-hand side in Fig. 5. In comparison with Fig. 4, it is clear in the amplitude image that a reflection at the metal can is weaker because of the ground surface influence. We can recognize a circular pattern in the phase image but it is more indistinct than that in Fig. 4.

The right part shows the clustering result. It does not show a circular pattern while the result in Fig. 4 does. But the central area is classified into a single class. The clustering is appropriately performed.

4.4. *Mock plastic mine on the ground surface*

We replace the metal can with a plastic mock mine. In general, imaging of plastic mines is more difficult than that of metal cans. First, we observe the mock plastic mine put on the ground surface. The result is given in Fig. 6. It shows a more indistinct pattern than that in Fig. 4 or Fig. 5.

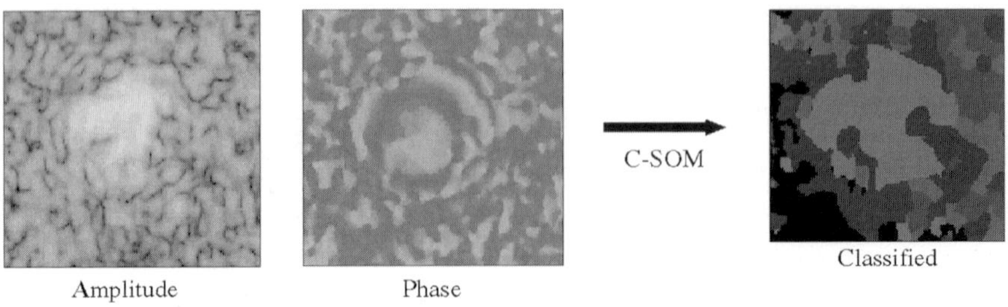

Fig. 5. Classification result of metal can buried near the ground surface.

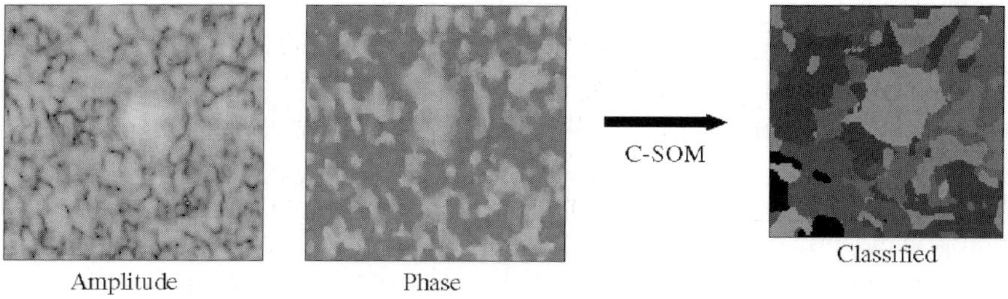

Fig. 6. Classification result of plastic mine put on the ground surface.

If we observe the multiple frequency phase images, the landmine area shows a clearer pattern variation depending on the frequency. Contrarily, the area without landmine shows a little more random change in the frequency domain. The result suggests the effectiveness to adopt a feature vector having frequency-domain information in the clustering.

The right part of Fig. 6 shows that a large area is segmented from its surroundings. We can say that the mine is visualized by the system when it is put on the ground.

4.5. *Mock plastic mine buried near the ground surface*

Finally, we observe a mock plastic mine buried near the ground surface. The observation is the left-hand side image in Fig. 7. It shows a quite indistinct pattern, in which we manage to recognize a certain kind of pattern only if we know in advance that there is something in the central area. In other words, we cannot recognize an object by just looking at the image.

The right-hand side image in Fig. 7 shows the clustering output. The result shows an object in the central area clearly. We consider the system works well to recognize a plastic mine buried near the ground surface.

At present, the successful imaging rate of shallowly buried plastic landmines is about 70%, which should be improved before practical application of our proposal. On the other hand, we also tried a real-valued SOM imaging. The successful imaging rate was, however, about 10%, which suggests the superiority of our method.

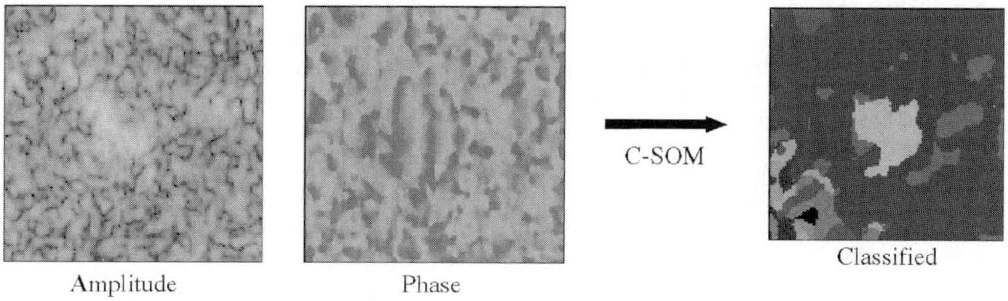

Fig. 7. Classification result of plastic mine buried near the ground surface.

5. Conclusion

We have first discussed the necessity to deal with objective phenomena by building proper models of them to construct safe, secure and reliable systems. As an example, we reported a successful imaging of a plastic anti-personnel landmine buried near the ground surface by dealing with both amplitude and phase information obtained at multiple frequencies. An appropriate segmentation without learning has been realized by the adaptive signal processing based on the complex-valued SOM. The proper clustering is performed since the feature vector in the complex-valued SOM reflects the property of the electromagnetic wave imaging physics. We have demonstrated the possibility of a fully automated mine detecting system.

Acknowledgments

A part of this work was financially supported by a grant from JSPS under Grant-in-Aid for Scientific Research (A) 15206047 to A. Hirose.

References

[1] A. Hirose, ed., *Complex-Valued Neural Networks: Theories and Applications*, World Scientific, Singapore (2003).

[2] M. Sato and M. Takeshita, *Estimation of subsurface fracture roughness by polarimetric borehole radar*, IEICE Trans. Electron. **E83-C(12)** (2000), 1881–1888.

[3] T. Moriyama, M. Nakamura, Y. Yamaguchi and H. Yamada, *Radar polarimetry applied to the classification of target buried in the underground*, Wideband Interferometric Sensing and Imaging Polarimetry. Proceedings of SPIE, Vol. 3210 (1997), 182–189.

[4] J.M. Bourgeois and G.S. Smith, *A complete electromagnetic simulation of the separated-aperture sensor for detecting buried land mines*, IEEE Trans. Antenna Propag. **46** (10) (1998), 1419–1426.

[5] T.P. Montoya and G.S. Smith, *Land mine detection using a ground-penetrating radar based on resistively loaded vee dipoles*, IEEE Trans. Antenna Propag. **47** (12) (1999), 1795–1806.

[6] L. Peters, Jr. and J.J. Daniels, *Ground penetrating radar as a surface environmental sensing tool*, Proc. IEEE **82** (12) (1994), 1802–1822.

[7] A. Hirose and T. Hara, Complex-valued self-organizing map dealing with multi-frequency interferometeric data for radar imaging systems. *International Workshop on Self-Organizing Map (WSOM) 2003 Hibikino*, September 2003, 255–260.

[8] T. Hara and A. Hirose, *Plastic mine detecting radar system using complex-valued self-organizing map that deals with multiple-frequency interferometric images*, Neural Netw. **17**(8–9), 1201–1210.

[9] A.B. Suksmono and A. Hirose, *Adaptive complex-amplitude texture classifier that deals with both height and reflectance for interferometric SAR images*, IEICE Trans. Electron. **E83-C(12)** (2000), 1905–1911.

CHAPTER 23

FDTD Simulation on Array Antenna SAR-GPR for Land Mine Detection

T. Kobayashi

Japan Science and Technology Agency, Tokyo, Japan
Tohoku University, Sendai 980-8576, Japan
E-mail: tak@cneas.tohoku.ac.jp

X. Feng and M. Sato

Tohoku University, Sendai 980-8576, Japan

Contents

Abstract

3D FDTD simulations of an array antenna SAR-GPR for mine detection were carried out under conditions of rough surface and inhomogeneous subsurface medium, which reproduced the dependence of the optimal antenna spacing on the ground surface roughness which had been found in laboratory experiments. This result implies that selection of array antenna spacing is essential to the optimal performance of SAR-GPR in mine detection.

SYSTEMS AND HUMAN SCIENCE – FOR SAFETY, SECURITY, AND DEPENDABILITY
Edited by Tatsuo Arai, Shigeru Yamamoto and Kazuhisa Makino

1. Introduction

In 2002, the Japanese government officially announced that Japan will support reconstruction of Afghanistan, which was followed by a humanitarian demining project of the Ministry of Education, Sport, Science and Technology. The project aims to develop a demining system in a few years in order to practice it in the demining action in Afghanistan [1–3].

Tohoku University joined the project and has developed an array antenna SAR-GPR for land mine detection focusing on anti-personnel (AP) mines. An AP mine is a difficult target for a metal detector because it contains little metal. A SAR-GPR visualizes buried objects which have a dielectric contrast to the ambient soil while a metal detector senses the secondary magnetic field of a metal part. Therefore, a SAR-GPR is expected to be an effective alternative method to a metal detector in the detection of AP mines.

In parallel to the developing of a SAR-GPR system, we have also developed a 3D-FDTD simulation code for evaluation of the SAR-GPR performance. The primary purpose of the simulation is to evaluate the SAR-GPR performance under wet conditions which are impossible to control in a laboratory.

In this chapter, we report the preliminary result of the FDTD simulations of the SAR-GPR performance which were carried out in order to confirm a hypothesis that had been drawn from the result of laboratory experiments.

2. Array antenna SAR-GPR

Since the primary target of the GPR is an AP mine which is deployed at shallow subsurface, attenuation of radar pulse during subsurface propagation is not the primary concern. Thus, a wide frequency band operation of the GPR is possible. On the other hand, a wide frequency band is necessary to achieve a fine spatial resolution lest the surface echo should mask the weak echo signal of a shallow target.

The operation frequency range of the SAR-GPR system is from 30 kHz to 6 GHz and the system is a stepped frequency radar. The array antenna system shown in Fig. 1 was introduced to the SAR-GPR system in order to reduce the surface clutters which are the most serious problem in landmine detection. An antipodal Vivaldi antenna is a wide frequency range antenna [4–6]. Since an antipodal Vivaldi antenna has a flat shape, and requires no balance–unbalance transformer, constructing an array of Vivaldi antennas is a rather simple task. For these reasons, we developed a Vivaldi antenna array system in which five pairs of transmission-receiving antennas were arranged so as to make a Common Mid-Point (CMP) array.

The array antenna scans over mine field two dimensionally. CMP stacking of measured data is carried out at every measurement point. The image of a subsurface object is reconstructed by diffraction stacking of CMP stacking data.

Fig. 1. The array antenna system of the SAR-GPR. The array is constructed with 10 pieces of Vivaldi antennas.

3. Laboratory experiment

3.1. *Experimental conditions*

Laboratory experiments were conducted under a dry condition but for two different ground conditions. One was a slightly rough surface condition with a homogeneous subsurface medium and another was a very rough surface condition with an inhomogeneous subsurface medium. Simulated mine fields were made in a sand box whose dimensions were $40 \times 70 \times 40$ cm^3. A model mine of Type-72, one of the most proliferated AP mines in Afghanistan, was buried at a depth of 5 cm below the mean surface in the sand box mine field. A Type-72 AP mine has a pancake shape with a diameter of 78 mm which is as thick as 40 mm.

The antenna scanned over the mine field at 5 cm above the mean surface. Measurement points were taken at grid points in the scanning surface at spatial intervals of 1 cm.

We took the array antenna spacing as the experimental parameter and evaluated the effect of the antenna spacing on the performance of the SAR-GPR. The spacing of the array antenna elements was changed from 1 to 5 cm with an interval of 1 cm.

No serious antenna coupling was observed at any antenna spacing.

The performance of the SAR-GPR is evaluated by an index that we introduced: the target echo contrast. The target echo contrast is defined by the ratio of strength of target echo to the standard deviation of clutter noises (Fig. 2). The strength of target echo is defined as relative strength to the mean clutter noise strength.

3.2. *Experimental results*

Slightly rough surface condition. Fig. 3 shows the sand box mine field of the slightly rough surface condition and Fig. 4 shows reconstructed horizontal slice images of

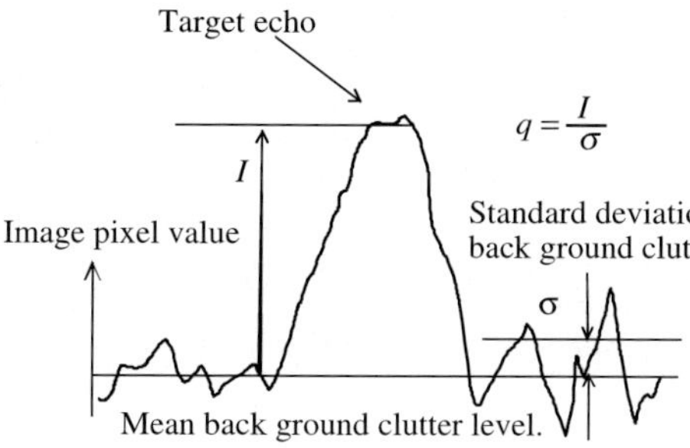

Fig. 2. A schematic of the definition of the target echo contrast.

subsurface target. The sand box was filled with crushed stone of the size of 7 mm. The RMS height of the surface was 1.8 mm, and the correlation length of the surface height distribution was 10 mm. The derived target echo contrasts are plotted in Fig. 7 along with those of the very rough surface condition case.

Very rough surface condition. Fig. 5 shows the sand box mine field of the very rough surface condition and Fig. 6 shows reconstructed horizontal slice images of subsurface target. Gravels of the size of 40 mm were added to the sand box and were mixed to realize a very rough surface. The RMS height of the surface was 15 mm and the correlation length of the surface height distribution was 20 mm. The derived target echo contrasts are plotted in Fig. 6.

Optimal antenna spacing. From experimental results presented in Fig. 7, we can conclude that the performance of the SAR-GPR is subject to the antenna spacing depending on the ground surface roughness. In these particular cases, we can also conclude that there is an optimal antenna spacing to realize the best performance of the SAR-GPR depending on the surface roughness, i.e., 1 cm for the slightly rough surface and 3 cm for the very rough surface condition.

Fig. 3. Simulated mine field with a slightly rough surface.

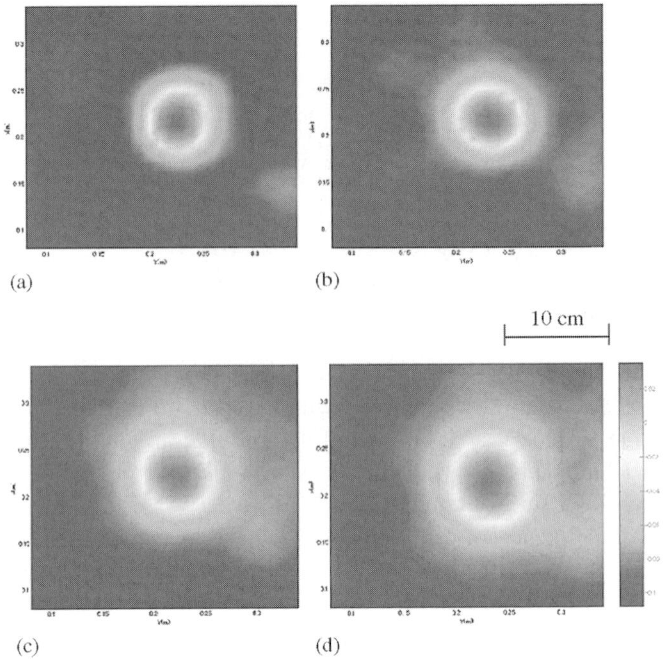

Fig. 4. Reconstructed target image. The RMS height and the correlation length of the surface are 1.8 and 10 mm, respectively. The antenna spacing is 1 cm (a), 2 cm (b), 3 cm (c), and 5 cm (d). The buried target is recognized as the circular image.

4. FDTD simulation

However, there is still some room for the possibility that this optimal antenna spacing is merely a result of the fluctuation of a random process since a random rough surface itself is a realization of a random process. In order to confirm the conclusion described above, we conducted FDTD simulations of the SAR-GPR for the case of very rough surface.

Fig. 5. Simulated mine field with a very rough surface.

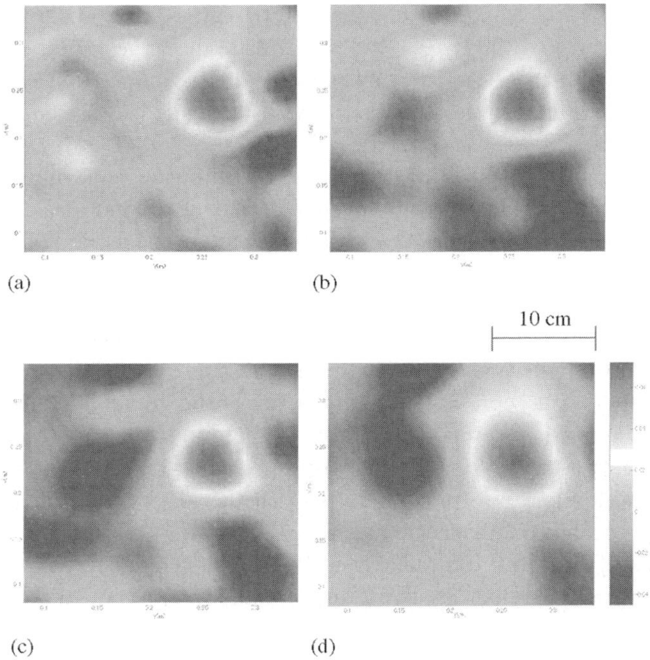

Fig. 6. Horizontal slice images of the buried target in the sand box. The antenna spacing is 1 cm (a), 2 cm (b), 3 cm (c), and 5 cm (d). The image of circular target is deformed but still recognizable.

4.1. *Simulation code*

The simulation code is a newly developed 3D-FDTD code for which the primary objective is the performance of the SAR-GPR in the detection of buried mines under various conditions including wet ones. The simulation code is run on the super computer of

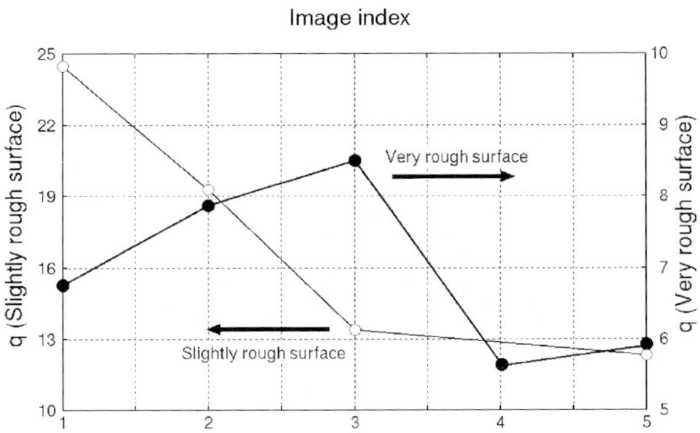

Fig. 7. The target echo contrast as a function of antenna spacing. Open circles are from the result of the slightly rough surface condition and the solid circles are of the result of the very rough surface condition. Note that they are referring different axes.

Tohoku University, NEC SX7, that enables a full scale 3D FDTD simulation of mine detection SAR-GPR with $1000 \times 1000 \times 1000$ grids at the largest. In the present study, a simulation space of $500 \times 500 \times 175$ grids was used to save calculation time. The grid size was 2 mm. This large scale simulation space was surrounded by Berenger's PML [7] of 10 layers.

The simulation space consists of two regions, air-space and subsurface space. A Gaussian random rough surface was employed to define the ground surface. The roughness parameters were chosen so that they coincided with those of laboratory experiments: the RMS height and the correlation length were 15 mm and 20 mm, respectively (Fig. 8).

The subsurface material was assumed to be a dry soil whose dielectric constant was 4. In this dry soil were scattered gravels whose dielectric constant was 5.3. The shape of the gravel is three axes elliptic body. The length of each axis was independently decided via Monte Carlo method. The representative dimension of the gravel is 40 mm. Monte Carlo method was also applied to define the position of the gravels.

The buried target was Type-72 AP mine whose dielectric constant was assumed to be 3. The target was buried and put horizontally so that the mass center of the target was at 10 cm below the mean ground surface.

In the simulation, the SAR-GPR radar system was assumed to be a pulse radar. A 38 mm dipole antenna was modeled as the transmission antenna of the SAR-GPR. The transmission antenna was put 10 cm off the mean ground surface and was excited by a first derivative Gaussian pulse. Figure 9 presents the excitation pulse of the transmission antenna and Fig. 10 presents the spectra of the transmitted pulse at several points off the transmission antenna.

The receiving antenna was not modeled in the simulation. Instead, the electric field at receiving points was regarded as the receiving signals.

The antenna scans over the mine field two dimensionally in the simulation space. The measuring points were taken as those in the laboratory experiments, i.e., 41×41 points at 1 cm spatial interval.

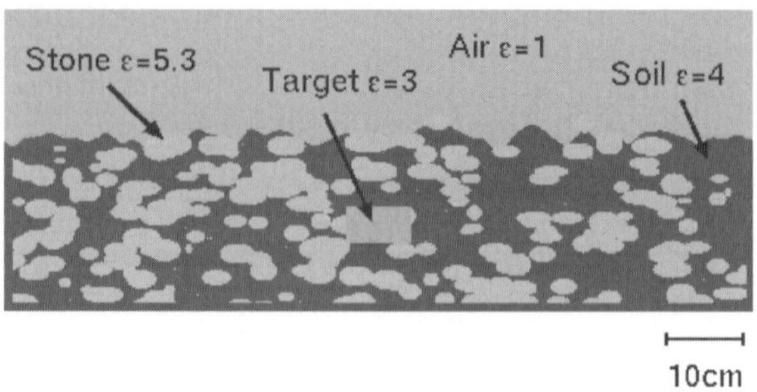

Fig. 8. A cross section of the simulation space. The ground surface was given a Gaussian random rough surface of which the RMS height and the correlation length were 15 and 20 mm, respectively. The subsurface material was assumed to be dry soil whose dielectric constant is 4. In the dry soil were scattered gravels whose size, shape and position were determined via Monte Carlo method. Gravel was given a dielectric constant of 5.3. The buried target is Type-72 AP mine.

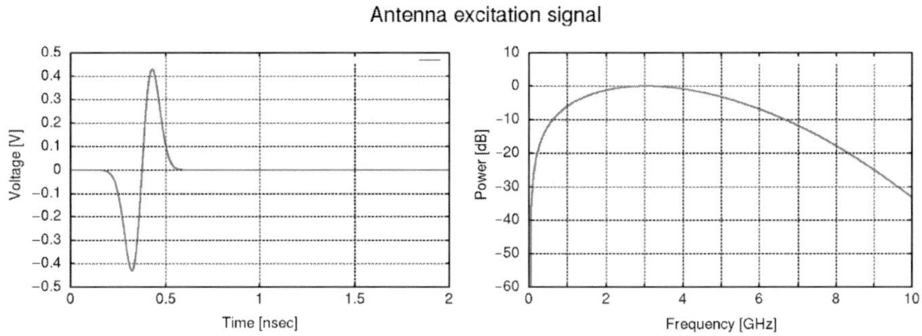

Fig. 9. Antenna excitation pulse. A first derivative Gaussian pulse was used to excite the transmission antenna. The left panel shows the wave form of the pulse in the time domain and the right panel shows the power spectrum of the excitation pulse.

The CMP stacking and the diffraction stacking were applied to the measured data to reconstruct the image of the subsurface target as had been done in the laboratory experiments and the results were evaluated by the target echo contrast.

4.2. *Simulation result*

Figure 11 presents the reconstructed horizontal slice images of the buried target. The image changes as the antenna spacing changes as was seen in Fig. 6. However, more clutter echoes are seen in Fig. 11 than in Fig. 6. This is attributed to the difference of antenna design.

In the simulation, the transmission antenna was modeled as a simple dipole antenna whose radiation pattern is isotropic around the antenna axis, and the received signal was assumed to be the electric field at the receiving point. These together allow that surface clutters from various ranges in any direction can be received with the same gain, thus resulting in surface clutters appearing in the reconstructed image at various depths. On the

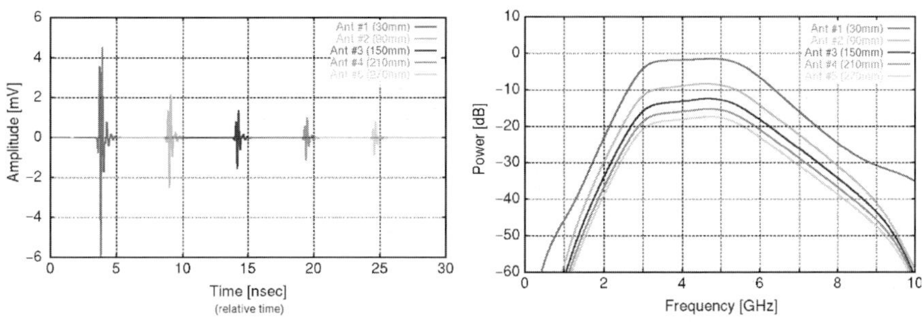

Fig. 10. Transmission pulse at different ranges (30 mm, 90 mm, 150 mm, 210 mm, and 270 mm). The left panel shows the waveform of the transmitted pulses and the right panel shows the power spectra. The frequency range of the pulse is estimated about 3 GHz (3–6 GHz).

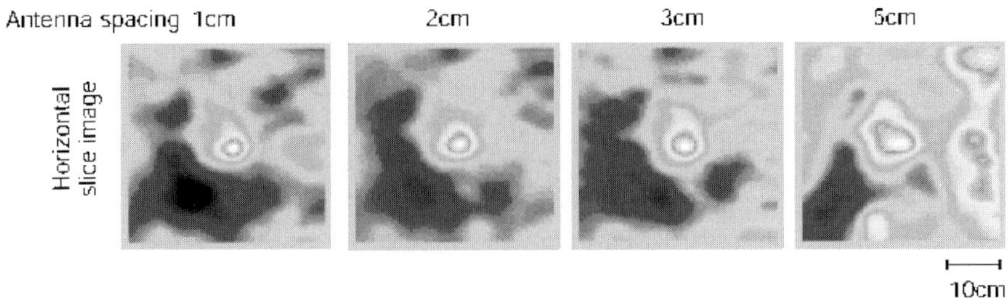

Fig. 11. The reconstructed images of horizontal slice of buried target, which were obtained after processing the FDTD simulation result data. Note that the images look very similar to those images of Fig. 4. The target echo contrast of these images was plotted in Fig. 10.

other hand, in the laboratory experiments, the antennas are Vivaldi antennas, which have a narrower beam pattern compared to a dipole antenna, and thus received surface clutters from more limited surface area (smaller area). Therefore, the reconstructed images of Fig. 6 have much less clutters than those of Fig. 11.

The target echo contrast of each image was plotted in Fig. 12 along with the result of the laboratory experiment of the rough surface condition. Although values of the contrast are smaller than those of experiment results, the behavior of the target echo contrast as a function of antenna spacing is similar to that of laboratory experiments in spite of different antenna types.

Therefore, we can conclude that the FDTD simulation of the mine detection of SAR-GPR reproduced the behavior of target echo contrast as a function of antenna spacing of laboratory experiment, that the antenna spacing is an essential factor in the SAR-GPR performance and that there is an optimal antenna spacing of the array antenna depending on the ground surface roughness.

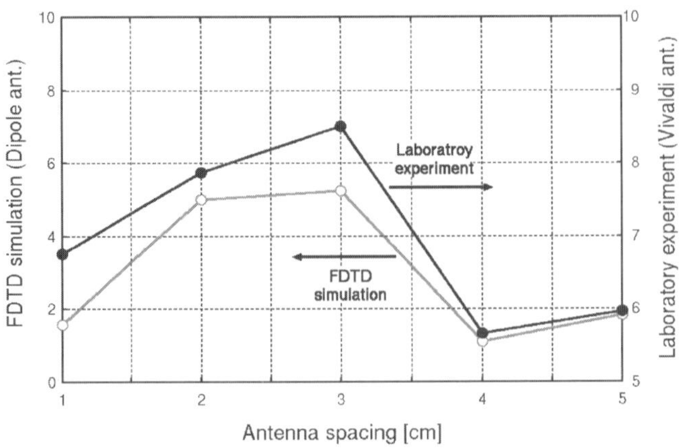

Fig. 12. The target echo contrast of the simulation result (Fig. 11). The target echo contrast of the laboratory experiment results under very rough surface condition is also plotted.

5. Conclusion

We have conducted laboratory experiments of mine detection SAR-GPR under dry condition and its 3D-FDTD simulation. Despite the difference of antenna design, the FDTD simulation well reproduced the variation of the SAR-GPR performance as a function of antenna spacing, which was observed in the laboratory experiments. From comparison of laboratory experiments and FDTD simulations, we have concluded that the antenna spacing is an essential factor in the SAR-GPR performance and that there is an optimal antenna spacing of the antenna array depending on the ground surface roughness.

Acknowledgments

This work was supported by the Humanitarian Mine Detection/Removal Project of Japan Science and Technology Agency. The 3D-FDTD code was developed in collaboration with Super Computing System, Information Synergy Center, Tohoku University.

References

[1] http://www.mext.go.jp/english/news/2002/05/020601.htm.

[2] http://www.jst.go.jp/pr/report/report264/index.html.

[3] M. Sato, *The state of the art of the abandoned land mines by GPR*, Proceedings of the Workshop on Humanitarian Demining of Anti-Personnel Mines, Science council of Japan, Japan (2001), April 2001, pp. 49–54.

[4] E. Gazit, *Improved design of the Vivaldi antenna*, Proc. Inst. Electron. Eng. **135** (Pt.H, 2) (1988), 89–92.

[5] E. Guillanton, J.Y. Dauvignac, Ch. Pichot and J. Cashman, *A new design tapered slot antenna for ultra-wideband applications*, Microwave Opt. Technol. Lett. **19** (4) (1998), 286–289.

[6] J.D.S. Langley, P.S. Hall and P. Newham, *Novel ultrawide-bandwidth vivaldi antenna and low crosspolarisation*, Electron. Lett. **29** (23) (1993), 2004–2005.

[7] J.P. Berenger, *A perfectly matched layer for the absorption of electromagnetic waves*, J. Comput. Phys. **114** (1994), 185–200.

PART V

Hybrid Systems Modeling of Human Behavior

CHAPTER 24

Modeling of Driver's Collision Avoidance Behavior Based on Expression as Hybrid Dynamical System

J.H. Kim

Department of Electronics and Information Engineering, Graduate School of Engineering, Nagoya University, Furo-cho, Chikusa-ku, Nagoya, Japan

S. Hayakawa

Toyota Technological Institute, Hisakata, Tempaku-ku, Nagoya, Japan

T. Suzuki and K. Hayashi

Department of Electronic-Mechanical Engineering, Graduate School of Engineering, Nagoya University, Furo-cho, Chikusa-ku, Nagoya, Japan

S. Okuma

Department of Electronics and Information Engineering, Graduate School of Engineering, Nagoya University, Furo-cho, Chikusa-ku, Nagoya, Japan

N. Tsuchida

Toyota Technological Institute, Hisakata, Tempaku-ku, Nagoya, Japan

M. Shimizu and S. Kido

Toyota Motor Corporation, Toyota-cho 1, Toyota, Japan

Contents

SYSTEMS AND HUMAN SCIENCE – FOR SAFETY, SECURITY, AND DEPENDABILITY
Edited by Tatsuo Arai, Shigeru Yamamoto and Kazuhisa Makino

Abstract

This chapter presents the development of the modeling strategy of the human driving behavior based on the expression as Piecewise Polynomial (PWP) model focusing on the driver's collision avoidance behavior. The driving data are collected by using the three-dimensional driving simulator based on CAVE, which provides stereoscopic immersive vision. In our modeling, the relationship between the driver's sensory information and the operation of the driver such as braking and/or steering amount is expressed by PWP model, which is a class of Hybrid Dynamical System. The identification problem for the PWP model is formulated as the Mixed Integer Linear Programming by transforming the switching conditions into binary variables. From the obtained results, it is found that the driver appropriately switches the "control law" according to the sensory information. These results enable us to capture not only the physical meaning of the driving skill, but also the decision-making aspect (switching conditions) in the driver's collision avoidance behavior.

1. Introduction

Recently, the modeling of driving behavior has attracted great attention by many researchers [1–3]. Since the driving behavior usually includes high nonlinearity, some nonlinear dynamics-based modeling is promising [4]. From this viewpoint, nonlinear regression models, neural network and fuzzy systems have been used [6,7]. These techniques, however, have some problems as follows: (1) the obtained model often results in a complicated model; (2) this makes it impossible to understand the physical meaning of the driver's maneuver. When we look at the driving behavior, it is often found that the driver appropriately switches the simple control laws instead of adopting the complex nonlinear control law. The switching mechanism can be regarded as a kind of driver's decision making in the driving behavior. Therefore, it is highly recommended that the model of the driving behavior involves both physical skill (operation) and the decision-making aspect (switching condition). This kind of expression can be categorized into a class of Hybrid Dynamical System (HDS). HDSs are systems which consist of both continuous dynamics and logical conditions. The former are typically associated with the differential (or difference) equations, the latter with combinatorial logics, automata and so on. Although many literatures have dealt with the expression, stability analysis, control, verification and identification of the HDS in the control and computer science communities [5], the application of the HDS model to the analysis of the human behavior has not been fully discussed yet.

In this chapter, the Piecewise Polynomial (PWP) model, which is a class of HDS, is adopted to understand human driving behavior especially focusing on the driver's collision avoidance behavior. The driving data are collected by using the three-dimensional (3D) Driving Simulator (DS) based on CAVE, which provides stereoscopic immersive vision. Although our DS does not have motion generator, thanks to the effect of the stereoscopic immersive vision, the examinee can feel the pseudo-acceleration. In our modeling, the relationship between the driver's sensory information such as the longitudinal distance between cars, longitudinal relative velocity and lateral displacement between cars, and the output of the driver such as the braking and steering amount are expressed by the PWP model. Then, we formulate the identification problem for the PWP model as the Mixed Integer Linear Programming (MILP) by transforming the logical conditions into inequalities [8,9]. By applying the developed strategy, it becomes possible to find not only coefficients in the polynomials but also parameters in the switching conditions from the measured driving data. This implies that both the physical meaning of the driving skill and the decision-making aspect (switching condition) in the driving behavior can be identified simultaneously. This chapter is organized as follows. In Section 2, configuration of the developed DS based on the CAVE is introduced. In Section 3, the scenario of our examination is described. Based on the setup described in Section 3, driver's collision avoidance behavior is investigated in Section 4. In Section 5, the modeling of the collision avoidance behavior based on the expression as the PWP model is introduced, and identification results based on the MILP are shown.

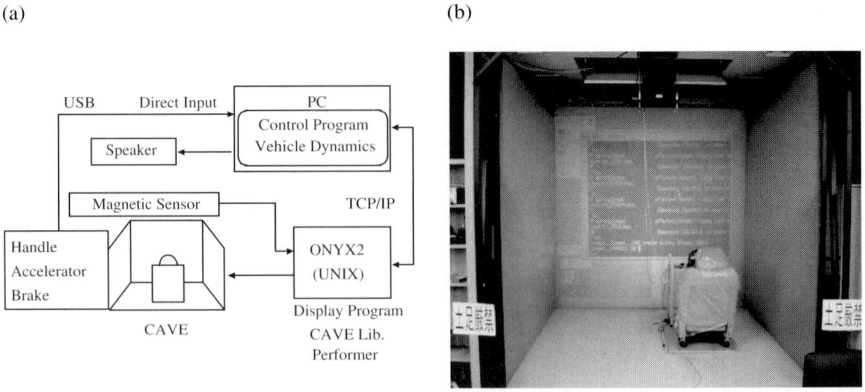

Fig. 1. The developed driving simulator. (a) Configuration of the DS (b) CAVE system.

2. Configuration of driving simulator

The configuration and appearance of the developed DS based on the CAVE are shown in Fig. 1(a) and (b). The display unit in the CAVE system provides the 3D virtual environment, and is controlled by ONYX2. The display program was developed by making use of the CAVE library and the Performer. The cockpit is built by installing a real steering wheel, an accelerator and a brake in the CAVE system. The information on the driver's output to the steering wheel, accelerator and brake is transferred to the PC through the USB terminal, and the vehicle position and motion are calculated based on these inputs and vehicle dynamics implemented on the PC using the CarSim software. The results of the calculation are transferred to ONYX2 through the Internet (TCP/IP), and the 3D visual image based on the position and motion of the vehicle is displayed on the screen.

3. Data acquisition in collision avoidance

3.1. *Experimental environment and conditions*

In this chapter, we focus on the driver's collision avoidance behavior at the instance of the sudden stopping of the preceding vehicle. The driver's collision avoidance behavior is considered to include not only physical operation but also the decision-making aspect. In order to model the driver's collision avoidance behavior, the following sensory information is captured as inputs:

(1) longitudinal distance between cars ($x_{1,k}$),
(2) longitudinal relative velocity ($x_{2,k}$),
(3) acceleration of the following vehicle ($x_{3,k}$),
(4) lateral displacement between cars ($x_{4,k}$),
(5) lateral relative velocity ($x_{5,k}$),
(6) lateral relative acceleration ($x_{6,k}$),
(7) yaw ($x_{7,k}$),

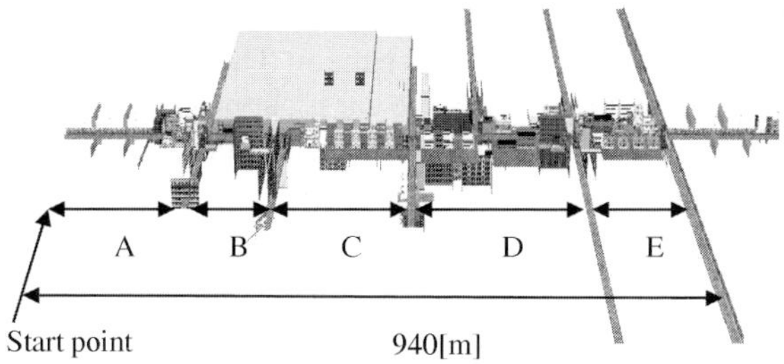

Fig. 2. Road environment for experiment.

(8) yaw rate ($x_{8,k}$),
(9) yaw acceleration ($x_{9,k}$),
(10) steering and braking amounts ($x_{10,k}$).
The outputs of drivers are also specified as follows:
(1) braking amount ($y_{1,k}$),
(2) steering amount ($y_{2,k}$).

In these definitions, $k \in Z$ denotes a discrete time. Note that no acceleration operation is necessary in the collision avoidance behavior. Fig. 2 shows the overview of the road environment developed for the experiment.

It has four intersections and two T-type junctions. The road is 1 km long and 7 m wide, and the pedestrian way is 1.5 m wide. The friction coefficient of the road was set to be 0.8. The scene around the start point is shown in Fig. 3. The vehicle moves from the left-hand side to the right-hand side in Fig. 2. The scene at 940 m point is same as the one at the start point. After the 940 m point, the same environment from the start point shows up again. Therefore, the driver feels that this virtual environment is a straight road without any end point. There exist only two vehicles in this environment. One of them is a sedan-type car

Fig. 3. Road image at start point.

driven by the examinee. The other one is the big truck, which runs in front of the examinee and is controlled by the operator of the experiment. The car used in the simulator has an engine with 3000 cm^3 displacement. Also, the car is supposed to have an ABS. The truck in front of the examinee runs at a constant speed of 50 km/h. The maximum deceleration of the truck is supposed to be 7 m/s^2.

3.2. *Procedure of experiment*

The examinee drives the car keeping constant distance (26 m) from the preceding truck. The operator sets the red or green parking vehicles on the right-hand side at the intersection. The examinee is supposed to take a look at the right-hand side at each intersection and then the examinee answers what color the parking vehicle is. When the examinee looks to the right-hand side at some intersection, the preceding truck is supposed to stop suddenly with maximum deceleration. Then, the collision avoidance behavior of the examinee is measured. Three trials have been made by each examinee. Before doing the experiments, all examinees practiced avoiding the stopped truck to get used to the DS in advance. Then, each driver took about 10 min to complete all the trials.

4. Experimental results and modeling framework

Based on the setup described in Section 3, six drivers carried out the experiment under virtual environments. First, the collision avoidance behavior at the instance of the sudden stopping of the preceding vehicle was measured and analyzed. This behavior is characterized by the profile between the beginning and ending of the steering operation.

The profiles of the driving data of the eighth trial of the driver E6 are depicted in Fig. 4. Fig. 4(a) illustrates the overview of the collision avoidance behavior. Also, Fig. 4(b) shows the trajectory in $x_1 - y_2$ space. The label $*$ in the trajectory Fig. 4(a) represents the following vehicle position when the preceding vehicle stops. When we look at the trajectory in Fig. 4(b), roughly speaking, the collision avoidance behavior can be regarded as the series of the following four sub-maneuvers: (1) the first period of avoidance, (2) the second period of avoidance, (3) the first period of recovery and (4) the second period of recovery. In the following, we denote these four periods by "Interval A", "Interval B", "Interval C", and "Interval D". The more formal algebraic expression of this behavior based on the PWP model is described as follows:

The interval A (the first period of avoidance)

$$y_{2,k} = a_0 x_{1,k} + a_1 x_{2,k} + a_2 x_{4,k} \qquad \text{if } x_{1,k} > e_1 \tag{1}$$

The interval B (the second period of avoidance)

$$y_{2,k} = b_0 x_{1,k} + b_1 x_{2,k} + b_2 x_{4,k} \qquad \text{if } e_1 \geq x_{1,k} > e_2 \tag{2}$$

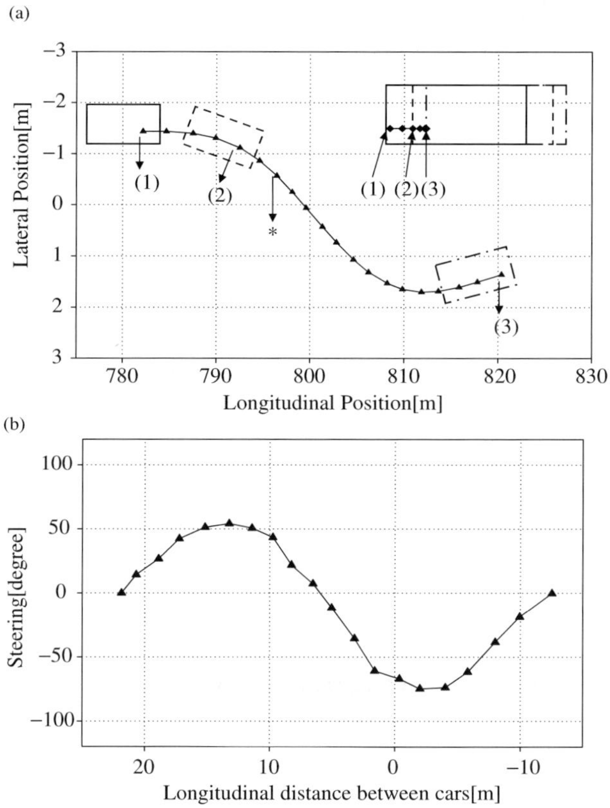

Fig. 4. Behavior at the avoiding.

The interval C (the first period of recovery)

$$y_{2,k} = c_0 x_{1,k} + c_1 x_{2,k} + c_2 x_{4,k} \qquad \text{if } e_2 \geq x_{1,k} > e_3 \tag{3}$$

The interval D (the second period of recovery)

$$y_{2,k} = d_0 x_{1,k} + d_1 x_{2,k} + d_2 x_{4,k} \qquad \text{if } e_3 \geq x_{1,k} \tag{4}$$

Also, the graphic representation of this behavior is depicted by Fig. 5. In (1)–(4), $x_{1,k}$, $x_{2,k}$ and $x_{4,k}$ represent the longitudinal distance between cars, longitudinal relative velocity and lateral displacement between cars, respectively. e_1 to e_3 are parameters to specify the switching condition between intervals. Note that only $x_{1,k}$, $x_{2,k}$ and $x_{4,k}$ appear on the right-hand side in (1)–(4). In our past study, we have clarified that $x_{1,k}$, $x_{2,k}$ and $x_{4,k}$ play important roles in the collision avoidance behavior by applying the Group Method of

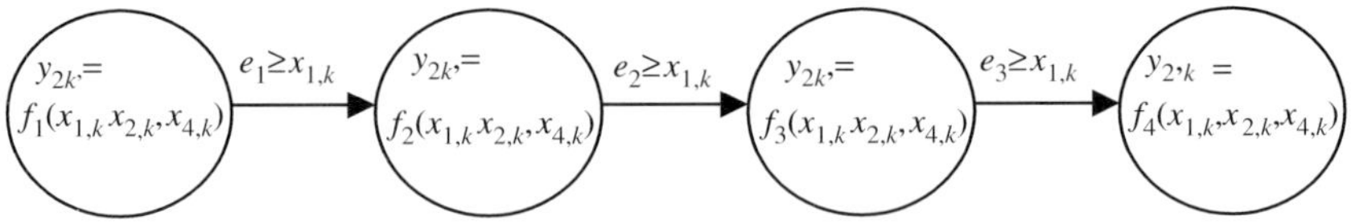

Fig. 5. Graphical representation of PWP model.

Data Handling (GMDH) technique [2]. Also, note that the braking profile did not show some specific characteristics in the collision avoidance behavior compared with the steering profile, and was excluded from our modeling.

Since the structure of this model contains both the continuous dynamics (polynomials) and the logical conditions (switching of polynomials), the proposed model belongs to a kind of HDS. This kind of HDS model enables us to capture not only the physical meaning (polynomials), but also the decision-making aspect (logical conditions) in the driving behavior. Note that the switching conditions between each interval are not specified in advance in our model. The parameter specifying switching condition (e_1 to e_3) and coefficients appearing in each polynomial (a_i to d_i) must be found simultaneously from the measured data. In Section 5, the strategy to solve this simultaneous identification problem is introduced. Note that our model in the continuous part represents a static mapping from the sensory information to the steering operation; the main reason for this is to reduce the computational burden required for the MILP. However, the PWP model can easily include the dynamics in the continuous part by introducing the Autoregressive (AR) model. The same formulation is also available in this case.

5. Modeling of driver's behavior based on PWP model and MILP

5.1. *Useful tools for identification of PWP model*

The goal of our modeling is to find not only coefficients in the polynomials a_i, b_i, c_i and d_i but also parameters in the "switching conditions" e_i from the measured driving data. Although this identification problem is not straightforward to handle, the idea developed in the Mixed Logical Dynamical Systems framework [8,9] makes it tractable. The key idea is to transform the logical condition into some inequalities by introducing auxiliary binary variables $\delta \in \{0, 1\}$ and auxiliary continuous variables z, and to formulate the problem as the MILP.

In the following, some useful tools to transform the logical condition into inequalities are introduced. First, the logical relationship given by

$$[f(x) \geq a] \Leftrightarrow [\delta = 1] \tag{5}$$

can be transformed into inequalities (6).

$$-f(x) + (a - m)\delta + m \leq 0, \qquad f(x) - (M - a + \varepsilon)\delta - a + \varepsilon \leq 0 \tag{6}$$

where $M = \max_x f(x)$, $m = \min_x f(x)$, and $\varepsilon > 0$ is a small tolerance. Also, in our setup, the product term of binary and continuous variables such as $\delta f(x)$ often appears. Since it is undesirable to handle this nonlinear term, we secondly introduce another auxiliary variable $z = \delta f(x)$, which satisfies the following two logical relationships.

$$[\delta = 0] \Rightarrow [z = 0], \qquad [\delta = 1] \Rightarrow [z = f(x)] \tag{7}$$

These relationships can be transformed into the following equivalent inequalities.

$$z \leq M\delta, \quad -z \leq -m\delta, \quad z \leq f(x) - m(1-\delta), \quad -z \leq -f(x) + M(1-\delta) \tag{8}$$

5.2. *Identification of PWPS model by MILP*

In order to transform the four logical conditions involved in (1)–(4) into the equivalent inequalities, binary variables $\delta_{1,k}$, $\delta_{2,k}$ and $\delta_{3,k}$ are introduced as follows:

(1) $[x_{1,k} > e_1] \Leftrightarrow [\delta_{1,k} = 0, \delta_{2,k} = 0, \delta_{3,k} = 0]$
(2) $[e_1 \geq x_{1,k} > e_2] \Leftrightarrow [\delta_{1,k} = 1, \delta_{2,k} = 0, \delta_{3,k} = 0]$
(3) $[e_2 \geq x_{1,k} > e_3] \Leftrightarrow [\delta_{1,k} = 0, \delta_{2,k} = 1, \delta_{3,k} = 0]$
(4) $[e_3 \geq x_{1,k}] \Leftrightarrow [\delta_{1,k} = 1, \delta_{2,k} = 1, \delta_{3,k} = 1]$

By applying the transformation rules and introducing the auxiliary variables, (1)–(4) can be rewritten as follows

$$\begin{aligned} y_{2,k} = {} & a_0 x_{1,k} + a_1 x_{2,k} + a_2 x_{4,k} + x_{1,k} z_{1,k} + x_{2,k} z_{2,k} + x_{4,k} z_{3,k} + x_{1,k} z_{4,k} \\ & + x_{2,k} z_{5,k} + x_{4,k} z_{6,k} + x_{1,k} z_{7,k} + x_{2,k} z_{8,k} + x_{4,k} z_{9,k} \end{aligned} \tag{9}$$

where the auxiliary variables, $z_{i,k}$, are defined as follows:

$$z_{i,k} = \delta_{1,k}(b_{i-1} - a_{i-1}) \ (i = 1\text{–}3), \qquad z_{i,k} = \delta_{2,k}(c_{i-4} - a_{i-4}) \ (i = 4\text{–}6) \tag{10}$$

$$\begin{aligned} & z_{i,k} = \delta_{3,k}(a_{i-7} - b_{i-7} - c_{i-7} + d_{i-7}) \ (i = 7\text{–}9), \\ & z_{i,k} = \delta_{1,k} e_{i-9} \ (i = 10\text{–}11) \end{aligned} \tag{11}$$

$$z_{i,k} = \delta_{2,k} e_{i-11} \ (i = 12\text{–}14), \qquad z_{i,k} = \delta_{3,k} e_{i-14} \ (i = 15\text{–}17) \tag{12}$$

Also, as stated in Section 5.1, some linear inequalities that come up with the introduction of $\delta_{i,k}$ and $z_{i,k}$ must be accompanied with (10)–(13). Now, the problem to find the coefficients in the polynomials and the parameters in the switching condition from the measured input/output data is formulated as the following MILP.

$$\text{known } y_{2,k}, x_{1,k}, x_{2,k}, x_{4,k}$$

$$\text{find } \{a_0, a_1, a_2, b_0, b_1, b_2, c_0, c_1, c_2, d_0, d_1, d_2, e_1, e_2, e_3, \delta_{1,k}, \delta_{2,k}, \delta_{3,k}\}$$

$$\text{which minimize } J = \sum_{k=1}^{N} |y_{2,k} - \hat{y}_{2,k}| \tag{13}$$

subject to

$$z_{i,k} \leq M_i \delta_{j,k}, \qquad -z_{i,k} \leq -m_i \delta_{j,k} \tag{14}$$

$$z_{i,k} \leq f_{i,k} - (1 - \delta_{j,k}) m_i, \qquad -z_{i,k} \leq -f_{i,k} + (1 - \delta_{j,k}) M_i \tag{15}$$

$$\delta_{1,k} = \{0, 1\}, \quad \delta_{2,k} = \{0, 1\}, \quad \delta_{3,k} = \{0, 1\}, \quad 0 \leq \delta_{1,k} + \delta_{2,k} - \delta_{3,k} \leq 1 \tag{16}$$

$$0 \leq \delta_{1,k} - \delta_{3,k} \leq 1, \quad 0 \leq \delta_{2,k} - \delta_{3,k} \leq 1, \quad \delta_{2,k} \leq \delta_{2,k+1}, \quad \delta_{3,k} \leq \delta_{3,k+1} \tag{17}$$

$$x_{1,k} \leq (1 - (\delta_{1,k} + \delta_{2,k}) + \delta_{3,k}) M_e + z_{10,k} + z_{13,k} - z_{15,k} - z_{16,k} + z_{17,k} \tag{18}$$

$$x_{1,k} \geq e_1 - z_{10,k} + z_{11,k} - z_{12,k} + z_{14,k} + z_{15,k} - z_{16,k} - z_{17,k} + \varepsilon + \delta_{3,k}(m_e - \varepsilon) \tag{19}$$

$$\begin{aligned} \hat{y}_{2,k} = {} & a_0 x_{1,k} + a_1 x_{2,k} + a_2 x_{4,k} + x_{1,k} z_{1,k} + x_{2,k} z_{2,k} + x_{4,k} z_{3,k} + x_{1,k} z_{4,k} \\ & + x_{2,k} z_{5,k} + x_{4,k} z_{6,k} + x_{1,k} z_{7,k} + x_{2,k} z_{8,k} + x_{4,k} z_{9,k} \end{aligned} \tag{20}$$

where M_i and m_i ($i = 1$–17) are the maximum and minimum values of $z_{i,k}$, and M_e and m_e represent the maximum and minimum values of e_1 to e_3, respectively. ε is a small tolerance. There are several ways to solve the MILP. One of the efficient algorithms is a branch-and-bound method. Although it requires some heuristic rules in the decision of the branching and bounding operation, it can guarantee the optimality, and can reduce the computational burden with the assistance of appropriate heuristic rules. Note that the computational burden strongly depends on the number of binary variables since this specifies the size of the search space. In our case, the number of measurement points affects the computational burden significantly.

5.3. *Identification results of collision avoidance behavior*

Based on the formulation of the identification of the PWP model described in Section 5.2, the identification of coefficients in the polynomials and parameters in the switching conditions was carried out. The 20 sampling data of the eighth trial of E6 driver were used for the identification. These data were selected by culling from the measured data with longer sampling interval. Before applying the MILP to the measured data, all input and output data were normalized as follows:

$$\bar{x}_i = \begin{cases} \dfrac{x_i}{x_{i\max}} & (x_i \geq 0) \\ -\dfrac{x_i}{|x_{i\max}|} & (x_i < 0) \end{cases} \qquad x_i \in [\,x_{i\min} \quad x_{i\max}\,] \tag{21}$$

$$\bar{y}_i = \begin{cases} \dfrac{y_i}{y_{i\max}} & (y_i \geq 0) \\ -\dfrac{y_i}{|y_{i\max}|} & (y_i < 0) \end{cases} \qquad y_i \in [\,y_{i\min} \quad y_{i\max}\,] \tag{22}$$

All numerical experiments have been performed by PC (CPU 4 3.06 GHz and Memory 1024 MB). It took about 10 h to find the solution of the MILP. In order to verify the validity of the obtained PWP model, the reproduced steering profile generated by the estimated parameters is plotted together with the measured steering profile in Fig. 6.

In Fig. 6, the horizontal and vertical axes represent the longitudinal distance between cars and the steering amount, respectively. In the steering amount, the right and left turn take positive and negative values, respectively. Also, the estimated switching points between polynomials (e_i) are designated by vertical lines. As shown in Fig. 6, the measured steering profile and reproduced steering profile agree well with each other. This result verifies the validity of the modeling based on the PWP model. In order to understand the characteristics in the collision avoidance behavior, the identified parameters for E6 examinee are analyzed in the following. The identified coefficients in the polynomials, a_i, b_i, c_i, d_i and the parameters in the switching conditions, e_i in (1)–(4) are listed in Table 1. As shown in Table 1, the most dominant input information (designated by underline in Table 1) in the intervals A and B were the longitudinal relative velocity ($x_{2,k}$) and the longitudinal distance between cars ($x_{1,k}$), respectively. On the other hand, the longitudinal relative velocity ($x_{2,k}$) and the lateral displacement between cars ($x_{4,k}$) were found to be dominant input information in both intervals C and D. In this experiment, we could not see

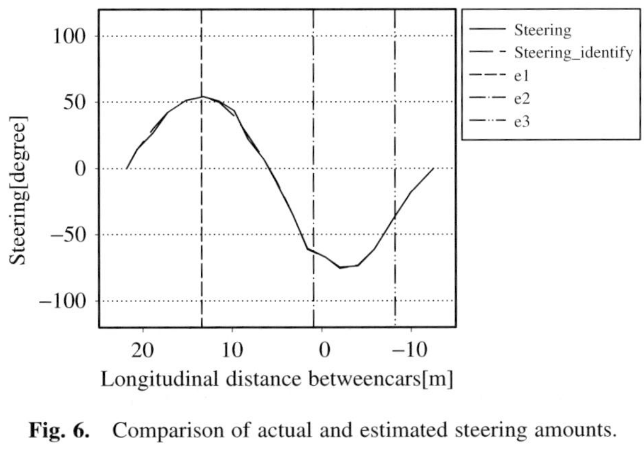

Fig. 6. Comparison of actual and estimated steering amounts.

Table 1. Identified parameters for E6

Parameters	Values	Parameters	Values
a_0	−0.429	d_0	0.283
a_1	1.369	d_1	2.632
a_2	0.968	d_2	−2.839
b_0	5.212	e_1	13.422
b_1	−3.195	e_2	0.926
b_2	1.321	e_3	−8.190
c_0	0.688		
c_1	5.144		
c_2	−5.158		

any significant difference in the behavior between the intervals C and D. A similar tendency has been found in the identified results of other drivers.

From these observations, we can conclude that the driver appropriately switches the "control law" according to the following scenario: at the beginning of the collision avoidance maneuver (just after finding the brake lamp of the preceding vehicle), the driver perceives the sudden stopping of the preceding vehicle, and then begins to avoid the preceding vehicle based on the longitudinal relative velocity information (Interval A). As the driver gets close to the preceding vehicle, the driver completes the avoidance by switching to another control law based on the longitudinal distance between cars (Interval B). After that, the driver starts to regulate the state of the driver's vehicle based on the longitudinal relative velocity and lateral displacement between cars, and finally, overtakes the preceding vehicle. Although the switching points depend on the driver's characteristics, qualitatively speaking, the scenario described above can be found as common characteristics in all drivers. These results clearly demonstrate the usefulness of the modeling based on the PWP model, which enables us to capture not only the physical meaning of the driving skill, but also the decision-making aspect (switching conditions) in the driver's collision avoidance behavior.

6. Conclusions

The modeling strategy of human driving behavior based on the expression as PWP model has been developed focusing on the driver's collision avoidance behavior. In our modeling, the relationship between the measured sensory information and the operation of the driver has been expressed by the PWP model. The MILP-based identification technique was adopted to find the coefficients in the polynomials and the parameters in the switching conditions simultaneously. As a result, it was found that the driver appropriately switches the "control law" according to the following scenario: at the beginning of the collision avoidance maneuver (just after finding the brake lamp of the preceding vehicle), the driver perceives the sudden stopping of the preceding vehicle, and then begins to avoid the preceding vehicle based on the longitudinal relative velocity information (Interval A). As the driver gets close to the preceding vehicle, the driver completes the avoidance by switching to another control law based on the longitudinal distance between cars (Interval B). After that, the driver starts to regulate the state of the driver's vehicle based on the longitudinal relative velocity and lateral displacement between cars, and finally, overtakes the preceding vehicle. Our proposed approach enables us to capture not only the physical meaning of the driving skill, but also the decision-making aspect (switching conditions) in the driving behavior. The analysis in a more complicated situation, and the application of the obtained results to the design of the collision avoidance support system are our future works.

Acknowledgment

This work was supported by the Space Robotic Center of the Toyota Technological Institute, where CAVE is installed. The authors would like to thank the researchers involved in the Space Robotic Center for their helpful suggestions.

References

[1] M.C. Nechyba and Y. Xu, *Human control strategy: abstraction, verification and replication*, IEEE Control Syst. Mag. **17** (5) (1997), 48–61.
[2] K. Jong-Hae, Y. Matsui, S. Hayakawa, T. Suzuki, S. Okuma and N. Tsuchida, *Acquisition and Modeling of Driving Skill Using Three-Dimensional Virtual System*, Proceeding of ICASE/SICE Joint Workshop, Vol. 1, (2002), 49–53.
[3] H. Uno and K. Hiramatsu, *Aged driver's avoidance capabilities in an emergent traffic situation*, SAEJ **32** (1) (2001), 113–118.
[4] J. Sjoberg, Q. Zhang, L. Ljung, A. Benveniste, B. Deylon, P.Y. Glorenner, H. Hjalmarsson and A. Juditsky, *Nonlinear black-box modeling in system identification: a unified overview*, Automatica **31** (12) (1995), 1691–1724.
[5] F.W. Vaandrager and J.H. Van Schuppen (Eds.), *Lecture notes in computer science, hybrid systems: computation and control*, Proceedings Second International Workshop, HSCC'99, Berg en Dal, The Netherlands (March 1999).
[6] S.J. Farlow, *Self-Organizing Method in Modeling*, Marcel Dekker, USA (1984).
[7] I. Hayashi and H. Tanaka, *The fuzzy GMDH algorithm by possibility models and its application*, Fuzzy Sets Syst. **36** (1990), 245–258.
[8] A. Bemporad and M. Moarari, *Control of systems integration logic, dynamics, and constraints*, Automatica **35** (1999), 407–427.
[9] A. Bemporad, J. Roll and L. Ljung, *Identification of Hybrid Systems via Mixed-Integer Programming*, Proceedings of the 40th IEEE Conference on Decision and Control, (2001), 786–792.

CHAPTER 25

A Case Study in Human Error Modeling Based on a Hybrid Dynamical Systems Approach

K. Uchida and S. Yamamoto

Department of Systems Innovation, Osaka University, Machikaneyama, Toyonaka, Osaka 560-8531, Japan

Contents

Abstract

In this paper, we propose a modeling method of a human operator who manipulates a switched dynamical system using highly practiced actions. The system is controlled by discrete inputs in on/off manners. The identified model is a hybrid dynamical system containing probabilistic properties. By using the model, we can detect faults resulting from the actions of a human operator.

SYSTEMS AND HUMAN SCIENCE – FOR SAFETY, SECURITY, AND DEPENDABILITY
Edited by Tatsuo Arai, Shigeru Yamamoto and Kazuhisa Makino

1. Introduction

Most accidents in manual control systems operated by humans are caused by human error. To prevent such accidents, it is important to detect the human error dynamically and to recover the system fault caused by the error.

Human errors can be classified by relating an action and its consequences to the intention that initiates and guides the performance. As proposed by Norman [1], an error is classified as a *mistake* if the action is carried out as intended, but the intention is not appropriate to the environment and/or the plan itself and the intention to be served by the plan does not fulfill the goals to be achieved. On the contrary, a *slip* is an error that occurs when a person does an action that is not intended. Although the intention of a slip fits the goals and the environmental situation, the action is not carried out as planned. In a classification of human errors (GEMS, Generic Error Model System) proposed by Reason [2], the slip–mistake distinction is combined with the so-called *SRK model*. The SRK model proposed by Rasmussen [3] is a hierarchical model of human behavior based on three levels of operation: skill-based, rule-based and knowledge-based behavior. The skill-based slip is related to routing tasks, requiring little or no conscious attention during operations.

In this paper, we model operations by an operator controlling a system by sequentially switching manipulations (Fig. 1). In manual control systems, simple sequential tasks may appear. In such tasks, skill-based slips possibly occur. For example, skill-based errors appear in well-organized and highly practiced actions which are served by subroutines of a human operator. Based on a hybrid system framework, we model the system controlled by the human operator as a hybrid dynamical system to detect the occurrence of such human error or to prevent errors from occurring. This approach conspicuously captures a feature of manual control that is a mixture of discrete-event processes and continuous dynamics. In general, hybrid dynamical systems are those which combine continuous and discrete behavior with both continuous and discrete states variables (see, e.g., [4]). The term hybrid is also used to generally characterize systems that combine time-driven and event-driven dynamics. The former are represented by differential (or difference) equations, while the latter may be described through various frameworks used for discrete-event systems, such as automata, max-plus equations, or Petri nets. In manual control systems, these dynamics show nondeterministic features to a greater or lesser extent. Hence, in this paper, we adopt hybrid models with transition conditions which are described by certain probability density functions. Additionally, since the behavior of human operators depends on plant dynamics, we will model manual control systems containing both human operations and plant dynamics.

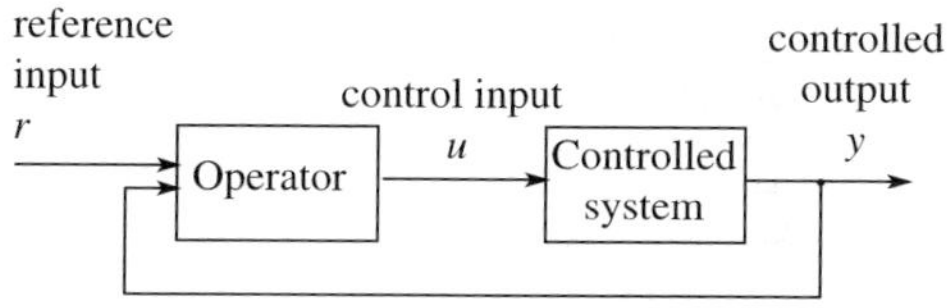

Fig. 1. Manual control system.

This paper is organized as follows. Section 2 describes a modeling method for discrete actions in manual control systems. In Section 3, as a case study, we apply the proposed method to modeling of control actions of operators manipulating a three-tank system. In addition, we show the results of fault detection of the operators.

2. Modeling of discrete actions for human error detection

To detect faults of human operations in manual control systems, we identify a hybrid model representing normal behavior of human operators. To this end, we cast the modeling problem into the identification of hybrid systems from observing data $\mathcal{O}$ including normal operations of a human operator. Once we obtain a hybrid system model, we can use it to determine that some faults occur when a new observation rejects the model.

2.1. *Hybrid system models of discrete actions*

A hybrid system under consideration can be described by

$$\dot{x}(t) = f(x(t), l(t)), \tag{1}$$

where $x \in \Re^n$ is the continuous state of the controlled system, $f : \mathcal{H} \rightarrow \Re^n$ is the continuous dynamics, and $l \in Q := \{l_1, \ldots, l_l\}$ is the *discrete states* (or also called *locations* of *modes*). The discrete state $l(t)$ is assumed to be piecewise continuous from the right (the notation t^- indicates $l(t^-) := \lim_{h \rightarrow t-0} l(h)$). In addition, the discrete state $l(t)$ is assumed to be changed by the human operator. Hence, the continuous state trajectory $x(\cdot)$ evolves according to $\dot{x}(t) = f(x(t), l(t))$ until l changes to l'. In this case, the human operator changes the discrete state $l(t)$ according to the value of x as if the continuous state x hits a boundary X. The boundary that causes such *transitions* is called *guard*. In manual control systems, the boundary may be time varying. In some cases, it is natural to capture it probabilistically. Hence, in this paper, the continuous state x, which causes the transition from l to l', is called the guard $X_{l \rightarrow l'}$, and the guard is assumed to be a random variable. Then, we define the probability $P(X_{l \rightarrow l'} \leq x)$ that the event $\{X_{l \rightarrow l'} \leq x\}$ occurs by using the probability density function $p_{l \rightarrow l'}(x)$ as follows:

$$F_{l \rightarrow l'}(x) = P(X_{l \rightarrow l'} \leq x) = \int_{-\infty}^{x} p_{l \rightarrow l'}(x) \mathrm{d}x.$$

2.2. *Nonparametric estimation of guards*

To identify the model of human operations, we need to estimate the probability density function $p_{l \rightarrow l'}(x)$ from a given observed data $\mathcal{O} = \{(x(t), l(t))\}$. First, we find a minimum cycle of sequence of locations $l_a, l_b, \ldots, l_k$ from the observed data $\mathcal{O}$ (in general, periodic operations can be observed in discrete input control systems).

Then, Q is given by $\{l_a, l_b, ..., l_k\}$. Collecting guards $X_{l \to l'}$, we estimate the probability density function $p_{l \to l'}(x)$ by a kernel smoothing technique (see [5] for details) which is a nonparametric statistical technique. Kernel smoothing is a useful method to estimate an unknown probability density function $f(z)$ from a finite random sample $Z = \{z_1, ..., z_n\}$ [5]. By using a kernel estimator, a kernel density estimate $\hat{f}$ at a certain point z is locally fitted to Z. For the random sample Z, the kernel density estimator is given by

$$\hat{p}(z) = \frac{1}{nh} \sum_{i=1}^{n} K\left(\frac{z - z_i}{h}\right),$$

where *kernel* $K(\cdot)$ is a function satisfying

$$\int K(x)\mathrm{d}x = 1, \qquad \int xK(x)\mathrm{d}x = 0, \qquad \int x^2 K(x)\mathrm{d}x > 0;$$

and *bandwidth* h is a positive number.

In this paper, the kernel function is chosen to be the Gaussian kernel

$$K(z) = \frac{1}{\sqrt{2\pi}} \exp\left(-\frac{z^2}{2}\right).$$

When f, which is to be estimated, is the normal distribution $N(\mu, \sigma^2)$, the optimal bandwidth h in the meaning of asymptotic mean integrated squared error (AMISE) is known to be $h = 1.059\sigma n^{-1/5}$.

Once we obtain an estimate $\hat{p}$, for each element of $g(l, l')$, we find a $(1 - \alpha)$ confidence interval $[z_{\min}, z_{\max}]$ in the meaning that

$$\int_{-\infty}^{z_{\min}} \hat{p}(z)\mathrm{d}z = \alpha/2 \qquad \text{and} \qquad \int_{z_{\max}}^{\infty} \hat{p}(z)\mathrm{d}z = \alpha/2.$$

Then, we can define a region of the continuous state $G_{l \to l'}(\alpha)$ where a transition from l to l' occurs with probability $1 - \alpha$.

2.3. *Fault detection*

We can diagnose human operations based on the identified hybrid system model with $G_{l \to l'}(\alpha)$ to check whether new observation $\mathcal{O}_{\text{new}}$ validates the model or not in real time. The simplest procedure to detect faults is summarized as follows: for $(x, l) \in \mathcal{O}_{\text{new}}$,

(1) Observe a transition $l \to l_{\text{new}}$ from a new observation (x, l).
(2) Check whether the transition $l \to l_{\text{new}}$ exists in the model. If it does not, then a fault is declared.
(3) If the transition occurs outside $G_{l \to l'}(\alpha)$, then a fault is declared.

3. Experiments and results

3.1. *Manual control of multiple tank systems*

In the manual control problem under consideration, the control objective is to maintain the levels of several tanks connected with each other in a multiple tank system (Fig. 2) [6]. The valves can be manipulated to be open or closed, whereas the pipes are always open. More precisely, general multiple tank systems are modeled as follows:

$$\dot{y} = \sum_{i=1}^{M} A_i u_i \delta_i + Bw, \tag{2}$$

$$\delta_i = \begin{cases} 1 & \text{if valve } i \text{ is open} \\ 0 & \text{if valve } i \text{ is closed,} \end{cases} \tag{3}$$

where M is the total number of valves, $y = [y_1, \ldots, y_L]^{\mathrm{T}} \in R^L$ is water levels of each tank, $A_i \in R^L$ and $B \in R^{L \times N}$ are defined by the relation of tanks, valves and pipes. When the ith valve is open, water is discharged at u_i unit/s from it. From each pipe water is always supplied at $w = [w_1, \ldots, w_N]^{\mathrm{T}} \in R^N$ unit/s. $\delta = [\delta_1, \ldots, \delta_M] \in \{0, 1\}^M$ is the valve state and means this system has 2^M modes. Using δ, we define each mode index as $I = \sum_{i=1}^{M} 2^{i-1}\delta_i + 1$.

The control objective of the human operator is to maintain the water levels of each tank y around a given reference level $r = [r_1, \ldots, r_L]^{\mathrm{T}} \in R^L$ under full observation of all tank levels. In other words, the human operator aims to make $e = r - y$ stay between $e_{\min}$ and $e_{\max}$ by manipulating only one valve at a time.

3.2. *Experimental task*

Four subjects took part in the following experiment. The subjects had to control a computer-simulated three-tank system with four valves and one pipe shown in

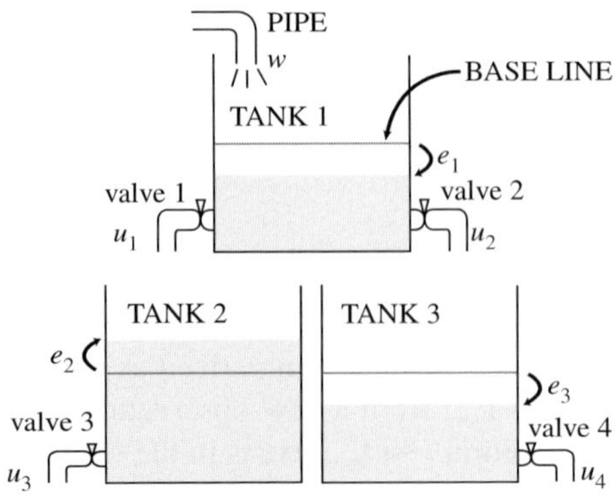

Fig. 2. An experimental setup.

Fig. 2. The system can be modeled, in terms of the water tank level error $x := e = r - y$, as

$$\dot{x} = \sum_{i=1}^{4} A_i u_i \delta_i + Bw,$$

where

$$A_1 = \begin{bmatrix} -1 \\ 1 \\ 0 \end{bmatrix}, \quad A_2 = \begin{bmatrix} -1 \\ 0 \\ 1 \end{bmatrix}, \quad A_3 = \begin{bmatrix} 0 \\ -1 \\ 0 \end{bmatrix}, \quad A_4 = \begin{bmatrix} 0 \\ 0 \\ -1 \end{bmatrix}, \quad B = \begin{bmatrix} 1 \\ 0 \\ 0 \end{bmatrix}.$$

Since the tank system has four valves, the hybrid system model has $2^4 = 16$ modes.

The task of the subjects is to keep water levels between $x_{\min} = [-20, -20, -20]^{\mathrm{T}}$ and $x_{\max} = [20, 20, 20]^{\mathrm{T}}$. That is, $x_{\min} \preceq x \preceq x_{\max}$ by changing only one valve to on or off at a time. The subjects were trained to control the computer-simulated tank system until they could achieve the control task.

All subjects manipulated the computer simulator under conditions where the system parameters are set to be $u_1 = 8$, $u_2 = 12$, $u_3 = 8$, $u_4 = 12$, $w = 10$. The initial condition is $x = 0$ and *mode 1* (that is, $\delta_i = 0$, all valves are closed).

3.3. *Identification results*

In the experiments, subjects periodically operated valves by observing one or more water levels of the tanks when they successfully achieved the task. As space is limited, we only show the results of Subject No. 1 and No. 4.

3.3.1. *Results of Subject No. 1.* Figure 3 shows a sequence of manipulations by Subject No. 1. The error of the water tank levels are kept between −23 and 23 by a sequence of a cycle formed by *mode 6*, *mode 8*, *mode 16* and *mode 14* as shown in Fig. 4. Hence, the hybrid dynamical model of Subject No. 1 has $Q = \{l_6 := \mathit{mode}\ 6, l_8 := \mathit{mode}\ 8, l_{16} := \mathit{mode}\ 16, l_{14} := \mathit{mode}\ 14\}$ and

$$f(x, l_6) = \begin{bmatrix} w - u_1 \\ 0 \\ 0 \end{bmatrix}, \quad f(x, l_8) = \begin{bmatrix} w - u_1 - u_2 \\ 0 \\ u_2 \end{bmatrix}$$

$$f(x, l_{16}) = \begin{bmatrix} w - u_1 - u_2 \\ 0 \\ u_2 - u_4 \end{bmatrix}, \quad f(x, l_{14}) = \begin{bmatrix} w - u_1 u_2 \\ 0 \\ u_2 \end{bmatrix}.$$

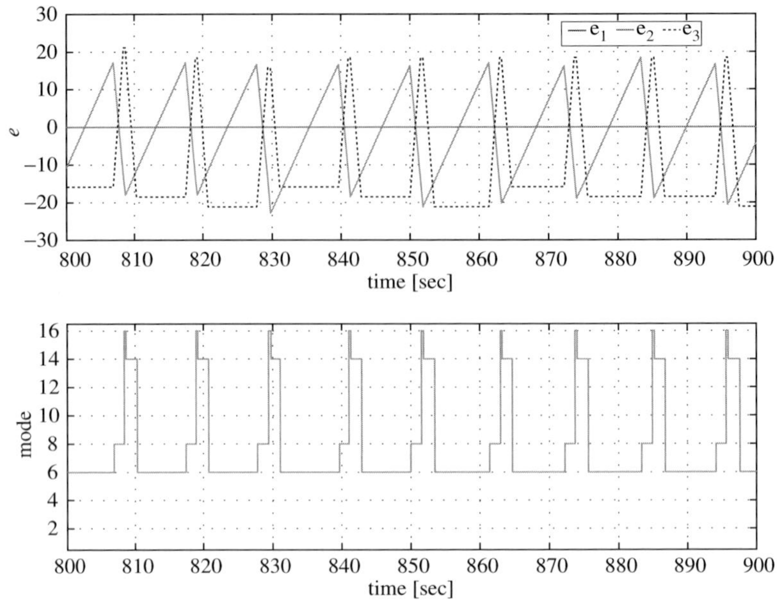

Fig. 3. A result of manipulations by Subject No. 1.

Next, to identify the guard, we decided which element of the continuous state x in the transitions is dominant. The dominant elements differ in every transition and they correspond to the water level that the subject monitored most closely. The decision was made by subjects' self-assessment about observations of their own operations.

Next, we applied the kernel smoothing method to each identified dominant element x_i. Figure 5 shows the resulting kernel density estimates of the water level where the subject switched the valves. From Fig. 5, it is obvious that the subject changes the valves when the error between the water level and the reference is in the neighborhood of -20 or 20.

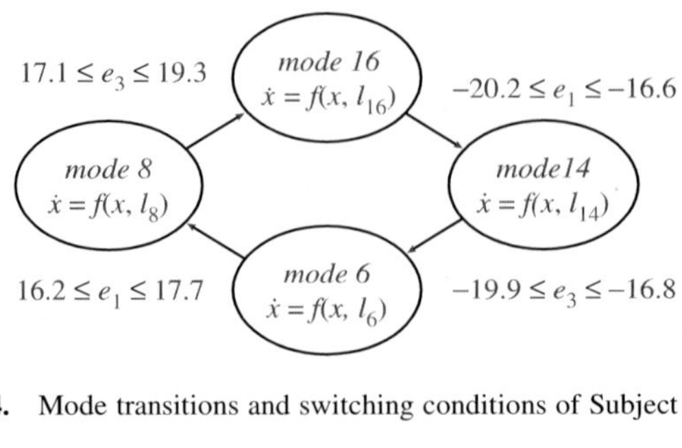

Fig. 4. Mode transitions and switching conditions of Subject No. 1.

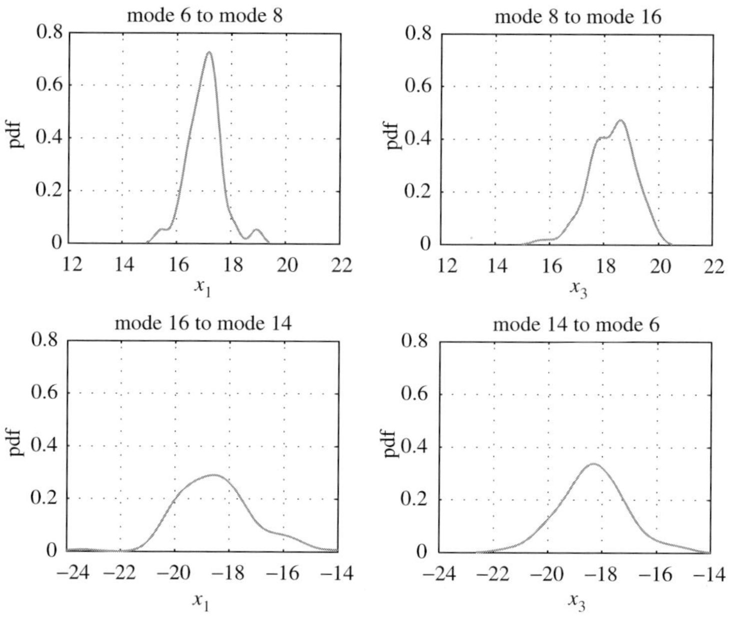

Fig. 5. Kernel density estimation of guards of Subject No. 1.

As a result of kernel smoothing, we found

$$
\begin{aligned}
G_{l_6 \to l_8}(0.1) &= \{x \in \Re^3 |\ 16.2 \leq x_1 \leq 17.7\},\\
G_{l_8 \to l_{16}}(0.1) &= \{x \in \Re^3 |\ 17.1 \leq x_3 \leq 19.3\},\\
G_{l_{16} \to l_{14}}(0.1) &= \{x \in \Re^3 |\ -20.2 \leq x_1 \leq -16.6\},\\
G_{l_{14} \to l_6}(0.1) &= \{x \in \Re^3 |\ -19.9 \leq x_3 \leq -16.8\}.
\end{aligned}
\tag{4}
$$

Based on the guards (4), we applied the fault detection procedure to new observations. The result is shown in Fig. 6. In Fig. 6, *error* is indicated in the time history of the fault detection when the water levels go out of the normal ranges which are specified by the guards (4).

Furthermore, for choosing $\alpha = 0.2$, we obtained the guards

$$
\begin{aligned}
G_{l_6 \to l_8}(0.2) &= \{x \in \Re^3 |\ 16.5 \leq x_1 \leq 17.5\},\\
G_{l_8 \to l_{16}}(0.2) &= \{x \in \Re^3 |\ 17.5 \leq x_3 \leq 19.0\},\\
G_{l_{16} \to l_{14}}(0.2) &= \{x \in \Re^3 |\ -19.7 \leq x_1 \leq -17.3\},\\
G_{l_{14} \to l_6}(0.2) &= \{x \in \Re^3 |\ -19.7 \leq x_3 \leq -17.3\}.
\end{aligned}
\tag{5}
$$

Figure 7 shows the result of fault detection for the same observed data used in Fig. 6 by using the guards (5). It follows from these results that larger α leads to more sensitive fault detection results. Hence, by the different values of α, we can adjust

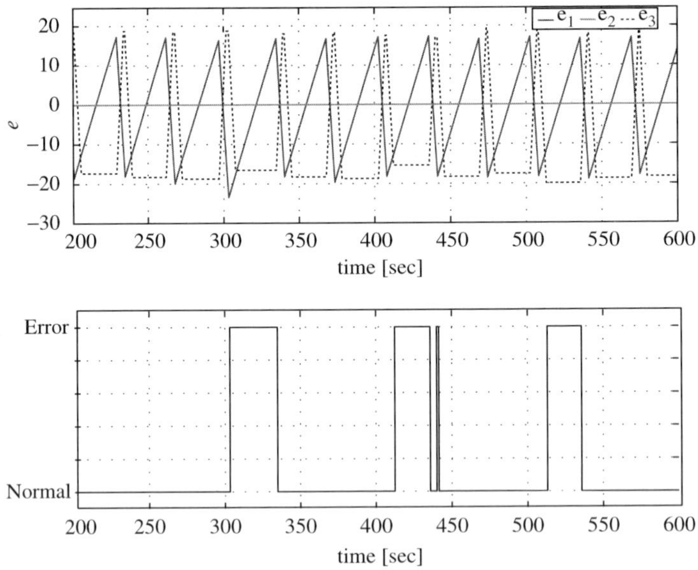

Fig. 6. A result of fault detection for Subject No. 1 ($\alpha = 0.1$).

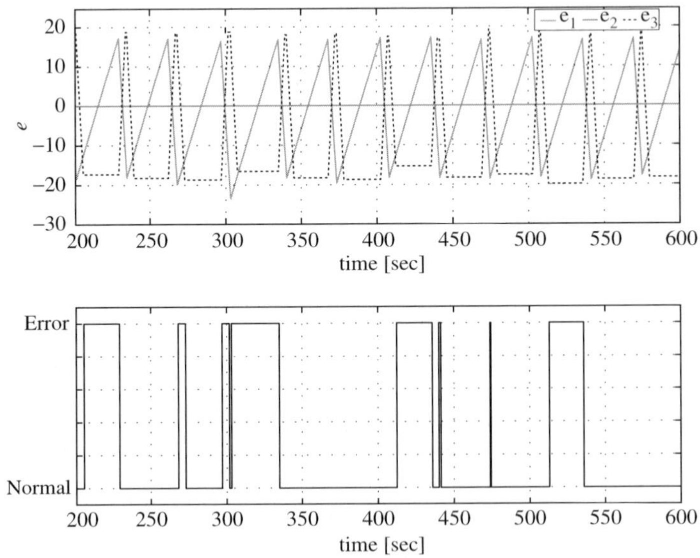

Fig. 7. A result of fault detection for Subject No. 1 ($\alpha = 0.2$).

the level of fault detection. It is useful in design for an alarm warning error of human operations.

3.3.2. *Results of Subject No. 4.* Subject No. 4 showed more complicated operations. He used 12 modes (*mode 1*, *mode 2*, *mode 3*, *mode 4*, *mode 5*, *mode 8*, *mode 9*, *mode 12*, *mode 13*, *mode 14*, *mode 15*, and *mode 16*). However, it follows from the investigation of kernel density estimation that there exist guard sets G having common regions. In fact, $G_{l_1 \to l_2}(\alpha)$, $G_{l_2 \to l_4}(\alpha)$, $G_{l_1 \to l_3}(\alpha)$, and $G_{l_3 \to l_4}(\alpha)$ are very similar. This is caused by the fact that there exist two sequences from l_1 to l_4, and two transitions in each sequence have almost the same event time. Hence, we can approximate transitions $l_1 \to l_2 \to l_4$ and $l_1 \to l_3 \to l_4$ to be simply $l_1 \to l_4$. The same argument leads to the approximated transition $l_4 \to l_{16}$, $l_{16} \to l_{13}$, and $l_{13} \to l_1$. This approximation reduces the number of locations (the resulting model has $Q = \{l_1, l_4, l_{13}, l_{16}\}$) as shown in Fig. 8. To this reduced model we applied the kernel smoothing technique to the transitions. As a result, we obtained kernel density estimates as shown in Fig. 9 and identified guard sets are given by

$$
\begin{aligned}
G_{l_{16} \to l_{13}}(0.1) &= \{x \in \Re^3 | \ -14.7 \le x_1 \le -22.7\},\\
G_{l_{13} \to l_1}(0.1) &= \{x \in \Re^3 | \ -13.2 \le x_3 \le -18.0\},\\
G_{l_1 \to l_4}(0.1) &= \{x \in \Re^3 | \ 20.1 \le x_1 \le 13.9\},\\
G_{l_4 \to l_{16}}(0.1) &= \{x \in \Re^3 | \ 17.4 \le x_3 \le 13.2\}.
\end{aligned}
$$

Based on the model, we applied the fault detection procedure to new observations from the operations of Subject No. 4. The result is shown in Fig. 10. It is obvious that the proposed method can detect faults of operations of Subject No. 4 similar to the results of Subject No. 1.

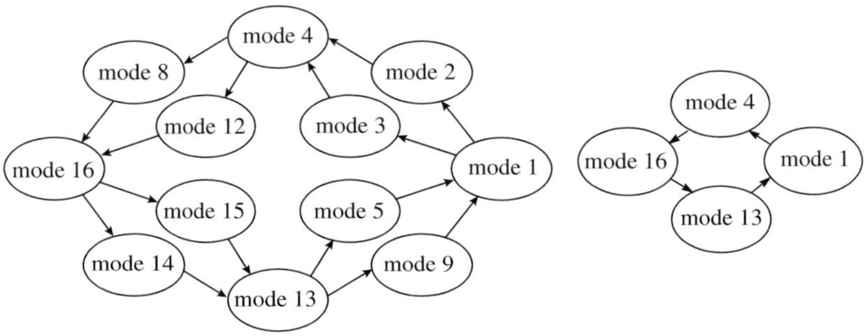

Fig. 8. Normal mode transitions of Subject No. 4 and its approximation.

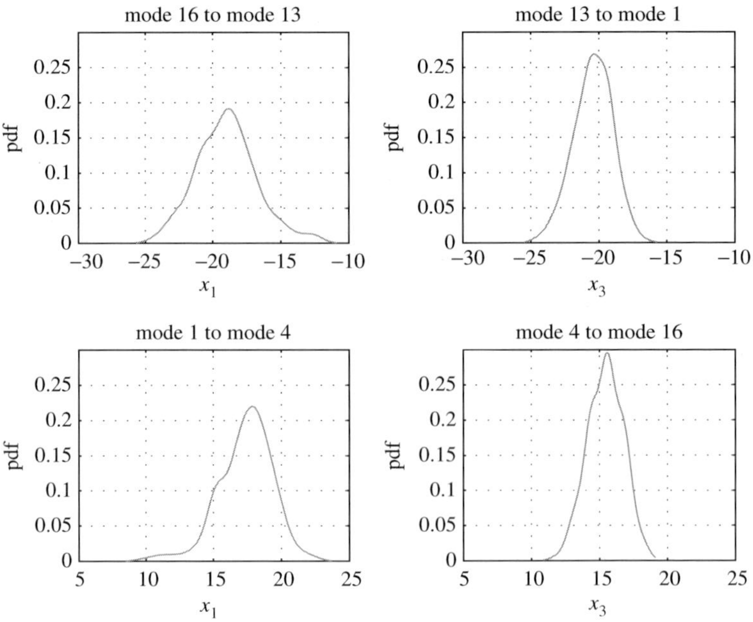

Fig. 9. Kernel density estimation of guards of Subject No. 4.

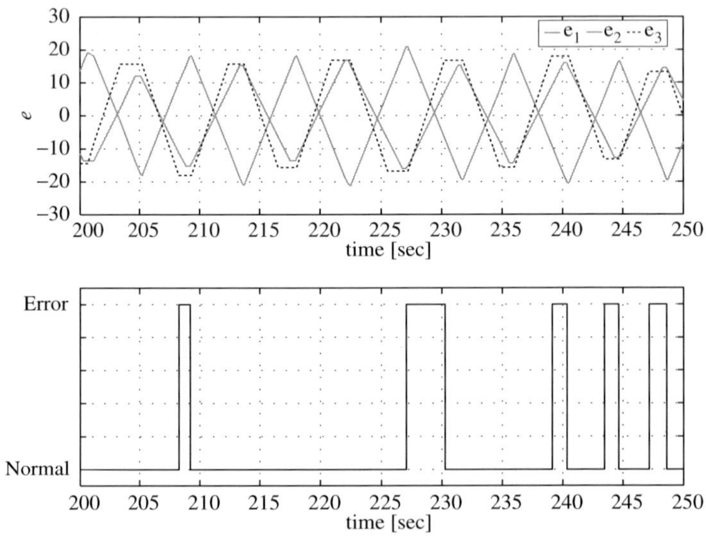

Fig. 10. A result of fault detection for Subject No. 4.

4. Conclusions

In this paper, the focus was mainly on a specific example. In spite of this, it is possible to summarize the following conclusions:

- In Section 3, we observed probabilistic properties of operations in a switching control system. It shows that they depend highly on the ability of the operator controlling the system. In addition, obtained probability density functions are different from the Gaussian distribution.
- We can detect faults of actions by the human operator based on the model derived from his or her own probability density function.

The practical relevant issue is a modeling problem under unobservable mode transitions and control by continuous inputs.

Acknowledgment

This research was supported by MEXT under Grant-in-Aid for Creative Scientific Research (Project No. 13GS0018).

References

[1] D.A. Norman, *Categorization of action slips*, Psychol. Rev. **88** (1) (1981), 1–15.

[2] J. Reason, *Human Error*, Cambridge University Press, Cambridge, MA (1990).

[3] J. Rasmussen, *Information Processing and Human–Machine Interaction*, Elsevier, Amsterdam (1986).

[4] A. van der Schaft and H. Schumacher, *An Introduction to Hybrid Dynamical Systems*, Springer, Berlin (2000).

[5] J. Simonoff, *Smoothing Methods in Statistics*, Springer, Berlin (1996).

[6] J. Imura, *Well-posedness analysis of switch-driven hybrid systems*, Proceedings of American Control Conferences (2001), 862–867.

PART VI

Robotics for Safety and Security

CHAPTER 26

Development of a UMRS (Utility Mobile Robot for Search) and a Searching System for Casualties Using a Cellphone

Toshi Takamori

Department of Computer and System Engineering, Kobe University, 1-1, Rokkodai, Nada, Kobe 657-8501, Japan

Shigeru Kobayashi

Department of Mechanical Engineering, Kobe City College of Technology, 8-3, Gakuenhigashimachi, Nishi, Kobe 651-2194, Japan

Takashi Ohira

Adaptive Communications Research Laboratories, Advanced Telecommunications Research Institute International, 2-2-2, Hikaridai, Keihanna Science City, Kyoto 619-0288, Japan

Masayuki Takashima, Akihiko Ikeuchi and Shiro Takashima

Department of Computer and System Engineering, Kobe University, 1-1, Rokkodai, Nada, Kobe 657-8501, Japan

Contents

SYSTEMS AND HUMAN SCIENCE – FOR SAFETY, SECURITY, AND DEPENDABILITY
Edited by Tatsuo Arai, Shigeru Yamamoto and Kazuhisa Makino

Abstract

For use during rescue activities in an urban disaster, we propose a sufferer searching system using a group of robots and are currently developing this system. In this chapter, five robots of the crawler type of different sizes and functions are described; in addition, the cellphone detection system is explained as there is a high probability a sufferer has his or her cellphone at hand.

1. Introduction

One of the key operations in any rescue activity in a large-scale earthquake is to find the sufferers as quickly as possible in destroyed buildings and houses at the disaster site. These search operations are very difficult, dangerous and time consuming. The places where the rescue teams have to enter in order to search are usually very messy, sometimes very narrow due to debris, and there is a possibility of the buildings' sudden collapse and the leakage of explosive and/or hazardous gases. To cope with these difficulties and dangers encountered by the human rescue teams, we are currently developing a rescue system to search for casualties using a group of robots. First, the whole rescue system we are attempting to create is explained, then robots for this activity currently being built are described briefly. Finally, search systems using cellphones and ESPAR (Electronically Steerable Passive Array Radiator) antennae [1] are reported in this chapter.

2. Sufferer search system

We are aiming to create an efficient sufferer searching system using a group of robots to carry out rescue operations [2,3]. A schematic view of this entire system is as shown in Fig. 1. Mobile information bases are used to gather information about each search site and to calculate the most effective operators' formation. In addition, this mobile base is the station to send this local information to the headquarters and *vice versa*. In this chapter, we focus on a local search system with a group of robots. As time is very limited and the areas that one rescue robot operator has to search are usually wide and discontinuous, one operator handles a group of robots and covers an area of about 100×100 m^2. One group

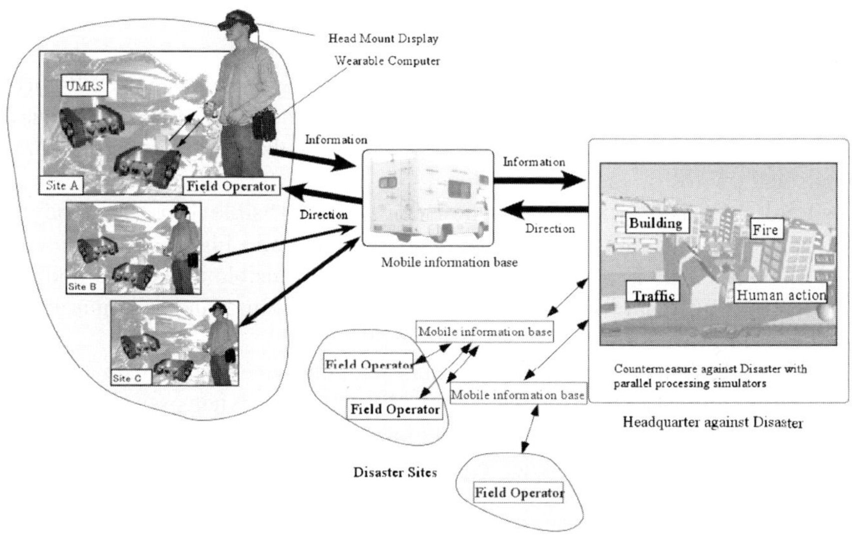

Fig. 1. Over view of sufferer searching system.

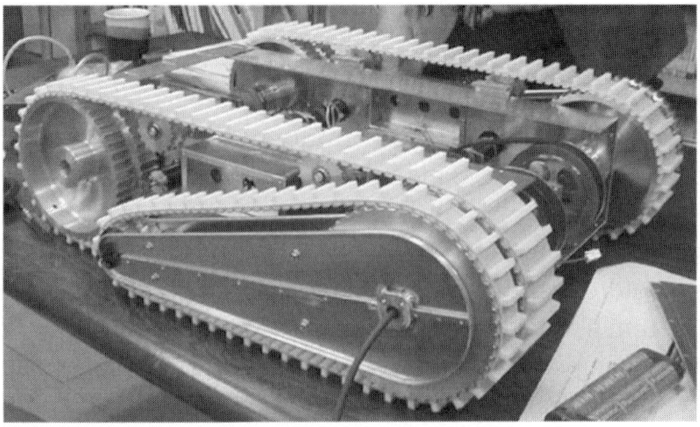

Fig. 2. UMRS-V-M1.

consists of about 10 robots and these robots search in a dispersion formation to increase the probability of finding a sufferer. Once one robot has a problem it cannot cope with, as one robot cannot overcome the obstacle, other robots will gather and work together and so on. Regarding the robots; we are now developing actual small size robots as explained in Section 3. If any clues are found, these are very helpful in finding the victims. For instance, many people these days have a cellphone, so if a sufferer's cellphone emits a special coded signal at the necessary time, we can easily identify the positions of sufferers. At this stage, a small robot may approach and confirm the conditions even when a human cannot approach directly. We will describe this procedure and the system utilizing the cellphone in Sections 4 and 5.

3. Robots for searching

We have named the robots that we use in our sufferer searching system UMRS (Utility Mobile Robot for Search). Our current model is the fifth generation of UMRS, so we call it UMRS-V. Five varieties of UMRS-V were developed for this study. Following are brief descriptions and photos of each robot.

(a) UMRS-V-M1. This is a crawler type robot with extensible arms. The body size is $582 \times 500 \times 176$ mm and weight is 21.4 kg as shown in Fig. 2.
(b) UMRS-V-S1. This is a crawler type robot with extensible arms. The body size is $300 \times 250 \times 100$ mm when assistant crawlers are retracted, and weight is about 9 kg as shown in Fig. 3.
(c) UMRS-V-M2. This is a crawler type robot with the travel mechanism at the robot's center of gravity. The body size is $558 \times 340 \times 163$ mm when assistant crawlers are retracted, and the total weight is 20.3 kg as shown in Fig. 4.
(d) UMRS-V-S2. This is a crawler type robot with extensible arms. The length of the arm is almost the same as that of the main body. The body size is $510 \times 470 \times 210$ mm when assistant crawlers are retracted, and the total weight is 20 kg.

(e) UMRS-V-M3. This is a four-wheel crawler type able to generate maneuverable movement on debris. The body size is 530 × 345 × 180 mm and the total weight is 18 kg as shown in Fig. 5.

Each UMRS-V has two types of sensor. One is a human detection sensor such as a CCD camera, IR sensor or CO_2 sensor and a distance measuring sensor that can detect the distance of a signal emitted by a cellphone as described in Section 4. The other is the robot's self position recognition sensors such as encoders and motion sensors with gyroscopes for the dead reckoning method. In addition, we plan to use the ESPER antenna that ATR Japan developed to identify the three-dimensional location of the robot as explained in Section 5. An outline of the control and communication system for the robot is shown in Fig. 6.

Fig. 3. UMRS-V-S1.

Fig. 4. UMRS-V-M1.

Fig. 5. UMRS-V-M3.

4. Development of SDSCP

One of the most effective ways of searching for sufferers with a group of UMRS is to use the system of cellphone sensing. There is a high probability that the cellphone is beside its owner even while he or she is in bed, and we could gain important clues to help find a sufferer if we could make his or her cellphone active by remote access and then physically search for it at a time of disaster. Currently, the cellphone is already popular, with about 80,000,000 units in use in Japan, and still increasing. Because the present population of Japan is around 120,000,000, it can be estimated that approximately 65% of Japanese have a cellphone. This number indicates the effectiveness of this sufferer search system. In this study, we propose the following two systems as the searching system.

(1) Distance measuring system (DSMS)

(2) Direction measuring system (DRMS)

DSMS is a measuring system used to determine the distance between the cellphone and the UMRS in which sound, light and radio waves are used as sensor signals, while DRMS

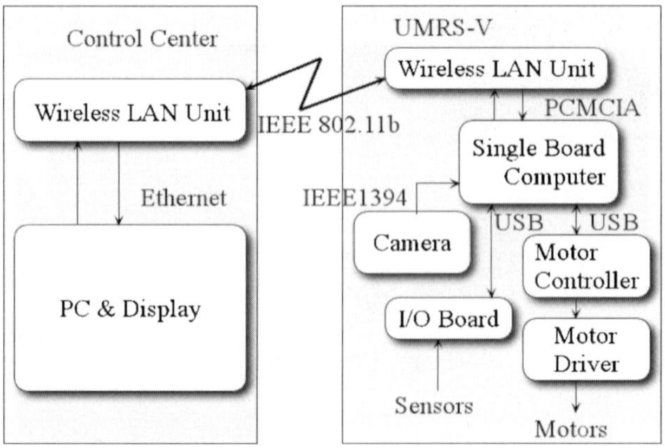

Fig. 6. Control and communication system of UMRS-V.

is a direction detection system using an ESPAR antenna, in which the directivity is rotating. It is also important that at the same time the sound and light signals can be used by the search party to alert them to the existence of sufferers.

4.1. *Distance measuring system*

When a cellphone receives a special code from the cellphone base station, this code triggers the cellphone to transmit a sound signal, a light signal and a radio wave signal simultaneously as shown in Fig. 7.

The receiver installed in the UMRS receives these three different kinds of signals and the distance between the cellphone and UMRS is determined by the following processes. The light or radio wave signal is received; it triggers the start of counting by the receiver's counter circuit.

(a) The sound signal is received; it triggers a stop to the counting of the receiver's counter circuit.
(b) The sound signal arrival time from the cellphone to the UMRS is calculated from the counted number.
(c) The distance between the cellphone and the UMRS can be calculated from the arrival time and the sound velocity at the disaster site.

At least three units of UMRS with receivers make it possible to determine the position of the cellphone using the above-mentioned system. The principle of this

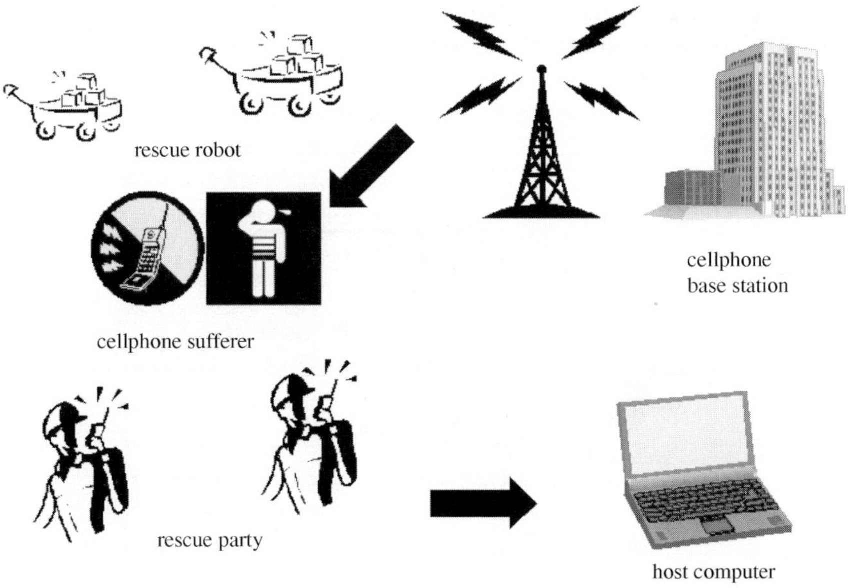

Fig. 7. Over view of SDSCP.

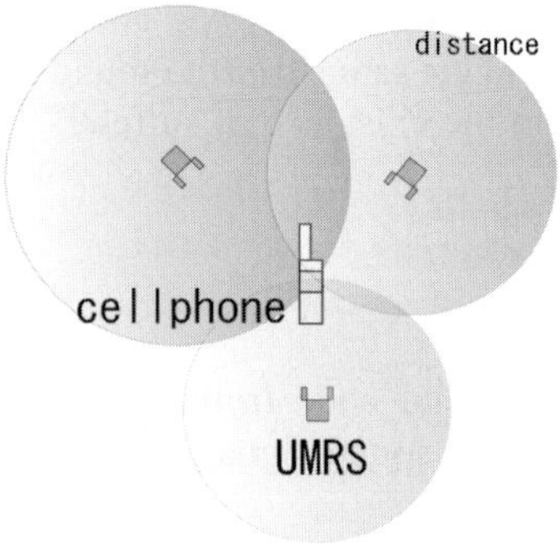

Fig. 8. Principle of DSMS.

measurement system and an example of the block diagram of the receiver system are shown in Figs. 8 and 9, respectively.

4.2. *Direction measuring system*

In this system, an ESPAR antenna is installed in the UMRS. The directivity is rotated electronically in the ESPAR antenna, and the strongest direction of radio wave magnitude is scanned at high speed, thus the direction of the vertical plain that contains the position of the UMRS and the position of the radio wave transmitted by the cellphone can be determined quickly. Figure 10 illustrates the principle of an ESPAR antenna and the procedure of data processing [1]. Currently, the resolution of the Prototype ESPAR antenna is 30°. The nearer the robot approaches to the cellphone, the smaller the distance error becomes.

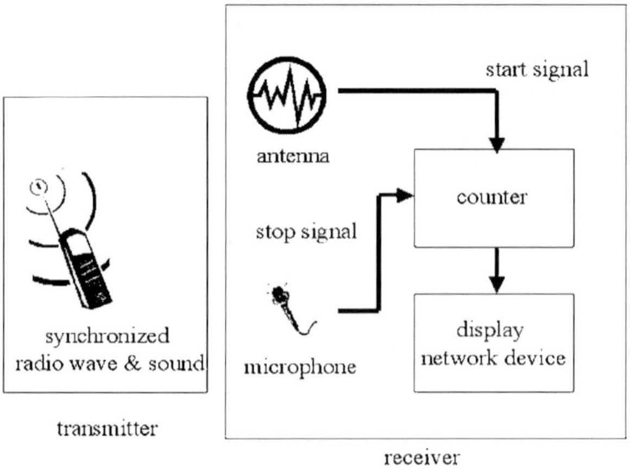

Fig. 9. Block diagram of DSMS.

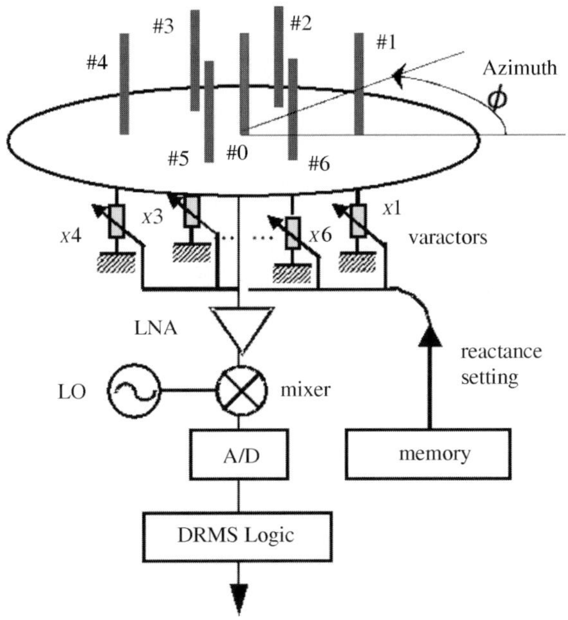

Fig. 10. Direction finding principle of the ESPAR antenna [1].

4.3. *Configuration of SDSCP*

A practical sufferer searching system for times of disaster will be composed of a combination of DSMS and DRMS (Figs. 11 and 12). We call this combination system SDSCP (sufferer detecting system based on cellphone). The SDSCP, in other words, both these two systems installed together in a UMRS, makes it possible for just one UMRS to determine the position of the cellphone even though three units of UMRS are required when just one measurement system is used. Figure 13 shows the measurement method with this combination system. In actual searching operations, it is necessary to search effectively for more than one cellphone at a disaster site. To make this possible, it is planned to design the system so that just one cellphone is chased by not more than one

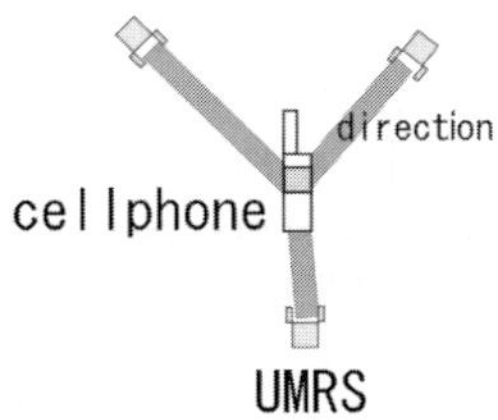

Fig. 11. Principle of DRMS.

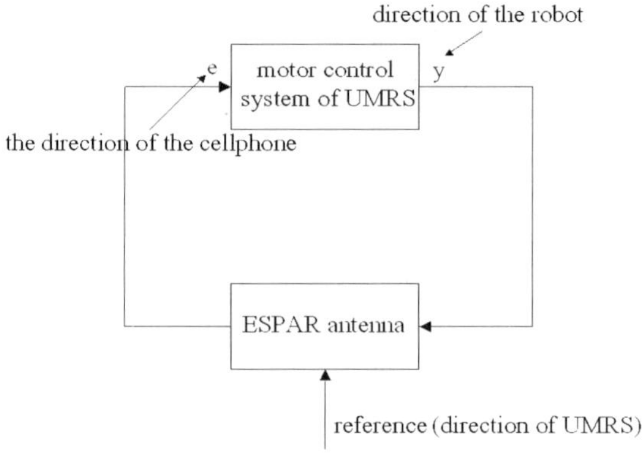

Fig. 12. Autonomous driving system of UMRS.

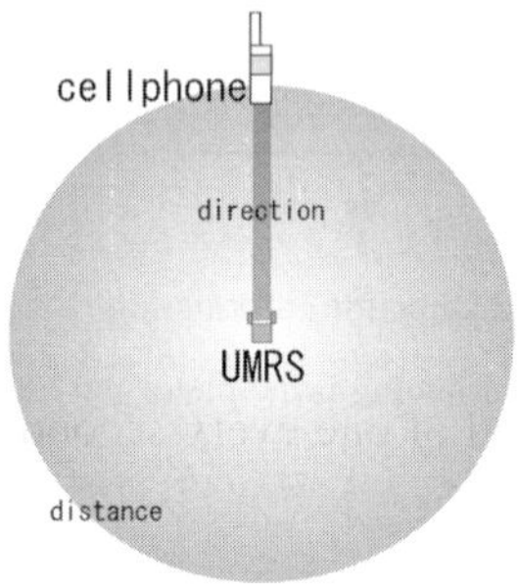

Fig. 13. Measurement way of SDSCP.

UMRS recognizing the modulated radio wave code that is transmitted from each cellphone using SDSCP.

5. Experiment and discussion

The transmitter circuit shown in Fig. 14 was developed as a pseudo-cellphone. This transmits sound, light and radio waves according to a special code signal from the experimentally set up cellphone base station, and the DSMS receives those signals. The key features of this receiver circuit are the filter structures that prevent the sensed 3 KHz sound signal from being influenced by other sound disturbances; this receiver was successfully developed. To experimentally compose the DRMS, we utilized the prototype direction-of-arrival finder with an ESPAR antenna as its receiver and a micro beacon as its transmitter, both developed by ATR [1]. An experimental search using the DSMS was conducted in this study, as one of the simulations to verify the SDSCP. The specifications of the DSMS used in this experiment are shown in Table 1.

Fig. 14. Transmitter circuit as the pseudo-cellphone.

5.1. *Experimental setup*

The experimental setup consisted of one set of DSMS, one unit of UMRS, the monitor system, and a block of debris. Figure 15 shows an outline of the experimental setup. The transmitter is buried under the debris, and transmits the sound signal, the light signal, and the radio wave signal at an interval of one every second. The UMRS with DSMS catches those signals and measures the distances at three different positions. In this experiment, the function and performance of the DSMS could be confirmed experimentally, even though this is not real-time.

5.2. *Experimental results of the DSMS*

The experiment was carried out in indoor conditions at a temperature of 15 °C.

(1) *Distance characteristics*. The distance was measured using 3 KHz pulses of sound emitted from the transmitter under the debris of the experimental setup. The variation of the count numbers in accordance with the distance between the transmitter and the UMRS is shown in Fig. 16. As the concept of this study, we planned to search a $100 \times 100\ m^2$ area with 10 units of UMRS; we believe that one set of DSMS in a UMRS is required to detect a distance of around 10 m.

Table 1. Specifications of DSMS

Magnitude of radio wave (μV/m)	500
Magnitude of light (mcd)	1800
Frequency of radio wave (MHz)	76.6
Frequency of sound (kHz)	3.0
Sound level (dB)	90

Figure 16 shows that the characteristics are almost linear up to 10 m, and this proves the effectiveness of this system.

(2) *Statistical error.* Figure 17 shows the experimental results concerning statistical error. The effective sensing distance is determined to be valid to about 10 m, shown by the characteristics of (1); we achieved the same results in the experiment concerning statistical error, confirming our earlier findings.

(3) *Monitoring of experiment.* At an actual rescue operation using our currently developing system, few operators would be required to use about 10 units of UMRS. In addition, it is necessary to develop a system that contains a raw data processing system from each UMRS and a display system with an easy-to-read monitor to help the operator understand the rescue activities by the group of UMRS. In this study, a monitoring system is developed that is able to display the information from various kinds of sensors on a meshed screen.

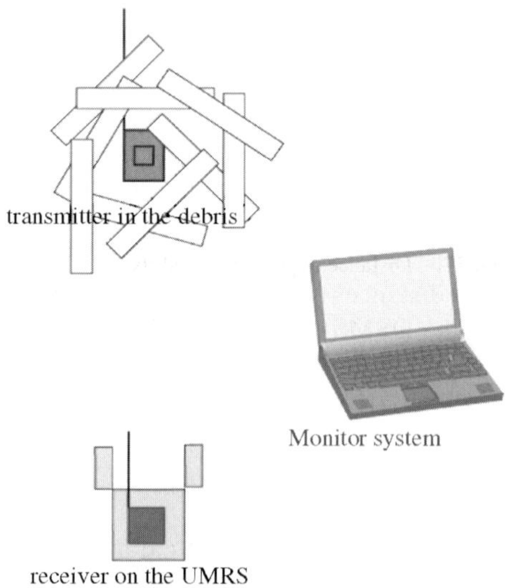

Fig. 15. Experimental setup.

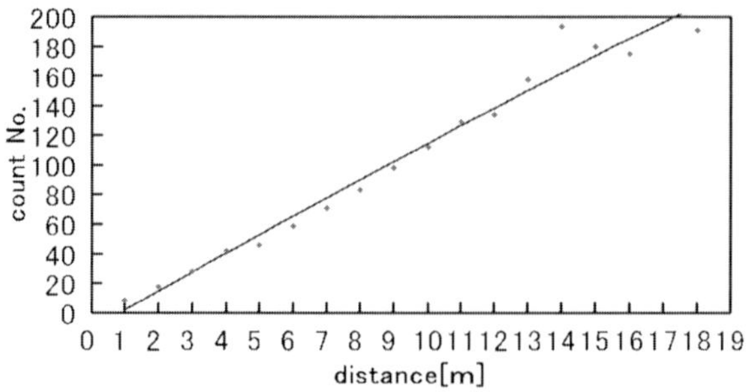

Fig. 16. Distance characteristics of DSMS.

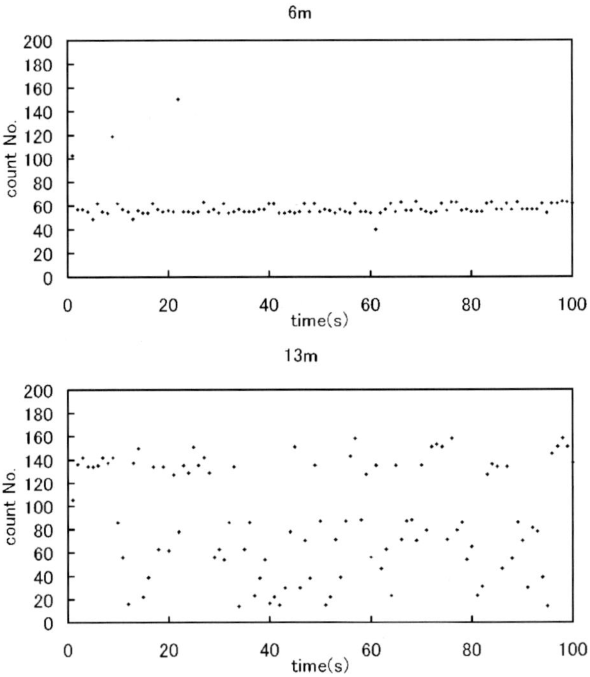

Fig. 17. Distance dependency and its variance.

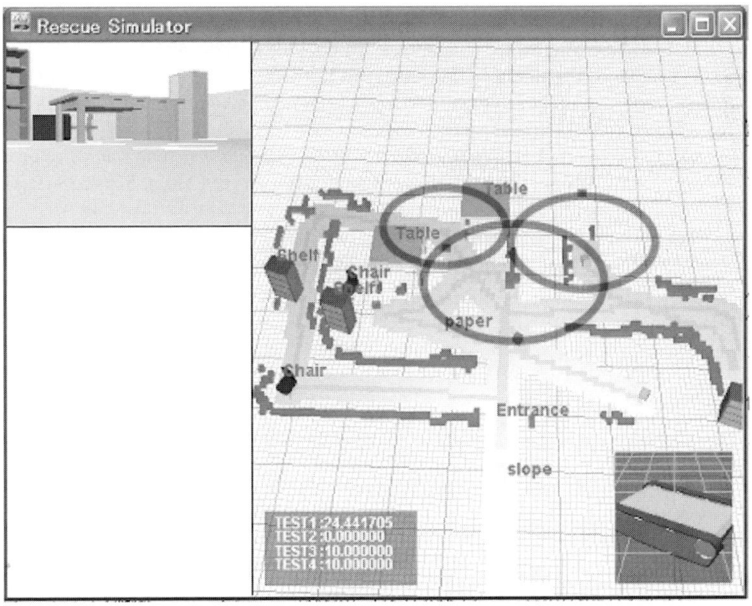

Fig. 18. View of monitoring system.

Figure 18 shows an example of the monitor display indicating the position of the cellphone in accordance with the principle of DSMS.

6. Conclusions

This chapter introduced the following research and development:

(1) The concept of the whole schematic view of our system for rescue operation.
(2) The development of a UMRS series with a variety of mechanisms.
(3) The development of a SDSCP that contains subsystem of DSMS and DRMS to find the sufferer directly.
(4) An experiment using the DSMS and monitoring system for operating the group of robots.

Acknowledgments

This research and development was performed as a part of the Special Project for Earthquake Disaster Mitigation in Urban Areas in cooperation with the International Rescue System Institute and the National Research Institute for Earth Science and Disaster Prevention.

References

[1] T. Ohira and K. Gyoda, *Handheld microwave direction-of-arrival finder based on varactor-tuned aerial beamforming*, Asia-Pacific Microwave Conference, Taipei (2001), 585–588.
[2] T. Takamori, S. Tadokoro, T. Kimura, Y. Masutani and K. Osuka, *Development of sufferer searching system by mobile robots, report of study group on development of rescue robots in huge disaster RS150*, Jpn Soc. Mech. Engng. (1999), 149–196 (in Japanese).
[3] S. Kobayashi and T. Takamori, *A human body search system by a man-machine controlled group of robots in a rescue operation*, Adv. Robotics, Cutting Edge Robotics Jpn **16** (6) (2002), 525–528 (Disaster Response Robots).
[4] A. Ikeuchi, T. Takamori, S. Kobayashi, M. Takashima, S. Takashima and M. Yamada, *Development of mobile robots for search and rescue operation systems*, The Fourth International Conference on Field and Service Robotics, (2003), 321–326.

CHAPTER 27

Proposal of a Wheelchair User Support System Using Humanoid Robots to Create an SSR Society

Kotaro Sakata, Kenji Inoue, Tomohito Takubo, Tatsuo Arai and Yasushi Mae

Department of Systems Innovation, Graduate School of Engineering Science, Osaka University, 1-3 Machikaneyama, Toyonaka, Osaka 560-8531, Japan
E-mail: sakata@arai-lab.sys.es.osaka-u.ac.jp

Contents

Abstract

For creating a safe, secure and reliable (SSR) society, the concept of a human support system using humanoid robots is proposed; humanoid robots which can exist in our environment and help us to perform some tasks to allow us an SSR life. This chapter discusses the need for a human support system by analyzing a questionnaire survey of ordinary people on the web. We then propose a wheelchair user support system using humanoid robots as an example of human support, and show fundamental experiments on pushing objects using the mobile manipulation control method proposed previously.

SYSTEMS AND HUMAN SCIENCE – FOR SAFETY, SECURITY, AND DEPENDABILITY
Edited by Tatsuo Arai, Shigeru Yamamoto and Kazuhisa Makino

1. Introduction

For the purpose of creating a safe, secure and reliable (SSR) society, an integrated system of monitoring and supporting functions is important. The monitoring system finds signs of a problem quickly in the environment by watching a wide area in detail using many fixed or moving cameras. The supporting system prevents the danger from occurring or copes with the occurring danger rapidly, thus reducing damage to the minimum; in the present project, humanoid robots are used as supporting devices. In this way, this integrated system can offer us a safe environment, allowing us to feel secure and comfortable in the environment [1,2]. This is because humanoid robots can move in our environment and use some tools and machines as humans do. This project aims at the conceptual design of such a monitoring and supporting system and the making of a prototype of the system.

This chapter is organized as follows: Section 2 describes the outline of a human support system using humanoid robots. Section 3 shows the need for such a system using humanoid robots as described in Section 2. Taking this need and the technical limitations of current humanoid robots into account, (in Section 4) we propose a wheelchair user support system using humanoid robots as a concrete application of this system. Finally, we show fundamental experiments on pushing objects using the mobile manipulation control method proposed previously. It is essential for humanoid robots to perform this task in order to create this proposed system.

2. Outline of a human support system using humanoid robots

"Human support" means "to help humans perform tasks leading to an SSR life" and "to help humans perform tasks in safety". Hence some kinds of physical interactions with the environment or humans are required of supporting devices. It is impossible to predict when and where problems may occur. Accordingly, this project disposes multiple robots as supporting devices in our environment. They move around us at normal times and are always ready to cope with problems. Thus, the robots are required not only to support us but also to make us feel secure in daily life. Humanoid robots are useful as robots coexisting with humans and working with/for humans, because they have human-like structures and can behave like humans. Hence the authors have chosen humanoid robots as supporting robots.

A conceptual image of a human support system using humanoid robots is shown in Fig. 1. Multiple humanoid robots move around in our environment. They continuously monitor the environment and us in cooperation with fixed or moving cameras. If some problems are detected, the robots nearest to the source protect us from the problems.

Humanoid robots can also help us perform some tasks which we cannot do in safety alone. This will be important for an aged society in the future.

Accordingly, two kinds of motion are required of humanoid robots used as human supporting robots:

(1) Human-like motions which do not frighten us at normal times.
(2) Supporting motions for protecting us from dangers or helping us do some kinds of tasks in safety.

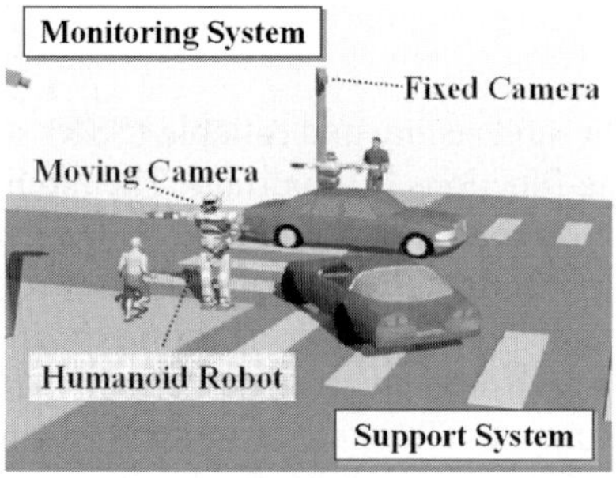

Fig. 1. Human support system using humanoid robots.

3. The need for a human support system for creating an SSR society

In order to create a human support system using humanoid robots as proposed in Section 2, it is important for the authors to clarify the following three points:

- What factors make society unsafe, and what makes people feel insecure?
- What do people think about humanoid robots working around them?
- What kinds of jobs do people want humanoid robots to do, assuming that they work around us?

However, no-one has carried out a survey to address these three points, although a survey concerning the need for rehabilitation robots [3] was carried out. The authors, therefore, carried out a questionnaire survey for ordinary people on the web. An analysis of this, ways in which to apply a human support system using humanoid robots and the requirements of such a system are discussed.

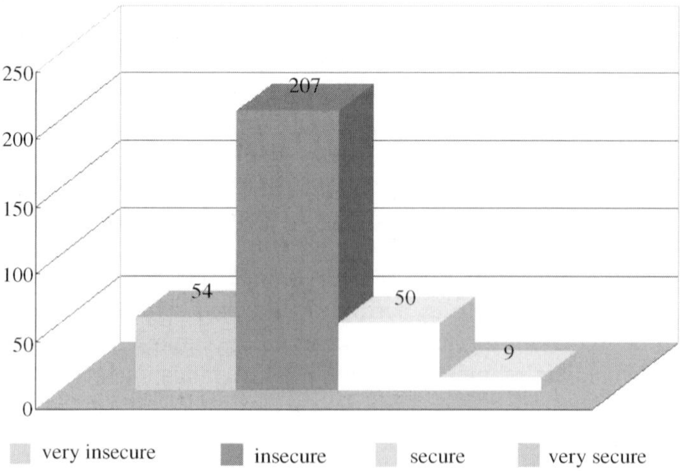

Fig. 2. (Q1) Do you feel insecure nowadays?

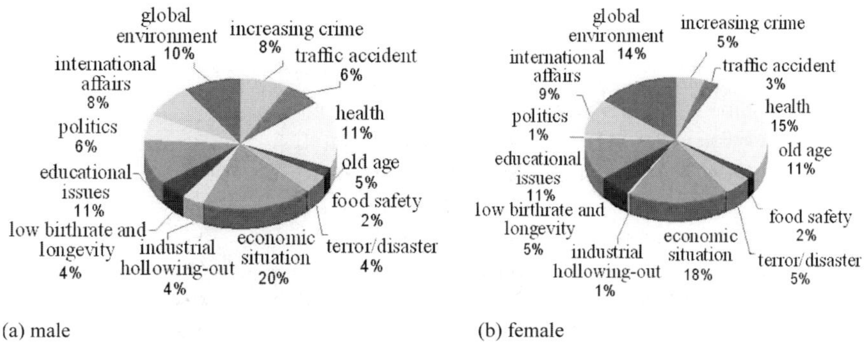

Fig. 3. (Q1) About what do you feel insecure? (a) Male, (b) female.

3.1. *Questionnaire*

The survey received a total of 335 responses from November 26 until December 31, 2002, of which 324 were valid. 60% of the valid respondents were male, and 55% were experienced in programming. The age structure is as follows: 26.2% are in their teens, 57.7% in their 20s, 4.3% in their 30s, 3.4% in their 40s, 4.0% in their 50s and 0.9% in their 60s and over.

Figures 2–13 show the results of the questionnaire. The result analysis is as follows.

3.1.1. *Anxiety in present-day life.* Figure 2 shows that the majority of people feel insecure nowadays. Figure 3 explains that they feel insecure mainly about the "economic situation" and "health", regardless of gender. On the other hand, the number concerned about "increasing crime", "traffic accident" and "terror/disaster" is small. This is why they are concerned with their daily life. Incidentally, we observed differences between the sexes on several counts. Males answered "increasing crime", "traffic accident", "industrial hollowing-out" and "politics" more than females, while females answered "health", "old age" and "global environment" more than males. In other words, females have a greater tendency to worry about their daily life than males.

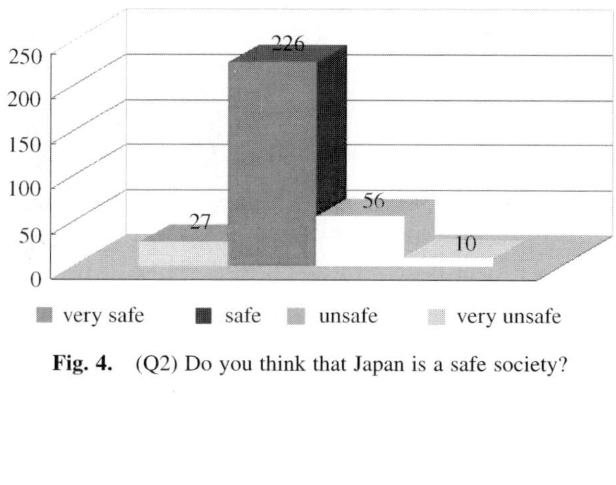

Fig. 4. (Q2) Do you think that Japan is a safe society?

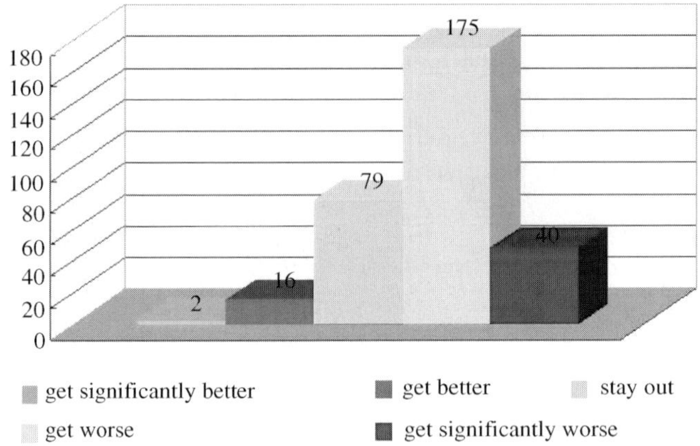

Fig. 5. (Q3) Will Japan be safe in the future?

Figure 4 shows that the majority of people recognize our present-day society is safe to some extent. On the other hand, Fig. 5 shows that they think Japan will not be safe in the future. Thus, we believe that creating an SSR society will become more important in the future. Figure 6 shows that participants think the main factors which will make society unsafe are "rising crime", "moral degeneration", and "economic depression", regardless of gender.

3.1.2. *Humanoid robots as human support robots.* The answers "yes (real robot)" and "yes (on TV or paper)" making up about 90% of the answers to the survey question illustrated in Fig. 7 suggest that the respondents to this questionnaire have a tendency to be interested in humanoid robots. Figure 8 shows that people experienced in programming tend to be well-disposed towards humanoid robots. For this reason, people who understand the mechanism of robot motion do not feel extra fear. Thus, it is required that robots give us notice and warning through eye contact and verbal communication, so that we can anticipate robot motion without fear. Figure 9 shows that many people regard the idea of humanoid robots as human support robots with favor.

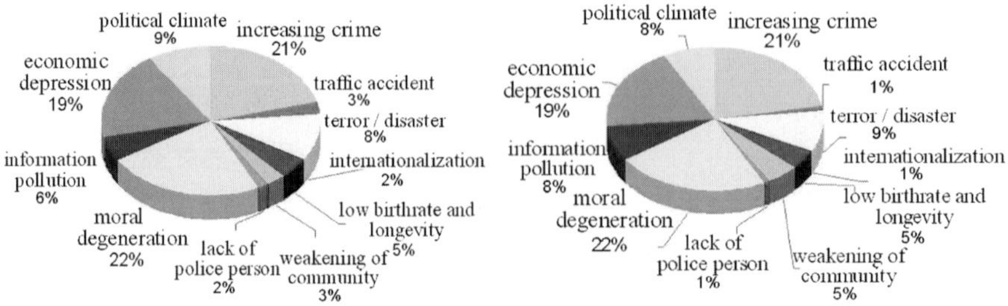

(a) male (b) female

Fig. 6. (Q4) What factor will make society unsafe? (a) Male, (b) female.

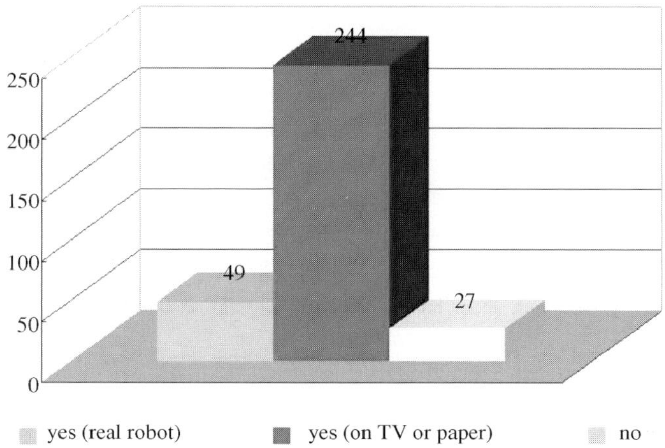

Fig. 7. (Q5) Have you ever seen humanoid robots?

Fig. 10 shows that people want humanoid robots to be shorter than people, and think white is suitable for their body color, assuming that they work around us. This is because white is regarded as a safe color for our environment, and the body color of the Honda ASIMO robot [4,5], the most popular humanoid robot, is white.

3.1.3. *Applications of humanoid robots.* Figure 11 shows that the majority of people want humanoid robots to carry out home services—"home security", "housework", "nursing-care"—and maintenance of security—"patrol", "janitor"—regardless of gender. It is desirable for even one humanoid robot to carry out "home security", "housework" and "nursing-care" tasks unsupervised, so the versatility of humanoid robots is a key point when they are introduced into our daily life.

Figure 12 shows that many people want humanoid robots to be introduced into our daily life as soon as possible.

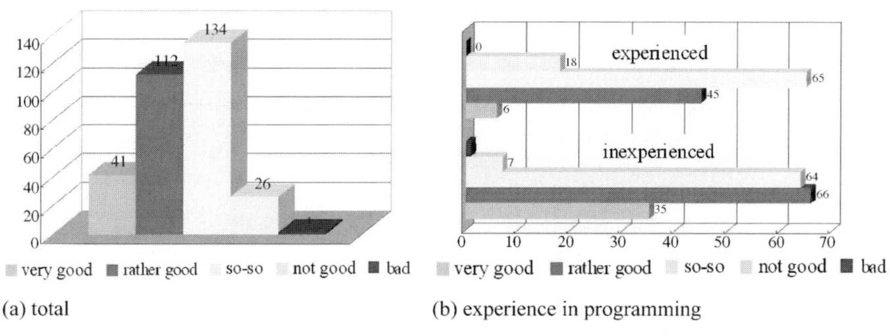

Fig. 8. (Q6) How do you feel about humanoid robots? (a) Total, (b) experience in programming.

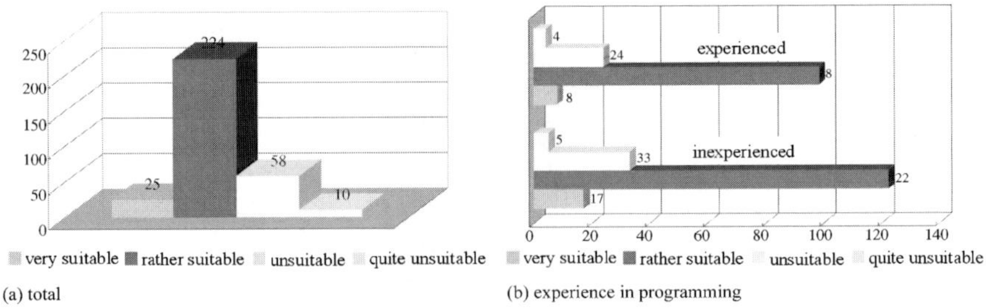

Fig. 9. (Q7) What do you think about humanoid robots working around us? (a) Total, (b) experience in programming.

4. Proposal of a wheelchair user support system

From the results of the questionnaire survey described above, it can be seen that people feel insecure about "old age" and "health", and they want humanoid robots to perform home services such as home security and nursing-care, as well as maintenance of security such as patrol and janitor. Furthermore, it is important for us to include everyone such as elderly people and handicapped persons, when planning for an SSR society. In particular, elderly people and handicapped persons require life support. Taking these points into account, in this section we propose a wheelchair user support system using humanoid robots as a concrete application of humanoid robots.

4.1. *Present condition and challenges facing wheelchair user support*

In proportion to the rapid aging of the population, the number of wheelchair users [6,7] is also increasing. Thus, it is important to create an environment in which they can get around safely, securely and actively in a wheelchair. To that end, we need to improve infrastructures, address the lack of care-givers and make the care service complete.

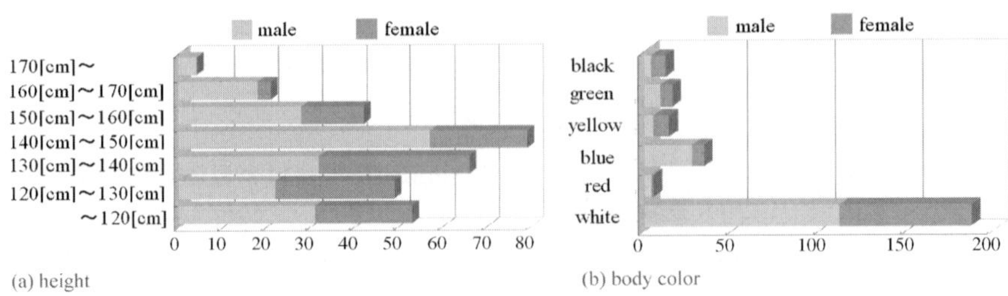

Fig. 10. (Q8) How tall will humanoid robots be or what body color will be suitable, assuming that they work around us? (a) Height, (b) body color.

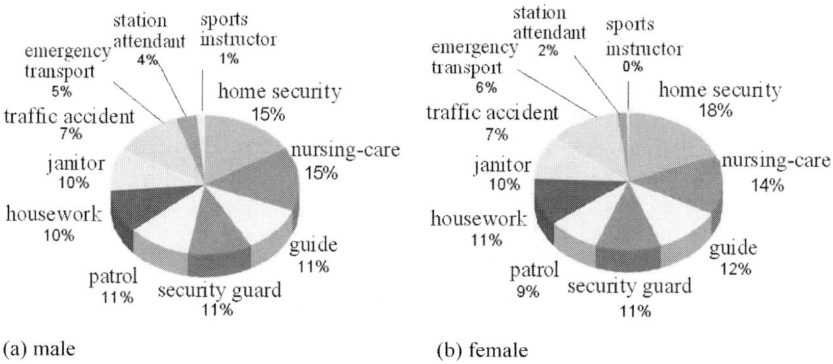

Fig. 11. (Q9) What kind of jobs do you want humanoid robots to do, assuming that they work around us? (a) Male, (b) female.

Wheelchair users need care in the following situations:

- irregular terrain
- step
- ditch
- ramp
- stair

In addition to this locomotion support, they need manipulation support. This is because their arms cannot reach over a wide space. Therefore, in the next section we propose a wheelchair user total support system of locomotion and manipulation using humanoid robots.

4.2. *Proposal system*

An electromotive wheelchair is one of the solutions for the lack of a care-giver. However, it provides only locomotion support and cannot move everywhere. Besides, in response to the diversification of values among people, several alternatives for users

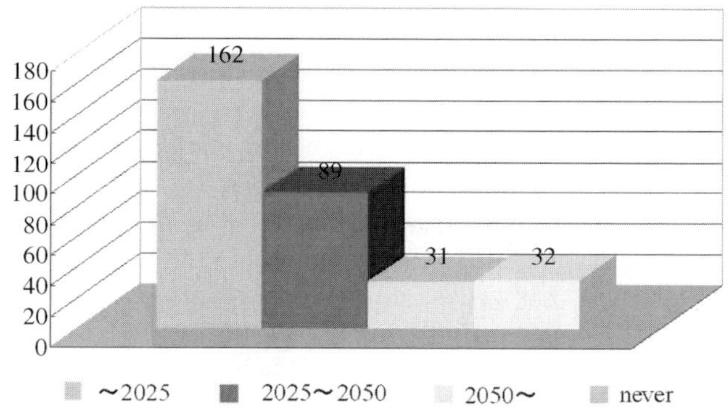

Fig. 12. (Q10) When do you want humanoid robots to be introduced in our daily life?

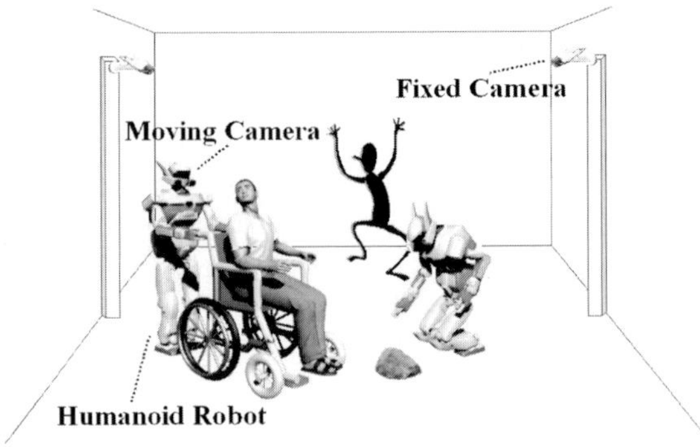

Fig. 13. The concept of a wheelchair user support system using humanoid robots.

are required. Thus, we propose a system in which humanoid robots support people in wheelchairs in cooperation with fixed or moving cameras (Fig. 13). Humanoid robots are a multiple degree of freedom system, so they can provide locomotion and manipulation support using their redundancy (Fig. 14). Also, humanoid robots gather information about a wide area in detail from many fixed or moving cameras, taking account of the environment.

In a human support system for creating an SSR society, it is important for humanoid robots to consider the users and the environment. Therefore, this system covers the following points by using fixed or moving cameras, in addition to the situation discussed in Section 4.1.

- Control of robots' hand vibration caused by robot motion
- Control of wheelchair vibration over irregular terrain or steps
- Avoidance of obstacles in our environment
- Notice and warning of robot motion
- Motion planning in consideration for psychology.

This system provides a suitable service for users with a software upgrade through which they communicate with humanoid robots. In addition, as the care-giver is not a person, they are able to care without feeling any constraints.

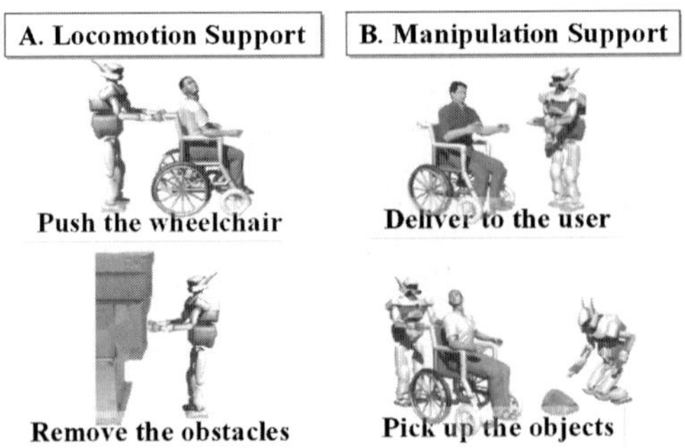

Fig. 14. A wheelchair user support system: integration of locomotion and manipulation.

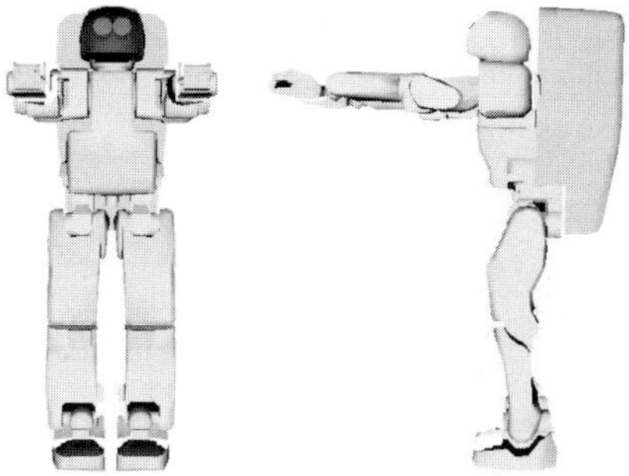

(a) Front view (b) Side view

Fig. 15. Humanoid Robot: HRP-1S (a) front view, (b) side view.

5. Fundamental experiments on a pushing task

5.1. *Problems*

In a wheelchair user support system using humanoid robots, it is a basic task for humanoid robots to push objects safely and reliably. Therefore, we performed computer simulations on pushing objects using the mobile manipulation control method previously proposed.

Figures 15 and 16 show the model of the humanoid robot HRP-1S dealt with in this simulation; this robot is developed by the Humanoid Robotics Project (HRP) [8] which is sponsored by the Ministry of Economy, Trade and Industry of Japan and runs from 1998 to 2002 JFY (Japanese fiscal year). The robot is 1.6 m in height, 130 kg in weight and has 30 DOF.

5.2. *Control method*

The authors have developed a control method for humanoid robots [9–11]; this method will be the basis for generating human support motion. This method autonomously

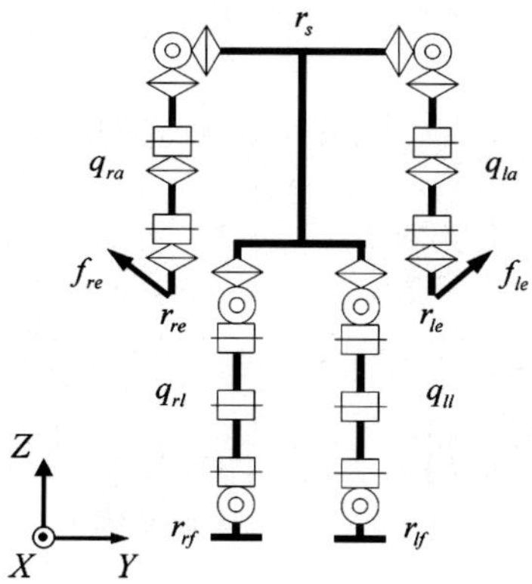

Fig. 16. Mechanism of HRP-1S.

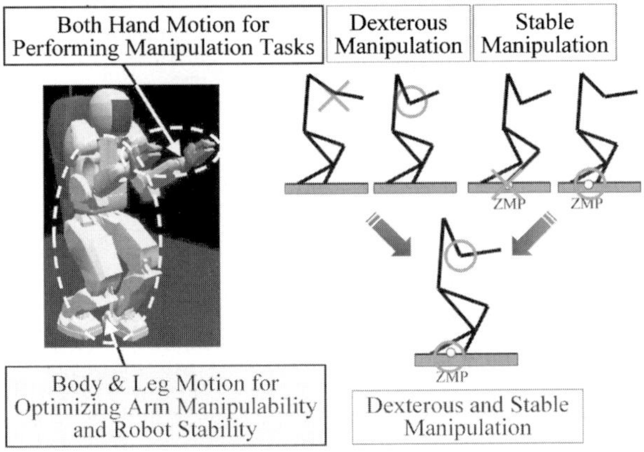

Fig. 17. Mobile manipulation control method.

generates the whole motion of the robot in real time, if only the desired motion of the hands is input; it does not require preset walking patterns. If the hands move in a wide area, the robot steps accordingly.

When the humanoid robots support humans, unexpected external forces or disturbances act on the robots. The proposed method allows the robots to perform tasks with their hands dexterously and stably in such situations (Fig. 17).

5.3. *Simulation results*

We show computer simulation results on pushing objects by the mobile manipulation control method previously proposed. OpenHRP [12–16] which is a dynamic simulator of

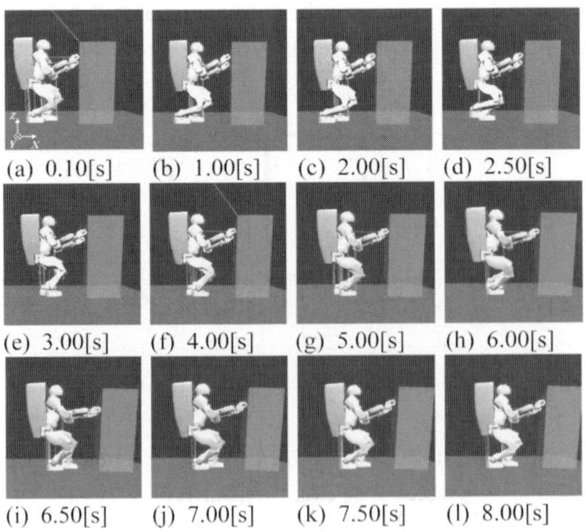

Fig. 18. Simulation results on pushing task (side view).

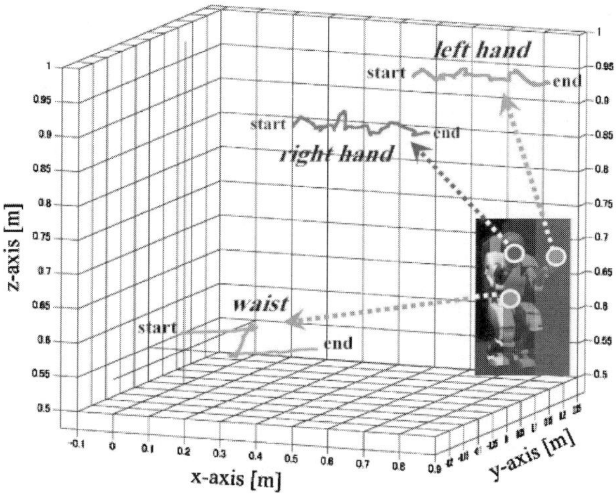

Fig. 19. Hand and waist path (3D view).

humanoid robots is used. Figure 18 shows the results of this simulation, and Fig. 19 shows the hand and waist paths. Although the robot's hand path shakes as shown in Fig. 19, it is ascertained by computer simulations that the mobile manipulation control method can adopt pushing tasks. The impact of a foot landing causes vibration of the whole body of the robot, and feet slip on the ground. This vibration of the whole body of the robot propagates to their hands.

As the next step, because a wheelchair propagates vibration on irregular terrain or steps and the user may suffer damages, it is important to tackle these problems.

6. Conclusion

For creating an SSR society, the concept a human support system using humanoid robots is proposed; humanoid robots which will exist in our environment and help us perform some tasks allowing us an SSR life. This chapter discussed the need for a human support system by analyzing a questionnaire survey of ordinary people on the web. Next, we proposed a wheelchair user support system using humanoid robots as an example of human support using humanoid robots. In this proposed system, humanoid robots provide locomotion and manipulation support for the wheelchair users. Finally, we showed fundamental experiments on pushing objects by the mobile manipulation control method proposed previously. In future, we aim to develop a wheelchair user total support system of locomotion and manipulation, using the real humanoid robot HRP-2 which is the final version of the humanoid robotics platform of HRP [8]. The robot is 1.54 m in height, 58 kg in weight, has 30 DOF including 2 DOF at the waist and contains computers and batteries within its body.

Acknowledgments

This research was supported by the Japan Society for the Promotion of Science under Grant-in-Aid for Creative Scientific Research (Project No. 13GS0018). The authors would like to express sincere thanks to this organization for financial support.

References

[1] K. Inoue, T. Arai, Y. Mae and Y. Nishihama, *Fundamental study on human support system using humanoid robots for creating SSR society*, Proceedings of the SICE Annual Conference (SICE 2002) (2002).

[2] K. Sakata, K. Inoue, Y. Mae and T. Arai, *Human support system using humanoid robots for safe, secure and reliable society: feasibility study on robotics application for safety and security*, Proceedings of the 20th Annual Conference of the Robotics Society of Japan (RSJ 2002) (2002).

[3] N. Tejima, *Survey of the needs about rehabilitation robotics*, JLSTS **4** (3) (1992), 106–115.

[4] M. Hirose, Y. Haikawa, T. Takenaka and K. Hirai, *Development of humanoid robot ASIMO*, Proceedings of the Workshop on Explorations towards Humanoid Robot Applications of IEEE/RSJ International Conference on Intelligent Robots and Systems (2001).

[5] Y. Sakagami, Y. Yoshida, K. Takahashi, N. Sumida, T. Ohashi, T. Yokoyama, M. Takeda and S. Hashimoto, *ASIMO touches on a human activity*, Proceedings of the Third IARP International Workshop on Humanoid and Human Friendly Robotics (2002), 110–115.

[6] H. Kamenetz, *The Wheelchair Book: Mobility for the Disabled*, C.C.Thomas, Springfield, IL (1969).

[7] R.A. Cooper, *Wheelchair Selection and Configuration*, Demos Medical Publishing, New York (1998).

[8] H. Inoue, S. Tachi, K. Tanie, K. Yokoi, S. Hirai, H. Hirukawa, K. Hirai, S. Nakayama, K. Sawada, T. Nishiyama, O. Miki, T. Itoko, H. Inaba and M. Sudo, *HRP:Humanoid robotics project of METI*, Proceedings of the First IEEE-RAS International Conference on Humanoid Robots (2000).

[9] K. Inoue, H. Yoshida, T. Arai and Y. Mae, *Mobile manipulation of humanoids: real-time control based on manipulability and stability*, Proceedings of the IEEE International Conference on Robotics and Automation (ICRA 2000) (2000).

[10] K. Inoue, Y. Nishihama, T. Arai and Y. Mae, *Mobile manipulation of humanoid robots: body and leg control for dual arm manipulation*, Proceedings of the IEEE International Conference on Robotics and Automation (ICRA 2002) (2002).

[11] Y. Nishihama, K. Inoue, T. Arai and Y. Mae, *Mobile manipulation of humanoid robots: control method for accurate manipulation*, Proceedings of the IEEE/RSJ International Conference on Intelligent Robots and Systems (IROS 2003) (2003), 1914–1919.

[12] Y. Nakamura and K. Yamane, *Dynamical computation of structure-varying kinematic chain and its application to human figures*, IEEE Trans. Robotics Automat. **16** (2) (2000), 124–134.

[13] F. Kanehiro, N. Miyata, S. Kajita, K. Fujiwara, H. Hirukawa, Y. Nakamura, K. Yamane, I. Kohara, Y. Kawamura and Y. Sankai, *Virtual humanoid robot platform to develop controllers of real humanoid robots without porting*, Proceedings of the IEEE/RSJ International Conference on Intelligent Robots and Systems (IROS 2001) (2001).

[14] H. Hirukawa, F. Kanehiro and S. Kajita, *OpenHRP: open architecture humanoid robot platform*, Proceedings of the ISPR 2001 (2001).

[15] F. Kanehiro, K. Fujiwara, S. Kajita, K. Yokoi, K. Kaneko and H. Hirukawa, *Open architecture humanoid robot platform*, Proceedings of the IEEE International Conference on Robotics and Automation (ICRA 2002) (2002).

[16] H. Hirukawa, F. Kanehiro, S. Kajita, K. Fujiwara, K. Yokoi, K. Kaneko and K. Harada, *Experimental evaluation of the dynamic simulation of biped walking of humanoid robots*, Proceedings of the IEEE International Conference on Robotics and Automation (ICRA 2003) (2003), 1640–1645.

CHAPTER 28

A Study on Localization of a Mobile Robot Based on ID Tags

Weiguo Lin, Songmin Jia and Kunitatsu Takase

Takase Laboratory Graduate School of Information System, University of Electro-Communications, Chofu, Tokyo 182-8585, Japan

Contents

Abstract

Localization is a feature of fundamental importance for mobile robots. A localization system which is low cost, easily accomplished, simple effective and robust is the continuous aim of researchers. Here, we propose a novel method for localization of a mobile robot using only an ID Tag. We propose this method based on two considerations. Firstly, a mobile robot can move straight and safely on the central line of a passage for at least 2 or 3 m, it is only necessary to adjust its position and orientation at a specified location such as a corner, passage crossing, an intermediate position of a long corridor, or where it meets with other mobile robots. Secondly, the absolute positioning and relative positioning can be separated. If the identification of absolute position can be implemented by RF communication, that will be very simple, effective and robust. Relative positioning can be implemented with other methods. In this chapter, the advantages of our method compared with others are discussed, the scheme of localization is described in detail, the

SYSTEMS AND HUMAN SCIENCE – FOR SAFETY, SECURITY, AND DEPENDABILITY
Edited by Tatsuo Arai, Shigeru Yamamoto and Kazuhisa Makino

localization conditions and results are presented and the factors that influence the accuracy and stability of the system are analyzed in detail. Finally, strategies for improving the system are discussed; two feasible methods have been proposed. We believe that localization using only ID Tags is possible after additional strategies have been adopted.

1. Introduction

In mobile robot navigation, there are four major areas: map building, self-localization, path planning, and obstacle avoidance. Among them, self-localization is of key importance.

There are a large number of systems and methods for indoor mobile robot self-localization, which can be classified from many different points of view. A common classification is relative positioning and absolute positioning.

Odometry is usually used in relative positioning because it is simple, inexpensive and easily accomplished in real-time [1], but it fails to accurately position over long traveling distances because of wheel slippages, mechanical tolerances and surface roughness [2]. Therefore, many mobile robots use odometry accompanied with other measures, such as conventional sensors, additional hardware and exploiting of prior information, to obtain an absolute position [3,4].

Beacon systems have also been widely applied to the localization of mobile robots. In this kind of system, ultrasonic sensors [5] and laser components [6] are two widely used devices. Absolute localization is usually implemented by trilateration (distance measurement) or triangulation (angle measurement). Wireless communication has also been used to achieve high precision [7].

Probabilistic methods (Kalman filtering, topological and grid-based Markov localization, Monte Carlo localization) are the third type of localization widely used to localize mobile robots precisely using noisy sensors [8]. When teams of robots localize themselves in the same environment, probabilistic methods are employed to synchronize each robot's information whenever one robot detects another.

Nowadays, landmark based localization is extensively used. In these systems, two kinds of landmarks are used: natural landmarks (for unknown environments) [9] and artificial landmarks (for known environments) [10]. Map matching is also used to localize robots [11].

Natural landmark recognition and map matching based localization techniques are very ambitious. They are designed to retrieve the position of a robot by relying exclusively on the detection of geometrical or photometrical features (such as "corner" points and lines in the scene [12], or regions of high edge density [13]). However, it is a formidable task to reliably and continuously extract landmarks in complex environments.

In contrast, artificial landmark recognition is a very simple and powerful tool for self-localization in indoor environments. Artificial landmark-based localization, using systems such as barcode [14], Intelligent Data Carrier (IDC) [15] and digital patterns [16] have been proposed.

From the point of view of map description, artificial landmarks would be accepted more easily. Most existing maps represent the environment using occupied cells, or geometric features such as points, lines and regions. If the map is described using nodes, as shown in Fig. 1, only moving orders and the directional relationship between two successive nodes are needed, the distance between two successive nodes and any obstacles on the path need not be considered. In this case the problem is simplified. If one node is detected, the absolute position of a mobile robot is determined, the only work remaining to be done are

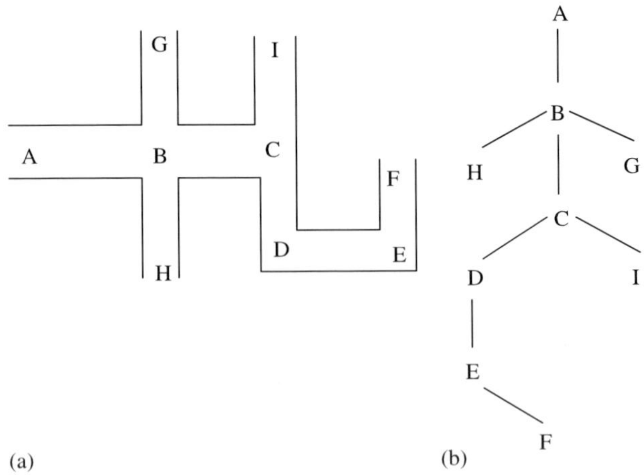

Fig. 1. Path representation with node tree.

determining the position and orientation relative to this node, and detecting the next node easily and correctly.

Moreover, we consider that it is acceptable to make the mobile robot move on the central line of passage, adjusting its position and orientation only at special locations, such as corners, passage crossings, an intermediate position of a long corridor, or where more than two mobile robots meet each other. From this point of view, localization using artificial landmarks is more simple and effective.

In this chapter, we propose to localize a mobile robot using only an ID Tag. We propose this idea based on the consideration that a successful mobile robot localization system should be simple, low cost and easily accomplished, robust and effective.

Some methods have previously been proposed which are somewhat similar to that using ID Tags. One is the digital pattern method proposed by Lee [16]. In this method, three kinds of sensors are used: a rotary encoder, a gyroscope and a CCD camera. The rotary encoder and gyroscope are used for relative positioning using a dead reckoning algorithm; the CCD camera is used for absolute positioning. Whether there is a digital pattern is estimated by the distance moved obtained from the rotary encoder. After it is estimated that there should be a digital pattern, the camera platform is turned using the position information obtained from the gyroscope for the camera to aim at it. After the camera has captured the digital pattern, the zoom is adjusted automatically to enlarge the pattern so that it occupies 80% of the image. Then, measuring the camera yaw angle and reading the binary code on it are used to calculate the position. For system robustness, the background around the digital pattern should be white and the time used for image processing must be at least 2 s.

The second method is proposed by Aoyagi [14]. In his method, barcodes are used as landmarks. The absolute position can be ascertained by reading the barcode with a camera, then the relative position and orientation can be obtained by processing the image of two spaced barcodes. In this system, a lamp is also used for lighting the barcode when it is necessary.

The third method is proposed by Arai [15]. In his method, an intelligent Data Carrier (IDC), a CCD camera and a compass module are used for localization. The absolute position is obtained using RF communication. After an IDC is detected, image processing is used for recognition of the IDC by turning the CCD camera. The orientation of the robot is obtained from the compass module. Using the orientation information and image processing, the relative position can be calculated.

In these methods, Aoyagi [14] and Lee [16] used a CCD camera to detect the absolute position by reading a digital pattern or barcode combined with image processing. This kind of method may be unstable and difficult to use in varying light conditions. In our system, the absolute positioning is implemented by RF communication between an ID Tag and a Tag Reader, which is very easy, effective and robust. Of course, at this point, it is somewhat similar to that proposed by Arai [15], but, in our system, only ID Tags are used for relative positioning. Moreover, the ID Tag is very light, it is powered with a small battery and it can be easily attached on the ceiling without causing damage to the environment. So the rearrangement of the path map is very easy and ID Tags can be used for years. Furthermore, if movable obstacles, such as movable chairs or equipment, are labeled with ID Tags and even every human being has an ID Tag, it will be very easy for a mobile robot to know whether there is an obstacle around or whether it should slow down.

2. Scheme of localization using ID Tags

2.1. *System diagram*

ID Tags are usually used in parking and dormitory management. As every ID Tag has an unique ID, it is a good choice for indicating an absolute position in an environment. Every ID Tag as a node and all the nodes make up a map of the environment.

The system diagram is shown in Fig. 2. The Tag Reader is mounted on the mobile service robot, ID Tags are affixed to the ceiling and every four ID Tags constitute a node.

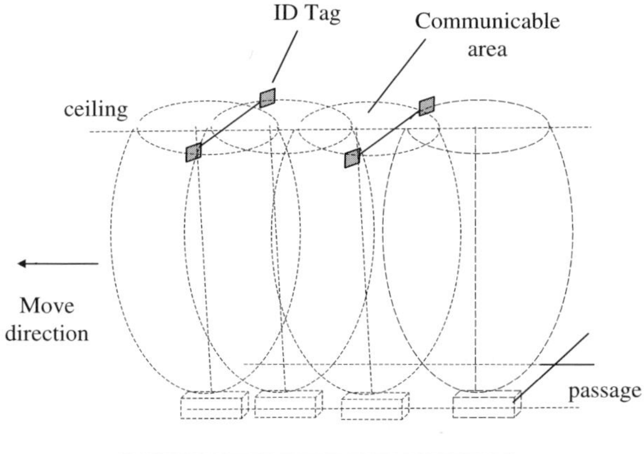

Fig. 2. System diagram.

Here, we use the middle point of four ID Tags to represent the absolute position of a node in the environment. Assume x_N, y_N are the absolute position of a node, x_r and y_r are the positions of a mobile robot relative to the node, x_c, y_c and α are the absolute position and heading angle of the mobile robot. Then the absolute position of the mobile robot can be expressed:

$$x_c = x_N - x_r \tag{1}$$

$$y_c = y_N - y_r \tag{2}$$

So, after a node has been detected and the relative position and orientation have been measured, the absolute position of the mobile robot can be calculated.

2.2. *Absolute positioning with RF communication*

Detection of ID Tags uses microwaves. The microwave Tag Reader is a sphere-like shape, as shown in Fig. 3. As the Tag Reader is mounted on a mobile robot, ID Tags are affixed to the ceiling, so that section is cut near the ceiling. This section is a circular-like plane; we refer to it as the communicable area.

If an ID Tag moves into the communicable area as the mobile robot moves forward, the Tag Reader can detect it. As soon as one ID Tag is detected, the absolute position of the node is obtained. The remaining work is to determine the relative position and orientation. As the detection of ID Tags is implemented using RF communication, it is stable and easier than that using a camera.

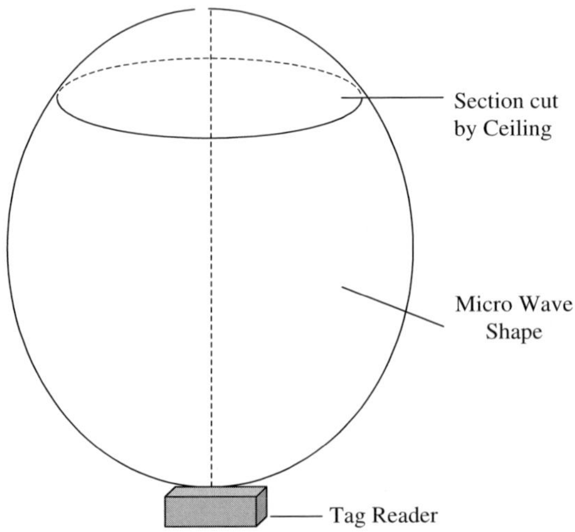

Fig. 3. Shape of the microwave Tag Reader.

2.3. *Relative positioning with four ID Tags*

Relative positioning using only ID Tags is shown in Fig. 4. In this method, we have divided four ID Tags into two lines: the fore line and the hind line. Tags L_1 and R_1 construct the fore line, Tags L_2, R_2 construct the hind line; which is the fore line and which is the hind line are defined according to the direction of motion.

As shown in Fig. 4, there are two coordinate systems, one is the Local Coordinate Frame (Reference Coordinate System), named {R}, where the origin O_r is the center of four ID Tags; the other one is the Objective Coordinate System {B} (service mobile robot coordinate system), where the origin O_b is the reference point of the Tag Reader. When a service mobile robot enters one node with a heading angle α, the Objective Coordinate System regards the motion as though it was rotated through an angle α around the z-axis of the Local Coordinate Frame.

Assume that there is a point P on the edge of the communicable area, its coordinates in the Objective Coordinate System are (x_{pb}, y_{pb}), and (x_{pr}, y_{pr}) are its coordinates in the Local Coordinate Frame. When the mobile robot moves with a heading angle α, the coordinates of P in the Objective Coordinate System can be regarded as though there are not only a rotation around the z-axis, but also translations along both the x-axis and the y-axis of the Local Coordinate Frame

$$\begin{pmatrix} x_{pr} \\ y_{pr} \end{pmatrix} = \begin{pmatrix} \cos\alpha & -\sin\alpha \\ \sin\alpha & \cos\alpha \end{pmatrix} \begin{pmatrix} x_{pb} \\ y_{pb} \end{pmatrix} + \begin{pmatrix} x_r \\ y_r \end{pmatrix} \tag{3}$$

x_r and y_r are the translations of the Origin of the Objective Coordinate System relative to the Local Coordinate Frame.

When one ID Tag is detected, we can show that x_{pr} and y_{pr} are in fact the coordinates of that ID Tag in the Local Coordinate System of the node it belongs to, which are

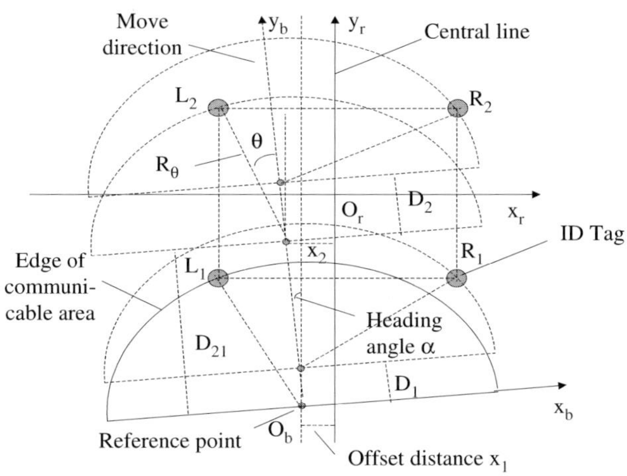

Fig. 4. Separation of distance moved with offset position and heading angle.

fixed and known. x_r and y_r are the coordinates of the reference point in the Local Coordinate Frame, While x_r is also the offset distance of the mobile robot.

From (3), we find that if we want to calculate x_r and y_r, we must first determine α, x_{pb} and y_{pb}. However, it is impossible to determine x_{pb} and y_{pb} first using unidirectional microwaves. Conversely, if we can obtain the values of α and x_r first, we can express x_{pb} with y_{pb} as $x_{pb} = f(y_{pb})$ according to (3). Furthermore, if the communicable area of microwave $R(\theta)$ can be obtained, then x_{pb} can be expressed with y_{pb} as $x_{pb} = tg(\theta)y_{pb}$. Finally the angle θ of point P in the Objective Coordinate System $\{B\}$ can be calculated. From Fig. 4 we can expand such a relationship further:

$$y_r = y_{pr} - R(\theta)\cos(\theta + \alpha) \tag{4}$$

If θ, α and the coordinate y_{pr} are known, we can calculate y_r. So the necessary conditions for calculating x_r and y_r are these:

(1) A model of the communicable area of the Tag Reader $R(\theta)$ is available.

(2) Heading angle α and offset position x_r must be obtained first.

In ideal conditions, if a mobile robot moves on the central line of a passage, two ID Tags in the same line (for example, Tag L_1 and Tag R_1) will be detected at the same time, so the distance moved (denoted with D) from the time that Tag L_1 is detected for the first time to that at which Tag R_1 is detected for the first time is zero. But in practical applications, the mobile robot does not always move on the central line, it may offset the central line, and/or have an heading angle, such that the value of D cannot be zero. There are two special cases when the motion of a mobile robot is perfectly straight: one is that there is only offset distance, no heading angle when one ID Tag in the fore line is the earliest detected for the first time (Fig. 5). The distance moved in this case is denoted with D_x. The other case is that there is no offset distance (Tag Reader is on the central line), but a heading angle when one ID Tag in the fore line is the earliest detected for the first time (Fig. 6); the distance moved in this case is denoted with D_α.

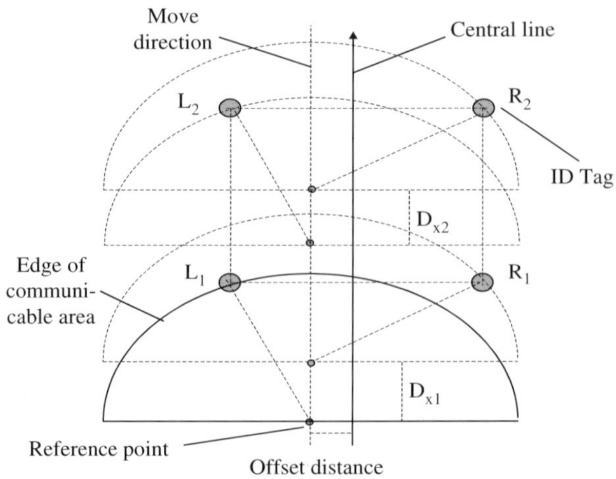

Fig. 5. Mobile robot moves with only offset distance.

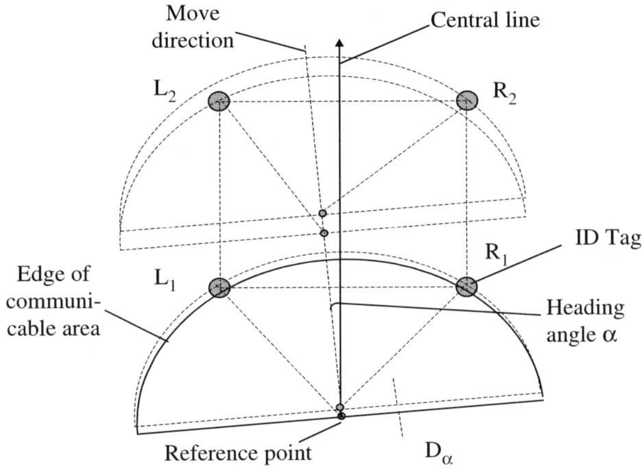

Fig. 6. Mobile robot moves with heading angle.

Assume that the move distance D_x varies with the offset distance x singularly (denoted with $D_x = f(x)$), and the move distance D_α varies with heading angle α singularly as well (denoted with $D_\alpha = g(\alpha)$). Furthermore, it is assumed that the distance moved D has a relationship with the elements D_x and D_α, i.e.:

$$D_1 = a_1 + a_2 D_{x_1} + a_3 D_{\alpha_1} \tag{5}$$

$$D_2 = b_1 + b_2 D_{x_2} + b_3 D_{\alpha_2} \tag{6}$$

Here,

D_1, D_2 : the total distance moved of the fore line (D_1) and the hind line (D_2);

D_{x_1}, D_{x_2} : the distance moved of the fore line and the hind line caused only by offset distance;

$D_{\alpha_1}, D_{\alpha_2}$: the distance moved of the fore line and the hind line caused only by heading angle;

a_1, a_2, a_3 and b_1, b_2, b_3 : the fitting coefficients of the fore line and the hind line.

Assuming that the service mobile robot moves straight, then (5) and (6) have the same heading angle α. As the structure of a node is a square, so both the elements caused by the heading angle in the fore line and the hind line should be the same because they are made up of the same angle and the same model $D_\alpha = g(\alpha)$. That is $D_{\alpha_1} = D_{\alpha_2}$. Then, D_{x_2} can be expressed by D_{x_1}. According to Fig. 4, it can be shown that there is such a relationship between x_1, x_2, D_{21} and heading angle α:

$$D_{21} \sin(\alpha) = x_1 - x_2 \tag{7}$$

D_{21} is the distance moved from the position where one ID Tag in the fore line is detected earliest for the first time to the position where one ID Tag in the hind line is detected earliest for the first time.

With (5)–(7), and the models $R(\theta)$, $D_\alpha = g(\alpha)$ and $D_x = f(x)$, it is possible to calculate the offset distance x_1, x_2, and the heading angle α.

3. Modeling, localization and discussion

In our system, the length of a squared node is 60 cm; the distance between the cart mobile robot and the ceiling is 2.0 m, so it is appropriate to use the ID Tags and Tag Reader produced by Kenwood Company. These are the S1500 Tag Reader and S1251/00 ID Tags; their greatest communicable distance is 4.5 m; the speed of the mobile robot is 20 cm/s; and the timeout of the Tag Reader is 167 ms, which means that every 167 ms, any ID Tag in the communicable area is only read once.

3.1. *Modeling*

The model developing the communicable area only uses one ID Tag. The ID Tag is affixed to the ceiling right over the central line. Making the mobile robot move on the central line, and making the Tag Reader a desired angle θ with the central line, the mobile robot stops when the ID Tag is detected. The distance between the ID Tag and the Tag Reader in a horizontal direction is R_θ. When the experiment is repeated with a different angle θ, part of the communicable area $R(\theta)$ is obtained (we only used the front part of the communicable area for detection).

Developing models D_x and D_α uses two ID Tags in the fore line. Making the mobile robot move along the central line with different offset distances and a zero heading angle, a set of move distances D_x is obtained, that is the model $D_x = f(x)$. Making the Tag Reader a desired angle θ with the central line and making the mobile robot move on the central line, the position where one ID Tag in the fore line is the earliest detected for the first time is obtained. After that, making the mobile robot move on a line which passes through that position with a heading angle α equal to θ and making the angle θ zero, a move distance at a specified heading angle α is obtained. By repeating this experiment with different angles of θ, a set of positions are obtained. Finally, a set of move distances D_α are obtained, that is the model $D_\alpha = g(\alpha)$. These are shown in Figs. 7 and 8.

3.2. *Calibration and localization*

Before localization, the coefficients a_i and b_i in (5) and (6) should be calibrated. From these two equations, it can be seen that sets of D_1, D_2, α, x_1 and x_2 are needed for calibration of the coefficients. Assuming that the mobile robot moves straight, then D_1 and D_2 can be found from the encoder and the heading angle α can be measured before moving. As the mobile robot stops when the last ID Tag in the node has been detected, so the offset distance at that position can be measured. With the information α and move distances D_2 and D_{21}, the offset distances x_1 and x_2 can be calculated. By using multiple regression in MatLab with sets of D_1, D_2, α, x_1, x_2 and models $D_x = f(x)$, $D_\alpha = g(\alpha)$, we have calculated the coefficients as follows:

Fore line a_1, a_2, a_3: -4.4267, 0.9009, 0.3640;

Hind line b_1, b_2, b_3: 17.6319, 1.7317, 1.1235.

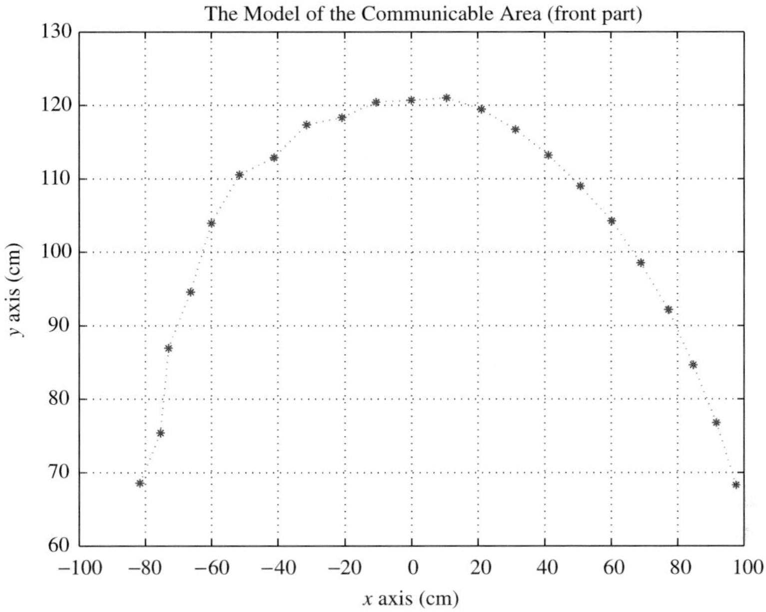

Fig. 7. The model of the communicable area.

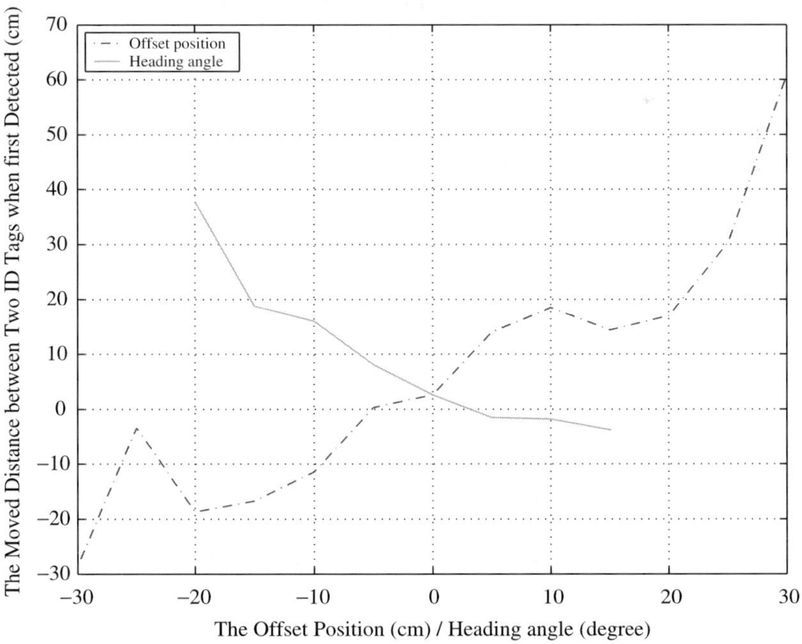

Fig. 8. The models of the offset position and heading angle.

Table 1. Experimental results of relative positioning

Index no.	*X* coord. (cm)			*Y* coord. (cm)			Angle (deg.)		
	Meas.	True	Error	Meas.	True	Error	Meas.	True	Error
1	18.8	14.0	4.8	−19.8	−22.0	2.3	−11.2	−5.3	−5.8
2	14.8	5.5	9.3	−37.7	−40.0	2.3	−19.5	−11.2	−8.3
3	1.5	−5.7	7.2	−58.1	−46.0	−12.1	−1.2	2.8	−4.0
4	6.8	18.5	−11.7	−24.1	−9.2	−14.9	1.1	3.0	−1.9
5	−22.5	−22.3	−0.2	−47.2	−57.5	12.3	0.0	5.5	−5.5
6	15.7	24.0	−8.3	−14.2	−24.0	9.8	−6.8	−5.1	−5.1

Using these coefficients for localization, some of the results obtained are listed in Table 1. These are the x coordinate and y coordinate of the reference point and the heading angle needed for adjusting the position and attitude of the service mobile robot. From these data we can see that sometimes the data are accurate, but sometimes errors are large and the method is unreliable.

3.3. *Discussion*

To explain why the localization is unreliable, we propose three main reasons. Firstly, we have used three models: the offset distance model, the heading angle model and the communicable area model. They are all developed experimentally, so three error sources are all introduced into the calculation. Secondly, the data flow between the ID Tag and the mobile robot controller limits the stability and accuracy of the system. Figure 9 shows the data flow. Data collection uses serial communication between the controller and the Tag Reader, and RF communications between the Tag Reader and the ID Tags. There is a time delay from calling for data to data arrival. The time delay will result in position errors, especially when the controller calls for data but the Tag Reader is busy reading microwave

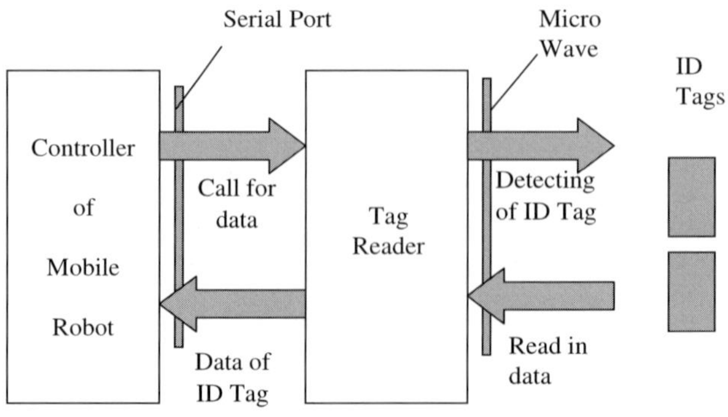

Fig. 9. Diagram showing data collection by the controller from ID Tags.

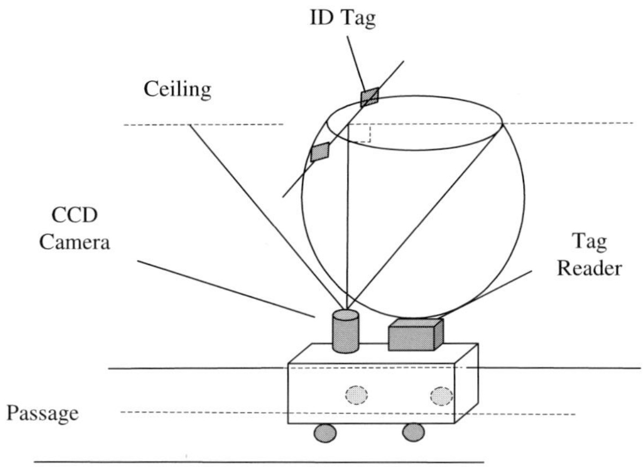

Fig. 10. Localization using an ID Tag and a camera.

data for the last call. Finally, from Fig. 8 we can see that the offset distance model is not ideally singular and that may result in multisolution. All these reasons result in large errors and instability.

For more precise localization and system stability, additional strategies should be adopted. Firstly, it is better to reduce the number of ID Tags in every node. Secondly, for the purpose of reducing the error sources, it is useful to reduce the number of models. Thirdly, the data collection of the system should be modified. If the Tag Reader reads ID Tags periodically and sends data to the controller autonomously, then the influence of any time delay will be greatly reduced.

Among these reasons, the time delay in data collection is considered the most important error source in the system, but it may be difficult to solve. There are two alternative methods for improving the system: one is using two ID Tags in every node; the other one is using an ID Tag and a camera (Fig. 10). We believe that either method will greatly improve the system.

4. Conclusions

In this chapter, a new method for localization of mobile robots in an indoor environment using only ID Tags has been proposed. This method determines the absolute position and measures relative position and orientation with only RF communication between the ID Tag and the Tag reader. Therefore it is simple, cheap, easily accomplished and robust. Although the experiment results are not sufficiently exciting, analysis shows that this method can be improved and be effectively applied in an environment with wide passages, such as a factory or warehouse. Furthermore, using ID Tags, a mobile robot will be able to avoid obstacles easily.

References

[1] B. Barshan and H.F. Durrant-Whyte, *Inertial sensing for mobile robotics*, IEEE Trans. Robotics and Automation **3** (1995), 328.

[2] J. Borenstein and L. Feng, *Measurement and correction of systematic odometry errors in mobile robots*, IEEE J. Robotics and Automation **6** (1996), 869.

[3] L. Kleeman, *Optimal estimation of position and heading for mobile robots using ultrasonic beacons and dead reckoning*, Proceedings of IEEE International Conference on Robotics and Automation, (1992), 2582–2587.

[4] J. Borenstein and L. Feng, *Gyrodometry: a new method for combining data from gyros and odometry in mobile robots*, Proceedings of IEEE International Conference on Robotics and Automation, (1996), 423–428.

[5] H. Lin, C. Tsai, J. Hsu and C. Chang, *Ultrasonic self-localization and pose tracking of an autonomous mobile robot via fuzzy adaptive extended information filtering*, Proceedings of IEEE International Conference on Robotics and Automation, (2003), 1283–1290.

[6] S. Hernandez, C.A. Morales, J.M. Torres and L. Acosta, *A new localization system for autonomous robots*, Proceedings of IEEE International Conference on Robotics and Automation, (2003), 1588–1593.

[7] S. Aoyagi, H. Noto, H. Kishimoto and M. Takano, *Development of a position and orientation localization system for an indoor mobile robot using non-directional ultrasonic sensors and radiofrequency wireless communication*, J. Prec. Eng. **8** (2000), 1241.

[8] S.I. Roumeliotis and G.A. Bekey, *Bayesian estimation and Kalman filtering: a unified framework for mobile robot localization*, Proceedings of IEEE International Conference on Robotics and Automation, (2000), 2985–2992.

[9] C.B. Madsen and C.S. Andersen, *Optimal landmark selection for triangulation of robot position*, Int. J. Robotics and Autonomous Syst. **4** (1998), 277.

[10] H.F. Durrant-Whyte, *An autonomous guided vehicle for cargo handling applications*, Int. J. Robotics Res. **5** (1996), 407.

[11] S. Thrun and A. Bucken, *Integrating grid-based and topological maps for mobile robot navigation*, Proceedings of the 13th National Conference on AI, (1996), 128–133.

[12] G. Hager, D. Kriegman, E. Yeh and C. Rasmussen, *Image-based prediction of landmark features for mobile robot navigation*, Proceedings of IEEE International Conference on Robotics and Automation, (1997), 1040–1046.

[13] R. Sim and G. Dudek, *Mobile robot localization from learned landmarks*, Proceedings of IEEE/RSJ International Conference on Intelligent Robots and Systems, (1998), 1060–1065.

[14] S. Aoyagi, Y. Kiguchi, K. Tsunemine and M. Takano, *Position and orientation measurement of a mobile robot*, Trans. IEE Jpn **2** (2001), 375.

[15] Y. Arai, T. Fuji, H. Asama, T. Fujita, H. Kaetsu and I. Endo, *Self-localization of autonomous mobile robots using information buried in environment*, J. Jpn. Mech. **619** (1998), 207.

[16] J. Lee, Y. Ogawa, C. Kasuga, A. Takagi, S. Mori and H. Hashimoto, *Study on hierarchical localization system for mobile robot*, The 16th Conference on Japanese Robotics Society, (1998), 789–790.

PART VII

Safety Recovery Systems

CHAPTER 29

Nuclear Safety Ontology—Basis for Sharing Relevant Knowledge among Society

K. Furuta

Institute of Environmental Studies, The University of Tokyo, 7-3-1, Hongo Bunkyo-ku, Tokyo 113-0033, Japan

T. Ogure

Research Institute of Science and Technology for Society, 2-5-1, Atago, Minato-ku, Tokyo 105-6218, Japan

H. Ujita

Institute of Applied Energy, 1-14-2, Nishishinbashi, Minato-ku, Tokyo 105-0003, Japan

Contents

SYSTEMS AND HUMAN SCIENCE – FOR SAFETY, SECURITY, AND DEPENDABILITY
Edited by Tatsuo Arai, Shigeru Yamamoto and Kazuhisa Makino

Abstract

Ontology is a basis for communication and knowledge sharing among society, which are prerequisites for successful risk deliberation. Having reviewed conventional subject classifications of safety studies, requirements for appropriate ontology in socio-technological contexts were discussed, and then nuclear safety ontology was constructed in accordance with general safety principles using an ontology authoring tool, OntStar.

1. Introduction

Nuclear safety is an area where long and hard arguments have continued in society. Smooth communication between specialists and the public was sometimes hampered, because relevant physical processes are hardly understandable from everyday senses, and because nuclear engineering is a highly specialized and complex domain. The public is usually irritated by technological arguments and becomes skeptical about specialists.

Along with the maturity of democratic society, a technocratic model of risk communication, where specialists teach the ignorant public and the latter accepts the decision, does not work anymore, not only in nuclear safety but also in every domain. Instead, a new model of risk communication is being accepted, where every interested party attends the decision process, and both risk analysis and risk deliberation are repeated reciprocally [1]. Risk deliberation is a process where participants exchange opinions and understand the interests of each other through communication to develop consensus.

The basis of risk deliberation is to share the common terms, notions, and knowledge among participants. Otherwise, smooth communication is unexpected and risk deliberation will fail. Specialists, therefore, are obliged to provide a structured specification of basic notions in a technological domain as a social infrastructure, through which the public can freely access any domain-specific knowledge it needs. Such a specification includes maps and definitions of technical terms, issues, subjects, topics, or academic areas, which can guide non-specialists to access relevant knowledge and to communicate with specialists.

The aim of this work is to provide a structured specification of notions in nuclear safety that is useful for risk deliberation on the issue. We can already find many classification schemes of issues and subjects on nuclear safety or on safety in general, but these schemes are inappropriate in that they are constructed from specialists' needs. Some specification of notions is desired, therefore, that is understandable to the public. Such a structured specification of notions is called ontology following the literature of knowledge engineering.

2. What is ontology?

The term "ontology" is used with different meanings in different contexts. It is originally a term in philosophy that stands for the idea that "every being in the world exists independent of human cognizance". Following philosophers, researchers of knowledge engineering or Artificial Intelligence (AI) have adopted the term to discuss methodologies for construction, reuse, or trans-utilization of a knowledge base. Gruber [2] defined ontology as a specification of a conceptualization, which is like a description of notions and relations to be shared among agents or an agent community. Mizoguchi [3] argued that ontology in engineering contexts deals not only with general being in philosophy, but also with tangible entities including artifacts and that ontology stands for explicit specification of notions and relations in a specific domain. He also raised terminology, vocabulary, and taxonomy as notions similar to ontology.

While AI researchers and knowledge engineers discussing ontology are interested in the ability to use knowledge for mechanized reasoning, ontology in socio-technological contexts is a structured specification of notions that can be the basis for communication or knowledge sharing in society. This ontology is an extension of the ontology in engineering contexts, but it focuses more on social acceptability rather than formality. The ontology in this work follows the socio-technological notion of ontology and it has the following features.

(1) It is a structure composed of notions mutually linked by relations among them.
(2) It is widely accepted by a particular community.
(3) It is to cover all notions relevant to the domain of interest in an appropriate granularity.
(4) It is related to a particular domain.

In the above, the first and the second features are common to the ontology in engineering contexts.

3. Ontology authoring tool

Since construction of ontology is a labor-intensive task, several supporting tools have been developed. Mizoguchi et al. developed an ontology utilization environment, Hozo, that consists of three modules of an ontology editor, ontology construction support system, and ontology server. Each concept in Hozo is to be defined by label, super-concept, axiom, definition, and slots [4]. The axiom is to describe declarative features and constraints that the concept obeys in a particular domain. OntoEdit is an ontology editor developed by Staab et al. [5]. OntoEdit provides an intuitive graphical user interface to deal only with ontology that can be described as formal axioms. Noy et al. [6] developed another ontology editor, Protégé-2000, to be used for construction of ontology for Semantic Web. Semantic Web is an idea to make web documents readable to automatic processing systems by adding concept identification tags to web documents. As explained above, previous works were interested in the construction of ontology that can be processed by AI applications, but ontology editors to specify ontology as formal axioms are not required for the present purpose.

An ontology editor for socio-technological contexts must be usable to non-specialists who have little knowledge on ontology. Description of ontology must not be much restricted so that intuitive and simple taxonomy is acceptable. Description is to be restricted to some extent, however, because restriction provides guidance to non-specialists to construct structured ontology easily. To what extent the tool restricts description of the user is a delicate trade-off in designing a tool of this kind.

An ontology authoring tool called OntStar was developed for conventional Windows PCs. In OntStar, ontology is defined as a network of concepts linked by various relations. The primary relation is hierarchical super-sub relation of concepts. The user is allowed to define other relations between concepts. Each concept is to be defined by the following slots.

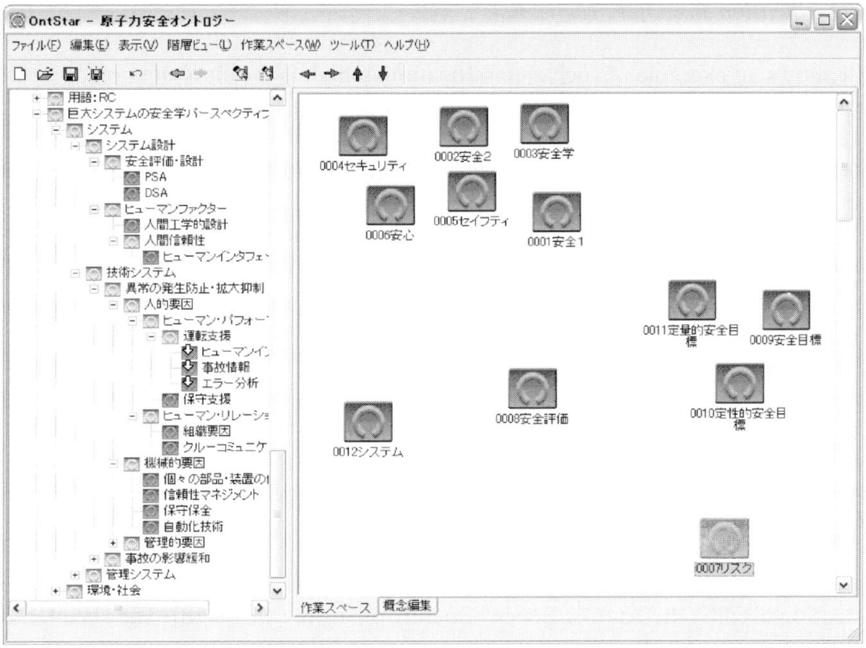

Fig. 1. Screen shot image of OntStar.

Title	A simple label for identification.
Description	Definition of the concept in natural language.
Comment	Auxiliary comment or detailed explanation.
Linguistic labels	Technical terms used to represent the concept.

An example interface of OntStar is shown in Fig. 1. It is very similar to the outlook of Windows Explorer; concepts are represented as icons in the right pane, the concept hierarchy as a tree in the left pane, and the interface provides direct manipulation functions with a pointing device. OntStar can also be used as an idea processor.

4. Conventional subject classifications in safety studies

Before discussing what nuclear safety ontology is appropriate in socio-technological contexts, conventional subject classifications in safety studies are to be reviewed for the basis of discussion. Although explicit considerations might not have been made, there are many classifications or taxonomies of subjects currently used in safety studies, which reflect how specialists view safety issues. Some of such classifications appear as subject lists in instructions for academic journals or call-for-papers of conferences, and others as tables of contents in books.

4.1. *Classification for safety regulation*

Table 1 shows an example of such a classification, which is the classification of researches on nuclear safety which appeared in a working paper presented at the Subcommittee on Safety Researches, the Nuclear Safety Commission (NSC) of Japan [7]. This classification reflects a typical view of specialists on nuclear safety. The top level is made up of six items. Two of them correspond to classes of hazards, environmental radiation and radioactive wastes; another two are classes of facilities, fission and fusion, one activity, disaster prevention, and one academic area, health physics. At a glance, no systematic idea can be found. Just "Safety of nuclear facility" contains many sub-items: facilities and activities. It seems this classification is primarily based on the classification of nuclear facilities, and then some subjects relating to all facilities in common are added. Since NSC is an organization to discuss regulatory issues and regulation is basically effected by the class of facility, it is natural that the classification is based on the class of facility.

4.2. *Classification in academy*

Such a viewpoint is not necessarily unique in safety regulation. Table 2 shows the subject classification used by the Atomic Energy Society of Japan (AESJ) [8]. The skeleton of this classification is also based on the classification of facilities, i.e., fission reactors, fuel cycle facilities, and fusion devices. Subcategories include components or objects composing

Table 1. Classification of safety researches in NSC [7]

Safety management of environmental radiation
Safety of nuclear facility (fission)
Framework of safety regulation
Nuclear reactor facility
Light water reactor
Fast reactor
Advanced reactor
Safety of nuclear fuel
Nuclear fuel cycle
Reprocessing plant
Fabrication facility of uranium fuel
Fabrication facility of mixed oxide fuel
Transportation
Advanced recycle system
Upgrade of safety level
Operation
Radiation control
Analysis and remedy of unfavorable events
Decommissioning
Disposal of radioactive wastes
Disaster prevention
Health physics
Safety of fusion reactors

Table 2. Subject classification in AESJ [8]

General issues	Nuclear fuel cycle and nuclear materials
Philosophical and ethical aspects	Basic properties
Justice and political aspects, international relations	Nuclear fuels
...	Reactor materials
	Irradiation behaviors, irradiation technology
Radiation, accelerator and beam technologies	...
Nuclear physics, nuclear data	Fusion energy engineering
Radiation behaviors, radiation shielding	Plasma technology
Radiation physics, detection and measurement	...
...	Health physics and environmental science
Fission energy engineering	Medical and biological application
Reactor physics, nuclear data, criticality safety	Radiation and radioactivity measurement
Advanced reactor, nuclear design, transmutation	...
Research reactor, application of neutron	
Nuclear fuel cycles, nuclear energy strategy	
Reactor instrumentation, reactor control	
...	

these facilities such as reactor instrumentation, nuclear fuels, and reactor materials. It is, however, characteristic that much more subjects are directly related to academic disciplines or physical processes such as philosophy, nuclear physics, health physics, and radiation behaviors, than the classification of NSC, because AESJ is an academic society. Other subjects correspond to activities, e.g., reactor design, operational management, and decommissioning. Anyway, subjects are also a combination of academic areas, classes of facilities, components, objects, and activities. Although this subject classification is not just for safety researches but also for nuclear science and engineering as a whole, it suggests a similar taste of specialists.

4.3. *Classification in general safety studies*

Now let us have a look at the preference of specialists in general safety or risk studies. Table 3 lists the chapters in a handbook of risk research [9]. The handbook has eight chapters and the first chapter is an introductory one. Chapters 2–5 are related to classes of latent or elicited hazards. Terminology is not well defined; hazard, risk, and damage are

Table 3. Chapters in a handbook of risk research [9]

(1) Academic disciplines and practices in risk research
(2) Countermeasure to health hazard and environmental risk
(3) Countermeasure to natural and urban disaster
(4) Coping with technological risks and civilization
(5) Socioeconomic risk in a society
(6) Science and method of risk assessment
(7) Risk perception and communication
(8) Risk management and risk policy

used but the distinction is not clear between potential, consequence, and expectancy of harm. Chapters 6–8 are dedicated to various levels of activities for risk governance: Chapter 6 deals with technological aspects, Chapter 7 with social aspects, and Chapter 9 with managerial aspects. Although this classification reflects a framework clearer and more general than the previous two examples, it also seems academic discipline is dominating as suggested by the title of Chapter 1. The chapters are organized in such a way that each chapter corresponds to a community of specialists, and it will be the result of writing and editing requirements in a publication of this kind.

4.4. *Drawbacks of existing classification*

The classifications presented so far will be suitable for specialists on nuclear safety or general safety studies, because they reflect the recognition accepted in specialists' communities. It is, however, doubtful that they are also accepted by lay people who are unfamiliar with academic disciplines. The primary reasons are twofold.

Firstly, a classification too specific to a particular domain is not applicable to different domains. The classification of NSC and that of AESJ contain many items related to facilities, components, and activities specific to nuclear industry. Most of these items are not applicable to other domains. If this manner is also followed by other domains, ontology of different domains will be made up of different concepts. Such discrepancy will give the public misleading recognition that principles of safety should be different in different domains, and it will result in the imbalanced perception of risks and then unfair risk trade-off between different domains. Domain-specific concepts, of course, must appear at lower levels of abstraction in ontology, but the argument here is on the top levels of ontology. Safety ontology of any specific domain should be based on the common basic principles, so that unfair risk trade-off will be prevented. Nuclear safety ontology must, therefore, be an extension of general safety ontology.

Secondly, disciplines or domains of academic researchers are not only incomprehensible to the public but also of little importance in socio-technological contexts. What the public is most interested in is by what principles safety of something is achieved. Ontology must show such basic principles that are understandable to the ordinary people by their common sense. This requirement is different from those requested by domain specialists. Of course it does not mean that domain specialists have to abandon their own ontology, but ontology in socio-technological contexts and that in academic contexts can coexist in parallel. What we need nowadays for effective risk communication is ontology in socio-technological contexts.

5. Nuclear safety ontology

We tried to build up nuclear safety ontology considering the requirements discussed above. The ontology to be created is not only an instantiation of general safety ontology, but also it represents a conceptual view of how the safety of nuclear power can be achieved.

The ontology authoring tool OntStar, which was presented in Chapter 3 was used for the job. We had several sessions for brain storming and discussion with specialists on nuclear safety, general safety studies, human factors, disaster prevention, and risk communication.

5.1. *Basic concepts*

In this section, basic concepts in safety will be presented on which the ontology is based. Fig. 2 illustrates basic concepts and their relations in safety. Each concept is explained below.

Hazard is an act, substance, or phenomenon that has the potential to produce harm or other undesirable consequences to humans or what they value [1]. It is the source of any harm and is sometimes called latent danger or latent risk. It includes various kinds of natural phenomena, poisonous chemicals, organisms, artifacts, and human behavior.

Harm is undesired consequences caused by hazard. They take various forms of damage or loss of what humans value: death, injury, illness, loss of money, contamination of land, air, or water, extinction of species, loss of traditional culture, breakdown of community, and so on.

Existence of hazard does not always result in damage or loss, but some *realization process* must occur for damage or loss to actually arise. The process consists usually of a sequence of many events starting from the initiating event. Damage or loss occurs if what humans value is exposed to hazard as a consequence of realization process.

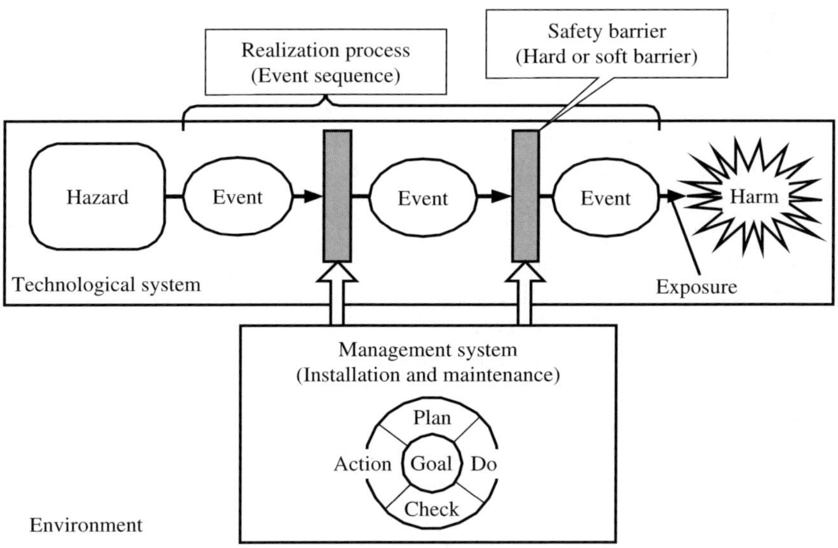

Fig. 2. Basic concepts in safety.

Risk is a concept used to give meaning to things, forces, or circumstances that pose danger to people or they value [1]. Risk is described quantitatively in terms of likelihood that harm will occur and magnitude of harm, but it is also a societal construct that is affected by various factors.

A *safety barrier* is an act, substance, or phenomenon that intervenes the realization process and prevents harm from occurring. Safety barriers can be classified into hard (physical or functional) barriers or soft (symbolic or conceptual) barriers. Hard barriers are further classified into natural or man-made barriers.

Installation and maintenance of safety barriers are the central issues of safety assurance, and the barriers have to be installed and maintained in a Plan–Do–Check–Action cycle. In order to organize these activities, we believe a human–machine systems view is essential. A human–machine systems view considers the target system as a complex combination of hardware (artifacts) and humanware (management) working within the environment. While hardware usually intervenes the realization process directly and promptly in safety assurance, installation and maintenance are done by humans. Both hardware and humanware are, therefore, essential concepts to be considered in safety assurance.

The environment surrounding the system is also an essential concept, because it affects the functioning of safety barriers built in the system. The boundary between the system and the environment is sometimes contingent, but it is usually easy to distinguish the part that is directly involved in and responsible for safety assurance from the rest. In the nuclear power industry, for instance, it is natural to consider the body of business and what are placed within the facility site should be included in the system, and the others outside the facility site should be included in the environment.

5.2. *Nuclear safety ontology*

An overview of the created nuclear safety ontology is shown in Table 4. This table lists just the items down to the third level of hierarchy. Although the items are described here in a hierarchical tree, some items have more than one super-concepts like "Safety barrier" in the table and the ontology is actually a network.

The basic concepts in safety are grouped under a node entitled "Basic concepts". The other two top-level concepts are "System" and "Environment" following the human–machine systems view. Below the "System" node "Technological system" and "Management system" exist, which respectively correspond to hardware and humanware. "System design" was added to deal with concepts relating to both technological system and management system, i.e., the system as a whole.

While the third level items shown here are not necessarily complete, the second level items are almost complete. At present the ontology contains more than 1500 items and is still growing. Technical term dictionaries on nuclear engineering available on the Internet include in general 2000–3000 words [10]; around 4000 items will be enough to cover relevant concepts, but 1500 items are already useful to a lesser extent.

The merits of this ontology compared with conventional classifications are twofold. Firstly, it is so general that it is applicable to any other domain than nuclear safety.

Table 4. Top-level items of nuclear safety ontology

- Basic concepts
  - Safety
    - Safety studies
    - Assurance
    - Security
  - Risk
    - Health risk
    - Environmental risk
    - Economic risk
    - Personal risk
    - Societal risk
    - Background risk
  - Hazard
    - Radioactivity
    - Poisonous chemical
    - Flammable material
    - Internal energy
  - Harm
    - Death and health damage
    - Economic loss
    - Environmental damage
    - Reputational loss
  - Realization process
    - Event sequence
    - Exposure
  - Safety barrier
- System
  - System design
    - Systems approach
    - Safety goal
    - Safety assessment
    - Safety barrier
    - Human factor
  - Technological system
    - Subsystem, equipment, and component
    - Human interface
  - Management system
    - Operation
    - Maintenance
    - Radiation control
    - Control of radioactive materials
    - Management of documents and rules
    - Total quality assurance
    - Education and training
    - Organizational culture
    - Crisis management
    - Public relations
- Environment
  - Safety regulation
    - Institution
    - Guideline
    - Licensing
    - Inspection
  - Safety standards
    - Technical standards
    - Authentication
  - Disaster prevention
    - Basic concepts of disaster prevention
    - Related body
    - Initial action
    - Protective action
    - Aftercare
    - Disaster information
    - Education on disaster prevention
    - Emergency drill
  - Risk communication
    - Risk perception
    - Risk message
    - Communication skill
    - Consensus development
  - Social safety culture
  - Safety research

Concepts specific to the domain appear just below the concepts common to almost every process industry and it provides a common view of safety issues. Secondly, it is based on the firm principle of safety management that clearly shows how safety can be attained in complex socio-technological systems. Since conventional classifications are organized by facilities, activities, or academic areas specific in the domain, those who are not familiar with the domain can neither understand the roles of concepts in safety nor access concepts of concern. Although the ontology proposed in this work is normative and does not necessarily reflect intuitive understanding of lay people, it can provide a comprehensive view of the roles and access routes to relevant concepts. It thereby contributes to effective communication between experts and non-experts.

6. Conclusion

Nuclear safety ontology was discussed in this chapter. Ontology is a basis for communication and knowledge sharing in society, which are prerequisites for successful risk deliberation. Having reviewed conventional subject classifications of safety studies, requirements for appropriate ontology in socio-technological contexts were discussed. Ontology for the purpose must be based on the principles common to every specific domain of safety, and it must be understandable to lay people for smooth communication. We then proposed the nuclear safety ontology based on the fundamental concepts of general safety and the human–machine system's view of safety assurance.

The ontology constructed in this work will be helpful for the public to access domain-specific knowledge in terms of the basic principles of general safety. A concrete example of its use is to use it as a directory of a web site for providing relevant information on safety to the public. Another possibility is an information retrieval engine that can provide non-specialists relevant documents based on the ontology. Such an information retrieval engine will be more useful than conventional ones, which are based on a simple keyword match algorithm. In addition to the extension of the present ontology, development of such supporting methods will be the next work to be performed.

References

[1] P.C. Stern and H.V. Fineberg, *Understanding RISK*, National Academy Press, Washington, DC (1996).

[2] T.R. Gruber, What is an Ontology? http://www-ksl.stanford.edu/kst/what-is-an-ontology.html.

[3] R. Mizoguchi and M. Ikeda, Trans. Jpn. Soc. Artificial Intell. **12** (1997), 559, in Japanese.

[4] K. Kozaki, Y. Kitamura, T. Sano, S. Matsumoto, S. Ishikawa and R. Mizoguchi, Trans. Jpn. Soc. Artificial Intell. **17** (2002), 407, in Japanese.

[5] S. Staab, A. Maedche, *Ontology Engineering beyond the Modeling of Concepts and Relations* (2000), Proc. ECAI2000 Workshop on Ontologies and Problem-Solving Methods, Berlin, Germany.

[6] N.F. Noy, M. Sintek, S. Decker, M. Crubezy, R.W. Fergerson and M.A. Musen, IEEE Intelligent Systems (2001), 60.

[7] Nuclear Safety Commission of Japan, http://nsc.jst.go.jp/senmon/shidai/senkaisi_kensaku_f.htm.

[8] Atomic Energy Society of Japan, http://wwwsoc.nii.ac.jp/aesj/meeting/call-2003fall.pdf.

[9] The Society for Risk Analysis: Japan-Section, Handbook of Risk Research, TBS Britanica, Tokyo (2000), in Japanese.

[10] ATOMICA, http://mext-atm.jst.go.jp/dictionary_search/index.html.

CHAPTER 30

Excavation of Non-Stockpile Munitions in China

Hiroshi Niho

Project Management Consultant PCI/JGC Joint Venture, ATTN: No. 23 Building, 1-23-7 Toranomon, Minatoku, Tokyo 105-0001, Japan
E-mail: nihoh@pcitokyo.co.jp

Contents

Abstract

The international treaty of abandoned chemical weapons and the memorandum of understanding by Japan and China call for recovery of nearly 670,000 abandoned chemical munitions that were buried and abandoned in Haerbaling. The Abandoned Chemical Weapon Office (ACW Office) of Japanese Cabinet Office proceeds with the Destruction Project of Abandoned Chemical Weapon in China and the system for excavation and recovery for abandoned munitions with the remote and automatic control subsystem was designed. In this chapter, the outline of the ACW destruction project, excavation machine and soil removal system are reported from the standpoint of the Project Management Consultant who is supporting the ACW Office.

SYSTEMS AND HUMAN SCIENCE – FOR SAFETY, SECURITY, AND DEPENDABILITY
Edited by Tatsuo Arai, Shigeru Yamamoto and Kazuhisa Makino

1. Introduction

The International Treaty of Chemical Weapons Convention and the Memorandum of Understanding by the Government of Japan and the Government of China regarding the abandoned chemical munitions in China call for recovery of approximately 670,000 munitions from two burial pits in the Haerbaling area of Dunhua in Jiling Province, China (Fig. 1) [4]. Since the amount of munitions buried is extremely large and the munition removal operation must be completed safely in a short span of time, an automated tele-robotic system has been proposed and designed to pick up and recover those buried munitions with a minimum exposure risk to the workers at the site. The tele-robotic system utilizes an excavation robot and a soil removal system.

The most challenging task is to develop precise equipment for picking up highly explosive munitions buried in the ground under dirty and dusty conditions. It is our intention to safely excavate the abandoned munitions by the automated and robotic system as a main system, but utilize human intervention whenever the conditions call for it. Two types of grabbing hand have been selected as candidate systems for the recovery robot, and testing has been conducted to validate their function to pick up munitions from the ground safely and effectively. By taking advantage of recent technical innovations in the field of the robotic system, technologies of all functions that are needed in our proposed recovery robots are readily available and we believe that a reliable robotic system can be developed within a short period.

Since the munitions are buried deep in the ground, the soil removal system is also one of the critical elements of the excavation system that had to be demonstrated before announcing the system to be ready for its practical deployment. Recently, we successfully demonstrated the performance of the soil removal system of a suction type and confirmed its function.

Fig. 1. Location of Haerbaling.

With recent technical innovations in the field of the tele-robotic system, the technologies of all functions needed in our design of recovery robots are now readily available and a reliable tele-robotic system can be developed and demonstrated shortly. In this chapter, the basic design concept, present plan and verification test results for excavation of buried ordinance are reported.

2. Conditions of buried munitions

In the 1950s, approximately 670,000 abandoned chemical munitions, among which a few conventional munitions are included, were collected and buried by the local government in the two burial pits that are located 43 km southeast of Dunhua City. These pits are relatively small in size and the distance between the two pits is about 65 m. Two-thirds of 670,000 munitions are buried in Pit No. 1 and the remaining one-third are buried in Pit No. 2 [3].

According to the past survey on the abandoned chemical munitions in China, more than 90% of munitions are expected to be small in size and light in weight, and hence are relatively easy to handle with robotic systems. The percentages of the number of munitions in sizes and weights are as shown in Table 1.

The percentages of the number of munitions in chemical agent types are expected to be as shown in Table 2. As indicated, 88% are of the chemical munitions type and 12% are of the conventional munitions type.

The following munitions have a high potential risk for explosion:

- munitions with a fuse; and
- munitions on which a metal picrate is adhered.

We expect to encounter munitions from which the chemical agents have leaked into the pits. Those munitions with high potential risks will be identified with industrial television (ITV) and/or other sensors before being picked up by the recovery robot (Fig. 2).

Table 1. Sizes and weights of munitions

Diameter (mm)	Length (mm)	Weight per munition (kg)	Percentage in number
75	302.5	5–6	22.4
90	392	5–6	70.9
105	485.5	16	4.9
150	556	32	1.8

Table 2. Percentage of chemical munitions

Chemical agent	Percentage in number
Mustard/lewsite	60.4
Diphnylcyanoarsine	27.6
None (conventional)	12.0

Fig. 2. Burial pit.

3. Entire system of abandoned chemical munitions

The entire system to retrieve and dismantle abandoned munitions is composed of two sequential processes: recovery process and destruction process. In the recovery process, processing will be performed over three facilities: the excavation area, the recovery area and the temporary storage area. In the excavation area, the soil removal from the pit, the excavation of munitions, the decontamination, chemical agent detection and numbering are performed. Classification, sorting and packing are then performed in the recovery area (Fig. 3).

In the temporary storage area, the munitions which are packed into the containers are stocked for subsequent shipment to the destruction process. The excavation process is addressed in this chapter.

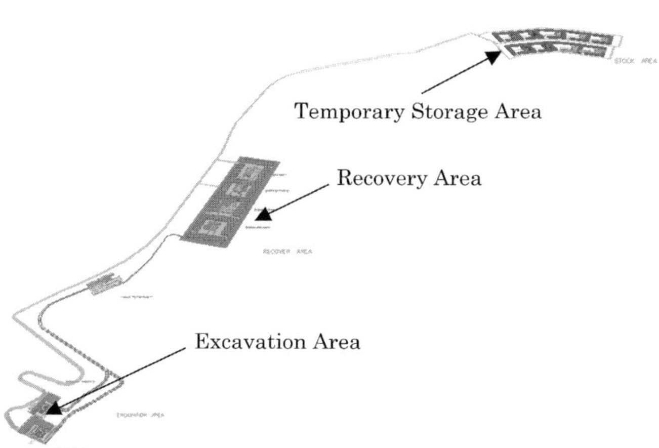

Fig. 3. Bird's eye view of excavation and recovery system.

4. Basic design concept for excavation and recovery of buried ordnance

The basic design concepts of the excavation and recovery facilities are as follows:

- to adopt a robotic system to reduce manual excavation work as much as possible;
- to adopt a remote control system to ensure the safe excavation and recovery work; and
- to carry out the excavation and recovery work by humans only for special cases when the use of a robotic system becomes inappropriate (Fig. 4).

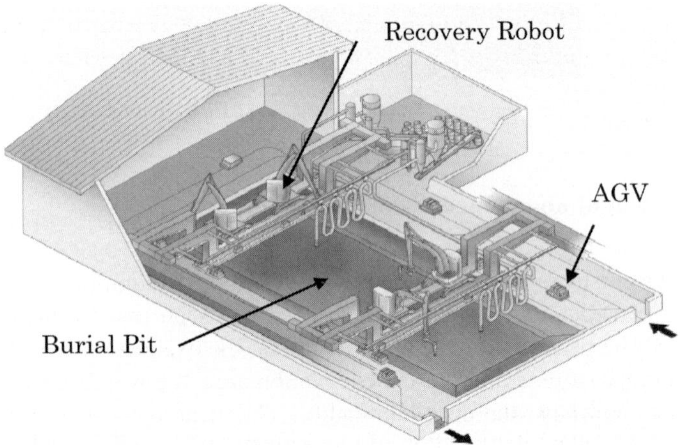

Fig. 4. Bird's eye view of excavation facility.

Even though a small number of abandoned chemical munitions in China have been excavated and recovered by humans in the past, the robotic system can be utilized to remove munitions in Haerbaling safely and efficiently since a large amount of munitions is buried in a relatively small area. By applying a high-performance tele-robotic control to the robotic system, the excavation and recovery work becomes safer and more efficient, and can minimize human errors and reduce potential risks. Buildings will be constructed at each burial pit to keep leaked chemical agents from being scattered into the air, thus making the environmental condition suitable for excavation and recovery work with a robotic system. Two sets of a robotic system will be installed at Pit No. 1 and one at Pit No. 2. Munitions removed from the burial pit by the recovery robot are transferred onto the auto-guided vehicle (AGV), which travels around the pit, and transported to the next facility for classification, sorting and packing. The recovery robots and AGV are controlled from the remote control center.

5. Functions of the robotic system

There are several design features, which have to be examined in detail before robotic systems can be considered to be ready for practical use in Haerbaling burial sites.

(1) *Firm gripping of munitions*. The metal picrate adhered on the shell is very sensitive to shock. Thus, it is very important that munitions once picked up will not be

dropped back into the burial pit to avoid the impact. Special attention must be taken to grip munitions firmly until they are placed onto the recovery box.

(2) *Gentle handling during gripping operation.* It is also important not to create any shocks to munitions during gripping operations for the same reason as described above. The robotic systems are already recommended for not handling munitions with fuse and/or metal picrate.

(3) *Removing soil.* The layer of soil, 2–3 m in thickness, that covers munitions must be removed manually before commencing the excavation and recovery work. Soil beside the buried munitions is removed with the soil removing system under manual remote control before gripping and picking up the munitions from the pit.

(4) *Tele-robotic operation.* We believe that a tele-robotic system combined with the operator's judgments is the most appropriate and reliable way to pick up the munitions from the pit in terms of safety and efficiency. It is clearly evident that the recovery robot with tele-robotic system cannot pick all buried ordnance. Small numbers of special ordnance, which cannot be handled by the tele-robotic system, will have to be handled under manual control. However, if a majority of buried munitions can be removed from the pit by the tele-robotic system, it has a great advantage to ensure the safe and efficient operation.

(5) *Sensing equipment.* Various sensors and ITV are needed to check conditions of burial pits and buried ordnance remotely before starting excavation and recovery operations by the recovery robot. They are:
   - sensor to detect the chemical agents;
   - sensor to detect the position of munitions;
   - ITV to confirm the absence of fuse and metal picrate; and
   - other sensors for the srobotic system.

6. Present plan of robotic systems

The robotic systems are composed of recovery robots, a traveling deck on which recovery robots are mounted, a soil removing system and a control system.

(1) *Recovery robot.* A recovery robot for excavation and recovery of burial ordnance is composed of gripping hands, manipulators and a platform. Taking the reliability and cost performance into consideration, it is planned to adopt a power shovel as the platform with some modification. An initial positioning of a gripping hand can be achieved by driving, traveling, revolving and luffing devices of the platform. The manipulator is installed at the tip of the lever of the platform for fine positioning of the gripping hands. The gripping hand is equipped at the tip of the manipulator. The gentle gripping operation of buried munitions can be achieved by the synchronized control of the gripper and the manipulator (Fig. 5).

(2) *Traveling deck.* A traveling deck with the recovery robots mounted on it travels alongside the pit and is composed of a steel structure of a deck, a traveling device and a conveyor. Its function is to receive empty boxes from the AGV and to unload the boxes with munitions to AGV.

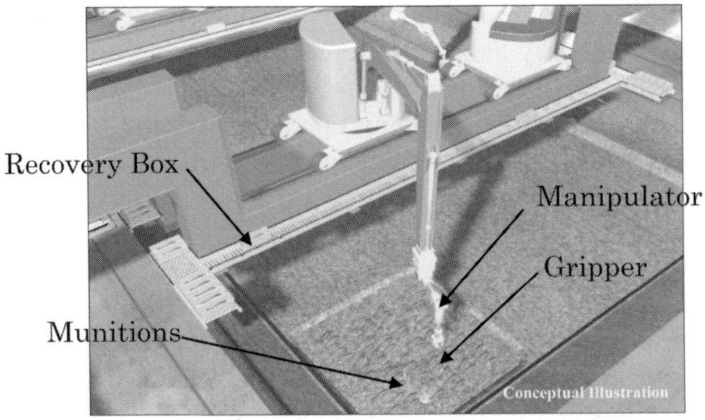

Fig. 5. Bird's eye view of excavation robot.

(3) *Soil removal system.* The soil removal system is under remote control and its function is to remove the soil beside the munitions and enable the recovery robot to pick up the munitions.

(4) *Control system.* The robotic system for excavation and recovery is operated from a control desk in the remote central control room. An operator operates the robotic systems by checking the site condition with ITV and several other sensors and judging the correctness of the tele-robotic operation of robotic systems. When the operator judges that he should stop, change or modify the tele-robotic operations, he can interrupt the tele-robotic operations at any time and correct them. The operator can also operate the robotic system under remote control mode with a joystick for any occasions when he feels that manual remote control is better suited for picking up the buried munitions than tele-robotic control.

7. Gripping hands

7.1. *Testing of gripping hands*

There is no past experience for excavation and recovery of the large number of buried munitions within the limited time frame. The existing gripper and control system, which handles the explosive ordnance, cannot be used in this case and should be modified and tailored to fit this special case. For this purpose two kinds of gripping hands have been selected and tested during the fiscal year 2001 to get the data to confirm the function needed as a gripper and to finalize its specification [1].

(1) *Magnet with flexible gripper.* The concept of this type is to integrate the two different functions into one gripper to meet the requirement of adopting the autonomous control, gentle handling and reliability not to drop the munitions. The magnet is the easiest way to pick up the object and accordingly the easiest way to attain the autonomous control. After picking up the munitions by the magnet, three fingers, which are activated by the motor and wire, rap up the munitions gently by fitting its shape so as not to drop it during the shifting

motion to the recovery box. The technical items which we have to confirm through the testing is whether the magnet of reasonable size can pick up the streamlined munitions covered with soil and rust and whether the flexible gripper can grip the munitions gently and tightly. Testing has been carried out for munitions of small size, which account for the majority of the buried munitions.

Figure 6 shows the magnet with its flexible gripper and Fig. 7 shows the sequence of the gripping operation.

The specification of magnet and flexible gripper is as follows.

- Size of electromagnet: 50 mm width × 150 mm length.
- Flexible gripper: three fingers, three joints, electric drive with wire rope.
- Magnetic force: 235 N with 3 mm gap by soil between magnet and munition.

(2) *Picking gripper.* The picking gripper has been used in every industrial field including the robots handling explosives. The construction is simple and reliable. This type of gripper is workable to grip the munitions under the special burial condition by remote control. The testing was carried out to find out the best mechanism, shape of gripping finger and gripping procedure for each munition.

The testing was carried out by manufacturing the gripping hand of actual size and fitting it to the tip of the link of the power shovel as shown in Fig. 8. Munitions of actual size and weight are also manufactured for this test and buried in the soil. Figure 9 shows the picking gripper and Fig. 10 shows the sequence of the gripping operation.

The specification of the picking gripper is as follows:

- Degree of freedom: 5 degrees of freedom.
- Gripping force: eight times shell weight.
- Drive system: hydraulic drive.

Fig. 6. Magnet with flexible gripper.

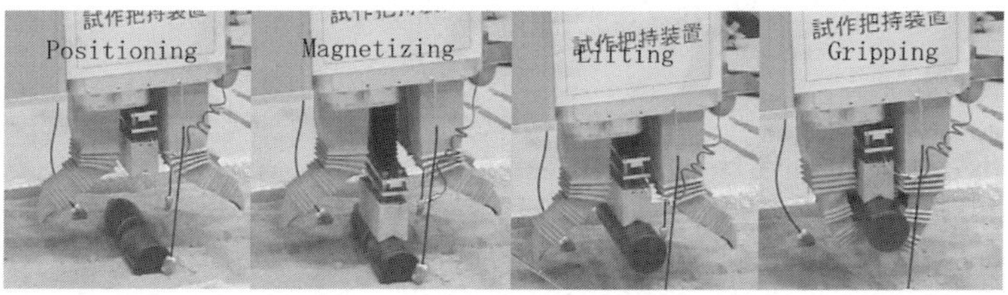

Fig. 7. Sequence of gripping operation.

Fig. 8. Testing facility.

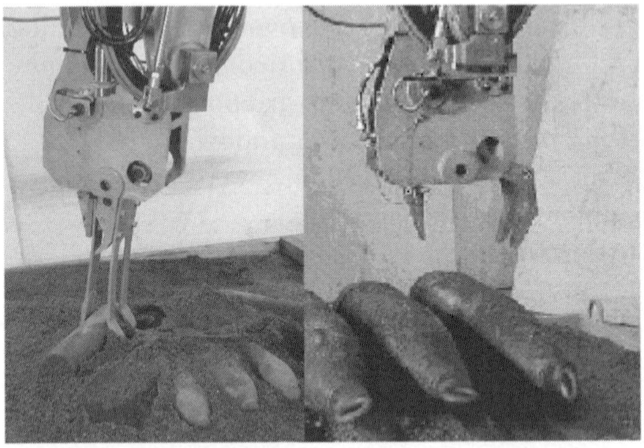

Fig. 9. Picking gripper.

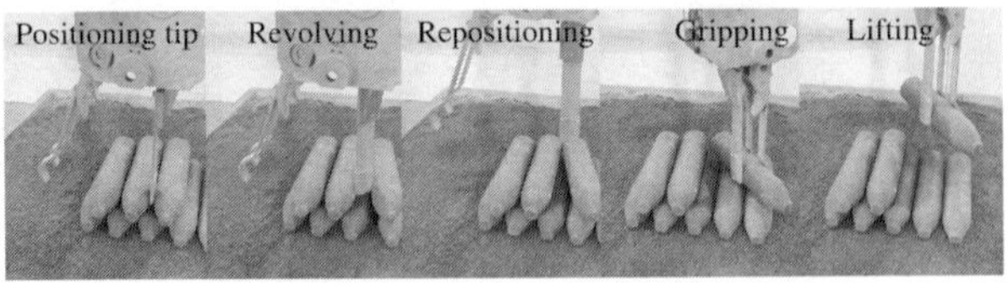

Fig. 10. Sequence of gripping operation.

7.2. *Test results*

Several kinds of testing have been performed to get the data to examine the effectiveness of the gripping hand. The test results for two kinds of gripping hands are as described below.

(1) Magnet with flexible gripper

- Enough magnetic force can be attained with a reasonable size of magnet. The size of magnet is 50 mm in width and 150 mm in length, and the magnetic force is

235 N with 3 mm gap between the magnet and the munitions surface, which corresponds to about four times the weight of small-size munitions.
- The magnet does not extract the surrounding object, not even by gem clip.
- The magnet can pick up the munitions of which the lower half is buried in the soil. This means that the upper half's surrounding soil should be removed by the soil removal system.
- The flexible gripper can grip the munitions gently and tightly.
- This gripper can pick up the munitions, which are buried at any direction from 0 to 90° on the condition that the surrounding soil has been removed.
- The requirements for the accuracy for positioning magnet are confirmed.

(2) Picking gripper
- The construction of two types of gripper is confirmed. One is a rigid type, which is suitable for gripping the larger munitions, and another is a flexible type, which is suitable for gripping the smaller munitions.
- Both types of gripper can grip the munitions tightly.
- The suitable gripping methods are confirmed for each case of burial condition and munitions type.

The test was carried out by manufacturing the gripping hand of actual size and fitting it to the tip of the link of a power shovel. The munitions of the actual size and weight are also manufactured for this test and buried in the soil. During verification, it was found that both types of gripper are effective in terms of gripping the munitions. However, the picking type was chosen over the magnetic type since there is a slight possibility of the magnet inadvertently creating induced electrical current on the proximity fuse, which in turn may cause munitions to explode. (The proximity fuse was not developed by the old Japanese army, but still there is a slight possibility of foreign-made proximity fuses being buried in the pits.)

8. Soil removal system

8.1. *Testing soil removal system*

There is no past experience for removing the soil under the conditions that are applicable in this project. The soil removal system must be designed to function to meet the conditions described below.
- Munitions are buried in the sandy soil of weathering granite.
- Munitions are randomly placed.
- Soil should be removed with a tele-robotic system.
- Soil should be removed without applying any shock to the munitions and to such an extent that types and positions of munitions can be recognized with the automatic sensing system.

The soil removal system of a vacuum type, which is composed of a vacuum nozzle, a hose and a pipe, a soil separator, a dust collector and a blower, was selected to meet such conditions [2]. The vacuum nozzle is composed of a compressed air injection nozzle and an air extraction vacuum nozzle. The soil is first loosened by injecting compressed air and then extracted through the vacuum nozzle.

The verification test has been conducted in the following sequential steps:

(a) Select the sandy soil having the same grain distribution found in Haerbaling.
(b) Compact the testing soil to simulate the same burial condition of munitions found in Haerbaling.
(c) Conduct the fundamental test of soil removal under various conditions of air injection and extraction.
(d) Examine the effect of water spray on the performance of the soil removal system.
(e) Construct the vacuum nozzle with a specific size.
(f) Confirm performance of a collision prevention system between the nozzle and munitions during the operation.
(g) Conduct the total testing using mock-up munitions buried under various conditions.

Figure 11 shows the flow diagram of the soil removal system and Fig. 12 shows the conceptual figure of the soil extracting nozzle.

The specification of the soil removal system is as follows:

- size of injection nozzle: 5 mm in diameter, three nozzles;
- pressure of injection air: 7 kg/cm^2;
- size of extraction nozzle: 100 mm in diameter;
- extraction air volume: 40–60 m^3/min;
- moving speed of nozzle: 50 mm/sec.

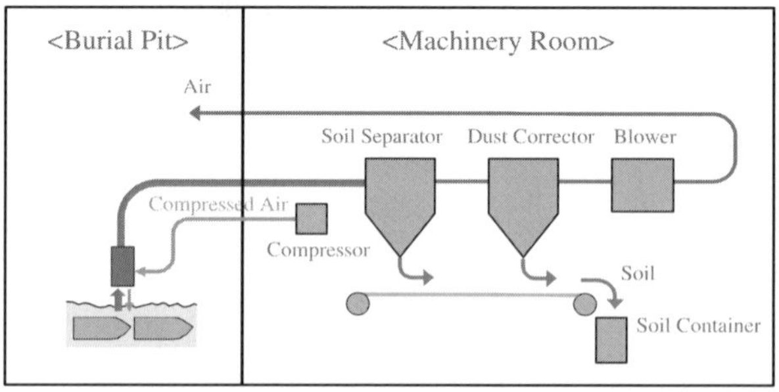

Fig. 11. Flow diagram of soil removal system.

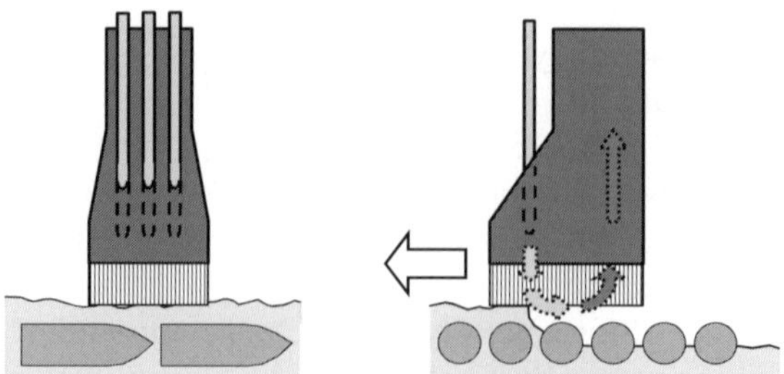

Fig. 12. Soil extracting nozzle.

8.2. *Test results*

With this test setup, the performance of the soil removal system of a suction type was successfully demonstrated. Figure 13 shows the soil extracting test and Fig. 14 shows the burial condition of munitions after removing the soil. Results of the test are as described below.

- By the combination of an injection nozzle and an extraction nozzle, the sandy soil of weathering granite can be removed effectively. It is less effective for the clay soil.
- The soil can be removed without any disturbance or shock to buried munitions.
- The water spray of small quantity is effective to loosen the compacted soil and to make the soil removal system function more effectively.

Fig. 13. Soil extracting test.

Fig. 14. Munitions after extracting soil.

9. Conclusion

A useful database had been obtained for the design of the gripping hand and the soil removal system through the experiments. These test data will be reviewed in more detail by taking the actual site conditions into consideration. Further, we will continue to work on the validations of a control system so as to enable the gripping operation by the tele-robotic system. Through those tests and validations, we believe that we can develop a safe, reliable and efficient robotic system that can be used for the recovery of abandoned munitions from the two burial pits at the Haerbaling area of Dunhua in Jiling Province, China.

References

[1] Hiroshi Niho, Tele-robotic system for recovery of non-stockpile munitions in China, The International CW Demil Conference, May 2002.
[2] Hiroshi Niho, Tele-robotic system for recovery of non-stockpile munitions in China, The International CW Demil Conference, May 2003.
[3] The Conditions of Abandoned Chemical Weapons in China, An Aggregated Report of the Results of Investigations (1991–1996), Japan Institute of International Affairs, March 1998.
[4] Outline of the Project for the Destruction of Abandoned Chemical Weapons in China, October 2002.

PART VIII

Services for Human

CHAPTER 31

A Human-Safe Control for Collision Avoidance by a Redundant Robot Using Visual Information

Jian Huang and Isao Todo

Graduate School of Engineering, Yokohama National University, 79-5 Tokiwadai, Hodogaya-ku, Yokohama 240-8501, Japan

Contents

Abstract

With the rapid development of service robots, avoiding collisions with human beings is a most important requirement of robot control. In this chapter, we propose a method in which a virtual potential field around a robot is established by stereovision to implement collision avoidance by using its redundant joints, while simultaneously completing a contact task with its hand. The effectiveness of the proposed method has been demonstrated by experiments.

SYSTEMS AND HUMAN SCIENCE – FOR SAFETY, SECURITY, AND DEPENDABILITY
Edited by Tatsuo Arai, Shigeru Yamamoto and Kazuhisa Makino

1. Introduction

With the rapid development of service robots to support various tasks in our daily lives, safety strategies of the service robots are primarily concerned [1,2]. Unlike the conventional industrial robot, service robots must coexist and interact with human beings in a common space. As a result, the possibility of collisions between service robots and human beings has increased. Therefore, it is expected that a robot can complete a specified task with its end effector and simultaneously avoid a possible collision by its potential capability.

Obstacle avoidance using a redundant robot has been widely discussed [3–15]. Among those studies, approaches on developing a real time algorithm [3,5–7,9,10], off-line path planning [6], obstacle avoidance in a narrow and unknown environment for a hyper redundant planar manipulator [8] and virtual potential methods [10,11] have been proposed. Recently, obstacle avoidance based on visual information was also reported [14,15]. However, the method of completing stereovision-based collision avoidance as well as taking into account the robot manipulability has not been reported.

In this chapter, we propose a method of avoiding a robot–human collision using stereo visual information. When someone is detected moving into a previously established virtual potential field around the robot, a virtual torque is generated to drive the robot's redundant joints so as to avoid a possible collision. We present a criterion function by considering the robot manipulability so as to determine which redundant joints will be used. A control method is proposed for a redundant robot to simultaneously perform a contact task with its hand and collision avoidance with its redundant joints.

2. Collision avoidance by joint virtual impedance control

The total number of joints of a robot is n, the number of degrees of freedom (expressed as DOF) required for a task with its hand is assumed to be m, and the robot control sampling period is $T(= 5\text{ ms})$. When n is larger than m, the robot is called a redundant robot. The difference $n - m$ is r, where r is the redundant degrees of freedom. Generally, m joints of the robot are used to perform the primary task at hand, and r joints are used for a secondary task. To facilitate the detection of a human's location by image processing, a marker is attached to the person's body as a feature point.

2.1. *Definition of a virtual potential field*

In order to detect a collision with a human in all possible directions, a virtual potential cylinder around a robot is defined in a computer as shown in Fig. 1. The radius of the virtual potential cylinder is r_v. At time $t = kT$, a position vector $\mathbf{e}_v(k) \in R^{3\times1}$ detected by stereovision quantitatively describes the feature point in the defined field. $\mathbf{e}_v(k)$ is

$$\mathbf{e}_v(k) = \mathbf{p}_b(k) - \mathbf{p}_v(k) \tag{1}$$

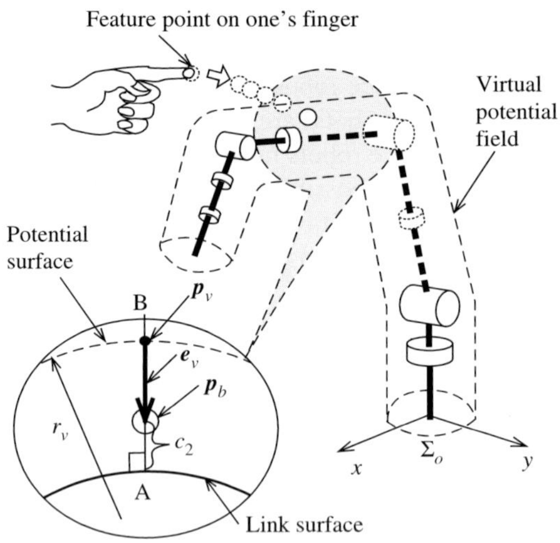

Fig. 1. A defined virtual potential cylinder around a manipulator.

where $\mathbf{p}_b(k) \in R^{3\times1}$ is the position of the feature point, and $\mathbf{p}_v(k) \in R^{3\times1}$ is the position on the potential surface where the feature point impinges the surface and enters into the field.

2.2. *Generation of a virtual torque*

When a human being is detected inside the previously established potential field by stereovision, a virtual torque is generated to drive the redundant joints to move away from the human. In this chapter, a virtual force $\mathbf{f}_v(k) \in R^{3\times1}$ is generated by

$$\mathbf{f}_v(k) = \mathbf{D}_v e_v(k) + \mathbf{K}_v \mathbf{e}_v(k) \tag{2}$$

where $\mathbf{D}_v \in R^{3\times3}$ is the virtual damping matrix, $\mathbf{K}_v \in R^{3\times3}$ is the virtual stiffness matrix.

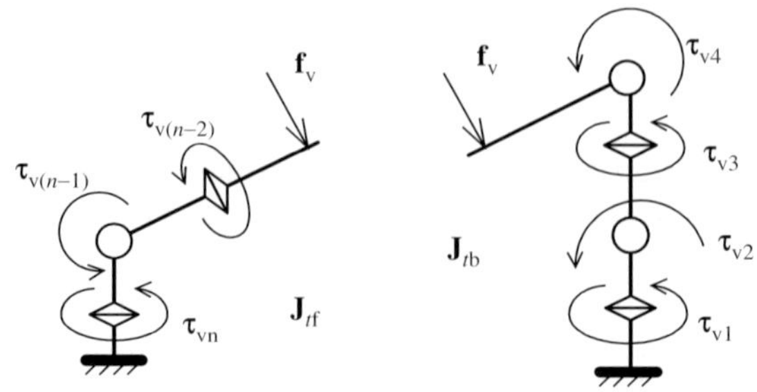

Fig. 2. The generated virtual torques.

As shown in Fig. 2, the generated virtual force $\mathbf{f}_{\mathrm{v}}(k)$ can be converted to the joint virtual torque $\boldsymbol{\tau}_{\mathrm{v}}(k) \in R^{n\times 1}$ by

$$\boldsymbol{\tau}_{\mathrm{v}}(k) = [\, \tau_{\mathrm{v}1} \quad \tau_{\mathrm{v}2} \cdots \tau_{\mathrm{v}n} \,]^{\mathrm{T}} = \begin{bmatrix} \mathbf{J}_{tb}^{\mathrm{T}} \\ \mathbf{J}_{tf}^{\mathrm{T}} \end{bmatrix}_{n\times m} \begin{bmatrix} \mathbf{f}_{\mathrm{v}}(k) \\ 0 \end{bmatrix}_{m\times 1} \tag{3}$$

where $\mathbf{J}_{tb}$ is the Jacobian of the links from the robot base to the link activated by the virtual force, $\mathbf{J}_{tf}$ is the Jacobian of the links from the robot hand to the link activated by the virtual force.

2.3. *Joint compliance control*

According to the virtual torque $\boldsymbol{\tau}_{\mathrm{v}}(k)$ computed by (3), a joint virtual torque $\boldsymbol{\tau}_{\mathrm{vr}}(k) \in R^{r\times 1}$ acting on redundant joints is

$$\boldsymbol{\tau}_{\mathrm{vr}}(k) = \mathbf{S}_{\mathrm{r}} \boldsymbol{\tau}_{\mathrm{v}}(k) \tag{4}$$

where $\mathbf{S}_{\mathrm{r}} \in R^{r\times n}$ is the given matrix. According to the compliance control algorithm [4,5], the desired joint velocity $\dot{\boldsymbol{\theta}}_{\mathrm{r}}(k+1) \in R^{r\times 1}$ of the redundant joints is generated by using the computed virtual torque $\boldsymbol{\tau}_{\mathrm{vr}}(k)$ as

$$\dot{\boldsymbol{\theta}}_{\mathrm{r}}(k+1) = (\mathbf{I} - T\mathbf{M}_{\mathrm{r}}^{-1}\mathbf{D})\dot{\boldsymbol{\theta}}_{\mathrm{r}}(k) + T\mathbf{M}_{\mathrm{r}}^{-1}\boldsymbol{\tau}_{\mathrm{vr}}(k) \tag{5}$$

where $\mathbf{M}_{\mathrm{r}} \in R^{r\times r}$ is the virtual mass matrix of the redundant joints, $\mathbf{D}_{\mathrm{r}} \in R^{r\times r}$ is the virtual damping matrix of the redundant joints, and $\mathbf{I}$ is the unity matrix.

3. Control of a redundant robot

3.1. *Image processing and interpolation*

In order to detect an invasion into the given potential field of a human being, two CCD cameras (CV-M40, JAI Co.) were used. The cameras output images at a rate of 60 frames per second. An image processor board (GENESIS, Matrox Co.) was used for image input and processing. On this board there is an embedded DSP C80 with which image input and processing can be carried out simultaneously. Therefore, real-time image processing can be achieved. Here, the image processing sampling period is assumed to be $T_{\mathrm{c}}(= 1/60\ \mathrm{s})$. As shown in Fig. 3, position ${}^{c}\mathbf{p}_{\mathrm{v}}(i)$ of a feature point attached to a person's body can be detected in real time.

Although image processing can be completed at the camera frame rate, T_{c} is still longer than T. Here, we assume that a human being moves smoothly along a continuous trajectory without sudden change in his movement direction. In order to apply the image results to robot control, it is necessary to interpolate them at every T so as to convert ${}^{c}\mathbf{p}_{\mathrm{v}}(i)$ to

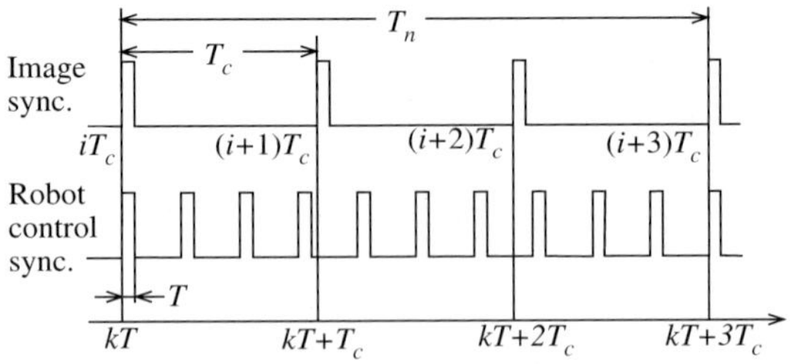

Fig. 3. Time chart of the proposed image processing method.

$\mathbf{p}_{\mathrm{v}}(k)$ by

$$\mathbf{p}_{\mathrm{v}}(k)=\begin{cases} {}^{c}\mathbf{p}_{\mathrm{v}}(i-1)+(kT-(i-1)T_{\mathrm{c}})\dfrac{{}^{c}\mathbf{p}_{\mathrm{v}}(i-1)-{}^{c}\mathbf{p}_{\mathrm{v}}(i-2)}{T_{\mathrm{c}}} & (iT_{\mathrm{c}}\leqq kT<(i+1)T_{\mathrm{c}}),\\ {}^{c}\mathbf{p}_{\mathrm{v}}(i)+(kT-iT_{\mathrm{c}})\dfrac{{}^{c}\mathbf{p}_{\mathrm{v}}(i)-{}^{c}\mathbf{p}_{\mathrm{v}}(i-1)}{T_{\mathrm{c}}} & ((i+1)T_{\mathrm{c}}<kT<(i+2)T_{\mathrm{c}}),\\ {}^{c}\mathbf{p}_{\mathrm{v}}(i+1)+(kT-(i+1))T_{\mathrm{c}},\ \dfrac{{}^{c}\mathbf{p}_{\mathrm{v}}(i+1)-{}^{c}\mathbf{p}_{\mathrm{v}}(i)}{T_{\mathrm{c}}} & ((i+2)T_{\mathrm{c}}<kT<(i+3)T_{\mathrm{c}}),\\ \vdots & \\ (k=0,1,2,\ldots),\ (i=0,1,2,\ldots) & \end{cases} \tag{6}$$

3.2. *Desired joint velocity generation of a redundant robot*

Unlike earlier studies in which a known obstacle was assumed, the human's location is unspecified in the present study. Therefore, a virtual potential field is defined by image processing so as to avoid a possible collision. During the action of collision avoidance, the robot is generally expected to carry out the primary task with its hand and, if possible, the primary task should not be interrupted by the avoidance action. To achieve this goal, a control technique has been proposed in this chapter by which a robot can carry out a compliance control with its hand and simultaneously avoid a possible collision by using its redundant joints.

At time $t = kT$, the hand position of the robot is given as $\mathbf{p}_{\mathrm{h}}(k) \in R^{6\times 1}$ from its kinematics, and its desired position is assumed to be $\mathbf{p}_{\mathrm{hd}}(k) \in R^{6\times 1}$. According to the compliance control law, the desired hand velocity $\dot{\mathbf{p}}_{\mathrm{h}}(k+1) \in R^{6\times 1}$ is generated by

$$\begin{aligned}\dot{\mathbf{p}}_{\mathrm{h}}(k+1) = {} & (\mathbf{I} - \mathbf{M}_{\mathrm{h}}^{-1}\mathbf{D}_{\mathrm{h}}T)\dot{\mathbf{p}}_{\mathrm{h}}(k)\\ & + T\mathbf{M}_{\mathrm{h}}^{-1}(\mathbf{f}_{\mathrm{d}}(k) - \mathbf{f}_{\mathrm{e}}(k)) + T\mathbf{M}_{\mathrm{h}}^{-1}\mathbf{K}_{\mathrm{h}}(\mathbf{p}_{\mathrm{hd}}(k) - \mathbf{p}_{\mathrm{h}}(k))\end{aligned} \tag{7}$$

where

$\mathbf{M}_{\mathrm{h}} \in R^{m\times m}$: virtual mass matrix of the robot hand,

$\mathbf{D}_{\mathrm{h}} \in R^{m\times m}$: virtual damping matrix of the robot hand,
$\mathbf{K}_{\mathrm{h}} \in R^{m\times m}$: virtual stiffness matrix of the robot hand,
$\mathbf{f}_{\mathrm{d}}(k) \in R^{m\times 1}$: desired force,
$\mathbf{f}_{\mathrm{e}}(k) \in R^{m\times 1}$: force measured by a F/T sensor,
$\dot{\mathbf{p}}_{\mathrm{h}}(k) \in R^{m\times 1}$: hand velocity of the robot hand at $t = kT$,
$\mathbf{p}_{\mathrm{hd}}(k) \in R^{m\times 1}$: desired hand position of the robot hand,
$\mathbf{p}_{\mathrm{h}}(k) \in R^{m\times 1}$: hand position of the robot hand.

It is known that the relation between the hand velocity $\dot{\mathbf{p}}_{\mathrm{h}}(k)$ and the joint velocity $\dot{\boldsymbol{\theta}}_n(k) \in R^{n\times 1}$ at $t = kT$ can be expressed as

$$\dot{\mathbf{p}}_{\mathrm{h}}(k) = \mathbf{J}_n\dot{\boldsymbol{\theta}}_n(k) \tag{8}$$

where $\mathbf{J}_n \in R^{n\times m}$ is the Jacobian and $n = m + r$. If the Jacobian $\mathbf{J}_n$ is separated into two parts, (8) can be rewritten as

$$\dot{\mathbf{p}}_{\mathrm{h}}(k) = \mathbf{J}_m\dot{\boldsymbol{\theta}}_m(k) + \mathbf{J}_{\mathrm{r}}\dot{\boldsymbol{\theta}}_{\mathrm{r}}(k) \tag{9}$$

where

$\mathbf{J}_m \in R^{m\times m}$: Jacobian of non-redundant joints, $\dot{\boldsymbol{\theta}}_m(k) \in R^{m\times 1}$: non-redundant joint velocity,

$\mathbf{J}_{\mathrm{r}} \in R^{r\times r}$: Jacobian of redundant joints, $\dot{\boldsymbol{\theta}}_{\mathrm{r}}(k) \in R^{r\times 1}$: redundant joint velocity.

In order to avoid a possible collision using the redundant joints of the robot, the desired joint velocity $\dot{\boldsymbol{\theta}}_{\mathrm{r}}(k+1)$ of its redundant joints can be obtained by (5). Therefore, the desired joint velocity $\dot{\boldsymbol{\theta}}_m(k+1)$ of the non-redundant joints in (9) can be calculated by

$$\dot{\boldsymbol{\theta}}_m(k+1) = \mathbf{J}_m^{-1}\dot{\mathbf{p}}_{\mathrm{h}}(k+1) - \mathbf{J}_m^{-1}\mathbf{J}_{\mathrm{r}}\dot{\boldsymbol{\theta}}_{\mathrm{r}}(k+1) \tag{10}$$

Using $\dot{\boldsymbol{\theta}}_{\mathrm{r}}(k+1)$ and $\dot{\boldsymbol{\theta}}_m(k+1)$ generated by (5) and (10), respectively, the desired joint velocity $\dot{\boldsymbol{\theta}}_n(k+1)$ can be written as

$$\dot{\boldsymbol{\theta}}_n(k+1) = \mathbf{I}_m\dot{\boldsymbol{\theta}}_m(k+1) + \mathbf{I}_{\mathrm{r}}\dot{\boldsymbol{\theta}}_{\mathrm{r}}(k+1) \tag{11}$$

where

$$I_m = \overbrace{\begin{bmatrix} 1 & \cdots & 0 \\ \vdots & \ddots & \vdots \\ 0 & \cdots & 1 \\ 0 & \cdots & 0 \\ \vdots & \ddots & \vdots \\ 0 & \cdots & 0 \end{bmatrix}}^{m} \begin{matrix} \left.\vphantom{\begin{matrix}1\\ \vdots\\ 0\end{matrix}}\right\} m \\ \left.\vphantom{\begin{matrix}1\\ \vdots\\ 0\end{matrix}}\right\} r \end{matrix}, \quad I_r = \overbrace{\begin{bmatrix} 0 & \cdots & 0 \\ \vdots & \ddots & \vdots \\ 0 & \cdots & 0 \\ 1 & \cdots & 0 \\ \vdots & \ddots & \vdots \\ 0 & \cdots & 1 \end{bmatrix}}^{r} \begin{matrix} \left.\vphantom{\begin{matrix}1\\ \vdots\\ 0\end{matrix}}\right\} m \\ \left.\vphantom{\begin{matrix}1\\ \vdots\\ 0\end{matrix}}\right\} r \end{matrix}.$$

Compared with the method using the pseudoinverse of Jacobian, the proposed method shown in (11) has a merit of less computation so as to increase the processing speed [13].

3.3. *A criterion function to determine the redundant joints*

The desired joint velocity $\dot{\boldsymbol{\theta}}_n(k+1)$ of the redundant robot is generated by (11) in terms of the computed joint velocities $\dot{\boldsymbol{\theta}}_r(k+1)$ and $\dot{\boldsymbol{\theta}}_m(k+1)$. However, the specific joints that are redundant have still not been selected. As stated above, because in the present study it is unspecified just where and when a human being may enter the defined potential field, the person's location is an important factor to be considered when determining which joints should be the redundant joints.

In this study, a criterion function is proposed to determine the redundant joints. The criterion function $P(k)$ at time $t = kT$ is defined by

$$P(k) = w_1 c_1(\theta(k)) + w_2 c_2(k) \tag{12}$$

where w_1 and w_2 are the given weighting coefficients. $c_1(\boldsymbol{\theta}(k))$ is defined as the manipulability [16–18] of the robot at time $t = kT$, and it is computed by n joint angles as

$$c_1(\boldsymbol{\theta}(k)) = \sqrt{\det(\mathbf{J}_n(\boldsymbol{\theta}(k)) \cdot \mathbf{J}_n^{\mathrm{T}}(\boldsymbol{\theta}(k)))} \tag{13}$$

$c_2(k)$ is defined as the distance between the detected feature point and the nearest link of the robot at time $t = kT$ as indicated in Fig. 1. The distance $c_2(k)$ can be calculated by

$$c_2(k) = r_v - |e_v(k)| \tag{14}$$

When the feature point is outside of the defined potential field, $c_2(k)$ is set equal to 0.

The next steps for deciding the redundant joints are as follows:

(1) Select a possible redundant joint, and calculate $\dot{\boldsymbol{\theta}}_r(k+1)$ by (1)–(5).
(2) Compute $\dot{\boldsymbol{\theta}}_m(k+1)$ by (10). Then we obtain $\dot{\boldsymbol{\theta}}_n(k+1)$ by (11).
(3) Calculate $\hat{\boldsymbol{\theta}}_n(k+1)$ by $\hat{\boldsymbol{\theta}}_n(k+1) = \boldsymbol{\theta}_n(k) + T\dot{\boldsymbol{\theta}}_n(k+1)$. Then we obtain c_1 by (13).
(4) Calculate $P(k)$ by (12) for all possible ways of selecting the redundant joints.
(5) Select the redundant joints so as to obtain the maximum $P(k)$.
(6) Repeat from step (1) to step (5) at every sampling instant to decide which joints are the redundant joints.

The computation time of the proposed method is mostly concerned when a robot has more than one redundant joint. However, the computation time can be definitely reduced with the development of high speed computer or applying parallel processing method.

Using the proposed method explained in Sections 3.2 and 3.3, the primary task performed by the robot hand and the secondary task of avoiding a collision with a human being by using the redundant joints can be carried out simultaneously.

3.4. *Applying the control algorithm to a redundant robot*

In this chapter, a 7-DOF robot (PA10, Mitsubishi Heavy Industry Co.) was used in the experiments. A force/torque sensor (F/T 10/100, BL AUTOTEC Ltd) was set up at its end-effector. The robot hand was required to perform a contact task with 6-DOF control, and the single remaining joint was used as a redundant joint to avoid a collision. Therefore, we have $n = 7$, $m = 6$, and $r = 1$. According to (4), the virtual torque $\tau_{\mathrm{vr}}(k)$ is expressed as

$$\tau_{\mathrm{vr}}(k) = \mathbf{s}_{\mathrm{r}}^{\mathrm{T}} \boldsymbol{\tau}_{\mathrm{v}}(k) \tag{15}$$

where vector $\mathbf{s}_{\mathrm{r}}^{\mathrm{T}}$ is given by

$$\mathbf{s}_{\mathrm{r}}^{\mathrm{T}} = \overbrace{[0 \quad \cdots \quad \underset{\substack{\uparrow \\ \text{redundant joint}}}{1} \quad \cdots \quad 0]}^{n}$$

The joint compliance control generated by (5) is rewritten as

$$\dot{\theta}_{\mathrm{r}}(k+1) = (1 - TM_{\mathrm{r}}^{-1}D)\dot{\theta}_{\mathrm{r}}(k) + TM_{\mathrm{r}}^{-1}\tau_{\mathrm{vr}}(k) \tag{16}$$

A block diagram for controlling the 7-DOF robot is proposed as shown in Fig. 4, where $\boldsymbol{\Lambda}$ is robot kinematics, and $\mathbf{R}_{\mathrm{f}}$ is the coordinate transformation matrix.

In Fig. 4, after position ${}^{c}\mathbf{p}_{\mathrm{b}}(i)$ of the feature point attached to a human subject's body is detected by image processing, an interpolation is performed by (6) to convert ${}^{c}\mathbf{p}_{\mathrm{b}}(i)$ to $\mathbf{p}_{\mathrm{b}}(k)$. A virtual torque $\tau_{\mathrm{vr}}(k)$ is computed with (3) and (15), and then the joint compliance control is generated by (16). At the same time, the desired hand velocity $\dot{\mathbf{p}}_{\mathrm{h}}(k+1)$ is computed by (7) based on the compliance control law. The desired joint velocity $\dot{\boldsymbol{\theta}}_{n}(k+1)$ is generated by calculating $\dot{\boldsymbol{\theta}}_{m}(k+1)$ and $\dot{\boldsymbol{\theta}}_{\mathrm{r}}(k+1)$ by (11). Finally, the computed joint velocity $\dot{\boldsymbol{\theta}}_{n}(k+1)$ is sent to the servo drivers to control the robot.

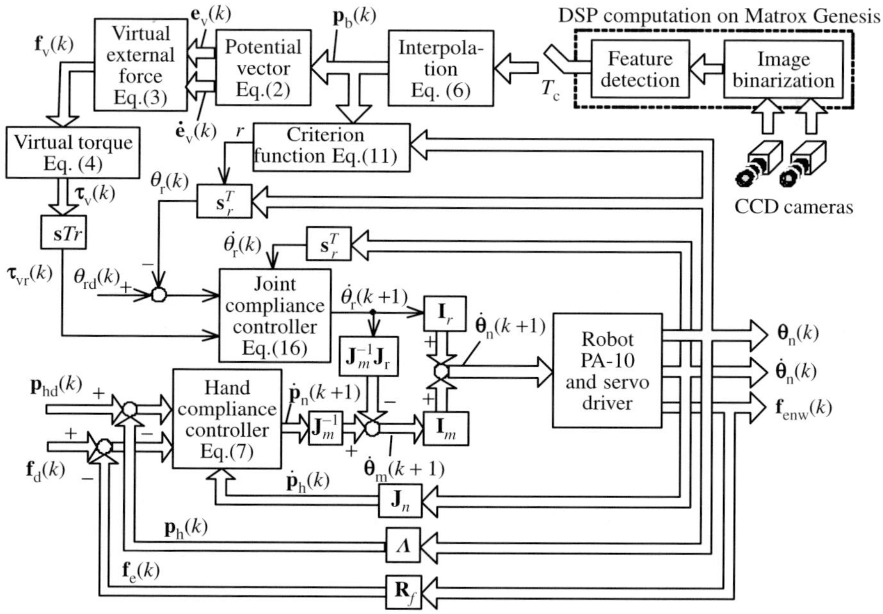

Fig. 4. A control diagram for a 7-DOF robot PA-10 ($n = 7$, $m = 6$, $r = 1$).

Since the robot used in the experiments had only one redundant joint, a perfect obstacle avoidance cannot be achieved. However, an efficient avoidance can be theoretically expected if a robot with more redundant joints is used.

4. Experiments

4.1. *Task descriptions*

Experiments were carried out to confirm the effectiveness of the proposed method. A lighting ball was made with a plastic ball in which a light bulb was inserted. It was used as the feature point attached to the human subject's body. The diameter of the ball was 0.05 m. The parameters used in the experiments are shown in Table 1. Parameters used in the potential field, the virtual torque, the joint compliance control were determined by trial and error.

As depicted in Fig. 5, seven joints of the robot are named as S1, S2, S3, E1, E2, W1 and W2 while joint S3 is the redundant joint. While the robot hand was required to perform the task of tracing a given 2D half-circle in $x-y$ plane with a specified force in the z axis based on the compliance control law given by (7), the lighting ball moved slowly into the potential field and came close to the link between joint S3 and joint E1. Collision with the lighting ball was avoided by use of the redundant joint S3.

4.2. *Experiments and discussions*

Two experiments were carried out. In the first experiment, the lighting ball did not enter the defined potential field when the robot carried out the given task with its hand. Position and

Table 1. Parameters used in the experiments

Potential field and virtual impedance parameters		
$r_v = 0.3$ m,	$\mathbf{K}_v = \text{diag}[2 \quad 2 \quad 2]$ N/m,	$\mathbf{D}_v = \text{diag}[1 \quad 1 \quad 1]$ N s/m,
Weight coefficients defined in (12)		
$w_1 = 1.0$,	$w_2 = 0.0$,	for no obstacle,
$w_1 = 0.2$,	$w_2 = 0.8$,	for obstacle detected,
Joint compliance control parameters in (16)		
$\mathbf{M}_r = \text{diag}[m_{j1} \quad m_{j1} \quad m_{j1} \quad m_{h2} \quad m_{h2} \quad m_{j2}]$,	$m_{j1} = 0.3$ kg,	$m_{j2} = 0.3$ kg m^2,
$\mathbf{D}_r = \text{diag}[d_{j1} \quad d_{j1} \quad d_{j1} \quad d_{j2} \quad d_{j2} \quad d_{j2}]$,	$d_{j1} = 8$ N s/m,	$d_{j2} = 8$ N m s/rad,
$\mathbf{K}_r = \text{diag}[0 \quad 0 \quad 0 \quad 0 \quad 0 \quad 0]$,		
Hand compliance control parameters in (7):		
$\mathbf{M}_h = \text{diag}[m_{h1} \quad m_{h1} \quad m_{h1} \quad m_{h2} \quad m_{h2} \quad m_{h2}]$,	$m_{h1} = 1.2$ kg,	$m_{h2} = 0.7$ kg m^2,
$\mathbf{D}_h = \text{diag}[d_{h1} \quad d_{h1} \quad d_{h1} \quad d_{h2} \quad d_{h2} \quad d_{h2}]$,	$d_{h1} = 310$ N s/m,	$d_{h2} = 110$ N m s/rad,
$\mathbf{K}_h = \text{diag}[K_{h1} \quad K_{h1} \quad 0 \quad K_{h2} \quad K_{h2} \quad K_{h2}]$,	$K_{h1} = 670$ N/m,	$K_{h2} = 400$ N m/rad,
$\mathbf{f}_d = [0 \quad 0 \quad f_{zd} \quad 0 \quad 0 \quad 0]^T$,	$f_{zd} = -4$ N	
Description of the desired trajectory:		
Center of the circle $[0.7 \text{ m} \quad 0 \quad 0.435 \text{ m}]^T$,	Radius of the circle 0.15 m	

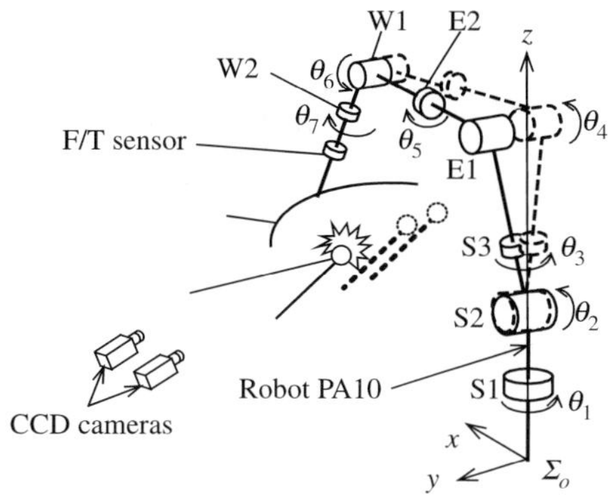

Fig. 5. Setup of the collision avoid experiment.

force results obtained in the first experiment are shown in Fig. 6. Force f_z shown in Fig. 6 was almost exactly controlled at the desired force f_{zd}, which suggests that the desired compliance control was achieved.

In the second experiment, the lighting ball entered the potential field several times while the robot carried out the given task with its hand. In this experiment, only contact force was controlled in z direction so that f_z was exactly kept at f_{zd} as shown in Fig. 7(a). The values of c_1 and c_2 are shown in Fig. 7(b), and joint angles are shown in Fig. 7(c).

The force result in Fig. 7(a) shows that the desired compliance effect was also achieved in the second experiment even if the lighting ball entered the potential field several times while the hand performed the tracing task. In Fig. 7(b), the c_2 curve falls below the boundary of the potential field at three places, which shows that the lighting ball entered the potential field three times. At the moment, we observed from video cameras that the possible collision between the link and the ball had been avoided as shown by dotted lines in Fig. 5. The joint angles θ_1, θ_3, θ_5 and θ_7 responded as soon as the lighting ball entered the virtual potential field as shown in Fig. 7(c). The above results suggest that the proposed method has enabled the robot to simultaneously trace a given curve with its hand and to avoid a collision by using its redundant joints.

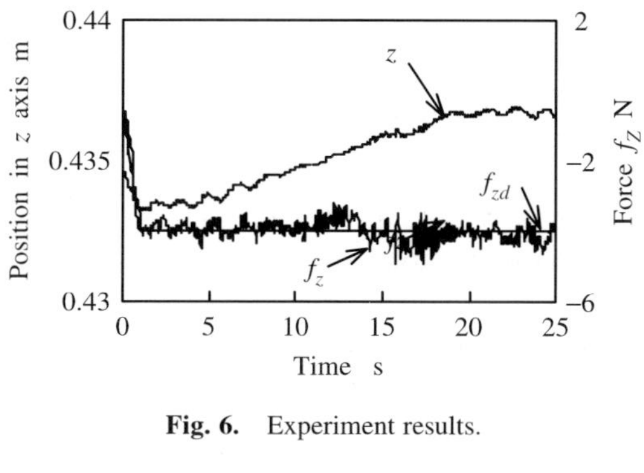

Fig. 6. Experiment results.

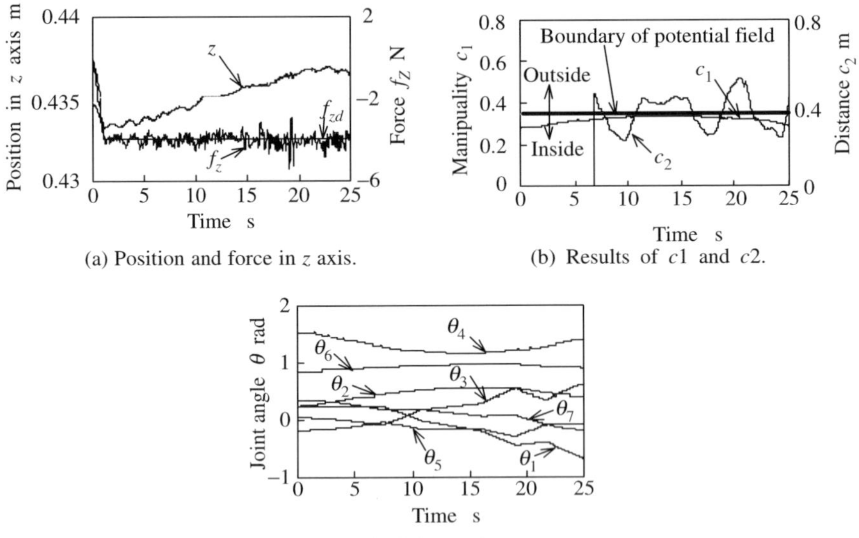

(a) Position and force in z axis.

(b) Results of $c1$ and $c2$.

(c) Joint angles

Fig. 7. Experimental results.

Camera measurement error caused by calibration and image processing delay should be considered. The calibration error was 5 mm in the experiments. If a human moves at a speed less than 1 m/s, a possible measurement position error caused only by image processing delay (without considering the proposed interpolation) will be less than $1000/60 = 16.67$ mm, while the potential cylinder's radius r_v was 300 mm. Because the total possible camera measurement error was a smaller quantity compared with r_v, the robot had a sufficient time to take an avoidance action.

Another concerned problem is that the two cameras cannot cover all the spaces around the robot. For such case, control strategies are possibly applied by using a visual system with more cameras or by introducing intelligent algorithms to estimate position of the feature point when it enters a field out of the camera's view range. Further discussions remain for future study.

5. Conclusions

(1) This chapter proposes a control method by establishing a virtual potential field around a robot to avoid collisions between a human being and the robot by the redundant joints of the robot. The greatest advantage of the proposed method is that a possible collision can be avoided automatically without requiring any action by nearby human beings.

(2) A control method is also proposed for a redundant robot to simultaneously carry out a contact task with its hand and perform collision avoidance with its redundant joints. The effectiveness of the proposed method has been demonstrated by experiments.

References

[1] V.J. Traver, A.P. del PoBil and M. Pérez-Francisco, *Making service robots human-safe*, Proc. IEEE/RSJ, Int. Conf. IROS (2000), 696–701.

[2] B. Martínez-Salvador, A.P. del PoBil and M. Pérez-Francisco, *A hierarchy of detail for fast collision detection*, Proc. IEEE/RSJ, Int. Conf. IROS (2000), 745–750.

[3] L.A. Loeff and A.H. Soni, *An algorithm for computer guidance of a manipulator in between obstacles*, Trans. ASME, J. Eng. Ind. **97** (3) (1975), 836–842.

[4] J.O. Kim and P.K. Kholsa, *Real time obstacle avoidance using harmonic potential functions*, IEEE Trans. Robotics Autom. **8** (3) (1992), 338–349.

[5] K. Glass, R. Colbaugh, D. Lim and H. Seraji, *Real-time collision avoidance for redundant manipulators*, IEEE Trans. Robotics Autom. **11** (3) (1995), 448–457.

[6] Z.Y. Guo and T.C. Hsia, *Joint trajectory generation for redundant robots in an environment with obstacles*, J. Robotics Syst. **10** (2) (1993), 199–215.

[7] L. Zlajpah and B. Nemec, *Kinematic control algorithms for on-line obstacle avoidance for redundant manipulators*, Proc. IEEE/RSJ, Int. Conf. IROS (2002), 1898–1903.

[8] H. Tani, K. Inoue, T. Arai and Y. Mae, *Shape adaptation of planner hyper-redundant manipulators to narrow and unknown environment using proximity sensors*, Proc. 11th Int. Conf. Adv. Robotics, IEEE/RAS (2003), 482–487.

[9] A.A. Maciejewski and C.A. Klein, *Obstacle avoidance for kinematically redundant manipulators in dynamically varying environments*, Int. J. Robotics Res. **4** (3) (1985), 109–117.

[10] O. Khatib, *Real-time obstacle avoidance for manipulators and mobile robots*, Int. J. Robotics Res. **5** (1) (1986), 90–98.

[11] A. MacLean and S. Cameron, *The virtual springs method: path planning and collision avoidance for redundant manipulators*, Int. J. Robotics Res. **15** (4) (1996), 300–319.

[12] M. Minami, Y. Nomura and T. Asakura, *Preview and postview control system for trajectory tracking and obstacle avoidance to unknown objects for redundant manipulators*, J. RSJ **15** (4) (1997), 573–580.

[13] S. Ma, S. Hirose and H. Yoshinada, *Efficient redundancy control of redundant manipulators*, J. RSJ **14** (5) (1996), 703–709.

[14] M. Mikawa, K. Yoshida, M. Tano and M. Matsumoto, *Vision-based redundancy control and image feature estimation of robot manipulators for obstacle avoidance*, J. RSJ **17** (4) (1999), 534–539.

[15] K. Hosoda, K. Sakamoto and M. Asada, *Trajectory generation for obstacle avoidance of uncalibrated stereo visual servoing without 3D reconstruction*, J. RSJ **15** (2) (1997), 290–295.

[16] Y. Nakamura, H. Hanafusa and T. Yoshikaswa, *Task-priority based on redundancy control of redundant robot manipulators*, Int. J. Robotics Res. **6** (2) (1987), 3–15.

[17] J. Furusho, H. Usui and A. Sano, *Manipulability of robotic manipulators considering the influence of obstacles*, J. RSJ **6** (3) (1988), 12–20.

[18] M. Uchiyama, K. Shimizu and K. Hakomori, *Performance evaluation of robotic arms using the Jacobian*, J. SICE **21** (2) (1985), 190–196.

CHAPTER 32

Management System for Cameras' Video Data in Emergency

Y. Wang, Y. Hijikata and S. Nishida

Division of Systems Science and Applied Informatics, Graduate School of Engineering Science, Osaka University, 1-3 Machikameyama, Toyonaka, Osaka 560-8531, Japan

Contents

Abstract

In case of emergency, we need to grasp the situation and make correct assessment quickly. The video data taken from the monitoring cameras are important information in emergency situations. In our research, we built a support system for identifying video data of monitoring cameras. The system collects video data from the net-cameras through the Internet and deals with them as spatio-temporal data. To search video data, we proposed an intuitive search method for users. In this method, we assume a virtual wall in the city. This method allows

SYSTEMS AND HUMAN SCIENCE – FOR SAFETY, SECURITY, AND DEPENDABILITY
Edited by Tatsuo Arai, Shigeru Yamamoto and Kazuhisa Makino

users to search for the video data, which is recorded during a period, and records a virtual wall in a certain direction. The users set the above search-key on the map, and it will be transformed to the search-key for the spatio-temporal access structure to proceed with the search. When the system shows the search result, the video data, which is easy to understand the whole scene, will be displayed first. As the horizontal direction of the screen corresponds to the virtual wall's direction in the real world, the user can narrow down the search result in the horizontal direction of the screen. We built a prototype in Java, Javaservlet and C++.

1. Introduction

Recently, the research on advanced disaster prevention systems has become increasingly important. When a large-scale disaster happens, the video data taken from monitoring cameras are one of the sources of information for us to grasp the situation and to make correct assessment. In many countries, there is a local disaster prevention center, which is established by the government to prepare for a large-scale disaster. In the case of emergency, the video data, taken from the disaster scene, are carried to the local disaster prevention center, and are displayed on some monitors. In future, with the spread of net-cameras, many private cameras will connect to the local disaster prevention center through the Internet when a disaster takes place.

It is necessary for us to check these video data to find problems in the disaster scene or to investigate the cause of the disaster. However, if there are a lot of video data, the above task will become hard for people to manage. Hence, the work to search for video data should be done by a computer. In fact, there are the following three methods to search video data: (1) image recognition, (2) using the index of video contents, and (3) using the information of cameras, while the video data are taken. Here, we define the recording information of cameras as the position, the recorded time and the recording direction. These data can be considered as a capsule of spatio-temporal data. Since these data can be obtained by using some sensors, the last method is easier than the other two types of methods.

In general, two types of query, which are range-search and nearest-neighbor search, are often used in spatio-temporal data search. However, the query should be more intuitive and simpler for the operator of the local disaster prevention center to grasp the scene situation quickly. Note that the contents of video data are dependent on not only the position/recorded time of the camera, but also the recording direction which plays an important role. One type of query comes to mind straightaway: "look at a certain place in a certain direction". For example, the operator may want to look at the building on the other side or want to look at the city from the seaside to know the situation of the disaster. The above query is practical to perform these demands. In our research, we deal with video data as spatio-temporal data. We aim to build a system that supports the above type of query for the fast search of video data of monitoring cameras, which record video of a place seen from a certain place during some period and display them in a simple way.

In this chapter, we will explain the system's outline, the method of search-key transformation and the method to display video data. Then we introduce the prototype system, which is built based on the above methods.

2. Analysis of video data

In the following subsections, we will analyze the ways to use video data in the disaster prevention center. Then we will explain what kind of data are the spatio-temporal data of the video data.

2.1. *How to use the video data*

In the disaster prevention center, the purposes of making use of video data are focused on the following two points:

- for discovering the potential problems; and
- for analyzing the problems that have occurred.

In the first case, such as the security system with monitoring cameras, the video data are monitored all the time to check whether there is something wrong or not.

In the second case, we search video data for investigating the cause/process/influence of the disaster. In addition, it is practical to grasp the situation of the scene too. We focus our research on this case and our goal aims to build a situation–grasp support system against a large-scale disaster.

2.2. *Spatio-temporal data of video data*

The first type of camera we discuss here is the fixed camera. The feature of a fixed camera is that the camera's position is located, which can be spotted in some buildings, stations and roads. Also there is a different type of a camera, a so-called moving camera. While the moving camera records video data, it changes its position. As a typical example, we can think of the type of camera which is set in front of emergency vehicles such as police cars.

The recording information of cameras plays an important role to describe the spatio-temporal data of video data, because the contents of the video data are difficult model to the real world. Indeed, the recorded contents of the video data are dependent on the status information of the camera (e.g., position). We know, when a large-scale disaster occurs, the video data that we get will have a close relation to the geographical information. Hence for grasping the whole or local situation of the scene, the spatial query is an important key for us to search video data. For instance, if a fire happens, we can check the video data taken by the cameras set in the surrounding area of the location to get knowledge about the situation (e.g., the scale, the expanse). In addition, since the situation changes with the temporal attributes, checking the video data in an interval time from the problem-occurred time is a choice to grasp how the situation changed.

We can record a camera's status information by using sensors, which are:

- Temporal information: the video data's recorded time.
- Spatial information: the camera's position.
- The other information: the camera's direction and zoom rate.

Here, let us image the scene of a camera's recording video data. At time t_0, the camera lies initially at position (x_0, y_0). During the period (t_0, t_1), it takes video data, and finally it lies at (x_1, y_1). Hence it can model the spatio-temporal data of the video data during (t_0, t_1) by a 3D (2D spatial space and 1D temporal space) segment $(x_0, y_0, t_0) - (x_1, y_1, t_1)$.

In our research, we use a spatio-temporal data structure to manage the spatio-temporal data of video data to manage the video data indirectly.

As other attributes of video data, there are the camera zoom rate, the resolution degree and so on. We consider the camera position, the recording time and the direction are the

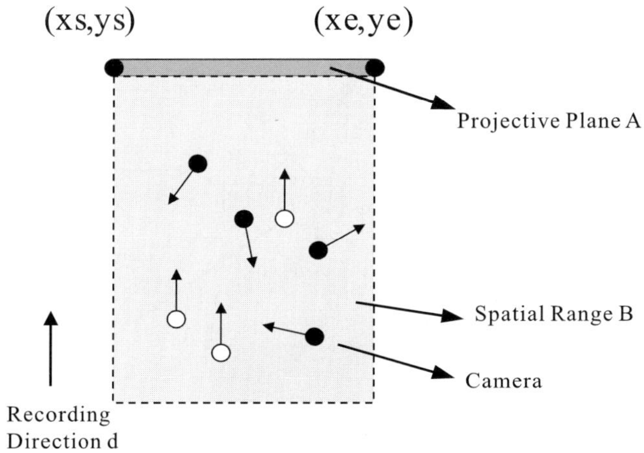

Fig. 1. Operator's spatial search-key.

most important factors to identify the target of recording. The other attributes are not so important as the above attributes and we do not use other attributes in our methods and system.

3. Problem setting and approach

Our research defines the operator's search-key as "search for the video data, which is recorded during a period, and records a certain plane in a certain direction". Considering the spatial query of the above search-key, it contains a certain plane and a certain direction (Fig. 1).

In Fig. 1, the projective plane *A* and the projective direction *d* are used to represent "a certain plane" and "a certain direction". The coordinates, (x_s, y_s) and (x_e, y_e), give the location and the length of the projective plane. And in the range *B*, cameras can record video data about the projective plane *A* in the projective direction *d*. To perform the above search-key, it equals the searching for the video data of the cameras with ○ mark in the range *B*. However, the range *B* is not clear for performing the general spatial range search.

The next problem is how to display the video data. When a large-scale disaster happens, we will get a lot of video data in a short time. According to the user's search request, sometimes there are too much video data in the search result. In that case, if those video data are outputted at a time, it is hard for the operator to understand. Hence, it is necessary to show them in a simple way for understanding.

According to the above problems, our research approaches are as follows:

(1) Not only the spatio-temporal information of the camera, but also the camera's direction is used for indexing video data.
(2) The search-key of the operator will be transformed to the search-key for the data structure that manages the video data.

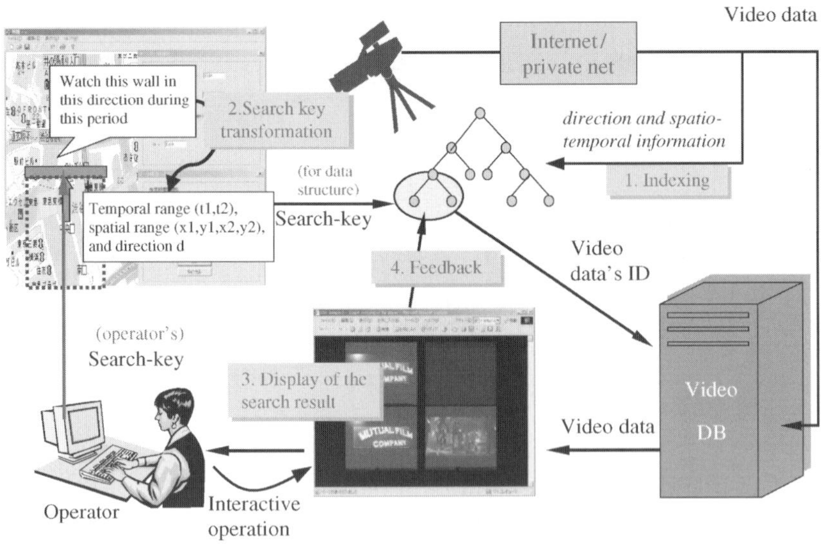

Fig. 2. Outline of the system.

(3) To show the result, at first the system will display the video data taken farther from the projective plane, which makes it easy to grasp the whole scene, and then show the closer video data interactively according to the user's operation.
(4) The search-key transformation (described in (2)) will also be phased in for realizing the function described in (3). (Feedback of the user's operation to the search-key transformation.)

The outline of the system is shown in Fig. 2. When a large-scale disaster happens, the video data and the information from cameras will be sent to the local disaster prevention center through the Internet, which are recorded by many net-cameras. These video data will be stored in the video database, and indexed by the direction and the spatio-temporal information of the camera. These indexes of video data will be managed by a spatio-temporal data structure. For searching the video data, the operator gives the operator's search-key on the map window, which is a part of GUI of the system to display map. Then the operator's search-key will be transformed to a spatio-temporal search-key, which is the search-key of the data structure. Based on the search results, the video data are requested from the database, and displayed in the view-screen, which is also a part of GUI of the system. The search query can be changed with the operator's interactive operation on the view-screen.

4. Data structure

4.1. *Design concept*

In the research, we developed a data structure for managing video data by considering the spatial and temporal attributes of cameras. The components of the idea are: (1) to manage video files' ID by using the spatio-temporal data structure; (2) to prepare two types of data structure to manage the video data of fixed cameras and moving cameras; and (3) to sample the recording direction of camera into eight directions, and to construct spatio-temporal structures in every direction.

As mentioned in the above section, the video data can be indexed by the spatio-temporal data that record time, camera's position and camera's recording direction. Therefore, we can use a spatio-temporal data structure, which serves the spatio-temporal query of the type "in which objects were located within a specific area during a period", to manage the video data's ID. According to the spatio-temporal search, the video files' ID will be outputted as the search result.

Generally, regarding the spatio-temporal data management, it can treat the fixed object as a special type of moving object. In other words, the spatio-temporal data structure for moving objects can also manage the fixed objects. However, compared to the spatio-temporal data structure for fixed objects, the spatio-temporal data structure for moving objects costs more memory and query processing. Despite the fact that the number of fixed cameras is larger than the moving cameras, it is not efficient to manage all of them by using the spatio-temporal data structure for moving objects. Hence, in our research, we design two types of data structure for the fixed cameras and moving cameras, respectively.

Furthermore, in the operator's search-key, it uses the recording direction of the cameras. For fast search for video data, the information of recording direction of cameras should be reflected in the data structure.

4.2. *Details of data structure*

Figure 3 outlines the data structure. Given the search-key for data structure, the request will be performed through the data structures for fixed cameras at first. The data structure for the fixed cameras consisted of the basic spatio-temporal data structures, which are

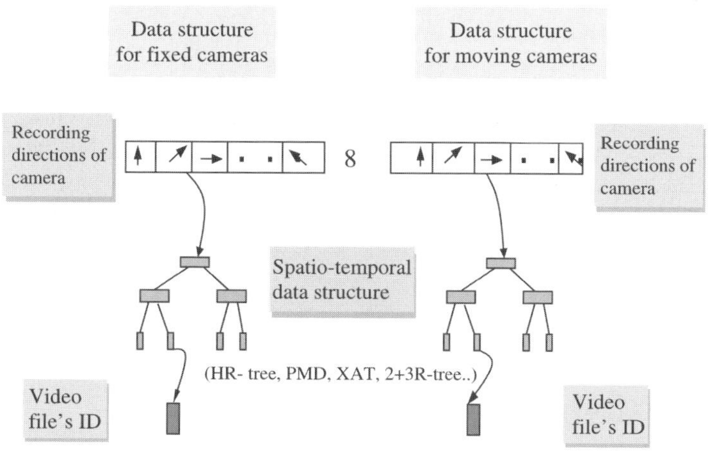

Fig. 3. Outline of the structure.

constructed based on the recording direction of the camera. According to the direction d, the data structure will be selected, and then the spatio-temporal range search is done. The same process is also done through the data structures for moving cameras as well.

To handle spatio-temporal data, many methods have been proposed, such as RT-Tree [1], HR-tree [2], 3D R-Tree [3] and so on. The former researches evaluated the performance of the above spatio-temporal data structures in query processing and memory cost. To our knowledge, there is no absolute best one. Our research proposed the framework of the data structure for managing video data by using the existing basic spatio-temporal data structure.

5. Search-key transformation and display

In this section, first we will explain the method of search-key transformation between the operator's search-key and the data structure search-key. Then we will describe the method for displaying the video data.

5.1. *Method of search-key transformation*

Recall that the operator's search-key defined in our research is "temporal search range, projective plane and projective direction". Before the system performs the search through the spatio-temporal data structure, the operator's search-key will be transformed to the temporal search range, the spatial search range and the camera's direction index. Figure 4(a-1) and (a-2) shows the transformed spatial search ranges of the operator's search-key. This method gets the approximate solutions by arranging spatial search range

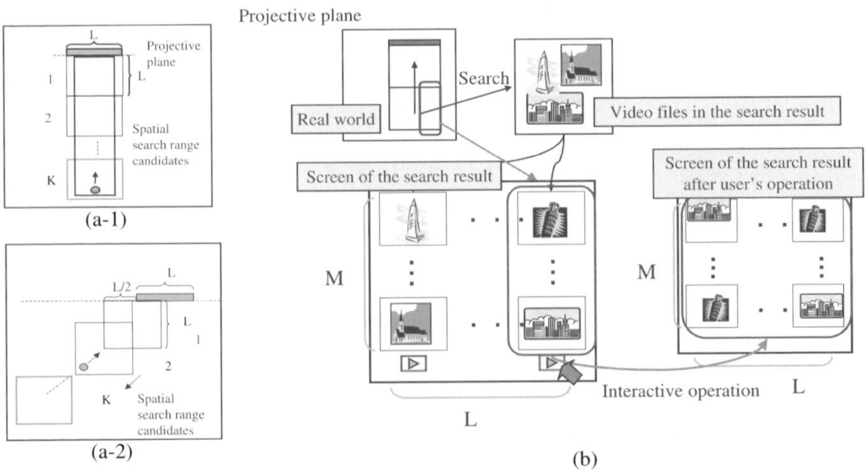

Fig. 4. Search-key transformation and view-screen of the system.

forward the projective plane. Concretely, the spatial search range is a square, set with length L that equals to the projective plane.

When the projective direction faces the projective plane in the vertical direction, the rectangle area, completed by several squares line-up, represents a set of spatial search range candidates to the data structure. And Fig. 4(a-2) outlines the case that the projective plane is seen from the direction of an oblique 45°.

The number of the transformed spatial search ranges is determined by the operator. And one of these ranges will be selected to perform the spatio-temporal range search. According to the interactive operation of the operator (see Section 5.2), the spatial search range will be changed to search the other video data.

5.2. *Method to display video data*

To understand the situation, the operator needs to check lots of video data, which are the results of spatio-temporal search. Hence, it is important for the system to display a limited number of video files to the operator at a time, and provide a function to narrow down the area to display video data according to the operator's request. In our research, the system shows the search result by using the method shown in Fig. 4(b).

In the method, the view-screen has $M * L$ areas to display video data. In each area, a video-data player is embedded for displaying video data. Because of the limitation of the view-screen's size, the number of divisions of the view-screen should also be limited. To reduce the number of video data to display, we notice the following facts:

- if two cameras record video data in the same direction and they are close to each other, the contents of the video data will be similar; and
- if two cameras record video data in the same direction and at the same zoom rate, it is easier to get a rough image for the whole scene from the video data, which is recorded by the camera that lies farther from the projective plane in the vertical direction.

In the system, the areas in the side direction in the view-screen are equivalent to the areas in the actual space. Before showing the search results to the operator, all the video data will be sorted by the cameras' coordinate at first. Then according to the number L, determined by the operator, video data are grouped into L groups. Instead of showing all the video data to the operator, it will select M video data in the order of the vertical direction from each group.

Furthermore, on the view-screen, the system provides the following functions.

(1) To request for the other video data, which is not shown in the current view-screen.
(2) To request for nearer (farther) cameras' video data. It is to reset search-key for data structure by selecting nearer (farther) spatial search range from the spatial search range candidates and then to perform the new query.
(3) To narrow down video data in the horizontal direction of the projective plane.

In Fig. 4(b), the operator performs the function (3) to request the other video data, which are taken from the cameras that existed in the right-hand side of the spatial search area. In this way, the operator can get the rough image of the situation from some representative video data.

6. Prototype implementations

The prototype of the system was built. The implementations consisted of three modules: map viewer, search engine and request manager. The map viewer is the GUI part of the system. It works on the client computer. The search engine and the request manager are implemented as server programs.

6.1. *Map viewer*

This module was written by Visual C++6.0. It provides the functions to select the map and set the search-key. The operator can draw the projective plane and the projective direction on the map directly to search video data. The spatial data of the given projective plane and the projective direction are set to correspond to the real world (Fig. 5).

The operator's search-key will then be transmitted to the server side to call the search engine to perform the query.

6.2. *Search engine*

Because 3D R-tree can provide uniform performance for spatial search and temporal search, it is the most conventional method in the proposed spatio-temporal data management. Hence, we use 3D R-tree to construct the data structure to manage the spatio-temporal data of the video data. The source is written by C++. When the spatio-temporal range search is processed, the search result, including the video data ID, will be saved as a file, and sent to the web application server.

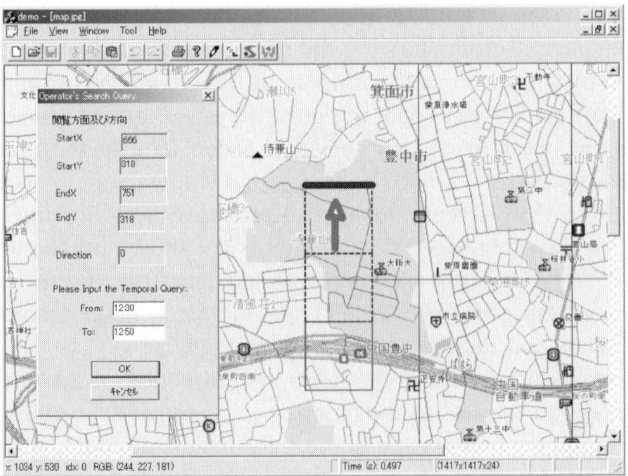

Fig. 5. Map viewer.

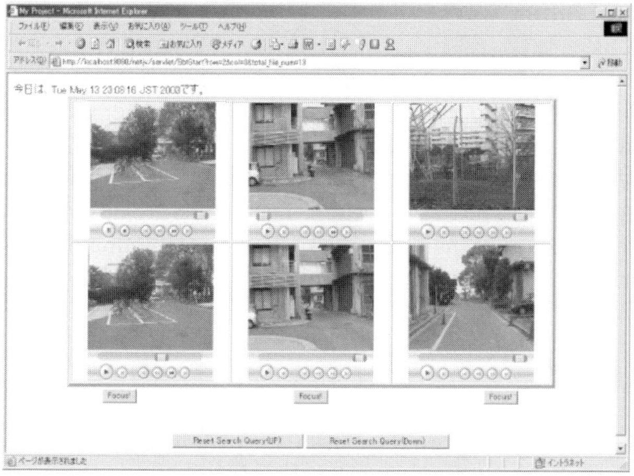

Fig. 6. Web page for displaying video data.

6.3. *Request manager*

The request manager is implemented by Javaservlet and JSP. When the request comes from the client, it governs the search engine to perform the query, then generates a web page for displaying video data according to the search result. The web page is shown in Fig. 6. This page embeds the Microsoft Media Player plug-in 7.0, so it can support many decode types of video data. We use Tomcat4.1 as our web server. And all the video files are stored in the Windows Media Server. The generated web page provides the functions that are described in Section 5.2.

7. Discussion

In our research, we proposed a new type of spatial query for video data, with a concept of using "virtual wall" and "projective direction", to grasp the disaster situation. Also we know one general way to query video data is to use a spatial range query; the user can define the search range directly to find the video data, which are recorded by the cameras in the range. But we can notice the fact that the user uses this type of query with some questions unconsciously, where the set cameras are and how the search area is set can help him to get good solutions. Sometimes it may be a burden to the user. Perhaps the user focuses his interest to a spatial area and he wants to get a different view from a different direction. This query type works well when the target area is clear and thin; if it is large enough, it can be considered to regard this query type as our proposed one. Recall the above-mentioned approaches of our research; our method shows the user the video data, which can grasp the whole scene more easily, and allow the user narrow down the solutions. We think, by this means, the user can get some hints first from the query of our method, then the other types of query will be carried out according to his demand.

8. Conclusions and future works

In this chapter, we proposed a data management system for monitoring cameras in an emergency. The basic idea is to treat the video data as spatio-temporal data and by using a general spatio-temporal data structures to manage them indirectly. In this chapter, we explained the method of search-key transformation and the method to display video data. We also built a simple prototype of the system. The details are described, and the next steps of our research are to construct the video data DB for completing the whole system and to do the computer simulation to evaluate the system.

Acknowledgments

This research was partly supported by the Japan Society for the Promotion of Science under Grand-in-Aid for Scientific Research (No. 13GS0018).

References

[1] X. Xu, J. Han and W. Lu, *RT-tree: an improves R-tree index structure for spatio-temporal databases*, Proceedings of the Fourth International Symposium on Spatial Data Handling, (1990), 1040–1049.

[2] M.A. Nascimento, J.R.O. Silva and Y. Theodoridis, *Access Structures for Moving Points*, Technical Report 33, Time Center, (1998).

[3] Y. Theodoridis, M. Vazirgiannis and T. Sellis, *Spatio-temporal indexing for large multimedia applications*, Proceedings of the Third IEEE Conference on Multimedia Computing and Systems, (1996), 441–448.

PART IX

Visual Surveillance and Monitoring

CHAPTER 33

Visual Object Tracking Based on a Multi-Viewpoint 3D Gradient Method

Takayuki Moritani, Shinsaku Hiura and Kosuke Sato

Graduate School of Engineering Science, Osaka University, 1-3 Machikaneyama, Toyonaka, Osaka 560-8531, Japan

Contents

Abstract

A method for 3D motion tracking without feature extraction is necessary for monitoring human action in a normal civil-life scene. To create a fast and robust object tracking method, we propose a model-based method using intensity images taken with a multiple viewpoint camera connected to a PC cluster system. First, the whole 3D shape and reflectance model of the object are prepared using several rangefinders. Each rangefinder is constructed with a camera, projector and PC, and all PCs are connected via network to each other. For tracking the object, several CG images with varied object pose and position are generated in each PC using the object model, and then compared to the input intensity image in parallel. The result of the comparison is transferred to a master PC, and the pose and position of the object are estimated by minimizing the residual of the CG and input images. We made a special CG generator, which is a precise simulator of the real camera to generate a CG image identical to the input image. We confirmed the ability of our method and achieved a 3DOF real-time object tracking system at the rate of 4.5 frames/s, and 6DOF tracking using four cameras at 5 frames/s.

SYSTEMS AND HUMAN SCIENCE – FOR SAFETY, SECURITY, AND DEPENDABILITY
Edited by Tatsuo Arai, Shigeru Yamamoto and Kazuhisa Makino

1. Introduction

Object motion tracking is a problem involving estimating the position and orientation of an object using a temporal sequence of images. In particular, not only planar motion estimation in a 2D image but also spatial 3D motion estimation is a very important problem. Both range and intensity images are used in existing methods of motion analysis. Range image is very efficient for 3D scene analysis [1], but real-time range sensors are not popular. Intensity image sensors are much more popular than rangefinders and many studies have been performed. However, this does not provide explicit information on depth, therefore, a predetermined assumption about the object or simultaneous estimation of the object shape is necessary for tracking the motion of the object. In particular, for objects with curved surfaces it is much more difficult to estimate the motion of the object than for a polyhedral object, because the extraction of the feature point is not robust. Therefore, we aim to create an object tracking method under the following conditions:

- Tracking of a rigid object in motion in 3D space
- Real-time tracking using intensity images
- Robustness against the shape of the object

In general, image analysis methods can be classified as bottom-up or top-down strategies. We selected the top-down method because information on the object shape can be employed easily and explicitly. First, CG images with varied object pose and position are generated. Then, the input image is compared with the generated CG images and the object motion is calculated. Such a method needs to measure the 3D object shape off-line, but the range information is not necessary in the tracking phase.

In contrast to the range images, the motion towards the optical axis cannot be measured robustly using intensity images. To compensate for this weakness of the intensity image, we used a multi-viewpoint camera system with a PC cluster system. In such a system, the overhead network transfer is a great nuisance. To avoid this problem, calculations of image comparison are done in each PC, and the minimized data are transferred and merged to estimate the object's motion. This idea is based on a distributed least square method.

2. Principle of estimating object motion

2.1. *Gradient method*

The image of a moving object changes with the pose and position of the object. If we can assume that the radiance of the object surface at each point is constant, the intensity value of each image is constant at the corresponding point. Therefore, the well-known gradient constraint equation proposed by Horn [2] is described as

$$I(x, y, t) = I(x + \delta x, y + \delta y, t + \delta t). \tag{1}$$

To solve this equation for determining optical flow, the Taylor expansion gives

$$\frac{\partial I}{\partial x}\frac{\delta x}{\delta t} + \frac{\partial I}{\partial y}\frac{\delta y}{\delta t} + \frac{\partial I}{\partial t} \simeq 0. \tag{2}$$

This equation only gives us a constraint between optical flow (δx, δy) and the intensity change $\partial I/\partial t$, and it is obvious that this equation cannot be solved without any additional constraint. Many studies are performed for estimating optical flow by giving some constraints on an image plane, but it is not essential to solve the problem because such constraints are only for convenience and are not related to the object motion itself. Therefore, we propose a direct estimation method of object motion based on the gradient method.

In contrast to (1), we can denote the image by the parameter of the object pose and position as

$$I = I(p_1, \ldots, p_n). \tag{3}$$

Here n is degrees of freedom of the object's motion. Similar to (2), we can also expand (3) as

$$\frac{\mathrm{d}I}{\mathrm{d}t} \simeq \sum_{i=1}^{n} \frac{\partial I}{\partial p_i} \frac{\mathrm{d}p_i}{\mathrm{d}t}. \tag{4}$$

At first sight, (4) appears more difficult to solve than (2) because it has many unknown parameters. However, this constraint is common to the whole area on the image of the object, because the motion parameter p_i is common to all the pixels of the object image if the object is a rigid body. Theoretically, if the number of pixels on the image of the object exceeds the degrees of freedom n, this equation can be solved using the least squares method. In fact, the number of pixels is much larger than the DOF, therefore, the motion can be directly estimated using (4).

To solve (4), we must prepare the derivative of the image with respect to the motion parameter $\partial I/\partial p_i$. This derivative cannot be calculated except on the image plane because the shape of the object (depth of the scene) affects the relationships between optical flow and the motion of the object. Therefore, we use a finite difference to calculate it as

$$\frac{\partial I}{\partial p_i} \simeq \frac{I(\ldots, p_i + \frac{1}{2}\delta, \ldots) - I(\ldots, p_i - \frac{1}{2}\delta, \ldots)}{\delta}. \tag{5}$$

If we have a precise CG model of the object and environment, we can generate images of any pose by rendering the object using it. The way to prepare the model is described in Section 3.2.

In this chapter, we describe a method of tracking the motion of a rigid object. Therefore, the number of parameters is 6, and (5) can be denoted as

$$\begin{aligned} I_{\mathrm{input}} - I_0 \simeq{} & \frac{I_{+X_\mathrm{t}} - I_{-X_\mathrm{t}}}{\delta} \Delta X_\mathrm{t} + \frac{I_{+Y_\mathrm{t}} - I_{-Y_\mathrm{t}}}{\delta} \Delta Y_\mathrm{t} + \frac{I_{+Z_\mathrm{t}} - I_{-Z_\mathrm{t}}}{\delta} \Delta Z_\mathrm{t} \\ & + \frac{I_{+X_\mathrm{r}} - I_{-X_\mathrm{r}}}{\delta} \Delta X_\mathrm{r} + \frac{I_{+Y_\mathrm{r}} - I_{-Y_\mathrm{r}}}{\delta} \Delta Y_\mathrm{r} + \frac{I_{+Z_\mathrm{r}} - I_{-Z_\mathrm{r}}}{\delta} \Delta Z_\mathrm{r}. \end{aligned} \tag{6}$$

where I_{+X_t} denotes the vector of a CG image with a slight shift of the object position along the X axis, and I_{+X_r} is rotation, respectively. I_0 is a CG image of the original position of the object and I_{input} is the input image from the camera. Therefore, $\Delta X_t, \ldots, \Delta Z_r$ can be calculated as the motion from the original position of the CG image to the real object.

To solve (6), we can use the least squares method as follows. First, each variable is denoted in matrix form as

$$D = I_{\text{input}} - I_0 \tag{7}$$

$$G = \left[\frac{I_{+X_t} - I_{-X_t}}{\delta}, \ldots, \frac{I_{+Z_r} - I_{-Z_r}}{\delta} \right] \tag{8}$$

$$E = [\Delta X_t, \Delta Y_t, \Delta Z_t, \Delta X_r, \Delta Y_r, \Delta Z_r]^{\mathrm{T}} \tag{9}$$

and then we can rewrite (6) as

$$D \simeq GE. \tag{10}$$

Since the number of the row of matrix G is the same as the number of pixels in the region of the object and it is much larger than the degrees of freedom of the object's motion, we can therefore solve this equation using the least squares method as

$$E = (G^{\mathrm{T}}G)^{-1}G^{\mathrm{T}}D. \tag{11}$$

The principle of estimating object motion is illustrated in Fig. 1.

2.2. *Extension for multiple camera system*

Theoretically, the full rigid motion of the object can be estimated using a single camera as described in Section 2.1. However, it is not so stable when the number of motion parameters increases because some differing movements look similar to the camera. Therefore we use multiple cameras to estimate the full motion of the object.

Here we assume a system with m cameras in this section. Each image from the camera is captured by a PC which is connected *via* LAN with every other. To estimate the object pose

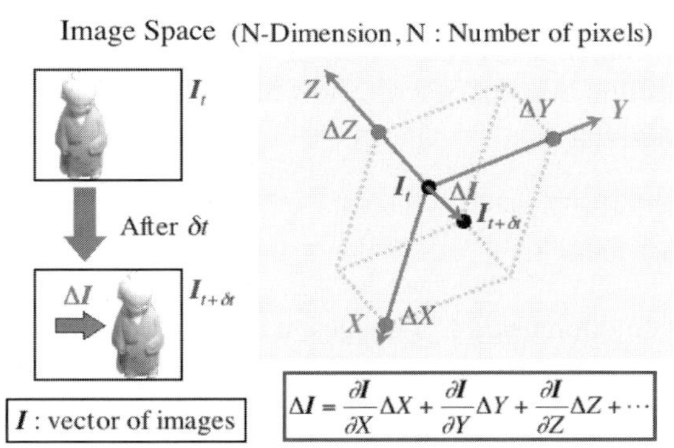

Fig. 1. Relation in image space.

and position, the sum of the least square error calculated from all images must be minimized. In other words, the images taken by m cameras are simply connected to each other, as

$$\begin{bmatrix} D_1 \\ \vdots \\ D_m \end{bmatrix} \simeq \begin{bmatrix} G_1 \\ \vdots \\ G_m \end{bmatrix} E. \tag{12}$$

Here D_1 is the result of subtraction between images from camera No.1 and the corresponding CG image at the original motion parameter; D_2 etc. are calculated accordingly.

From a practical point of view, the calculation cost to solve (12) is not small because the number of rows in each matrix is much larger than (10). The communication cost between PCs is also large, because each CG image generated must be transferred to the master PC. Therefore, we expand the equation of least squares method as

$$E = \left(\begin{bmatrix} G_1 \\ \vdots \\ G_m \end{bmatrix}^{\mathrm{T}} \begin{bmatrix} G_1 \\ \vdots \\ G_m \end{bmatrix} \right)^{-1} \begin{bmatrix} G_1 \\ \vdots \\ G_m \end{bmatrix}^{\mathrm{T}} \begin{bmatrix} D_1 \\ \vdots \\ D_m \end{bmatrix} = \left(\sum_{i=1}^{m} G_i^{\mathrm{T}} G_i \right)^{-1} \sum_{i=1}^{m} G_i^{\mathrm{T}} D_i \tag{13}$$

Here the 6×6 matrix $G_i^{\mathrm{T}} G_i$ and 6×1 vector $G_i^{\mathrm{T}} D_i$ is calculated on each PC and the results are small enough to transfer *via* the usual LAN. The master PC only calculates the sum and inversion of the small matrices.

3. Tracking system

The proposed method utilizes a CG model which contains information on the shape and reflectance of the object. This CG model must be prepared by 3D measurement of the object prior to motion tracking. In the motion-tracking phase, several CG images with varied object poses and positions are generated. Then, the pose and position parameters are converged to the real object using minimization of the residual between CG images and input image. In this section, we will describe how to prepare the model of the object and the rendering phase of tracking.

3.1. *3D shape measurement*

For calculating object motion using CG images, it is necessary to measure the shape of the object precisely. We use an active rangefinder system, which consists of a camera and a projector. It is based on a Glay-coded pattern light projection method [3], and requires a full calibration of the camera and projector with a fixed world coordinate (X,Y,Z) defined by a reference object. (x_c, y_c) and (x_p, y_p) denote coordinates on an image from a camera and a projector respectively, and the relationships of these coordinates to a world coordinate are represented as

$$h_c \begin{bmatrix} x_c \\ y_c \\ 1 \end{bmatrix} = C \begin{bmatrix} X \\ Y \\ Z \\ 1 \end{bmatrix}, \quad h_p \begin{bmatrix} x_p \\ y_p \\ 1 \end{bmatrix} = P \begin{bmatrix} X \\ Y \\ Z \\ 1 \end{bmatrix} \tag{14}$$

where the 3×4 matrices C and P are called system parameters.

3.2. *Generating aligned CG images*

To properly calculate object motion using the method described in Section 2.1, the CG images generated must satisfy these conditions:

(1) CG images with any pose and position can be generated.

(2) A CG image with the same pose and position as the real object must coincide with the real image.

In particular, condition 2 has two factors, geometric and photometric. The geometric factor means that each point on the object must be projected on the same coordinate on the input image and the generated CG image, and the photometric factor means that the brightness of these two points must coincide each other. To satisfy these conditions, we use the system parameters, described in Section 3.1. First, we calibrate the camera and projector geometrically and acquire the system parameters. Then the 3D shape of the object is measured using a rangefinder system. An intensity image is also captured to acquire textural data. In the phase of generating a CG image, the system parameters are used to calculate the projection from the 3D coordinates to the 2D image coordinates to satisfy the geometric condition. The photometric condition is also satisfied using the textural mapping.

Figure 2 shows the comparison of an input image and a CG image generated with the same pose and position to the real object. Separation of the object region from the background is done using the intensity of the texture image, therefore, the generated CG image lacks some concave or dark regions. When calculating motion using several CG images, only valid pixels for all generated CG images are used. In general, the number of pixels is much larger than six degrees of freedom and (13) can be solved stably.

3.3. *Real-time tracking and convergence*

The principle of estimating the object pose and position is based on an assumption of the validity of linear approximation. However, the image changes caused by object motion are nonlinear, and the estimation contains some error. Therefore, we use a real-time iterative method to converge the pose and position to the real-object (Fig. 3). In the tracking phase, the input image is taken continuously, and several CG images are generated based on an estimated object pose and position. The input image is compared to the generated CG

Fig. 2. Comparison of input image and generated CG image.

images and the new object pose and position are calculated as described above. Then new CG images are generated using new parameters. If the object is stationary, the pose and position parameters will converge to the real parameter.

4. Experiments

For our experiment, we used a Sony EVI-G20 camera, but we did not use the pan-tilt-zoom feature of this camera. The projector we used was an EPSON ELP-7700, which has a brightness of 3000 [ANSI lm] and XGA resolution. The host processor is a PC with dual Pentium-III 500 MHz processors and a GeForce2 graphics card. The performance of the graphics card is very important for generating CG images fast enough. These were

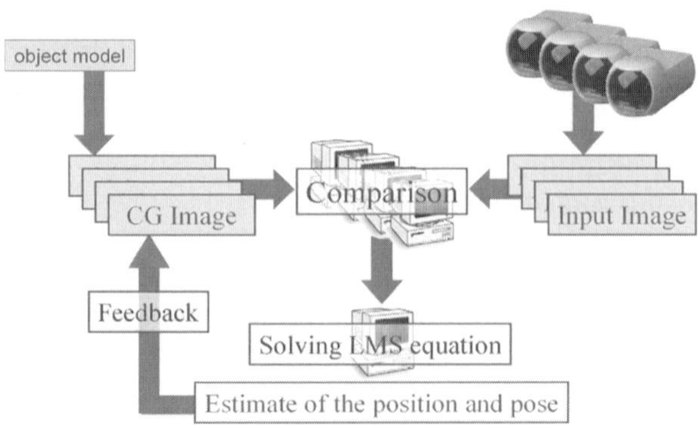

Fig. 3. Flow of object tracking.

controlled by Linux and OpenGL. For our experiment, we limited object motion in a plane (X, Y), therefore only the 2-DOF translation (X and Y axis) and 1-DOF rotation (around Z axis) were estimated.

Figure 4 shows the sequence of the input images and the overlaid wire-frame CG which displays the estimated motion. The object is moved left and rotated counterclockwise. The cycle time of the tracking process is about 220 ms (4.5 frames/s). The proposed method is very robust against the background of the image because the subtraction between input image and generated CG images are calculated only on valid pixels of the CG image.

Next, we constructed the multi-viewpoint measurement and tracking system shown in Fig. 5. This system consists of four sets of a camera (Sony EVI-G20), projector (EPSON ELP-703) and PC (dual Pentium-III 1.26 GHz, GeForce4MX). All PCs are connected *via* 100Base-T Ethernet to each other. As described in Section 2.2, each PC captures an image and generates CG images independently. From these data, the PC calculates two matrices of (13) then transfers the matrices to the master PC. The master PC calculates the motion of the object and sends the pose and position of the object to all the client PCs for generating CG images with proper pose and position for the next step. The result of the tracking is shown in Fig. 6. We confirmed that the robustness of tracking is much improved without any degradation of tracking speed.

Figure 7 shows the result of precision evaluation of tracking translation. We placed the object on a slide stage and recorded the estimated position of the object when the

(a) (b) (c) (d)

Fig. 4. Tracking result (single camera, 3DOF).

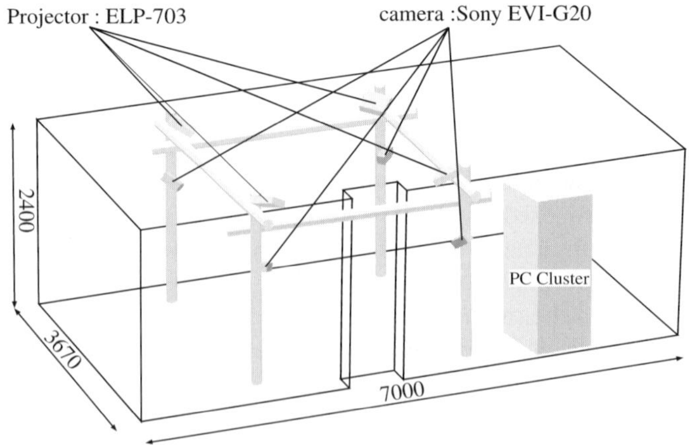

Fig. 5. Object measurement and tracking system.

Fig. 6. Tracking result (four cameras, 6DOF).

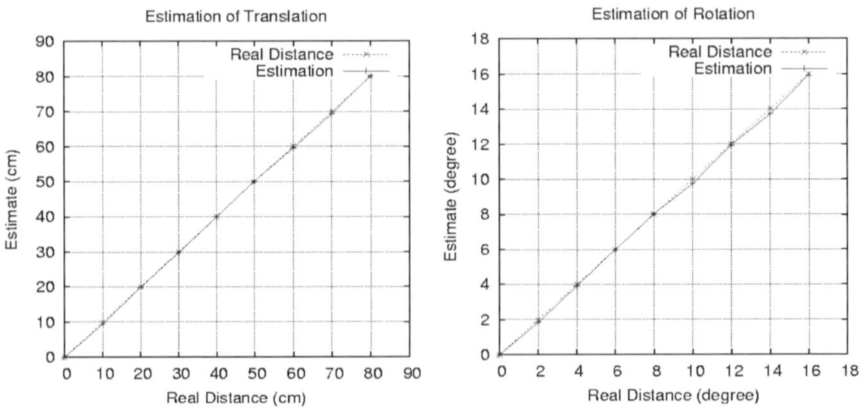

Fig. 7. Evaluation of precision of rotation and translation.

optimization is converged. Figure 7 also shows the result of tracking rotation. Both results show this method is very precise when considering the size of the object and the distance between the camera and the object.

5. Conclusions

We propose a simple principle of motion estimation based on a model-based method. Our method can be understood as a multi-factorial Newton optimization of a raw image, but the essentials of the system are the precision of the CG generator as a simulator of the scene, and the camera. We used a projector and a camera to build a rangefinder, and calibrated them to achieve alignment of the CG image to the input image.

We then developed a system with four cameras and four projectors to measure the whole shape of the object, and confirmed that the robustness is much improved without degradation of tracking speed. Now we are making a system for more robust 6-DOF real-time tracking of objects using multiple cameras and a high-speed network.

Acknowledgments

This research was supported by the Japan Society for the Promotion of Science under Grant-in-Aid for Creative Scientific Research (Project No. 13GS0018).

References

[1] S. Hiura, A. Yamaguchi, K. Sato and S. Inokuchi, *Real-time tracking of free-form objects by range and intensity image fusion*, Syst. Comput. Jpn **29** (8) (1998), 19–27.

[2] B.K.P. Horn and B.G. Schunck, *Determining optical flow*, Artif. Intell. **17** (1981), 185–203.

[3] K. Sato and S. Inokuchi, *Range-image system utilizing nematic liquid crystal mask*, Proceedings of 1st ICCV (1987), 657–661.

Further Reading

M. Yamamoto and K. Koshikawa, *Human motion analysis based on a robot arm model*, Proceedings of CVPR'91 (1991), 664–665.

D. Hogg, *Model-based vision: a program to see a walking person*, Image Vis. Comput. **1** (1) (1983), 5–20.

M. Armstrong and A. Zisserman, *Robust object tracking*, Proceedings of ACCV95, Vol. 1 (1995), 58–62.

L. Dreschler and H.H. Nagel, *Volumetric model and 3D trajectory of a moving car derived from monocular TV-frame sequences of a street scene*, Proceedings of the International Joint Conference on Artificial Intelligence (1981), 692–697.

T. Drummond and R. Cipolla, *Real-time visual tracking of complex structures*, IEEE Trans. on PAMI **24** (7) (2002), 932–946.

E. Marchand, P. Bouthemy, F. Chaumette and V. Moreau, *Robust Real-Time Visual Tracking Using a 2D–3D Model-Based Approach*, IEEE International Conference on Computer Vision ICCV99, Vol. 1, (1999), 262–268.

Y. Sumi, Y. Ishiyama and F. Tomita, *Hyper frame vision: a real-time vision system for 6-DOF object localization*, Proceedings of ICPR02, III (2002), 577–580.

CHAPTER 34

Invariant Image Information and Face Detection in Unrestricted Posture

Jun'ichi Yamaguchi and Hiroshi Seike

Faculty of Engineering, Kagawa University, 2217-20, Hayashi-cho, Takamatsu 761-0396, Japan

Contents

Abstract

The authors propose a method for recognition of a three-dimensional posed face, using invariant image information which is obtained by Fourier transform and polar transform of the edge data of the face. It has been possible to track the face of the person during unrestricted behavior in a general environment. The method is explained and the experimental result is demonstrated.

SYSTEMS AND HUMAN SCIENCE – FOR SAFETY, SECURITY, AND DEPENDABILITY
Edited by Tatsuo Arai, Shigeru Yamamoto and Kazuhisa Makino

1. Introduction

Studies on human measurement or human recognition have been increasing in the fields of welfare, medical care and security. In face recognition, recent topics of study are face verification, face expression, gesture, etc. and some of these are put to practical use. These studies produced new methods for face detection, extraction of facial parts, handling of facial features, etc. [1–5]. The high applicability of these methods makes possible the development of new applications using facial images. On the other hand, it is important to realize a high convenience of the utilization of the image. Then it is needed to eliminate a burden of the person. In conventional study, full-face image or near full-face image is used in general. Furthermore, the face image is generally of a fixed size in many cases. In particular, eyes, nose and mouth are usually located from the upper part to the lower part of the input image. Recently, some studies have shown a way of recognizing a rotating face in the image [6–8]; however, they are unable to handle a three-dimensional posed face (e.g., an inverted or oblique face) at any place in the field of vision. The authors consider that a method which can detect the facial position of a person in various postures in three-dimensional space has not been reported. Regarding face detection, we know of a method for the detection of skin color (race, suntan, makeup, etc.). When using that method, it must be judged whether the colored skin region is a feature of the face or not, in order to prevent detection error. Candidates for error are other body parts (hands, feet) and any skin color region in the background. In addition, the method must recognize the face skin color automatically, to account for changes to the person (e.g., a patient in hospital). To detect the face skin color of a new person in an undetermined posture with unknown skin color is a difficult problem. We consider that skin color will be a difficult criterion to apply to this problem.

It is important that an invariant feature of the face is used for face detection. In a monochrome image, the gray level of the facial image is changed by lighting intensity or direction. By opening and closing the eyes and mouth, face parts are changed in area and shape. In order to decrease the influence of these changes, it is considered that the edge of a feature is a useful measure. But shape distortion and size changes of the face parts still occur, because an edge provides geometric information which varies with posture. Therefore, a processing method which can decrease the influence of geometric change, is required. The authors propose a method for detecting the posed face in an undetermined posture, using a shift-invariant and rotation-invariant pattern obtained by calculating an input image. First, we show that a spectrum, which is obtained by polar transform and Fourier transform of the edge data of the face image, is shift-invariant and rotation-invariant and is shift-invariant with regard to depth. We show the invariant pattern is useful enough for face detection in three-dimensional space. We also describe a limitation of the utilization of the pattern in a general environment, where a distribution obtained by the calculation of correlation is shown. This shows the degree of face likelihood. It also shows that there are high correlation areas in the background, the clothes, etc. which are not the face. Further, the correlation on a posed face is low. Next, we describe a way of solving these problems and detecting the position of the face, using an adaptive correlation.

This consists of rationalization of the local edge extraction and correlation using a three-dimensional rotated image of a reference face. The face is detected by the position of the highest correlation obtained through the adaptive correlation, using the invariance of the face image.

In this chapter, the proposed method is explained and an experimental result, which is performed to verify the efficacy of the method, is demonstrated.

2. Face detection algorithm

2.1. *Invariant pattern of face*

In order to carry out detection of the face in an undefined posture, it is necessary to utilize three-dimensional invariant image information on the face. In this method, an invariant pattern is made by a two-step calculation on the extracted edge data. First, using a center of the edge image as an origin, polar transform $P(r, \theta)$ is calculated by an argument θ and a distance r from the origin to the edge data (Fig. 1) where the sum of the edge data on argument θ_n is calculated by (1). By calculating the omni-directional sum, $f(\theta)$ shown in Fig. 1 is obtained:

$$f(\theta_n) = \sum_{r=0}^{R} \sum_{\Theta=\theta_n-\sigma}^{\theta_n+\sigma} P(r, \Theta) \tag{1}$$

where R is a radius of a region of the face and σ shows the argument range for the sum. Next, the power spectrum $|F(\tau)|^2$ of $f(\theta)$ is calculated by the following equation (τ is defined by number of argument resolution).

$$|F(\tau)|^2 = \left| \frac{1}{N} \sum_{n-0}^{N-1} f(\theta)\exp\left\{-j2\pi\frac{n\tau}{N}\right\} \right|^2 \tag{2}$$

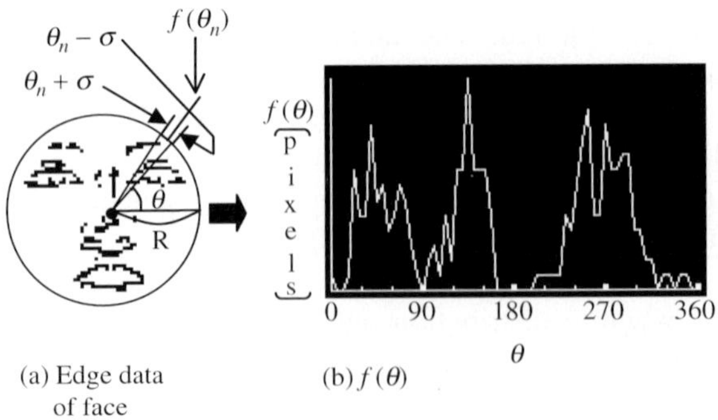

Fig. 1. An example of $f(\theta)$.

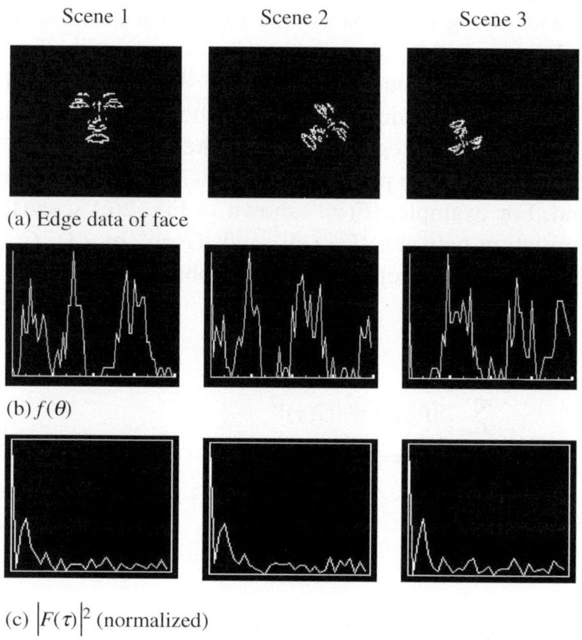

Fig. 2. Shift-invariant and rotation-invariant pattern.

where n is number θ and N is total number defined by argument resolution. Normalization of $|F(\tau)|^2$ obtained by (2) is shift-invariant and rotation-invariant in a plane which is orthogonal to the camera axis, and is also shift-invariant with regard to depth. Figure 2 shows an example using an actual face. The patterns of $|F(\tau)|^2$ shown in Fig. 2(c) are compared with each other. These appear to be slightly different to each other. The difference is caused due to noise and strain of facial parts. Thus, they are not in exact accord; however, they are approximately the same. We can confirm their similarity using the calculation of correlation. Accordingly, the pattern obtained by (1) and (2) is sufficiently useful for analyzing invariant image information in three-dimensional space [9,10].

2.2. *Local edge extraction and correlation map*

In order to apply the invariant pattern described in Section 2.1 to face detection, it is necessary to know a value of R which shows the size of the facial region. In this study, a stereo view is used and R is determined by a parallax that is calculated by template matching. The calculation of matching is applied not only to the edge point but also around the edge point. Thus, if an edge is present in the template at the coordinate, the calculation is applied to the coordinate. The operation around the edge point is necessary to prevent a problem that the method cannot be adapted to deal with, when the edge is not detected at the center of the facial image. Parallax is obtained at the coordinate to which the matching operation is applied. On the other hand, a relation between the value of R and the parallax is prepared beforehand. Using this relation, the value of R at the coordinate in the input image is determined.

In this method, the power spectrum $|F_{a,b}(\tau)|^2$ of the edge data (shown in Fig. 3(a)) extracted by the radius R is calculated. (a, b) shows a coordinate position in the computational region, that is the region excluding the black region in the case shown in Fig. 3(b). As described above, the power spectrum $|G(\tau)|^2$ of a reference facial image is prepared beforehand. For example, $|F(\tau)|^2$ shown in Fig. 2(c) scene1 is used as $|G(\tau)|^2$. Calculating the correlation between $|F_{a,b}(\tau)|^2$ and $|G(\tau)|^2$ by (3), $C_{a,b}$ which shows the degree of face likelihood at the coordinate (a, b) is obtained.

$$c_{a,b} = \frac{\sum_{\tau=0}^{(N-1)/2} |F_{a,b}(\tau)|^2 |G(\tau)|^2}{\sqrt{\sum_{\tau=0}^{(N-1)/2} (|F_{a,b}(\tau)|^2)^2 \sum_{\tau=0}^{(N-1)/2} (|G(\tau)|^2)^2}} \quad (3)$$

Then, applying this operation to the area of parallax, a correlation map such as that shown in Fig. 3(b) is obtained. Features of the map are as follows:

(1) Both $|F_{a,b}(\tau)|^2$ and $|G(\tau)|^2$ compress the face information, resulting in high areas of correlation at the background, clothing region, etc.

(2) If the difference between the input face and the reference face is large with regard to shape or location of the facial parts, the correlation between $|F_{a,b}(\tau)|^2$ and $|G(\tau)|^2$ is low.

Due to this feature, the coordinate with the highest correlation does not always show the center of the face. Consequently, the map shows the distribution of the degree of facial likelihood and cannot be used for deterministic face position data. Thus, the face position is detected by Section 2.3, using the region of high correlation (white region is high in Fig. 3(b)).

As a threshold for extraction of the face likelihood region, a minimum correlation value at the center of the face in input images should be used for elimination of the possibility of missing the face. In our experiment (Chapter 3), 0.8 is used following a confirming test beforehand (correlation is expressed from 0 to 1.0).

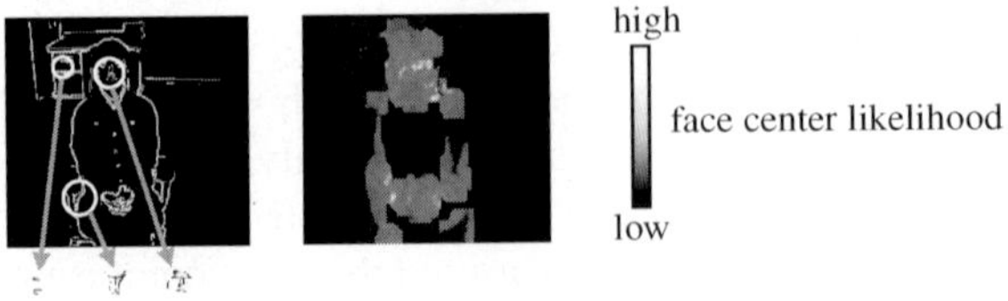

(a) Ex. of the extracted edge (b) Correlation map

Fig. 3. Examples of the extracted edge data and correlation map.

2.3. *Adaptive correlation*

If this influence of facial direction changes can be reduced, it can be expected that the highest correlation will be obtained at the face position in the input image. Problems to solve are as follows: The change in shape of the facial parts, the distortion of the relative location of the parts and the facial contours in the extracted edge data. To address the changes of shape and location, a power spectrum $|G_{\phi,\varphi}(\tau)|^2$ is prepared beforehand by rotation of the reference face (Fig. 4). Calculating again the correlation between $|G_{\phi,\varphi}(\tau)|^2$ and $|F_{a,b}(\tau)|^2$ the highest value is detected in:

$$c_{a,b,r,\phi,\varphi} = \frac{\sum_{\tau=0}^{(N-1)/2} |F_{a,b,r}(\tau)|^2 |G_{\phi,\varphi}(\tau)|^2}{\sqrt{\sum_{\tau=0}^{(N-1)/2} (|F_{a,b,r}(\tau)|^2)^2 \sum_{\tau=0}^{(N-1)/2} (|G_{\phi,\varphi}(\tau)|^2)^2}} \tag{4}$$

parameter ϕ and φ. In this method, an operation regarding the incline to the right or left side by a third parameter is not needed. The reason why the operation of a third rotation is not needed is that $|G_{\phi,\varphi}(\tau)|^2$ cannot receive information on the influence of the rotation of the face in a plane because of the invariance of shift in Fourier transform. Thus, the method handles the face direction change in three-dimensional space using two operations on the rotation of the reference face image. This results in a useful reduction of processing time. To address the influence of the facial contours, subtracting 1 (pixel) from R, the edge data of a smaller region is extracted. Then the correlation between $|F_{a,b,r}(\tau)|^2$ and $|G(\tau)|^2$ is calculated. Iterating the operation from R to a certain radius, the highest correlation is detected. In this method, parameter ϕ, φ and r are changed and $C_{a,b,r,\phi,\varphi}$ is calculated by (4). Then the value at the coordinate (a, b) is determined using the maximum value in $C_{a,b,r,\phi,\varphi}$. Figure 5 shows an example of correlation using ϕ, φ and r. The coordinate is at the center of the face. In the example, the radius R is decided by parallax and is 21. The contour of the face is included in the extracted edge data (Fig. 5(a)). Figure 5(b) shows the result of correlation using the edge data extracted by the radius from 21 to 15. The size of the white circle corresponds with the correlation power. In this method, it is important to eliminate the facial contours and to leave the face parts. For this operation, the most

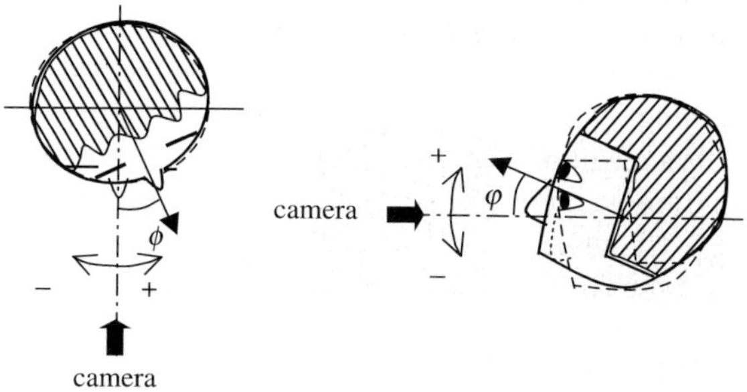

Fig. 4. Rotation of the reference face.

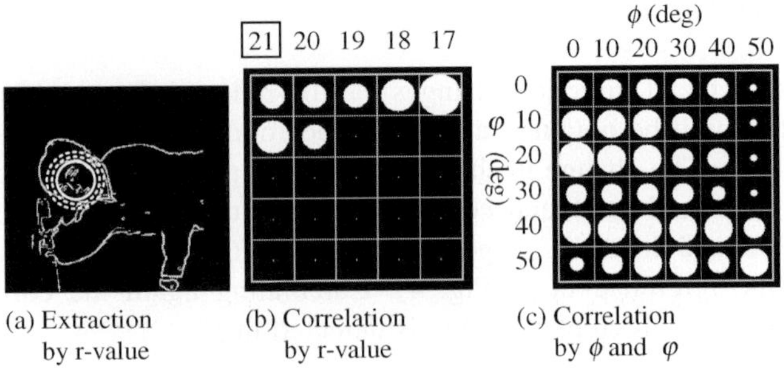

Fig. 5. Correlation by r-value and correlation by ϕ and φ.

appropriate radius was 17 (pixels). Figure 5(c) shows the result of the correlation between the face edge data extracted by 17 on the radius and the rotation of the reference face edge data. It also shows that the most proper ϕ is 0 degrees and φ is 20 degrees.

In this method, the face position is detected by the highest correlation using ϕ, φ and r. Consequently, it has been possible to apply the method to a bold posed face in a general environment. Figure 6 shows the flow of the detection algorithm.

3. Experiment

In this experiment, the input image is 256×256 in size and 256 in gradation. The argument resolution θ is 360/64 degrees and σ is $\theta/2$. The reference image shown in Fig. 6 is used as the reference face image in the experiment. Both ϕ and φ are every 10 degrees from -50 to $+50$ degrees. For the threshold value for determination of high correlated regions, we use a value, which is about 90 percent of the highest threshold value under a condition resulting in no miss on the face region in a test beforehand. The subject is watching TV. A camera is installed at the top of the TV and captures the subject. The detection result of the face position is plotted with white points on the edge image generated from the input image. Then the second degree of correlation is plotted with white points smaller than the points for the highest correlation.

Figure 7 shows an example of the experimental result. This is a sample of behavior when the subject is changing position for watching TV. In the correlation map, the gray degree shows correlation power and the face center likelihood is shown in white. It is confirmed that correlation is high for all areas except the face (rails of the bed side, painted part on the shirt, wrinkles in clothing, etc.) (Section 2.2).

The face position, as a result of detection, is approximately correct in (a), (d), (e), (f), (g) and (h). However, an improvement will be needed to detect the center of the face precisely. Regarding this point, we consider that it will be solved by improvements in the detection accuracy of the edge of the face parts and improvements in elimination of the influence of facial contours. In (b) and (c), the detection results are incorrect and the actual face positions assigned second highest correlation. It is considered that the quality of the facial parts, edge is not good enough. The edge data of (b) and (c) are shown in Fig. 8. In Fig. 8(a), the shape of the parts is insufficient and the face contour is in contact with

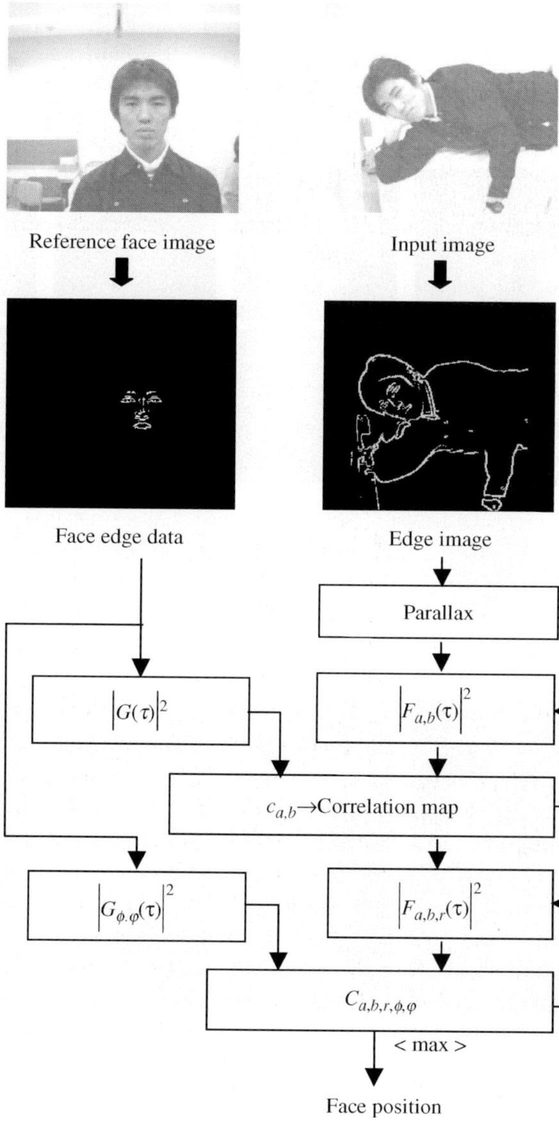

Fig. 6. Flow.

the parts. In this case, the invariance of $|F_{a,b}(\tau)|^2$ failed and the correlation is too low. Therefore, it is necessary to improve the function of edge detection and improve accuracy of separating the parts from facial contours. Figure 8(b) shows an example of noise on the face. The correlation is low in this case as well. It is necessary to improve the accuracy of noise reduction. Regarding θ, ϕ and φ, their values were determined by a test beforehand. We consider that their values are appropriate, because error resulting from these was not confirmed in the experiment. However, higher resolution argument will be needed for

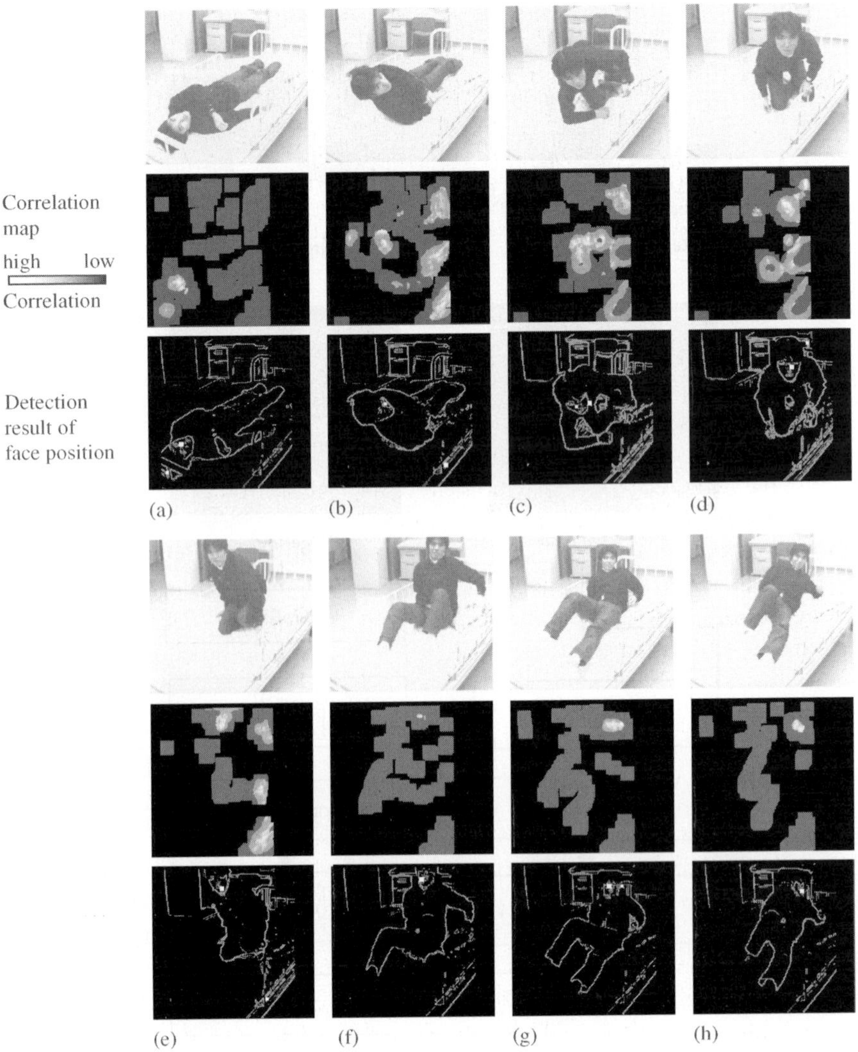

Fig. 7. Experimental result.

further improvements in detection accuracy. The process is made up of three steps. The first step detects parallax from a stereo view. The ratio of the first step to all steps is about 70 percent of processing time, though it is changed by the number of edge points. In this step, template matching consumes time. The second step makes a correlation map by polar transform, Fourier transform and calculation of the correlation. The processing time for polar transform and Fourier transform is 95 percent in this step. For calculation of the correlation, data of a power spectrum is used. The number of data points is small (32 points in the experiment) and processing time is minimal. In the third step, face position is detected using the high correlated region. Processing time is changed according to the area

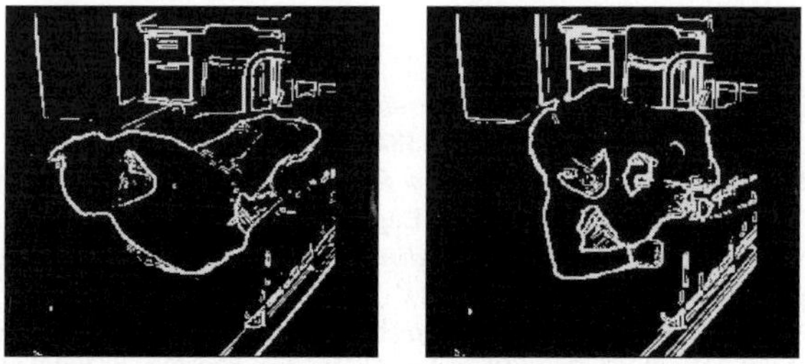

(a) (b)

Fig. 8. Edge images of Fig. 7(b) and (c).

of the high correlated region and is approximately less than 50 percent of the second step. In the result, the detection of parallax, as a first step, consumes most of the time. For example, for the input image of Fig. 7(e) whose high correlated area seems average, processing time by PC (CPU: Celeron, 800 MHz) was about 10 min. The Improvements in hardware and software are needed to reduce time.

From this experimental result, we have confirmed that the method functions usefully, though room for improvement remains. Consequently, it has been possible to recognize a face in various postures as well as any posed face. The utility of the method has been demonstrated.

4. Conclusion

In this chapter, the authors propose a method for face recognition in undefined postures and positions, and the utility of the method was showed by the experimental result. In the method, a spectrum pattern is made by polar transform and Fourier transform of the edge data of the facial image. We showed that the pattern is shift-invariant and rotation-invariant in a plane that is orthogonal to the camera axis, and is shift-invariant toward depth. By extending the idea to face recognition in three-dimensional space, we also explained the detection of the posed face position. In the experiment, the subject changed his posture on the bed and then not only full face but also various facial positions (inverted face, oblique face, etc.) were handled. In many scenes, the position of the face according to the detection result was correct. Thus, it was confirmed that the algorithm functioned usefully. On the other hand, the detection result of some of the scenes was incorrect due to insufficiency of edge data, noise, or face contour. We consider that these problems can be solved by improving the accuracy of edge detection and the ability of contour reduction. Consequently, the utility of the method has been shown, though room for improvement remains.

In future work, we aim to improve realization of higher performance of this method. In particular, we consider it is necessary that detection accuracy is improved and processing time is reduced. We also consider a combination with other methodological techniques will be useful.

References

[1] T. Kato, Y. Mukaigawa and T. Shakunaga, *Cooperative distributed registration for robust face recognition*, Trans. Inst. Electron., Inf. Commun. Engrs. D-II **J84-D-II** (3) (2001), 500–508.

[2] O. Yamaguchi and K. Fukui, *Smartface—a robust face recognition system under varying facial pose and expression*, Trans. Inst. Electron., Inf. Commun. Engrs. D-II **J84-D-II** (6) (2001), 1045–1052.

[3] T. Hirano and O. Nakamura, *A robust personal identification system for angled facial images*, Trans. Inst. Electrical Engrs. Jpn **120-C** (6) (2000), 800–808.

[4] Y. Mitsukura, M. Fukumi and N. Akamatsu, *A detection method of face region in color images by using the lip detection neural network*, Trans. Inst. Electrical Engrs. Jpn **120-C** (1) (2001), 112–117.

[5] Y. Shiga, H. Ebine, M. Ikeda and O. Nakamura, *Extraction of facial area and facial parts based on color and motion information and detection of its movements*, Trans. Inst. Electrical Engrs. Jpn **121-C** (5) (2001), 912–920.

[6] A. Khotanzad and Y.H. Hong, *Invariant image recognition by Zernike moments*, IEEE Trans. Pattern Anal. Mach. Intell. **12** (5) (1990), 489–497.

[7] T. Kazaana, S. Kaneko and S. Igarashi, *Fast and rotation picture matching based on circular zernike moments*, Tech. Rep. Inst. Electron., Inf. Commun. Engrs., PRMU99-143 (1999), 75–80.

[8] A. Ono, *Face recognition with zernike moments*, Trans. Inst. Electron., Inf. Commun. Engrs. D-II **J85-D-II** (7) (2002), 1149–1156.

[9] H. Seike, A. Takeuchi and J. Yamaguchi, *Detection of face position in unrestricted posture*, Proceedings of the Eighth Symposium on Sensing via Image Information, H-2, (2002), pp. 349–354.

[10] H. Seike and J. Yamaguchi, *Face recognition position in unrestricted posture using invariant image information*, Proceedings of the SICE System Integration Division Annual Conference SI2002, 1A92-01, (2002), pp. 177–178.

CHAPTER 35

Head Detection and Tracking for Monitoring Human Behaviors

Y. Mae, N. Sasao, Y. Sakaguchi, K. Inoue and T. Arai

Graduate School of Engineering Science, Osaka University, 1-3 Machikaneyama, Toyonaka, Osaka 560-8531, Japan

Contents

Abstract

This chapter describes a mobile manipulator for monitoring and support of human activity in home and office to maintain security. The mobile manipulator is equipped with cameras at the end of an arm. The camera pose can be changed flexibly for monitoring by controlling both mobile platform and manipulator. The trajectory of a person's head is detected for recognizing his/her behaviors.

SYSTEMS AND HUMAN SCIENCE – FOR SAFETY, SECURITY, AND DEPENDABILITY
Edited by Tatsuo Arai, Shigeru Yamamoto and Kazuhisa Makino

1. Introduction

For the purpose of creating a safe, secure and reliable (SSR) society, an integrated system of monitoring and supporting functions is important [1]. The monitoring system finds the first sign of danger in the environment quickly by watching a wide area in detail using many fixed or moving cameras. The supporting system prevents the danger from occurring or copes with the occurring danger rapidly, thus reducing damage to the minimum; in the present project, humanoid robots are used as supporting devices [2]. In this way, this integrated system can offer a safe environment to us, and we feel secure and comfortable in the environment. The project aims at a conceptual design of such a monitoring and supporting system and making a prototype of the system.

There have been many studies on person detection and pose estimation from the images of cameras [3–5]. By using not only fixed cameras but also moving cameras [6,7], the monitoring system increases its monitoring performance; the moving camera can eliminate blind spots of fixed cameras and monitor persons in detail by moving according to the persons' motions (Fig. 1).

We designed and developed a mobile manipulator equipped with a camera at the end of an arm which is used as a moving camera [8]. Various kinds of mobile manipulators have been developed [9–12] for various applications. However, there are no studies on mobile manipulators equipped with cameras at the arm end for the purpose of monitoring. The developed mobile manipulator has high degrees of freedom for camera motion. It increases the flexibility of monitoring motion. Our final goal is to establish a methodology of motion generation of the mobile manipulator for monitoring.

In the present chapter, we introduce the developed mobile manipulator with camera at the arm end, and describe a method of detecting head position using a silhouette of a bust of a human. Simple behaviors of a person are recognized by the detected head positions. Experimental results of detecting head trajectory for walking, standing, and sitting motions are shown.

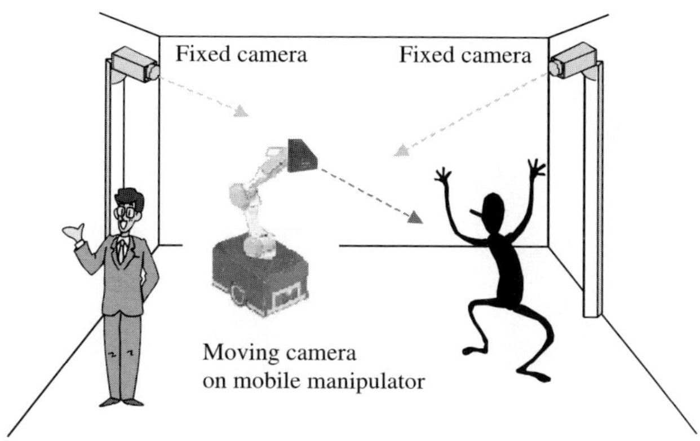

Fig. 1. Monitoring by fixed cameras and moving cameras attached to mobile manipulators.

2. Mobile manipulator for monitoring and support

We design a mobile manipulator which can be used for both monitoring and supporting persons. If not only cameras but also hand tools are attached to the end of the arm, the mobile manipulator has both monitoring and supporting functions. Considering mobile manipulators that coexist with humans and working with/for humans, we determine the size of the mobile manipulator is about human scale.

Figure 2(a) shows an overview of the developed mobile manipulator. We adopt a general purpose robot arm PA-10, a product of Mitsubishi Heavy Industries Ltd, as a manipulator. We adopt a mobile platform customized by PATNA Corporation. The specifications of the mobile platform are in Table 1.

To find danger from the person's motion, it is important to measure the person's pose, motion, and his/her neighborhood in high precision. It requires high precision localization of moving cameras. If the camera can change its position without moving its mobile platform, adequate views can be selected to observe adequate environmental features for localization without increasing the error of dead reckoning. Then we attach a camera at the end of the arm of a mobile manipulator. The effectiveness of using multi-camera units for range measurement has been revealed in recent studies [13]. We use a pre-calibrated trinocular camera unit, Digiclops Stereo Vision, as a camera attached to the arm end. Figure 2(b) shows the camera unit attached to the arm end.

The three cameras in the unit are arrayed at the vertices of a right-angle triangle. The three cameras are called *right*, *left*, and *top* cameras. The *right* camera is set at the vertex at right angle. The *top* camera is above the *right* camera. The camera unit calculates the range for every pixel based on the sum of absolute differences (SAD) matching method. The *right* camera is used as a reference camera. Three images of *right*, *left*, and *top* cameras are denoted by I_1, I_2, I_3, respectively. The image coordinate is denoted by $x = (x, y)$. The horizontal disparity d at a pixel (x, y) is obtained by

$$d = \arg \min_{d=d_{\min}}^{d_{\max}} \sum_{i=-m/2}^{m/2} \sum_{j=-m/2}^{m/2} |I_1(x+j, y+i) - I_2(x+j+d, y+i)|, \tag{1}$$

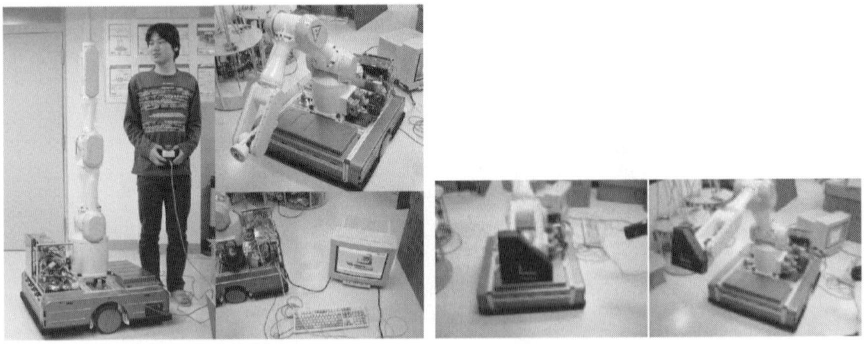

(a) Mobile manipulator (b) Camera unit mounted on the arm

Fig. 2. Developed mobile manipulator.

Table 1. Specifications of mobile platform

Size	(W)700 × (D)700 × (H)215
Weight	40 kg
Speed	max 0.6 m/s
Turning radius	495 mm (diagonal length of the frame)

where $d_{\min}$ and $d_{\max}$ indicate minimum and maximum disparities for search, m indicates the mask size for SAD matching. The vertical disparity is obtained in the same way. The disparity with a smaller SAD value is selected for calculation of the range.

Figure 3 shows a depth map of an environment obtained by a viewpoint. Since the camera pose can be changed by both mobile platform and arm motions, a detailed three-dimensional shape of the environment can be obtained by the integration of depth maps obtained by multiple viewpoints.

3. Monitoring by mobile manipulator

3.1. *Overview of monitoring*

Monitoring for safety and security has two main tasks:

(1) detection of unknown persons,

(2) detection of danger for persons.

In both tasks, detection and tracking of persons are required functions for monitoring persons. We focus on a method of detection and localization of persons.

We assume the faces of persons who regularly use a monitoring space are previously stored in the database for authentication. The mobile manipulator moves to find and authenticate the faces of detected persons. If the face region is detected in high enough resolution, the detected face may be matched to the registered face. Otherwise, the mobile manipulator moves to an adequate position to obtain the face region in high resolution. A person whose face is not matched to the registered faces is tracked as an unknown person until his/her face is matched to a registered face.

While the registered persons walk through a monitoring space, the faces will be authenticated. On the other hand, unregistered persons will not be authenticated for a

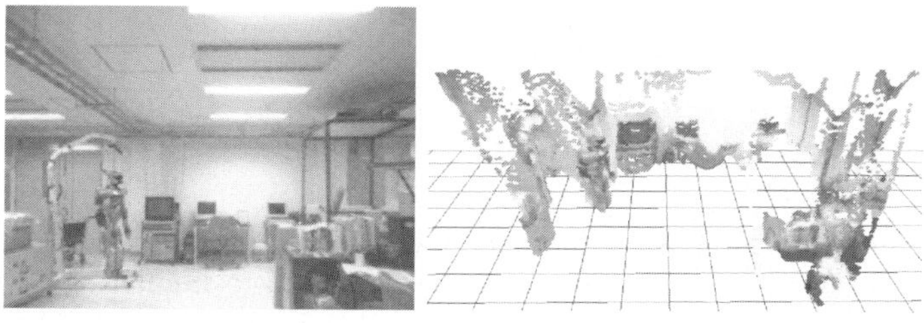

(a) Environment image (b) Depth map

Fig. 3. Example of detected depth map.

long time. Such unknown persons will be monitored by human operators to confirm if they are outsiders or not.

If the distance between a camera and a person is large, the error of the measured range is large. Thus, it is difficult to detect a head position from the difference of ranges. Besides, the features of a face cannot be detected when a person is far from a camera. To detect the head position of a person, even in this case, we use a silhouette of a bust of a person, since a bust silhouette is a simple and rough representation of a human.

An outline of the process of person detection and localization by the mobile manipulator is as follows. First, the mobile manipulator detects regions with motion on the image from the input images. Second, regions corresponding to persons' heads are detected by a bust silhouette of a person. Third, the persons' positions are obtained by calculating average ranges in the detected head region.

3.2. *Extraction of motion region*

To find persons from the images of monitoring cameras, we first extract regions with motion caused by persons' motions in the image.

To simplify the algorithm for person detection, we assume the camera does not move when the camera detects regions with persons' motions. We detect such motion regions by background subtraction or frame subtraction methods. When no moving objects are in the view for a long time, the view is recorded as a background image for background subtraction. In the other cases, the consecutive input images are used for frame subtraction. An absolute value at (x, y) after subtraction of images is denoted by $\Delta I_n(x, y)$. A binarized image $S_n(x, y)$ is obtained by thresholding $\Delta I_n(x, y)$ for all pixels

$$S_n(x, y) = \begin{cases} 1 & \text{if } \Delta I_n(x, y) \geq \text{threshold} \\ 0 & \text{otherwise} \end{cases}. \tag{2}$$

A set of pixels with $S_n(x, y) = 1$ represents the regions with motion. The suffix n indicates one of the *right*, *left*, and *top* cameras. The detected regions will include the regions corresponding to persons.

If the background motion caused by camera motion can be distinguished from the other objects' motion, the regions with persons' motions can be extracted by some sort of motion analysis methods.

3.3. *Detection of person's head*

We detect a head of a person as the first cue of detecting a whole body. A silhouette of a bust including the head and shoulders is a shape unique to humans. The shape of the silhouette does not change much depending on the head orientation and the difference in individuals. Thus, we use a silhouette of a bust to detect the head region of a person. The image of the detected motion regions $S_1(x, y)$ is used as the input image to search for a

(a) Silhouette (b) 3.5m (c) 2.0m

Fig. 4. Detected head region overwritten on original images.

silhouette of a bust of a person. We previously make a template of a typical bust silhouette. The shape of the bust silhouette is obtained by making the silhouette of a person symmetrical which is detected by the background subtraction of a person. Figure 4(a) shows an example of the bust silhouette template.

The bust silhouette template is represented by a binarized image like detected motion regions

$$T(j,i) = \begin{cases} 1 & \text{if } (j,i) \text{ is on a silhouette} \\ 0 & \text{otherwise} \end{cases} \tag{3}$$

where (j, i) indicates the coordinates on the template.

We detect a part corresponding to a head from the detected motion regions by matching with the bust silhouette template. The size of the bust silhouette template is denoted by $M \times N$. The head position on the image $x_{\mathrm{h}} = (x_{\mathrm{h}}, y_{\mathrm{h}})$ with the smallest SAD value which is lower than the predetermined threshold is obtained by

$$x_{\mathrm{h}} = \arg\min_{x} \sum_{i=-M/2}^{M/2} \sum_{j=-N/2}^{N/2} |T(j,i) - S_1(x+j, y+i)|. \tag{4}$$

The template size changes in the search for the best matching position of the template. For a template with s magnified size of the original template, $T(sj, si)$ and $S_1(x + sj, y + si)$ are used for calculation in (4). The adequate template size is selected automatically by changing s, which has the minimum SAD value.

3.4. *Calculation of a person's position*

The distance of a person from the camera is determined from the range of the detected head position. The distance is determined by the average of the range in the neighborhood of the center of the template at the matched position. The neighborhood is determined by $M' \times N'$ rectangle region, whose center corresponds to the center of the template. The neighborhood region $M' \times N'$ is set to 25×25 in the experiments. The results are not subject to the size.

Let n denote the number of the pixels, where $S_1(x, y) = 1$ in the neighborhood. Let $Z(x, y)$ denote the range at the pixel (x, y). The distance to the person Z_p is obtained by

$$Z_p = \frac{1}{n} \sum_{i=-M'/2}^{M'/2} \sum_{j=-N'/2}^{N'/2} S_1(x_h + j, y_h + i) Z(x_h + j, y_h + i). \tag{5}$$

4. Experiments

4.1. *Detection of a person*

The experimental results of person detection using a bust silhouette template are shown.

Figure 4(b) and (c) shows detected head positions by rectangles overwritten on the original images. The rectangle indicates the outline of the matched template. In this case, the motion regions are detected by the background subtraction method. Figure 5(a) and (b) shows motion regions extracted by background subtraction. Figure 5(c) and (d) shows motion regions extracted by frame subtraction. In Fig. 5, a person is 3.5 and 2.0 m in front of the camera in the left and right figures, respectively. A detected head position is represented by a rectangle in every figure. By changing template size, template matching using a bust silhouette works even when the distance between the person and the camera changes in both subtraction methods (Fig. 5).

In both subtraction methods, motion regions are detected which correspond to shadows of persons. In fact, regions corresponding to shadow are detected by a simple background subtraction method (Fig. 5(a) and (b)). In the experiments, however, the template matching using a bust silhouette does not detect the shadows as a head. This shows the template matching using a bust silhouette is effective for person detection. From the detection results, the method can detect a head part even when the resolution of the face part is low.

In the experiments, we set the mask size m for calculation of range to 15 experimentally. The size m does not affect the results crucially. We set the original template size for person detection to 15×15 pixels. The original size is determined by the minimum size which can be recognized experimentally as the silhouette of a person by a human. The template is magnified to different template size. The magnification changes from 3 to 5 for detecting persons at different distances from a camera. Thus, the template size M changes from 45 to 75. In calculation of SAD for a magnified template, 15×15 pixels are used at

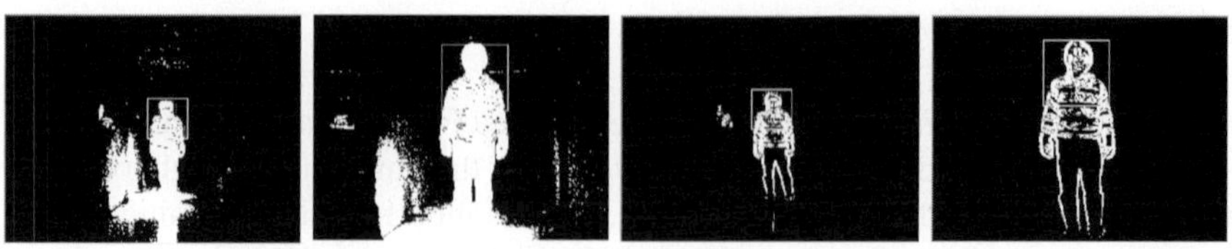

(a) 3.5m (b) 2.0m (c) 3.5m (d) 2.0m

Fig. 5. Detected head for background (a,b) and frame (c,d) subtraction methods.

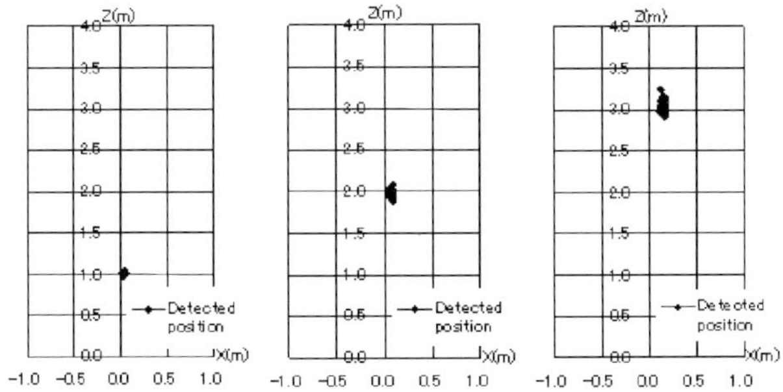

(a) 1m (b) 2m (c) 3m

Fig. 6. Detected positions while a person faces to the camera.

the magnified positions and the other pixels are skipped. It reduces the calculation time of template matching.

4.2. *Evaluation of the detected position*

The localization accuracy of a person depends on the distance between the person and the camera, and the orientation of the head. The detected positions of a person in several situations are shown and evaluated below.

We evaluate the detected position of a standing person. The person stands at about 1, 2, 3 m distances from the camera and facing the camera. The detected positions are shown by black points in Fig. 6. The positions are sampled in about 10 s. We can see from the figures, the variance of the detected positions becomes larger as the distance becomes larger, especially in a depth direction (Z axis). This is because detected motion regions corresponding to a bust become small in the image and the shape of the detected bust becomes different from the bust silhouette template.

4.3. *Trajectory of detected head*

Simple behaviors such as walking, standing, and sitting can be recognized by the change of detected head positions. In the experiment, a person walks from about 4 to 2 m distances from the camera crossing the line of sight diagonally. The views of the camera are shown

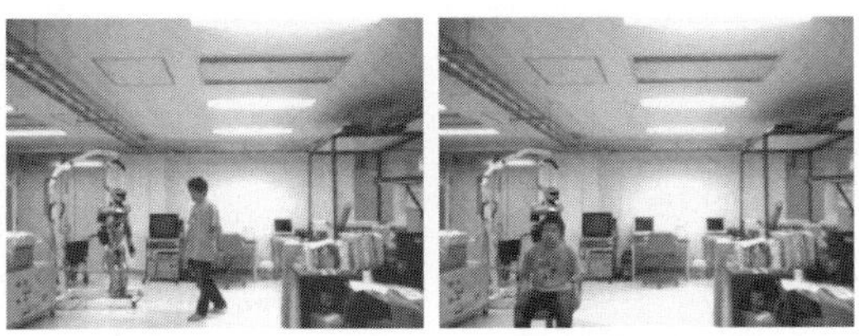

(a) Walking person (b) Sitting person

Fig. 7. A walking and sitting person.

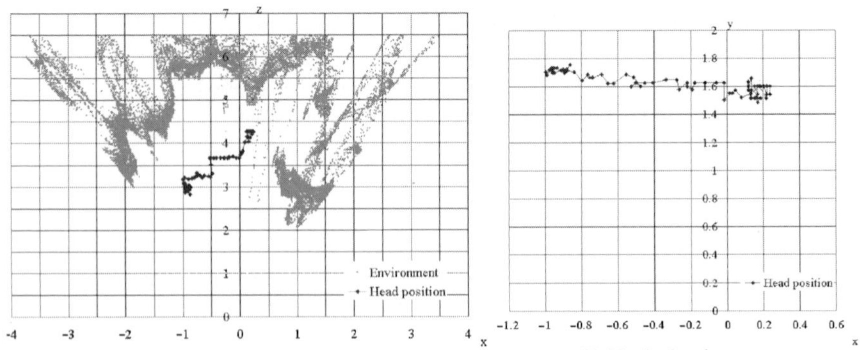

(a) Horizontal trajectory (b) Vertical trajectory

Fig. 8. Walking and standing trajectory.

in Fig. 7. We call the start and goal positions of walking as A and B, respectively. We show detected head trajectories for two cases: (1) a person walks from A to B, and stands at B, (2) a person walks from A to B, and sits on a chair at B. Figure 7(a) shows a walking person, and Fig. 7(b) shows a sitting person at B. The person faces to the walking direction during walking. In the experiments, motion regions are detected by the background subtraction method.

Figure 8(a) shows an overhead view of a trajectory of detected head positions in the first case (1). The detected positions are plotted by black points. The consecutive measured positions are connected by a line segment. The measured environmental points are represented by gray points. In the figure, they are projected onto the horizontal plane. The camera is fixed at the origin in the figures. Figure 8(b) shows a vertical trajectory of the detected head positions. When the person is standing at B, the head position is detected around $(x, y) = (-1.0, 1.7)$ (m). It shows the height of a person is almost 1.7 m.

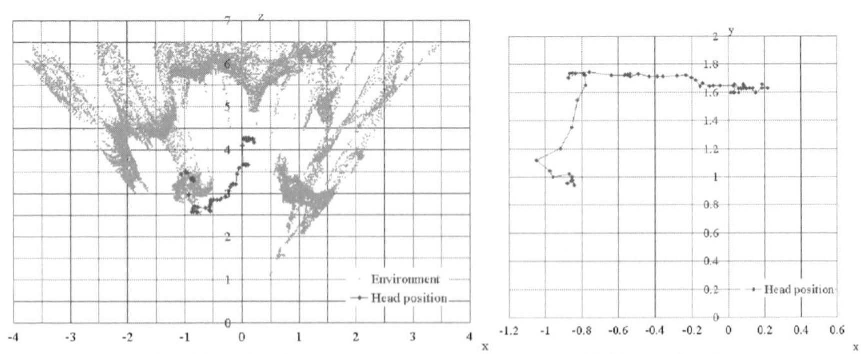

(a) Horizontal trajectory (b) Vertical trajectory

Fig. 9. Walking and sitting trajectory.

Figure 9(a) shows an overhead view of a trajectory of the detected head positions in the second case (2). Environmental points corresponding to the chair are seen around B. Figure 9(b) shows a vertical trajectory of the detected head positions. Trajectories of the head positions of Fig. 9 show the person is sitting on the chair at B.

5. Conclusions

This chapter describes a developed mobile manipulator with camera at the arm end for monitoring, and describes a method of detecting head position using the silhouette of a bust of a human. The experimental results of detecting a head position are shown and the trajectories of detected head positions in walking, standing, and sitting behaviors are also shown.

In future, we will develop a method of combining color and range information to estimate motions of persons in detail. Dangers such as falling and collision will be detected based on the measured behaviors and the environmental shape. Our aim is to generate adequate motions of the mobile manipulator according to persons' motions. For example, the mobile manipulator moves the camera for zooming in on a person to observe the person's face in high resolution or to measure the person's motions in high precision.

References

[1] T. Arai, *Initiative of systems and human science for safe, secure, and reliable society. Creative of new science and its social contribution by integrating the systems science and the human science*, SICE (2002).

[2] K. Inoue, T. Arai, Y. Mae and Y. Nishihama, *Fundamental study on human support system using humanoid robots for creating SSR society*, SICE (2002).

[3] T. Darrell, G. Gordon, M. Harville and J. Woodfill, *Integrated person tracking using stereo, color, and pattern detection*, Int. J. Comput. Vision **37** (2) (2000), 175–185.

[4] C. Wren, A. Azarbayejani, T. Darrell and A. Pentland, *Pfinder: real-time tracking of the human body*, IEEE Trans. Pattern Anal. Mach. Intell. **19** (2) (1997), 780–785.

[5] M. Covell, A. Rahimi, M. Harville and T. Darrell, *Articulated-pose estimation using brightness- and depth-constancy constraints*, Proc. IEEE Conf. Comput. Vision Pattern Recognit. (2000).

[6] P.J. Burt, J. Bergen, R. Hingorani, R. Kolczyaski, W. Lee, A. Leung, J. Lubin and H. Shvaytser, *Object tracking with a moving camera*, Proc. IEEE Workshop Visual Motion (1989), 2–12.

[7] Y. Rosenberg and M. Werman, *Real-time object tracking from a moving video camera: a software approach on a PC*, IEEE Workshop Appl. Comput. Vision (1998), 238–239.

[8] Y. Mae, K. Inuoue, N. Sasao and T. Arai, *Mobile-manipulator for monitoring-support system*, SICE Syst. Integrat. Div. Annu. Conf. **2** (2002), 235–236 (in Japanese).

[9] M. Mason, D. Pai, D. Rus, L.R. Taylor and M. Erdmann, *A mobile manipulator*, Proc. IEEE Int. Conf. Robotics Autom. **3** (1999), 2322–2327.

[10] S.H. Murphy, J. Wen and G. Saridis, *Simulation of cooperating robot manipulators on a mobile platform*, IEEE Trans. Robotics Autom. **7** (4) (1991), 468–478.

[11] Y. Yamamoto and X. Yun, *Coordinating locomotion and manipulation of a mobile manipulator*, IEEE Trans. Autom. Control **39** (6) (1994), 1326–1332.

[12] J. Imamura and K. Kosuge, *Handling of an object exceeding load capacity of dual manipulators using virtually unactuated joints*, Proc. IEEE Int. Conf. Robotics Autom. (2002), 989–994.

[13] T. Kanade, A. Yoshida, K. Oda, H. Kano and M. Tanaka, *A video-rate stereo machine and its new applications*, Proc. 15th Comput. Vision Pattern Recognit. Conf. (1996).

CHAPTER 36

Adaptive Background Estimation and Shadow Removal in Indoor Scenes

Junya Morita, Yoshio Iwai and Masahiko Yachida

Graduate School of Engineering Science, Osaka University, Toyonaka, Osaka 560-8531, Japan

Contents

Abstract

Background subtraction algorithm is susceptible to both global and local illumination changes such as shadows, sunlight, and reflection. These changes sometimes cause failures in object tracking, gesture recognition, or posture estimation. In this chapter, we propose a method for detecting objects casting shadows in an indoor scene by modeling a pixel value as the total energy received from light sources. Our proposed method can also estimate the rate of illumination change in order to improve background subtraction. Experimental results demonstrate the usefulness and performance of the method.

SYSTEMS AND HUMAN SCIENCE – FOR SAFETY, SECURITY, AND DEPENDABILITY
Edited by Tatsuo Arai, Shigeru Yamamoto and Kazuhisa Makino

1. Introduction

Background subtraction is one of the most effective methods for the detection of moving objects in static scenes because of its fast processing [1]. The method is, however, susceptible to both global and local illumination changes such as shadows, sunlight, and reflection. In order to stably track moving objects, the object region should be correctly extracted against the effects of such illumination changes. Moreover, light conditions easily change when lights are turned on/off in actual indoor scenes, so the method must be able to deal with changes in light.

Many methods for removing illumination effects have been proposed. In outdoor scenes, there are object tracking methods using an object's 3D geometric model [2] and object detection methods using 3D geometric relations between objects and the sun [3]. As opposed to these methods using geometric information, Gordon *et al.* used stereo images and color information for object detection. This method integrates depth estimation with background subtraction [4]. However, the method has some disadvantages, i.e., multiple cameras are needed and the depth of a scene cannot be estimated from dark images. Matsuyama *et al.* [5] used a normalized distance between a block of an input image and that of a background image. This method can stably detect objects under various illuminations, but the spatial resolution for object detection is very low because the processes are performed per block.

On the other hand, many statistical approaches have also been proposed [6]. The relation between reflection on an object surface and the value of a pixel is often statistically modeled by using mixture of Gaussian [7]. Stauffer and Grimson [8] used a mixture Gaussian model for changes in background pixel values. Ohta [9] uses a chi-square test to detect outliers. These methods implicitly assume that there is one light source in a scene, or that there is one color of light in a scene. However, real indoor scenes contain many kinds of colored light: tungsten light (3500 K) and natural daylight colors (5000 K). Therefore, we need a method that can deal with multiple colored light conditions in order to apply background subtraction to indoor scenes.

Under a condition with multiple lights, the values of background pixels are often modeled with a linear combination of the energy received from light sources [10,11]. Methods that use a certain number of basic images (axes of illuminated image space) to express arbitrary illuminated images are often applied to object recognition [12]. Shashua [13] shows that arbitrary illuminated images are represented by the linear combination of three basic images when their reflection model is Lambertian. Shingu *et al.* [14] have proposed a method for synthesizing background images by using such a reflection model. However, this method requires the parameters of a light's brightness at each frame, so such parameters must be controllable and observable by another method. In this chapter, we too assume that light sources can be controlled by dimmers or switches since our goal is object detection in indoor scenes. However, our method estimates light conditions at each frame by using background components, so we estimate background components only once in advance. The advantage is that our method can be simply applied to light conditions that frequently vary, such as stage illumination.

In this chapter, we propose a method for detecting objects that cast shadows in an indoor scene by modeling a pixel value as the total energy received from lights. Our proposed method can deal with multiple lights and multiple colored lights as well. In order to deal with illumination changes, our method initially estimates the ratio between the radiance of input image and that of the background image estimated in advance.

2. Background model

In this section, we model the relationship between a pixel value captured by a camera and total energy received from lights. We then introduce a parameter in order to deal with shadows. Here, we assume that a camera and lights are relatively static in the background scene. Therefore, a complex reflection model including the surface normal, light direction, and camera direction is not needed. This means that we can use a simple reflection (background) model expressed with a few parameters, and we can estimate these parameters more stably than those of a complex reflection model.

Let the reflection coefficient matrix of an object surface be $\mathbf{r}_j$, and the intensity of the illumination at that point j from controllable light source i be $\mathbf{I}_{ij}$. We assume that a pixel value $\mathbf{E}_j$ is given by the following equation:

$$\mathbf{E}_j = (R_j, G_j, B_j)^{\mathrm{T}} = \mathbf{r}_j \mathbf{I}_{ij}, \tag{1}$$

where $\mathbf{r}_j$ includes albedo and specular reflection of an object surface, $\mathbf{r}_j$ is a diagonal matrix, and $\mathbf{I}_{ij}$ also includes rays reflected by walls and the ceiling (see Fig. 1). Here, we also assume that the relationship between a camera's total energy received from lights and a pixel value is linear.

Next, we introduce a parameter S_{ij} to deal with shadows and illumination changes. (1) is rewritten as follows:

$$\mathbf{E}_j = \mathbf{r}_j S_{ij} \mathbf{I}_{ij}, \tag{2}$$

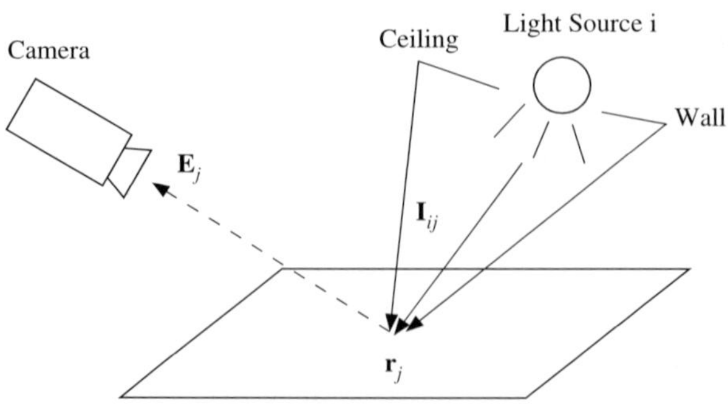

Fig. 1. Relation between energy from light sources and pixel values.

where S_{ij} expresses the degree of brightness of light source i at point j and the range of S_{ij} is from 0 to 1. The ray of light source i is obstructed at point j, or light source i is lit off if S_{ij} is 0. If S_{ij} is 1, all rays of light source i reach at point j.

In the case of multiple light sources, the relation between lights and pixel value $\mathbf{E}_j$ is defined as $\mathbf{E}_j = \mathbf{r}_j \sum_i S_{ij}\mathbf{I}_{ij}$. The equation can be rewritten by substituting $\mathbf{L}_{ij}$ for $\mathbf{r}_j\mathbf{I}_{ij}$ as follows:

$$\mathbf{E}_j = \sum_i S_{ij}\mathbf{L}_{ij}. \tag{3}$$

By using the above equation, we can use the background subtraction method on indoor scenes illuminated by multiple lights. We call $\mathbf{L}_{ij}$ a background component of pixel j received from light i. An estimate $\mathbf{L}_{ij}$ can be preliminary calculated for indoor scenes, because the lights in a room can often be controlled by dimmers or switches, and S_{ij} can be treated as a known parameter. Once $\mathbf{L}_{ij}$ is known, we can estimate S_{ij} from (3). We explain the estimation processes in the next section.

3. Background subtraction that accounts for illumination changes

In this section, we explain countermeasures against illumination changes and shadows. As described in Section 2, $\mathbf{L}_{ij}$ is estimated in advance and then background subtraction is performed by using this estimation.

For simplicity, we only describe the proposed algorithm with two light sources. However, our algorithm can be used with three or more light sources. The flow of the estimation processes is shown in Fig. 2. Each process is described in the following section.

3.1. *Estimation of initial background components*

With two light sources, (3) can be written as $\mathbf{E}_j = S_{1j}\mathbf{L}_{1j} + S_{2j}\mathbf{L}_{2j}$. As described in Section 2, $\mathbf{L}_{1j}$ and $\mathbf{L}_{2j}$ are required to synthesize background images. From the above equation,

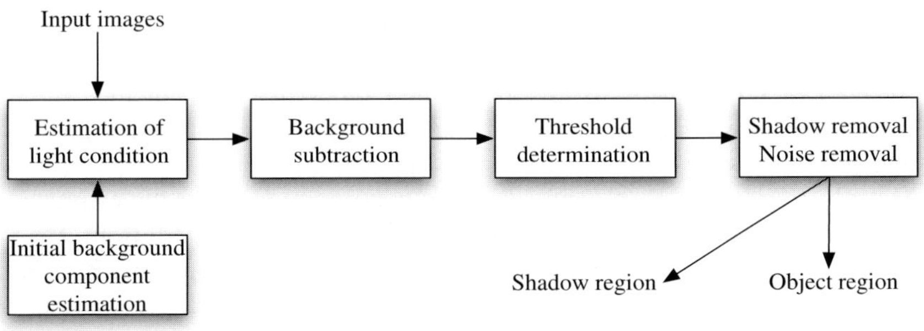

Fig. 2. Outline of process.

when we get two or more different pairs of (S_{1j}, S_{2j}), we can estimate the background components: $\tilde{\mathbf{L}}_{1j}$, $\tilde{\mathbf{L}}_{2j}$.

The shutting parameter, S, is also considered as the parameter of brightness for a light source in an indoor scene. We can estimate $\mathbf{L}_{1j}$ and $\mathbf{L}_{2j}$ from two or more background images where the brightness of each light source is controlled by a dimmer or a switch. In short, we can estimate $\mathbf{L}$ under the condition that S is given. When the switch of light i is turned off, we can clearly determine that S_i is 0, and, likewise, S_i is 1 when the switch of light i is turned on and there is no object obstructing the light. Generally, in the case of N light sources, we can estimate N background components when we get N background images illuminated by the various known degrees of brightness of light sources.

3.2. *Estimation of light condition*

The algorithm must be able to deal with changes in light condition since this condition easily changes when lights are turned on or off in actual indoor scenes. There are actually two types of light condition changes: color and brightness. We only deal with the change in brightness in this chapter.

S_{1j} and S_{2j} uniformly change at each pixel and can be written as S_1 and S_2, respectively, when the brightness of the lights is changed and there is no obstructing object. Therefore, when two or more pixels at arbitrary points are selected from an input image, we can estimate $\tilde{S}_1$ and $\tilde{S}_2$ from the estimated background components, $\tilde{\mathbf{L}}_{1j}$ and $\tilde{\mathbf{L}}_{2j}$, that were estimated in Section 3.1. However, there is the problem of selecting pixels from an input image for estimation when there is an obstruction, because the assumption that S_1 and S_2 uniformly change at each pixel is not satisfied in shadow regions and object regions. When the light condition is estimated by using the whole input image, the effect of outliers is small if the obstruction is small, but the effect cannot be ignored if the object is large.

In order to reduce the chance of an incorrect selection, we use the RANSAC [15] algorithm to select the pixel pairs. Our algorithm is shown below:

(1) Randomly select two pixels ($j = 1, 2$) from an input image.

(2) Calculate S_1 and S_2 by using the following equation:

$$T_1 = S_1\tilde{T}_{11} + S_2\tilde{T}_{21}, \qquad T_2 = S_1\tilde{T}_{12} + S_2\tilde{T}_{22}, \tag{4}$$

where T_{ij} is the intensity of the background components, $\tilde{\mathbf{L}}_{1j}$ and $\tilde{\mathbf{L}}_{2j}$, of selected pixel j. T_j is the intensity of the pixel value, $\mathbf{E}_j$, at selected pixel j.

(3) Accept (S_1, S_2) if $0 \leq S_1, S_2 \leq 1$ is satisfied, otherwise reject them.

(4) Iterate the above process until the number of accepted points is greater than a threshold.

(5) Make histograms of S_1, S_2 and select the maximum point for the estimates.

After the estimation of S_1 and S_2, $\tilde{\mathbf{L}}'_{1j}$ and $\tilde{\mathbf{L}}'_{2j}$ are calculated from $\tilde{\mathbf{L}}'_{1j} = \tilde{S}_1\tilde{\mathbf{L}}_{1j}$, $\tilde{\mathbf{L}}'_{2j} = \tilde{S}_2\tilde{\mathbf{L}}_{2j}$, respectively. We can synthesize a background image by $\tilde{\mathbf{E}}_j = \tilde{\mathbf{L}}'_{1j} + \tilde{\mathbf{L}}'_{2j}$. By using this synthesized background adjusted to an input image, we can perform background subtraction and use a simple criterion for object detection so that the difference between the background and an input image is larger than a certain threshold value, T_a. Since this simple criterion detects shadow regions as well as object regions, we need a method for removing shadows, as will be explained in the next section.

3.3. *Background subtraction and shadow removal*

When there are two light sources, an input image is classified into four regions:

(1) background illuminated by two lights: $\mathbf{L}_1$, $\mathbf{L}_2$
(2) shadow illuminated by $\mathbf{L}_1$ ($\mathbf{L}_2$ is blocked)
(3) shadow illuminated by $\mathbf{L}_2$ ($\mathbf{L}_1$ is blocked)
(4) object.

The background and shadow vectors can be expressed by using the background components, $\tilde{\mathbf{L}}'_{1j}$ and $\tilde{\mathbf{L}}'_{2j}$ described in Sections 3.1 and 3.2. The object vector is different from these vectors. Soft shadows are expressed by the linear combination of $\tilde{\mathbf{L}}'_{1j}$ and $\tilde{\mathbf{L}}'_{2j}$.

In real scenes, it is difficult to clearly classify an input image into four regions because the size of an actual light source is not zero, and soft shadow regions, dim shadow regions lit partially by a light source, are generated by a light that has a certain size. Therefore, we must deal with soft shadows in real scenes. Many soft shadows are distributed around the edge of the parallelogram of $\tilde{\mathbf{L}}'_{1j}$ and $\tilde{\mathbf{L}}'_{2j}$. We can distinguish object regions from shadow regions by using the Euclidean distance in RGB space between an observed pixel value and the parallelogram, the plane determined by $\tilde{\mathbf{L}}'_{1j}$ and $\tilde{\mathbf{L}}'_{2j}$; however, the chance of error in detecting objects increases when the region determined as shadow is larger. Moreover, the possibility of error in calculating increases when the angle between $\tilde{\mathbf{L}}'_{1j}$ and $\tilde{\mathbf{L}}'_{2j}$ is smaller. Therefore, we assume that soft shadows exist around the four segments of the parallelogram.

Above all, we classify pixels into object, shadow, and background according to the following rules:

(1) background if $\|\mathbf{E}_j - (\tilde{\mathbf{L}}'_{1j} + \tilde{\mathbf{L}}'_{2j})\| \leq T_a$ is satisfied.
(2) shadow if $\|\mathbf{E}_j - (\tilde{\mathbf{L}}'_{1j} + \tilde{\mathbf{L}}'_{2j})\| > T_a$, $f \leq T_b$ and $\|\mathbf{E}_j\| > T_c$ are simultaneously satisfied.
(3) otherwise pixels are classified into object.

We calculate feature value f as follows:

$$d_m = \min_{0\leq\alpha\leq 1, 0\leq\beta\leq 1}\Big[\|\mathbf{E}_j - \alpha\tilde{\mathbf{L}}'_{1j}\|, \|\mathbf{E}_j - \beta\tilde{\mathbf{L}}'_{2j}\|,$$
$$\|\mathbf{E}_j \times -(\alpha\tilde{\mathbf{L}}'_{1j} + \tilde{\mathbf{L}}'_{2j})\|, \|\mathbf{E}_j - (\tilde{\mathbf{L}}'_{1j} + \beta\tilde{\mathbf{L}}'_{2j})\|\Big].$$

$$f = \frac{d_m}{\|\mathbf{E}_j\|}, \tag{5}$$

where $\mathbf{E}_j$ is a pixel value of an input image and $\|\mathbf{E}_j\|$ is a distance from the origin.

With multiple light sources, the above criterion can be applied by using the distance between a pixel value and the segment calculated from each background component. The area of shadow regions is larger in RGB space when the light sources increase, so the error of object detection must be considered.

T_a, T_b and T_c should be assigned to valid values in order to correctly distinguish objects from the background. The distribution of feature f's histogram is double peaked with object and background (shadow). We use Otsu's [16] method for automatic threshold determination of T_b. This method is used to binarize gray level images, but it is also used to determine the threshold of features used for our method by regarding feature values as gray level images. Valid values of T_a and T_c are changed slightly under various indoor scenes and we use the values determined empirically.

4. Theoretical analysis of proposed algorithm

As mentioned in Section 3.2, the correct selection of pixel pairs is required to accurately estimate $(\tilde{S}_1, \tilde{S}_2)$ since our algorithm chooses the mode (S_1, S_2) for its estimates. In the case of two light sources, the combination of pixel pairs is shown in Table 1. A_i in the table expresses a correct pair, and B_i and C_i express incorrect pairs that make a noise. Let R_1, R_2, and R_3 be the acceptance probability of pixel pairs: A_i, B_i, and C_i, respectively. The acceptance probability expresses that a pixel pair accidentally satisfies the constraints. The condition that the proposed algorithm works well with is when the number of correct pairs is larger than that of incorrect pairs. This condition is expressed by the following equation:

$$\sum_i R_1 P(A_i) \geq \sum_i R_2 P(B_i) + \sum_i R_3 P(C_i). \tag{6}$$

For further analysis, we assume that P_1, P_2, P_3, and P_4 are the probability of background, shadow, soft shadow, and object, respectively. P_1, P_2, and P_3 can be estimated from the number of pixels of background, shadow, and soft shadow in an input image, respectively. R_i cannot, however, be easily estimated because it depends on each pixel value, so R_i is empirically estimated in the next section and is analyzed further.

5. Experiments

We conducted experiments to evaluate the performance of the algorithm. The light source used in the experiments has three fluorescent lights that can be turned on/off independently. Brightness is changed by switching on/off one or more of the fluorescent lights. The differences in color are made by using colored cellophanes. The direction and position of the lights and camera are fixed. The input images used in the experiments are

Table 1. Patterns of pair selection

	Background	Shadow	Soft shadow	Object
Background	A_1	B_1	B_2	B_3
Shadow	B_1	A_2	C_1	B_4
Soft shadow	B_2	C_1	C_2	B_5
Object	B_3	B_4	B_5	B_6

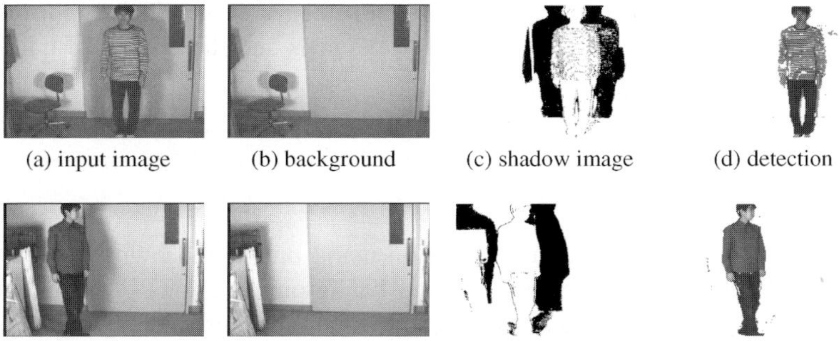

(a) input image (b) background (c) shadow image (d) detection

(e) input image (f) background (g) shadow image (h) detection

Fig. 3. Results of test images: (a)–(d) two lights, (e)–(h) two lights of the same color.

720×480 pixels and the depth of RGB planes is 8 bits. The experiments were conducted at night to avoid any other light sources.

Figure 3 shows an experimental result by using the background components. The results show that the effects of shadows are largely removed and the object is correctly extracted. Moreover, even though each light is a different color, the object regions are accurately detected.

5.1. *Stability of light estimation*

We conducted an experiment to evaluate light estimation under various light conditions. We calculated the difference between the input image shown in the top row of Fig. 4 and the synthesized image shown in the bottom row of the figure. The values of $(\tilde{S}_1, \tilde{S}_2)$ are estimated by the proposed method described in Section 3.2. D_r is the average of the difference between a synthesized background and a background in an input image (excluding objects).

These results show that even though object and shadow regions occupy large areas in an input image, our proposed method can accurately estimate background components.

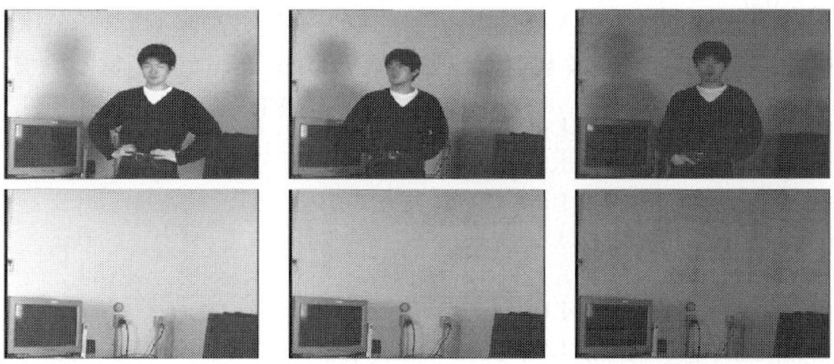

(a) (b) (c)

Fig. 4. Estimated background images under various light conditions (top: input image, bottom: estimated background): (a) $(\tilde{S}_1, \tilde{S}_2) = (0.99, 0.98)$, $D_r = 1.83$, (b) $(\tilde{S}_1, \tilde{S}_2) = (0.65, 0.69)$, $D_r = 3.27$, (c) $(\tilde{S}_1, \tilde{S}_2) = (0.33, 0.36)$, $D_r = 3.71$.

The accuracy of estimation is worse when an input image is darker. This is because when an input image is darker, the SNR of the image worsens and the chance of quantization error becomes relatively larger.

5.2. *Accuracy of object extraction*

We compare the results of automatic extraction using our method with that of manual extraction. Let A and B be object regions and background regions determined by our method, respectively. Let C and D be object regions and background regions determined by hand, respectively. Object detection rate R_D and incorrect detection rate R_I are calculated from the following equation:

$$R_D = \frac{\#\{A \cap C\}}{\#C}, \qquad R_I = 1 - \frac{\#\{B \cap D\}}{\#D}, \tag{7}$$

where # is the number of pixels in a region. Table 2 shows the results using 20 images illuminated by two lights and three lights. In the case of two light sources, the average object detection rate and incorrect detection rate are 90.3 and 2.99%, respectively. Shadow removal is correctly performed by using the proposed method. In the case of three light sources, the average R_D and R_I are 85.8 and 0.97%, respectively. Shadow removal is also correctly performed. However, note that the results are worse in comparison with the case of the two light sources. This is because the area of regions with overlapping soft shadows is larger than that of the case of the two light sources.

5.3. *Effectiveness of light estimation*

We conducted an experiment to verify how effective the light estimation was. We used the same 10 images illuminated by two lights that were used in the accuracy estimation in the

Table 2. Accuracy of object extraction: two lights and three lights

Two lights			Three lights		
Image	$R_D \times 100(\%)$	$R_I \times 100(\%)$	Image	$R_D \times 100(\%)$	$R_I \times 100(\%)$
(a)	96.2	1.49	(k)	84.6	1.88
(b)	89.1	1.39	(l)	89.4	0.29
(c)	92.4	1.64	(m)	86.8	0.38
(d)	94.1	3.16	(n)	80.2	0.39
(e)	89.5	2.12	(o)	84.2	1.08
(f)	90.8	1.08	(p)	75.1	0.70
(g)	90.1	1.94	(q)	82.6	3.09
(h)	89.0	7.80	(r)	91.2	0.60
(i)	87.1	4.99	(s)	88.5	0.53
(j)	85.1	4.30	(t)	95.8	0.79
Average	90.3	2.99	Average	85.8	0.97

previous section. We calculated R_i of each image: $R_1 = 0.408$, $R_2 = 0.109$, $R_3 = 0.274$. We assume that $P_2 > P_3$, in other words the area of shadow regions is greater than that of soft shadow regions. This assumption is reasonable because soft shadows exist around shadows. Under this assumption, we finally get

$$(-0.816P_0^2 + 1.632P_0 - 0.299)P_1^2 \geq (0.816P_0^2 - 1.632P_0 + 0.794)P_2^2 + 0.109, \quad (8)$$

where P_0 is the ratio between the area of an input image and that of regions affected by illumination.

P_1^2 is equal to 0.2 in the case of $P_0 = 1.0$. This result shows that the algorithm works well if the background illuminated by lights covers about 45% of an input image. This means that the algorithm can estimate background components even though object and shadow regions occupy areas as large as half the size in an input image. This fact also proves the effectiveness of our proposed algorithm. When P_0 comes down to 0, the area of the region where the algorithm works well is small and $P_0 = 0.3$ is a limit to our algorithm.

6. Conclusion

Many methods have been proposed for addressing problems caused by shadows that lead to failure in the background subtraction method, but most of these methods assume that there is one light source or there is one color of light in a scene. In this chapter, we have proposed a background model that takes into account illumination changes and shadows with multiple colored lights. We have also proposed a method for automatic background estimation and have analytically estimated the domain where our algorithm works well for illumination changes. We conducted experiments with real images and confirmed the effectiveness of our proposed method.

As pre-processing, our method can be applied to various situations, such as tracking individuals, recognizing gestures, and detecting objects. This method can improve the accuracy of these processes. Moreover, it has the salient feature in that shadow regions can be divided into sub-regions because the method can detect object and shadow region separately even when illumination changes. Furthermore, the method can calculate the ratio of energy received from each light source at each pixel.

References

[1] M. Takatoo, T. Kitamura and Y. Kobayashi, *Vehicles extraction using spatial differentiation and subtraction*, IEICE Trans. **J80-DII** (11) (1997), 2976–2985.

[2] D. Koller, K. Daniilidis and H.-H. Nagel, *Model-based object tracking in monocular image*, Intl. J. Comput. Vision **10** (3) (1993), 257–281.

[3] S. Watanabe, K. Miyajima and N. Mukawa, *Detecting changes of man-made structures using shading model in aerial images*, MIRU **II** (1998), II-373–II-377.

[4] G. Gordon, T. Darrell, M. Harville and J. Woodfill, *Background estimation and removal based on range and color*, International Conference on Computer Vision and Pattern Recognition, (1999), 459–464.

[5] T. Matsuyama, T. Wada, H. Habe and K. Tanahashi, *Background subtraction under varying illumination*, IEICE Trans. **J84-DII** (10) (2001), 2201–2211.

[6] T. Horprasert, D. Harwood and L.S. Davis, *A statistical approach for real-time robust background subtraction and shadow detection*, Proceedings of the IEEE ICCV'99 Frame-rate Workshop, Greece (1999).
[7] X. Gao, T.E. Boult, F. Goetzee and V. Rmaesh, *Error analysis of background adaption*, International Conference on Computer Vision and Pattern Recognition, South California, USA (2000).
[8] C. Stauffer and W.E.L. Grimson, *Adaptive background mixture models for real-time tracking*, Proc. CVPR (1999), 246–252.
[9] N. Ohta, *A statistical approach to background subtraction for surveillance systems*, International Conference on Computer Vision, Vancouver, Canada (2001), 481–486.
[10] I. Sato, Y. Sato and K. Ikeuchi, *Illumination distribution from shadows*, IPSJ Trans. CVIM **41** (SIG-10) (2000), 31–40.
[11] E. Hayman and J.-O. Eklundh, *Probabilistic and voting approaches to cue integration for figure-ground segmentation*, European Conference on Computer Vision, Copenhagen, Denmark III (2002).
[12] A.S. Georghiades, D.J. Kriegman and P.N. Belhumeur, *Illumination cones for recognition under variable lightning: faces*, International Conference on Computer Vision and Pattern Recognition, (1998), 52–58.
[13] A. Shashua, *On photometric issues in 3d visual recognition from a single 2d image*, Int. J. Comput. Vision **21** (1/2) (1997), 99–122.
[14] J. Shingu, Y. Kameda, K. Kakusho and M. Minoh, *A dynamic lighting control method based on foreground extraction with background image synthesis*, PRMU, IEICE (2001), 101–569.
[15] M.A. Fischer and R.C. Bolles, *Random sample consensus: a paradigm for model fitting with applications to image analysis and automated cartography*, Commun. ACM **24** (6) (1981), 381–395.
[16] N. Otsu, *A threshold selection method from gray-level histograms*, IEEE Trans. Syst., Man, Cybern. **9** (1) (1979), 62–66.

CHAPTER 37

Tracking People and Action Recognition from Omnidirectional Images

Akari Matsumura, Yoshio Iwai and Masahiko Yachida

Graduate School of Engineering Science, Osaka University, Toyonaka, Osaka 560-8531, Japan

Contents

Abstract

In this chapter, we propose methods for tracking people and recognizing their actions through indoor scenes captured with an omnidirectional image sensor. They can be used to detect and track people to extract their trajectories of movement and their actions are then recognized by using extracted trajectories. Recently, stochastic algorithms have frequently been used for action recognition because they require non-linear and non-Gaussian models of action. Action models prepared from trajectories, however, include movements that are almost the same, so they are redundant. We have, therefore, assumed that human actions can be classified into action primitives, which are modeled by transitions of discrete states considered as action primitives. The methods we propose combine continuous state models and discrete state models by stochastic sampling generated from state transition probabilities.

SYSTEMS AND HUMAN SCIENCE – FOR SAFETY, SECURITY, AND DEPENDABILITY
Edited by Tatsuo Arai, Shigeru Yamamoto and Kazuhisa Makino

1. Introduction

In recent years, the social environment has become more complex and people's personal lives have become more varied, so the development of security systems that detect hazards and allow us to avoid these has become necessary for us to be safe and secure. Such a system would need facilities to detect unusual situations automatically and inform system administrators of unusual situations by sensing and recognizing our environment. To insure safety, person authentication and the detection of unusual situations would also be important. To detect suspicious action, the system needs to detect and track people surreptitiously. Cameras have usually been utilized as environmental sensors because they do not make us feel uncomfortable. People are detected and tracked through input images by image processing, and our purpose is to do this and recognize their actions by using trajectories of movement.

In monitoring the environment, image sensors with a normal range of view cannot capture many people simultaneously. We, therefore, used an omnidirectional image sensor with a wide range of view [1].

Numerous methods using various features for specific purposes have been proposed to recognize human actions. Bobick *et al.* [2] proposed a method using temporal templates to recognize behavior. Trajectories are generally used to recognize positional movement [3]. Models of action to recognize positional movement are mainly classified into two models: the first is used to construct continuous human actions and the other is used to define human actions as discrete state transition. To recognize continuous actions, stochastic methods have frequently been used recently, such as the CONDENSATION algorithm [4] and particle filters [5]. These methods require non-linear and non-Gaussian models to distinguish them from methods using a linear model like the Kalman filter.

However, a method using a hidden Markov model [6] has been considered to be a typical example for recognizing the discrete state of actions. This model has been researched in the field of gesture and speech recognition. In addition, a method proposed by Wada *et al.* [7] uses a finite-state automaton. Trajectories of movement often include movements that are almost the same. We, therefore, assumed that human actions could be classified into action primitives. Actions are modeled by discrete states considered as action primitives such as HMM. The method we propose combines continuous state models and discrete state models by stochastic sampling generated from state transition probabilities.

Figure 1 is a flow chart of the proposed system. It is divided into two modules: a tracking and an action-recognition module. It extracts human regions from input images through a skin color and a background model. The system then estimates the position of a person on the world coordinate system from their foot points in input images. The planar trajectories of objects are obtained from positional information in consecutive frames, and compared to action models learned from examples in advance.

2. Omnidirectional image sensor

We use an omnidirectional image sensor for observation in our system. This sensor covers a wide range of view and has the same optical characteristics of a common camera, so we

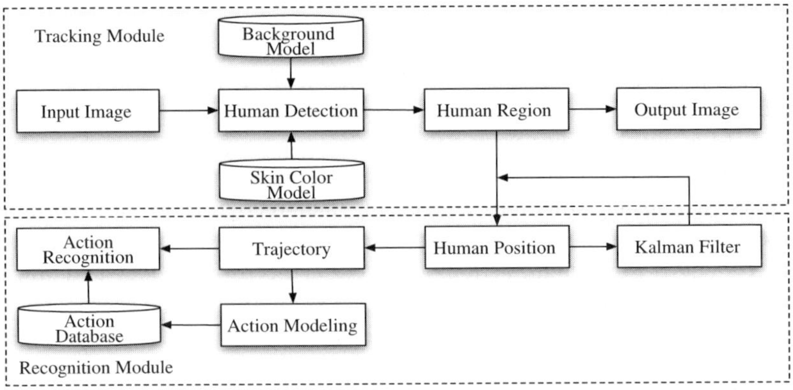

Fig. 1. System diagram.

can easily estimate positions of people from the input images. We briefly explain the sensor below.

The sensor consists of a camera fixed upward and a hyperboloidal mirror fixed downward. The relation between the camera and the world coordinate system is shown in Fig. 2.

A hyperboloidal plane has two focal points: $(0, 0, +c_\mathrm{h})$ and $(0, 0, -c_\mathrm{h})$. The focal point of a hyperboloidal mirror is fixed at the upper focal point, $(0, 0, +c_\mathrm{h})$, and the focal point of a camera is fixed at the lower focal point, $(0, 0, -c_\mathrm{h})$. The image plane representing the xy-plane is parallel to the XY-plane of the world coordinate system and the image plane is fixed at $(0, 0, f - c_\mathrm{h})$. f is the focal length of the camera. The point (x, y) on the image plane is calculated from the 3D point (X, Y, Z). Our system can be used to estimate human positions in the panoramic image shown in Fig. 2(a). A point on the panoramic image is denoted by (x', y').

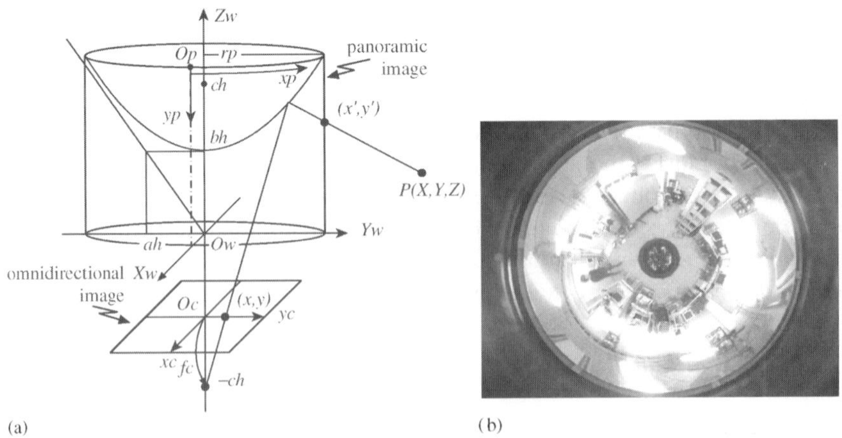

Fig. 2. Omnidirectional image sensor: (a) coordinate systems, (b) input image.

3. Tracking module

3.1. *Detecting a person*

Skin color regions are extracted from input images by using skin color and background models. We can, therefore, detect people standing in front of the camera with the skin color model and can also remove objects whose color is similar to the skin color using background model, so the extraction process can be correctly done.

Skin color regions are extracted from input images by comparing a color, $C(\mathbf{p})$, of a sampling point, $\mathbf{p}$, with the skin color distribution. The parameters for skin color distribution are calculated through preliminary experiments. We assume that the distribution for skin color would have a Gaussian distribution in the normalized rg-space. The average μ_c and covariance matrix Σ_c of the distribution are calculated from the colors of the sampling points. Here, we exclude sampling points whose intensity is less than a certain threshold, T_R. Dissimilarity $\phi(\mathbf{p})$ is defined by

$$\phi(\mathbf{p}) = \exp\left\{-\tfrac{1}{2}[C(\mathbf{p}) - \mu_c]^T \Sigma_c^{-1} [C(\mathbf{p}) - \mu_c]\right\}.$$

Finally, the similarity, $s(\mathbf{p})$, of the skin color is defined by using a skin color model, $\phi(\mathbf{p})$, and a background color model, $b(\mathbf{p})$, as $s(\mathbf{p}) = \phi(\mathbf{p})(1 - b(\mathbf{p}))$. We can define human face region as $R_f \equiv \{\mathbf{p} | s(\mathbf{p}) \geq T_p\}$.

When a human region is detected, the foot point in the input image is searched for, and the position in the world coordinate system can be estimated. We also calculate the height of the subject at the same time. When a foot point is occluded by other objects, we estimate its position from the height and the head position. The information we extracted in each frame is in Table 1.

3.2. *Tracking human*

The positions of human regions are predicted with a Kalman filter. We assume that these regions would move linearly in the panoramic images because people only move slightly within 1/30 s. We define $\mathbf{X}_t \equiv (x', y', \dot{x}', \dot{y}')$ to be the *a priori* state estimated at time t. Parameter $\mathbf{X}_t$ is predicted by a Kalman filter.

Table 1. Human information

Information	Symbol
Face point in input images	(x', y')
Position in world coordinates	(X_F, Y_F)
Human height	h_p
Human status	S_t
Parameters of Kalman filter	$\mathbf{X}_t, \mathbf{P}_t$
Human template	T_{image}

The equation for the time update is expressed by the following equation:

$$\mathbf{X}_{t+1} = \mathbf{A}\mathbf{X}_t + \mathbf{B}\omega_t, \qquad \mathbf{A} = \begin{bmatrix} \mathbf{I} & \mathbf{I} \\ \mathbf{0} & \mathbf{I} \end{bmatrix}, \qquad \mathbf{B} = \begin{bmatrix} \mathbf{0} \\ \mathbf{I} \end{bmatrix}, \tag{1}$$

where ω_t is white system noise such that $E[\omega_i \omega_j^{\mathrm{T}}] = \mathbf{Q}\delta_{ij}$. The procedure for the measurement update is expressed by the following equation:

$$\mathbf{Y}_t = \mathbf{C}\mathbf{X}_t + \varepsilon_t, \qquad \mathbf{C} = [\mathbf{I} \quad \mathbf{0}], \tag{2}$$

where ε_t is white observation noise such that $E[\varepsilon_i \varepsilon_j^{\mathrm{T}}] = \mathbf{R}\delta_{ij}$.

As the system can estimate the next position, (x', y'), of a skin color region and estimate the error covariance, $\mathbf{P}_t$, with the Kalman filter, it searches for the skin region within the predicted area. When no skin color region within the area, a histogram of the area is generated. A face point is obtained from the maximum point of the histogram. If the value of the maximum point is less than the threshold value, T_{h}, the system considers that the human region is lost. When occlusion occurs, it is easy to distinguish a human with our system because the distance between objects and the camera is known. Trajectories of moving points in the world coordinate system are generated by the results of tracking.

4. Recognition module

Our system assumes that human actions are sequences of action primitives. Transitions of action primitives between the first detection considered as status S and the disappearance of people considered as status E are modeled in Fig. 3(a). Actions are recognized using transition probabilities. The system has action primitive models and transition probabilities for each action model. Action models and action primitive models are denoted by $\{M^{\eta}\}_{\eta=1}^{\mathcal{M}}$ and $\{\mathbf{m}^{\mu}\}_{\mu=1}^{m}$.

A stochastic dynamic model is constructed to recognize non-linear movement. This model estimates state variables of action primitive models through observed values. State and observed values up to time t are denoted by $\mathcal{X}_t = \{\mathbf{x}_1, \ldots, \mathbf{x}_t\}$ and $\mathcal{Z}_t = \{\mathbf{z}_1, \ldots, \mathbf{z}_t\}$.

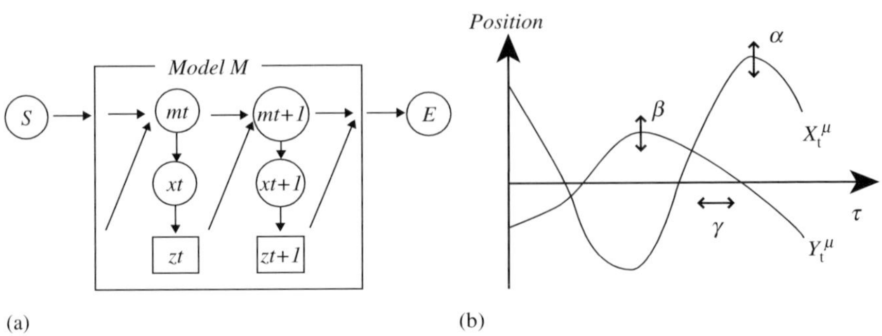

Fig. 3. (a) Transition model, (b) action primitive model.

The propagation of state conforms to a Markov chain, so the new state depends only on the prior state and is independent of the earlier states, as expressed by $p(\mathbf{x}_t|\mathcal{X}_{t-1}) = p(\mathbf{x}_t|\mathbf{x}_{t-1})$.

4.1. *Action primitive model*

Action primitive models, $\{\mathbf{m}^\mu\}_{\mu=1}^{m}$, have information on the human's position, (X^μ, Y^μ), at each phase in the world coordinate system. An example of action primitive models is shown in Fig. 3(b). The value of a human position at phase τ is denoted by (X_τ^μ, Y_τ^μ). The relation between an action primitive model, $\mathbf{m}^\mu$, and a state, $\mathbf{x}_t$, is defined as follows. The state, $\mathbf{x}_t$, at time t has four parameters: action model $\eta = 1, \ldots, \mathcal{M}$, action primitive model $\mu = 1, \ldots, m$, time in primitive model $\tau \in [0, \tau_{\max}^\mu]$, and scale in time dimension $\gamma \in [\gamma_{\min}, \gamma_{\max}]$. The value of $\tau_{\max}^\mu$ depends on action model $\mathbf{m}^\mu$.

Given state $\mathbf{x}_t$, a position obtained from an action primitive model is denoted by $(X_{\mathbf{x}_t}, Y_{\mathbf{x}_t})^{\mathrm{T}} = (X_\tau^\mu, Y_\tau^\mu)^{\mathrm{T}}$.

4.2. *Automatic generation of action primitives*

We use Shintaku's algorithm [8] for automatic generation of action primitives. Input trajectories are automatically classified into action primitives by the algorithm. To use the algorithm, we need a distance function, D_{se}, as a metric for comparing two trajectories. The transition probability, $p(\mathbf{m}^i|\mathbf{m}^j)$, the first occurrence probability, $p(\mathbf{m}^j|M_{t=0})$, and the probability of an action model, $p(M_t|\mathbf{m}^i)$, are also calculated when the action primitive is generated.

4.3. *Stochastic action recognition*

An action that has the maximum posterior probability in response to observed values is selected as optimal recognized action M_{s}.

$$M_{\mathrm{s}} = \arg\min_{M_t} P(M_t|z_t), \tag{3}$$

where $M_t = M^\eta$, η is the action model of state $\mathbf{x}_t$. By using Bayes rule,

$$\begin{aligned} P(M_t|\mathbf{z}_t) &= \int p(M_t, \mathbf{x}_t|\mathbf{z}_t)\, \mathrm{d}\mathbf{x}_t \\ &= \int \frac{p(\mathbf{z}_t|\mathbf{x}_t, M_t)p(\mathbf{x}_t, M_t)}{p(\mathbf{z}_t)}\, \mathrm{d}\mathbf{x}_t \propto \int p(\mathbf{z}_t|\mathbf{x}_t, M_t)p(\mathbf{x}_t|M_t)\, \mathrm{d}\mathbf{x}_t. \end{aligned} \tag{4}$$

A Monte Carlo method is used to calculate the above equation quickly and approximately. If samples, $\mathbf{s}_t = \{\mathbf{s}_t^{(n)}\}_1^N$, are generated from probability distribution

$p(\mathbf{x}_t|M_t)$, then we get the following equation:

$$P(M_t|\mathbf{z}_t) \propto \sum_{i=1}^{N} p(\mathbf{z}_t|\mathbf{x}_t = \mathbf{s}_t^{(i)}, M_t)p(\mathbf{x}_t = \mathbf{s}_t^{(i)}|M_t). \tag{5}$$

$p(\mathbf{x}_t|M_t)$ is a probability density of state as action model M_t occurs and can be written as follows:

$$\begin{aligned} p(\mathbf{x}_t|M_t) &= \int p(\mathbf{x}_t|\mathbf{m}^i)p(\mathbf{m}^i|M_t)\,\mathrm{d}\mathbf{m}^i \\ &\times \propto \int p(\mathbf{x}_t|\mathbf{m}^i)p(M_t|\mathbf{m}^i)p(\mathbf{m}^i|\mathbf{m}^j)p(\mathbf{m}^j|M_{t-1})\mathrm{d}\mathbf{m}^j\,\mathrm{d}\mathbf{m}^i, \end{aligned} \tag{6}$$

where $p(\mathbf{x}_t|\mathbf{m}^i)$ is an uniform distribution. $p(\mathbf{m}^i|M_t)$ is an occurrence probability of action primitive $\mathbf{m}^i$ when action model M_t is obtained. $p(\mathbf{m}^i|\mathbf{m}^j)$ is a transition probability from action primitive $\mathbf{m}^j$ to $\mathbf{m}^i$, calculated from learned data. Furthermore, the first occurrence probability $p(\mathbf{m}^j|M_0)$ is extracted by learning, and $p(\mathbf{m}^i|M_t)$ is calculated recursively. $p(M_t|\mathbf{m}^i)$ is also learned.

In the same way, estimation of the human state, $\hat{\mathbf{x}}$, can be expressed by the following equation:

$$\hat{\mathbf{x}} \equiv E[\mathbf{x}_t|\mathbf{z}_t, M_t] = \int \frac{\mathbf{x}_t p(\mathbf{z}_t|\mathbf{x}_t, M_t)p(\mathbf{x}_t|M_t)}{\int p(\mathbf{z}_t|\mathbf{x}_t, M_t)}\mathrm{d}\mathbf{x}_t \approx \sum_{i=1}^{N}\left[\frac{\mathbf{s}_t^i p(\mathbf{z}_t|\mathbf{x}_t = \mathbf{s}_t^i, M_t)}{\sum p(\mathbf{z}_t|\mathbf{x}_t = \mathbf{s}_t^i, M_t)}\right]. \tag{7}$$

4.4. *Sampling*

The sample set denoted by $\{(\mathbf{s}_t^{(n)}, \pi_t^{(n)})\}_{n=1}^{N}$ is generated from probability distribution $p(\mathbf{x}_t|M_t)$. $\pi_t^{(n)}$ is the weight of a sample and calculated with observed values, $\mathbf{z}_t = (z_t^X, z_t^Y)$, for d frames i.e., a temporal window:

$$\begin{aligned} \pi_t^{(n)} &= p(\mathbf{z}_t|\mathbf{x}_t = \mathbf{s}_t, M_t) \\ &= \frac{1}{\sqrt{2\pi}\sqrt{(\sigma_X^\mu)^2 + (\sigma_Y^\mu)^2}} \\ &\quad \times \exp\left\{-\frac{1}{2d}\sum_{i=0}^{d}\frac{(z_{t+i}^X - X_{\tau+\gamma i})^2}{(\sigma_X^\mu)^2} + \frac{(z_{t+i}^Y - Y_{\tau+\gamma i})^2}{(\sigma_Y^\mu)^2}\right\}, \end{aligned} \tag{8}$$

where σ_X^μ and σ_Y^μ are variances of positions X and Y depending on action primitives $\mathbf{m}^\mu$.

The new sample set $\{(\mathbf{s}_t^{(n)}, \pi_t^{(n)})\}_{n=1}^{N}$ is constructed from prior sample set $\{(\mathbf{s}_{t-1}^{(n)}, \pi_{t-1}^{(n)})\}_{n=1}^{N}$. We will now describe how to predict sample $\mathbf{s}_t^{(n)}$. First, random value $u \in [0, 1]$, a uniform distribution, is chosen and the smallest n such that $C_{t-1}^{(n)} \geq u$ is found. $C_{t-1}^{(n)}$ is calculated with the following equations:

$$C_{t-1}^{(0)} = 0, \qquad C_{t-1}^{(n)} = C_{t-1}^{(n-1)} + \pi_{t-1}^{(n)} \qquad n = 1, ..., N.$$

An action model of sample $\mathbf{s}_t^{(n)}$ is defined as an action model of sample $\mathbf{s}_{t-1}^{(n)}$ and an action primitive model is selected by $p(\mathbf{x}_t|M_t)$ expressed by (6). Note that $p(\mathbf{m}^i|m^j)$ in (6) varies according to phase τ of action primitive model m^j. Therefore, $p'(\mathbf{m}^i|\mathbf{m}^j)$ is defined as follows:

$$p'(\mathbf{m}^i|\mathbf{m}^j) = \begin{cases} p(\mathbf{m}^i|\mathbf{m}^j)\exp\left\{-\dfrac{(\tau_{\max}^j - \tau)^2}{2\sigma_\tau^2}\right\} & \text{if } i \neq j \\ p(\mathbf{m}^i|\mathbf{m}^j)\left[1 - \exp\left\{-\dfrac{(\tau_{\max}^j - \tau)^2}{2\sigma_\tau^2}\right\}\right] & \text{otherwise} \end{cases}.$$

When a selected action primitive model is equal to that of sample $\mathbf{s}_{t-1}^{(n)}$, parameters of sample $\mathbf{s}_t^{(n)}$ are predicted as follows:

$$\mu_t^{(n)} = \mu_{t-1}^{(n)}, \qquad \tau_t^{(n)} = \tau_{t-1}^{(n)} + \gamma_{t-1}^{(n)} + \varepsilon_\gamma, \qquad \gamma_t^{(n)} = \gamma_{t-1}^{(n)} + \varepsilon_\gamma, \tag{9}$$

where ε is Gaussian noise. Otherwise, when a selected action primitive model is not equal, other parameters are selected randomly. Finally, weight $\pi_t^{(n)}$ is calculated by $\pi_t^{(n)} = p(\mathbf{z}_t|\mathbf{x}_t = \mathbf{s}_t^{(n)}, M_t)$. After the new sample set is generated, weight $\pi_t^{(n)}$ is normalized.

4.5. *Improvements of sampling method*

In MCMC method, Metropolis-Hastings sampling algorithm has a disadvantage that sampling points have a tendency to converge one local minimum [9] as shown in Fig. 4. In this method, some action models have the same transition and its transition probability is almost the same, so the probability has a local minima. To avoid a local minimum, one solution is that we increase the number of sampling points to approximate the probability distribution accurately, but the computation time would increase.

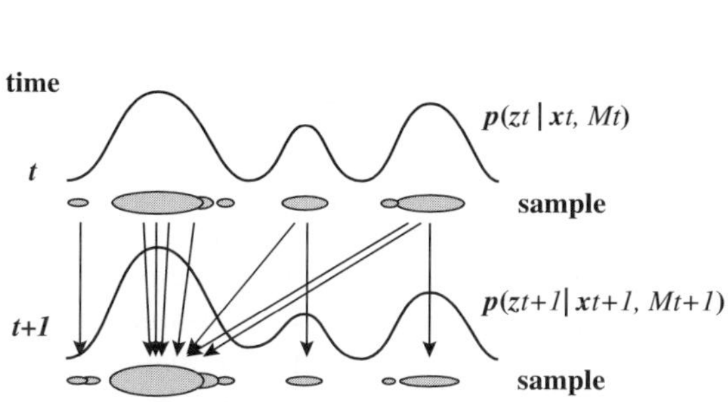

Fig. 4. Convergence to the local minimum.

In this chapter, we use Dispersing Deterministic Crowdings method [10] to avoid local minimum. Our method samples a point according to $p(\mathbf{x}_t|M_t)$, so model M_t of sampling point $\mathbf{x}$ is never changed once sample $\mathbf{x}_t$ chooses model M_t. We, therefore, improve the sampling method to avoid to converge one action model as follows:

$$P_t^* = \frac{\pi_t^*}{f(\mathbf{s}_t^*)}, \qquad P_t^{(n)} = \frac{\pi_t^{(n)}}{f(\mathbf{s}_t^{(n)})}, \qquad \mathbf{s}^{(n)} = \begin{cases} \mathbf{s}_t^* & \text{if } P_t^* \geq P_t^{(n)} \\ \mathbf{s}_t^{(n)} & \text{otherwise} \end{cases}, \tag{10}$$

where $f(\cdot)$ indicates the maximum of the sample's local distribution. The comparison of the weights is performed by using the value relative to the local maximum. In this method, we use a model distribution, $p(\mathbf{x}_t|M_t)$, as a local distribution, $f(\cdot)$. To smooth the distribution, we sample $N_{\min}$ points for each action model.

5. Experimental results

The size of the input images is 1300×1030 pixels and the input rate is 12 Hz. First, trajectories of human movement were extracted with a tracking module. The recognition module recognized actions through these trajectories. The extracted trajectories contained 12 movements following the action models and one movement that was different from the action models. These modules were processed with a SGI workstation (Onyx2). The room was 7×7 m^2. The camera was fixed at the center of the room at a height of 188.9 cm. The results of the tracking people are in Fig. 5.

The action models and action primitive models described in Section 4.2 were generated from trajectories of movements. We used 15 input trajectories and the system automatically outputs nine action models and 11 action primitives. Figure 6 shows the input trajectories and extracted action primitives.

We conducted experiments to evaluate the performance of the algorithm. As action models and action primitive models, we use automatically generated models as shown in Fig. 6(b). The number of action models, $\mathcal{M}$, is nine and the number of action primitive models, m_{N}, is 11. The temporal scale parameters, $\kappa_{\min}$ and $\kappa_{\max}$, are 0.5 and 2.0, respectively. An example of recognition results by using the trajectory following action model $M7$ is shown in Fig. 7(a). In this experiment, we use 750 sampling points. Action models $M7$ and $M2$ partially have the same transition. The results for the recognized action model, therefore, are ambiguous up to the 17th frame. After the 17th frame, the input trajectory is correctly recognized as model $M7$.

The relation between the number of sampling and recognition rates is shown in Fig. 7(b). We use 37 trajectories in this experiment. The recognition rate of our proposed method described in Section 4.5 is about 70% and higher than that of Metropolis-Hastings sampling algorithm. Moreover, our method can recognize actions correctly even though a few sampling points are used. This fact proves the effectiveness of our proposed algorithm.

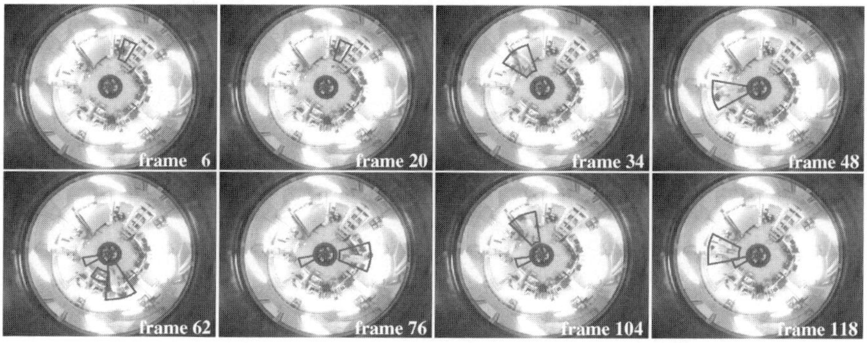

(a)

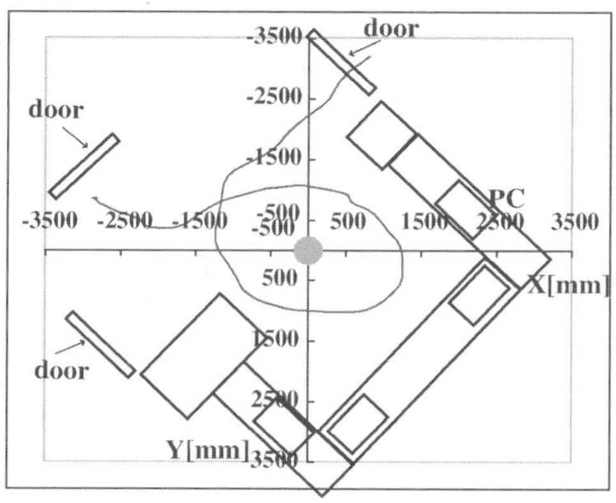

(b)

Fig. 5. Tracking results: (a) input image, (b) extracted trajectory.

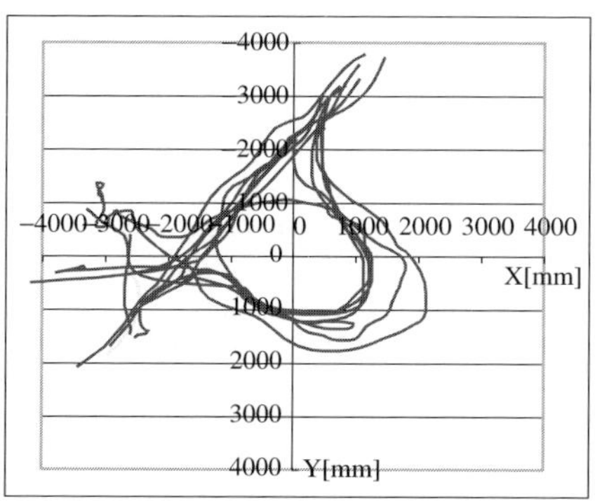

(a)

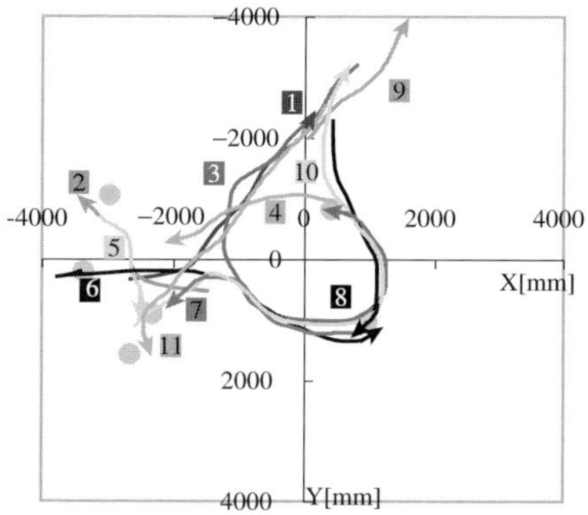

(b)

Fig. 6. Automatic action primitive generation: (a) input trajectories, (b) extracted action primitives.

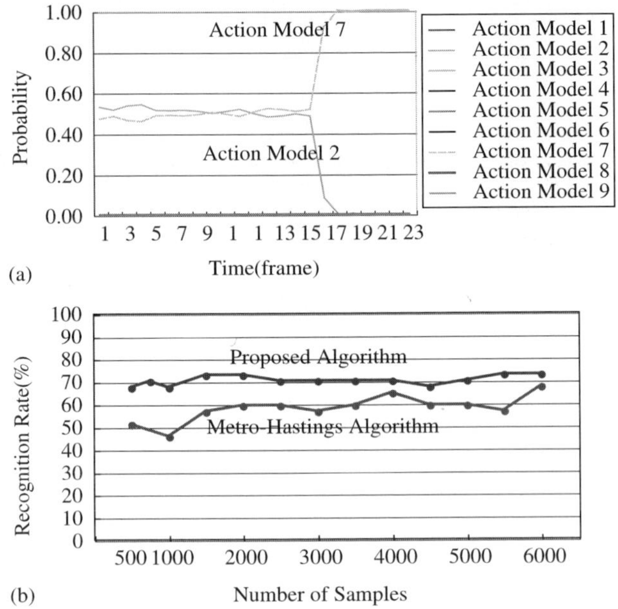

Fig. 7. Action recognition results: (a) probabilities of recognized action models, (b) relation between the number of sampling and recognition rate.

6. Conclusion

We proposed methods of tracking people and recognizing their actions from indoor scenes captured with an omnidirectional image sensor. Because human actions include very similar movements, we assume that human actions could be classified into action primitives. They are modeled by continuous parameters, and actions are modeled by discrete states considered as action primitives. Experiments proved that our proposed method could recognize input trajectories as learned action models and detect suspicious actions.

References

[1] K. Yamazawa, Y. Yagi and M. Yachida, *Omnidirectional imaging with hyperboloidal projection*, Proceedings of the International Conference on Intelligent Robots and Systems (IROS-93), 2, (1993), 1029–1034.

[2] A.F. Bobick and J.W. Davis, *The recognition of human movement using temporal templates*, IEEE Trans. PAMI **23** (3) (2001), 257–267.

[3] R. Rosales and S. Sclaroff, *3D trajectory recovery for tracking multiple objects and trajectory guided recognition of actions*, Proceedings of IEEE Conference on CVPR, (1999), 2117–2123.

[4] M. Isard and A. Blake, *Condensation—conditional density propagation for visual tracking*, IJCV **29** (1998), 5–28.

[5] H. Sidenbladh, M.J. Black and L. Sigal, *Implicit probabilistic models of human motion for synthesis and tracking*, ECCV **1** (2002), 784–800.

[6] N.M. Oliver, B. Rosario and A.P. Pentland, *A Bayesian computer vision system for modeling human interactions*, IEEE Trans. PAMI **22** (8) (2000), 831–843.
[7] T. Wada and T. Matsuyama, *Multiobject behavior recognition by event driven selective attention method*, IEEE Trans. PAMI **22** (8) (2000), 873–887.
[8] S. Shintaku, *A Study for Gesture Primitive Extraction*, Graduation Thesis, Faculty of Engineering Science, Osaka University (2002) (in Japanese).
[9] M. Isard and A. Blake, *Icondensation: unifying low-level and high-level tracking in a stochastic framework*, Proceedings of the Fifth European Conference on Computer Vision, 1, (1998), 893–908.
[10] M. Himeno and R. Himeno, *The effect of crossover and mutation to DC in early generations for multimodal function optimization*, IEICE (D-I) **J85-D-I** (11) (2002), 1015–1027.

PART X

Transportation Systems for Safety and Security

CHAPTER 38

An Evacuation Problem in Tree Dynamic Networks with Multiple Exits

Satoko Mamada and Kazuhisa Makino

Division of Mathematical Science for Social Systems, Graduate School of Engineering Science, Osaka University, Toyonaka, Osaka 560-8531, Japan
E-mail: mamada@inulab.sys.es.osaka-u.ac.jp (S.M.), makino@sys.es.osaka-u.ac.jp (K.M.)

Satoru Fujishige

Research Institute for Mathematical Sciences, Kyoto University, Kyoto 606-8502, Japan
E-mail: fujishig@kurims.kyoto-u.ac.jp

Contents

Abstract

In this paper, we consider an evacuation problem in dynamic networks as one of the basic studies on crisis management systems for evacuation guidance of residents against large-scale disasters. We restrict our attention to tree networks and flows such that all the supplies going through a common vertex are sent to a single sink, since everyone has to evacuate fairly and without confusion. We show that the evacuation problem can be solved in polynomial time if the number of sinks is bounded by some constant.

SYSTEMS AND HUMAN SCIENCE – FOR SAFETY, SECURITY, AND DEPENDABILITY
Edited by Tatsuo Arai, Shigeru Yamamoto and Kazuhisa Makino

1. Introduction

Recently, it has been widely recognized how important it is to establish crisis management systems against large-scale disasters such as big earthquakes. It is one of the most important issues in the crisis management against disasters to secure evacuation pathways and to effectively guide residents to safe places.

Mathematical models for evacuation problems are classified into two groups: microscopic models and macroscopic models. Microscopic models are used for experimental analyses by simulation of behaviors of individual residents. Such typical microscopic models are cellular automata simulation models [1] and probabilistic models [4] for pedestrians and traffic movement. In macroscopic models behaviors of individual residents are not directly treated but residents are regarded as a homogeneous group. There are several classes of mathematical macroscopic models such as static networks, dynamic networks, and traffic assignments [2,3,7,10,11].

In this paper, we adopt dynamic networks as a model for evacuation. Namely, we regard evacuation problems as flow problems on dynamic networks. A dynamic network is defined by a directed graph $G = (V, A)$ with capacities $u(a)$ and transit times $\tau(a)$ on its arcs $a \in A$. For example, if we consider building evacuation, vertices $v \in V$ model workplaces, hallways, stairwells, and so on, and arcs $a \in A$ model the connection between these parts of the building. For an arc $a = (v, w)$, $u(a)$ represents the number of people which can traverse the component corresponding to a per unit time and $\tau(a)$ denotes the time it takes to traverse a from v to w.

The quickest transshipment problem is defined by a dynamic network with several sources and sinks; each source has a specified supply and each sink has a specified demand. The problem is to send exactly the right amount of flow out of each source and into each sink in the minimum overall time. Here, sources and sinks can be regarded as places where the people to be evacuated are staying and emergency exits, respectively. Hoppe and Tardos [6] constructed the only known polynomial time algorithm for the problem.[1] However, their algorithm is not practical at all.

In this paper, we restrict our attention to tree networks and flows such that all the supplies going through a common vertex are sent to a single sink, since everyone has to evacuate fairly and without confusion. From this assumption, if we have k sinks, V can be partitioned into k sets $V_1, V_2, \ldots, V_k$ such that the subgraph induced by V_i is connected and V_i contains a single sink t_i, where all the supplies in V_i are sent to t_i. The problem when $k = 1$ can be solved in $O(n \log^2 n)$ time [9], where n is the number of vertices in the given network. Note that the assumption on flows is automatically satisfied when $k = 1$. Moreover, it can be easily seen that the problem is solvable in $O(n^k \log^2 n)$ time by using $O(n \log^2 n)$ time [9] for each possible partition of V. This paper shows that the problem can be solved in $n(c \log n)^{k+1}$ time for some constant c.

The rest of the paper is organized as follows. Section 2 formally defines the problem and introduces some notations. Section 3 briefly reviews the algorithm for our evacuation

---

[1] The continuous version of the quickest transshipment problem was solved by Fleischer and Tardos [5] in polynomial time.

problem with a single sink. Sections 4 and 5 consider our evacuation problem for $k = 2$ and a constant k, respectively. Finally, we conclude the paper in Section 6.

2. Evacuation problem

We consider a dynamic tree network $\mathcal{N} = (T = (V, A), u, \tau, d)$, where V is a set of vertices, A is a set of arcs, $u : A \to \mathbf{R}_+$ is the upper bound for the rate of flow that enters each arc per unit time, $\tau : A \to \mathbf{R}_+$ is a transit time function, and $d : V \to \mathbf{R}_+$ is a supply function. Here, the undirected graph obtained from T by ignoring the direction of arcs and then identifying parallel edges is a tree and $\mathbf{R}_+$ denotes the set of all non-negative reals.

The problem in this paper is to compute a quickest flow which sends given initial supplies $d(v)$ ($v \in V \backslash S$) to a given sink set $S \subseteq V$. Here, we assume that all the supplies going through a common vertex are sent to a single sink. It follows from the assumption that T can be partitioned into $k(= |S|)$ trees $T_i = T[V_i]$, $i = 1, 2, \ldots, k$ such that V_i contains a single sink $t_i \in S$, where $T[W]$ denotes the subgraph of T induced by $W \subseteq V$.

For any arc $a \in A$, any $\theta \in \mathbf{R}_+$, we denote $f_a(\theta)$ as the flow rate entering the arc a at time θ which arrives at the head of a at time $\theta + \tau(a)$. We call $f_a(\theta)$ ($a \in A, \theta \in \mathbf{R}_+$) as a *continuous dynamic flow* in T (with a sink set S) if it satisfies the following three conditions: (a) capacity constraints, (b) flow conservation, and (c) demand constraints.

(a) *Capacity constraints*: For any arc $a \in A$ and $\theta \in \mathbf{R}_+$,

$$0 \leq f_a(\theta) \leq u(a).$$

(b) *Flow conservation*: For any $v \in V \backslash S$ and $\Theta \in \mathbf{R}_+$,

$$\sum_{a \in \delta^+(v)} \int_0^{\Theta} f_a(\theta) \mathrm{d}\theta - \sum_{a \in \delta^-(v)} \int_{\tau(a)}^{\Theta} f_a(\theta - \tau(a)) \mathrm{d}\theta \leq d(v).$$

(c) *Demand constraints*: There exists a time $\Theta \in \mathbf{R}_+$ such that

$$\sum_{a \in \delta^-(S)} \int_{\tau(a)}^{\Theta} f_a(\theta - \tau(a)) \mathrm{d}\theta - \sum_{a \in \delta^+(S)} \int_0^{\Theta} f_a(\theta) \mathrm{d}\theta = \sum_{v \in V \backslash S} d(v).$$

Here, $\delta^+(S) = \{(v, w) \in A | v \in S, w \notin S\}$ and $\delta^-(S) = \{(v, w) \in A | v \notin S, w \in S\}$. For simplicity, we write $\delta^+(v)$ and $\delta^-(v)$ instead of $\delta^+(\{v\})$ and $\delta^-(\{v\})$, respectively.

Based on the above assumption, we consider continuous dynamic flows that satisfy

(d-1) For any arc $a = (v, w) \in A$ with $v \in S$ and $\theta \in \mathbf{R}_+$,

$$f_a(\theta) = 0.$$

(d-2) For any arc $a = (v, w) \in A$ and $\theta \in \mathbf{R}_+$,

$$f_a(\theta) = 0$$

if $f_{a^*}(\theta^*) > 0$ for some $a^* \in \delta^+(v)$ $(a^* \neq a)$ and $\theta^* \in \mathbf{R}_+$.

We call the flow satisfying (d-1) and (d-2) as *feasible*.

For a feasible (continuous dynamic) flow f, let θ_f denote the completion time for f, i.e., the minimum Θ in condition (c). Our problem is to compute a feasible flow f with minimum θ_f.

3. Single-sink case

This section reviews our evacuation problem when $k = 1$. Here, we describe the algorithm proposed in [8].

For a sink t, we regard T as an in-tree with root t. The algorithm keeps two tables, *Arriving Table* A_v and *Sending Table* S_v for each vertex $v \in V$. Arriving table A_v represents the sum of the flow rates arriving at the vertex v as a function of time θ, i.e.,

$$\sum_{a \in A : a = (v,w)} f_a(\theta - \tau(a)) + \eta_\theta(v),$$

where $\eta_\theta(v) = d(v)/\Delta$ if $0 \leq \theta < \Delta$; otherwise 0. Here, Δ denotes a sufficiently small positive constant. Sending table S_v represents the flow rate leaving the vertex v as a function of time θ, i.e.,

$$f(v, w)(\theta),$$

where w is a parent of v.

Algorithm SINGLE-SINK.

Input: A tree network $\mathcal{N} = (T = (V, A), u, \tau, d)$ and a sink $t \in V$.

Output: A quickest dynamic flow f and the completion time $C(t)$.

Step 0: Put $T' := T$.

Step 1: If T' consists of t alone, then go to Step 3.

For each leaf vertex v of T', construct, Sending Table S_v from Arriving Table A_v by bounding A_v by $u(v, w)$, where w is a parent of v in T'.

Step 2: For each non-leaf vertex w whose children are all leaves, construct Arriving Table A_w from Sending Tables S_v of its children v by shifting A_v right by $\tau(v, w)$ and adding all such shifted tables and $\eta_\theta(w)$.

Remove all the leaves $v(\neq t)$ from T' and denote the resultant tree by T' again.

Go to Step 1.

Step 3: Compute a quickest flow f from A_v, $v \in V$ and the completion time $C(t)$ from A_t.

Return f and $C(t)$, and halt. □

Note that Algorithm SINGLE-SINK tries to send out as much amount of flow as possible from each vertex to its parent.

Let us consider a table $g : \mathbf{R}_+ \rightarrow \mathbf{R}_+$, which represents the flow rate in time $\theta \in \mathbf{R}_+$. A time θ is called a *jump time* of g if $\lim_{x\rightarrow -0} g(\theta + x) \neq \lim_{x\rightarrow +0} g(\theta + x)$. Here, we assume $g(\theta) = 0$ for $\theta < 0$. Note that all the tables used in the algorithm can be decomposed by intervals $[\theta_i, \theta_{i+1})$, $i = 1, 2, ..., k - 1$, i.e.,

$$g(\theta) = \begin{cases} 0 & \text{if } \theta < \theta_1 \\ g(\theta_i) & \text{if } \theta_i \leq \theta < \theta_{i+1} \text{ for } i = 1, ..., k - 1 \, . \\ 0 & \text{if } \theta \geq \theta_k \end{cases}$$

Thus, we represent such tables g by a set of intervals (with their height), i.e.,

$$([\theta_i, \theta_{i+1}), g(\theta_i)), \qquad i = 1, 2, ..., k - 1.$$

Figure 1 shows such a table g, where filled circles denote $g(\theta_i)$'s at jump time θ_i's.

Note that Algorithm SINGLE-SINK computes tables by handling three basic operations, *Add-Table* (i.e., adding tables), *Shift-Table* (i.e., shifting a table), and *Ceil-Table* (i.e., ceil a table by some capacity c). It is not difficult to see that all these operations can be handled in $O(n^2)$ time in total, and hence Algorithm SINGLE-SINK can be executed in $O(n^2)$ time.

In order to make the algorithm faster, Mamada *et al.* [9] proposed sophisticated data structures for the tables. Although we skip the details, we have an $O(n \log^2 n)$-time algorithm for our problem.

4. Two-sink case

We consider the problem for evacuating all residents to two facilities (or sinks) $t_1, t_2 \in S$ as quick as possible. As mentioned in Section 2, our problem is to find an optimal partition V into two components (V_1, V_2) with $t_i \in V_i$, $i = 1, 2$ such that all the supplies $d(v)$ $(v \in V_i)$ are sent to t_i. For example, see Fig. 2 that depicts a tree structure dynamic network $\mathcal{N} = (T = (V, A), u, \tau, d)$. The filled circles represent two sinks t_1 and t_2.

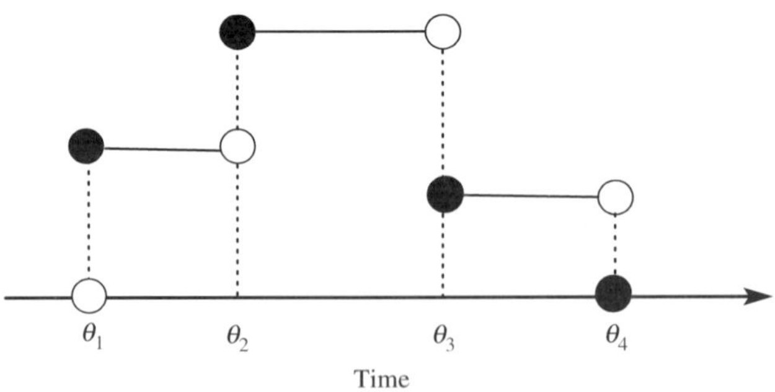

Fig. 1. An example of a table that can be decomposed into intervals.

Let $\hat{T}$ denote the undirected tree obtained from T by ignoring the direction of the arcs and then identifying parallel edges. Let $P = (V_P = \{v_1(= t_1), v_2, \ldots, v_\ell(= t_2)\},\ E_P = \{(v_i, v_{i+1}),\ i = 1, 2, \ldots, \ell - 1\})$ denote the unique path from t_1 to t_2 in $\hat{T}$. By removing all edges in E_P, we have ℓ trees $\hat{T}_i$ (with v_i). Note that any supplies in $\hat{T}_i$ are sent to either t_1 or t_2 by way of v_i. Thus, we first sent all the supplies in $\hat{T}_i$ to v_i by using Algorithm SINGLE-SINK. This means that our problem can be reduced to the problem for partitioning V_P into $V_1 = \{v_1(= t_1), \ldots, v_h\}$, $V_2 = \{v_{h+1}, \ldots, v_\ell(= t_2)\}$ such that the supplies (corresponding to given arriving tables) A_{v_i} can be sent to t_1 if $i \le h$, and t_2 if $i > h$ as quick as possible. Such an optimal partition can be found as follows. For each $j = 1, 2, \ldots, \ell - 1$ we consider two quickest flows f_{1j} and f_{2j} such that f_{1j} (resp., f_{2j}) sends supplies A_{v_i}, $i = 1, \ldots, j$ (resp., $i = j+1, \ldots, \ell$) as quick as possible. $C(f_{1j})$ and $C(f_{2j})$ denote the completion times of flows f_{1j} and f_{2j}, respectively. An optimal partition corresponds to j that attains the minimum of $\max\{C(f_{1j}), C(f_{2j})\}$. Since $C(f_{1j})$ (resp., $C(f_{2j})$) is monotone non-decreasing (resp., non-increasing), we can determine the minimum of $\max\{C(f_{1j}), C(f_{2j})\}$ by a binary search.

Figure 3 shows the path from v_1 to v_6 in the network $\mathcal{N}$ which is depicted in Fig. 2. Each v_i has A_{v_i} $(i = 1, \ldots, 6)$ and f_1 (resp., f_2) is sent to t_1 (resp., t_2) based on $A_{v_1}, \ldots, A_{v_5}$ (resp., $A_{v_2}, \ldots, A_{v_6}$).

Algorithm DOUBLE-SINK.

Input: A tree network $\mathcal{N} = (T = (V, E), u, \tau, d)$ and sinks t_1 and t_2.
Output: A quickest flow f and the minimum completion time $C(\{t_1, t_2\})$.

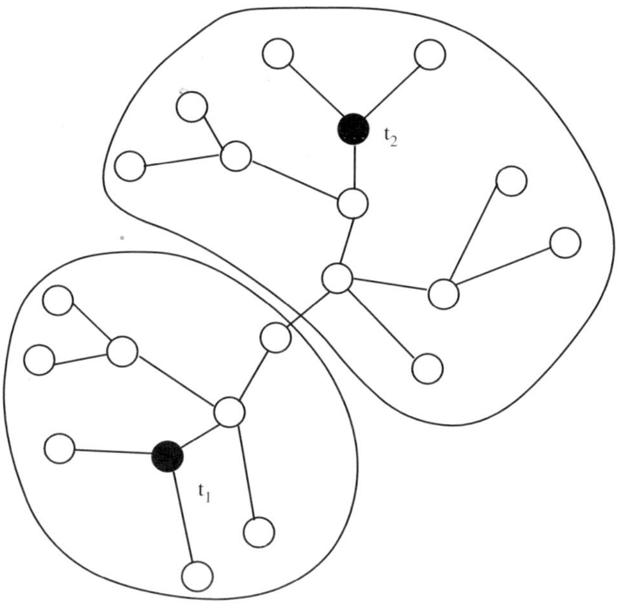

Fig. 2. The two components.

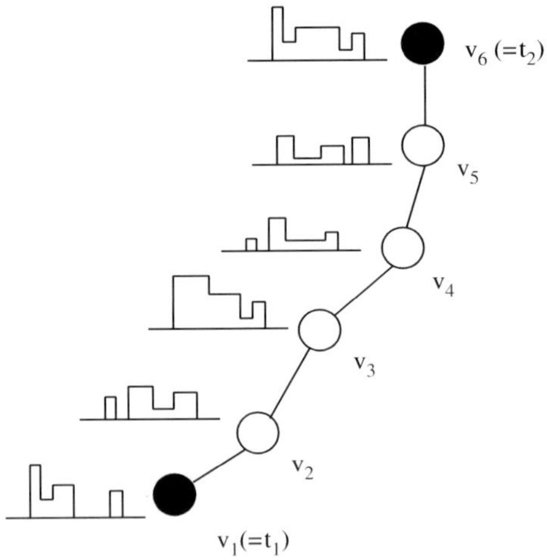

Fig. 3. The path from v_1 to v_6 in the network $\mathcal{N}$.

Step 1: For each $v_i \in V_P$, we sent all the supplies in $\hat{T}_i$ to v_i to construct the Arriving Table A_{v_i}.

Step 2: By means of the binary search find $j \in \{1, 2, \ldots, \ell - 1\}$ that attains the minimum of $\max\{C(f_{1j}), C(f_{2j})\}$. Denote the obtained j by j^*.

Step 3: Let f be a flow given by a direct sum of f_{1j^*} and f_{2j^*} and put the completion time $C(\{t_1, t_2\}) = \max\{C(f_{1j^*}), C(f_{2j^*})\}$. Return f and $C(\{t_1, t_2\})$, and halt. □

Step 1 requires $O(n \log^2 n)$ time by using Algorithm SINGLE-SINK. Step 2 can be done in $O(n \log^3 n)$ time by the algorithm similar to SINGLE-SINK and by the binary search. Hence, Algorithm DOUBLE-SINK computes a quickest flow and the completion time in $O(n \log^3 n)$ time.

THEOREM 4.1. *Algorithm DOUBLE-SINK solves the evacuation problem for two-sink case in* $O(n \log^3 n)$ *time.*

5. *k*-Sink case

This section considers an evacuation problem with k sinks. Consider two sinks t_1, t_2 and the unique path $P(t_1, t_2)$ between t_1 and t_2. From Section 4, it seems that this problem is solved by finding an optimal partition of path $P(t_1, t_2)$ by induction. However, in the multiple-sink case the problem does not have the monotonicity property as noted in Section 4, so that the binary search as in Section 4 does not work.

Figure 4 shows the case when $k = 3$, where a partition is determined by removing two edges in $\hat{T}$.

Let T denote a tree rooted at an arbitrary node $r \in V$, and let $\{t_1, t_2\}$ be a pair of sinks such that their nearest common ancestor is the deepest in T. Let s denote the

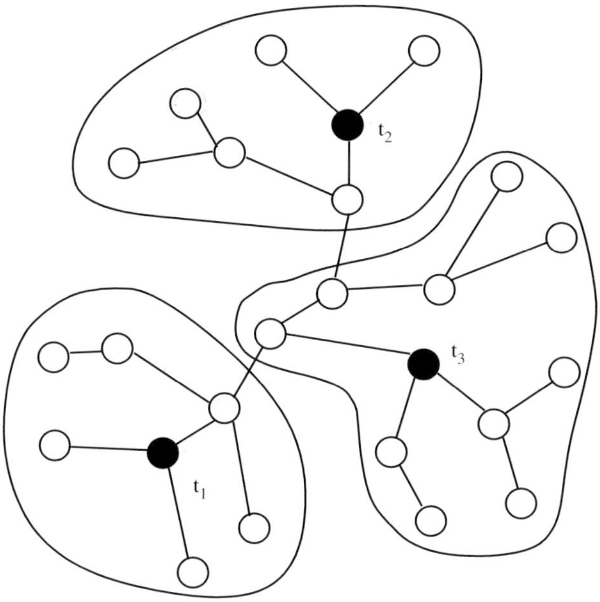

Fig. 4. The case when $k = 3$.

nearest common ancestor of such a pair $\{t_1, t_2\}$. Any dissection of path $P(t_1, s)$ (resp., $P(t_2, s)$) partitions the sink set S into $\{t_1\}$ (resp., $\{t_2\}$) and the rest. Among these dissections, we can find an optimal one by a binary search based on the monotonicity for each of $P(t_1, s)$ and $P(t_2, s)$. Hence, an optimal dissection of $P(t_1, t_2)$ can be found by two binary searches on $P(t_1, s)$ and $P(t_2, s)$.

Let $A(n, k)$ denote the time to compute our evacuation problem with n vertices and k sinks. The argument in the previous sections shows that $A(n, 1) = O(n \log^2 n)$ and $A(n, 2) = O(n \log^3 n)$. In the following we show by induction that $A(n, k) \le n(c \log n)^{k+1}$ for any $k \ge 2$ and some constant $c \ge 4$. Assuming that this holds for any $k \le h - 1$ with some $h \ge 3$, we consider the case when $k = h$. From the above discussion we have

$$A(n, h) \le 2 \log n \max\{A(n_1, 1) + A(n_2, h - 1)\} \le n(c \log n)^{h+1}.$$

This shows the following.

THEOREM 5.1. *The evacuation problem for $k \ge 2$ can be solved in $n(c \log n)^{k+1}$ time for some constant c.*

6. Concluding remarks

We have presented dynamic networks as a model for evacuation. When we restrict our attention to tree networks and flows such that all the supplies going through a common vertex are sent to a single sink, the problem is to determine an optimal partition

$V_1, V_2, \ldots, V_k$ of V such that the subgraph induced by V_i is connected and V_i contains a single sink t_i, where all the supplies in V_i are sent to t_i. We showed that the problem can be solved in $n(c \log n)^{k+1}$ time for some constant c, where n is the number of vertices in the given network. Further improvement over the complexity given here will be discussed elsewhere.

Finally, we note that the evacuation problem for dynamic flows can be further extended in many directions. Some of them are (1) to find a sink to which we can send a flow of maximum value from sources within given fixed time and (2) to consider the partition problem on general (non-tree) dynamic networks. These are left for future research.

Acknowledgment

This research was supported by the Japan Society for the Promotion of Science under Grant-in-Aid for Creative Scientific Research (Project No. 13GS0018).

References

[1] C. Burstedde, A. Kirchner, K. Klauck, A. Schadschneider and J. Zittartz, *Cellular automaton approach to pedestrian dynamics—applications*, Pedestrian and Evacuation Dynamics, M. Schreckenberg and S.D. Sharma, eds, Springer, Berlin (2002), 87–97.

[2] M. Carey and E. Subrahmanian, *An approach to modelling time-varying flows on congested networks*, Transport. Res. B **34** (2000), 157–183.

[3] H.K. Chen and C.F. Hsueh, *A model and an algorithm for the dynamic user-optimal route choice problem*, Transport. Res. B **32** (1998), 219–234.

[4] E.R. Galea, *Simulating evacuation and circulation in planes, trains, buildings and ships using the EXODUS software*, Pedestrian and Evacuation Dynamics, M. Schreckenberg and S.D. Sharma, eds, Springer, Berlin (2002), 203–225.

[5] L. Fleischer and É. Tardos, *Efficient continuous-time dynamic network flow algorithms*, Oper. Res. Lett. **23** (1998), 71–80.

[6] B. Hoppe and É. Tardos, *The quickest transshipment problem*, Math. Oper. Res. **25** (2000), 36–62.

[7] B.N. Janson, *Dynamic traffic assignment for urban road networks*, Transport. Res. B **25** (1991), 143–161.

[8] S. Mamada, K. Makino and S. Fujishige, *Optimal sink location problem for dynamic flows in a tree network*, IEICE Trans. Fundam. **E85-A** (2002), 1020–1025.

[9] S. Mamada, T. Uno, K. Makino and S. Fujishige, *An $O(n \log^2 n)$ algorithm for the optimal sink location problem on dynamic tree-networks*, to appear.

[10] Y. Sheffi, H. Mahmassani and W.B. Powell, *A transportation network evacuation model*, Transport. Res. A **16** (1982), 209–218.

[11] D.J. Zawack and G.L. Thompson, *A dynamic space–time network flow model for city traffic congestion*, Transport. Sci. **21** (1987), 153–162.

CHAPTER 39

A Proposal of Both a Concept and a Prototype of a Driver Secure System

S. Washino

Faculty of Environmental and Information Studies, Tottori University of Environmental Studies, 1-1-1, Wakabadai-Kita, Tottori, Japan

Contents

Abstract

This chapter deals with a concept to assure both security and safety while driving a car. Based on analysis of statistics on traffic accidents from a viewpoint of cognitive or traffic psychology, a model to explain the causes of traffic accidents is proposed. In addition, a system to assure security while driving a car is also proposed.

SYSTEMS AND HUMAN SCIENCE – FOR SAFETY, SECURITY, AND DEPENDABILITY
Edited by Tatsuo Arai, Shigeru Yamamoto and Kazuhisa Makino

1. Introduction

Automatic transmission systems were introduced into the Japanese market as easy driving systems from around 1980. At that time, automatic transmission systems were claimed to be useful for driving in safety because they were able to reduce the workload of driving by eliminating operations such as changing the gear ratio of the manual transmission, and as a result drivers could focus their attention on the action of driving. As a more advanced system than the automatic transmission system, an automatic driving system without drivers was proposed to represent driver assistance systems in intelligent transport systems (ITS).

It was considered that automatic driving systems without drivers would be the most promising forms of driver assistance system in the early stages of ITS. Therefore, many experiments on automatic driving systems were performed at several locations, for example, at Komoro in Japan and San Diego in the USA. These experiments demonstrated the technical potential of automatic driving systems, but ironically also highlighted issues related to deploying such systems.

In this chapter, issues related to deploying automatic driving systems are first mentioned to show the importance of driver assistance systems which will work alongside the drivers, like automatic transmission systems. Then overviews of statistics on both the diffusion rate of vehicles equipped with automatic transmission (VAT) systems and traffic accidents involving vehicles equipped with manual or automatic transmission are shown, and it is confirmed that only a driver assistance system, which can operate alongside the driver can be put into the market very widely. Finally, discussion of a model of driving behavior is mentioned leading to consideration of the concept of a driver secure system which could be put into the market easily.

2. Issues to deploy automatic driving system

Becker et al. summarized the legal and social issues of deploying an automatic driving system as shown in Fig. 1 [1].

The author does not have enough space to explain all issues in Fig. 1, so only three important issues—"Product Perception & Use", "System Safety & Controllability", and "Responsibility & Product Liability" are briefly explained here.

The first issue, "Product Perception & Use", concerns how we can make users recognize minutely both the performance and the use of an automatic driving system. If we fail to do that it may cause new and unexpected types of traffic accidents. Therefore, this issue is one of the most serious issues involved in deploying an automatic driving system.

The second issue, "System Safety & Controllability", is also a big issue. It is not necessary to explain "System Safety", so we will explain only "System Controllability". In other words, this means the ability to override the system when it does not work well. In conjunction with the first issue the second issue is also important in preventing system failures because every system is certain to have some problems in its operation.

The last issue, "Responsibility & Product Liability" is a different type of problem involving legal issues, but is still a basic issue when deploying an automatic driving system. The question is: "Which is responsible, driver or system, for traffic accidents when the automatic driving system causes a traffic accident?"

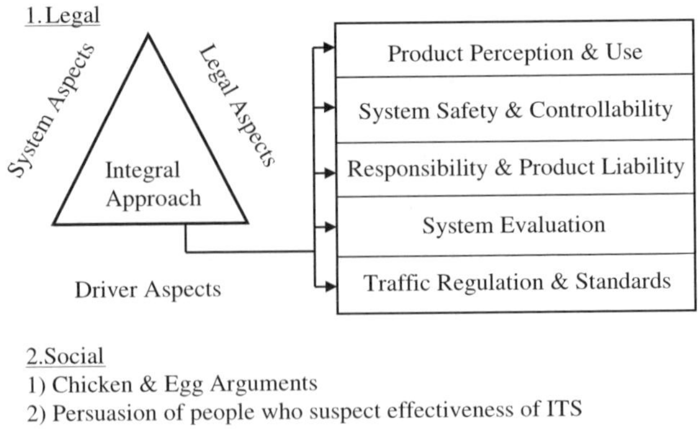

Fig. 1. Legal and social issues [1].

Considering only these three issues, the automatic driving system is far from ready for deployment. That is, we have to rebuild the concept of a driver assistance system instead of an automatic driving system.

It can be considered that there are two types of driver assistance systems. One is a driver assistance system which can assist drivers by compensating for drivers' faults or errors. The other is a driver assistance system which can assist drivers by operating in parallel with drivers. Automatic driving systems belong to the former, but automatic transmission systems, for example, belong to the latter type of driver assistance system because the automatic transmission system is completely integrated with the driver. Therefore, it is very important to investigate both how many VAT diffuse into the market and how many accidents involving VAT do happen, because this investigation can confirm whether the latter type of driver assistance system can be widely accepted into the market. Unfortunately, there are no data on the diffusion rate of VAT, so we can obtain it by extrapolation from VAT on sale. Data on traffic accidents involving VAT are supplied by the Institute for Traffic Accident Research and Data Analysis (ITARDA). Both the rate of traffic accidents involving VAT and vehicles equipped with manual transmission systems (VMT) were estimated by comparison of the rates of road traffic accidents (RTAs) between VAT and VMT.

3. Results of analysis of the rate of traffic accidents

3.1. *Definition of RTA and diffusion rate of VAT*

In order to calculate the rate of traffic accidents (RTAs) defined by the next equation we need to know the total number of VAT running on the actual roads.

$$\mathrm{RTA} = \frac{\mathrm{NTA}}{\mathrm{VAT\ or\ VMT}} \times 100 \tag{1}$$

where NTA is the number of traffic accidents involving VAT or VMT.

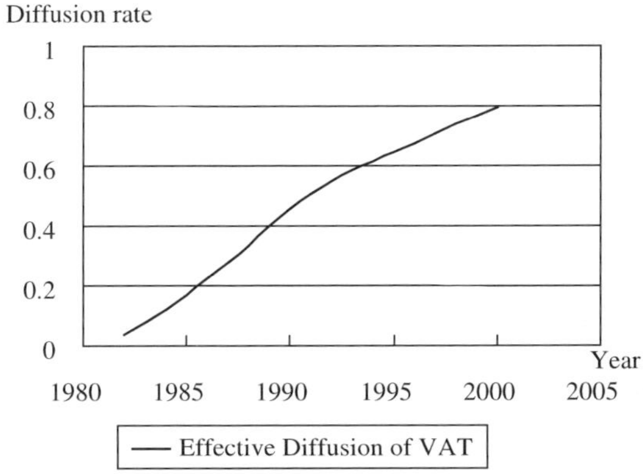

Fig. 2. Calculated diffusion rates of VAT (calculated based on the data from JAMA) [2].

Unfortunately, we do not have statistics regarding the numbers of VAT and VMT. Therefore, we estimated these two numbers by integrating the number of passenger cars sold equipped with automatic transmissions (VAT). We then calculated the number of passenger cars equipped with manual transmissions (VMT) from the statistics of the total number of passenger cars. Figure 2 shows the result of the diffusion rate of VAT. We can easily see that VAT are now widespread, as shown in Fig. 2.

3.2. *Macroscopic results of RTAs*

In order to get an overview of the macroscopic characteristics of RTAs we show the data on RTAs involving both VAT and VMT. Figure 3 shows the results of the calculations. The abscissas in Fig. 3(a) and (b) represent physical years. We need an explanation of RTAs calculated based on (1) because RTAs are calculated on the basis of the number of vehicles. In general, the RTA rate, which is calculated on the basis of the mileage of all vehicles, is more accurate when discussing RTAs involving both VAT and VMT. However, (2) uses the summation of mileages of all vehicles and the number of all vehicles.

$$\sum_{i=1}^{M} X_i = M[X]_{\mathrm{AVE}} \tag{2}$$

where M is the total number of vehicles, X_i the mileage of every vehicle, and $[X]_{\mathrm{AVE}}$ the average mileage of every vehicle. Therefore, we can estimate the degree of safety using the rate of RTAs calculated based on the number of vehicles if the average mileages $[X]_{\mathrm{AVE}}$ of both VAT and VMT are equal. In our calculation, the number of both VAT and VMT vehicles is distributed between 10 million and 25 million. Therefore, it is natural to assume that both VAT and VMT are in similar use. This means that we can assume that the average mileages of both VAT and VMT are similar.

One of the distinct features in Fig. 3 is that the proportion of RTAs involving VAT in all types of traffic accidents is greater than the proportion involving VMT, where all traffic

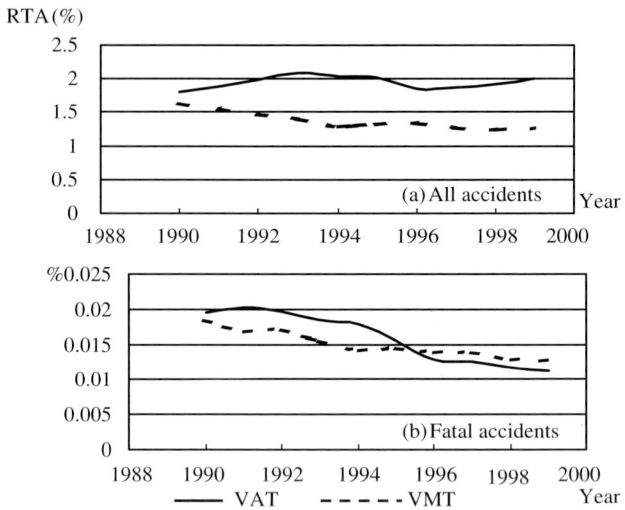

Fig. 3. Comparison of road traffic accidents (calculated based on the data from ITARDA) [3].

accidents are composed of injuries and fatal accidents. In contrast with this, the proportion of RTAs involving VAT in fatal accidents is nearly equal to those involving VMT, in particular, in recent years. In both figures accidents include drivers who were primarily, secondarily and thirdly responsible for the traffic accidents.

Apparently, we can see that the number of RTAs involving VAT is not always smaller than for VMT, as shown in Fig. 3. We originally believed that VAT would be safer than VMT because automatic transmissions can decrease the workload of drivers compared with manual transmissions. Nevertheless, the results show the opposite effect. We show the results of a microscopic analysis of RTA in the next section.

3.3. *Microscopic results of RTA*

In this section, all accidents are confined to those involving drivers with primary responsibility for the accident.

3.3.1. *RTA analyzed by type of accident.* Figure 4 shows the results of analysis of RTA by type, including all accidents and fatal accidents.

In Fig. 4, the ordinates represent the classification of the pattern of accidents, for example, head-on collision, rear-end collision, crossing collision, left turn collision, and right turn collision in ascending order on the left side of the ordinates. The following features are observed.

(1) From Fig. 4(a), the number of RTAs involving VAT in all accidents is almost double independent of the type of accident such as right turn, crossing collision at an intersection, and so on, except in the case of head-on collisions.

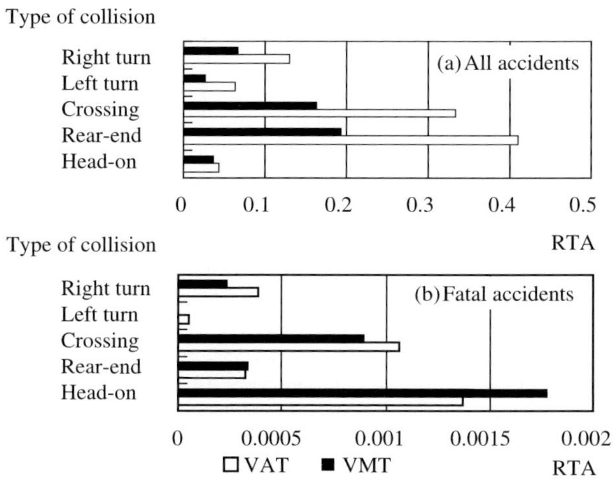

Fig. 4. RTA by type (calculated based on the data from ITARDA) [3].

(2) In contrast, from Fig. 4(b), it is obvious that the number of RTAs involving both VAT and VMT are very similar, and that the number of RTAs involving VMT in cases of head-on collision is even larger than that of VAT.
(3) In cases of head-on collision shown in Fig. 4(a) we can see another distinct feature which is that the RTAs involving both VAT and VMT are remarkably small compared with those of all other collision types.
(4) In contrast with this, in the case of fatal accidents shown in Fig. 4(b), the number of RTAs involving head-on collision is relatively large.

3.3.2. *RTA analyzed by human factors.* Figure 5 shows the results of analyzing RTAs by human factors from the data on all accidents and fatal accidents. In Fig. 5 the ordinates represent the classification of the human factor that caused the accident, for example, #1, represents aimless operation induced by a mental factor of the driver; #2, operation while looking away; #3, lack of safety confirmation; #5, lack of attention to the surrounding, and #6, the mistake of predicting the movement of a nearby vehicle, in ascending order on the left side of the ordinates. The following features show similarity to the results of analysis of the type of accident as observed in Fig. 4, as follows:

(1) From Fig. 5(a) the proportion of RTAs involving VAT in all accidents is almost two times larger, independently of human factors such as aimless operation induced by a mental factor of the driver, operation while looking away, lack of safety confirmation, lack of attention to the surroundings, and so on.
(2) On the other hand, from Fig. 5(b), it can be seen that the number of RTAs involving both VAT and VMT are very close in the case of fatal accidents.

3.3.3. *RTA analyzed by the range of drivers' ages.* Figures 6(a) and (b) shows the results of analyzing RTAs with respect to the range of driver age of all accidents and fatal accidents, respectively. In Fig. 6 the ordinates represent the ranges of drivers' ages: #1

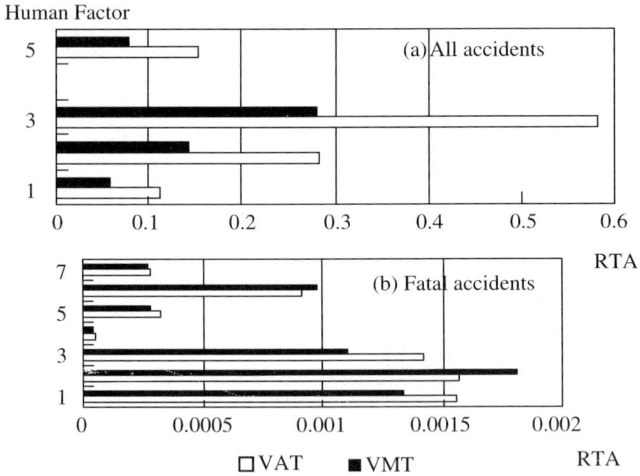

Fig. 5. RTA by human factors (calculated based on the data from ITARDA) [3].

indicates that the drivers' age is lesser than 17 years, #2 the age ranges from 18 to 19, #3 from 20 to 24, #4 from 25 to 29, #5 from 30 to 39, #6 from 40 to 49, #7 from 50 to 59, #8 from 60 to 64, #9 from 65 to 69, #10 from 70 to 74, #11 from 75 to 79, and #12 more than 80 years, in ascending order of the left side of the ordinates.

Features similar to those observed in Figs. 3–5 are also seen in Fig. 6. That is, the number of RTAs involving VAT in all accidents is almost twice that of VMT independent of the range of drivers' age. On the other hand, from Fig. 6(b), it can be seen that the number of RTAs involving both VAT and VMT is very close in the case of fatal accidents.

3.3.4. *RTA analyzed by the range of drivers' age in head-on collision.* Figures 7(a) and (b) shows the results of analyzing RTAs by the range of drivers' age involving head-on collision in all accidents and fatal accidents, respectively. In the case of head-on collisions,

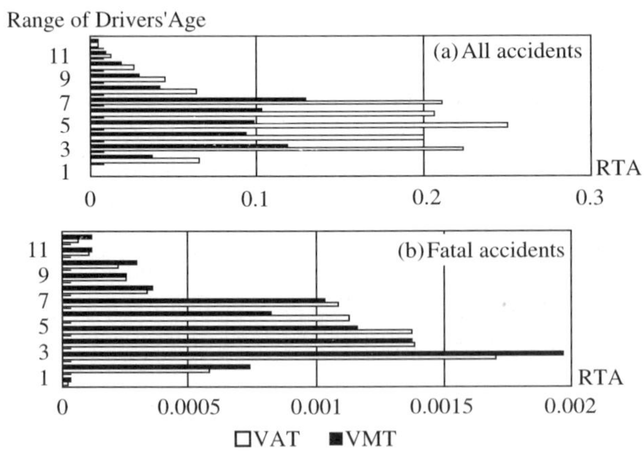

Fig. 6. RTA by range of drivers' age (calculated based on data from ITARDA) [3].

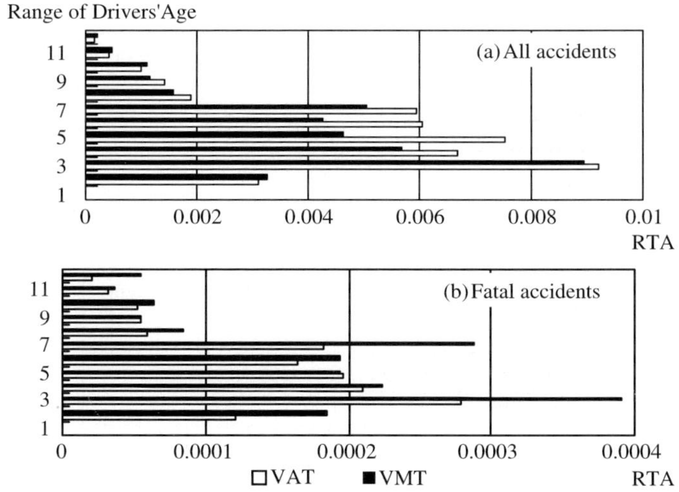

Fig. 7. RTA by range of drivers' age in head-on collisions (based on data from ITARDA) [3].

the following remarkable feature is observed, that is, the number of RTAs in both all and fatal accidents are close. These differences will be discussed later in the next section.

3.3.5. *RTA analyzed by the range of drivers' age in rear-end collision.* Figures 8(a) and (b) shows the results of analysis of RTAs by the range of drivers' age in rear-end collision of all accidents and fatal accidents, respectively.

3.3.6. *RTA analyzed by the range of drivers' age in crossing collisions at intersections.* Figures 9(a) and (b) shows the results of analysis of RTAs by the range of drivers' age in crossing collisions of all accidents and fatal accidents, respectively.

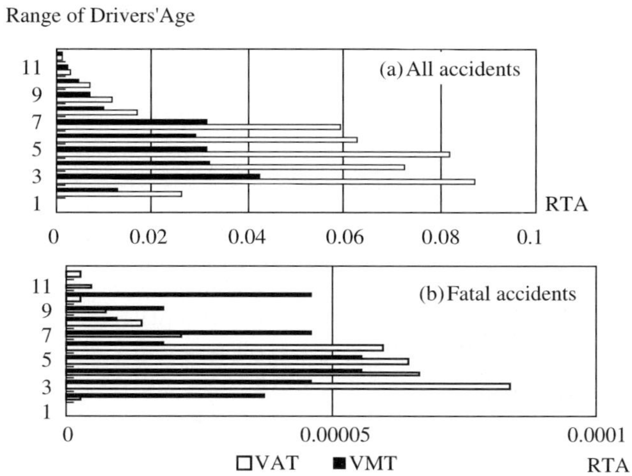

Fig. 8. RTA by range of drivers' age in rear-end collisions (calculated based on ITARDA data) [3].

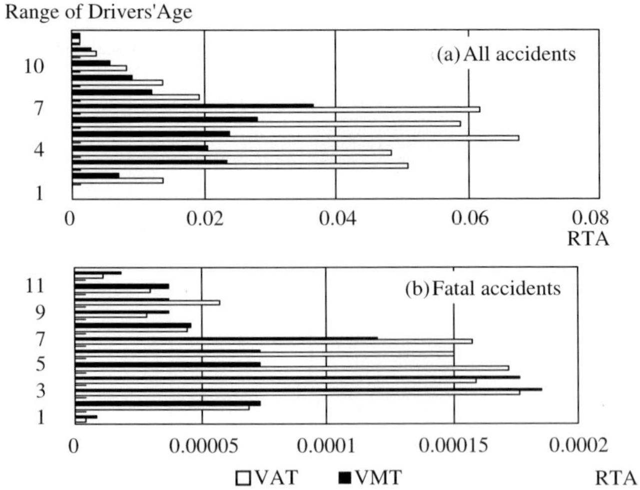

Fig. 9. RTA by range of drivers' age in crossing collisions (calculated based on ITARDA data) [3].

In cases of both rear-end and crossing collisions the following feature, as mentioned previously, is seen again. That is, the proportion of RTAs involving VAT is greater than those involving VMT in all accidents, but are close in fatal accidents.

4. Discussion

Summarizing the driving process we can generate an idea as shown in Fig. 10. Attention is the first process required in driving a car, followed by perception, decision, and operation processes. In all these processes, some delays or mistakes, called human errors, are caused very often by all the human factors shown on the right side in Fig. 10. I would like to suggest that a driver assistance system could reduce traffic accidents by working on human factors, but on the contrary an alternative system such as an automatic driving system could reduce accidents by working on human errors by force.

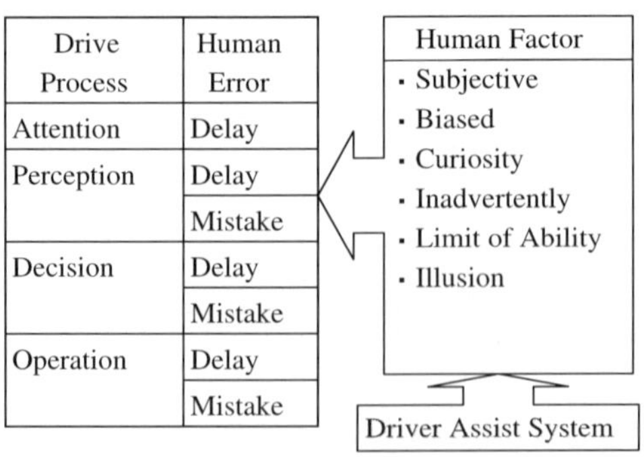

Fig. 10. Driving processes [4].

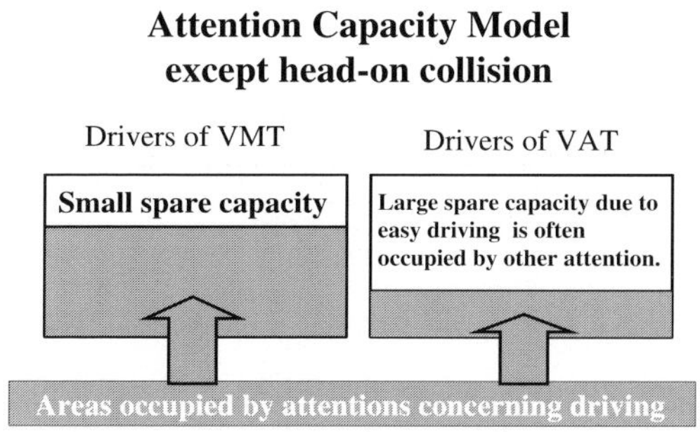

Fig. 11. Attention capacity model [5].

Now the process of attention is located in the first step of the driving process. If we apply the idea of spare capacity to this first process and summarize all the results on RTA we can derive an idea shown in Fig. 11:

In Fig. 11 the same two rectangles indicate the attention capacities of drivers of both VMT and VAT, respectively. The shaded areas in both attention capacities indicate the area occupied by the work of driving a car. For drivers of VAT the driving is easier and a smaller area is occupied by driving attention. In response to this the spare capacity in the attention of the driver of VAT becomes larger compared with that of drivers of VMT.

In contrast with this, it can be considered that the spare capacity of the attention of VAT drivers becomes very close to that of VMT drivers when VAT are driving facing the oncoming traffic. As a result, spare capacity in this situation can be shown in Fig. 12 because drivers become nervous in such a driving situation.

This model shows that the larger the spare capacity of the attention the larger the probability of traffic accidents. Therefore, we could reduce traffic accidents by controlling the spare attention capacity using some means, for example, providing drivers with information concerning driving, information on the vehicle control system, and so on. That is, we propose that the less the spare attention capacity, the less the traffic accidents. By using this model we can explain an experimental result showing that traffic accidents were reduced on a road where the central line discriminating up and down flow was erased from the surface.

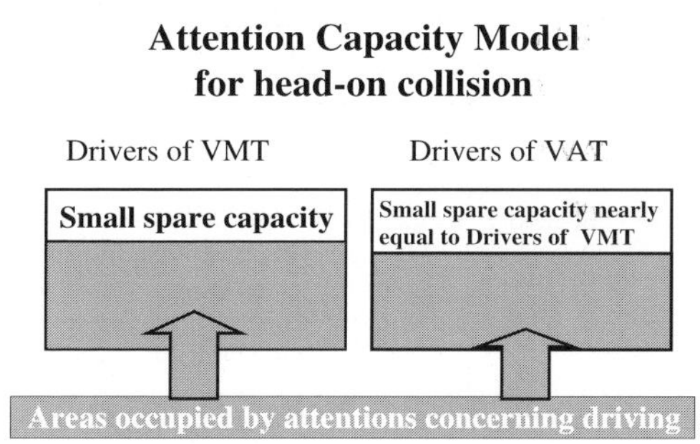

Fig. 12. Attention capacity model for head-on collisions.

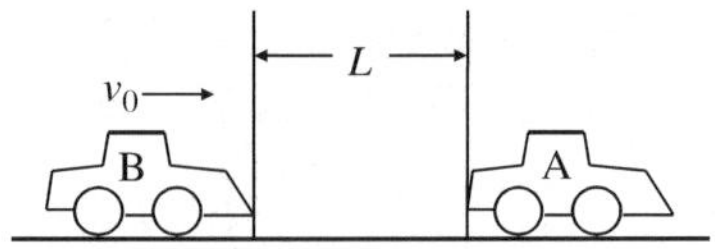

$$v_0\delta + \frac{v_0^2}{2\mu g} = L$$

Fig. 13. A driver secure system to avoid rear-end collisions.

Now consider rear-end collisions, where the RTAs comprise 25% of all traffic accidents in Japan. In such cases as rear-end collisions the spare capacity of the driver of the following car becomes larger because their attention to driving reduces. In general, there are many cases where drivers of preceding cars notice the behavior of the following cars. Therefore, drivers of preceding cars can control the spare capacity of drivers of the following cars by sending them messages.

From this we propose an idea of a driver secure system for preventing rear-end collisions using a communication system from the driver of a preceding car to the driver of a following car. That is, the driver of the preceding car can send some messages to the following car through a display device to prevent a rear-end collision. This system is a kind of driver assistance system, so to speak, a driver secure system which can reduce rear-end collisions using both drivers and systems to control the spare capacity of the driver of the following car through the messages. When the driver of the preceding car notices the possibility of a rear-end collision with the following car, the driver is able to avoid the danger by sending messages to the driver of the following car and thus feels a sense of security. In this sense, we can call this system a driver secure system.

5. Proposal and trial of a driver secure system

A driver secure system is proposed as shown in Fig. 13 to avoid rear-end collisions using driver communication. Suppose that the driver of vehicle A stops his vehicle. The driver of vehicle B with the initial velocity of v_0 is approaching vehicle A from behind.

The driver of vehicle A will probably fear having a rear-end collision caused by the driver of vehicle B. In such a situation he could eliminate this fear by sending a signal to driver B making him take action to stop vehicle B such as "Please stop your car". If driver B stops his or her car within the length L the driver would feel mental security. That is, this

Table 1. Specification of the LED dot-matrix display [6]

Vertical side length	64 mm	96 mm
Size of the dot emitting light	$\phi 3.2$	$\phi 5.3$
Number of dots	16 × 16	
Dot spacing	4 mm	6 mm
Wavelength	660 nm (red), 567 nm (green)	

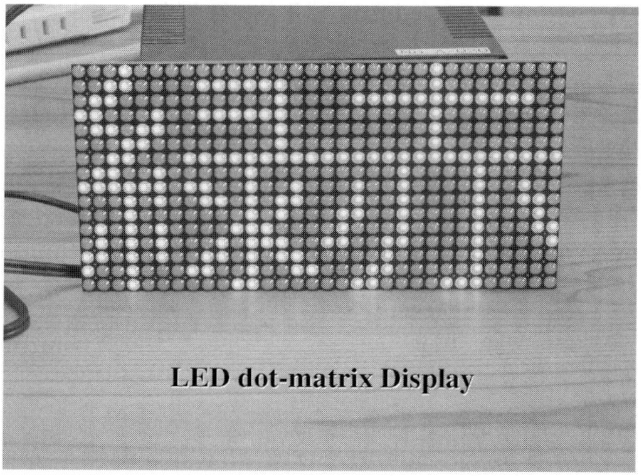

Fig. 14. An example of LED dot-matrix display.

system could provide mental security free from the fear of having a rear-end collision. In this sense, we can call this system a driver secure system.

Suppose that the inter-vehicle distance is L when driver A sends a signal to driver B and after δ seconds driver B takes braking action with deceleration rate μg, this driver secure system is valid if there exists an area where δ is positive in the equation in Fig. 13. We determined the distance L by a preliminary experiment. In this experiment, we determined the longest values of L where a given LED dot-matrix display was visible. The specification of a conventional LED dot-matrix display for indoor use is listed in Table 1, and the external view of the LED dot-matrix display used in this experiment is shown in Fig. 14. The experimental procedure was as follows: We set the display on the trunk of a vehicle outdoors, then we moved away from the vehicle and determined the longest distance at which we could recognize letters displayed on the LED dot-matrix display. When an LED dot-matrix 64 mm^2 is used the distance is 10 m, and 25 m in the case of an LED dot-matrix 96 mm^2. These values are for red color LEDs.

When a green color is displayed, the distance is reduced compared to a red color. The weather was cloudy when the experiments were performed. The eyesight of the people

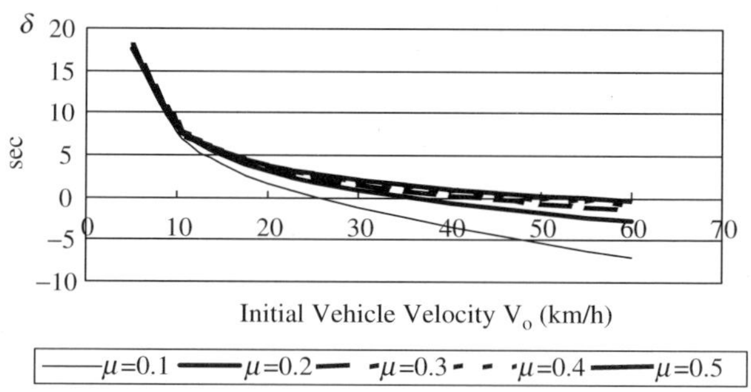

Fig. 15. Calculation results of δ in Fig. 13.

who took part in the experiment ranged from 0.7 to 1.0. Several calculation results of δ are shown in Fig. 15.

Fig.15 shows the areas where δ is positive. Therefore, our concept of the driver secure system is valid. We are currently making a prototype of our driver secure system. A similar system to ours is available using an inter-vehicle electronic communication system to communicate between drivers. In that system, both vehicles A and B in Fig. 13 have to be equipped with the inter-vehicle electronic communication systems. In contrast with this, our system does not need vehicle B to be equipped with our communication system.

6. Conclusion

Our conclusions can be summarized as follows:

(1) A driver assistance system, which can work alongside the driver, can be put into the market very widely.
(2) The proportion of RTAs involving VAT in all accidents except head-on collisions are almost two times larger than those of VMT.
(3) The proportion of RTAs involving VAT in fatal accidents is close to that of VMT.
(4) These results can be explained with an attention capacity model.
(5) A driver secure system to avoid rear-end collision is proposed and basic experiments were performed to produce an experimental system.

References

1. S. Becker, D. von Randow and J. Feldges, *Driver assistance system*, Proceedings of Intelligent Vehicle '98, (1998), pp. 694–698.
2. Statistics on data of distribution of vehicles equipped with automatic transmission by Japan Automotive Dealers Association.
3. Statistics on traffic accidents supplied by the Institute for Traffic Accident Research and Data Analysis (ITARDA).
4. Y. Nagayama, Textbook of Training Course on Traffic Psychology (1992) (in Japanese).
5. I.D. Brown, *Effect of a car radio on driving in traffic*, Ergonomics **8** (1965), 475–479.
6. Technical data of LED dot-matrix display provided by Sanyo Electric Co., Ltd (2003) (in Japanese).

Author Index

Subject Index